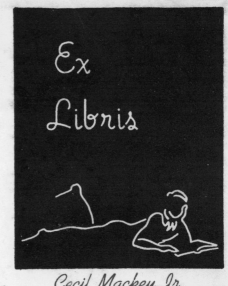

ECONOMICS

An Introductory Analysis

BY PAUL A. SAMUELSON

Professor of Economics

Massachusetts Institute of Technology

SECOND EDITION
SECOND IMPRESSION

McGraw-Hill Book Company, Inc.

NEW YORK   TORONTO   LONDON   :   1951

ECONOMICS

THE MAPLE PRESS COMPANY, YORK, PA.

Preface

THIS book is designed for a one-semester or two-semester course in introductory economics. It is intended for the intelligent citizen interested in a general education, and it tries to supply a theoretical understanding of the economic institutions and problems of American civilization in the middle of the twentieth century.

The book concentrates on the big, vital, and interesting problems: on inflation and depression; on family income and national income; on wages, prices and profits; and most important of all, on the conditions that will lead to rapid economic progress and security, and to efficient use of all our resources.

No previous knowledge of economics is assumed. Each topic is developed leisurely and at length in recognition of the principle: "Short writing makes long reading." No use is made of mathematical equations or symbols. Even the currently fashionable use of geometric diagrams has been subordinated to an unusually extensive application of arithmetical examples, supplemented by pictorial charts.

The present work represents a complete rewriting of the first edition. The revision is based upon experience gained from widespread use of the book in colleges and universities both here and abroad. (1) New material has been added: *e.g.*, Part Four represents a whole new group of chapters on the principles of income distribution; and the space devoted to topics like labor and agriculture has been tripled. (2) Minor rearrangements in chapter order have been made, and the material has been organized in six rather than three parts. On careful reexamination, the general structure of the original plan seemed to be essentially sound; but the changes will, I hope, increase the reader's understanding and the teacher's flexibility. (3) Because of a personal phobia against books whose facts are already a few years old by time of publication. I have strained (perhaps sometimes to an almost ridiculous degree) to bring factual material up to as late a date as possible, so that the reader will be dealing with the world of the 1950's and not some earlier age. (4) The emphasis has been shifted throughout, away from the problem of mass unemployment and toward this next decade's problems of inflation and a national-security economy. (5) The national income approach has been retained, but it has been subordinated to the over-all goal of synthesizing *aggregate* concepts with economic analysis of the *component parts*. This, I am convinced, is the ideal goal for the textbook of the future.

An author never knows his own book. Literally hundreds of teachers and other readers have written me detailed letters of comment and criticism. All these have been of incalculable benefit to me in this revision. They have enabled ıne to post a Stop, Look and Listen sign at any point where the discussion becomes (1) difficult to understand or (2) controversial as far as policy is concerned. If the result is a more teachable and objective book—and I hope it is—the credit must go to this legion of helpful critics.

The present book should provide material enough for a full year's course. It can be supplemented if desired, and the material has been arranged in such a way that chapters and appendixes can be omitted without breaking the continuity. Many institutions will want to use the book for a one-semester course; a suggested table of contents for such a course (like that used at my own institution, the Massachusetts Institute of Technology) is included.

Each chapter has been planned to constitute a unit of understanding; each is provided with a detailed analytic summary and with discussion questions. Where a chapter tends to become long, it has been broken up into sections A, B, and so forth; these can be assigned like chapters. In several places, material has been put in chapter appendixes. A straw vote showed that most instructors have approved of the extra flexibility provided by this method: such material is not necessarily more difficult, but it is usually something that can be eliminated if time is short, or at a first reading.

The discussion has been carefully arranged so that the instructor can, if he wishes, alter the order of assignments. Thus, although at M.I.T. we prefer not to do so, there is no reason why Part Three on Pricing Theory could not precede Part Two on Income Determination. In fact we often assign Part Three's introductory chapter on Supply and Demand as soon as the first three introductory chapters of Part One have been covered.

To make this new edition understandable and teachable, my coworkers and I have spared no pains. Every diagram has been carefully drawn, labeled, captioned, and integrated with the text and with the numerical tables. In addition, the McGraw-Hill Book Company has available a set of a dozen silent filmstrips to provide a valuable classroom supplement.

When it comes to acknowledgments for help received, I am a hopeless bankrupt. I cannot even begin to enumerate the names of those who have helped in this revision. My greatest debt is to Mr. Romney Robinson for his extensive collaboration in the revising. In addition, I have been particularly indebted for help to my M.I.T. colleagues Professors E. Cary Brown, George P. Shultz, Douglass V. Brown, John R. Coleman, Morris A. Adelman, and Robert L. Bishop; also to Professor Arthur G. Ashbrook, Jr., of Duke University. And the influence of Professors Charles A. Myers, Richard M. Bissell, Jr., John G. Turnbull, John T. Wheeler, Daniel C. Vandermeulen and George N. Halm, all of whom gave critical aid in preparation of the first edition, is still present in this revision. The editorial assistance of Miss Beatrice A. Rogers, the secretarial help of Mrs. Gloria Wiggin, and the research assistance of Sumner M. Rosen and Francis M. Bator are all gratefully acknowledged. Above all, I am indebted to Professor Ralph Evans Freeman, chairman of the Department of Economics and Social Science at M.I.T., who first suggested that this book be written. Neither he nor any of the above should be blamed for the result.

PAUL A. SAMUELSON

CAMBRIDGE, MASS.
February, 1951

Contents

PART ONE: BASIC ECONOMIC CONCEPTS
AND NATIONAL INCOME

PART TWO: DETERMINATION OF NATIONAL INCOME
AND ITS FLUCTUATIONS

PART FOUR: DISTRIBUTION OF INCOME:

THE PRICING OF THE PRODUCTIVE FACTORS

SUGGESTED OUTLINE FOR
A ONE-SEMESTER COURSE

PART ONE

Basic Economic

Concepts and

National Income

Chapter 1: INTRODUCTION

FOR WHOM THE BELL TOLLS

A well-known college administrator used to address the entering class: "Take a good look at the man on your right and the man on your left, because next year one of you won't be here."

If the future should be like the past, then of any three readers of this book, a similar statement may be made: There is a strong probability that one, at some period of his life, will be hard hit by a depression or he may have his lifetime savings wiped out by price inflation. And all three will find that economic events play a dominant role in their everyday lives.

From a purely selfish point of view, then, it is desirable to gain understanding of the following overwhelmingly important problems of modern economics: the causes of depression, unemployment, and inflationary booms; and the causes of prosperity, full employment, and rising standards of living. But no less important is the fact—clearly to be read from the history of the twentieth century—that the political health of a democracy is tied up in a crucial way with the successful maintenance of stable high employment and living opportunities. It is not too much to say that the widespread creation of dictatorships and the resulting World War II stemmed in no small measure from the world's failure to meet this basic economic problem adequately.

POVERTY MIDST PLENTY

Modern economics tries to explain, among other things, how it is that nations are alternately afflicted with the dizzy ups and downs of business activity. Back in the old days, before science and the Industrial Revolution had developed our tremendous technology, there were often periodic famines. The statistics of marriages varied inversely with the price of bread. Thousands or millions would die as a result of floods, droughts, or other easily recognized natural catastrophes. Everyone knew the causes of disasters, but nobody could do much about them.

Today it is just the opposite. Now we know how to produce a fair abundance of goods, but we are subject to periodic depressions of obscure causation.

3

Bread is cheap in depression; but present-day marriages follow job opportunities rather than the cost of food. Famine due to crop failure in one part of the world can now be relieved by shipments from elsewhere. People go hungry in modern slumps, not because we can produce too little, but seemingly because we can produce too much.

A man from Mars or a Rip Van Winkle from an earlier century would have been at a loss had he returned to the world of the 1930's. He would have thought that everybody had lost his senses. Little pigs were plowed under while families did without meat. Because we had new efficient factories, we did without production. Because we had too many skilled and willing hands, unemployment prevailed. Everybody tried to save and hoard money, with the result that everyone got poorer and poorer. So it might have seemed.

The man from Mars would have been even more surprised to observe that the onset of history's most destructive and bloody war, instead of depressing American business conditions further, had just the opposite effect. Despite shortages, the American civilian standard of living surpassed all previous levels. And since the war, he would have observed all over the world mad inflationary spirals, in which wages chased after prices and prices chased after wages.

ECONOMIC DESCRIPTION AND ANALYSIS

It is the first task of modern economic science to describe, to analyze, to explain, to correlate these fluctuations of national income. Both price inflation and depression unemployment are our concern. This is a difficult and complicated task, but still an obvious one. A second task is equally difficult, but perhaps not so obvious. We must study the economic principles that tell us how productivity can be kept high and that tell us how people's standards of living can be improved. It is not enough to make jobs plentiful so that economic resources do not go unemployed. We must also make sure that our economic resources are fruitfully employed in such a way as to be efficiently producing the goods and services that people really want and need. So fully half of this book is concerned with the composition of national production and not simply with its total.

Because of the complexity of human and social behavior, we cannot hope to attain the precision of a few of the physical sciences. We cannot perform the controlled experiments of the chemist or biologist. Like the astronomer we must be content largely to "observe." But economic events and statistical data observed are, alas, not so well behaved and orderly as the paths of the heavenly planets. Fortunately, however, our answers need not be accurate to several decimal places; on the contrary, if only the right general *direction* of cause and effect can be determined, we shall have made a tremendous step forward.

Knowledge and understanding of nature and society are worth while for their own sake. Just as it is interesting to know the paths of planets and the antics of atoms, it is worth while to know how banks create money, how inflations behave, how supply and demand help to determine prices. But in addition to knowledge for its own sake—and, to most people, of far greater importance —there is the hope that the findings of physics may help engineers make useful technological improvements, that the study of physiology may promote medical advancement, and that dispassionate analysis of the economic facts will enable society to devise ways to keep some of the more unpleasant ones from happening.

ECONOMIC POLICY

This brings us to the important problem of economic policy. Ultimately, understanding should aid in control and improvement. How can the business cycle be diminished? How can economic progress be furthered? How can standards of living be made more equitable?

At every point of our analysis we shall be seeking to shed light on these policy problems. But to succeed in this, we must all try to cultivate an objective and detached ability to see things as they *are*, regardless of our likes or dislikes. The fact must be faced that economic subjects are close to everybody emotionally. Blood pressures rise and voices become shrill whenever deep-seated beliefs and prejudices are involved, and some of these prejudices are thinly veiled rationalizations of special economic interest.

We know that a doctor passionately interested in stamping out disease must first train himself to observe things as they are. His bacteriology cannot be a different one from that of a mad scientist out to destroy the human race by plague. Wishful thinking is bad thinking and leads to little wish fulfillment.

In the same way, there is only one valid reality in a given economic situation, however hard it may be to recognize and isolate it. There is not one theory of economics for Republicans and one for Democrats, not one for workers and one for employers. On the basic economic principles concerning prices and employment, most economists are in pretty close agreement.

This does not mean that economists always agree in the *policy* field. Economist *A* may be for full employment at any cost. Economist *B* may not rank it of primary importance. Basic questions concerning right and wrong goals to be pursued cannot be settled by economists as such. Each citizen must decide them for himself, and an expert is entitled to only one vote along with everyone else. All the expert can do is point out the true costs that may be involved in the different decisions.

COMMON SENSE AND NONSENSE

Economics is not an easy subject. True, it does not require the mental application of, say, mathematics. But there is a definiteness in mathematics despite its complexity. So most people feel that, by gritting their teeth and applying themselves sufficiently, they can learn to solve such things as quadratic equations just as other ordinary mortals have done.

Economics at first seems less definite. The world of prices, wages, interest rates, stocks and bonds, banks and credit, taxes and expenditure is a complicated one. Every question seems to have two (or more!) sides, and often the right answer seems to be only that of the last man to buttonhole you.

Now no one can understand a complicated subject like chemistry prior to long and careful study. This is an advantage and a disadvantage. The man on the street or behind a newspaper desk cannot possibly consider himself a final authority on these subjects—which is all to the good. On the other hand, the new student of chemistry must be made familiar with all the basic concepts for the first time, all of which takes a good deal of time.

From childhood days on, everyone knows something about economics. This is both helpful and deceptive: helpful, because much knowledge can be taken for granted; deceptive, because it is natural and human to accept uncritically the truth of superficially plausible views. Everyone of college age knows a good deal about money, perhaps even more than he realizes. Thus he rightly laughs at the child who prefers the large nickel to the small dime or the shiny quarter to the paper dollar bill; and at the Basque peasants who murdered the visiting artist for his book of blank checks.

But a little knowledge may be a dangerous thing. On closer examination common sense may prove to be really nonsense. Because a union leader has successfully negotiated several labor contracts, he may feel that he is an expert on the economics of wages. A businessman who has "met a payroll" may feel that his views on price control are final. A banker who can balance his books may conclude that he knows all there is to know about the creation of money. And an economist who has studied the business cycle may be under the illusion that he can outguess the stock market.

Each individual naturally tends to look only at the immediate effects upon himself of an economic event. A worker thrown out of employment in the buggy industry cannot be expected to reflect that new jobs may have been created in the automobile industry. But we must be prepared to do so.

In an introductory survey, the economist is interested in the workings of the economy as a whole rather than in the viewpoint of any one group or unit. Social and national policies rather than individual policy are his goals. Too often, everybody's business is nobody's business. It is just as well, therefore, to understand at the beginning that an elementary course in economics does not pretend to teach one how to run a business or a bank, how to spend one's money wisely, or how to get rich quick from the stock market. However, it is to be hoped that general economics will provide a useful background for many such activities.

Certainly the economist must know a good deal about how businessmen, consumers, and investors behave and think. This does not mean that those individuals must use the same language and methods in coming at their decisions as economists find useful in describing their behavior—any more than the planets need know that they are following the elliptical paths traced by the astronomer. Just as many of us have been speaking prose all our lives without knowing it, so many businessmen would be surprised to learn that their behavior is capable of systematic economic analysis. This unawareness is not necessarily to be deprecated. It does not help a baseball pitcher to know the laws of aerodynamics; in fact, if we become self-conscious about how to button our shirts, we may find it harder to do.

THE TYRANNY OF WORDS

Peculiarly in a field where such an everyday concept as "capital" may have ten or more different meanings, we must watch out for the "tyranny of words." The world is complicated enough without introducing further confusions and ambiguities because (1) two different names are unknowingly being used for the same thing, or because (2) the same one word is being applied to two quite different phenomena. Jones may call Robinson a liar for holding that the cause of depression is oversaving, saying, "Underconsumption is really the cause." Schwartz may enter the argument with the assertion, "You are both wrong. The real trouble is underinvestment." They may continue to argue all night; but really if they stopped to analyze their language, they might find that there were absolutely no differences in their opinions about the real facts and that only a verbal confusion was involved.

Similarly, words may be treacherous because we do not react in a neutral manner to them. Thus a man who approves of a government program to ration housing will call it a program of "sensible planning" while an unsympathetic opponent will describe the same activity as "totalitarian bureaucratic regimentation." Who can object to the former, and who could condone the latter? Yet they refer to the same thing. One does not have to be an expert in semantics—the study of language and its meaning—to realize that scientific discussion requires us to avoid such emotional terminology, wherever possible.

THEORY VERSUS PRACTICE

The economic world is extremely complicated. As we noted, it is usually not possible to make economic observations under controlled experimental conditions characteristic of scientific laboratories. A physiologist who wishes to determine the effects of penicillin on pneumonia may be able to "hold other things equal" by using two test groups who differ only in the fact that they do and do not get penicillin injections. The economist is less fortunately placed. If he wishes to determine the effect of a gasoline tax on fuel consumption, he may be vexed by the fact that, in the same year when the tax was imposed, pipe lines were first introduced. Nevertheless, he must try—if only mentally—to isolate the effects of the tax, with "other things being equal." Otherwise, he will understand the economic effects neither of taxation, nor of transportation improvements, nor of both together.

The difficulty of analyzing causes when controlled experimentation is impossible is well illustrated by the confusion of the savage medicine man who thinks that both witchcraft and a little arsenic are necessary to kill his enemy, or that only after he has put on a green robe in spring will the trees afterward do the same.[1] As a result of this limitation and many others, our quantitative economic knowledge is far from complete. This does not mean that we do not have great amounts of accurate statistical knowledge available. We do. Bales of census data, market information, and financial statistics have been collected by governments, trade associations, and business concerns.

Even if we had more and better data, it would still be necessary—as in every science—to *simplify*, to *abstract* from the infinite mass of detail. No mind can apprehend a bundle of unrelated facts. All analysis involves abstraction. It is always necessary to *idealize*, to omit detail, to set up simple hypotheses and patterns by which the mass of facts are to be related, to set up the right questions before we go out looking at the world as it is. Every theory, whether in the physical or biological or social sciences, distorts reality in that it oversimplifies. But if it is a good theory, what is omitted is greatly outweighed by the beam of illumination and understanding that is thrown over the diverse empirical data.

Properly understood, therefore, theory and observation, deduction and induction cannot be in conflict. And the test of a theory's goodness is its usefulness in illuminating observational reality. Its logical elegance and fine-spun beauty are irrelevant. Consequently, when a student says, "That's all right in theory but not in practice," he really means "That's not all right in theory," or else he is talking nonsense.

[1] In logic this is sometimes called the *post hoc, ergo propter hoc* fallacy (after this, therefore because of this).

BRIEF SUMMARY

Let us sum up what we can all agree on. (1) Economics concerns us all; depressions and inflations hit us where it hurts. (2) Beyond the problem of maintaining a high-level total output, we are all equally concerned that the detailed composition of output shall be in line with what people really want. Efficient work and not leaf raking is what we are after. (3) By its nature, economics is an inexact science in which emotions play an important role and controlled experiments play almost no role. (4) Nonetheless, we must undertake to formulate useful theories; these need not fit all the facts down to the last decimal place; their final worth must be reckoned in terms of the factual insight they give us and not their finespun beauty. Without sound principles or theories we can neither describe the economic system nor prescribe remedies for it.

But now let us go on to describe two special and strange features concerning economic principles: (1) the so-called "fallacy of composition" and (2) the fact that, in a world of great unemployment, the truth may be the reverse of what appears to be the simple truth.

THE WHOLE AND THE PART: THE "FALLACY OF COMPOSITION"

The first lesson in economics is: things are often not what they seem. The following true statements may illustrate this:

1. If all farmers work hard and nature cooperates in producing a bumper crop, total farm income *may fall*.

2. *One* man by great ingenuity in hunting a job or by a willingness to work for less may thereby solve his own unemployment problem; but *all* cannot solve their problems in this way.

3. Higher prices for one industry may benefit its members but, if the prices of everything bought and sold increased in the same proportion, no one would be any better off.

4. It may pay the United States to reduce tariffs charged on goods imported even if other countries refuse to do likewise.

5. It may pay a business firm to take on some business at much *less than full costs*.

6. Attempts of individuals to save more in depression *may lessen the total of* the community's savings.

7. What is prudent behavior for an individual or a single business firm may at times be *folly* for a nation or a state.

Let us emphasize: Each of the above statements is true. But they are paradoxical. In the course of this book, each of the seeming paradoxes will be resolved. Once explained, each is so obvious that you will wonder how anyone could ever have failed to notice it. This again is typical of economics. There are no magic formulas or hidden tricks. Anything that is really correct will seem perfectly reasonable once the argument is carefully developed.

At this point it is just as well to note that many of the above paradoxes hinge upon one single confusion or fallacy, called by logicians the "fallacy of composition." In books on logic, this is defined as follows:

> *A fallacy in which what is true of a part is, on that account alone, alleged to be also true of the whole.*

Very definitely, in the field of economics, it turns out that what seems to be true for each individual is not always true for society as a whole; and conversely, what seems to be true for all may be quite false for any one individual. For everybody to stand on tiptoes to watch a parade does no good, even though a single person may gain a better view in so doing. Countless similar examples could be given in the field of economics. You might amuse yourself by checking over the previous seven examples to see which are probably related to the fallacy of composition. Or better still, try your luck at finding some new examples.

THROUGH THE LOOKING GLASS

There is one very important situation in which any sensible person's beliefs are likely to turn out to be the reverse of the actual economic truth. When is that? It is not during times of high or substantially full employment; it turns out that at such times one's common-sense notions usually are confirmed by the facts. *It is when there is substantial unemployment that things often go exactly into reverse.* We then move into a topsy-turvy wonderland where right seems left and left is right; up seems down; and black, white.

Mathematicians tell us that in addition to ordinary Euclidean geometry there exist non-Euclidean geometries. In these non-Euclidean worlds, two parallel lines may meet—an example is the spherical surface of the earth where two "parallel" lines perpendicular to the equator meet at the pole. What is true of one kind of world may be false of another. Similarly, for a world of unemployment, the conclusions of the old classical or Euclidean economics may have to be carefully reformulated before they become applicable.

This difference between what is true when there is full employment and when there is unemployment may be illustrated by three examples, all of which will be fully explained later and need not be understood at this point:

1. Men mine gold from the bowels of the earth only to have it go back to the

earth in the vaults at Fort Knox, Kentucky. How good or bad is this strange procedure? The answer depends in an important way upon whether or not there is full employment.

2. Nations try in the worst way to raise their standards of living by exporting goods and by *not* importing them from other countries. This anxiety to give away goods would be merely stupid under conditions of full employment, but it does make some sense in a world of unemployment.

3. Thriftiness and parsimony may be individual and social virtues during a war or boom period. During a depression these same individual virtues may be self-defeating social vices that intensify our ills and represent the height of folly. Individual virtues can be restored to being social virtues, provided we are able to restore a healthy environment of adequate aggregate demand for the product of business.

After one has thoroughly mastered the analysis of national income determination, it is not hard to steer one's way with confidence in these seemingly difficult fields. The important hard kernel of truth in the older economics of full employment can then be separated from the chaff of misleading applications. Moreover, as we shall see later, if modern economics does its task well so that unemployment and inflation are substantially banished from democratic societies, then its importance will wither away and the traditional economics (whose concern is *wise* allocation of fully employed resources) will really come into its own—almost for the first time.

A PREVIEW

Here in Part One we deal with the facts, institutions, and analysis necessary to an understanding of national income or output.

In Part Two we analyze the causes of prosperity and depression: how the processes of saving and investment interact to determine the level of monetary purchasing power, income, and employment all over the world and how monetary and fiscal policies can stabilize business activity at a healthy level of progressive growth.

Part Three is concerned with the forces of competition and monopoly which act through supply and demand to help determine the composition of the national income, in terms both of goods and services to be produced and of their prices.

Part Four deals with the distribution of income: of wages, rent, interest, and profits.

Part Five discusses international trade, in both its monetary and real aspects.

Part Six concludes with a brief survey of the alternative economic systems that we face in the world today. We study these, not to belittle our own, but to understand better the workings and merits of our own system and the direction in which its performance can be improved through remedying its defects.

QUESTIONS FOR DISCUSSION

1. If another major depression like that of the 1930's should occur, do you think you would be affected (*a*) very seriously, (*b*) moderately, or (*c*) not at all?

2. Why does the physicist often talk about a frictionless system, when there is no such thing? Is there any justification for this?

3. Discuss the emotional content of the following words: regimentation, planning, usury, monopolist, gambling, speculation, American way of life, free enterprise, cartels, thrift, hoarding.

4. Give an example of the fallacy of composition.

5. Give an example of an economic principle which is valid when there is full employment but misleading when there is unemployment.

6. Could a policy that was deemed bad one month before the outbreak of the war in Korea in June of 1950 be deemed good two months later?

Chapter 2: CENTRAL PROBLEMS

OF EVERY ECONOMIC SOCIETY

AT THE foundations of any community there will always be found a few universal economic conditions. Certain background problems hold as much for our present-day economy as they did in the days of Homer and Caesar. And they will continue to be relevant in the "brave new world" of the years ahead.

In this chapter we shall see what some of these universal conditions are: (A) how every society must meet a triplet of *basic problems of economic organization;* (B) how technological knowledge together with limited amounts of economic resources defines the available choices between goods and services open to a community, and how these *production possibilities* are subject to changing costs and to the law of diminishing returns; (C) finally, the *underlying population or human basis of any economy.*

The above topics form the three parts of this chapter. We leave to Chapter 3 those important special economic features characteristic of our own mixed system of private and public enterprise.

A. *PROBLEMS OF ECONOMIC ORGANIZATION*

Any society, whether it consists of a totally collectivized communistic state, a tribe of South Sea Islanders, a capitalistic industrial nation, a Swiss Family Robinson or Robinson Crusoe—or, one might almost add, a colony of bees—must somehow meet three fundamental economic problems.

1. *What* commodities shall be produced and in what quantities? That is, how much and which of many alternative goods and services shall be produced?

2. *How* shall goods be produced? That is, by whom and with what resources and in what technological manner are they to be produced?

3. *For Whom* are goods to be produced? That is, who is to enjoy and get the benefit of the goods and services provided? Or, to put the same thing in another way: How is the total of national product to be *distributed* among different individuals and families?

These three questions are fundamental and common to all economies.[1] In a primitive civilization, custom may rule every facet of behavior. *What*, *How*, and *For Whom* may be decided by reference to traditional ways of doing things. To members of another culture, the practices followed may seem bizarre and unreasonable; the members of the tribe or clan may themselves be so familiar with existing practices as to be surprised, and perhaps offended, if asked the reason for their behavior. Thus, some tribes consider it desirable not to accumulate wealth but to give it away in the *potlatch*—a roisterous celebration. But this deviation from acquisitive behavior will not surprise anthropologists; from their studies they know that what is correct behavior in one culture is often the greatest crime in another.

In the bee colony, all such problems, even those involving an extraordinarily elaborate cooperative division of labor, are solved automatically by means of so-called "biological instincts."

At the other extreme we can imagine an omnipotent, benevolent or malevolent, dictator who by arbitrary decree and fiat decides just What, How, and For Whom economic activity is to be carried on. Or we might imagine economic organization by decree, but with decrees drawn up by democratic vote, or, what is more likely in view of the multiplicity and complexity of economic decisions, with decrees drawn up by selected legislative or planning authorities.

Finally, as Chapter 3 develops at length, in a so-called "capitalist free enterprise economy," a system of prices, of markets, of profits and losses primarily[2] determines What, How, and For Whom goods and services shall be produced.

BOUNDARIES AND LIMITS TO ECONOMICS

The study of economics can provide part of the material necessary to answer these questions. But many specialists other than economists are also needed to help provide relevant facts and analysis. Thus, psychology (the study of mental behavior), sociology (the study of group behavior), anthropology (the

[1] This viewpoint, with minor adaptations, corresponds to that worked out some years ago by Frank H. Knight of the University of Chicago, a distinguished American economist. See his *Social Economic Organization* (syllabus for second-year course in the social sciences, University of Chicago Press, 1933, 2d ed.).

[2] There never has been a 100 per cent purely automatic enterprise system. Even in our capitalistic system, the government has an important role in modifying the workings of the price system.

study of human races and cultures), and even physiology (the biological study of how organisms function) might cast light on What people want in the way of goods and services: why men sometimes like nourishing food and sometimes do not, why people often seem to find it as necessary to have a shiny automobile as a wife or a baby, and so forth.

Then, too, such noneconomic studies as the physical sciences and engineering are needed to help provide the basis for the second question of How goods are to be produced. It is not the task of the economist to deal with the precise technological laws that determine how certain resource *inputs* are *transformed* into output of goods and services. By a division of labor common to all sciences, he takes much of the technological groundwork for granted—just as he must often take psychological tastes and social institutions for granted. Moreover, even in the technological sphere, his interests are not those of the physicist. The economist may regard a certain process as more efficient than another even though the first law of thermodynamics asserts that no energy can be created or lost in any process whatsoever. And he may choose to disregard the physical fact that one process has a greater ratio of useful work (less useless heat and energy dissipation according to the second law of thermodynamics) than a second, provided the second is using up a cheaper source of energy. We must also guard against the muddled thinking that results from an attempt to reduce all values to ergs or energy units, as retired engineers (*viz.*, the short-lived technocrat movement of the early 1930's) are so often tempted to do.

When we come to the third question of the desirable distribution of wealth and income between individuals, we leave the field of science altogether. *De gustibus non est disputandum:* there is no disputing (scientifically!) tastes; and the same goes for ethics. We must leave the definition of social *ends* to the philosopher, the theologian, the statesman, and to public opinion.

To summarize the results of this section:

Economics cannot try to cover every fact of the universe. It must take certain things for granted as having been established by workers in other scientific fields. The institutional framework of society, the tastes of individuals, the ends for which they strive—all these must be taken as being given. These and more. For the character and quantity of resources and the technological facts about their combinations and productive transformations must also be taken as given.

Economics can, then, pursue the positive task of describing, analyzing, and understanding the processes that take place within the above framework. More than that, economics—and here it becomes "political economy"—can hope to appraise, and improve, the efficiency with which a community mobilizes its *means* to achieve the prescribed *ends*.

Fortunately, there is some underlying agreement with respect to social ends. Most western peoples profess to prefer (1) a measure of individual freedom of choice and action, (2) a high and improving standard of living, (3) an equitable distribution of income between classes so that gross inequalities are to be tolerated only if there is some strong and compelling reason.[1]

THE LAW OF SCARCITY

What to produce, How, and For Whom would not be problems if resources were unlimited: if an infinite amount of every good could be produced, or if human wants were fully satisfied, it would not then matter if too much of any particular good were produced. Nor would it then matter if labor and materials were combined unwisely. Since everyone could have as much as he pleased, it would not matter how goods and income were distributed among different individuals and families. There would then be no *economic goods*, *i.e.*, no goods that are relatively scarce; and there would hardly be any need for a study of economics or "economizing." All goods would be *free goods*, like water or air.

In the world as it is, even little children are supposed to learn in growing up that "both" is not an admissible answer to a choice of "which one." Compared with backward nations or compared with previous centuries, modern industrial societies seem very wealthy indeed. But even the richest of such nations, the United States, would have to be hundreds of times more productive than it now is to give everybody as comfortable a standard of living as is enjoyed by our most fortunate few.

Higher production levels always seem to bring in their train higher consumption standards. People feel that they want and "need" steam heat, indoor plumbing, refrigerators, education, movies, radios and television, books, automobiles, travel, music, fashionable clothes, etc. The biological scientist may tell them that they can be well nourished on a thin porridge for a few cents a day,[2] but that leaves them as cold as the information that the chemicals in their bodies are worth only a couple of dollars. Anyone who has kept a family

---

[1] The careful reader will note that some of these ends may be in partial conflict. Thus, shall a man be free to water milk? Or to exploit "his" patented invention so as to earn more in a year than most men can earn in a century? Freedom and equality may come into partial conflict. In itself "equality of opportunity" is an ambiguous slogan. What does it mean to treat equally people who have different amounts of property and different abilities? Moreover, a lottery or sweepstake provides equality of opportunity but a very bad distribution of income.

[2] Statisticians have shown that the best modern standards of adult nutrition (vitamins A, B, . . . , calories, proteins, etc.) could be bought in 1951 for less than $100 per year! But what a diet this implies: kidneys, lima beans, and not much else.

budget knows that the necessities of life—the absolute musts—have little to do with the minimum physiological needs of food, clothing, and shelter necessary to keep life flickering.

During the Great Depression that followed the stock-market crash of 1929, it was fashionable for popular writers to announce the repeal of the "law of scarcity." They claimed we had moved into a new scientific era in which the economic system knew how to produce more than could be consumed. This was dead wrong. Such observers were perfectly right in pointing out that the system could produce more than we were then consuming. They were right that the problem of *technological unemployment* could not be shrugged off lightly. They were also right in pointing out that "freedom from (physical) want" could be achieved for the more productive parts of the globe if only unemployment could be banished. But they should also have realized what the postwar period has since helped to confirm: Even with all resources working at top efficiency, the average standard of living would be a quite moderate one compared with what we please to call the "American way of life," as revealed, for example, in rosy magazine advertisements. It is shown later that dividing up equally our highest full-employment income among every man, woman, and child would still yield less than an average of $40 per person per week. Releasing atomic energy will still not bring us near to the state of "bliss." You need never fear that no useful work remains to be done. An infinite number of tunes are still to be written. If ever consumption needs should be sated—which is unlikely—there would always remain the alternative of leisure, recreation, and the other elements that go to make up the good life.

B. *THE TECHNOLOGICAL CHOICES OPEN TO ANY SOCIETY*

THE PRODUCTION-POSSIBILITY OR TRANSFORMATION CURVE

We have discussed the basic economic fact that *limitation* of the total resources capable of producing different commodities necessitates a choice between relatively scarce commodities. This can be illustrated quantitatively by simple arithmetic examples and by means of geometrical diagrams. Students have found that diagrams and graphs are important visual aids in many parts of economics. A little care at the beginning in understanding them will be rewarded manyfold later on.

Consider an economy with only so many people, only so much technical knowledge, only so many factories and tools, only so much land, water power, and natural resources. In deciding What shall be produced and How, the economy must really decide just how these resources are to be allocated among the thousands of different possible commodities. How much land should go into wheat cultivation? Or into pasturage? How many factories are to produce hairpins? How much skilled labor should go into machine shops?

These problems are very complicated even to discuss, much less to solve. Therefore, we must simplify. So let us assume that there are to be produced only two economic goods (or classes of economic goods). For dramatic purposes, we can concentrate on the famous pair, guns and butter. These two commodities are commonly used to illustrate the problem of choosing between civilian and war goods. But the same analysis applies to any choice of goods; *e.g.*, the more resources the government uses to build public roads, the less will be left to produce private houses; and the more the public chooses to consume of food, the less it can consume of clothing.

But let us stick to the example of guns and butter. Now, suppose that all resources are thrown into the production of civilian goods, or butter. There will still be at most some maximum amount of butter that can be produced per year. The exact amount depends upon the quantitative and qualitative resources of the economy in question and the technological efficiency with which they are used. Let us suppose that 5 million pounds of butter is this maximum amount which can be produced in the existing state of the technological arts.

At the other extreme, imagine that 100 per cent of society's resources were to be devoted to the production of guns.[1] Only some maximum number of guns could then be produced: 15,000 guns of a certain description can perhaps be produced if we are willing to produce no butter.

TABLE 1. *Alternative Possibilities in the Production of Butter and Guns*

	A	B	C	D	E	F
Butter, millions of pounds............	0	1	2	3	4	5
Guns, thousands....................	15	14	12	9	5	0

These are extreme possibilities. In between there are still others. If we are willing to give up some butter, we can have some guns; if we are willing to give up still more butter, we can have still more guns. A schedule of a number of possibilities is given in Table 1, with *F* being the extreme where all butter

[1] Of course, this could not really happen. Without some civilian production society could not live. But we are considering possibilities—the subjunctive mood not the indicative.

and no guns are produced, and *A* being the opposite extreme where all resources go into guns. In between, at *E*, *D*, *C*, and *B*, butter is increasingly

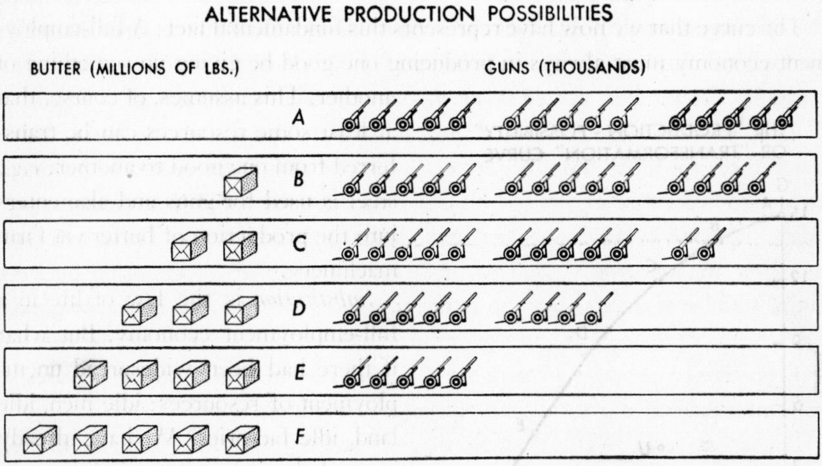

ALTERNATIVE PRODUCTION POSSIBILITIES
BUTTER (MILLIONS OF LBS.)
GUNS (THOUSANDS)
A
B
C
D
E
F

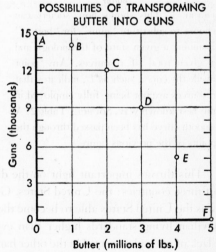

FIGURE 1.

being given up in return for more guns. Butter is "transformed" into guns, not physically but by diverting resources from one use to the other.

Our numerical schedule can also be represented diagrammatically by Figure 1, which should be self-explanatory.

It may be even more illuminating to represent this same production-possibility or production-transformation schedule by measuring butter along the horizontal axis and guns along the vertical, as in Figure 2.

The student should, of course, be able to go directly from the numerical table to the final diagram; by counting over 5 butter units to the right in *F* and going up 0 gun units; in *E*, by counting over 4 butter units to the right and going up 5 gun units; and finally in *A* by going to the right 0 butter units and up 15 gun units.

POSSIBILITIES OF TRANSFORMING BUTTER INTO GUNS
Guns (thousands)
Butter (millions of lbs.)
15
12
9
6
3
0
0
1
2
3
4
5
A
B
C
D
E
F

FIGURE 2. Each point shows the maximum amount of guns obtainable at full employment when different amounts of butter are to be produced.

We may fill in all intermediate positions, even those involving fractions of a million pounds, or of a thousand guns, as in the so-called production-possibility curve shown in Figure 3.

The curve that we now have represents this fundamental fact: A full-employment economy must always in producing one good be giving up something of another. This assumes, of course, that at least some resources can be transferred from one good to another; *e.g.*, steel is used for guns and also enters into the production of butter via farm machinery.

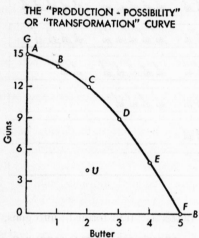

THE "PRODUCTION - POSSIBILITY"
OR "TRANSFORMATION" CURVE

Substitution is the law of life in a full-employment economy. But what if there had been widespread unemployment of resources: idle men, idle land, idle factories? We have already warned that our economic laws may then be quite different. And this is one such instance.

FIGURE 3. This shows how society can choose to substitute "guns" for "butter," assuming a given state of technology and a given total of resources. Any point inside the curve, such as *U*, indicates that resources are not being fully employed in the best known way. SOURCE: Table 2. A smooth curve has been passed through the points of the previous figure.

With unemployment we are not on the transformation or production-possibility curve at all, but somewhere *inside* it; say at *U*, producing only 2 million pounds of butter and 4 thousand guns. If resources are idle, by putting them to work we can have more butter *and* more guns. We can move from *U* to *D* or *E*, thereby getting more butter and more guns.

This throws important light on the different historical wartime experience of three countries: the United States, Germany, and Russia. After 1940, how was the United States able to become the "arsenal of democracy" and to enjoy civilian living standards higher than ever before? Largely by taking up the slack of unemployment. On the other hand, Hitler Germany's war effort began in 1933, long before any formal declaration. It stemmed from a period of unemployment acute enough to win him the votes necessary to get into power peacefully. Almost all the total extra output made possible by taking up unemployed workers and plants was siphoned into German war goods rather than into higher civilian consumption. Still a third case is that of the Soviet Union in World War II. The Russians had little unemployment before the war and were already on their rather low production-possibility curve. They had no choice but to substitute war goods for civilian production—with consequent privation.

Two questions will help to emphasize that the production-possibility curve is drawn up as of (1) fixed totals of resources and (2) given technological knowledge. First, what will happen to the production-possibility curve if a country's population and labor force grows over the years? And second, what will happen to it if scientists and engineers discover better ways of producing guns and butter? It is clear that, in both of these cases, the production-possibility curve will shift outward. More guns and more butter will be possible, as the last few centuries of economic history confirm. (The student should pencil in a new curve on Figure 3 showing the effect of growth in productivity.)

If a third world war were to break out in the near future, the United States would face a quite new problem. Employment is already full; in terms of a normal labor force and work week we are already *on* our production-possibility curve—not inside it. If the war effort required additional billions of dollars of goods and millions of men, civilian living standards would *have* to fall. Civilians would have to do without automobiles and numerous other goods; and note, too, they would have to give up *leisure*, having to work longer hours per week.

INCREASING COSTS

Our production-possibility curve, sloping as it does rightward and downward (*i.e.*, from northwest to southeast), summarizes the fact of substitution and choice between commodities at full employment. But curving out as it does, it depicts a further important economic principle: *As we want more of any good, we must usually pay a higher cost for it; we must give up more and more of other goods.*

Table 1 and Figures 1, 2, and 3 will illustrate this law of increasing cost. A very first unit of butter requires a sacrifice of only one unit of guns. But how much of guns must we sacrifice to get one more unit of butter? A full *two* units of guns! Our numerical table shows that each extra unit of butter becomes more and more expensive in terms of necessary extra sacrifices of guns.

This law of increasing extra cost applies in the case of butter production. Does it also apply in the case of gun production? The bloated, or convex, shape of the curve in Figure 3 shows that the law of extra cost does apply to guns too. It applies perfectly symmetrically to either good. A first extra gun requires the sacrifice of very little butter when we are near the point *F*. But after this we have got to the point where we are producing lots of guns and little butter; this can be seen if one bothers to measure off the distances carefully around the point B or A.

What is the common sense of this law of increasing cost? We must note that the first few guns can be produced in part with the kind of resources that are no good for butter anyway. But if more guns are wanted, we must use resources that are quite valuable for butter production. And if we insist upon having all guns, we must be prepared to take farm land and farmers, which are very efficient in the production of butter, and transform them to the production of guns even though they can produce only very little in this sphere. Thus increasing costs are to be expected.[1]

ECONOMIES OF SCALE: MASS PRODUCTION AND DECREASING COSTS

The above figure and reasoning assume that increasing costs set in from the very beginning. Actually, at first, there will be a countertendency that must be overcome before increasing costs will set in. This is the widely appreciated technological fact that many processes *increase in efficiency as their scale increases*. Among the causes of such "economies of mass production," to which we owe the great productivity of modern industries, are (1) use of nonhuman and nonanimal power sources (water and wind power, steam, electricity, turbines and internal-combustion engines, internal atomic energy); (2) automatic self-adjusting mechanisms (lathes, jigs, servomechanisms); (3) use of standardized, interchangeable parts; (4) breakdown of complex processes into simple repetitive operations; (5) specialization of function and division of labor; and many other technological factors. The automobile-production assembly line or the historical development of modern textile spinning and weaving typify these diverse factors.

Upon thought it will be obvious that each of these economies or savings comes into full play only if a large enough number of units is being produced to make it worth while to set up a fairly elaborate productive organization. If only a few guns are to be produced, they might just as well be produced by hand; but if resources are available to produce many thousands, it will pay to make certain elaborate initial preparations which need not be repeated when still more units are to be produced. Thus, it might come about that, unlike our simplified picture above, we would have to pay two butter units for our first gun unit; but to get still another gun unit we would have to pay only one

---

[1] Even if resources could be divided into two uniform classes, such as homogeneous land and homogeneous labor, increasing costs would still result from the fact that guns and butter do not require the same proportion of these resources, butter taking more land and guns requiring relatively more labor. But such an explanation goes beyond the scope of an introductory work.

butter unit because of the efficiency of mass production. This would be a case of decreasing rather than increasing costs.

Economies of scale are very important in explaining why so many of the goods we buy are produced by large companies. They raise questions to which we shall return again and again in later chapters.

THE FAMOUS LAW OF DIMINISHING RETURNS

Underlying the previous discussion of increasing costs is a well-known technological economic relationship—the so-called "law of diminishing returns." The validity of this law is twice blessed: by the theorists who think they have proved it deductively on a priori grounds, and by the empiricists who regard it as a universally observed technological fact!

The law of diminishing returns refers to the amount of extra *output* obtained when we add to a fixed input more and more of some one input, or class of inputs. Thus, suppose food is produced by the cooperation of two resources: labor and land. If we add 1 man-year of labor to 100 acres of land, we may get a number of thousands of bushels of corn at harvest time. But if, on the same plot of land, we add still another man-year of labor, we shall probably get *not quite so many extra* bushels of corn. Adding a third man-year of labor to the same land will result in a still smaller increase in production.

Table 2 provides an arithmetical illustration of the law of diminishing returns.

TABLE 2. *Showing How Returns in Terms of Output Diminish When Successive Units of Labor Are Added to 100 Acres of Land*

No. of man-years of labor	Amount of product, bu.	Extra output added by additional unit of labor
0	0	2,000
1	2,000	1,000
2	3,000	500
3	3,500	*
4	3,800	100
5	3,900	

* To be filled in by reader.

Why have diminishing returns set in? Primarily because when more workers are added, each has less and less acres of land to work with. The fixed factor of production, land, has decreased in proportion to the variable input, labor. If we crowd the land even further, we may by intensive cultivation of the soil still get some extra corn; but the amount of extra corn will become less and less. We may summarize the law of diminishing returns as follows:

> *An increase in some inputs relative to other comparatively fixed inputs will cause output to increase; but after a point[1] the extra output resulting from the same additions of input will become less and less; this falling off of extra returns is a consequence of the fact that the new "doses" of the varying resources have to work with less and less of the constant resources.*

C. THE UNDERLYING POPULATION BASIS OF ANY ECONOMY: PAST AND FUTURE POPULATION TRENDS

THE MALTHUS THEORY OF POPULATION

There is an important and interesting application of this law in the field of population. Around 1800, Thomas Robert Malthus, a young English clergyman, used to argue at breakfast against his father's view that "every day in every way, the human race is getting better and better." Finally the younger Malthus became so agitated that he wrote a book about it. His famous *Essay on the Principle of Population* (1st ed., 1798) was an instantaneous best seller. It went through several editions and for a century influenced the thinking of people all over the world (including Charles Darwin, the expositor of the famous doctrine of biological evolution). It is still a living influence today. Malthus' views depend directly on the law of diminishing returns, and they continue to have relevance.

Malthus first took the observation of Benjamin Franklin that, in the American colonies where resources were abundant, population tended to double every 25 years or so. Malthus postulated, therefore, *a universal tendency for population—unless checked by food supply—to grow at a geometric progression.* Now anyone who lets his imagination roam knows how rapidly geometric progressions grow— how soon 1, 2, 4, 8, 16, 32, 64, 128, 256, 512, 1,024, . . . , becomes so large that there is not space in the world for all the resulting offspring to stand.[2]

---

[1] At first the countertendency of increasing mass-production efficiencies may outweigh the tendency toward diminishing returns. But ultimately diminishing returns will win out.

[2] At 6 per cent compound interest, money doubles in value every 12 years. It has been

To all this Malthus, Sr., said only, "So what?" Consequently, at this point Malthus in effect unleased the devil of the law of diminishing returns. As population doubles and redoubles, it is exactly as if the globe were halving in size until finally it has shrunk so much that food and subsistence fall below that necessary for life. Because of the law of diminishing returns, food tends *not* to keep up with the geometric progression rate of growth of population.

Mind you, Malthus did not say that population *would* increase at these rates. *Exploit* This was only its *tendency* if unchecked. He considered it an important part of his argument to demonstrate: In all countries in all times, checks were operating to hold population in. In the first edition of his work he put emphasis on *positive* checks that operate to increase the death rate: pestilence, famine, war, etc. Later he relented from this gloomy doctrine to hold out hope for the human race through *preventive* checks operating on the birth rate. Although the birth-control movement is often called Neo-Malthusianism, Malthus, himself an early nineteenth-century clergyman, advocated only *moral restraint* with prudential postponement of early marriages until a family could be supported. In fact, to him the struggle for existence was an illustration of the wisdom of · the Creator, and we can picture him discussing over a hearty breakfast with his own daughter how diminishing returns keep poor people from getting soft and lazy and how great are the advantages of "virtuous celibacy."

This important application of diminishing returns illustrates what profound effects a simple theory can have. Malthus' ideas had widespread repercussions. His book was used to support a stern revision of the English poor laws, whereby destitution was considered a result of laziness and unemployment a state to be made as uncomfortable as possible. Also he bolstered the argument that a trade-union could not improve the welfare of workers, since any increase in their wages would only cause them to reproduce until there was again barely enough to go around.

Despite the tons of statistics in later editions covering many countries, it is today recognized that his views were oversimplifications. In his discussion of diminishing returns, he never fully anticipated the miracles of the Industrial Revolution. In the next century technological innovation *shifted* production-possibility curves *outward* and made possible better standards of living for more people. At the same time medical advances were prolonging human life and further lessening the positive checks to population. Nor did he realize that after 1870 in most Western nations, including the United States, family *fertility*

---

estimated that the $24 received by the Indians for the island of Manhattan would, if deposited at compound interest, be today worth at least as much as all real property on the island. At 6 per cent, Sir Francis Drake's plunder of Spanish gold would have grown to equal Britain's modern wealth.

as measured by actual number of children would begin to fall far short of family *fecundity*, or biological reproductive capacity.

Nevertheless, the germs of truth in his doctrines are important still for understanding the population behavior of India, China, and other parts of the globe where the balance of numbers and food supply is a vital factor.

TABLE 3. *Estimated Population of the World and Its Distribution*

Sections of the world	Population, millions		
	1800	1939	1947
Europe (including all of U.S.S.R.).................	188	542	579
North, South, and Central America................	29	273	310
Asia, Africa, and Oceania.......................	702	1,265	1,441
World.......................................	919	2,080	2,330

SOURCES: Figures for 1800 and 1939, W. S. Thompson, *Plenty of People*, (Cattell and Company, Incorporated, Lancaster, Pa., 1944). Figures for 1947, United Nations, *World Population Trends 1920–1947*, December, 1949.

Table 3 shows how the population of the world has more than doubled since 1800, while the population of the New World has increased tenfold. This increase was made possible mainly through the declining death rate resulting from scientific advances in medicine and from the improved living standards made possible by the Industrial Revolution. Life expectancy has increased from 18 years in 1800 to about 68 years at present,[1] and standards of living far exceed those of any previous century. Moreover, the parts of the world where population is held in by food supply are shown in the table to have been of declining percentage importance. But will the Malthus devil of overpopulation stay chained? In India alone, one of the fruits of modern science has been a great increase in average life expectancy. In the 20 years from 1921 to 1941, India's population grew by about 83 million, an amount equal to the combined populations of France and England! What if modern medicine were to keep people free of disease only to let them face starvation?

DO AMERICA AND EUROPE FACE DEPOPULATION?

At the end of World War I men still feared the Malthusian curse of overpopulation. They wrote books with such alarming titles as *The World Faces Over-population* and *Standing Room Only!* But just as these books were coming

[1] LOTKA, DUBLIN, and SPIEGELMAN, *Length of Life* (Ronald, New York, 1949).

off the presses, Western Europe and the United States were undergoing a profound revolution in population.

Only a generation later was this beginning to be understood. The pendulum then swung to the other extreme; the best sellers carried such flashy titles as *The Twilight of Parenthood* and *England without People*.

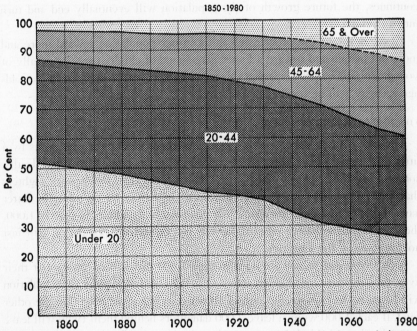

PROPORTION OF POPULATION IN EACH AGE
DISTRIBUTION OF TOTAL POPULATION
1850-1980

FIGURE 4. This shows clearly the decreasing proportion of children in the population and the present-day swollen numbers of adults. It also indicates the growing importance of older people. SOURCE: *The Problems of a Changing Population* (National Resources Committee, 1938). Events since 1938 suggest that this understates both the aged and the very young.

How can we account for this sudden change of tune? Have births fallen below deaths in modern England, France, Sweden, Germany, or the United States? The records show they have not. Why then were the experts afraid, before World War II, that a decline in population was just around the corner?

The answer is not hard to find. Since 1870—even earlier in France—birth rates began to drop in most countries of Western European civilization. After World War I, and especially after the Great Depression of the 1930's, the drop became precipitous. But curiously enough, the alarming nature of the crisis in births was hidden for a time.

Why did a comparison of births and deaths give a misleading feeling of security. Crude births and deaths were misleading because they ignored the fact that the United States and Western Europe *temporarily* have had an unusually large number of women in the childbearing groups. This is because our grandparents had larger families than we are now having. With so many women of the age to be a mother, births may now be considerable; and yet the number of births per mother may be low—so low that, if the same rate continues, the future growth of the population will eventually end and turn into a decline.

Figure 4 shows the progressive shifts in our population toward more and more old people and toward a lower percentage of children and eventually of young adults. The problems that this trend will create for the financing of old-age security will be touched upon later.

THE NET REPRODUCTION RATE

The true state of affairs as to population trends can be revealed to us by a little arithmetical trick. Instead of concentrating on crude births and deaths, someone got the bright idea of asking, "What is the total number of daughters that will have been born to 1,000 newborn girl babies by the time the latter have all completed their life spans?" If this total of daughters is exactly 1,000, then we say that the *net reproduction rate* is 1.0, and the population will just hold its own in the long run.

If only 900 girl babies are born to each 1,000 girl babies throughout their lives, then the net reproduction rate is only 0.9—and ultimately the population will begin to decrease at the rate of 10 per cent per generation. On the other hand, if each 1,000 women leave 2,000 daughters behind them (who will leave 4,000 daughters behind them, etc.), then the net reproduction rate is equal to 2.0 and the population will ultimately grow at a rate of 100 per cent increase per generation. (A "generation" is about 30 years, the average age of a mother.)

The computation of the net reproduction rate for a given group is not too difficult if the necessary statistical data are available. From past mortality data collected by insurance companies, we know what fraction of the original 1,000 women are likely still to be alive at the ages of 15, 20, 25, . . . , and 50 years. From data on the number of likely births to women of each of these ages—data that this country has often neglected to collect—we are able to calculate just how many babies our group of women will have throughout their entire lives. A little less than half of these will be girls, and this number of girls divided by 1,000 is the net reproduction rate.[1]

---

[1] The net reproduction rate can increase only if the birth rate per woman of each age rises or if fewer women die in infancy and prior to the completion of the childbearing ages. Keep-

The population crisis of our age may be summarized in the statement that before World War II the net reproduction rate dropped far below unity in England, France, Germany, Sweden, and many other countries. The United States was balanced just under unity. South America, Eastern Europe, and Russia continue to have very high net reproduction rates. India and the Orient tend to have high fertility rates, but so few girls survive to adulthood and through the years of childbearing that until recently their net reproduction rate did not greatly exceed unity.

OUR AMAZING POPULATION UPSURGE

Before World War II there was every good reason for the population expert to despair for the future of the population of Western nations. Moreover, the problem did not appear to be directly economic. Everyone knows that the rich seem to have fewer children than the poor. Before the war, Harvard and Vassar students were not reproducing themselves. Neither were Michigan State and Oberlin students or high-school graduates or urban groups generally.[1]

But then something remarkable happened to jar the expert. Nobody yet knows quite how to explain it. During and after World War II the pattern of fertility began steadily to climb, reaching new heights. Some of the reasons are, of course, obvious. With the war came prosperity, and with prosperity the backlog of depression-deferred marriages began to melt. Also the Selective Service Act had something to do with the increase in marriages. With many more recent marriages, it was only natural to expect the birth rate to leap upward. Moreover, prosperity and the war seem to have stepped up the rate at which newly married couples have children.

For a long time, the population expert tended to pooh-pooh the new trend. He kept insisting that the increases in births represented only a flash in the pan. He argued that most of these births represented either the backlog of the depression or a borrowing against the future: Instead of having their

---

ing older people alive or having the *same* number of babies at an earlier age will increase the population in the short run, but it cannot alone raise the NRR above 1 and check an ultimate declining trend in population.

[1] Most authorities believe that the decline is to be explained by social rather than biological factors. Thus, the French Canadians, who have high birth rates, came from just those rural regions of France with the lowest rates. Second-generation Italian and Jewish city dwellers show greatly reduced rates, as do Negroes who move from the South to the North. Some of the highest net reproduction rates are among the white people in the Southern hillbilly regions of the Appalachian Plateau. Ironically, the highest rates of all are to be found among —of all peoples—the American Indians, suggesting that we may yet give the country back to the Indians.

children in the 1930's or 1950's, people were having them in 1946. For a long time, too, it looked as if the increases in births were primarily increases in first and second children. The expert argued that the net reproduction rate could be lifted above unity only if married couples averaged more than two or three children during their years of childbearing.

But finally the expert had to admit that at least temporarily there was an important break in the falling trend of the net reproductive rate. All over the Western world, in the neutral as well as the warring countries, there was this same increase in fertility. Part could be explained by full employment and marriages. But to explain the increased fertility of marriages, one had to explore deeper psychological factors such as fear of death in battle and a desire to achieve a kind of personal immortality by leaving behind offspring. In the face of a world grown more dangerous, people's attitudes and values seemed to turn inward toward the home. Moreover, man is a very imitative animal. Once it began to be fashionable for a middle-class family to have numerous children, many began to do the same. A glance at any college faculty—young, old, and middle-aged—will show the changing trends in this regard. Still other factors are important, such as accumulated wartime savings, unavailability of automobiles during the war, lessened fear of childbirth now that its pains and dangers have diminished, government encouragement, and family allowances.

As a result of the new trend, many countries of Western Europe whose net reproductive rates were far below unity are now hovering around the critical level of unity. The United States, temporarily at least, has a net reproductive rate that is considerably in excess of unity.[1] Table 4 shows some interesting contrasts in net reproductive rates.

Will the present American trend continue? This nobody knows. It depends upon whether the number of *un*married adults continues to remain at the present low levels, never before reached in the modern history of any country. It depends upon whether the typical married couple thinks that a boy and a girl are enough or aspire toward having several children.

The economic impact of population changes is already very noticeable. The emptiness of rooms in junior and senior high schools contrasts with the tremendous overcrowding in the lower grades. The slump in movie attendances is directly related to the number of families who must find a baby-sitter before they can go out; the demand for television sets is also vitally affected, but in the opposite direction. The future size of the labor force and its percentage

---

[1] The present fashion among experts is to recognize the volatility of net reproductive rates. They prefer to analyze the trends in the ages at which people get married and the trends in the patterns of fertility of marriages of different ages. The 1949 report of the British Royal Commission on Population reflects this change of approach.

importance in comparison with the aged will be critically affected by the future trends in births.

TABLE 4. *Net Reproduction Rates for Various Countries*

Country	Year	NRR
U.S. (total)	1930–1940	0.98
U.S. (total)	1945	1.14*
U.S. (total)	1946	1.36
U.S. (white)	1945	1.11*
U.S. (nonwhite)	1945	1.38*
France	1935–1937	0.87
France	1941	0.77
France	1944	0.94
Germany	1933	0.70
Germany	1936	0.93
Sweden	1933–1934	0.73
Sweden	1945	1.15
United Kingdom	1934–1936	0.76†
United Kingdom	1948	1.07*
U.S.S.R.	1926	1.72†
U.S.S.R.	1938	1.54†
Japan	1930	1.57
Japan	1937	1.44*

* Provisional.
† Approximate.
SOURCE: *Population Index*, April, 1950, Office of Population Research, Princeton University, and Population Association of America, Princeton, N.J.

From the military manpower viewpoint, time seems to be working against the countries of Western Europe and North America. Table 5 shows estimates of future populations for certain countries. Note the high estimate for the Soviet Union, where net reproduction rates have a long way to fall until they reach unity; and note the remarkably pessimistic figures for France and England.[1]

[1] The interested reader may consult the following books: T. R. Malthus, *Essay on the*

TABLE 5. *Estimated Future Population of Different Countries in 1970 (All data in millions)*

Country	1940	1970
United States................	132	175
England and Wales	41	37
France.....................	41	37
Soviet Union................	174	251
Sweden.....................	6.3	5.8
Italy.......................	44	49
Europe and U.S.S.R...........	572	668

SOURCE: All data except those for the United States taken from Frank W. Notestein, *The Future Population of Europe and the Soviet Union: Population Projections 1940–1970*, League of Nations, 1944. United States estimate made by the author with the help of Joseph S. Davis, *The Population Upsurge in the United States* (Food Research Institute, Stanford, 1949).

SUMMARY

A. PROBLEMS OF ECONOMIC ORGANIZATION

1. Every economy must somehow solve the three fundamental economic problems: What and how much shall be produced of all possible goods and services; How shall economic resources be used in producing these goods; For Whom shall the goods be produced; *i.e.*, what is the distribution of income among different individuals and classes.

2. Different societies meet these problems in different ways—by custom, instinct, fiat and decree, and in our own system partially through a price and market system. Other subjects than economics are involved in each of these questions: psychology and sociology, science and engineering, ethics, and even theology.

3. The basic problems are important because of the fundamental fact of all economic life: with limited resources and technology, standards of living are limited. Economic goods are scarce rather than free; society must choose between them because not all needs and desires can be fulfilled.

Principle of Population, 1798; R. R. Kuczynski, *The Balance of Births and Deaths*, (Macmillan, New York, 1928), Vol. 1, a short readable explanation of the causes of the future underpopulation crisis: W. S. Thompson, *Plenty of People*, (Cattell and Company, Incorporated, Lancaster, Pa., 1944), a recent popular survey.

B. TECHNOLOGICAL CHOICES OPEN TO SOCIETY

4. With given resources and technology, the production choices open to a nation between two such goods as butter and guns can be summarized in the production-possibility curve or schedule. This indicates how butter can be transformed into guns by transferring resources from butter to gun production.

5. Usually there will be increasing costs (in terms of sacrificing one good) of getting more of another good; but at first, economies of scale may reverse this tendency.

6. The law of diminishing returns asserts that, after a point, as we add more and more of a variable input (like labor) to a fixed input (like capital), the amount of extra product will fall off. This law is really just a matter of proportions—the varying input has less and less of the fixed input to work with.

C. UNDERLYING POPULATION BASIS OF ANY ECONOMY

7. The Malthus theory of population rests on the law of diminishing returns. He thought that a population—if unchecked!—would tend to grow in geometric rate, doubling every generation or so. However, each member of the growing population would have less resources to work with. Therefore, because of diminishing returns, income would have a tendency to fall so low as to lead to starvation and pestilence.

8. For a century and a half after Malthus, populations grew by leaps and bounds everywhere. But so successful were the improvements of technology and in medicine that improved death rates are responsible for most of the increase.

9. Since 1870, birth rates have begun to fall. Today, western European nations and the United States are at a population crisis: unless social habits cause net reproduction rates to stay firm at 1.0 or more, each of these countries faces ultimate population decrease in the near or distant future.

QUESTIONS FOR DISCUSSION

1. Without looking at the next chapter, can you anticipate how our price system through supply and demand solves the three problems of economic organization?

2. Attack or defend the social creed: "From each according to his ability. To each according to his need." What is your philosophy on the third question of For Whom?

3. Instead of choosing between war goods and peace goods, society may choose between *consumption* goods and capital goods. Draw a hypothetical production-possibility or transformation curve indicating this choice.

4. What would happen to society's production-possibility curve if all services (population, land, etc.) increased in amount? What would happen to it if scientific inventions increased the productivity of given resources? What if these improvements were only in butter production and not in guns?

5. If land were increased in a number of steps and labor were held constant, would the law of diminishing returns hold? Illustrate and tell why.

6. How many were there in your grandparents' family? In your parents' family? How many do you think there will be in your own family?

7. "Population pressure doesn't cause war as is commonly believed. Careful study suggests that cause and effect are just the reverse. Nations which want to expand try to persuade their citizens to grow in numbers so that the nation will be militarily strong and will have a pretext for expansion. Examples are Italy, Germany, and Japan." Discuss.

Chapter 3: FUNCTIONING OF A "MIXED" CAPITALISTIC ENTERPRISE SYSTEM

A MIXED ENTERPRISE SYSTEM

Most of our attention will be devoted to the special features of economic life found in twentieth-century industrial nations (with the exception of Soviet Russia). In most of these countries, there was a trend in the past few centuries toward less and less direct governmental control of economic activity: gradually feudal and preindustrial conditions were replaced by greater emphasis on what is loosely called "free private enterprise" or "competitive capitalism." Long before this trend had approached a condition of *laissez faire* (*i.e.*, of complete governmental noninterference with business), the tide began to turn the other way.

Since some time in the nineteenth century, in almost all the countries under consideration there has been a steady increase in the economic functions of government. We must leave to historians the task of delineating the important factors underlying this significant and all-pervasive development. Suffice it to say here that ours is a mixed free-enterprise economic system in which both public and private institutions exercise economic control.

The first part of this chapter shows how our mixed system tackles the three problems of economic organization that must be answered by all societies. The last section of this chapter deals with some fundamental characteristics of the present economic order.

A. HOW A FREE ENTERPRISE SYSTEM SOLVES THE BASIC ECONOMIC PROBLEMS

In a system of free private enterprise no individual or organization is consciously concerned with Chapter 2's triad of economic problems: What, How, and For Whom. This is really remarkable. To paraphrase a famous economic example, consider the city of New York. Without a constant flow of goods in and out of the city, it would be on the verge of starvation within a week. More than a variety of the right kinds and amounts of food is involved; from the surrounding hinterland, from 48 states, and from the far corners of the world, goods have been traveling for days and months with New York City as their destination.

How is it that 8 million people are able to sleep easily at night without living in mortal terror of a breakdown in the elaborate economic processes upon which the city's existence depends? For all this is undertaken without coercion or centralized direction by any conscious body!

Everyone notices how much the government does to control economic activity—tariff legislation, pure-food laws, utility and railroad regulations, minimum-wage regulations, fair-labor-practice acts, social security, price ceilings and floors, public works, national defense, national and local taxation, police protection and judicial redress, zoning ordinances, municipal water or gas works, etc. What goes unnoted is how much of economic life goes on without direct government intervention. Hundreds of thousands of commodities are produced by millions of people more or less at their own volition without central direction or master plan.

NOT CHAOS BUT ECONOMIC ORDER

This alone is convincing proof that a competitive system of markets and prices—whatever else it may be, however imperfectly it may function—is not a system of chaos and anarchy. There is in it a certain order and orderliness. It works. It functions. Without intelligence it solves one of the most complex problems imaginable, involving thousands of unknown variables and relations. Nobody designed it. Like Topsy, it just growed; and like human nature, it is changing; but at least it meets the first test of any social organization—it is able to survive.

A dramatic example of the importance of a pricing system is postwar

Western Germany. In 1946–1947 production and consumption had dropped away to almost nothing. Neither wartime bombing damage nor postwar reparation payments could account for this breakdown. The paralysis of the price mechanism was clearly to blame: Money was worthless; factories closed down for lack of materials; trains could not run for lack of coal; coal could not be mined because miners were hungry; miners were hungry because peasants would not sell food for money and no industrial goods were available to give them. Prices were legally fixed, but little could be bought at such prices; a black market characterized by barter or fantastically high prices existed. Then in 1948 a "miracle" happened. A thoroughgoing currency reform set the price mechanism back into effective operation. Almost immediately production and consumption soared; again the What, How, and For Whom were being resolved by markets and prices.

The fact to emphasize is that such so-called miracles are going on all around us all the time—if only we look around and open our eyes to the everyday functioning of the market. A revolutionist out to destroy the capitalistic system could ask nothing better than a great inflation or deflation that would paralyze the price mechanism.

THE INVISIBLE HAND

Students of economics must avoid the error of thinking that a price mechanism has to work chaotically if it is not controlled by somebody. Having learned this lesson, they must not go to the other extreme and become enamored of the beauty of a pricing mechanism, regarding it as perfection itself, the essence of providential harmony and beyond the touch of human hands.

Adam Smith, the canny Scot whose *Wealth of Nations* (1776) represents the beginning book of modern economics or political economy, was thrilled by the recognition of an order in the economic system. Smith proclaimed the principle of the "invisible hand"; each individual in pursuing only his own selfish good was led, as if by an invisible hand, to achieve the best good of all, so that any interference with free competition by government was almost certain to be injurious. But Smith recognized its realistic limitations.

Actually much of the praise of perfect competition is beside the point. As has been discussed earlier, ours is a mixed system of government and private enterprise; as will be discussed later, it is also a mixed system of monopoly and competition. It is neither black nor white, but gray and polka-dotted.

A cynic might say of perfect competition what Bernard Shaw once said of Christianity: The only trouble with it is that it has never been tried. Historians quarrel over whether there ever was a golden age of free competition, and certainly competition is not now perfect in the economist's sense; perhaps it is becoming less so every day, because of the fundamental nature of large-scale production and technology, consumers' tastes, and business organization. But this does not mean that we must accept as inevitable the trend toward big business, mergers, trusts, and cartels that began to swell in the 1890's. The challenge is to work out laws and customs which help to improve the working of our less than perfect competitive system.

THE PRICE SYSTEM

Just how does the unconscious automatic price mechanism operate? The bare outlines of a competitive profit-and-loss system are simple to describe. *Everything has a price*—each commodity and each service. Even the different kinds of human labor have prices, usually called "wage rates."

Everybody receives money for what he sells and uses this money to buy what he wishes. If more is wanted of any one good, say shoes, a flood of new orders will be given for it. This will cause its price to rise and more to be produced. Similarly, if more is available of a good like tea than people want, its price will be marked down as a result of competition. At the lower price people will drink more tea, and producers will no longer produce so much. Thus equilibrium of supply and demand will be restored.

What is true of the markets for consumers' goods is also true of markets for *factors of production* such as labor, land, and capital goods. If welders rather than glass blowers are needed, job opportunities will be more favorable in the former field. The price of welders, their hourly wage, will tend to rise while that of glass blowers will tend to fall. Other things being equal, this will cause a shift into the desired occupation. Likewise an acre of Puerto Rican bottom land will go into sugar cultivation if the sugar producers bid the most for its use. In the same way, machine-tool production will be determined by supply and demand.

In other words, we have a vast system of trial and error, of successive approximation to an equilibrium system of prices and production. We shall see later that the matching of supply and demand and price and costs helps to solve our three problems simultaneously. The bare outlines of the process can be briefly sketched.

1. What things will be produced is determined by the votes of consumers—not every 2 years at the polls but every day in their decisions to purchase this item and not that. Of course, the money that they pay into business cash registers ultimately provides the payrolls, rents, and dividends that consumers receive in weekly income. Thus the circle is a complete one.

2. How things are produced is determined by the competition of different producers. The method that is cheapest at any one time, because of

both physical efficiency and cost efficiency, will displace a more costly method. The only way for producers to meet price competition and maximize profits is to keep costs at a minimum by adopting the most efficient methods. For example, synthetic rubber will be made from petroleum rather than from grain alcohol if the price of the one is in a certain relation to the price of the other, or electric power will be generated by steam rather than water power if the price of coal is below some critical level. The large, tractor-operated farm will displace the family-size farm if this leads to lower costs of production.

3. For Whom things are produced is determined by supply and demand in the markets for productive services: by wage rates, land rents, interest, and profits, all of which go to make up everybody's income—relative to everyone else and relative to the whole. The character of the resulting distribution of income is highly dependent upon the initial distribution of property ownership and acquired or inherited abilities.

A competitive system is impersonal but not completely so. The consuming families face business enterprises on two fronts, with only prices in between. One front is the widely dispersed one, the retail market on which consumers buy thousands of small items from a score of different retail establishments: grocery, drug, and department stores; movie theaters; gasoline stations; and electric-power companies, government post offices, landlords, railroad lines, and insurance companies.

On the other front—the market for labor and other productive services— relations are not always so peaceful. To the family breadwinner his wage is not simply another price. It is the difference between luxury and comfort, between comfort and privation. The laborer feels inferior to the large corporation in bargaining power, and he may turn to collective bargaining by means of trade-unions. By doing this he may at times be helping to restore competition, while at other times he may be causing conditions to deviate still further from competition.

The above picture of competition tending toward lowest costs is a highly oversimplified one. Even if the system worked perfectly as described above— which everybody knows to be far from the case—many would not consider it ideal. In the first place, goods go where there are the most votes or dollars. A rich man's dog may receive the milk that a poor child needs to avoid rickets. Why? Because supply and demand are working badly? No. Because they are doing what they are designed to do, putting goods in the hands of those who can pay the most, who have the most money votes.

Or, to take another example, suppose the invention of automatic machines should cause the competitive price of labor to fall and thereby reduce incomes of the poor. Is there anything necessarily right in that? And should the fact that a man inherited 500 square miles of range land, for which oil companies offer a million dollars per year, necessarily justify so large an income? Whether incomes should be completely determined by a competitive struggle—the survival of the survivors—is an ethical question that goes beyond the mechanics of economics.

IMPERFECTIONS OF COMPETITION

As we said earlier, an equally serious drawback to the picture of the price system as described above is the fact that, in the real world, competition is nowhere near perfect. Firms do not know when consumer tastes will change; therefore, they may overproduce in one field and underproduce in another. By the time they are ready to learn from experience, the situation has again changed. Also, in a competitive system many producers simply do not know the methods of other producers and costs do not fall to a minimum. One can sometimes succeed in the competitive struggle as much by keeping knowledge scarce as by keeping production high.

An even more serious deviation from perfect competition results from *monopoly elements.* These—as we shall see more fully later on—may result in wrong pricing, incorrect and wasteful resource allocation, and monopoly profits. We shall also see later how strict is the economist's definition of a "perfect competitor"; the mere presence of a few rivals is not enough for perfect competition. But the economic definition of an "imperfect competitor" is this: *anyone who buys or sells a good in large enough quantities to be able to affect the price of that good.* To some degree that means almost every businessman, except possibly the millions of farmers who individually produce a negligible fraction of the total crop. All economic life is a blend of competitive and monopoly elements. Imperfect, or monopolistic, competition is the prevailing mode, not perfect competition.

Of course, as we shall later see, a businessman cannot set his prices completely as he pleases and still make profits. He must take into account the prices of goods that are substitutes for his own. Even if he produces a trademarked coal with unique properties, he must reckon with the prices charged for other coals, for oil and gas, and for house insulation. But he is not compelled to keep his price from rising above the prevailing market price for fear of selling nothing.

Businessmen, farmers, and workers both like and dislike competition. Anyone likes it when it enables him to expand his market, but he may be the first to label it as "chiseling," "unfair," or "ruinous" when the knife cuts the other way. The worker whose livelihood depends on how the market prices his labor may likewise be the first to howl when competition threatens to depress wages. Farm groups, aware of what competition can do to agricultural prices, have brought pressure to bear on the government to restrict production and thereby raise prices.

Some of the basic factors responsible for bigness in business may be inherent in the economies of large-scale production. This is especially true in a dynamic world of technological change. Atomistic competition by numerous producers would simply not be efficient in many fields and could not last. Trade-marks, patents, and advertising are often responsible for still other market imperfections. It would be humanly impossible, therefore, to attempt to create *perfect* competition by law. The problem is one of achieving reasonably effective "workable competition."

We shall return in Part Three to a more microscopic examination of supply and demand. After that discussion we shall be in a position to appraise the workings of the price system more judiciously. We have seen enough already to avoid the errors of both extremes. A competitive price system is one way of organizing an economy, but it is not the only way. Still it is of interest that some socialists plan to continue to use a price mechanism as one part of their new society. It is not perfect, but neither are its alternatives.

ECONOMIC ROLE OF GOVERNMENT

It was said earlier that ours is not a pure price economy but a mixed system in which elements of government control are intermingled with market elements in organizing production and consumption. The economic role of government is so important now that Chapters 7 and 8 are devoted to it.

The broad outlines of its influence can be briefly indicated here. Democratic countries are not satisfied with the answers to the three questions, What, How, and For Whom given by a perfectly unrestrained market system. Such a system might dictate that certain people starve from lack of income and that others receive inadequate or excessive incomes. Therefore the government steps in with its own expenditure to supplement the real or money incomes of some individuals; *e.g.*, it may provide hospital beds for its citizens or may present the more needy of them with monthly allowances in times of unemployment or old age. Minimum standards of life are widespread as goals of government in this century.

More than this, government provides certain indispensable *collective* services without which community life would not be thinkable, and which by their nature cannot appropriately be left to private enterprises. Included in these are the maintenance of national defense, of internal law and order, and the administration of justice. By and large in its expenditure of money, it is behaving exactly like any other large spender. By casting sufficient votes in the form of dollar bids in certain directions, it causes resources to flow there. The price system works much as if these were individual rather than collective needs.

If governments financed all their expenditure by printing paper money or by endless borrowing, that would be almost the whole story. Actually most government expenditure is paid for out of taxes collected. It is here that an important element of *coercion* enters in. It is true that the citizenry as a whole imposes the tax burden upon itself; also each citizen is sharing in the collective benefits of government. But there is not the same close connection between benefits and tax payments as holds when the individual citizen puts a nickel into a gum machine or makes an ordinary purchase. I need not smoke Luckies or buy Nylon stockings if I do not wish to, but I must pay my annual taxes whether or not I choose to.

Moreover, a second important form of coercion is involved in the universal custom of passing governmental laws: thou shalt not smoke opium, thou shalt not sell false weight, thou shalt not employ child labor, thou shalt not set a house on fire, thou shalt not charge more than the ceiling price for food, and so forth. This set of rules provides the framework within which private enterprise functions; it also modifies the direction of that functioning. Together with government expenditure and taxation, the decrees of government are hardly less important than the price system itself in determining the economic fate of the nation. It would be fruitless to try to decide whether public enterprise or private enterprise is the more important—as fruitless as to debate heredity versus environment. Without either our economic world would be an entirely different one.

Finally, as we shall see in Part Two, it is part of the government's function to alleviate one of the most important causes of acute and chronic cycles in unemployment or inflation. Especially in wealthy communities like our own, individuals as a whole may try to save much more or much less than the private enterprise can profitably or usefully invest in new real capital goods. Defense and war may require more output than civilians will voluntarily give up. We shall see that this will result in inflation or deflation and a distortion of the economy's long-run rate of progress. Clearly the government must try to use its constitutional fiscal and monetary powers to enable private enterprise to maintain a steady level of high employment and rising productivity.

B. THE CAPITALISTIC CHARACTER OF MODERN SOCIETY

There are three further important features of modern economic society:

1. Modern advanced industrial technology rests upon the use of vast amounts of capital: elaborate machine equipment, large-scale factories and plants, stores and stocks of finished and unfinished materials. Our economy receives the name "capitalism" because this capital, or "wealth," is primarily the private property of somebody—the capitalist.

2. The present-day economic system is characterized by an almost incredibly elaborate degree of *specialization* and intricate *division of labor*.

3. Finally, ours is a system that makes extensive use of *money*. The flow of money is the lifeblood of our system. It also provides the measuring rod of values.

All these features are interrelated—with each other and with the price mechanism previously described. Thus we shall see that, without the great facility for trade and exchange which money provides, an elaborate division of labor would be impossible. Money and capital become related through the credit activities of the banking system and through the organized capital markets upon which securities can be transformed into money by sale or vice versa. And of course the relationship between the price mechanism and money is immediate and obvious.

CAPITAL AND TIME

First, let us survey the important economic role of capital. If men had to work with their hands on barren soil, productivity and consumption would be very low indeed. But gradually over time our economic system has been able to amass a tremendous stock of instruments of production, of factories and housing, of goods in process.

Men learned very early that the simple, direct methods of production can be improved upon by using time-consuming indirect methods. We who are inside the economic system are not conscious of how roundabout modern productive processes are. An outside observer would be struck with the fact that almost no one in our system is producing *finished* goods. Almost everyone is doing work of a preparatory nature, with final consumption a distant future goal. The farmer spends his time in fattening hogs, the truck driver in carrying them toward market, the packer in advancing them further toward the last stage of consumption. A steel worker prepares pig iron, part of which will become a hammer to build a house; another bit will become part of a pig-iron furnace, which in turn will prepare pig iron to be used in making further hammers and more pig-iron furnaces, and so forth.

And so the economic process goes—around and around like air inside the pipes of a French horn, or like the egg-chicken-egg-chicken-egg sequence of biological evolution.

Each person is unconscious of the roundabout character of production: all he has to do is to perform his own job and not worry himself as to where his output will ultimately go or whence come the raw materials to which his activity has added value. Once all the circular paths had become established and activity became synchronized, even an outside observer of the system might not notice its complexity. In such a steady state each day would look like the previous one, and it would appear that the work of each day was producing the output of that same day.

But this is an optical illusion. Time was required to get the process going in the first place. Human and nonhuman resources had to be put to work for a long time before any output came out from each new process. It is as if one had to blow into a huge French horn for some time to get the air pressure up before the note could be sounded. Gradually a steady state is reached when one is pumping air constantly in and receiving out a constant tone. Finally, if one stopped pumping air in, one would not incur the penalty of losing the note for some time. So in the economic world, we can stop replacing capital and begin to loaf for a while and still can hope to leave output undiminished for a spell while "milking capital."

The fact that it takes time to get things started and synchronized is important. It explains why society does not automatically replace all direct processes by more productive indirect ones; and all indirect processes by still more indirect processes. The advantage in doing so is balanced by the initial disadvantage of having *to forego present consumption goods* by directing resources from current production to uses that will bear fruit only after some time.

To the extent that people are willing to save—to abstain from present consumption and wait for future consumption—to that extent society can devote resources to new capital formation.[1] And to the extent that people are irresponsible as to the future, they may at any time try to "dissave"—to snatch present pleasures at the expense of the future. How? By diverting resources away from the endless task of replacing and maintaining capital and to the job

---

[1] We shall later see that, *sometimes* in our modern monetary economy, the more people try to save, the less capital goods are produced and, paradoxically, the more people spend on consumption, the greater the incentive for businessmen to build new factories and equipment.

of producing extra present-day consumption goods. There is an old Chinese proverb: "He who cannot see beyond the dawn will have much good wine to drink at noon, much green wine to cure his headache at dusk, and only rain water to drink for the rest of his days."

We may summarize as follows: The bulk of all economic activity is directed toward the future. By the same token, the bulk of current economic consumption is the consequence of past efforts. *It is the primary role of current productive efforts to produce for the future, so as to repay the past for present consumption.* Also, in progressive societies some fraction of current productive efforts is devoted to the new or net capital formation, in which current consumption is sacrificed to increase future production.

FIXED AND CIRCULATING CAPITAL

Even the cave man used some capital in the form of primitive hunting axes; his cave dwelling, too, was also a form of capital and wealth, whether he dug it out himself or whether he had acquired possession of it by discovery and conquest. These two items of capital are precursors of factory productive equipment and residential housing. Both would come under the heading of what is called "fixed capital."

When primitive man reached the stage of domesticating animals and cultivating the growth of plants, a new form of capital came into existence: goods in process or so-called "circulating capital." A grain of wheat in the spring is the progenitor of a cup of wheat in the fall and of a loaf of bread in the following winter; a litter of squealing pigs represents to the knowing eye a bundle of pork chops, hams, salt pork, and lard.

The names "fixed and circulating capital" are not very aptly chosen. Certainly fixity in space is not their distinguishing criterion: A locomotive represents fixed capital and a crop in the field represents circulating capital. The exact differentiation in borderline cases requires rather fine-spun and arbitrary distinction. An apple tree is treated as fixed capital, a stalk of corn as circulating capital; a milch cow is treated as fixed capital while a beef steer is treated as circulating capital. The distinction lies in the fact that the apple tree, like the cow and the locomotive, gives up its economic services *over a long period of time* while the cornstalk or the steer or the raw cotton in a textile mill gives up its economic services *all at once or in a short time.* Usually in giving up its services, the circulating capital changes its form; on the other hand, the fixed capital appears to keep its form.

However, to a careful observer it is obvious that the fixed capital too—the cow and locomotive—are really depreciating and getting nearer to the day when their economically useful life is over.

Just how long is a "long time"? How short is a "short time"? Obviously, one could split hairs indefinitely on such a problem. The modern financial community, very rightly, has no patience with such trifles. As we shall see, modern accountants simply apply a rough rule of thumb: Any asset that is to be liquidated within a year is considered as part of "current assets" and "working capital"; any that requires more than a year is part of fixed capital assets.

CAPITAL AND INCOME

Capital is essentially something in existence at a moment of time. It would be revealed, so to speak, by an instantaneous flash photograph or still picture of the economy at some instant of time. Its various components—machines, houses, warehouse inventories—could be listed on a balance sheet as of a given time, say December 31, 1955.

Income, on the other hand, is by its nature a flow over time: a flow of dollars received per week or year, a flow of goods produced per day or month, a flow of satisfaction enjoyed over time. A motion-picture camera would be necessary to register its amount.

Capital and income are dimensionally incommensurable. The rent income of a piece of land cannot be said to be greater or less than its capital value, any more than the length of a ship can be said to be greater than its speed. A ship $\frac{1}{4}$ mile long has a speed of $\frac{1}{2}$ mile per minute, 30 miles per hour, $\frac{1}{120}$ mile per second. How can we compare length and speed, since one is measured in distance and the other in terms of distance per unit time?

Similarly, an acre of land that yields a rent income of $5,000 per year or $50,000 per decade or $416.67 per month may have a capital value of $100,000. Can we conclude from this that its capital value must exceed its rate of flow of income? No. We must not forget that its income is equivalent to a rate of $500,000 per century. It all depends on our time units.[1] Under no circumstances can one add capital value, which has the dimension of dollars, to income flow which has the dimensions of *dollars per unit time*.

But the market place does relate capital and income. The factor that enables the market to do so is the *interest rate*. Thus a permanent source of income of $5,000 per year, from a corner lot or perhaps from a goose that never grows too old to lay golden eggs, can be bought at any one time for a fixed capital sum—say $100,000. This is called the "capitalized value" or "present discounted value" of such a "permanent income."

---

[1] It would only confuse the issue to point out that income would not remain constant over a century or that rents are usually paid by the month and not by the year. These are as irrelevant as the reply of Little Audrey, who when arrested for driving 75 miles an hour "just laughed and laughed, because she knew she had only been riding for 15 minutes."

To see why the interest rate is important in turning permanent income flows into capital values, ask the following question: Suppose I lend my money out at the ruling market rate of interest—say 5 per cent. Then $100,000 of principal will get me an annual income of $5,000 (= 5 per cent of $100,000). And in addition at the end of the year I will get my principal back, to be lent out again at interest.

How much then can I afford to pay for a piece of land that will always earn $5,000 per year over and above all expenses? At 5 per cent interest, the land must be worth exactly $100,000. If its price were more than $100,000, no one would buy it. The market interest rate of 5 per cent means that lending $100,000 will bring in an income of $5,000 yearly. Why pay more than that for an asset yielding only the same return? And no landowner would offer his property for less than $100,000, since everyone would jump at it, instead of lending his money at 5 per cent interest. Hence, under ideal conditions the equilibrium price of the land will have to be exactly $100,000.

The last two paragraphs show that the interest rate—expressed as a percentage per year—is the magic factor that relates permanent *income* flows and present capital value. When we lend our money out, arithmetic tells us

Permanent annual income = 5 per cent of capital value

or if the interest rate is 3, 4, 6, or i per cent per annum, we can always say

$$\text{Permanent annual income} = \frac{i}{100} \times \text{capital value}$$

But suppose we know the interest rate (per annum) and the permanent annual income. How do we use the above formula to find the unknown capitalized value of this future income stream? We must turn our formula around and say that capital value of a permanent income stream is *inversely proportional* to the interest rate, or

$$\text{Present capital value} = \frac{\text{permanent annual income}}{i/100}$$

Thus, if the interest rate is 5 per cent, I will pay for each $1 of permanent income exactly $1 ÷ $\frac{5}{100}$ = $20. Often this is described as follows: At 5 per cent interest, things will sell for "20 years' purchase"; at 4 per cent, they will sell for 25 years' purchase; at 10 per cent for 10 years' purchase; by definition, the number of years' purchase goes up as the interest rate goes down, being the reciprocal of the interest percentage or $1 ÷ \frac{i}{100}$.

The interest rate is peculiar; it enables you to have your principal and live on it too. If you wait long enough your principal will have brought you in an indefinitely large number of income dollars. If interest permits a principal to do this, then it must follow that you will not pay 1 million dollars for a piece of land just because it will pay you $1 a year in each of the next million years. Dollars in hand are worth more than dollars in the future. Why? Because dollars in hand will earn interest and can accumulate at compound interest. It follows that future dollars must always be "discounted." The amount by which we discount future dollars to arrive at their present-day value will depend on the interest rate: The higher the interest rate, the more we must discount future dollars. This explains why capital value depends *inversely* on the interest rate.

In Chapter 29 on Interest and Capital, all this will be explained at greater length. An important qualification is needed here. Most assets—such as a bond or truck or annuity—give rise to dollar receipts for only a finite amount of time, rather than permanently. Our simple formula for capital value cannot be applied to them; instead we must use bond tables. Thus, when the interest rate is cut in half, the price of a bond will go up some; but the bond will not fully double in value because it is not of perpetual duration.[1]

INTEREST AND THE REAL NET PRODUCTIVITY OF CAPITAL

Lying behind the dollar relationships of capital and interest, there are certain fundamental real relationships. Capital goods contribute toward the production of a flow of current goods and services. Not only have capital goods the productivity just described; in addition they must have over their lifetime a greater cumulative productivity than the resources that went to produce them, or they will not be replaced when worn out. In other words, capital goods have a real net productivity (over and above replacement costs)—and we shall see later that this net productivity, when expressed as a percentage, constitutes the real aspect of the rate of interest.

When we increase the quantity of all capital goods relative to fixed land or labor, the law of diminishing returns will set in. The interest rate or net productivity of capital may decline from 10 to 5, to 1 per cent, until either capital stops growing or some technological improvement comes along and raises capital's interest yield.

If a nation is to enjoy a high standard of living, it needs—in addition to manpower, natural resources, and know-how—a large quantity of the best capital equipment. Our own industrial society is very fortunate in this respect. So

---

[1] Whether an asset is perpetual or not, the general formula for its present value is shown in Chapter 29 to be the sum of all its future net dollar receipts *after* each such receipt has been discounted by means of the interest rate. In the special case of a permanent income stream, the above especially simple relations hold true.

efficient are our tools at producing new tools that we are likely to forget the plight of backward nations. They cannot get their heads above water because their production is so low that they can spare nothing for capital formation by which their standard of living could be raised.

The scarcity of capital among primitive communities is well illustrated by a story of a famous anthropologist. While traveling through a village, he noted the deep air of mourning and despondency. Upon inquiring as to whether a death had occurred, he received the reply, "Death, what is that? We have lost the needle!"

CAPITAL AND PRIVATE PROPERTY

Physical capital goods are important in any economy because they help to increase productivity. This is as true of Soviet communism as it is of our own system. But there is one important difference. By and large, private individuals own the tools of production in our capitalistic system.

What is the exception in our system—government ownership of the means of production—is the rule in a socialized state where productive property is collectively owned. The returns from such real capital goods accrue to the government and not to individuals directly. The government then decides how such income is to be distributed among individuals. The communist government also decides how rapidly resources are to be invested in new capital formation: by how much *present* consumption should be curtailed in order to add to the total of factories, equipment, and productive stocks of goods that are necessary if *future* output is to rise.

In our system individual capitalists earn interest, dividends, and profits, or rents and royalties on the capital goods that they supply. Every patch of land and every bit of equipment has a deed or "title of ownership" that belongs to somebody directly—or if it belongs to a corporation, then indirectly it belongs to the individual stockholders who own the corporation. Moreover, each kind of capital good has a money market value. Hence each claim or title to ownership of a capital good also has a market value. A share of common stock of General Electric is quoted at some certain price, a New York Central bond at another price, a mortgage on a house is valued at some amount, the deed to a house and lot is appraised by the real-estate market at some given level, etc.

Clearly, in taking a census of the nation's total capital, we must avoid fallacious double counting. Nobody could be so foolish as to declare that his total capital was $20,000 if he owned a $10,000 house on Main Street and also had under his mattress a $10,000 deed to that house. Nor would three brothers who owned a small corporation manufacturing electric toasters ever be under the illusion that the million dollars of stock of the company could be *added* to the million dollars' worth of capital goods (factory, machines, wire, etc.) held by the corporation.

These cases are too simple to give rise to confusion and need not be discussed further at this point. It is enough to point out that the everyday term "capital" has many different meanings. It may refer to a capital good; it may refer to a bond, stock, security or deed, or any document that represents a claim to an income-producing capital good. Often in everyday parlance, it is thought of as a sum of money. We say, "Jones is in need of $100,000 of capital which he hopes to raise from the bank." Actually, of course, when Jones borrows that sum from the bank, he will not continue to hold it in the form of a liquid cash asset. He will convert his assets into tangible capital assets, such as tools, or into intangible capital assets, such as an important patent.

It should be pointed out that the government does own a good deal of the national real capital; e.g., Hoover Dam. In addition, its agencies, such as the RFC (Reconstruction Finance Corporation) and the Defense Plant Corporation are important sources of capital loans for private business.

Also the legal property rights of an individual are relative and limited. Society determines how much of his property a man may bequeath to his heirs and how much must go in inheritance and estate taxes to the public treasury. Society determines how much the owners of public-utility companies—such as electric-light and gas companies—can earn and how they shall run their business.

Even a man's home is not his castle. He must obey zoning laws and, if necessary, make way for a railroad or slum-clearance project. Interestingly enough, most of society's economic income cannot be capitalized into private property. Since slavery was abolished, human earning power is forbidden by law to be capitalized. A man is not free to sell even himself.

C. *EXCHANGE, DIVISION OF LABOR, AND MONEY*

We turn now to the second of the three characteristic features of the present-day economy. The economies of mass production upon which modern standards of living are based would not be possible if production still took place in self-sufficient farm households or self-sufficient provinces. *Specialization* of function permits each person and each region to use to best advantage any peculiar differences in skill and resources. Even in a primitive economy men learn that, rather than have everyone do everything in a mediocre way, it is better to institute a *division of labor:* for fat men to do the fishing, lean men to do the hunting, and smart men to make the medicine.

Besides resting upon any interpersonal differences in ability, specialization accentuates and creates differences. Hunting makes a man thin and good at stalking prey; a region that has no resources especially adapted to hat making may nevertheless develop skills and know-how which give it advantages in this trade.

Finally, even with no natural or acquired differences in skills, specialization will sometimes pay: Often in this way alone can a large enough volume of activity be reached to realize all the economies of large-scale production mentioned in the preceding chapter.[1] Two identical Indian twins might find it better for one to make all bows and the other all arrows—even if they had to draw lots to see which would make which—because only in this way could each be making enough of each item to warrant introducing improved techniques.

The classical example illustrating the increased productivity of specialization is provided by the making of pins. One man could at best make a few dozen imperfect pins per day. But when a small group of men are subdivided with respect to function so that each performs simple repetitive operations, they can turn out hundreds of thousands of perfect pins in the same period of time.[2] Moreover, the simplification of function made possible by specialization

[1] In his famous work Adam Smith recognized that specialization and division of labor were limited by the extent of the market, *i.e.*, by the volume that can be sold.

[2] The following passage describing the extent of specialization in meat slaughtering has often been quoted: "It would be difficult to find another industry where division of labor has been so ingeniously and microscopically worked out. The animal has been surveyed and laid off like a map; and the men have been classified in over thirty specialties and twenty rates of pay, from 16 cents to 50 cents an hour. The 50-cent man is restricted to using the knife on the most delicate parts of the hide (floorman) or to using the ax in splitting the backbone (splitter); and, wherever a less skilled man can be slipped in at 18 cents, 18½ cents, 20 cents, 21 cents, 22½ cents, 24 cents, and so on, a place is made for him, and an occupation mapped out. In working on the hide alone there are nine positions, at eight different rates of pay. A 20-cent man pulls off the tail, a 22½-cent man pounds off another part where good leather is not found, and the knife of the 40-cent man cuts a different texture and has a different 'feel' from that of the 50-cent man. Skill has become specialized to fit the anatomy. . . .

"The division of labor grew with the industry, following the introduction of the refrigerator car and the marketing of dressed beef, in the decade of the seventies. Before the market was widened by these revolutionizing inventions, the killing gangs were small, since only the local demands were supplied. But when the number of cattle to be killed each day increased to a thousand or more, an increasing gang or crew of men was put together; and the best men were kept at the most exacting work." From J. R. COMMONS, *Quarterly Journal of Economics*, vol. XIX, 1904, pp. 3, 6.

lends itself to mechanization and the use of labor-saving capital. At the same time it avoids the wasteful duplication of tools that would be necessary if every man had to be a Jack-of-all-trades, and it also saves time lost in going from one job to another. The modern conveyer system of automobile assembly illustrates the efficiency of specialization. In the years ahead, we may see an advance in the art of automatic self-controlling electronic servomechanisms that may revolutionize modern industry.

Clearly, however, specialization and division of labor involve one serious problem—that of *interdependence*. A single-celled low form of life such as the amoeba or paramecium is not particularly efficient, but it can live alone and like it. In higher animals such as man, every cell will die if once the heart cells fail. When all goes well, the extreme specialization of cells is very efficient, but at the cost of extreme interdependence.

In modern economic society this process is carried to the nth degree. No one man makes the smallest fraction of the commodities that he consumes. In medieval times the artisan made one article and exchanged it for many others. Today a worker produces not even a single good; he may make only shoe tongues or simply turn bolt 999 on the Chevrolet assembly line. Such may be his whole life work. For performing this he will receive an income adequate to buy goods from all over the world, but hidden costs are involved. Specialization may breed half men—anemic clerks and brutish truck drivers.

Also, specialization involves complete mutual dependence. A bank in Austria fails, and the natives in Fiji, who carry water in empty Standard Oil cans and clothe their infants in Pillsbury flour bags, lose their livelihood—yes, and may even starve. In the backwash of a war a breakdown in transportation and the economic fabric of exchange reveals how perilously modern economic life depends upon exchange. Would we, if we could, turn the clock back to a simpler and poorer life? Or can we keep the advantages of division of labor and find policies that will prevent breakdown?

BARTER VERSUS THE USE OF MONEY

Without the use of money our present division of labor would be impossible. But we could imagine a state of *barter*, where one kind of merchandise is traded directly for another. In primitive cultures it is not uncommon for food to be traded for weapons or aid in the building of a house exchanged for aid in clearing a field. Even in the most advanced industrial economies, if we strip down exchange to its barest essentials, peeling off the obscuring layer of money, we find that trade between individuals or nations really boils down to barter—transforming one good into another by exchange rather than by physical production.

Barter represents a great improvement over a state of affairs in which every man had to be a Jack-of-all-trades and master of none, and a great debt of gratitude is owed to the first two ape men who suddenly perceived that each could be made better off by giving up some of one good in exchange for some of another. Nevertheless, simple barter operates under such great disadvantages that a highly elaborate division of labor would be unthinkable without the introduction of a second great improvement—the use of money.

In all but the most primitive cultures men do not trade one good against another but instead sell one good for money and then use money to buy the goods they wish. At first glance this seems to complicate rather than simplify matters, to replace a single transaction by two transactions. Thus, if I have apples and want nuts, would it not be simpler to trade one for the other rather than to sell the apples for money and then use the money to buy nuts?

Actually the reverse is the case. The two transactions are simpler than one. Ordinarily there are always people ready to buy apples and always some willing to sell—at a price—nuts. But it would be an unusual coincidence to find a person with tastes just opposite to my own, with an eager desire to sell nuts and buy apples. Such a coincidence would be as unlikely as the chance of picking two winning horses in a row. Even if the unusual should happen—as occasionally it must—there is no guarantee that the desires of the two parties with respect to the exact quantities and terms of the exchange would coincide.

To use a classical economic phrase: Instead of there being a double coincidence of wants, there is likely to be a want of coincidence; so that, unless a hungry tailor happens to find a farmer who has both food and a desire for a pair of pants, neither can make a trade.

COMMODITY MONEY, PAPER MONEY, AND BANK MONEY

If we were to reconstruct history along hypothetical, logical lines, we would naturally follow the age of barter by the age of commodity money. Historically a great variety of commodities have served at one time or another as a medium of exchange: cattle (from which comes the Latin stem of "pecuniary" and also the words "capital" and "chattel"), tobacco, leather and hides, furs, olive oil, beer or spirits, slaves or wives, copper, iron, gold, silver, rings, diamonds, wampum beads or shells, huge rocks and landmarks, and cigarette butts.

Each of the above has some advantages and disadvantages. Cattle are not divisible into small change; but while it is being hoarded such money is likely to increase by reproduction, giving the lie to the doctrine of Aristotle that "money is barren." Wives and beer do not improve with keeping, although wine may. Olive oil provides a nice liquid currency which is as minutely divisible as one wishes. Iron will rust and is of so little value that one would need a cart instead of a pocketbook. The value of a diamond is not proportional to weight but varies with its square; therefore, if cut up into pieces it loses value. The yearly additions to (by mining) or subtractions from (by use in teeth or jewelry) the world's accumulated stock of precious metals is small in percentage terms; so that the total amounts and value of these substances do not fluctuate wildly. Silver has luster but will tarnish in air. Gold keeps its attractive sheen, but unless mixed with an alloy is very soft. Gold's high specific gravity makes detection of counterfeiting and admixture easy; but through most of historical time, gold's scarcity value has been so great per ounce as to require inordinately minute coins for small purchases.

Most kinds of money tended once to be of some value or use for their own sake. Thus, even wampum had decorative uses, and paper money began as warehouse or mint receipts for so much metal. But the intrinsic usefulness of the money medium is the least important thing about it.

The age of commodity money gives way to the age of paper money. The essence of money, its intrinsic nature, is typified by paper currency. *Money, as money rather than a commodity, is wanted not for its own sake but for the things it will buy!* We do not wish to use money up directly; but rather to use it by getting rid of it; even when we choose to use it by holding it, its value comes from the fact that we can spend it later on.

Money is an artificial, social convention. If for any reason a given substance begins to be used as money, all people will begin to value it even if they happen to be teetotalers or vegetarians or disbelievers in its intrinsic usefulness. As long as things can be bought and sold for a given substance, people will be content to sell and buy with it. Paradoxically, money is accepted because it is accepted!

The use of paper currency (dollar bills, fives, tens, etc.) has become widespread because it has many conveniences as a medium of exchange. Currency is easily carried and stored away. By the printing of more or fewer zeros on the face value of the bill a great or small amount of value can be embodied in a light, transportable medium of little bulk. By the use of decimal points it can be made as divisible as we wish. By careful engraving, the value of the money can be made easily recognizable and can be protected from counterfeiting and adulteration. The fact that private individuals cannot create it at will in unlimited amounts keeps it scarce, *i.e.*, an economic rather than a free good.

Given this limitation in supply, modern currencies have value—*i.e.*, can buy things—independently of any gold, silver, or governmental backing. The public neither knows nor cares—and needs not know or care—whether its currency is in the form of so-called "silver certificates," federal reserve notes, or in copper, silver, or nickel coin. So long as each form of money can be converted into any other form at fixed terms, the best is as good as the worst.[1]

Along with the age of paper money there is finally also the age of bank money, or bank checking deposits. Today at least nine-tenths of all transactions, by value if not number, take place by checks. An executive will have his salary paid directly into his bank account, after income and social security taxes have already been withheld at the source by his employer. His rent or dentist bills will be paid by check, which his wife may not even give him the privilege of signing. Except then for a little petty cash for lunches, tobacco, and carfare, he may hardly handle any hard cash at all in the course of a year's time.

PRICE RATIOS AND MONEY PRICES

In every transaction, whether for barter or money, each person gives something up and receives something in exchange. If 5 apples are traded for 25 nuts, the price of apples in terms of nuts is 25 to 5 or, briefly, 5 to 1; the price of nuts in terms of apples is 5 to 25 or 1 to 5, or $\frac{1}{5}$, or in terms of decimals 0.2. Similarly, if 5 apples sell for 25 cents, then the price of apples in terms of money is 5 cents. It would be equally true, but not very customary or familiar, to say that a penny costs $\frac{1}{5}$ or 0.2 of an apple.

Every price is really a price ratio involving a numerator and a denominator. Each depends upon the way in which the two quantities are measured; thus, eggs are quoted at 5 cents apiece, 60 cents a dozen, or $7.20 a gross; likewise we may say that eggs sell for $\frac{1}{20}$ dollar, "get-away automobiles" for $1\frac{1}{2}$ "G's," and haircuts for "6 bits."

If we relied completely on barter, we should have to keep in mind a great number of price ratios—as many as the number of pairs that could be formed mathematically from the number of commodities. Thus, for only 5 different goods there would be 10 different price ratios to remember, just as there are 10 different tennis matches which must be played in a round robin of 5 different individuals. For 1,000 commodities, there would be almost 500,000 price ratios to remember.[2]

A little reflection will convince us that many of these price ratios are unnecessary, being deducible from a much smaller number. For example, if the price of apples in terms of nuts is 5 and the price of oranges in terms of nuts is

[1] A century ago it was the exception rather than the rule for bank notes and coins to exchange for each other at par. Each had different prices which varied from day to day so that it was necessary for storekeepers to keep daily lists of values; and it became a profession in itself to change money, buying and selling it at a profit.

[2] By elementary algebra, the number of pairs that can be selected from n different objects is no less than $n(n-1)/2$, or about $\frac{1}{2}n^2$ all together.

10, then it is not necessary for us to be told what the price of oranges is in terms of apples. Because 10 nuts is twice 5 nuts, we know already that 2 apples must be paid for 1 orange.

By use of the elementary axiom that things equal to the same thing are equal to each other, the reader can convince himself that, once he knows the price ratios of all goods in terms of any *one* good, he can easily get the price ratio between *any two goods* by division. For 5 commodities we need only remember 4 price ratios, not 10; the other 6 price ratios are redundant, being deducible from these 4. For 1,000 commodities, only 999 price ratios are needed, not 500,000.[1]

MONEY AS A MEDIUM OF EXCHANGE OR AS A UNIT OF ACCOUNT

There are two distinct functions of money: as a medium of exchange and as a standard unit of value. This distinction is illustrated by a perfect clearing system, where careful record of all transactions is kept and where finally what each person has coming to him is canceled against what he owes, with the balance credited to his account. In such a system no medium of exchange whatever is needed! But a common denominator of value, telling us how to compare and weigh such diverse items as a stick of gum and an automobile, would certainly still be necessary. Actually an African tribe once existed which used as its unit of money the so-called "macute." This was not a shell or commodity; it had no corporeal existence as a medium of exchange but represented simply a standard unit of value or money of *account*. Until recently the Paraguayan unit of money was based upon a long-obsolete, extinct Argentine coin.

Similarly, fashionable London shops quote prices in terms of "guineas" even though that coin no longer exists. I buy a 1-guinea hat by actually paying 21 shillings; it is fashionable to pretend that guineas still exist. Americans can thank Franklin and Jefferson that the decimal system was adopted for our

---

[1] This is only one illustration of a general principle applying to all price ratios. When we come to examine the exchange rate at which the moneys of different countries can be converted into each other, we find the same principle applies. If 4 dollars make 1 British pound sterling and $1/50$ of a dollar equals 1 Italian lira, then the number of lira in a pound is perfectly determinate (equal to $4 \div 1/50$ or 200). When the Allied military authorities first took over Italy in World War II, they overlooked this fundamental economic truth and set three independent rates. The result was what one might expect: by using currency *A* one could buy currency *B* which could then be exchanged for an amount of currency *C*—an amount that would buy more than the initial amount of *A*. This is just what happened. *Arbitragers* (*i.e.*, people who speculate on a sure thing) went round and round the circuit making a profit at each whirl. Of course, the military authorities suffered a corresponding loss. Finally they noticed what was happening and did what they should have done in the first place—set the third price ratio in proper relation to the other two.

money. Imagine doing arithmetic problems with heterogeneous English small coins such as the farthing, penny, shilling, half crown, etc. This is almost but not quite so bad as having to do long division with Roman rather than Arabic numerals.[1]

In earliest schooling, we are taught never to add apples to oranges or to combine dimensionally heterogeneous quantities. In economics it is the function of money prices to make all values commensurable. We cannot add apples to oranges. But if we multiply the number of apples by their price per apple, we get a dollar quantity. If we do the corresponding thing with respect to oranges and their price, we again get a dollar magnitude. And of course two dollar magnitudes can be added together. Aesthetically bread and flowers may be incommensurable, but from an economic standpoint money reduces them to comparability.

MONEY AND TIME

The two essential functions of money—(1) as a *medium of exchange* and (2) as a standard *unit of account* or common denominator of values—are both tied up with the passage of time.

First, there is always a time interval between receiving and spending money. Normally this is not more than a week or month. To hold any substantial amount of money idle for longer than a few months means you are earning no interest return. If there were any securities or bonds that were sure to pay a positive interest rate, no sensible man would long continue to use money as a store of value. Again and again we shall return to this important question in later chapters.

But whether the period be a day or a decade, it is clear that money must be held for some period of time. And what if prices should generally rise or fall during that time?

Also the use of money will always play an important role in serving as a *standard unit of reckoning* between financial transactions over time. When a man borrows $10,000 for 5 years, he is, of course, getting present money and agreeing to pay back future money. But suppose all prices have doubled in the meantime; or, what is another way of saying the same thing, suppose the value of money has halved? Is it not unfair that the lender should receive much less in real purchasing power than he has given to the borrower?

Obviously, when prices are very unstable over time, when there is extreme

---

[1] Of course, any system of reckoning which a child has been taught seems easiest to him, and it is natural for people to think their own methods best. But the real test is whether it would be easier for us to learn their system than for them to learn ours. The decimal system is an obvious winner in such a contest.

inflation or deflation, money serves very badly as a "standard of deferred payment" (over time). Inflation favors debtors at the expense of creditors; in deflation, when prices fall, debtors are hurt and creditors are benefited—if they can collect!

This completes the discussion of the way in which money performs its two essential functions between points in time. In Part Two, we shall examine in detail the monetary and credit operations of banks and the government to see how they bear on fluctuations in prices and production.

SUMMARY

Even though it deals with facts subconsciously familiar to every person, this is one of the most difficult chapters in the whole field of economics. We are too near our own system to appreciate how it works.

A. PRICING AND MIXED ENTERPRISE

1. In our mixed private enterprise system, the price mechanism, working through supply and demand in competitive markets, operates to answer the three fundamental problems of economic organization. The system is not perfect, but it works to solve the What, How, and For Whom.

2. The dollar votes of people affect prices of goods; these prices serve as guides on the amounts of the different goods to be produced. Whenever the price of a good exceeds its cost of production, a businessman can make a profit by expanding production of that good. Under competition, the businessman must find the cheapest method of production, using labor, land, and other factors that are relatively cheap and economizing on the use of relatively expensive factors. Otherwise he will make losses and be eliminated.

At the same time that the What and How problems are being resolved by prices, so is the problem of For Whom. The distribution of income is determined by competitive bidding up or down of prices of the factors of production—wages of each kind of labor, of each kind of land, royalties of books, etc. Anyone lucky enough to own much fertile well-located land or possess widely admired crooning ability will be supplied with many dollar votes for his use in the markets for consumer goods. Anyone without property and with skills that the market cares little about will receive a very low annual income.

3. Our system is mixed in at least two senses: Government action modifies private initiative, and monopolistic elements condition the working of perfect competition.

B. CAPITAL

4. Capital goods—such as machinery, housing, and inventories of goods in process—add tremendously to a nation's output. Roundabout, time-consuming methods take time to get started; hence, to add to the stock of capital goods requires a temporary sacrifice of present consumption goods.

5. The flow of income and the stock of capital are not dimensionally comparable. The interest rate, expressed as a percentage per annum, is the factor that relates capital and income. The *present discounted value* of any permanent income stream equals *annual income* $\div i/100$, where i is the percentage of interest per annum. (Nonpermanent incomes are evaluated by more complicated formulas, but the fundamental principle that dollars far off must be discounted by use of the interest rate always holds.)

6. Under a system of capitalism, capital goods are owned as private property and the incomes they produce belong to their owners. Under communism, ownership of capital goods is by the State.

C. DIVISION OF LABOR AND MONEY

7. Specialization and extreme division of labor characterize modern economies, thereby increasing productivity, but at the cost of accentuating interdependence.

8. Without exchange, division of labor could not be highly developed. Simple barter is quite inefficient and tends to be superseded by the use of money. Commodity money in its turn has become superseded by paper money. Unlike other economic goods, money is valued because of social convention, and people value it indirectly for what it will buy rather than for its direct utility.

9. The two main functions of money are (*a*) as a medium of exchange and (*b*) as a unit of account or common-denominator standard of value. Related to these two functions of money by the passage of time are two subsidiary functions: (*a*) while money is held, it is a "store of value" whose ultimate worth depends on the trend of prices; (*b*) contracts concerning the future are usually expressed in terms of money, which is why it is often called "a standard of deferred payment."

QUESTIONS FOR DISCUSSION

1. During World War II did we let consumers' dollar demand determine their sugar consumption? Why not? What did?

2. Could supply and demand for labor work so as to distribute to salesmen with a "gift of gab" ten times as much income as to competent surgeons? At other times could it operate so as to give surgeons ten times the income of accountants?

3. Do you think that an "instinct of craftsmanship" and a "sense of social responsibility" could ever replace the "profit motive"?

4. List a number of cases where the government modifies the working of an automatic price system. Also list a number of cases where monopoly elements modify the workings of the price system.

5. Assuming that she cannot borrow abroad, what must China do if she wishes to become an efficient industrialized nation within the next few generations?

6. Which is fixed and which circulating capital: pen and ink; safety razor and blade; bow and arrow; cup and saucer; flashlight case, bulb, and battery? Try to think of a difficult borderline case between the two categories.

7. At 2.9 per cent interest per annum, a victory bond paying $25 ten years from now costs $18.75 today. If the rate of interest doubled, would it cost more or less than $18.75? Why? What if the interest rate went down to 1 per cent?

8. Cross out the incorrect words in the following sentence: "When the rate of interest rises, bond prices go (up, down). The price of 20-year bonds will change (more, less) than the price of 5-year bonds."

9. "In 1862 Lincoln freed the slaves. With one stroke of the pen he destroyed a large fraction of the capital which the South had been able to accumulate over the years." Comment.

10. Would ice cubes make a good unit of money? Why not? What about radium? How would people's spending habits be changed if every dollar bill decreased 10 per cent in value with each month that has elapsed since its date of printing?

11. What are some of the advantages of using bank checks rather than paper or metal money? List some of the disadvantages.

12. Late in 1947, Russia called in old rubles and issued one new one for ten old ones. How do such actions affect people's desire to hold wealth in the form of money?

Chapter 4: INDIVIDUAL
AND FAMILY INCOME

ONE does not have to know anything about the laws of economics to have a lively appreciation of the importance of income. The expression "Clothes make the man" would be more nearly right if it were "Income makes the man." That is to say, if one can know but one fact about a man, knowledge of his income will prove to be the most revealing. Then a rough guess can be made as to his political opinions, his tastes and education, his age, and even his life expectancy. Furthermore, unless a steady stream of money comes into the family's hands every week, every month, and every year—even though it be made up of saints—that family is sick. Not only its materialistic activities, but its nonmaterialistic activities—the things that convert existence into living—must suffer: education, travel, health, recreation, and charity to say nothing of food, warmth, and shelter.

It is a commonplace to state that the American standard of living and level of family income are the highest in all the world. But few people have more than a hazy conception of just how small the average American income really is, or how great is the range between the highest and the lowest incomes, or even how great are the fluctuations over time in the levels of income.

DISTRIBUTION OF INCOME IN THE UNITED STATES

As a matter of fact any poll of students will show that they are not very certain as to what their own family incomes really are. Usually it turns out that students have a slightly exaggerated notion as to how much their fathers earn. And despite the recent (quite justified) claim of a prominent clubwoman that "women spend 70 per cent of the national income, and we soon hope to get hold of the rest," an astonishing number of wives have no conception of their husbands' pay checks. In addition there are some people so inept at keeping records and with such variable earnings that they do not themselves know how much they make. Even where income is known within the family, there is a quite natural reticence to reveal it to outsiders, so much so that investigators who made a recent survey of the birth-control habits of native white Protestants of Indianapolis often found it harder to get financial data than intimate personal information.

In the absence of statistical knowledge, it is understandable that one should form an impression of the American standard of living from the full-page magazine advertisements portraying a jolly American family in an air-conditioned home with a Buick and a station wagon and all the other good things that go to make up comfortable living. Actually, of course, this sort of life is far beyond the grasp of 95 per cent of the American public and even beyond the means of most families from which the selected group of college students comes.

In 1950, at the pinnacle of American prosperity, the amount of per capita income in the United States was around $1,600 per year per person, or less than $35 per week. Such an average figure has not very much meaning, inasmuch as it is derived by pretending that all the income in the United States is divided equally among every man, woman, and child. Of course, in real life income is distributed far from equally, as we shall see presently; furthermore, there is no guarantee that the attempt to divide income in this way would leave the total unchanged.

If the members of a classroom, or of the whole country, write down their family income on a card, these cards may be sorted into different income classes; i.e., some cards will go into the $0 to $1,000 class, some into the $1,000 to $2,000 class, and so forth. In this way we get the *statistical frequency* distribution of income. At one extreme will be the very poor, who have drawn a blank in life; at the other extreme, the very rich, who have hit the jack pot. In between will fall the vast majority of the population.

Table 1 summarizes recent statistics on this subject. Column (1) gives the *income class interval*. Column (2) shows the percentage of families and individuals in each income class. Column (3) shows the percentage of the total of all income that goes to the people in the given income class. Columns (4) and (5) are computed from (2) and (3), respectively. Column (4) shows what percentage of the total number of families and individuals belong to each income class *or below*. Column (5) shows what percentage of total income goes to the people who belong in the given income class or have still lower incomes.

Table 1 shows it would be a great mistake to think that the poor and the rich are equally distributed around the middle. The Biblical statement, "For ye have the poor always with you," gives no inkling of their vast numbers.

TABLE 1. *Distribution of Incomes of American Families and Individuals, 1948*

Income class	Per cent of all families and individuals in this class	Per cent of total income received by families and individuals in this class	Per cent of families and individuals in this class or lower ones	Per cent of income received by this class or lower ones
(1)	(2)	(3)	(4)	(5)
Under $1,000	10	2	10	2
$1,000–$2,000	17	5	27	7
2,000– 3,000	16	10	43	17
3,000– 4,000	18	15	61	32
4,000– 5,000	13	12	74	44
5,000–10,000	21	38	95	82
Over 10,000	5	18	100	100
	100	100		

Number of families and individuals: 47 million
Median income: $3,400
Average income: $4,200 (approximately)

SOURCE: Adapted from *Economic Report of the President*, January, 1950, and Census data (corrected for estimated underreporting of income).

Abraham Lincoln pointed up this fact picturesquely in his statement, "The Lord prefers common people . . . . He made so many of them." A glance at the distribution of income in the United States shows how pointed is the income pyramid and how broad its base. The statement. "There's always room at the top," is certainly true; this is so because it is hard to get there, not because it is easy. If we made such an income pyramid out of a child's play blocks with each layer portraying $1,000 of income, the peak would be far higher than the Eiffel Tower, but almost all of us would be within a yard of the ground.

Moreover, the middle, or "median," income class (around which most people fall and which divides the upper from the lower half) corresponds to low incomes. In 1948 the median income class, for an average American family of two adults and a number of children, was only about $3,400. Table 1 shows that such an income falls short of the average income per family of $4,200. This is primarily because the unequal distribution of incomes gives so much more to the families lying above the median.

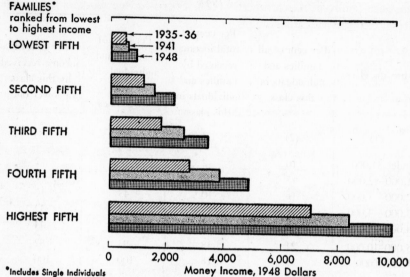

CHANGES IN AVERAGE FAMILY INCOME, 1935-1948

FIGURE 1. The average family income of all groups has increased greatly from the pre-war period. The fifth of all families having highest incomes received the largest increase in dollars but smallest relative increase. SOURCE: President's Report, January, 1950, from data of National Resources Planning Board (Department of Labor, Department of Commerce) and Council of Economic Advisers.

TABLE 2. *Per Capita Income of Different Countries, 1939**

United States	$554	Eire	$248
Germany	520	Argentina	218
United Kingdom	468	USSR	158
Switzerland	445	Italy	140
Sweden	436	Czechoslovakia	134
Australia	403	Japan	93
Canada	389	Mexico	61
Denmark	388	India	34
France	283	China	29

* In United States dollars. Most figures are official and differ in their reliability.

SOURCE: Per Capita National Income, *Foreign Assets and Liabilities of the United States and Its Balance of International Transactions;* Report to the Senate Committee on Finance by the National Advisory Council on International Monetary and Financial Problems, Dec. 18, 1947; and P. A. Baran, "National Income and Product of the USSR, 1940," *Review of Economic Statistics,* November, 1947, as quoted in P. T. Ellsworth, *The International Economy* (Macmillan, New York, 1950).

Let us see how adequate was the income level enjoyed by the typical American family in this prosperous year. Social-service workers have made careful estimates of certain minimum budgets as follows:

1. Bare subsistence—no movies, practically no meat, no dental care, no newspapers, little clothing, etc.
2. Minimum health and decency—occasional movie or recreational expenditure, cheap cuts of meat at intervals, some medical and dental care, etc.
3. Minimum comfort—adequate diet, occasional vacation and amusement, some tobacco and books, etc.

We may roughly estimate the cost of the first of these in 1948–1950 at $1,600. Now, if we examine the actual 1948 statistics rearranged in Table 1, it appears that 20 per cent of the population did not even reach this level of income and 30 per cent earned less than the $2,200 needed for the second budget. Even allowing for the fact that it costs less to live in the country than in the city, we see how justified was the public concern for the "lower third" of the population.

From the same table, we find that only half of the people have incomes reaching above the $3,500 needed for the comfort budget. If we revert to our typical American family of the slick-paper magazine ads, even after stripping them of their station wagons and mink coats, we still find that only 5 per cent of the population have the $10,000 income which we can conservatively estimate was the minimum necessary in 1948 to rough it out at such an existence. And the less said the better about the number of American families who have as much as the $25,000 per year which magazines assure us is absolutely necessary in order to make ends meet just east of Fifth Avenue in New York City.

WORLD COMPARISONS

To some, these statistics may come as a shock. But actually the present postwar picture is tremendously better than it was in the prewar 1930's. Figure 1 illustrates the changes in income distribution in the United States over the last 15 years.

Statistics show that the median family in the United States enjoys a standard of living which is higher than that of the median family anywhere else on earth or anything ever recorded in historical statistics. Table 2 gives a few illustrative estimates to show how great the differentials really are.

THE DECLINE OF POVERTY

It is now more than a century since Karl Marx and Friedrich Engels in 1848 issued the Communist Manifesto containing the lines: "Workers of the world, unite! You have nothing to lose but your chains." A number of the Marx predictions as to the future of industrial capitalism were proved to be only too correct in the intervening years, but one of the most famous has proved to be quite wrong. His assertion that the rich will become richer and the poor will become poorer has not been sustained by careful historical and statistical. research. In Western Europe and in North America there has definitely been a steady secular improvement in minimum standards of living whether measured by food consumption, clothing, housing, or length of life. This is clear from statistics to be presented shortly. It is also obvious from a comparison with more backward nations, two-thirds of whose inhabitants are badly under-nourished.

Not very long ago it was fashionable for economic historians to dwell on the evils of the Industrial Revolution and the poverty-ridden condition of the masses in the disease-producing cities. In point of fact no Dickens novel ever did justice to the conditions of child labor, length of the working day, and conditions of safety and sanitation in early nineteenth-century factories. A work week of 84 hours was the prevailing rule, with time out for breakfast and sometimes supper, as well as lunch. A good deal of work could be got out of a six-year-old boy or girl, so long as one didn't care about his health or existence beyond the age of twelve. If a man lost two fingers in a machine, he still had eight left.

However true their lurid picture of industrial factory towns, the earlier historians erred in thinking that conditions were worse than in the preindustrial era. The earlier "putting-out" or domestic system, in which wool or yarn was provided to workers for them to spin or weave in their homes, brought the worst conditions of the sweatshop into the home. Sleep and need battled for the week's 168 hours. The whole family, not just the breadwinner, was figuratively forced to run on the treadmill to keep alive. For these reasons labor unions have always opposed this system of production, even more than the factory with all its evils.

Furthermore, poverty is never so obvious in the country as in the industrial cities where it forces itself on the observer. The idyllic picture of the healthful happy countryside peopled by stout yeomen and happy peasantry is a mirage in most parts of the world. Even today, nothing in New York's Hell's Kitchen or east side, nothing in Boston's south or north end, nothing "behind the Yards" in Chicago or in its black belt can overshadow the poverty and squalor of our rural problem areas: the Tobacco Road of the deep South, the hillbilly regions of the Appalachian Plateau, the two dust bowls, the ghost mining towns of Pennsylvania, and the cutover region of the upper Michigan peninsula.

Modern historians therefore emphasize that the inadequate conditions of the industrial present are nevertheless great improvements over the previous periods of commercial enterprise and agrarian feudalism. How far we have come is illustrated by the following quotation describing a period that some men can still remember:

In the middle of the nineteenth century there lived in the parish of Marsham, Norfolk, a couple of poor people by the name of Thomas and Mary Edwards. It was on October 5th, 1850, that Mary Edwards bore her last baby boy. At the time of my birth my father was a bullock feeder, working seven days a week, leaving home in the morning before it was light, and not returning in the evening until it was dark. He never saw his children, at this time, except for a little while on the Sunday, as they were always put to bed during the winter months before his return from work. At this time my father's wage had been reduced to 7s. [about $1.40] per week, and had it not been that my mother was able to add a little to her husband's wages by hand-loom weaving the family would have absolutely starved. I have known my mother to be at the loom sixteen hours of the twenty-four, and for those long hours she would not average more than 4s. [80¢] a week, and very often less than that.

The cottage in which the child was born was a miserable one of but two bedrooms, in which had to sleep father, mother, and six children. The family at this time was in abject poverty. When lying in bed with the infant the mother's only food was onion gruel. As a result of the bad food, or, properly speaking, the want of food, she was only able to feed the child at her breast for a week. After the first week he had to be fed on bread soaked in very poor skimmed milk. As soon as my mother was able to get about again, she had to take herself again to the loom. . . . Food rose to famine prices. . . . The only article which did not rise to such a proportionately high figure was meat, but that was an article of food which rarely entered a poor man's home, except a little piece of pork occasionally which would weigh about 1½ lb., and would have to last a family of nine for a week! At the time of the Crimean War meat never entered my father's house more than once or twice a year! . . .

In order to save the family from actual starvation, my father, night by night, took a few turnips from his master's field. My father used to keep our little boots in the best state of repair he could. My sister and I went to bed early on Saturday nights so that my mother might be able to wash and mend our clothes, and we have them clean and tidy for the Sunday. We had no change of clothes in those days. This work kept my mother up nearly all the Saturday night, but she would be up early on the Sunday morning to get our scanty breakfast ready in time for us to go to Sunday School.

This was the only schooling I ever had![1]

[1] From the autobiography of George Edwards (1850–1934), quoted in Colin Clark, *National Income and Outlay* (Macmillan & Co., Ltd., London, 1938), pp. 262–264.

Figure 2 shows the great increase in United States real national product per capita during this century.

REGIONAL INEQUALITIES OF INCOME

The map in Figure 3 shows that the United States is by no means an area of uniform incomes. The South has much lower incomes than does the Northeast

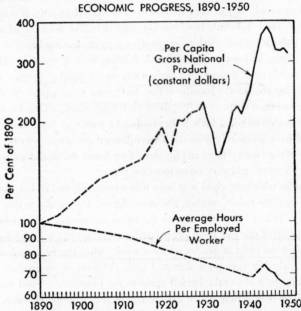

FIGURE 2. Rising per capita national product has been accompanied by a decline in working hours per day. The broken lines indicate estimates, based on fragmentary data, but indicating approximate trends. Note that this is a "ratio" chart: Vertical distances show, not the absolute figure for national product or hours worked for any year, but its percentage of the 1890 figure. SOURCE: Adapted from President's Report, January, 1950.

and the West Coast. States like Mississippi have scarcely yet attained per capita incomes equal to those reached in Pennsylvania and New York back in 1880. But it is interesting to note that the regional differentials in income are gradually narrowing and changing. The South is pulling up, and regions like New England that have long been above the average are returning toward the average; other states, such as California, are improving more rapidly than the average.

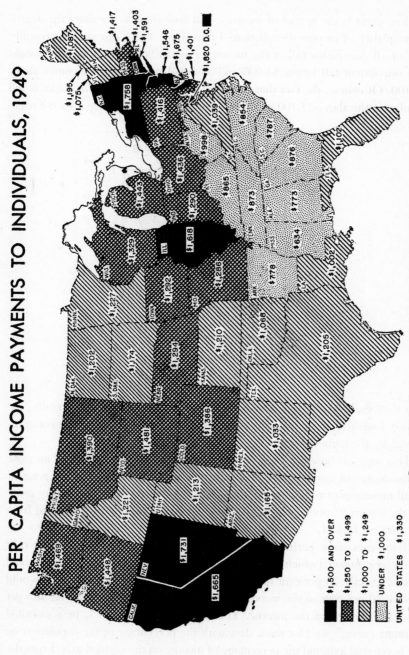

PER CAPITA INCOME PAYMENTS TO INDIVIDUALS, 1949

$1,500 AND OVER
$1,250 TO $1,499
$1,000 TO $1,249
UNDER $1,000

UNITED STATES $1,330

FIGURE 3. SOURCE: U.S. Department of Commerce, Office of Business Economics.

THE INEQUALITY OF INCOMES

How great is the spread of incomes, and how shall we measure the degree of inequality of income distribution? From Table 1, we can say that roughly half of all Americans fall in the income range $1,900 to $5,100. This means that one-fourth fall below $1,900 and an equal number have incomes above $5,100. Of course, the fact that there are the same number of individuals and families in the above-$5,100 group as in the below-$1,900 group does not mean

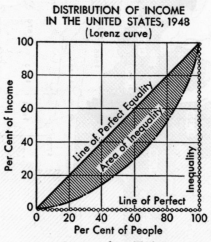

DISTRIBUTION OF INCOME IN THE UNITED STATES, 1948
(Lorenz curve)

FIGURE 4. SOURCE: from Tables 1 to 5.

that they each receive the same percentage of the total income. Actually, the lowest fourth of the population receives much less than half the income received by the highest fourth.

This suggests how we can go about the task of getting a numerical measure of the degree of inequality of income distribution. We can ask: What per cent of all income goes to the lowest 10 per cent? What to the lowest 50 per cent? To the lowest 95 per cent? And so forth. Such data can be easily derived from the data of Table 1.

If incomes were perfectly uniformly distributed, the lowest 20 per cent of the population (which in this case would mean *any* 20 per cent) would receive exactly 20 per cent of the total income, the lowest 80 per cent would receive 80 per cent of the income, and the highest 20 per cent would also get only 20 per cent of the income. This is typified by Table 3. In a so-called "Lorenz curve," we plot these data with the percentage of the population on the horizontal axis and the percentage of income on the vertical axis. From the data for equal distribution of income, we get the diagonal straight line shown in Figure 4.

TABLE 3. *Perfect Equality in Distribution of Income*

Per cent of the population...........	0	20	40	60	80	100
Per cent of income received..........	0	20	40	60	80	100

So much for the case of perfect equality. At the other extreme, we have the hypothetical case of perfect inequality, where everybody (say 99 out of 100 people) has no income, except for one person who has all the income. This is shown in Table 4.

TABLE 4. *Perfect Inequality in Distribution of Income*

Per cent of the population...........	0	20	40	60	80	100
Per cent of income received..........	0	0	0	0	0	100

Why? Because the lowest 0, 20, 80, and 99 people have no income at all. But the lowest 100 include the last man, and all the people, of course, have all the income. The lowest curve on the Lorenz diagram—the right-angled line—represents the case of perfect inequality.

Any actual income distribution such as that of 1948, of course, falls in between these extremes. The student can verify from Columns (4) and (5) of Table 1 that its table of values is given roughly by the numbers in Table 5. Its Lorenz curve is given in Figure 4 by the indicated intermediate curve, with the shaded area indicating the deviation from perfect equality, *i.e.*, the degree of inequality of income distribution.

TABLE 5. *Inequality in Actual Distribution of Income, 1948*

Per cent of the population...........	0	20	40	60	80	100
Per cent of income received..........	0	4	15	31	53	100

There are still other ways of measuring the degree of inequality of income. One of the most interesting of these will be mentioned but not discussed in detail here. The Italian-born Swiss professor of economics, Vilfredo Pareto, was often called, with somewhat questionable accuracy, the ideological precursor of fascism. By using a certain logarithmic chart[1] called the "Pareto chart," he found that the "upper tail" of the income data of many different countries and many different times fell along straight lines of almost the same slopes. He came to believe this to be a fundamental natural law. According to Pareto's Law, *there is an inevitable tendency for income to be distributed in the same way—regardless of social and political institutions and regardless of taxation.* In the past 50 years, more careful studies have cast doubt on the universality of Pareto's Law, and upon its inevitability.[2]

DIFFERENCES IN ABILITY AND INCOMES

In Part Four we shall study in detail the economic principles underlying the distribution of income. Our common sense enables us to anticipate part of that analysis and suggests that one factor helping to explain differences in income must be differences in people.

These differences in people may be physical, mental, temperamental, or even moral. They may be associated with biological inheritance through the genetic cells or with social and economic environment. They may be permanent —like being a man or a woman—or acquired, like educational advantage. These differences may even involve such artificial conventionalities as the possession or nonpossession of a union card and one's propensity to drop "(h)-aitches" in speaking or to pronounce "oil" with an "r" and "girl" without one.

These differences provide us with at least the beginning of an answer—but only a beginning. For we will find that most physical traits, such as height or hip girth, and most mental traits, such as intelligence quotient or tone perception, are not so different among people as are the differences in income distribution. Usually, by hook or crook, the scientist who measures these traits finds that they are "normally" distributed, with most people in the middle and fewer people at each end, as represented by Figure 5a. Whereas incomes—even those from work rather than property—are distributed *askew*, with a very long tail off in the direction of the highest paid, as in Figure 5b.

One could go on speculating on these fundamental questions. Probably it would be more scientific and more fruitful at this point to reserve judgment until we have looked at more facts about the earnings of different groups in

---

[1] VILFREDO PARETO, *Cours d'économie politique* (Lausanne, 1897), Tome 2, Livre 3, Chap. I. A critical account in English of Pareto's Law is given by F. R. Macaulay, *Income in the United States—Its Amount and Distribution* (National Bureau of Economic Research, Inc., New York, 1922), pp. 341–425.

[2] In Great Britain in the period following World War II, progressive taxation had gone so far as to leave only 70 people with incomes of more than $24,000 after taxes were paid.

different occupations and have analyzed them with the aid of logical theory. However, it may be as well to mention at this point that a recent careful study of wage inequalities in the Russian communistic economy[1] showed inequalities and dispersions between the best paid and the poorest paid workers which were surprisingly like those of our own society.

Perhaps a warning is in order at this point against jumping to the conclusion, as Pareto did, that there is something *necessary* and *inevitable* about this dispersion of income. Within the framework of our free competitive society fundamental changes in education have already made significant changes in inequality. Moreover, as no one knows better than the man at the top, our system of

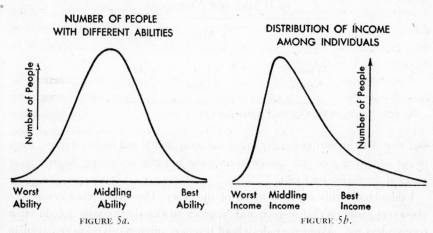

FIGURE 5*a*. FIGURE 5*b*.

progressive income taxation has already greatly changed the relative take-home and—what is more important—the "keep-at-home" of the high and lowly paid; and there is every indication that this will continue to be an abiding feature of American life.

THE POSITION OF MINORITIES

No discussion of the inequality of incomes would be complete without mention of the position of economic minorities. In a real sense this is the concern of everyone because we all belong to some minority. Yes, even the Smiths or, for that matter, the Lodges and the Cabots.

Of course the economically most important minorities consist of Negroes,

[1] ABRAM BERGSON, *The Structure of Soviet Wages* (Harvard University Press, Cambridge, Mass., 1944). The inequality of property incomes is, of course, less in a society hostile to private property. The inequality of political privilege among Soviet bureaucrats, military officers, Communist party members, and the Soviet public at large is not capable of precise numerical measurement.

women, and old people. Careful, competent observers have asserted again and again that outright sexual discrimination in the sense of paying men higher rates for the same kind and volume of work is not a common practice. Similarly it has been asserted that racial discrimination in the sense of unequal pay for the same work is not prevailing practice.

How can we reconcile these statements with the economic inequalities which every sophisticated person knows prevail between the sexes and races and which are shown in Table 6? The answer to the paradox lies partly in the

TABLE 6. *Comparative 1948 Median Wage Incomes of Men and Women and of Whites and Nonwhites*

	Male	Female
White..........	$2,711	$1,615
Negro..........	$1,615	$ 701

SOURCE: Bureau of the Census, February, 1950.

fact that discrimination usually takes the more subtle and more effective form of *not admitting men and women to the same jobs and in barring Negroes from many of the higher paid jobs.*

Undoubtedly this explains much of the story. However, other competent observers maintain that women and Negroes on exactly the same job do often receive less pay. Women grade-school teachers often receive lower pay than men on the grounds that their *needs are less and their classroom authority not so great.* Where Negro and white dishwashers work side by side, it is not impossible that the former should receive lower pay. In a large electrical-goods plant, job-evaluation experts divide all factory work into two parts: women's jobs and men's jobs. The pay of the lowest men begins about where the highest women's pay leaves off. Yet both management and the union will admit, off the record, that in many borderline jobs the productivity of women is greater than that of the men.

Now it cannot be denied that there are physical and temperamental differences between men and women. For example, a woman could not win the heavyweight wrestling championship or set a record for the 100-yard dash. On the other hand, the female sex is the stronger sex in the sense of life expectancy and also, perhaps, in being capable of sustained, painstaking effort. It is equally obvious that there are differences of skin color and hair texture between colored and white races.

Whatever one's views as to the biological and environmental differences between the races and sexes—and the views of the scientists who have studied the question most are very different from those of the man on the street—it is absolutely clear to any observer that there are numerous jobs which either sex or race can do equally well and is prevented from doing. This is shown by the experience of wartime and boom when the usual barriers are lowered.

Similarly the older worker in ordinary times finds himself at a disadvantage in our society. A man may be thrown on the scrap heap by the age of forty when many of his best years are still ahead of him. It is not true that an older worker is the first to be fired; usually his experience or seniority helps to protect him. But once he is fired, it is much harder for him to become reemployed. Paradoxically, the humanitarian measures adopted by corporations to aid older workers (retirement pension schemes, etc.) are one of the reasons for corporations' refusing to hire older men, since it then becomes more expensive to hire them.

Again, from the horror of war a few salutary lessons have been snatched. Women, Negroes, and older workers have shown that they are capable of holding down better jobs and earning more money than was thought possible before the war. The experience of the Federal and state Fair Employment Practice Commissions has not been that prejudice can be legislated out of existence overnight, but that steady improvement is possible if the people really want it. Nor can all of the blame be placed upon bigoted employers. Organized labor, particularly many unions of the AFL, must incur some of the blame or credit for Jim Crow legislation.[1]

The position of women shows steady improvement. In fact there is evidence that they are burrowing into those overhead white-collar jobs and service industries which are least sensitive to the ups and downs of the business cycle and which have more favorable long-run trends than the heavy capital goods sector of the economy in which men predominate. The war and postwar prosperity have improved the relative economic position of the Negro. From 1939 to 1948 nonwhite median wages more than tripled while white median wages little more than doubled. But just as the Negro is the last to be hired, he is the first to be fired when depression comes. When jobs become scarce, whites invade even the fields of domestic service usually abandoned to the Negro.

Still once again we are faced with the challenge of providing full employment. For it is in the wake of layoffs and economic insecurity that the disruptive cry against minorities—against Negro, Jew, Catholic, "Okie"—gathers the force to cause our democratic institutions to tremble.

[1] See H. R. NORTHROP, *Organized Labor and the Negro* (Harper, New York, 1944). Also GUNNAR MYRDAL *et al.*, *An American Dilemma* (Harper, New York, 1944), Vols. I and II.

ECONOMIC STRATIFICATION AND OPPORTUNITY

America has always been considered the land of opportunity where anyone with ability might get ahead in the world. The success legend of the Horatio Alger, Jr., "poor but proud" hero who worked his way to the top and married the boss's daughter—or vice versa—has no doubt been overdrawn. But it did have elements of truth as compared to the situation in older European countries, where an aristocratic tradition lingered on, and where free schooling beyond the primary grades was never established.

For example, the "old school tie" and, more important, the Oxford accent were until recently almost indispensable to political and social advancement in Britain; even with the free scholarship system, few members of the lower or middle class could jump this hurdle. In this country, few people outside the State Department even know how to recognize a "prep school" accent, and variations in speech are geographical rather than social. The American stenographer is almost indistinguishable in appearance from the blueblood debutante.

Moreover, ours has been rather a materialistic civilization in which success is interpreted in business terms. Because "money talks," it is easier for outsiders to break into the upper crust than it would be in a culture that puts greater emphasis upon tradition. The *nouveaux riches* of one generation, such as the Vanderbilts, become the social dictators of the next.

Nevertheless, a careful questionnaire investigation of the social origins of successful businessmen, namely, the directors and officers of corporations, turned up some surprising facts. The typical American business executive did not come off a farm or out of a workingman's home, but more likely his father was also a businessman or possibly in one of the professions. Table 7 summarizes the social origins of a large sample of businessmen as observed by Taussig and Joslyn. For comparison, the social origins of millionaires and of those listed in *Who's Who* are also presented.

It is not surprising that millionaires come from well-to-do business backgrounds because here we should expect inherited wealth to be an important element. But it is rather unexpected to learn that there is a hundred times greater probability[1] of a businessman's son becoming a successful businessman than a laborer's son, and twenty times greater probability than for a farmer's son. Moreover, the trend was even more pronounced for the younger generation of businessmen studied.

Does this mean that American economic society is hardening along caste

[1] The reader should be sure that he realizes why this statement is not inconsistent with Table 5: There are more than twenty times as many sons of laborers as of businessmen.

TABLE 7. *Per Cent Distribution, by Occupation of Fathers of American Business Leaders, of Millionaires, and of Persons Listed in "Who's Who"*

Occupation of father	American business leaders, 1928	American million-aires, living in 1925	Persons listed in *Who's Who*, 1912
Businessman.........	60.0	75.0	35.3
Professional man.....	13.4	10.5	34.3
Farmer.............	12.4	7.3	23.4
Laborer............	12.5	1.6	6.7
Other.............	1.7	5.6	0.3
Total............	100.0	100.0	100.0

SOURCE: F. W. TAUSSIG and C. S. JOSLYN, *American Business Leaders* (Macmillan, New York, 1932), Chap. XII.

lines?[1] Taussig and Joslyn are not sure. They point out that two diametrically opposite explanations are possible: (1) In the past there was high social mobility in America: all the cream rose to the top, leaving naturally less gifted people at the bottom. (2) There are strong, and perhaps growing, barriers to circulation between the economic classes.

Taussig and Joslyn incline rather to the first view, feeling that "you can't keep a good man down." Most sociologists would disagree. They would emphasize the thousand and one subtle psychological, social, economic, and educational disadvantages of the children of less fortunate families; that equal ability is not always able to give rise to equal achievement; that

> "Full many a flower is born to blush unseen,
> And waste its sweetness on the desert air."

Whichever view is right, the implications for policy are the same. Human beings are a nation's most important form of social capital—a form, moreover, in which we have invested too little in the past. Talent, wherever it may be, is worth being sought out and nurtured.

[1] When the first edition of this book was written, the author inclined toward the view that it was becoming increasingly difficult to go from the bottom to the top. Now he is not so sure. Recent careful studies of the origins of business leaders back before 1900 suggest that the present does not compare unfavorably with the good old days, which may not have been so good after all. Increasingly as organizations become bigger, the elements of personal favoritism seem to become less important, and the increasing emphasis upon civil-servant-like quasi-objective tests of performance suggests greater mobility among the elite.

SUMMARY

1. Factual studies of the American distribution of income show that median incomes are lower than popularly believed. Even though incomes today are higher than in any other country or in any past era, they are still not high in comparison with common notions as to what represents comfortable modern living.

2. The view that the poor are becoming poorer in modern industrial nations will not stand up under careful factual examination. Since the Industrial Revolution, average standards of life in Western Europe and America seem definitely to have been showing a rising secular trend. But even within the United States, the differentials in living standards are very great. However, there has been a trend toward narrowing the historical differentials between North and South.

3. The Lorenz diagram is a convenient device for measuring the spreads or inequalities of income distribution. It shows what percentage of total income goes to the poorest 1 per cent of the population, to the poorest 10 per cent, to the poorest 50 per cent, to the poorest 95 per cent, etc. The modern distribution of American income appears to be less unequally distributed than in the depressed days before the war, but it still shows a considerable measure of inequality. An interesting question is to relate the skew distributions of income with the various measures of differences in the mental and physical abilities of people.

4. Minority groups—such as the aged, women, Negroes, and various ethnic groups—pose important economic problems for any democracy. At the borders between economics and sociology, we run into the interesting questions concerning the "circulation of the elite." Such popular clichés as "shirt sleeves to shirt sleeves in three generations" appear to have a weak factual basis. There turns out to be a strong positive correlation between income and social status of a person's parents and grandparents and his own, but the exact direction of causation is hard to establish.

QUESTIONS FOR DISCUSSION

1. Let each member of the class write down on a slip of paper an estimate of his own family's income. From these, draw up a frequency table showing the distribution of incomes. What is the median income? The average income?

2. How much do you think it takes for a childless married couple to live comfortably in your community? How would the money be spent?

3. Were your parents better off than their parents? What does this suggest with respect to the advantages and disadvantages of capitalism?

4. Formulate some of your own ethical beliefs concerning how unequal incomes should be for people of different abilities and needs. How do you justify these beliefs? Would a nineteenth-century American agree? Would a present-day Russian? A South Sea Islander?

5. The *Federal Reserve Bulletin* for August, 1949 (page 15), gives the following data on the 1949 inequality of distribution of liquid-asset holding by "spending units" (*i.e.*, members of a family living together and pooling their incomes):

Percentage of spending units.	0	20	40	60	80	100
Percentage of total liquid asset holdings.	0	0	½	3	17	100

Draw the Lorenz curve, and explain why the distribution of wealth is always so much more unequal than the distribution of income.

Chapter 5: INCOMES FROM AGRICULTURE, PROPERTY, AND LABOR

NOW that we have seen what the distribution of money income is like, let us try to describe the various forms it may take. Economists like to divide income into two major parts: (*A*) income from *property*—rents received from land and real estate, interest on bonds and other loans, profits on so-called "equity-capital" which also shares the risk of losses, royalties, etc.; (*B*) income from *personal effort*, or work—wages and salaries, professional earnings, and earnings of the self-employed. Several chapters in Part Four will be devoted to the determination of these elements, which are usually referred to as rents, wages, interest, and profits or as the income returns to land, labor, capital, and risk-taking enterprise.

This chapter will be confined to a bird's-eye factual view of the principal facts concerning income from (1) agriculture, (2) interest and dividends, and (3) labor in various occupations and professions. We shall return in later chapters to a more detailed analysis.

A. *AGRICULTURAL AND PROPERTY INCOME*

RELATIVE DECLINE OF AGRICULTURE

Farming is still America's largest single industry. But the percentage of people engaged in farming has been declining steadily for the last two centuries. Why this relative shift away from farming?

The answer is simple: Country people prefer to move to town and city. Young people seek higher incomes in the city; they seek shorter hours; and finally, they seek what most of them seem to regard as a better social life in the urban centers.

Many social observers deplore the exodus away from the country, cities having a bad reputation among moralists. But this is a free country, and if people want to leave the farms, they simply pick up and go. This pattern is nothing new. It has been going on throughout our history. In each period of depression the cityward flow has slowed down, only to resume again in prosperity.

Differential Birth Rates.   In a way, it is lucky this is so. For, as we saw in Chapter 2, birth rates are much higher in rural areas than in cities. If it were not for this migration, cities would grow smaller and smaller; the rural share of total population would grow larger and larger. The law of diminishing returns tells us that this would have to mean a great reduction in the productivity of each man-hour spent on the farm. And what does our common sense tell us must then be the law of the market place if an increasing part of the nation's production were to take the form of food and fiber rather than other products? Obviously, the dollar prices of foods would go way down in comparison with the dollar prices of other things. The land would become crowded with many people, each producing little and each unable to buy many of the comforts of life with his produce.

Does this sound far-fetched? It is a true picture of about two-thirds of the globe. In Asia especially, standards of living are pitifully poor. With three out of every four persons engaged in producing the food necessary for life, only one out of four can be producing the bare comforts of life. Contrast this to the United States, where each farm family is efficient enough to feed six other families besides itself on a most expensive scale.

Technological Change and Patterns of Taste.   In addition to the differential in birth rates, there are two other reasons why agriculture is declining in relative importance: Technological progress has been greatly reducing the number of people needed to produce any given total of food and fiber. Use of the tractor, the combine, the cotton picker, irrigation, fertilizer, selective breeding of hybrid corn and livestock, and numerous other examples come to mind.

Coupled with the improvement in laborsaving technique is the unshakable fact that, as we get richer, we do not want to expand our food consumption by as much as we wish to expand our consumption of city products. This has been shown by almost every statistical investigation in this country and abroad. So birth rates, tastes, and technology dictate that agriculture must export people to industry.

POVERTY IN AGRICULTURE

An enduring American vision is that of the "family farm." This is run by father, mother, and children, with possibly a little outside help; it is a reasonably efficient unit and it produces at least a minimum income level, comparable to that of city living after taking account of the extra pleasures and duties that go with self-reliant country living.

Let us turn from vision to fact. Professor Theodore Schultz[1] of the University of Chicago has pointed out that this definition automatically excludes numerous sharecroppers; and from the $5\frac{1}{2}$ million remaining farms of 1940, Schultz eliminates country residences, large nonfamily farms, and about 1 million subsistence farmers who did not earn a cash income of even $600 in 1940. This leaves about 3 million farms that *might* be classed as family farms. But in Schultz's judgment about half of these, which had prewar farm incomes of less than $1,200 or $1,500, could not be regarded as representing a reasonably efficient use of resources. So in the end, he finds that only a fraction of all American farms are at all like the American dream.

The sad fact is that about half of all our farm products are produced on the 5 to 10 per cent most efficient acreage. This means that 90 per cent of all farm land is low producing. A hidden surplus of population exists in the form of low-productivity marginal farm residents.

The *paid farm laborer* was, before the war, one of the lowest paid of all workers. It is estimated that two-fifths of the $2\frac{1}{2}$ million farm laborers received less than $250 per year over and above their keep! And only one-fifth received more than $500. During the war, the drafting of farm hands and the upswing in farm earnings sent farm wages up. By 1951 farm wages had increased fourfold in comparison with the average before World War I but still averaged little more than $120 a month plus board. Even if the increase persists, this is still a low wage, considering the length of the working day and the exertion involved.

The Southern white or Negro *sharecropper*, who owns neither land nor tools and who lives during the year on credit and goods advanced from the company store, is a more complex case. In ordinary years, he is lucky if the cotton crop brings him enough cash to pay off the I.O.U.'s that he has incurred. Often he is chained to risking everything on a single crop—cotton—because it cannot be eaten or easily stolen. A week after the harvest, he is again in debt, again on the interminable annual treadmill. In exceptional years when the crop

[1] T. W. SCHULTZ, *Production and Welfare of Agriculture* (Macmillan, New York, 1949), pp. 33–34. See also Schultz's valuable Committee for Economic Development study, *Agriculture in an Unstable Economy* (McGraw-Hill, New York, 1945); and Gale Johnson, *Trade and Agriculture* (Wiley, New York, 1950).

sells for a high value, he may make a profit high enough to pay back past debts and still have something left over. He is therefore a capitalist in a certain sense, but usually he would gladly change this status for decent wages. This explains the influx of Southern Negroes and poor whites into the Northern cities during the two wars and throughout the prosperous 1920's.

The *tenant farmer* represents another intermediate case typical of all parts of the United States. Ordinarily, he will rent land for a fixed price or on some sort of sharing basis. He may live on the farm, provide all of the labor, occasionally own half of the equipment and half of the livestock, and quite commonly share 50-50 in the annual return. Under the most favorable circumstances, tenant farming represents the stepladder by which a young farmer is able to climb to ownership of his own establishment. But when agriculture is depressed for many years, as in the period between the two world wars, even independent farmers may be losing their holdings through widespread mortgage foreclosure, and the traffic on the ladder may be predominantly downward.

INSTABILITY IN AGRICULTURE

Farming is an up-and-down industry. Corn, wheat, beef, pork, and other farm products are sold in highly competitive markets whose prices change yearly, daily, hourly, and by the minute. The farmer swings at the very end of our seesawing economy. Good times, such as from 1941 to 1951, bring him great percentage increases in income. Depressions cause his cash income to drop away to very little. The farmer particularly benefits from wartime demand conditions; and unlike most of the community, the farmer can ride out an inflationary period of skyrocketing prices. To balance the gloomy prewar data already cited, consider the following estimate of Professor Gale Johnson:

Since 1942, commercial farmers have enjoyed real labor incomes as high or higher than comparable workers received in other employments. In 1947, the average farm labor income per worker on the roughly 3 million commercial farms was about $1,900. It was supplemented by about $500-$600 of labor income from nonagricultural sources, giving a net labor income of about $2,500. This was equal in dollar income to the income of the employed industrial worker and probably had a purchasing power of up to one-fourth more.[1]

If we look closely at farm statistics, we note a surprising fact. Farm *incomes* fluctuate between boom and bust to a greater degree than do nonfarm incomes, but farm *production* is remarkably more stable than is industrial production. Even the weather, which is a great threat to stability of income in any one farm region, does not cause sizable fluctuations in total farm crops

[1] JOHNSON, *op. cit.*, pp. 44-45, footnote 1.

over the whole nation. During the last quarter century, industrial production had an average year-to-year variation of about 15 per cent, while agricultural production had less than a 4 per cent average variation.

No wonder the farmer feels he is at the mercy of a fluctuating market. When demand for food falls off, he goes on producing anyway, perhaps even working harder in an attempt to bolster his falling income. The result: Unchanged out-

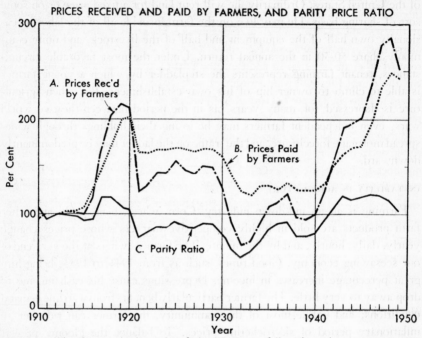

PRICES RECEIVED AND PAID BY FARMERS, AND PARITY PRICE RATIO

FIGURE 1. The C curve is the ratio of A to B. For a fuller discussion, see pp. 86–88. SOURCE: U.S. Department of Agriculture.

put and declining demand combine together to cause great drops in farm prices. Figure 1 shows that fluctuations in the prices received by farmers are greater than the fluctuations in the prices of the things they must buy. Note how in the Great Depression days of the early 1930's prices received by farmers dropped about twice as far as did prices elsewhere. Even in the prosperous 1920's the farmer did badly; and remember, to make things worse, he then carried a heavy burden of mortgage debt incurred during the tremendous land boom at the end of World War I.

GOVERNMENT AID TO AGRICULTURE

Agriculture may be the unlucky stepchild of nature, but it is certainly the favored foster child of government. Farmers have lots of votes, which both political parties ardently woo. Moreover, from the beginning of time, the public seems always to have hated a landlord and loved a farmer, and hence there is fairly widespread support among the electorate at large for aid to the farmer.

Prior to 1929, the principal government aid to agriculture came through our public land policy aimed at getting acreage into the hands of settlers and through the elaborate practical and scientific aids to improved agricultural methods and conservation. The work done in agricultural experiment stations at the so-called state land-grant colleges is well known; and in every farm district, the government-paid county agent is an important source of help toward efficient farming. In addition, the Farm Credit Administration (FCA) and the Rural Electrification Administration (REA) are government agencies set up to help the farmer borrow at low interest rates and to help bring electric power to new regions.

But in 1929 under the Hoover administration, the Federal Farm Board was set up and a new era of direct aid to farmers began. Subsequently under various alphabet agencies (the AAA, the CCC, etc.) the government has stepped in to "interfere with the natural laws of supply and demand" so as to increase the stability and level of farm incomes. In 1950 both political parties pledged themselves to a continuation and extension of such activities; the powerful American Farm Bureau Federation, the Grange, and the Farmers' Union maintain close contact with Washington to make sure that Congress is acquainted with the wishes of farmers.

DIRECT GOVERNMENT AIDS

Government aid programs are of a diverse nature, and the economic principles involved cannot be fully understood until the analysis of Part Three has been mastered. It is enough here to discuss the elements of such programs:

1. *Limiting farm production* by marketing agreements. The Secretary of Agriculture has the right to ask farmers to vote to control the acreage sowed of a given crop. The hope is that, if less tobacco, cotton, or wheat is produced, then the price will thereby rise sufficiently for farmers to receive a higher income.

2. *Increasing the demand for farm products.* Campaigns are waged to encourage better nutrition. Expensive meat and dairy products are substituted for low-cost starchy diets. The free or low-cost school lunch program has been of tremendous scope. Before World War II, people on relief in certain cities were given blue and orange stamps which permitted them to buy extra foodstuffs at lower prices. To increase the declining foreign market for farm exports, we have deliberately "dumped" cotton and other products abroad at

a price lower than they sell for at home, setting up tariff duties to ensure that they are not shipped back into this country.

3. *Stabilizing farm income through storage and loan programs* of the Ever-Normal-Granary type. In bad times, when demand for foods is low, the government steps in with a loan or with an outright purchase. The result is an addition of food to storage. The process supposedly goes into reverse in times of higher demand; the government then sells its stocks of staple commodities, thus keeping price down. It is hoped that the result will be steady prices to the consumer and steady incomes to the farmer; everybody will be better off.

In practice, things do not always work out so nicely. There is a tendency, notably revealed by the case of cotton, for the government to set too high a buying or loan price. An attempt is made to maintain price near the level of "parity"—a concept we shall discuss more fully in a moment. As a result, prices are not stabilized around their natural level; instead, the average level of prices is artificially raised and is maintained only by the government's adding more and more to its already excessive stores of cotton and similar products.[1] Were it not for the increases in demand caused by World War II and its aftermath, this problem would probably have become much more acute.

4. *Payment of an outright subsidy to farmers.* Such subsidies are paid from the general treasury like any other expenditure. If they are to be justified, it must be in terms of the electorate's belief that the needs of farm families have a high priority in comparison with the other needs of the community. In the opinion of many economists, this is the only effective and genuinely honest type of aid that can and ought to be given to any special group: the true costs are on the table for all to see, and if the American people do not consider them justified, then they may be changed.

But this is to neglect the human and political element. Farmers want aid from the government in earning a better living, but they are bitterly opposed to anything that smacks of what they consider charity or a "handout." They want to feel that they are "earning" the extra income, as opposed to the wicked "labor and business monopolists" who form pressure groups to raid the public. Consequently, farm aid rarely appears in the form of a direct subsidy. Yet if a plan such as type 3 fails to work out properly, the effects are the same as—or worse than—if a direct subsidy had been paid.

THE CONCEPT OF PARITY

Figure 2 shows how important was government aid for different farm crops even in a prosperous year like 1948. The typical 1948 program will illustrate how the preceding plans worked. Usually, farmers voted to participate in a

[1] But by 1950, cotton stocks were shrinking fast, as will be noted shortly.

control scheme limiting their acreage for a given crop to some agreed-upon total. In return, Congress agreed to support the price of such a farm product at 90 per cent of the magic figure called "parity."

The years 1910 to 1914 are often looked back upon as the golden age of American farming. Consequently, this is regarded as a "comparison period." The intention is to guarantee to the farmer an average price for the things he sells that will rise as much as the prices of the things he buys (including interest

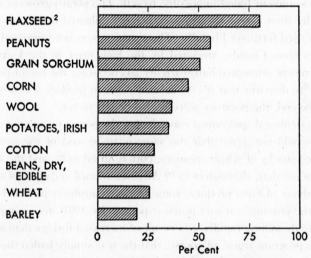

PRICE SUPPORT PAYMENTS AS A PERCENTAGE OF CASH RECEIPTS, 1948 FOR SELECTED COMMODITIES[1]

FIGURE 2. SOURCE: U.S. Department of Agriculture.

[1] Payments include loans outstanding, crops delivered on matured loans, and purchases for price support for 1948 crops, as of Sept. 30, 1949.

[2] Includes purchases for price support of linseed oil.

and taxes). Prices received and prices paid during 1910 to 1914 are the basis for comparison. No allowance is made for the fact that the real costs of production of farm products may have greatly declined since that time as a result of technological advance.

Thus, back in Figure 1, the A curve of prices received is divided by the B curve of prices paid, and the C curve results. If C is far below 100, then parity is not being achieved. Either the government must step in and buy up the crop out of public funds at the 90 per cent price; or, what is the same thing, through its Commodity Credit Corporation (CCC), it must "lend" the farmer 90 per cent of the parity price on his crop. If the price subsequently goes up, the farmer earns the profit and pays back the government loan from his receipts.

If the price does not go up, title to the stored commodity passes to the government.

The results of these programs are somewhat confusing and inconsistent. On the one hand, the Department of Agriculture is teaching the farmer how to produce more crops on each acre of land; and on the other hand, it is helping farmers to restrict the numbers of acres that can be planted to any one crop. The potato-marketing agreement is a painful example of what may result. In 1949, the average check received by farmers in one Maine county was $15,000; some individuals received as much as $100,000—for potatoes that the government found impossible to sell. The potato growers had abided faithfully by their acreage restriction, but they planted their rows closer together and used fertilizer liberally. The situation was not improved by a flow of potatoes from Canada, attracted by the high price in the United States. The government attempted halfheartedly to encourage the use of potatoes for flour, only to discover that it cost several cents to produce 1 cent's worth of flour. In the end, the potatoes were buried or left to rot.

Many agricultural spokesmen concede that the potato program was a fiasco. But they would not agree that the same is to be said of the government's accumulated stocks of wheat, peanuts, cotton, dried milk, and the like. They would point out that, although in 1939 America seemed in danger of smothering under surpluses of farm produce, some of those surpluses proved very useful indeed in the ensuing war and postwar period. By 1950, for example, cotton stocks were dwindling rapidly as a result of increased foreign demand. Critics of the farm program argue, of course, that the war simply bailed the advocates of parity out of a very embarrassing situation.

The "Brannan plan"—named for its author, President Truman's Secretary of Agriculture—would permit the government to sell these stored goods on the open market at prices *less* than those paid to farmers. This would lower prices to consumers; but as we shall later see, such sales would probably also cost the Treasury money. As of 1950, most farm groups are politically cool toward the plan—possibly because it smacks more closely of a direct subsidy to farmers. In Chapter 21 we shall examine some of its economic aspects.

THE LONG-RUN SOLUTION

It is important to understand how all these programs try to redistribute income in favor of agriculture. But they only scratch the surface of the long-run problem of instability and poverty in agriculture. The long-run solution is itself fundamentally simple:

1. The greatest help to agriculture will come from *a stabilization of the non-agricultural sector of the economy at a high-employment high-real-income level.*

That being the case, the demand for agricultural products will be optimally high.

2. Nonetheless, as the 1920's showed, it will probably still be desirable and necessary for people to move out of low-income farm areas into higher income urban jobs. This they will want to do because of existing income differentials. But unless the problem of urban mass unemployment is under control, they will not be able to move because no jobs will be available. So once again, we come back to the same basic solution: avoidance of mass unemployment outside of agriculture coupled with aids toward increased mobility out of low-income areas.

3. Finally, Congress and the people will give outright aid to deserving needy wherever they may be—on the farm or in the city. It is up to the electorate to define the priorities to be given to different needs and the conditions that must be met to qualify.

PROPERTY INCOMES: THE RENTIER CLASS

The number of people who throughout most of their lives depend principally on the earnings of their investments is very small indeed. When the census taker comes around each decade, he finds practically no American males of age twenty-five to fifty-five, of good health, who are not engaged in or seeking some kind of gainful occupation. The so-called *rentier* (rhymes with May) class, which depends for its primary support on interest income, is not large and at any one time tends to consist of older people who have retired from work or who are the surviving heirs of a previous generation of workers.

Moreover, for the last 20 years interest rates have been very low. Instead of being able to count on earning 5 or 6 per cent interest, a person who today clips bond coupons for a living is lucky if he (or more likely she) can count on earning much more than 3 per cent. Thus, a man who retired at forty in 1929 with a million dollars could then have counted on about $60,000 interest free of taxes. Today that same income would have shrunk to almost half even before taxes; and after paying more than $10,000 in taxes, and in view of the greatly increased cost of servants and of goods in general, it is quite clear he would have to lead an entirely different life in the 1950's.

Quite possibly he would be tempted to convert his million dollars into an annuity[1] rather than pass on to his heirs his capital intact, particularly if he is strongly opposed to having the government collect death or inheritance taxes on his estate. Almost certainly, too, he will have been tempted by the higher earnings on common stocks to take some of his money out of interest-earning

---

[1] This would guarantee his fixed earnings for a certain number of years or for life, but at the end of the period, his capital would be completely used up.

bonds and put it into dividend-paying common stocks. This has become so common that a case can be made for stretching the definition of the *rentier* class to include owners of common and preferred stocks, provided they have no controlling interest in the companies concerned.

The above example is rather unrepresentative in that it refers to a millionaire. But the same applies to some extent to people of more moderate means. With declining rates of interest, it is becoming increasingly difficult for any family head to set aside enough savings to provide for his old age and dependents—or at least to provide for them from interest earnings on capital kept intact.

We are perhaps returning to the conditions of an earlier age. When the poet Pope's father retired to the country to live, he took with him a chest of gold coins, from which all family expenditures were subsequently made. Such a chest could not, of course, be bottomless. In a later day, however, it became possible with the development of financial markets for a wealthy man to have his cake and eat it too; *i.e.*, one could live off the interest income of his capital *in perpetuity*. In fact, some men had such large fortunes that they could, so to speak, live on the income of their income and permit their fortunes to increase at compound interest.

Today at 3 per cent it is not so easy to accumulate a fortune out of interest earnings. According to a rough rule of thumb, to find out how long it takes for money to double at compound interest, divide 72 by the interest rate. Instead of having to wait 12 years, as at 6 per cent, today one must wait a quarter of a century! In making his life plans, every citizen must therefore reckon with the fact that his savings can earn only a moderate yield. Few can hope to live in retirement without depleting their capital. And because men marry women younger than themselves, and because women live longer on the average than men, the same problem must be faced in providing for one's widow.

A visitor to a small New England town in the past century once observed that a certain harmless-looking citizen was treated as a social pariah by all the other townfolk. After much importunate questioning as to what was wrong with the man, he was told in a shuddering whisper, "He dipped into his capital!" Such attitudes are changing. It is ironical that an epoch which no longer considers itself responsible for the care of its retired parents should at the same time be the one which can no longer afford to preserve and bequeath family inheritances.

Two important reservations to the above gloomy picture must be noted. First, the prophets of gloom who predict the gradual "euthanasia or extinction of the *rentier* class" should reserve their tears or gloating. The interest earned on each dollar invested has been declining. True enough. But the number of dollars that the American people have been able to accumulate as savings has increased more than the decline in yield. Much of these savings is in the form of war bonds. In any case, even in the prewar years, total interest income was not declining. For the postwar period, it is about 10 billion dollars per year as compared with the prewar figure of 5 billion, or about double the previous amount. An additional 8 billion dollars of dividends must be remembered also. Property income has, therefore, increased along with the postwar increase in national income, with the fraction of total national income going to property a rather stable one.

The second reservation involves the fact that within the past decade a more or less comprehensive social security system has been set up to cover most of the population. As Chapter 10 describes, this will provide for the old age of the bulk of our people more generously than individual savings and interest earnings ever were able to in the past, when the vast majority of citizens did not succeed in providing at all adequately for their old age.

B. *INCOME FROM WORK*

Let us turn now to the different forms of labor income. We may briefly classify jobs into the following approximate categories: (1) unskilled, (2) semiskilled, (3) skilled, (4) clerical and white collar, (5) professional and executive. These titles are mostly self-explanatory.

White-collar Jobs. For the most part the following listing is in order of relative goodness of pay and of status, but with an interesting exception—clerical and white-collar work may carry more social status with it than skilled or semiskilled work, but in the last 50 years it has declined from a position of equality with the skilled trades down to at least the level of the semiskilled. This may seem surprising in view of the fact that our modern economy has an increasing need for typists, bookkeepers, filing clerks, and counter attendants. To frame an explanation, therefore, we must not look to the demand side of the picture. Rather we must ask: What has been happening to the supply of people able and willing to perform such jobs?

Two facts immediately strike our eyes: (1) There has been a tremendous increase since 1900 in the number of people who finish high school; (2) there has been a great influx of women into these clerical positions. Thus the typewriter plus the growing custom of having women work prior to getting married has completely displaced men from the secretarial and related fields. Because clerical work is considered relatively clean and socially admirable, a plentiful supply of white-collar workers has continued to be available even though the earnings of this group have relatively declined.

Skilled Craftsmen. Again if we examine what has been happening to the labor market here and abroad since 1900, we are struck by the fact that the position of the highly skilled craftsman has deteriorated relative to that of the semiskilled laborer. The differential in pay between a highly skilled machinist and a man working on the automobile assembly line has been gradually diminishing over the years. In addition to the decline in the differential between the skilled and semiskilled, there has also been going on a relative decrease in the number of skilled jobs in comparison with the semiskilled. Artisans in such crafts as glass blowing and cigar making have been almost completely replaced by machine attendants. Unions organized along craft lines have attempted to slow down this process, but the widespread unionization since 1933 along industrial lines, we shall see in Chapter 9, has accelerated this drastic change.

The Semiskilled Worker. Perhaps the most important group in the labor market today is the semiskilled. The semiskilled laborer learns after a few months how to attend the loom or machine in the factory where he is employed. Unlike the skilled worker who has mastered a trade, if a semiskilled worker leaves a factory after 5 years of work, he usually has no transferable skill which will make him more valuable to a new employer. His destiny, therefore, tends to be closely tied up with his original employer, and in that sense he is in a vulnerable position. But working against this, and perhaps more important, is the fact that modern industry has an increasing need for factory workers without highly developed special skills. If a semiskilled worker is reasonably alert and has a general familiarity with machines and factory life, he can soon acquire the specialized knowledge needed on a new job. Thus, if the defense effort causes tank factories to boom, workers from a typewriter factory can be quickly trained to carry on in the new occupation.

No other group in the economy has shown such remarkable improvements in earnings since the days prior to World War I. When Henry Ford announced in 1914 his policy of paying $5 for an 8-hour day, it was considered revolutionary. Today, earnings of $2.50 per hour or $90 per week are above the average, but they are not uncommon. The sweatshop so characteristic of highly competitive industries like the garment trade is, in its worst forms, pretty much a thing of the past.

Two explanations are advanced to account for the improved status of factory labor. The first, and by far the more important, is the *steady increase in productivity and efficiency of labor resulting from technological improvements and large-scale production.* As a result, $1 spent on labor working in efficient American factories may be twice as worth while as $0.60 spent in England and

Germany and may be worth more than ten times $0.10 spent on Chinese coolie labor.

A secondary factor has been the *growth of trade-union collective bargaining and government legislation*. Since 1933 the unskilled and semiskilled workers have become increasingly unionized in such fields as automobiles, textiles, and electricity. Unions have zealously—sometimes too zealously—made sure that the increases in productivity were shared by management with labor. We shall return to this field of labor relations many times in the course of our later discussions.

A factory worker will ordinarily be paid in one of two ways: by *the hour* or by *piece rates*. Under provisions of the Fair Labor Standards Act the hourly rate cannot be less than 75 cents for factories engaged in interstate commerce. It may, of course, be much greater than this. As of 1950, average hourly rates were around $2.00 in bituminous coal mining, $1.80 in automobile manufacturing, $1.30 in Northern textiles, $1.20 in Southern textiles, $1.75 in the steel industry, and $1.35 in the men's clothing industry.

When a worker is on piece rates, he is paid according to how many units of product he is able to turn out. A woman who wraps 10,000 candy bars per hour will receive one-third more than one who wraps only 7,500, and so forth. Such a method of pay has an element of fairness in it, since those who work harder and more skillfully receive more. It also pleases the employer because it goads the workers into increasing production. On the other hand, workers claim that it leads to a fatiguing speed-up.

Moreover, it gives rise to endless debate concerning the fair piece rate. As workers are given better machines, their productivity increases even without increased effort and their earnings may become very great at the old rates. The employer not unnaturally, therefore, wishes to cut the piece rate. He may send a time-and-motion efficiency engineer (a modern disciple of Frederick Taylor's scientific management) around with a stop watch to clock the worker and set a new fair rate. Often the worker feels aggrieved and tries to slow down and magnify the difficulty of the new job. He feels that the incentive pay for increasing the number of pieces of output is an illusion; that whenever workers increase their speed, the rate is cut and they end up by getting no more than before, while working harder and with a number of their unluckier buddies being laid off.

The natural consequence is for unions and unorganized workers to discourage their more energetic comrades from working too hard and to reject the suggestions of the time-and-motion expert which would often result in saving of effort and fatigue and substantial increases in productivity. Thus part of the increases in efficiency, which come in after unions have forced management to pay workers well and use them more efficiently, may be lost by union "featherbedding" or "make-work" tactics.

The Labor Market's Basement. At the bottom of the labor market come the unskilled jobs that often require little more than the ability to hold a shovel, an ability which reaches its peak around the age of twenty and goes downhill from then on. Then too there are a wide range of dead-end jobs such as messenger, bus boy, elevator operator, etc. When a youth quits school to take such a job, he at first feels rich; but a few years later his pay is unchanged, and unless he moves on, it will never change by much. Studies of the labor market show that most people do begin by taking any job that comes to hand, but there follows a period of trial and experiment in which the individual gravitates toward a job more nearly suited to his abilities and tastes. Particularly when there is full employment in the community do people have the opportunity to upgrade themselves and leave low-productive low-paid jobs.

A dramatic case in point is that of domestic help, whose pay has increased spectacularly in the last decade of prosperity. We tend to think of the steel or automobile industries as being the great employers of people and follow the newspaper reports of their wage changes with great interest. We tend to forget that the number of domestic servants must also be expressed in seven digits and represents one of our most important occupations. The prewar facts made it amply clear to all but the harassed suburban housewife that the great American sweatshop is to be found in the American home. A factory worker grumbles if she is made to work 8 hours a day 5 days a week for $20 per week or $1,000 a year. Yet two-thirds of the household workers in such representative prosperous states as Connecticut and Michigan before the war earned less than $500; one-third earned less than $250 per year! During this period, a servant who lived off the premises was lucky if she finished the supper dishes within a 12-hour day. If she was unfortunate enough to live on the premises, only the sleeping hours were her own, and she was lucky to get off Thursday evening and every other Sunday. Nor were there many of the alleged comforts of a cozy home, as she had long since lost the old Yankee privilege extended to the "help" of eating with and being one of the family. Finally, but not least important, a maid's chance of meeting a marriageable prospect has always been at rock bottom.

It is no wonder then that, when the war opened up jobs in stores, offices, factories, and beauty parlors, women left domestic service, never to return voluntarily. Moreover, if reasonably high levels of employment opportunities are maintained in the years ahead, middle-class families must resign themselves to the new order. With immigration pretty much a thing of the past, and with the country girls being less available for domestic service, the odds are that wages for household help will continue to rise. Unless a family is willing to give up a significant fraction of its own income, it will not be able to find a reasonably intelligent person who will dedicate her life to raising other people's children. The moral: Sell that big house and buy an automatic washing machine.

INCOMES OF BUSINESS EXECUTIVES

During the decade of the prosperous 1920's, the prestige of the businessman was at an all-time high—much to the disgust and contempt of litterateurs isolated in Greenwich Village or expatriated in Paris. But despite the lampooning of Sinclair Lewis's "Babbitt" and H. L. Mencken's "Boobus Americanus," the businessman's go-getter philosophy was in the ascendancy. Even religion was promoted as good business and explained in accounting terms. With Calvin Coolidge in the White House and Andrew Mellon the Secretary of the Treasury, the businessman felt, quite rightly, that his was the dominant class.

It is now history how Herbert Hoover reaped the ensuing whirlwind. The fickle public, terrified by unemployment and resentful of depression, drove out its old idols from the temple. Like savages who must blame even the breaking of a fishline on some evil spirit, the American people began a great witch hunt for the crooked businessmen who had caused the Great Depression. As if honest concerns had not failed with the dishonest, and as if ignorance and stupidity were not infinitely more important than fraud!

The businessman has never fully returned to his previous position of prestige. Shaken of self-confidence by a decade of considerable losses, lampooned by novelists, harassed by government and labor, pounced upon by the courts for violation of antitrust laws he had forgotten existed, it is little wonder that he was dyspeptic before the war. But like the unemployed, he experienced during the emergency of World War II a feeling of being wanted and needed. The postwar period finds some of his status restored. In any event the class of business executives and managers constitutes, in many ways, the real aristocracy of our industrial society. As we shall see in the next chapter, corporation executives do not typically own any significant part of the corporation capital that they manage. In short, they are *bureaucrats* even though in ordinary times they have no connection with government. This is not used as a word of reproach or belittlement, for it has been claimed with some cogency that ours is essentially an age of bureaucracy.

Although the large corporation executive, like the Soviet commissar, wields infinitely more economic power than his own income would suggest, it would be a mistake to dismiss his earnings as negligible. Each year the SEC (Securities and Exchange Commission) requires corporations to list the amounts that they pay their top employees. Usually the list is headed by Louis B. Mayer of Metro-Goldwyn-Mayer movies, Thomas J. Watson of International Business Machines, Alfred P. Sloan of General Motors, E. G. Grace of Bethlehem Steel, Vincent Riggio of American Tobacco, and a number of movie executives. Mixed with these luminaries are usually such stars from Hollywood as Bing Crosby, Betty Grable, Ray Milland, Tyrone Power, Betty Hutton, and Alan Ladd.

Part of the reward of top executives comes in the form of bonuses, retirement pensions, and capital stock. Bonuses, in particular, go up sharply with improvements in business, so it is hard to say just how much the top executives of large companies can hope to get. Par may be set at somewhere below $1,000 a day or around $300,000 a year. Of course, few people can hope to shoot par; but during good times and wars, a few earn "birdies" and even "eagles."

Of course, these very highest salaries do not apply to all senior corporation executives, but only to those at the top of the largest companies. A more detailed study[1] of good-sized companies (60 to 200 million dollars of assets) shows that in 1941, under favorable circumstances, the top executive might earn $195,000, the second in command $122,000, the third $100,000, the tenth executive only $44,000, and the twentieth $28,000. In the middling generous companies, the top man received only $75,000, the fifth man $33,000, the tenth man $25,000, and the twelfth man only $16,000.

Among smaller companies with assets from 5 to 50 million dollars, salaries were $75,000 at the top of the generous companies, $25,000 for the fifth man, and $11,000 for the fourteenth man on the totem pole. In the small companies of only medium generosity, the top man received $50,000 but the fourteenth man is down to only $8,000.

We may summarize the study by saying that, aside from differences in the generosity of companies, a medium executive in a medium large company earned about $25,000 a year before taxes and a similar man in the small company field received about $12,000 a year. All the figures cited are *before* federal personal income tax; such taxes are considerable and must be subtracted in arriving at the executive's *disposable income*. By 1951, most of the figures would have to be increased upward 50 per cent or so.

[1] JOHN C. BAKER, "Payments to Senior Corporation Executives," *Quarterly Journal of Economics*, vol. LIX, February, 1945, pp. 170–185. See also the discussion in Chap. XII of R. A. Gordon, *Business Leadership in the Large Corporation* (Brookings, Washington, D.C., 1945), where further references are given.

PROFESSIONAL INCOMES

The various professions have this in common: They all require a great deal of education and training. In addition to undergraduate college training of 3 or 4 years, a doctor requires 4 years of medical-school training and 1 year or more of hospital internship. This is a far cry from the days when the new apprentice simply accompanied a doctor as he made his horse-and-buggy rounds. In lesser degree, the same trends are observable in the nonmedical professions. Even the preacher of the Gospel now requires increased training.

The professions differ in the extent to which their members are self-employed or employed for wages by others. About four out of five doctors "hang out their shingles," but only seven out of ten lawyers do. The engineer, on the other hand, although he started out as a private consultant, is today almost completely in the regular employ of somebody else. The same is true of about three-fourths of the registered nurses, almost one-half of the certified public accountants, and practically all teachers. Dentists, chiropodists, chiro-practors, and osteopaths, on the other hand, are self-employed in 95 per cent of the cases.

In one respect all the professions are alike. They all think that they are underpaid. This is understandable, since nobody gets enough of the good things in life. What is strange is the fact that the spokesmen for each—intelligent deans, editors, and heads of professional societies—all seem honestly to believe that other professions receive more money or that in some past golden age their own professions earned more. Harold F. Clark's work on life earnings[1] gives a number of amusing quotations showing how the doctors think that they make less than lawyers, engineers, and plumbers; how the dentists think that they are slipping behind in the financial race; and so forth.

This would be merely comical were it not for its serious side: the tendency for each profession to try to lessen competition by restricting its numbers. Not that such august bodies as the American Medical Association put matters in this way or think cynically in these terms. Rather an attempt is made to raise minimum standards of training, in itself a commendable thing. But carried to its logical extreme, this could provide an excuse for any amount of cutting down of numbers, until we reach the *reductio ad absurdum* of having only the single best doctor left in the profession.

According to competent observers, whose testimony went unheard before the war emergency, the medical needs of the American people could not ade-

[1] H. F. CLARK et al., *Life Earnings in Selected Occupations in the United States* (Harper, New York, 1937).

quately be met by the existing number of doctors. Few experienced college deans would quarrel with Clark's statement:

There is good reason to think that there are perhaps two or three million people in skilled and unskilled labor who have ability equal to that of the average individual in medicine. . . . The average salary in engineering, for instance, is some five and a half times the average income in unskilled labor and three times the average income in skilled trades. There seems to be no reason for such large differences except lack of information in regard to average incomes and lack of opportunity to enter engineering. . . . Much as . . . professional groups dislike to have larger numbers of people entering, on grounds of social welfare there seems to be no other alternative. If income data are any adequate test, the country needs far more people in all these professional groups.[1]

Let us turn now to the facts on professional earnings. In Table 1, comparative data are given for many different occupations. Column (2) gives estimated median annual earnings. (By the median man is meant the one just in the middle, with half the people above him and half below.) Column (3) gives average annual earnings; these exceed the medians because the extremely large earnings of the lucky few are divided equally among all members and swell the average. Column (4) gives the present (discounted) values of lifetime earnings.[2] Column (5) gives the age span of those who remain in the occupation in question.

A number of interesting relations appear from the tables. Of all the "genteel" professions, that of the ministry is by far the worst paid, even though its members must maintain a relatively expensive standard of living. Obviously, no one enters the ministry for its financial rewards in this life, and a surprising number of ministers leave the profession for other activities. All observers have commented upon the revolutionary decline in the percentage of college students aiming at the ministry today as compared to 75 or 40 years ago.

To supplement the above estimates, which Clark is the first to admit are only roughly accurate, we are fortunate in having some rather elaborate questionnaire surveys by the Department of Commerce of earnings in a

[1] *Ibid.*, pp. 16, 24.

[2] Thus, suppose the average doctor works from the ages of twenty-seven to sixty-nine, or 42 years in all. At $4,850 per year 42 years would give a total of lifetime earnings of about $203,700. But a dollar 10 years from now is not worth a dollar today. In fact, if the rate of interest is 2.9 per cent as in government victory bonds, $1 payable 10 years from now is worth only $0.75 today. At 4 per cent interest, as used by Clark in Table 1, even more would have to be deducted or "discounted" for interest. Now to a young student debating whether to be a doctor or not, part of his earnings in that profession will be even more than 10 or even 40 years away. This has been allowed for in the *discounted* value of lifetime *earnings*.

number of professions consisting primarily of independent practitioners.[1] In every case before arriving at net income we subtract from the professional man's gross income or cash intake all his expenses of doing business (rent, assistants' salaries, materials, etc.).

TABLE 1. *Income Data for Selected Occupations, 1920–1936*

Occupation	Median annual earnings	Average annual earnings	Present (discounted) value of lifetime earnings	Age span of occupation, years
(1)	(2)	(3)	(4)	(5)
Medicine............	$4,250	$4,850	$108,000	27–69
Law.................	3,600	4,730	105,000	
Dentistry............	3,760	4,170	95,400	24–69
Engineering...........	3,700	4,410	95,300	22–65
Architecture..........	3,190	3,820	82,500	22–65
College teaching.......	2,470	3,050	69,300	25–69
Social work...........	1,517	1,650	51,000	30–65
Journalism...........	1,600	2,120	41,500	23–69
Ministry.............	1,780	1,980	41,000	25–69
Library work..........	.....	2,020	35,000	23–69
Public-school teaching....	1,220	1,350	29,700	20–69
Skilled trades..........	.....	1,430	28,600	18–62
Nursing.............	.....	1,310	23,300	21–51
Unskilled labor........	.....	795	15,200	18–62
Farming.............	.....	580	12,500	51
Farm labor...........	.....	485	10,400	51

SOURCE: H. F. CLARK *et al.*, *Life Earnings in Selected Occupations in the United States* (Harper, New York, 1937), p. 5 and later chapters. All these figures should be increased by about 50 to 100 per cent to bring them up to date as of 1951.

Both median and average incomes are given for the 1929 boom year, the 1933 depression year, and for the latest available year, 1941. From the comparison let us eliminate certified public accountants as being a select sample of the best accountants and as being more comparable to members of the College of Surgeons than to the rank and file of physicians. It then appears that lawyers and doctors lead the list in earnings. Actually in recent years the physicians were beginning to forge ahead of the attorneys in earnings. Den-

[1] These are reported in eight articles on incomes in selected professions, *Survey of Current Business*, 1943, 1944, and 1949.

tists fall below both of the above groups, but well ahead of veterinarians and registered nurses.

The more detailed yearly figures from which the table is taken show clearly that all professions are hard hit by depression. Aside from consulting engineers, whose earnings are cut to the bone, dentists are most affected by the business cycle, probably because many people consider their treatments as postponable. Doctors are next hardest hit, presumably because they, like dentists, cannot

TABLE 2. *Average and Median Net Income of Nonsalaried Practitioners in Stated Professions, Selected Years, 1929–1941*

Professional group	Net income					
	1929		1933		1941	
	Median	Average	Median	Average	Median	Average
Certified public accountants.................	......	$7,300	......	$4,200		
Lawyers...............	......	5,500	......	3,900	$3,000	$4,800
Physicians.............	......	5,200	......	2,900	3,800	5,000
Dentists..............	$3,700	4,300	$1,900	2,200	3,300	3,800
Osteopathic physicians...	3,100	3,600	1,500	1,900		
Veterinarians..........	......	......	......	......	2,300	2,700
Chiropractors.........	2,100	2,500	1,100	1,300		
Chiropodists..........	......	......	1,200	1,500		
Nurses................	......	1,200	......	......	1,200	1,200

SOURCE: *Survey of Current Business*, May, 1944, p. 15. All data rounded off to nearest $100. For 1949, comparable figures are available for lawyers and dentists: lawyers' median $6,400, average $8,400; dentists' median $6,000, average $7,000. Using past relationships between gross and net incomes, we can estimate the 1949 average net income of physicians as being around $11,000.

collect all their bills during depression or cut down on their overhead expenses. Registered nurses, on the other hand, having no fixed expenses to speak of and working largely for cash, show rather steadier earnings over the cycle. However, if we allow for their unemployment for many days of the month as Clark does, we may estimate that their earnings fall 50 per cent in depression, which is a much less rosy picture.

What differences are there in professional earnings in cities of different sizes? The answer given by the Department of Commerce study is as follows: In all professions earnings increase as we go to larger towns and cities until we reach cities of about a one-quarter or one-half million population. Then earnings seem to drop in all professions except law. Possibly because most successful corporation lawyers are to be found in large metropolitan centers, *average* legal earnings continue to rise; but interestingly enough, median earnings—the more significant measure—do fall off in the large cities as in the case of the other professions.

Also, there are characteristic income differences according to regions of the country. The Pacific Coast states lead in every case. Usually the Middle Eastern states come next. Almost invariably the Southern and Mountain states are near the bottom, and New England seems to be below the country-wide average. Between 1941 and 1948, there were some striking regional changes in dentists' incomes: New England and the Middle Atlantic states fell compared to other regions because of the relative abundance of graduates in the former areas. The moral seems to be to go to a good-sized West Coast town, but not to the largest ones. However, a number of people have been doing just that during the war. So before you pack the family into the automobile, you had better check with the latest statistics on earnings and be sure that California will let you practice your profession there.

These average earnings figures must now be supplemented by data showing the dispersion around the average. Every one of the professions is characterized by considerable inequality of income. The spread between highest and lowest incomes is most marked in the case of law. This is in line with common-sense expectations, since experienced lawyers with wide contacts are known to have very high earnings. The least inequality holds in the case of nursing. Again this is in line with the ordinary observation that rates of pay do not vary much with the experience or ability of the registered nurse in question.

To show graphically the amount of inequality in the professions as of 1941, we use our old friend the Lorenz curve. It will be recalled that the heavy diagonal line represents perfect equality. The curve for nursing is therefore nearest to this line. Law, being most unequal of all, naturally has a curve farthest from this line. Since the spread in physicians' earnings is rather large, its curve comes near to that of lawyers. Dentistry, being by and large more of a routine profession, has its curve nearer to that of nursing, *i.e.*, with relatively little inequality.

Let us translate these inequality figures into concrete dollar terms. Because $5,900 is the dentists' 1948 median, half of them got less than that and half more. Twenty per cent earned more than $10,000 per year; only 3 per cent got over $15,000 per year. Most of these would be specialists (in teeth straightening, extractions, dental surgery), but a few might be "society dentists" with a good barber-chair manner.

With the growth of hospital care, private-duty nursing by both registered and practical nurses has been on the decline. Earnings in this field are about comparable to those of general staff nurses, counting in the latter's maintenance (food and lodging), but less than that of nurses engaged in public-health work. In other words, governments (state, local, and federal) are good employers. A nurse contemplating free lancing should be warned that only 1 in 20 private-duty nurses can hope to earn more than $3,000 a year. Even fewer can hope to win a rich and elderly husband.

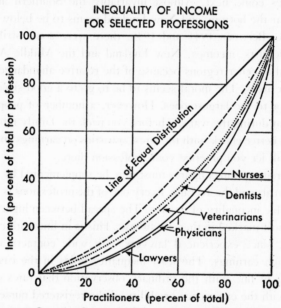

FIGURE 3. SOURCE: *Survey of Current Business*, May, 1944.

Of all physicians out on their own, about one-fourth earned less than $4,000 in 1941. A little more than one-fifth earned more than $7,000, and one in eight surpassed $10,000. Interestingly enough, physicians who worked for a salary averaged about $500 more per year than those on their own; while those part on salary and part on their own averaged almost $1,000 more. Moreover, those completely on salary hardly ever fell below the $2,000 level. They were grouped much more around the median. In view of the move toward clinical and socialized medicine, it is interesting to note that the best paid people seemed usually to lie in the category of being attached to some clinic or hospital and of receiving at least part of their income from that source. By 1951, doctors' incomes were double these prewar figures.

Before leaving the independent professional practitioners, we must observe that all of them possess the pleasing quality of having earnings that rise with age and experience. A ditchdigger at twenty-five has passed his prime, but a physician or lawyer continues to improve economically until past middle age. Table 3 gives in Column (2) the age at which earnings are at their peak. Column (3) gives the span of years in which earnings are within 10 per cent of the peak, or what has been called the "prime earning period."

TABLE 3. *Growth of Professional Earnings with Age*

Profession	Age of peak earnings	Prime earning period
(1)	(2)	(3)
Medicine.....................	Low 50's	35–54
Law.......................	Late 40's	45–59
Dentistry....................	Around 40	35–49
Veterinary practice............	Late 30's	35–39

SOURCE: *Survey of Current Business*, May, 1944, p. 16.

On the whole, lawyers seem to do best at the older ages. (In fact, the indicated peak around 50 years is followed by a long plateau in which earnings drop very little.) Physicians' earnings hold up well until the mid-fifties, and then drop rather rapidly. Presumably the strenuous character of a doctor's duties is the main reason. Dentists seem to reach their peak at the quite early age of forty. But veterinarians show even stranger behavior since the young men do better than the old. Probably this is misleading. Because of a virtual revolution in education requirements in recent years in this field, the younger men—many of whom have a profitable pet practice rather than a farm practice—receive more money. Presumably such a revolution will not be repeated; therefore, in time, the well-trained older men will show more normal earnings.

Incidentally, it is not true, as many people believe, that doctors do badly in their early years of practice. Once their training is really completed, their earnings greatly exceed those of most workers. However, there is a possible joker in all the above statistics. They refer to the earnings of *active* practitioners. They do not relate to all the people who were *trained* for this profession. Thus, they do not indicate how many lawyers become discouraged by low earnings and quit to go into other businesses with their fathers-in-law.

Let us turn very briefly to teaching. Increasingly a college bachelor's degree rather than a couple of years of normal school is becoming the prerequisite for grade-school teaching; for high-school teaching in city schools, a master's degree. In the college field, the universal trend is toward the doctor of philosophy degree.

There is a clear tendency for increases in teachers' salaries at all levels to be sticky and to fall behind the cost-of-living and wage increases elsewhere. In the late 1940's the average college teacher received a salary of only $4,100; in purchasing power this represented little improvement over 1905. This means that the quality and quantity of people going into the teaching field may fall. This was the case in World War I, in the 1920's, and during the recent war. At the college level the situation is most acute in the natural sciences and other fields (such as economics, surprisingly enough), where higher paid competitive offers from business and government threaten to drain off the best men.

We may close our discussion of professional incomes with a brief examination of engineering, a relatively new profession. Even today many of the older men designated as engineers have never had formal full-time college training. By 1950 about 330,000 individuals were classified as engineers; civil engineers, mechanical engineers, and electrical engineers each had about one-quarter of the total. Of the remainder the relatively newer branch of chemical engineering had outstripped that of mining and metallurgical engineering.

IS COLLEGE WORTH WHILE?

The answer to this question depends in only small measure upon economics. The social and cultural value of 4 years of collegiate life cannot be translated into exact dollar terms. If we consider the cost of a professional education and compare its earnings with less trained occupations, we should be able to reach some general conclusions about its purely economic advantages.

To evaluate each profession, imagine a number of members of a high-school graduating class. A hard-boiled accountant with a crystal ball gazes into the future and draws up a balance sheet showing the present value *as of that moment* of all future costs of each occupation's training. These figures are given in Column (2). Thus a boy without any resources who wished to have a medical education would have to borrow about $20,000 on the day he graduated from high school to pay for the extra costs of a medical education and to cover the income he foregoes while in school. A boy who desires only a college bachelor's degree would need $10,000 in the bank to be free of worries. One who quits at high school needs zero dollars by definition. A similar procedure of estimating extra costs must be followed for each profession or for a college education itself.

With what shall we compare the extra costs of professional training? With the *present discounted value of lifetime earnings* in that profession? No. Instead, we should compare the extra training costs with the *extra* value of lifetime earnings over and above lifetime earnings without professional training. Column (3) gives a rough estimate of the average extra value of professional lifetime earnings over and above nonprofessional work. This must be compared with the extra cost.

TABLE 4. *Illustrative Figures on Extra Cost and Value of Professional Training*

Kind of professional training	Cost*	Value†	Profit‡
(1)	(2)	(3)	(4)
High school only......................	0	0	0
College bachelor's degree..............	$10,000	$35,000	+$25,000
Master's degree......................	12,000	35,000	+ 23,000
Engineering degree...................	11,000	70,000	+ 59,000
Ph.D. degree........................	15,000	50,000	+ 35,000
Medical training.....................	20,000	85,000	+ 65,000
Legal training.......................	15,000	80,000	+ 65,000
Dental degree.......................	17,000	70,000	+ 53,000

* Discounted at 4 per cent interest back to day of high-school graduation and inclusive of expenditures for books, tuition, extra board and room costs, as well as foregone earnings.

† Present discounted value of (median) lifetime professional earnings discounted back to day of high-school graduation.

‡ How much of this algebraic difference between value and cost is due to training rather than ability or other factors cannot be said with confidence. Probably the figures for similar professions can be compared with the greatest accuracy.

SOURCE: In arriving at these estimates, consideration was given to the figures of H. F. Clark *et al.*, *Life Earnings in Selected Occupations in the United States*, (Harper, New York, 1937); J. R. Walsh, "The Capital Concept Applied to Man," *Quarterly Journal of Economics*, 1935, pp. 225–285; and the Department of Commerce, *Survey of Current Business*, 1943 and 1944. The quantitative results are very rough and should not be taken too seriously.

Column (4) shows whether or not the professional training was worth while. It gives the difference between Columns (3) and (2), or the algebraic profit or loss of an average individual going into the profession. As we should expect, it is profitable to go into most of the professions with the possible exception of teaching. Whether or not the nonpecuniary advantages of academic life overrule the money calculation will depend upon the individual in question. Certainly in all vocational decisions the net advantages of pleasantness, seniority rights, and continuity of employment must be given full weight.

Why does not competition wipe out the profit or loss from any profession? For example, why do not more people go into medicine and dentistry? In fact, why do not more individuals go into medicine instead of dentistry, since the returns are better and the prestige is greater? If competition does not set the right price for a spool of thread, the social loss is not catastrophic. But here in the most important aspect of getting a living we see that competition works far from perfectly. A number of obvious reasons suggest themselves:

1. Families have not the necessary knowledge to make wise plans for their children. In part this ignorance can be dispelled by vocational guidance and factual information. In part it stems from the fact that the choice of a profession involves a decision that will cover a half century in the future. Who can be sure of any forecast over such a period?

2. Many families have not the necessary capital to invest in their children even though the return in money, happiness, and national service would be very large. If people were property like horses or slaves and if a man could legally sell himself, shrewd speculators might invest in promising young people and share part of the return with them. But, quite properly, our laws do not permit this. Of course, the same desirable effects can be achieved in part if students of poor families can borrow from somebody and repay out of later earnings. Actually there is some of this, often on a semiphilanthropic basis. But it is primarily of importance in enabling students to finish their college training; it does not bring very many people to college who would not otherwise go. The same is true, but in lesser degree, of undergraduate scholarships. These rarely cover the full expenses of schooling and too rarely enable really poor boys and girls to go to school.

3. There is considerable evidence from the statistics of medical school and dentistry applications[1] that a considerable number of people *do* try to get such advanced training. Unlike a law student, a medical student does not cover most of his training costs when he pays tuition. With gifts and endowment earnings being limited, there are not new places in medical schools for more students even if they were willing to pay tuition. This fact, plus the natural desire of the profession to limit numbers by raising standards, has caused the American economy to have too few trained doctors as measured by three criteria: (1) national needs, (2) doctors' earnings, (3) the nation's stock of talented young people who are eager to be doctors or who would be eager if their economic situation did not make that out of the question. Since 1910 the number of medical schools has not increased and the output of doctors has failed to grow commensurately with population increases.

Thus a case can be made for government aid on a large scale to education, both for tuition and for extra capital facilities. A federal education program,

---

[1] See Milton Friedman and Simon Kuznets, *Income from Independent Professional Practice* (National Bureau of Economic Research, Inc., New York, 1945).

going beyond the G.I. Bill of Rights, would be an extrapolation of what has always been peculiarly an American trend at the state and local levels.

In conclusion, the individual must keep two important qualifications in mind before applying our figures to his own case: (1) It is a fact that those over forty with a Harvard degree earn $8,500, or twice as much as the average college graduate. But this does not necessarily mean that the Harvard sheepskin deserves all the credit. We know that Harvard students are already a select group with respect to wealth,[1] influence, and perhaps ability; no one can tell how much of their extra earnings were due to the degree. The same point holds for all professions. (2) An individual choosing a profession is not interested just in average figures, but in the spread. If two professions have equal average earnings but one has greater extremes at the top and the bottom, which will be chosen by the individual? This depends. Some people who value certainty will prefer dentistry to medicine even though its average earnings are less, because there is less chance that a dentist will earn starvation wages than a doctor. However, there is also less chance that he will hit the jackpot of very high earnings. Other individuals like to take a chance, particularly since they and their families are often biased in favor of their own capabilities and chances of coming out on top. Certain it is that, in professions like law and movie acting, the few rich plums held out at the top constitute an attraction for aspirants far beyond what is justified by any reasonable probability calculation. It is one of the more engaging traits of human nature to feel, "I am different." Alas, there result vast social wastage and endless heartbreak to would-be artists, musicians, and inventors. To these fields as to the Kingdom of Heaven—many are called but few are chosen.

A PROLETARIAT OF COLLEGE GRADS?

The previous figures are all based on the past. What of the future? With so many going to college now, any one ambitious person feels he cannot possibly miss going. But what will happen if the number of graduates swells beyond suitable job opportunities? Will college graduates willingly go into other occupations? Or will they insist upon following traditional careers, thereby creating low wages and much unemployment among the intellectuals? And if this condition materializes, as some think it did in Europe, will there result a politically disaffected and frustrated group?

No one knows the answer to these questions. Professor Seymour Harris, in *The Market for College Graduates* (Harvard, 1949) presents statistics and arguments that foretell a gloomy future. Others, impressed by the continuing

[1] For example, in 1946 the average family income of Harvard students was $9,000.

favorable economic position of college men, take a more cheerful view. Which is right the future will decide.

SUMMARY

1. Although the rural birth rate is higher than the urban, a persistent cityward migration means that the percentage of the population engaged in agriculture is declining. Improvements in agricultural techniques mean that the same total of food can be produced with fewer workers; and as incomes increase, the increase in demand for food is less than proportionate. Farm income is low and unstable; as a result, the government has undertaken a variety of programs to support farm-product prices and to maintain farm incomes.

2. The fall in interest rates has worked to the disadvantage of the *rentier* class; but countering this has been a great increase in the total of funds loaned, so that the total of interest payments has not fallen.

3. Within the labor market, white-collar-job incomes have suffered a relative decline, down to the level of semiskilled pay. Increased demand has been more than offset by increased supply, as a result of expanded secondary education and an influx of women workers. The differential of skilled labor pay over that of semiskilled has also narrowed.

4. Executive and professional earnings continue to be high relative to other earnings. But the professions differ widely both with respect to the average (or median) level of income and the spread of incomes around that average. With the exceptions of teaching and the ministry, the difference between professional and nonprofessional earnings is perhaps greater than that explainable in terms of ability differences. This raises problems concerning future public aid to education, to enable more bright young people to enter the professions. What the expansion of college enrollment following World War II will do to the future earnings of graduates is a question that remains to be answered.

QUESTIONS FOR DISCUSSION

1. Give reasons for past and future migration from country to town. Do noneconomic factors reinforce or work against the basic economic fact of relatively low farm income?

2. Contrast the cyclical pattern of agriculture and of industry.

3. Describe government indirect and direct aids to agriculture. What does "parity" mean?

4. What do you think must be the long-run solution for the agriculture problem?

5. How extensive is the *rentier* class? How does its prosperity depend on price levels, interest rates, and stock dividends? Did its day end in 1929?

6. Contrast the position today of skilled, semiskilled, and other categories of labor with their relative position 50 years ago. Give reasons for the change.

7. What are the economic and noneconomic rewards to a successful career as a business executive? Do you feel the public appreciates this class at its true worth?

8. How do earnings differ in the different professions with respect to age, place, and inequality of distribution?

9. How would you have to go about throwing light on the question: Is advanced training a good investment? Do you think America is sending the right people in the right numbers to college? Give your reasons.

Chapter 6: BUSINESS

ORGANIZATION AND INCOME

OURS is a business civilization. To understand it at all, we must first understand the organization and functioning of business enterprise. The first part of this chapter leads up to the analysis of the modern corporation, primarily by an extensive case study; the last half is concerned with the financial structure of corporations, particularly the modern large-scale or "giant" corporation. In an appendix there is presented a brief introduction to the fundamentals of accounting, without a comprehension of which there can be no real understanding of the economics of enterprise.

A. *THE FORMS OF BUSINESS ORGANIZATION*

THE POPULATION OF BUSINESS ENTERPRISES

There are some 4 million American business units in the early 1950's. All except a very small fraction of these enterprises consist of very small-scale units owned by a single person. Most businesses are here today and gone tomorrow, the average life expectancy of a business being only about half a dozen years. Some will terminate in bankruptcy; many more will be voluntarily brought to a close with sighs of regret for dashed hopes and an expensive lesson learned; still others will come to a joyous end when their "self-employed" owner finally lands a good, steady job or takes up a new line of endeavor.

As fast as old businesses die, others are born. The present population of business concerns grew up as a result of the cumulated excess of business births over business deaths during previous years. As the American economy grows, we may expect a steady further increase in the number of firms from a normal excess of business births over deaths.

During World War II few old businesses failed, but few new businesses could be born. At the end of the war there was a spectacular growth of new businesses to make up for lost time. The causes are obvious: extreme national prosperity, increasing supplies of civilian goods, wartime cumulations of savings by would-be businessmen, easy credit conditions, and government help to former servicemen.

BIG, SMALL, AND INFINITESIMAL BUSINESS

By number, the tiny, transient, self-owned "individual proprietorship" is overwhelmingly the dominant form of American business. But in terms of dollar value, political and economic power, payrolls, and employment, some few hundred "giant corporations" occupy a strategically dominant position in the modern American economy.

Let us glance briefly at the role in our economy of "infinitesimal businesses." There are almost 400,000 grocery-store owners in the United States, all trying to make a living. There are almost a quarter of a million automobile service stations; more than 50,000 drugstores; and so it goes through all types of retailing and service establishments.[1]

Some of these ventures are highly successful, but it is still true to say that

[1] Out of every 1,000 business establishments in the United States, approximately
  170 are retail food stores
  90 are eating and drinking establishments
  90 are in the real-estate, insurance, or finance fields
  70 are filling stations
  60 are motor-truck or taxicab owners
  60 are contractors, etc.
  60 are beauty or barber shops
  45 are wholesalers of various kinds
  35 are automobile dealers, repair shops or garages
  35 are clothing or general-merchandise stores
  30 are laundries, etc.
  20 are shops for shoe repair, shoeshines, etc.
  15 are food-manufacturing plants
  15 are drugstores
  15 are printing shops or publishing plants, etc.

All the data referred to thus far are from Department of Commerce and Bureau of the Census sources. In addition, reliance is placed throughout this chapter on data from The National Industrial Conference Board; The National Resources Planning Board; R. A. Gordon, *Business Leadership in the Large Corporation* (Brookings, Washington, D.C., 1945); *TNEC Report*, Temporary National Economic Committee, 1938–1940; W. L. Crum, *Corporate Size and Earning Power* (Harvard University Press, Cambridge, Mass., 1939).

most do not earn for their owners much more than they could get with less effort and risk by working for somebody else. Thus, a few chain stores do about 35 per cent of all the grocery business, the rest being divided among all the independents. Most of these independents consist of the so-called "Ma and Pa" stores, doing less than $50 of business every day. These are often started by people who have only a couple of thousand dollars of initial capital—less than half the amount necessary for an adequate grocery store that will do the $150 a day business necessary if the owner is to earn even minimum wages for his effort. Such small-scale efforts are doomed from their very beginning; they are finished when the owner's initial capital is used up. They help to illustrate why one-third to one-half of all retail businesses are discontinued before they are 2 years old.

Of course, different fields differ in the amount of capital that is required. To build a modern service station costs more than $40,000; but to lease one from a gasoline company brings the initial capital requirement down to around $5,000. Occupations with a high rate of turnover of inventory—like vegetable stores—obviously require less initial capital than drugstores, hardware, or jewelry stores where many items of stock will stay on the shelves for 3 to 5 years and where the average "turnover ratio" of annual sales to stock of inventory may be less than one.

Aside from the capital necessary to open a business, there is the tremendous amount of personal effort that is required. Self-employed farmers usually work from 60 to 70 hours per week as compared to about 58 for farm hands. Similarly, it has been estimated that the people in other trades who are their own bosses put in at least 8 hours more per week than wage earners. Who, on his Sunday ride in the country, has not had pity for some self-employed drudge, whose own efforts and those of all his family hardly suffice to cause him to break even? Still, people will always want to start out on their own. Theirs may be the successful venture. Even if they never do succeed in earning more than a couple of thousand a year, there is something attractive about being able to make your own plans and in performing the variety of tasks that a small enterpriser must tend to every day.

THE SINGLE PROPRIETORSHIP

We may gain insight into the principal forms of business organization—the single proprietorship, the partnership, and the corporation—by following the history of a particular business venture as it grows from a small beginning into a good-sized corporation. In the last part of this chapter, we shall turn to the subject of the giant corporation and its modern economic role.

Let us suppose that you decide to start a business to produce tooth paste.

You may have hit upon a good preparation in your chemistry class, or you may simply have looked up an old formula in the *Encyclopaedia Britannica* or the *U.S. Pharmacopoeia.* To be a single proprietor you need not get anybody's permission; you simply wake up one morning and say, "Today, I am in business!" And you are.

You may hire as few or as many laborers as you wish, borrow whatever capital you can. At the end of the day or month whatever is left over as profits, after all costs have been met, is yours to do with as you like. And there is nothing to stop you at any time from going to the cash register, taking out $800, and giving it to your wife to buy a fur coat or a piece of Chippendale furniture. Of course as an individual you must pay personal income taxes on all your earnings.

The losses of the business also are all yours. If your sales fail to cover the costs you have incurred, your creditors can ask you to dig deep into your personal assets: the war bonds put aside for junior's education, the old farmstead, and all the rest. In legal terms an individual proprietor has "unlimited liability" for all debts contracted by the business. All his property, beyond a small minimum, is legally attachable to meet those debts.[1]

BUSINESS GROWTH AND THE NEED FOR SHORT-TERM CAPITAL

Let us suppose that the business is prospering tremendously, perhaps because a chain of five-and-ten-cent stores has been induced by your low price to place a large order for tubes of paste to be marketed under its name. Although you are now making more money than you expected to, you find yourself harder pressed for cash than ever before. Why? Because you are not paid in advance for your sales, whereas you must pay your workers and suppliers promptly on the receipt of their services. For the moment you are putting out money and getting nothing for it, *i.e.*, nothing except the certainty of future payment on the sales orders which you have booked, nothing but a miscellaneous batch of "goods in process"—unfinished tooth paste, empty tubing, and so forth.

To some extent, the stringency of "working capital" can be relieved by your not paying for supplies until the end of the month or even longer. However, there is a limit to which your suppliers will let you run up bills. Furthermore, letting your so-called "accounts payable liabilities" pile up is an expensive way of raising capital. This is because goods are often billed at 2 per cent discount if paid within 30 days; when you do not take advantage of such

---

[1] An economics textbook cannot go into the legal details, which vary from state to state, concerning the minimum amount of household furniture and property that bankrupt proprietors or partners are allowed to keep.

discounts, you are, in effect, paying so high an interest rate that borrowing at any reasonable rate of interest would be better.

Where is such a single proprietor to borrow? A personal finance company will probably charge you something like 3 per cent per month or 40 per cent per year for a small personal loan, and even such a company will prefer to lend to a man with a steady wage, which can be legally "attached" or "garnisheed" in case of nonpayment. If you own a home without a mortgage, a loan at 4, 5, or 6 per cent might be raised upon it. To borrow in this way is clearly to risk your family's future well-being, but probably if you are sufficiently convinced of your business future you might assume the risk.

Someone will naturally ask why the local banker cannot be called upon for a commercial loan at 6 per cent or less. The answer is that, ordinarily, a commercial bank will not provide "venture capital" for an unproven enterprise. The bank's vice-president looks at your checking balance and finds that it has always been near the vanishing point; this is natural, since as fast as payments have come in, you have had to write checks to stave off the ever-insistent claims of your creditors. Ordinarily, the bank likes to make 3-month loans to be used for peak-season needs and to be canceled during the rest of the year. It is idle to pretend that 3 months from now your growing business will be any more flooded with cash than now, and that you will not at that time be applying for continuous renewal of the loan.

Even if the bank were emancipated from the old-fashioned prejudice against "term loans" of some years' duration, it could not conscientiously provide the capital to a business like yours. However certain and glorious the future of the business appears to you, to the banker you are only one of numerous would-be entrepreneurs, most of whom are destined for failure even in the best of times, and almost all of whom will certainly be wiped out when the first big depression comes along. For the bank really to protect the sums entrusted to it by its depositors, it would have to charge you an extra risk premium, in addition to, say, 4 per cent interest, of perhaps 10 per cent or more.[1] Otherwise, the successful ventures would not be meeting the losses of the unsuccessful ones.

There is probably only one possibility of your getting a loan from the bank. If you are a World War II veteran, one of the provisions of the G.I. Bill of Rights provides that the government, after surveying your business prospects,

---

[1] Another alternative, which has been used extensively in Germany but not in the United States or Great Britain, would be for the bank to buy part ownership in your business and share in the jack pot of profits. Such participation in ownership inevitably leads to management responsibilities by the banks and often to monopoly control of business by banking interests. For this reason, and others, such activity is legally forbidden to our banks.

may "guarantee" one-half of your bank loan, up to a guarantee by the government of $2,000. Since the banker's risk has been reduced, he is usually glad to lend you the money at the specified 4 per cent. It is to be emphasized that the whole transaction is a loan and not a gift, a loan that the veteran will have to make good out of his private assets. Furthermore, if a veteran has used up his borrowing provisions on a foolish venture, he is out of luck as far as future loans are concerned.

Despite your makeshift attempts to borrow capital, the business is still suffering from a bad case of growing pains. You have exhausted all possibilities of raising further loan capital. There is nothing for you to do but look around for a partner.

THE PARTNERSHIP

Any two or more people can get together and form a partnership. Each party will agree to provide some fraction of the work and capital, to share some percentage of the profits, and of course to share some percentage of any losses or debts. A purely oral agreement will do, but it will be more business-like and make for less misunderstanding if some sort of formal partnership agreement is drawn up by a lawyer.

In the case of the tooth-paste business, let us suppose that your brother-in-law is given a part ownership in the business in return for putting up $21,000 of capital. Like you, he is to work for the company, receiving, let us say, a salary of $4,000 per year as compared to your $7,000.[1] You are to receive two-thirds of all profits or losses and he one-third.

Your partner has put up $21,000 in cold cash. What have you brought into the venture? In the first place, you have, of course, some unfinished barrels of tooth paste to contribute, along with some uncollected accounts receivable for goods already delivered. This does not seem like much.

Actually, what you bring to the partnership is an intangible but valuable asset: the profitable sales orders, the know-how, or what is called "good will." In short, you are bringing with you a potential profit-earning power over all costs of, say, $9,000 a year. You are letting your partner have a $4,000 a year job—which we shall assume is about equal to what he can get elsewhere—and in addition for $21,000 he is purchasing a one-third slice of $9,000 every year.

To get this much per year from bond investments would cost him much

[1] It is customary to speak of these payments as "salaries," but strictly, they are not; they are *withdrawals*. The partners agree that each shall receive the specified sum—provided there is enough money in the business to pay it. A salary is a payment to a hired employee; as a claim, it would rank ahead of a partner's withdrawal account in the event of financial difficulties.

more than $21,000. He would have to buy $100,000 worth of 3 per cent government bonds to get such a return, or $50,000 worth of 6 per cent private bonds. Aside from the risk element, your partner is getting a good buy for his $21,000, since he will be collecting some 14 per cent on his investment every year. Clearly, therefore, your two-thirds share is justified by the good will that you are supplying.[1]

CAUSES OF BUSINESS GROWTH

So your business continues to prosper and grow. Each year, both partners agree to take out of the business only their salaries and about a fifth of their profits, plowing back the rest of the profits into the business.

Why do you decide to take out any profits from the business at all? Because you both need the cash to pay your federal personal income taxes, which are levied not only on your salaries but also *upon your respective shares of the partnership's earnings*. The government is a silent partner, sharing about one-third out of every extra dollar that you receive and out of every extra dollar of your partner's slightly smaller income.

The business has grown because (1) more orders for tooth paste have come in as a result of your trade name becoming advertised and better known and as a result of your sending out more salesmen. (2) As more tooth paste is produced, economies of large-scale production are realized so that you are able to cut your price. (3) A new factor of growth results from "vertical integration." You decide to buy a chemical factory so as to be sure of a cheap source of supply, and in addition you become your own wholesaler, thus operating three stages rather than only one "stage of production." (4) In addition, the company begins to grow by "horizontal integration"; you take advantage of a profitable opportunity to buy out a number of competitors producing similar tooth pastes in this and other areas. (5) New "complementary products," such as soap and lipstick are added. You feel that bringing in the new lines under the same roof will help to spread the overhead expenses, and your salesmen feel that they might just as well get many orders as few when making a call. (6) Finally, your business may grow just because you are producing a better tooth paste.

NEW NEEDS AND SOURCES OF CAPITAL

Once again, the enterprise finds itself in a paradoxical situation: The more successful it is and the faster it grows, the harder up it is for capital. The

[1] The problem of good will and capitalized earning power is discussed further in the Appendix to this chapter on accounting.

$21,000 of new "equity capital" brought into the business did not stay in the form of cash very long. It was quickly transformed in part into circulating assets such as goods in process and office supplies. In part it was used to pay off the most pressing liabilities of the concern, particularly the highly costly, undiscounted, accounts payable liabilities.

The remainder was used as a down payment on a factory building and equipment. The difference between the down payment and the purchase price of the factory was secured by a mortgage loan on the property. The mortgage money was advanced by a near-by life-insurance company and was to be amortized or paid off in installments over a period of 20 years along with $3\frac{1}{2}$ per cent interest per year on the actual principal still unpaid at any time. In case the loan should not be paid, the holder of the mortgage of course has the right to foreclose the mortgage, *i.e.*, to take over the ownership of the building and sell it for what it will bring. Since the down payment on the factory came to about one-fourth of its price, and since this price was a bargain price to begin with, and since each year the insurance company will be getting back part of its principal, the risk taken by the company is not very great. The only way it could lose would be if there were a disastrous real-estate crash within the first few years of the making of the contract.

Despite the continuous plowing of profits back into the business, the growth of the enterprise still leaves you in need of further capital. But now, having established your reputation, so to speak, some new avenues of borrowing are open to you. Your banker will be glad to lend you money to tide you over the busy pre-Christmas period. An industrial finance company, like the Commercial Credit Corporation, will lend you money on the basis of your safe, but as yet uncollected, "accounts receivable" (meaning by these two words the sums owed you for goods that you have sold and delivered but which have not yet been paid for). Finally, your bank, which was leary of lending you money for venture capital, becomes willing to make a "term loan" for 5 years. Or if the bank should still be unwilling, the government's Reconstruction Finance Corporation (RFC) can advance you the money on its own or guarantee a private bank loan, provided it considers your activity to be in the national interest and to be a good risk.

Let us suppose that, when all is said and done, you still need more capital than you can raise by any kind of borrowing. The painful necessity arises of getting more "equity" capital by letting some new people share in the profits (and losses) of the business. As a matter of fact, even if you could still find some institutions to borrow from, it would be unwise to do so. You have already superimposed too many liabilities and fixed charges on a narrow equity base. As long as things go well, it is lovely to earn 10 per cent profit on capital that costs you only 5. But if losses should occur, they will fall all the more heavily on the two partners who are the residual owners.

DISADVANTAGES OF THE PARTNERSHIP FORM

One possibility of getting more ownership capital is to admit new partners. There is no limit to the number of partners that you can admit; there have been partnerships in the brokerage and banking fields involving more than 100 people. However, every time a new partner is admitted, or one dies or resigns, a whole new partnership must be formed.

Moreover, as the number of partners increases, there comes to the fore a factor that has been soft-pedaled in our discussion up to now. Each partner is liable *without limit* to the full extent of his personal fortune for all debts contracted by the partnership. If he owns 1 per cent of the partnership and the business fails, then he will be called upon to foot 1 per cent of the bills, and the other partners will be assessed their 99 per cent. Should they be unable to pay any part of their assessment, then the 1 per cent partner may be called upon to pay *for all*, even if it means selling his fine etchings at auction or disposing of his home.

This feature of *unlimited liability* reveals why partnerships tend to be confined to small, homogeneous, personal enterprises. When it becomes a question of placing their personal fortunes in jeopardy, people are ordinarily very reluctant to put their capital into complex ventures over which they can exercise little control. According to the doctrine of "mutual agency" involved in the law of partnerships, each partner has rather broad powers to act as an agent to commit the whole partnership.

This explains why agriculture and retail trade are the only sectors of our economy where more than half of the business done is done by single proprietors and partnerships. In the field of investment banking, concerns like J. P. Morgan & Company used to advertise proudly "not incorporated" so that their creditors could have the extra assurance. But even these concerns have transmuted themselves into such corporate entities as Morgan, Stanley and Company, Inc., and J. P. Morgan, Inc.

Two further disadvantages—in addition to unlimited liability—are often said to characterize the partnership. First, and much less important than most textbooks would have us believe, there is the need to start a new partnership every time somebody new enters or when somebody dies. The trouble and nuisance of such reorganizations are rather trifling, as is well known in the investment banking field.

More weighty is the real disadvantage stemming from the fact that a partnership can be dissolved whenever any party finds the existing arrangement unsatisfactory and wishes to withdraw.[1] In any case, the law of partnerships makes it impossible for any partner to sell his share to a new party without the consent of his partners. If agreement cannot be secured, a costly liquidation of the assets of the partnership may be inevitable.

The giant brokerage partnership of Merrill, Lynch, Pierce, Fenner, and Beane handles a sizable fraction of all stock-market trading in this country. It has many major partners and scores of junior partners. It illustrates that the barriers put up by the partnership form to running a large enterprise are not insuperable. But except in the brokerage field, where corporations cannot belong to the New York Stock Exchange, such giant partnerships are rare.

B. *THE MODERN CORPORATION*

At this point, therefore—or even long before—you will probably decide to form a corporation rather than a partnership. Usually you will incorporate in the state in which you live and operate. However, if the corporation is of any size, you may prefer to establish token headquarters in some state like Delaware or New Jersey, where the regulations governing corporations are made much lighter than in other states in order to attract corporations.

Some centuries ago, corporation charters were awarded by governments very rarely and only by special acts of the king and legislature. Parliament or Congress would graciously permit a public-utility enterprise or railroad to form a corporation to do specific things and perform specific functions. The East India Company was such a privileged corporation. The early railroads here and abroad often had to spend as much money in getting a charter through the legislature as in preparing their roadbeds. Gradually within the past century, this procedure began to seem unfair and it became the practice to pass general incorporation laws granting almost anyone the privilege of forming a corporation for almost any purpose, without having to get a special vote of approval from Congress or Parliament.

Today, for a very small fee a lawyer will draw up the necessary papers of

[1] Perhaps the reader will remember how the novelist William Dean Howells has his famous title character, Silas Lapham, a rising self-made paint tycoon, present his partner with the ultimatum: "You buy me out or I'll buy you out." Silas' two excuses, that his were the real brains and energy responsible for the success of the business and that the proffered price exceeded his partner's original investment, were cleverly seen through by Mrs. Lapham. She pointed out that, without the partner's money at the critical time, the business could never have succeeded and that Silas' offer to sell was premised upon the knowledge that his partner was not in a position to buy the whole of the business.

incorporation and will write into the charter almost as wide powers and purposes as you could wish. Automatically and at small expense the state will grant the corporate charter.

Let us see how the incorporating procedure works in the case of your tooth-paste company. You decide to issue 20,000 shares of common stock in the corporation, 6,600 going to you, 3,300 to your partner, 100 to your wife, and the other 10,000 to be sold to outside interests. Although each share is to have an initial stated value of $10, your lawyer has advised you to make them no-par-value shares, since "par value" has no particular significance anyway.

The 10,000 shares to be sold to the public are to be marketed through a local *investment banking* firm. These firms are simply merchandisers of securities; and like any merchant, their profit comes from the difference between their buying and selling prices. Because yours is such a small business, they must drive a hard bargain, especially since they can claim that the costs of selling the securities are likely to be high. Thus the investment brokers may offer you $10 per share and plan to resell at a price of $12.50 per share. Had you been a large company, you might have held out for as much as $12.40, or even in some cases $12.45, out of the $12.50 selling price, because of the eager competitive bidding of the different investment banking syndicates.

Moreover, for a large company the investment banker would probably have agreed to underwrite the new issue of 10,000 shares. This means that he would have guaranteed the purchase of the full 10,000 shares at a set price. If the market then refused to buy all these shares from the investment banker at his announced price, he, not you, would have to absorb the loss. But he probably regards you as too small and untried a business to justify his assuming the underwriting risk. Consequently, if it should have been impossible for him to sell all the shares, you would have had to do with less capital.

Fortunately, all goes well and he pays you $100,000 in cash for the securities that he has sold. Unlike the case of the partnership, you need not concern yourself with the people to whom he has sold the shares, or with the fact that they may resell their shares to still someone else. The names of the owners of the shares are registered with the company just in case they get lost and so that you will know where to send the dividend checks or the announcements of stockholders' meetings. Ordinarily, each owner is given one vote and a share in the earnings of the corporation in direct proportion to the number of shares he owns. Someone with 100 shares has 100 votes and will receive correspondingly higher dividends.

The outside owners of 10,000 shares have paid in $100,000 of cash to the company. What have you and your partner paid in? Obviously not cash, but rather an equivalent amount of earning assets: plant, equipment, goods in process, and perhaps good will which is, as we have already seen, the capitalized value of the presumed "excess earning power" of the business, resulting from its trade-marks, patents, know-how, and so forth.

Back in the good old days before 1929, you and your investment banker might have evaluated the good will pretty much as liberally as you wished, possibly giving yourself 20,000 rather than 10,000 shares. This practice has been called "watering the stock." But today, you would have to submit any sizable new issue to the SEC. They would have to satisfy themselves that the public is not being invited to pay good cash for "useless water" before they would approve the new flotation. Moreover, they would try to make sure that there was no phony advertising or inspired false rumors, and that the salesman who peddles the shares leans over backward in providing advice and authentic accounting information. However, they do not pretend to pass judgment on or certify to the value of the stock.

ADVANTAGES AND DISADVANTAGES OF THE CORPORATE FORM

The corporation has solved most of the problems that bothered you about the partnership. It is an almost perfect device for the raising of large sums of capital. Most important, every stockholder now has *limited liability*. After paying $12.50 for a share of stock, the investor need not worry about his personal estate's being in jeopardy. If worse comes to worst and the business becomes bankrupt, the most that each shareholder could lose would be his original $12.50 per share. He cannot be assessed further.

Of secondary importance is the fact that the corporation is a fictitious legal person created by the state. It exists not by "natural right" but only at the pleasure of the state. The corporation, as distinct from its owners, can be sued in court and can sue. Any officer of the company, unlike any partner, is strictly limited in his legal ability to act as agent for the other owners and to commit them financially. Also, the corporation may have "perpetual succession" or existence, regardless of how many times the shares of stock change hands by sale or bequest, and regardless of whether there are 10,000 different stockholders. No group of shareholders can force any other group to sell or retain their holdings, and only a majority vote rather than unanimity is needed to reach any legitimate business decision. Usually the stockholders will be too numerous to meet for every decision; they will prefer to elect a board of directors consisting of a dozen or so members to represent them between annual meetings, in much the same way that democratic electorates select legislative representatives to act for them. However, as we shall see in a moment, the problem of keeping large corporations "truly democratic" is almost an insuperable one.

There is one disadvantage to incorporation that has become increasingly serious in recent years. The federal government (and many states) taxes corporate income and regulates corporate activities. Thus, during World War II a small and profitable corporation might have had to pay as much as 80 per cent of its income to the government in excess-profit taxation. In 1951 it would have to pay almost 45 per cent in ordinary corporate income taxes—and more if its excess profits become taxable. These corporate taxes are *in addition* to the personal income taxes which must later be paid on all dividends distributed to the share owners.

A number of intelligent businessmen are beginning to realize that this is a rather high price for a small business to pay for limited liability and greater ease of raising capital; many are deciding to continue business in the partnership form. However, their decision is complicated by the existence of tax *advantages* offered by the corporate form. There is a loophole in our present law whereby all *undistributed* corporate profits escape *personal* income taxes; only paid-out dividends are taxed by the personal-income-tax law. A very rich man who is taxed at about 85 cents on every dollar of personal income says to himself: "It would be better to invest in a corporation which distributes little of its earnings than to invest in a partnership and be taxed 85 per cent of all earnings whether they are plowed back into the business or paid out to me. Of course, the corporation has to pay 45 per cent on its earnings, and I must pay an additional 85 per cent on what they pay out to me in dividends. But if they don't pay out much in dividends, my effective tax rate is 45 rather than 85 per cent."

To some degree he is only putting off the evil day. For when he does come to collect his future dividends, they will be taxable. As we saw in Chapter 3, in a world of compound interest, time is money, and it is an important task of tax lawyers to find legal ways of putting off the evil day for their clients. The forgotten man who "gets it in the neck" is the relatively poor stockholder who is taxed personally perhaps 30 per cent on his dividend receipts and who already has indirectly paid a 45 per cent corporate tax. This is sometimes called "double taxation."[1]

Problems of taxation properly belong in the chapters on governmental finance and cannot be discussed further here.

---

[1] Another loophole used to avoid the disadvantages of double taxation under the corporate form is for the owners of a closely held corporation to vote most of its earnings to themselves and their relatives in the form of high salaries. The Treasury Department tries to check up on such ways of avoiding taxes by puffing up expenses; but it is always hard to know whether a given second cousin is or is not really worth $15,000 a year.

HOW A CORPORATION CAN RAISE CAPITAL

Let us suppose that the corporation continues to grow as a result of vertical and horizontal combination, addition of new products, economies of mass production, advertising promotion, and so forth. What new forms of financing are available to it in addition to borrowing on promissory notes or mortgages or buying on credit?

Bonds. First it may issue bonds. These are nothing but special kinds of promissory notes printed on fancy paper and issued in $100 or other denominations so as to be readily marketable for resale. A bond is a security promising to pay a certain number of dollars every 6 months for a number of years until it matures. At that time the borrowing company promises to pay off the principal of the bond at its face value. (Often the company has the right to call in the bond a few years before its maturity date by paying the bondholders some previously agreed upon price.) The dollar installments paid every 6 months, which represent the interest earnings of the bond, are usually called the "coupon payments," because the owner of the bond cuts off a certain little corner of the bond each 6 months, which little coupon he then mails and receives his interest payment.

Ordinarily, the coupons and principal must be paid on time regardless of whether the company has been making earnings or not. Otherwise the company is in default of its obligations and can be taken to court like any debtor. (Occasionally the bonds are also covered by a mortgage on the corporation's factories or equipment so as to give the lenders extra security.) Of course, there is no particular reason why a partnership could not borrow by the use of bonds; but ordinarily it would not be well enough known to succeed in interesting any lenders. For that matter a small corporation is rarely in a position to raise capital by issuing bonds.

Common Stocks. It will be clear that issuing bonds and issuing common stocks are exactly opposite methods of financing. The common stockholder is providing "equity" capital. He shares in all profits and in control of business decisions, but he must also share in all losses. His is a more risky venture, because he can never receive any dividends until the fixed charges owed to the bondholder are paid off. The bondholder gets a nominally lower but steadier income. Unless the corporation is bankrupt or in danger of being so, the bondholder has ordinarily no legal control over the decisions of the business; but a wise management will take care to stay on good terms with all sources of future capital.

Preferred Stocks. Intermediate between bonds and common stocks are so-called "preferred stocks." These are like bonds in that the buyer who puts up capital for them is limited in the percentage return that he can get from them—say, to a stipulated 4 per cent of the face value per share—no matter how profitable is the business in any year. However, he is more likely to get his fixed stock dividend than is the common stockholder, because his legal claim stands next in line after that of the bondholder and before that of the common stockholder.

If the tooth-paste company owes $2,000 per year in bond interest and has issued $50,000 worth of 4 per cent preferred stock, then the common stockholders will receive no earnings until the company's net profits (after all taxes!) are about $2,000 + $2,000. If net earnings are $5,000, then only $1,000 will be available for the common stockholders or only about $\frac{1}{2}$ per cent return on their $200,000 capital investment. Should the company have a good year and earn $40,000, then no less than $36,000 could be paid to the common stockholders without impairing the corporation's total assets.

Often "cumulative" preferred stock is issued rather than "noncumulative." The former term means that if for 5 years of depression there has not been enough in the way of earnings to pay any of the 4 per cent dividends on the preferred stock, then when good times come back again the "cumulated" $20 (5 × $4) of unpaid preferred stock dividends must be made good before the common stockholders can begin to receive any dividends. Often, too, preferred stock is "callable" or "convertible." The first term means that at some previously stated value, say $103, the company can buy back its outstanding preferred stock. The second term refers to the right given the preferred stockholder of converting each share into shares of common stock at some stipulated ratio.[1]

ADVANTAGES OF DIFFERENT SECURITIES

From the standpoint of the investor, bonds, preferred stocks, and common stock obviously form a sequence of increasing risk and decreasing security—balanced by an increased chance of making high earnings. Thus, today, a "gilt-edge" bond may yield about 3 per cent, a good preferred stock about 4 per cent, and a good common stock anywhere from 5 to 10 per cent.

To test his understanding of these three forms of securities, the reader should make sure that he understands why common stocks are better investments in time of inflation than the other two. Except for institutional investors, preferred stocks are not so popular as they used to be a few decades ago.

It would be a mistake to leave the reader with the impression that bonds

---

[1] Also some preferred stocks are made more attractive by being made "participating." This means that once profits exceed some agreed upon figure, they share with the common stockholder in any further profits.

are perfectly safe investments. On the contrary, during depressions many companies have gone bankrupt and their bonds have gone into default, paying off only a few cents on the dollar. Often a company will undergo reorganization in which the stockholders may be squeezed out completely; the courts may appoint a "receiver" or trustee to run the business and the bondholders may be given bonds (or even stocks!) equal only to some fraction of their original investments. Moreover, certain bondholders may have prior claims over holders of other issues, depending upon whether the bonds were backed by so-called "first," "second," or even "third" mortgages, etc. Many investors in railroad securities have learned of the above possibilities in the hard way.

From the standpoint of the corporation, bond borrowing creates low but inflexible fixed charges. These fixed charges may be highly embarrassing in bad times. Preferred stock is slightly better with respect to flexibility, and equity capital best of all.[1]

THE GIANT CORPORATION

We have now carried our successful tooth-paste enterprise far enough up the ladder of success. The rest of this chapter will be concerned with the economic position and power of the very large modern corporation, and the problems that they create for the American economy.

A list of the 200 largest nonfinancial corporations reads like an honor roll of American business, almost every name being a familiar household word. Among the 107 industrial companies will be found United States Steel, Bethlehem Steel, and the Aluminum Company of America; Standard Oil of New Jersey, of California, of Indiana; the Texas Company; General Motors, Chrysler, and Ford; Swift, Armour, and Cudahy meat packing; American Tobacco (Luckies), R. J. Reynolds (Camels), and Liggett and Myers Tobacco (Chesterfields); The Great Atlantic & Pacific Tea Company, Sears Roebuck, Montgomery Ward, F. W. Woolworth, and J. C. Penney; National Dairy Company (Kraft's), Borden's, Procter & Gamble, and Lever Brothers, and so forth.

Among the 39 railroads are such old stand-bys as Pennsylvania, New York Central, Southern Pacific, and many others. The public-utility list of 54 companies is headed by A.T.&T. and Commonwealth & Southern. This completes the three divisions of the 200 largest nonfinancial corporations.

[1] Bond interest charges can also be deducted from the corporation earnings for tax purposes. There is an incentive, therefore, other things being equal, to use this method of financing rather than either kind of stock financing. However, other things have not been equal, and the marked trend in the past 20 years has been away from fixed charges, or loan financing, and toward stock financing.

But if we go on to include in addition the 60 largest financial organizations, we bring in such giants as the Bank of America (California), and National City Bank (New York City), the Chase National Bank (New York City), the Continental Illinois National Bank (Chicago), and the First National Bank of Boston; the Metropolitan Life Insurance Company, the Prudential Life, New York Life, and so forth. Altogether there were in 1950 more than 56 companies whose assets had passed the billion dollar mark.

The tremendous concentration of economic power involved in these giant corporations may be gauged from the following facts: they alone own more than half of the total assets of all nonfinancial corporations, more than a third of all banking assets, and four-fifths of all life-insurance assets. In manufacturing alone, the 100 most important companies employed more than one-fifth of all manufacturing labor and accounted for one-third of the total value of all manufactured products.

Their power did not grow overnight. Up until the New Deal of 1933, their percentage importance steadily mounted. Throughout the 1930's and up to World War II, they grew some but, relatively speaking, just about held their own. During World War II, the largest 200 corporations operated more than half of all new war-plant facilities and had a slightly higher profit to sales ratio than the next smaller group of 800 companies. But small concerns showed an even greater percentage of profitability and growth. Large size breeds success, and success breeds further success,[1] but there are also economic and political barriers to largeness.

DIVORCE OF OWNERSHIP AND CONTROL IN THE LARGE CORPORATION

Let us begin to examine the internal workings of one of these giant corporations. *The most striking feature is the tremendous diversification of ownership among thousands and thousands of small stockholders.* In the postwar period, almost 700,000 different people had shares in A.T.&T., with one-quarter of the shares being held in blocks of less than 100 shares, and with no single owner possessing as much as 1 per cent of the total outstanding shares.

Berle and Means in a path-breaking study[2] pointed out that this wide diversi-

---

[1] The statistical evidence on profits suggests that profits increase with size but that the very biggest firms in an industry sometimes seem to show a slight dropping off of relative profits compared with the next to the largest. A larger percentage of small firms than of large firms falls in the class of firms making losses. However, as W. L. Crum's study, *Corporate Size and Earning Power* (Harvard University Press, Cambridge, Mass., 1939) has shown, within the class of firms that make profits, size and percentage profitability are negatively rather than positively correlated.

[2] A. A. BERLE, JR., and GARDNER C. MEANS, *The Modern Corporation and Private Property* (Commerce Clearing House, Inc., New York, 1932).

fication of stockholding has resulted in a *separation of ownership and control*. Recent studies have confirmed the fact that in the typical giant corporation, all management together—officers and directors—hold only about 3 per cent of the outstanding common stock. The largest single minority ownership groups typically hold only about a fifth of all outstanding voting stock. Such a small fraction is considered more than enough to maintain "working control."[1]

AMPLIFICATION OF CONTROL BY THE PYRAMIDING OF HOLDING COMPANIES

Even the figure of 5 to 1 amplification of the control exercised by minority stockholders is a gross understatement. In addition to the common stock outstanding, the corporation may have the use of as much capital again in the form of bond borrowing or preferred-stock issues. Moreover, there grew up during the 1920's the practice of selling nonvoting common stock to the public while retaining control of the voting stock for the insiders. Therefore a figure of 10 to 1 of assets controlled to assets owned is not at all unrealistic.

Nor is this all. With $100,000 I can hope to control a million-dollar company. But what if the million-dollar corporation is a holding company whose sole function is to control a 10-million-dollar company through its ownership of 10 per cent of that company's stock? And the latter is a holding company controlling a 100-million-dollar company in a similar way? A small amount of money at the apex of the inverted pyramid can be given tremendous leverage of control simply by adding more layers to the structure—the result being 1,000 to 1 amplification of control, or even more.

This use of holding companies is not a mere theoretical possibility. During the 1920's, vast and complex public-utility empires were built up by their use. Just to chart the organizational structure of such corporations as the Associated Gas & Electric system would take a number of ordinary sized book pages. The greatest losses to investors after the great 1929 stock-market crash came from such holding-company securities. The small and large investors who were eager to buy Middle Western Utilities from the highly respectable Chicago tycoon, Samuel Insull, lost every penny of their investments. It is for this and other reasons that Congress and the SEC have, by the Public Utility Holding Company Act (1935), passed a "death sentence" on such holding-company systems, and that they are in a gradual state of dissolving themselves.

A less dramatic case of pyramiding of control may be mentioned. The duPont family owns most of the shares of a holding company, Christiana

[1] See R. A. GORDON, *Business Leadership in the Large Corporation* (Brookings, Washington, D.C., 1945), Chap. II.

Securities Company. This company in turn owns about one-quarter of the voting stock of the great chemical concern E. I. duPont de Nemours, which in turn owns about one-quarter interest in GM. Although the direct participation by the duPonts in GM affairs appears to be lessening in recent years, it is clear that no management actually opposed to their interests and wishes would be able to get into office or maintain itself.

It should be added that in connection with neither GM nor the United States Rubber Company have the duPonts exercised their influence in a manner detrimental to the earnings of the other stockholders. On the contrary, anyone who put $1,000 into GM stock in 1920 would find himself with many, many times that wealth as a result of the repeated dividends of new shares of common stocks and the repeated split-ups of the common-stock shares.

LEADERSHIP AND CONTROL OF THE LARGE CORPORATION

The problem of keeping a large corporation truly democratic is a difficult one even to define. Until recent years, less than a dozen stockholders would turn up for the annual meeting. More recently, a few hundred have been attending such meetings, often drawn by free chicken salad and, it must be confessed, by the chance to heckle management.

Decisions at the annual meeting are really settled by the use of "proxies." Each stockholder is asked to mail in a proxy permitting the management to exercise his votes. Many do not reply. But enough usually do to establish a quorum and a comfortable plurality for management. The SEC has tried to improve the democratic structure of corporations by insisting that motions to be decided at the annual meeting be indicated on the proxy statement so that stockholders can indicate their preferences; also rival groups must be permitted mailing access to the stockholders, and so forth.

However, it still remains true that there is no fully effective democratic control of management by the stockholders. Political parties may go in and out of office, but most corporation managements are self-perpetuating. Occasionally there is a battle among giants, and one minority group is able to defeat another one. In 1929 John D. Rockefeller, Jr., led a spirited fight to oust from office Col. Robert W. Stewart, who had been allegedly engaged in some financial irregularities at the expense of Standard Oil of Indiana. After a titanic battle, Rockefeller won the day—proving that it takes tremendous initiative and power to turn out a well-entrenched management.

If not the stockholders, who do make corporate decisions? Primarily, the increasingly important class of *professional managers*. The old-time captain of industry, for all his creativeness and ability to calculate the risks necessary to build up a great enterprise, often had something of the buccaneer in his make-up and an irresponsible "the-public-be-damned" attitude. In company after company, the original founder has been replaced by a new type of executive, usually having a different surname; if he should be a completely self-made man, he will nevertheless probably have acquired special training and management skills. The new professional executive is more adept at public relations and in the handling of people. He is necessarily more the bureaucrat, interested as much in preserving the *status quo* as in taking extreme risks.

Typically, the dominant spirit will be the president of the corporation. As he begins to feel his years, he may have himself made chairman of the board of directors, while still serving as the chief executive officer (*e.g.*, Alfred Sloan in GM until 1946, or Sewell Avery in Montgomery Ward & Co., Inc.). More often, the chairman of the board is an elder statesman, who, together with a small executive or steering committee of the board of directors, gives advice and approval to the actions of the president and his many vice-presidents.

The exact role of the board of directors varies from company to company, and from group to group. Many directors are simply well-known men selected to give the company prestige. Others possess special knowledge and take an active part in determining policy. On the whole, it would be going too far to say that most boards of directors act simply as rubber stamps to approve the decisions already taken by the officers of the company. But it is true that, so long as management possesses the confidence of the board, that body will usually not actively intervene to dictate specific policies. This is the same sound administrative procedure usually followed by the board of trustees of a philanthropic foundation or college, and is not too unlike the parliamentary system of ministerial responsibility.

Generally speaking, there will be no clash of goals between the management and stockholders. Both will be interested in maximizing the profits of the firm. However, in two important situations, there may be a divergence of interests, not infrequently settled in favor of management. First, insiders may legally or illegally vote themselves and their friends or relatives large salaries, expense accounts, bonuses, and retirement pensions at the stockholders' expense. When many corporations do this, a vicious circle is introduced: every other corporation must follow suit under penalty of losing its better executives, and there is hardly any limit to the process. The wonder is not that executives' salaries are so high but that they are not higher.

A second conflict of interest may arise in connection with undistributed profits. The managers of every organization have an innate tendency to try to make it grow and perpetuate itself. The psychological reasons are subtle and by no means always selfish ones. There is reason to question whether profits are not plowed back into a company in some cases when the same capital could better be invested by the stockholders elsewhere, or be spent upon consumption. Indeed, the case occasionally arises when a company would be well advised to wind itself up and pay back its capital. But one need not be a cynic to doubt that management is likely to vote itself out of existence and out of jobs.

THE EVIL OF MONOPOLY

In view of the above facts, it is not surprising to find that most important American industries are characterized by a few large corporations whose

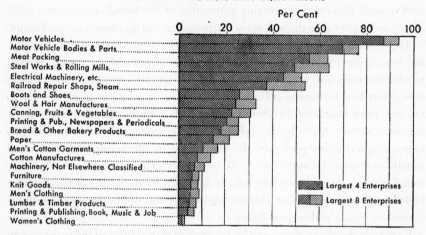

CONCENTRATION, MEASURED BY VALUE OF PRODUCTS, IN MANUFACTURING INDUSTRIES 1935

INDUSTRIES EMPLOYING MORE THAN 100,000 PERSONS

FIGURE 1. SOURCE: National Resources Committee, "Structure of the American Economy."

share of the output of that particular industry is vastly greater than their numerical importance would warrant. Figure 1 gives a list of the large American industries and depicts their degree of concentration by showing the relative proportion of total output controlled by the first four dominant corporations and by the next four.

Later, in Part Three, we shall analyze some of the problems raised by monopoly and imperfect competition. Within the past 60 years, particularly since the 1890 Sherman Antitrust Act, there has been great concern over the breaking down of free competitive markets under the encroachment of large-scale enterprise.

From an economic point of view it does not matter a great deal whether price is too high because of various of the following monopolistic devices:

(1) cooperative "pools" or "cartel agreements," (2) so-called "trusts" (involving selected "trustees" who "coordinate" pricing policy), (3) interlocking directorates, (4) "holding company" control, (5) tacit collusion and trade association action, (6) government "fair price" legislation (Robinson-Patman Act, etc.) and government sponsored "commodity agreements" (wheat, rubber, cotton, etc.). Too high a price, wastage of resources, and creation of monopoly profits are economic evils, however they are brought about and whatever the legal technicalities of the matter.

THE CURSE OF BIGNESS?

Is bigness itself a bad thing? Undoubtedly there is much popular hostility toward large corporations. Even if they could do so, General Motors or U.S. Steel would be most reluctant to swallow up competitors until they accounted for, say, nine-tenths of their respective industries. They would fear the effect on public opinion. Is this antagonism toward big business directed toward bigness itself? Or against the alleged evils of monopoly that are often supposed to be associated with bigness? What should public policy be toward a "benevolent, well-behaving, efficient" giant corporation?

The so-called "A and P" case provides an example. This chain of food stores is noted for its low prices. Yet the Department of Justice prosecuted it under the antitrust acts. Leaving aside certain minor irregularities that the company may have engaged in, the basic issue is clearly posed: Shall it be a crime to grow large as a result of efficiency and continued maintenance of low, competitive prices?

To produce a hydrogen atomic bomb, the government turned to the duPont Company and gave it a cost-plus-one-dollar contract. The scientific know-how of General and Western Electric are invaluable for peace as well as war. In the words of a recent world-famous economist:[1]

. . . the modern standard of life of the masses evolved during the period of relatively unfettered "big business." If we list the items that enter the modern workman's budget and from 1899 on observe the course of their prices not in terms of money but in terms of the hours of labor that will buy them—i.e., each year's money prices divided by each year's hourly wage rates, we cannot fail to be struck by the rate of the advance which, considering the spectacular improvement in qualities, seems to have been greater and not smaller than it ever was before. . . . Nor is this all. As soon as we go into details and inquire into the individual items in which progress was most conspicuous, the trail leads not to the doors of those firms that work under conditions of comparatively free competition but precisely to the doors of the large concerns—which, as in the case of agricultural machinery, also account for much of the progress in the

[1] J. A. SCHUMPETER, *Capitalism, Socialism, and Democracy* (Harper, New York, 1942).

competitive sector—and a shocking suspicion dawns upon us that big business may have had more to do with creating that standard of life than keeping it down.

This suggests that the future problem may not be one of choosing between large monopolistic corporations and small-scale competitors, but rather that of devising ways to improve the social and economic performance of large corporate aggregates. To channel the tremendously creative abilities of the modern large-scale corporation to the public good—that is the problem for the years ahead. We shall return to the problem of the maintenance of "effective and workable competition" after an analysis in Part Three of prices and cost under perfect and imperfect competition.

SUMMARY

A. FORMS OF BUSINESS ORGANIZATION

1. The present population of American businesses, which has grown up as a result of a cumulative excess of business births over business deaths, consists in the greater number of infinitesimal single proprietorships, largely in retail and service establishments. Their turnover is rapid.

2. The reader should understand how a small-scale enterprise grows, what are its needs and avenues for short-term or long-term capital, and what are the advantages and disadvantages of the corporate form over the single proprietorship and partnership.

B. THE MODERN CORPORATION

1. He should also be acquainted with the fundamental legal rights involved in the corporation, and with the general features of bonds, preferred- and common-stock corporate securities.

2. The problems created by the separation of ownership and control and by the great concentration of economic wealth and monopoly power in the modern giant corporation deserve serious study.

The best possible review of the economic principles discussed in this chapter is provided by a study of the fundamental principles of accounting presented briefly in the Appendix to this chapter. Accounting is an indispensable prerequisite to the understanding of economics.

QUESTIONS FOR DISCUSSION

1. Imagine that you are going to start a business of your own. Write a case history of its development.

2. Compare the advantages and disadvantages of (a) the single proprietorship, (b) the partnership, and (c) the corporation form of business organization.

3. What are the reasons underlying the growth of a business to large size?

4. Make a list of the ways of raising capital for small, medium, and large businesses.

5. What are the advantages and disadvantages of different kinds of securities?

6. Discuss the structure of the modern large corporation.

7. This chapter introduces such terms as holding company, investment banking, RFC, SEC, proxy, etc. Go through it to collect other such technical expressions. Give a definition of each.

8. What is meant by calling ours the age of the "Managerial or Bureaucratic Revolution"? Does this apply outside of government?

9. Give examples of divergent interests between stockholders and management. Of coincident interests.

10. Defend "bigness as such." Attack it. What evils often are thought to go along with bigness.

11. How might the economic evils of monopoly arise? Give examples.

APPENDIX TO CHAPTER 6
ELEMENTS OF ACCOUNTING

Ours is the Age of the Machine. Scarcely less important, it is the Age of Accounts. A little literacy in the elements of accounting is becoming a prime necessity in modern life.

THE BALANCE SHEET

It is necessary for every student of economics to have some understanding of the two fundamental accounting statements: the Balance Sheet and the Statement of Profit and Loss (or, as it is sometimes called, the Income Statement).

The balance sheet is presented in a report annually or oftener. It represents an instantaneous "still picture" of the condition of the enterprise as of some particular day, usually the last day of the year. Corresponding to the dollar value of every asset—tangible or intangible—there must necessarily be an exactly equal total amount of claims or ownership. The value of a $10,000 house is exactly matched by somebody's claim to ownership of that house, consisting, for example, of $7,000 owed to a creditor and $3,000 owned by the possessor of the house.

This is the fundamental identity underlying every balance sheet:

$$\text{Value of assets} = \text{value of claims or ownership}$$
$$= \text{value of liabilities (owed)} + \text{value}$$
$$\text{of proprietorship (owned)}$$

or

Assets = Liabilities + Net Worth

Let us illustrate this by considering a simple balance sheet as shown in Table 1. This is a new company whose operations have just got under way.

A question mark has been deliberately placed next to the Common Stock Net Worth item because the reader should realize for himself that the only correct entry compatible with our fundamental balance sheet truism is the number $200,000. A balance sheet must always balance—because Net Worth, *i.e.*, the ownership of the "residual claimants," always adjusts itself to make things balance.

To illustrate this, let us suppose that a thief steals all the cash, and a fire burns up one-fourth of the inventory. The accountant will learn of this sad news without turning a hair. "Total Assets are down $40,000 all told. Liabilities remain unchanged. Very well, I must write down Net Worth by $40,000, to the level of only $160,000." Such is the accountant's method of keeping score.

A number of interesting facts are revealed even by this simple balance sheet. First, it is customary to divide up assets according to whether they will be convertible into cash by normal operations within a year or not, the

TABLE 1. *Balance Sheet of Pepto-Glitter Co., Inc., as of December 31, 1955*

ASSETS		LIABILITIES AND NET WORTH	
		Liabilities	
Current Assets:		*Current Liabilities:*	
Cash...................	$ 20,000	Accounts payable.........	$ 20,000
Inventory...............	80,000	Notes payable............	30,000
Fixed Assets:		*Long-term Liabilities:*	
Equipment...............	130,000	RFC note................	50,000
Buildings................	170,000	Bonds payable............	50,000
		Net Worth	
		Capital:	
		Preferred stock...........	50,000
		Common stock...........	?.....
Total...................	$400,000	Total...................	$400,000

first category being called Current Assets and the second Fixed Assets. The liabilities can also be subdivided into Current and Long-term Liabilities depending upon whether they come due in less than a year. The difference between total Current Assets and total Current Liabilities,

$$\$50,000 = \$100,000 - \$50,000,$$

is usually termed "Net Working Capital"; also in more advanced discussions some attention is paid to the

$$\text{"Working-capital ratio"} = \text{Current Assets} \div \text{Current Liabilities}$$
$$= \$100,000 \div \$50,000, \text{ or 2 to 1.}$$

Another thing to be noticed about our balance sheet is this: Although its two sides must balance *in total*, yet no single item on one side is matched by an item on the other side. Thus, the Bonds do not correspond in value to the Equipment or Buildings, nor do the Capital items correspond to the Cash. The only correct statement about a balance sheet is that the creditors have a general claim of a definite value against the enterprise, and the owners have a residual claim against the rest.

Most of the specific items listed are more or less self-explanatory. Cash consists of coins, currency, and money on deposit in the bank. Cash is the only asset whose value is exact rather than an estimate. All other valuations involve some guesswork, albeit careful guesswork. Moreover, all accounting valuations must be made relative to the actual intended purpose or use of the asset in question. If a business is a going concern and not in the process of liquidation, the accountant will be careful not to value the assets at the low figure that they would bring at a forced sale, but he will rather value them at their worth to the company in its normal operation.

Inventory, consisting in the case of our tooth-paste company of sugar, chemicals, tubing, raw materials, and other goods in process, can be valued in many different ways. Many conservative companies use original cost of the inventories or present market value, whichever is lower. Especially difficult problems arise when the prices of materials vary from month to month. Should we figure the chemical cost of the tooth paste at the original price of the ingredients actually used, which of course were bought some time ago when prices were different? Or should we figure, as our cost, the price that must *now* be paid for the chemicals to replace those being used up? An elementary discussion cannot go into these two possible methods of inventory valuation.[1] Obviously, it will make a great difference in stated profits during a time of inflation or deflation which of these two methods is used. It also will make a difference in income taxes. Therefore, the government is compelled to say, "Use whichever method you wish, but having made up your mind, stick to it." So much for inventories.

If we assume that the Equipment and Buildings items were just bought at the end of 1955, then their balance sheet values will be listed equal to their purchase price. This follows a fundamental accounting rule or convention: "At time of purchase a thing is presumed worth what the enterprise pays for it." However, as we shall see in connection with the income statement and the next year's balance sheet, almost insuperable problems are involved in deciding how to evaluate exactly equipment and buildings that have depreciated through use and age.

On the liability side, Accounts Payable are, as their name implies, the sums owed for goods bought and charged. Notes Payable represent promissory notes owed to the banks or to a finance company. The RFC Note listed under the Long-term Liabilities is a 5-year loan advanced by, or guaranteed by, the RFC of the federal government. The Bonds Payable represent a long-term loan, floated at a 3 per cent coupon rate, and not due or callable for 15 years.

---

[1] Accounting texts refer to them as "First-in–first-out" (FIFO) and "Last-in–first-out" (LIFO) and analyze them in detail.

Turning now to the Net Worth items, we find that 500 shares of $100, 4 per cent, cumulative (nonparticipating) preferred stock have been issued. And finally 20,000 shares of no-par common stock were issued at $10 each. This completes our first glance at a simple balance sheet.

THE STATEMENT OF PROFIT AND LOSS, OR INCOME STATEMENT

Now let time march on. During the following months, the firm is profitably engaged in producing and selling tooth paste. To show its flow of income over the 12 months of the year, we must turn to its Income Statement, or, as many companies prefer to call it, the Statement of Profit and Loss.

TABLE 2. *Income Statement of Pepto-Glitter Co., Inc., from January 1, 1956, to December 31, 1956*

Net Sales (after all discounts and rebates)		$240,000
Less: Manufacturing cost of goods sold:		
Materials	$ 50,000	
Labor cost	100,000	
Depreciation charges	20,000	
Miscellaneous operating cost	5,000	
Total manufacturing cost	$175,000	
Add: Beginning inventory	80,000	
	$255,000	
Deduct: Closing inventory	85,000	
Equals: Manufacturing cost *of goods sold*	$170,000	170,000
Gross profit (or gross margin)		$ 70,000
Less: Selling and administrative costs		14,000
Net operating profit		$ 56,000
Less: Fixed interest charges and local taxes		6,000
Net earnings before income taxes		$ 50,000
Less: Corporation income taxes		13,000
Net earnings after taxes		$ 37,000
Less: Dividends on preferred stock		2,000
Net profits of common stockholders		$ 35,000
Less: Dividends paid on common stock		5,000
Addition to surplus		$ 30,000

This is a statement which reports the following: (1) Pepto-Glitter's income from sales in 1956, (2) the expenses to be charged against those sales, and (3) the profit remaining after expenses have been deducted. You will understand it better if at first you disregard the figures in the Manufacturing Cost of Goods Sold section (the indented figures) and look only at those in the right-hand column. Sales were $240,000; and the cost of manufacturing the goods sold came to $170,000. After deducting another $14,000 for selling and adminstrative costs, $56,000 remained in net operating profit. Out of this, a total of $19,000 in interest and taxes had to be paid, leaving $37,000 in net earnings. Dividends of $2,000 preferred and $5,000 common were paid, leaving $30,000 of net profit retained in the business.

Now turn to the indented Manufacturing Cost of Goods Sold section, which lists the costs incurred in this part of the business. The firm's outlays for materials, labor, and miscellaneous expenses are listed, together with an item for Depreciation. (Depreciation is worth a section to itself, and we shall consider it soon.) The sum of these four items, $175,000, is the Manufacturing Cost. Then follows what may seem a puzzling adjustment. The value of the inventory on January 1 is added, and that of the year-end inventory is deducted. The result, which differs from Manufacturing Cost by $5,000, is the Manufacturing Cost *of Goods Sold*. What is the difference between these terms, and why is this inventory adjustment needed?

Pepto-Glitter began the year with an inventory of $80,000 in raw materials and partly or wholly finished goods. During the year, it built up its inventories by an extra $5,000. In such a case, it would be quite false to attribute all of the manufacturing costs to *the goods actually sold*. Some of these costs are really attributable to goods to be sold *in the future*. To neglect this fact would be to overstate the Manufacturing Cost of Goods Sold in this year; it would be subtracting too much from this year's Net Sales; it would be understating this year's Profits.

If there had been no change in the value of inventory, then all would be simple; Manufacturing Cost and Manufacturing Cost of Goods Sold would be one and the same.

On the other hand, what if we had had less Inventory on hand at the end of the year than at the beginning? Pretty clearly we shall be fooling ourselves if we fail to recognize that the cost of the goods we have sold this year ought really to be greater than the money we have paid out to labor and to other firms. We shall have neglected the cost element of used-up and unreplaced inventory.

To summarize: In order to reach a valid figure for Manufacturing Cost of Goods Sold, we must adjust the Manufacturing Cost figure as follows: (1) If the year-end Inventory shows an increase over the beginning Inventory, deduct that increase; (2) if the year-end Inventory has decreased, add that decrease.

Instead of subtracting $5,000 directly from the $175,000 total of manufacturing expense, the accountant does it in two steps. Rather than working with the difference between the two, he first adds the total beginning inventory, then subtracts the closing inventory. This procedure has the advantage of being standardized; it is the same whether inventory is up or down, whereas a single change-in-inventory figure would in some cases be a subtraction, in others an addition. And the accountant's method also reveals the change in inventory relative to the size of the total inventory.

DEPRECIATION

At first, one may wonder why any Depreciation charges have been made for 1956. The buildings and equipment were newly bought at the beginning of the year, and surely they will not have been worn out already. (There will of course be need to spend money on men to maintain the equipment and keep the factories painted. But their wages are already included in Labor Cost or Miscellaneous Expense and are not included in Depreciation.)

Here is where the farseeing wisdom of the accountant comes to the fore. He points out that not a cent may have to be spent upon replacement of equipment for 10 years, at which time suddenly all the machines may have to be bought anew. It would be nonsense, he claims, (1) to charge nothing to depreciation for 9 years and fool yourself into thinking you are making a nice profit and then (2) suddenly in the tenth year to have to charge off all the value of the machines at once and think you have made a tremendous loss in that year.

Actually, he points out, the equipment is being used up all the time. A truer, undistorted picture of net income or profit will be learned if the costs of the equipment are spread more evenly over its lifetime. The value of equipment declines as a result of age and use; it depreciates from its price when new to its final scrap value. In recognition of this, the accountant depreciates the value of fixed capital items by some *gradual* formula. Here, we have not the space to go into the various methods that have been used. Suffice it to mention two widely used ones.

The first is called "straight-line depreciation." Suppose that you have a truck whose cost when new is $10,100, and whose economic life is 10 years; after this its physical life may continue but its economic life will be over, because of its unreliability and maintenance costs. Suppose that its scrap value at the end of 10 years is $100. According to the straight-line method you will each year charge off to depreciation one-tenth of the lifetime decline in its total value, $10,000 (new price minus scrap value). Thus, $1,000 will be charged in depreciation every year.

A second general method called the "service unit method"—or "unit of production method"—can be mentioned only briefly here. According to this we would estimate the number of miles, or loads, or service units that the truck will perform in its life. Thus, if the truck goes a million miles in 10 years and its loss of value during that time is $10,000, then each mile used up represents about 1 cent. This method has the virtue that during the first year of life of the truck, when presumably it will be used proportionately more than toward the end of its life, depreciation charges will be reckoned at perhaps $1,500 (for 150,000 miles) rather than at only $1,000 as in the straight-line method. Another advantage of this second method is that, during periods of depression when trucks are idle a good deal of the time, the calculated depreciation charges are less, and so the businessman may not be prevented from reducing prices by a misleading overestimate of his money costs.[1]

Although depreciation is usually figured by some apparently exact formula, every accountant knows that the estimates are really very rough, being subject to large and unpredictable errors, and involving arbitrary corrections and assumptions. He comforts himself with two thoughts: (1) A rough method of depreciation, like an imperfect watch, is often better than none at all. (2) Any mistakes in depreciation will ultimately "come out in the wash" anyway.

Let us see why a mistake in depreciation ultimately tends to correct itself. Suppose that the truck lasts 15 years rather than the predicted 10. We have been then overstating our depreciation expenses during the first 10 years. But in the eleventh and later years there will be no depreciation charged on the truck at all, since it has already been written down to its scrap value by the end of the tenth year. Our profits in these later years tend, therefore, to be overstated by about as much as they were understated in the earlier years. After 15 years, everything is pretty much the same after all.

Except for taxes. Different methods of depreciation result in a different apparent distribution of earnings over time, and therefore in a different pattern over time of corporation income taxes. Naturally a businessman prefers a method of depreciation that will make his income average out more steadily over time—so as to keep his effective tax rate as low as possible and permit him to cancel off losses against profits; and he also likes a method that will enable him to put off the evil day of taxes as far as possible.

---

[1] Many accounting books also describe a third still different method that permits of greater depreciation when an asset is new than when it is old. This is the constant percentage depreciation method, whereby the truck would be depreciated a constant percentage of remaining value each year until it reached its final scrap value. During the first year, the depreciation charged would be largest because of the truck's high initial value; during the later years, a constant percentage of the greatly reduced remaining value would result in low annual depreciation charges.

This explains why so many corporations took advantage of the government's wartime offer to let them amortize (or depreciate) their newly built war plants and equipment over 5 years. They were glad to be able, by charging high depreciation expenses, to reduce their stated profits during the war years when their profits were enormous. They much preferred to take advantage of this "accelerated depreciation" plan so as to shift their profits from war years to postwar years when corporation tax rates were expected to be much lower.

In ordinary times, the Treasury will not let a corporation manipulate its depreciation charges so as to avoid taxes. The company may select any reasonable method; but having once made its choice, it must stick to it. Mention may be made of the fact that economists are today worried about the harmful effects of taxation on "venture capital." They argue that we shall get more investment in new tools and create more jobs, if the Treasury is a little more liberal in letting companies depreciate their equipment more rapidly, thereby saving on their taxes.

THE RELATION BETWEEN THE INCOME STATEMENT AND THE BALANCE SHEET

Now we must relate the description by the Income Statement of what has happened during the year to the Balance Sheets at the beginning and end of the year. Table 3 shows the Balance Sheet of our tooth-paste corporation at the end of its first year of operation. It has prospered. Net Worth, the difference between Total Assets and Total Liabilities, has increased between the beginning and end of the accounting period by $30,000—from $250,000 to $280,000. The amount of this increase, as shown by a comparison of balance sheets, is just equal to the amount of earnings or profits *available* to the common stockholders but not paid out to them in dividends; or as we saw at the bottom of the Income Statement, just equal to $35,000 − $5,000, or $30,000 of undistributed profits.

Some Net Worth item must be written up by $30,000. It would clearly never do to increase the Preferred Stock Capital Account, because such stockholders are not the residual claimants to the profits of the corporation and no new stock has been sold. Theoretically, one could add the $30,000 to the Common Stock Capital Account. However, this is not done. Instead the Common Stock Capital Account is left at its original par value or value when issued.

It is more informative to create a new account called Surplus—or sometimes Earned Surplus—to show how much of the increase in "book value" or Net Worth has resulted from accumulated undistributed earnings plowed back through the years.

In many ways Surplus is a misleading word. It sounds like something extra or unnecessary; or too often like a nice spare chunk of cash which the company's workers or stockholders might hope to stage a raid against. Actually, Surplus is distinctly not an asset account, much less a pool of liquid cash. It simply indicates a part of the ownership—over and above liabilities to creditors and original subscribed capital ownership—in the polyglot assets of the corporation. A glance at Table 3 will convince us that the $30,000 of Surplus is not matched by an equivalent amount of cash on the asset side.

TABLE 3. *Balance Sheet of Pepto-Glitter, Inc., as of December 31, 1956*

ASSETS		LIABILITIES AND NET WORTH	
		Liabilities	
Current Assets:		*Current Liabilities:*	
Cash	$ 20,000	Accounts payable	$ 10,000
Inventory	85,000	Notes payable	17,000
Sinking Fund to Replace Equip-		Reserve for taxes	13,000
ment	5,000		
(U.S. Government Bonds)			
Fixed Assets:		*Long-term Liabilities:*	
Equipment $130,000		RFC note	50,000
Less allowance		Bonds payable	50,000
(or reserve)			
for deprecia-			
tion 15,000			
	115,000	Net Worth	
Buildings $170,000		*Capital:*	
Less allowance		Preferred stock	50,000
(or reserve) for		Common stock	200,000
depreciation 5,000		Surplus	30,000
	165,000		
Intangible Assets:			
Patents	10,000		
Good will	20,000		
Total	$420,000	Total	$420,000

We must once again issue a warning against trying to link up specific items on the two sides of the Balance Sheet. Only the totals correspond. That is all. It is not even possible to say exactly how the $30,000 plowed back into the business, or added to Surplus, has been used. Part of it was used to pay off some of the liabilities of the business, part to enable the corporation to add to its assets (patents, etc.).

It would be an equal mistake to think that the profits of a corporation accrue in the form of cash; so that on the last day of the year, just before the board of directors decided upon its dividend rate, there was some $35,000 of cash on hand, available either for the stockholders or to be invested back in the business. In the case of our tooth-paste company, the very handsome profit earned was largely embodied in the form of new assets and lowered liabilities; not very much more than $5,000 could have been paid out as cash dividends without forcing serious changes in the financial decisions of the company—decisions such as to borrow more, to grow more slowly, to sell off some of the equipment and inventory at a loss, or to operate with a ludicrously low cash balance.

Only very rarely can a company contemplate declaring a dividend in kind, rather than cash. One such famous example of this was the case of the American Distillery Company which paid out barrels of whisky as dividends during the war, sending the price of the stock up from $15 to more than $100 after the news got around. Even in that case, the dividend was paid out of an asset, Inventory; Surplus was simultaneously diminished to show a decrease in net worth.

SUMMARY OF ELEMENTARY ACCOUNTING RELATIONS

Before taking a last look at the new complexities introduced in the 1956 Balance Sheet over that of 1955, we may briefly summarize the relationship between balance sheets and income statements: (1) The Balance Sheet indicates an instantaneous financial picture. (2) The Income Statement shows the flow of sales, cost, and revenue over the year or accounting period time. (3) The change in total Net Worth between the beginning and the end of the period—as shown by comparing the new and old balance sheets—is also to be understood from an examination of the changes in Surplus as shown at the end of most modern income statements. If new common stock is sold, that will be revealed by comparing the two Balance Sheets.

There do remain, however, certain shifts in the balance-sheet items from their previous levels in the earlier period to which the intervening Income Statement gives us no clue. A closer look at the December 31, 1956, Balance Sheet will therefore prove instructive, although enough has been said already to introduce the reader to the fundamentals of accounting.

RESERVES, FUNDS, AND INTANGIBLE ASSETS

The new Balance Sheet looks much like the old for the most part; but some new items are present for the first time. The last of these new items, Surplus, we have already explained. Among the Liabilities there is a new item called Reserve for Taxes of $13,000. It is not hard to understand. The taxes that the corporation will have to pay the government on March 15, 1957, and succeeding quarterly dates are as much short-term liabilities as the Accounts Payable or Notes Payable.

Taxes Payable might have been a better title since the word "Reserve" suggests a pool of cash, which it decidedly is not. Instead the Reserve for Taxes is simply an earmarking of part of the total assets of the company for a special creditor, and a reminder that the Net Worth of the owners is less by the amount of owed taxes. In a moment we shall see that there are three main kinds of "reserves," and no one of them represents a pool of cash or liquid assets.

Let us turn to the Asset side for new items.[1] The first stranger, entitled "Sinking Fund to Replace Equipment" is listed midway between the Current and Fixed Assets. It is an asset consisting of, say, 2 per cent government bonds which are to be held for the purpose of ultimately providing part of the money to buy new machines when the old ones are to be replaced. Although the corporation could change its mind and use the Sinking Fund bonds for some other purpose, it presumably will not choose to do so. The nature of this Sinking Fund is very understandable; it is simply a pool of liquid assets set aside for a specific future purpose.

Turning to the Fixed Assets, we find ourselves in for a surprise. From our previous discussion of the Depreciation charges of the Income Statement, we should have expected the Building and Equipment items to total $280,000. Why? Because at the beginning of the year they added up to $300,000, because no new equipment was bought during the year, and because the Income Statement told us that $20,000 of depreciation accrued during the period as part of the necessary costs of production.

Why then are these Fixed Assets carried on the new Balance Sheet at the old $130,000 and $170,000 figure? Looking more closely we see that they really are not. From the $130,000 nominal Equipment valuation, there is subtracted an Allowance (or Reserve) for Depreciation, so that really only $115,000 is carried for Equipment. Similarly from the $170,000 original value of the Buildings, there is subtracted a $5,000 allowance for Depreciation. Our faith in the accountant's sanity is restored; but we may still wonder why he goes through this roundabout procedure of stating "two" as "four minus two" instead of simply as "two."

Actually, he has his good reasons. An honest accountant knows that his

[1] Neither this Balance Sheet nor the previous one contains a frequently met current asset item called Prepaid Expenses. Often an enterprise will pay its rent or buy some of its supplies a number of months in advance. Very properly, the enterprise is regarded as possessing on its Balance Sheet an equivalent asset.

depreciation charges are only the roughest of guesses. If he were simply to make his guess and put down the final figure of $115,000 for equipment, the public would not be able to know how much reliance to place upon the figure. So he puts down $130,000 of original value, which is firmly rooted in the solid fact of original cost; and he then carefully isolates his own guessed-at Allowance for Depreciation. Then the public is in a better position to evaluate the reliability of the final $115,000 figure. The roundabout procedure does no harm, and may do good.

Now we know the precise meaning of Depreciation Allowances or Reserves. They are not sums of money; they are not sinking funds of liquid assets that can be spent on replacement. They are simply *subtractions from overstated asset figures.* Thus, the Allowance for Depreciation of Buildings of $5,000 is simply an explicit correction to the original value of the Buildings, which would be an overstatement of the value left in them. This correction must be made to keep Assets and Net Worth from both being artificially inflated.

It must be made regardless of whether at the same time any money is or is not being set aside into sinking funds to replace the Depreciation asset. Note that there is no Sinking Fund for Buildings, and that the Sinking Fund for Equipment is only one-third as large as the estimated depreciation of equipment. As a matter of fact, American businesses rarely set aside any considerable sums of money in replacement Sinking Funds. This is because liquid gilt-edge bonds earn at most only a few per cent interest, whereas capital invested in the firm's own activities usually brings in much more.[1]

We have met two kinds of reserves: (1) a Liability Reserve, like that for taxes, which is really simply a liability of fairly certain amount, and (2) an Asset Valuation Reserve like that for Depreciation (or allowance for estimated uncollectible bills), which is really simply a subtraction from an overstated asset. A third so-called "Surplus Reserve," which is also not to be confused with a sum of money, may be briefly mentioned: Sometimes a firm takes part of its Surplus and sets it aside under a different name so that the stockholders will not be tempted to lobby for higher dividend payments. For example, our tooth-paste company might earmark one-third of its $30,000 Surplus account into a Reserve for Research and Development. This $10,000

---

[1] Where then will the money be coming from to replace any particular machine or building if no sinking funds have been set aside? Ordinarily, the equipment can be purchased with sales dollars earned by other equipment that is not currently calling for replacement expenditure. The selling price of the output of such other equipment contains an accounting allowance for depreciation expense, and this sum of money is available for investment elsewhere in the business. Speaking somewhat loosely, we may say that each asset not needing replacement lends its depreciation charges to those which need replacement, knowing that it too will be taken care of when the need arises.

Reserve would no more consist of cash or liquid funds than does Surplus itself, or than does any other kind of Reserve. It should never be confused with a fund.[1]

Never was it more important to emphasize these accounting fundamentals. Time and again a trade-union will claim higher wages to be paid out of the Surplus or Reserves of some big company. Except in terms of demagoguery, it is often weakening its own case when falling into such egregious and transparent errors.

INTANGIBLE ASSETS

Only one further new category of Assets can still be found on the December 31, 1956, Balance Sheet. To illustrate that an asset need not be a tangible commodity, a piece of equipment, or a sum of money, a Patent has been introduced into the picture. Let us suppose that it is a patent on a profitable new chemical process, which gives the company the exclusive production rights for 17 years.

Such a patent is obviously worth money. How much money? It is shown later in this book that the value of such an asset will be the sum of the "present discounted values" of all its future net profits over the next 17 years—with the more distant years' profits being more heavily discounted by compound interest. Of course, as 5, 10, 12, and 16 years pass, the patent will be coming near to the end of its life and will be declining in value. Therefore, some depreciation formula will be applied to it just as if it were a truck. Probably the ideal formula would be to recalculate each year its *present discounted value*, and charge to Depreciation the decline from the previous year; it should be remembered, however, that in practice this theoretical refinement is impossible to carry out.

GOOD WILL AND MONOPOLY POWER

So much for the Patent as an illustration of an intangible asset. Let us suppose that, at the same time we bought the patent, we also took over a rival tooth-paste company. This horizontal combination will presumably add to our monopoly position and earning power. Therefore, we were willing to buy the company for more than its trifling assets—which happened to consist solely of a little inventory—were worth. Perhaps part of the purchase price went as profits to the promoters who engineered this little monopolistic merger.

An example of the capitalization of earning power is J. P. Morgan's formation of the giant United States Steel Company at the turn of the century. He

[1] The problem of reserves becomes even more complicated in connection with contingencies that may or may not occur. Thus Reserve for Depression Contingencies or for Renegotiation would fall halfway between true Liability and Surplus Reserves.

bought out the Andrew Carnegie steel plants and combined them with half a dozen other holdings. But in economics, as in certain branches of atomic physics, the whole is equal to more than the sum of its parts. After Morgan had put the pieces together, he found himself with some 130 million dollars of extra capital value.

Who was hurt by this transaction? Certainly not Carnegie or Morgan. Even the people who bought the stock had no right to complain that it had been "watered," since for many years they continued to get more than a fair return on their investments. To have sold them the stock for its actual cost (without water) would be (1) to make them a free gift of the enlarged profits of the concern and (2) to give them the privilege of reselling the stock at the higher price that its earning power could earn for it in a competitive stock market.

In terms of standards at the time, there was nothing illegal or unethical about this merger. The company hoped to realize cost economies from the combination; and not even the Supreme Court (which later declared USS not to be a monopoly) can determine the degree to which their hope was realized. Other firms in the industry have been able to grow at an even faster pace and the present-day price policies of the industry have little connection with this bit of ancient history.

However, our practical-minded accountant is not concerned with such matters of public policy and political economy. He will tell our tooth-paste company or J. P. Morgan the same thing: "If you paid a certain sum of money for some assets, they must presumably be worth that much to you. If the assets don't exist, they must be created. 'Good Will' is their name." But since this term has come into bad repute in recent years, it is often lumped in with some other assets.

This explains our last intangible asset. Good Will is the difference between what a company pays in buying out another company and what it gets in the way of identifiable assets.

CONCLUSION[1]

Finally, some interesting relations between economics and accounting can be briefly mentioned. (1) All balance sheets depend on valuation of assets, which is one of the basic questions of the capital and interest theory discussed in Part Four. (2) All our national income statistics are founded on the accounting data of sales, cost, etc; this, too, is discussed in detail later. (3) As we shall see in a later discussion of how firms set price, accounting cost data play an important role.

The accountant deals with money magnitudes; the economist tries to probe

[1] This should be skipped by beginning students.

deeper to the underlying real magnitudes. Especially in periods of great inflation or deflation, the accountant realizes that his ordinary methods may give strange results. A good example is the problem of changing price levels and depreciation. Suppose prices are rising sharply. If I sell my goods for enough to cover labor and other costs and also to cover depreciation, you might think I am breaking even. What would an accountant say who figured depreciation on the basis of the past low prices originally paid for my machines and building? He, too, would say I am breaking even. But in actuality I can be said to have been selling my goods at a *real* loss; for when my machines and buildings have worn out, I shall not have enough money to *reproduce them* at the new higher price level. The same is true of a merchant who sells off his inventory at a price lower than reproduction cost. So we must beware of fictitious money overstatements of real profits during rising prices and of fictitious understatements of profits during falling prices. (Later in national income statistics, you will note that profits are "adjusted" for inventory revaluations.)

(4) A last interesting problem relates to "the flow of purchasing power or money spending" by business. Suppose that every corporation pays out all its 1956 earnings in dividends. Does that mean that corporations as a whole have paid out all the cash they have received in that year? The answer: Not necessarily. Money expenses that are entered in a year's Income Statement do not necessarily involve equivalent money expenditures. Thus, our tooth-paste company very properly listed Depreciation as an expense in 1956; yet no machinery or buildings were replaced in that year.[1]

The so-called flow of purchasing power is important for the problem of whether we shall have prosperity or depression. Later we shall discuss how it depends on investment, saving, consumption, etc. Here I need only warn that there is no simple relation between accounting statements and this intricate problem.

[1] During the Great Depression such phenomena were very important; charges to depreciation exceeded actual replacement expenditures by billions of dollars. On the other hand, in the years around 1950, new plant and equipment expenditure and replacements vastly exceeded depreciation charges. The investments were largely financed by undistributed profits. This serves to warn us that the mere act of paying out less dividends than earnings is *not* by itself a deflationary act that interrupts the flow of purchasing power.

SUMMARY TO APPENDIX

Instead of a lengthy recapitulation, this section presents only a check list of the accounting concepts that the student should understand:

1. The fundamental balance sheet relationship between Assets, Liabilities, and Net Worth; and the breakdown of each of these categories into Current and Fixed Assets, Current and Long-term Liabilities, Capital and Surplus.

2. The character of the Income Statement (or Profit-and-loss Statement), and the relationship between its final undistributed profits and the changes in Surplus on the new Balance Sheet.

3. The whole problem of Depreciation, both in its income statement aspect as a necessary expense, which need not be an expenditure, and in its balance sheet treatment as a deduction from a purposely overstated asset; also the logic of the two principal depreciation methods.

4. The difference between a Fund or a pool of liquid assets and the three kinds of so-called Reserves; also the meaning of such intangible assets as Patents or Good Will.

QUESTIONS FOR DISCUSSION

1. Describe the right-hand side of a balance sheet. Its left-hand side. What items must match as a result of the "fundamental identity"?

2. You are a banker deciding whether to lend money to the tooth-paste company. Why might you be interested in calculating its working capital or working capital ratio?

3. Write out a list of as many different assets as you can, describing the nature of each in a few lines. Do the same for liabilities.

4. Is an income statement a "still picture" at an instant of time? Is a profit-and-loss statement? What flows are shown by such a statement?

5. In 1956 a company has 10 million dollars of net sales and 9 million dollars of costs of all kinds (including taxes, interest, etc.) It rents its equipment, its inventory does not change in the year, and it has no preferred stock. It pays no dividends. Draw up its simplified income statement using at most half a dozen lines.

6. The same company as in (5) owes no money, having been completely equity-financed years ago. Fill in the following year-end balance sheets.

ASSETS			LIABILITIES AND NET WORTH		
	1955	1956		1955	1956
			Liabilities...........	0	0
			Net Worth...........	$50 mil.	....
Total............. $50 mil		....	Total...............	......	....

7. Redo problems 5 and 6 making the following changes: In addition to the other expenses, its buildings depreciate by 2 million dollars; also its inventory has fallen off by 3 million dollars. Draw up an income statement showing its loss for the year, and adjust its 1956 balance sheet accordingly.

8. Describe the two methods of calculating depreciation.

9. Differentiate between three different kinds of reserves. Which, if any, are also "funds"? Which cash?

10. Give an example of intangible assets.

11. Guess how much you would pay for a business that is sure of yielding a net profit of $10,000 per year with little risk of principal. Suppose its total assets exclusive of Good Will were valued at $100,000. What would you guess for the value of Good Will?

Chapter 7: THE ECONOMIC ROLE

OF GOVERNMENT: EXPENDITURE,

REGULATION, AND FINANCE

THE activities of the state are becoming an increasingly important part of the study of modern economics. This is reflected in the quantitative growth of government expenditure and in the great expansion of direct regulation of economic life.

THE GROWTH OF GOVERNMENT EXPENDITURE

Before World War I, federal, state, and local government expenditure amounted to little more than one-twelfth of our whole national income. During World War II, it became necessary for the government to consume about half of the nation's greatly expanded total output. Within the space of a third of a century, the cost of all government in the United States had risen from a paltry 3 billion dollars spent in 1913 to a temporary peak of around 110 billion dollars in 1945.

If this remarkable contrast were the result of only a temporary wartime condition, it could be shrugged off as being of but passing significance. Actually, the exact reverse is the case. For more than a century, national income and production have been rising. At the same time, in almost all countries and cultures, the trend of governmental expenditure has been rising even faster. Each period of emergency—each war, each depression—expands the activity of government. After each emergency has passed, expenditures never seem to go back to their previous levels.

Nor is the end in sight. With the end of World War II, government expenditure receded from its wartime peak, but it did not drop down as far as those prewar levels which, a few short years ago, were considered alarmingly high.

Before World War II, the annual federal budget never reached the 10-billion-dollar mark. In the years ahead, regardless of whether the Republican party or the Democratic party holds office, probably no man now alive will ever live to see the year when there is a federal budget of less than 30 billion dollars or a combined federal-state-local expenditure of much less than one-fifth of the national income. Figure 1 indicates the historical trend of total government expenditure and federal debt relative to the growth of national income.

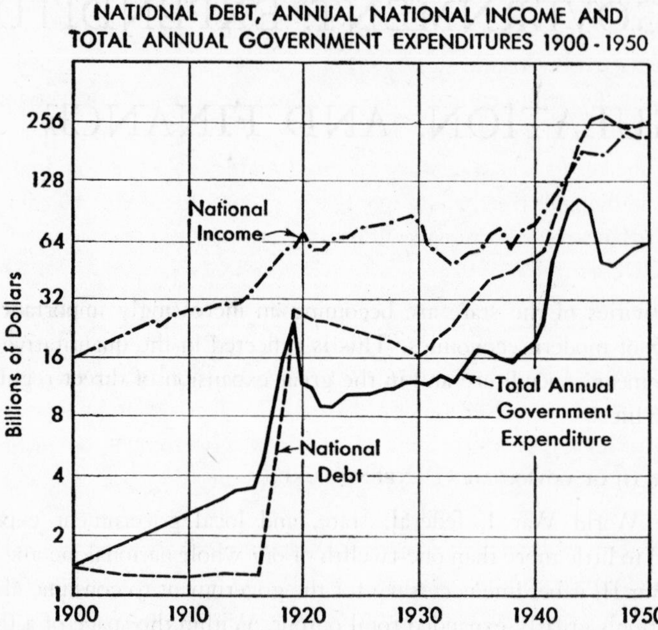

NATIONAL DEBT, ANNUAL NATIONAL INCOME AND
TOTAL ANNUAL GOVERNMENT EXPENDITURES 1900-1950

FIGURE 1. Government expenditure includes federal, state and local expenditures. Note that this is a "ratio" chart; equal vertical distances represent equal *percentage* changes. SOURCE: For the data up to 1944, National Industrial Conference Board, *The Economic Almanac*. 1945 and later figures are author's estimates from Department of Commerce data.

These are the hard, cold facts about public finance. Some may deplore them. Some may like them. But there they are. They make clear the increasingly important economic role of government. They explain why no modern economic textbook can relegate to an obscure corner the vitally important problems of public finance.

THE GROWTH OF GOVERNMENT CONTROLS AND REGULATION

The increase in collective expenditure is only part of the story. In addition to increased direct participation by government in national production, there has been a vast expansion in its laws and executive orders regulating economic activity.

No longer does modern man act as if he believed: "That government governs best which governs least." In a frontier society, when a man moved farther west as soon as he could hear the bark of his neighbor's dog, there was some validity to the view, "Let every man paddle his own canoe." But today, in our vast interdependent society, the waters are too crowded to make unadulterated "rugged individualism" tolerable. The emphasis is increasingly on "we're all in the same boat," "don't rock the craft," "don't spit into the wind," and "don't disregard the traffic signals."

Perhaps nineteenth-century America came as close as any economy ever has to that state of *laissez faire* which Carlyle called "anarchy plus the constable." The result was a century of rapid material progress and an environment of individual freedom. Also there resulted periodic business crises, wasteful exhaustion of irreplaceable material resources, extremes of poverty and wealth, corruption of government by vested interest groups, and too often the supplanting of self-regulating competition in favor of all-consuming monopoly.

Gradually, and in the face of continuing opposition, the methods of Alexander Hamilton began to be applied toward the objectives of Thomas Jefferson: the constitutional powers of central and local government were interpreted broadly and were used to "secure the public interest" and to "police" the economic system. Utilities and railroads were brought under state regulation; after 1887, the Federal ICC (Interstate Commerce Commission) was set up to regulate rail traffic across state boundaries. The Sherman Antitrust Act and other laws were invoked after 1890 against monopolistic combinations in "restraint of trade." Regulation of banking became thoroughgoing; after 1913, the federal reserve system was set up to serve as a central bank, aiding and controlling member commercial banks; and since 1933 most bank deposits have been insured by the Federal Deposit Insurance Corporation or by the Federal Savings and Loan Insurance Corporation.

Pure food and drug acts were passed following the revelations of the "muckraking era" of the early 1900's. Loan sharks came under regulation in many states. The abuses of high finance, before and after 1929, gave rise to ever more stringent regulation of the financial markets by the SEC and other bodies.

Humanitarian legislation to better factory conditions for children and women won at first only a grudging acceptance by the courts. But with the passage of time, the radical doctrines of one era became the accepted and even reactionary beliefs of a later era: state and federal legislation was expanded to include minimum-wage legislation, compulsory workmen's accident compensation insurance, compulsory unemployment insurance and old-age pensions, maximum-hour laws for children, women, and men, regulation of factory conditions of work, compulsory collective bargaining, fair labor relations acts, and so forth.

To understand this trend toward greater governmental authority one must maintain a sense of historical perspective. Each new step generated strong political feelings on both sides. Thus the "square deal" doctrines of the Republican Theodore Roosevelt, which today would cause no raising of eyebrows or fluttering of pulses, were considered dangerous and radical in their time. Our democracy cannot, and would not if it could, turn the clock back to the conditions of the nineteenth century as represented by Henry Ford's Greenfield Village and McGuffey's Reader. Nevertheless, it would be wrong to regard these historical processes as inevitable, to join Omar in his mournful chant:

> "The Moving Finger writes; and having writ,
> Moves on: nor all your Piety nor Wit
> Shall lure it back to cancel half a Line,
> Nor all your Tears wash out a word of it."

No immutable "wave of the future" washes us down "the road to serfdom," or to Utopia. Where the complex economic conditions of life necessitate social coordination, there can sensible men of good will be expected to invoke the authority and creative activity of government. But expansion of centralized power as a worthy end for its own sake is quite another matter—an end alien to the typical American citizen's credo.

Unfortunately, not until long after the event will history tell us—and perhaps not then—whether or not a given expansion of governmental authority was a good or bad policy; whether or not it should have the approval of all those genuinely interested in conserving and improving the good elements in our system. And in politics as elsewhere, it is only too true that the road to hell is paved with good intentions.

But this, past history does seem to suggest. Unyielding conservatism defeats its own purpose. Steel without "give" will rupture suddenly under strain. Brittle economic systems without the flexibility to accommodate themselves in an evolutionary manner to accumulating tensions and social changes—however strong such systems may appear in the short run—are in the greatest peril of extinction. For science and technology are constantly changing the natural lines of economic life. If the system is to continue to function well, our social institutions and beliefs must be capable of adjusting themselves to these changes. And without a sense of historical perspective neither radicals nor conservatives nor middle-of-the-roaders can effectively advance their own true long-run interests.

FEDERAL, LOCAL, AND STATE FUNCTIONS

If we return now to the over-all figures of expenditure, we find that they become more meaningful when we break them down to see just what activities they represent and by which branch of government they are administered.

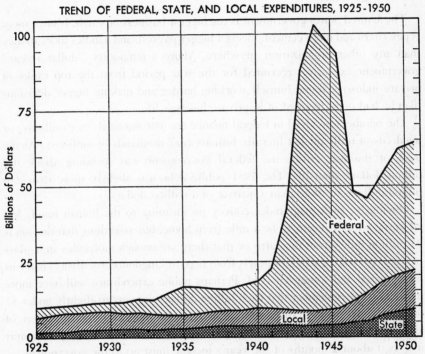

FIGURE 2. SOURCE: Data to 1944, *Economic Almanac for 1950* (National Industrial Conference Board, Inc., New York); 1945 to 1950 figures are author's estimates.

Primarily, each American is faced with three levels of government: federal, state, and local. It will surprise most people to learn that, of the three, the states have always been the least important with respect to government expenditure. This is still true, although, as we shall see, it is becoming less so.

Prior to World War I, local government was by far the most important of the three. The federal government did little more than pay for national defense, meet pensions and interest on past wars, finance a few public works, and pay the salaries of judges, congressmen, and other government officials. Almost all its tax collections came from liquor and tobacco excises and from tariff duties levied on imports. Life was simple in those days; local governments performed most functions and collected the most revenue, primarily from taxes on property owners.

In Figure 2, we see how different everything has been since World War I. The federal government now leads in total expenditure. The states are still last but are gradually gaining on the local governments.

Let us turn now to federal finance.

FEDERAL EXPENDITURE

The United States government is the biggest business on earth. It buys more typewriters and more cement, meets a bigger payroll, and handles more money than any other organization anywhere. Many a temporary "dollar-a-year" government executive, recruited for the war period from the top ranks of private industry, found himself working harder and making bigger decisions than he had ever dreamed of in private business life.

The numbers involved in federal finance are astronomical: not millions, or hundreds of millions, but literally billions (*i.e.*, thousands of millions). At the peak of the war effort, the federal government was spending about 100 billion dollars annually. The 1951 public debt was slightly more than 250 billion dollars, or more than a quarter of a trillion dollars.

Obviously, such magnitudes convey no meaning to the human mind. We all know what it means to be a mile from home, but assertions that the sun is 93 million miles from the earth or that there are enough molecules in a glass of water to make a string of pearls from here to kingdom come always leave us unimpressed and somewhat cold. Perhaps public expenditure will have more meaning if we remember that each billion dollars amounts to slightly under $7 per American man, woman, and child. A postwar federal annual budget of about 40 billion dollars would be equivalent, then, to about $260 per capita; it is as if about 2 months of the year's income must go to the government.

Table 1 illustrates the estimated importance of different categories of federal expenditure in the fiscal year 1952, *i.e.*, from July 1, 1951, to June 30, 1952.

In the main, the first four items represent the costs of past and future wars. Together they account for five-sixths of all federal expenditure and for most of the increase in federal expenditure over prewar levels. Naturally, these are only rough estimates. They take into account the planned increase in defense expenditures following the Korean war in 1950.

Much of the next item goes to the support of the Merchant Marine and atomic energy and is also intimately involved with national defense. Part refers to public highways and other civilian public works. If unemployment should grow in the years ahead, we may expect this particular item to grow also.

Item 6 represents aid to the farmer. Item 7 refers to the welfare aid to the needy, aged, etc., and to expenditure on labor, education, and housing.

The final category includes the costs of running Congress, the courts, and the general expenses of the executive branch of the government. In conclusion, it is to be emphasized that the bulk of postwar federal expenditure and debt is the consequence of war and not of depression.

TABLE 1. *Estimated Federal Expenditure in Fiscal Year 1952*

Items	Estimate in billions	Percentage of total
1. National defense	$41.4	58
2. Veterans' services and benefits	4.9	7
3. Interest on public debt	5.9	8
4. International affairs and finance	7.5	10
5. Natural resources and transportation	5.7	8
6. Agriculture and agricultural resources	1.4	2
7. Social security, welfare, and health	3.4	5
8. Other, including general government	1.4	2
Total expenditure	$71.6	100

SOURCE: Estimates based on the President's 1951 Budget Message.

EFFICIENCY AND WASTE IN GOVERNMENT

The above estimates represent large sums of money. Undoubtedly, we should all be better off if the government were to increase its efficiency so as to give us the same services for lower costs or, what is equally important, if it were able to give us more and better services for the same dollar of expense.

Every effort should be made toward these ends. Having said this, one must go on to add: It is easier to preach economy than to practice it. It is easy to speak of cutting public expenditure to the bone, but when it becomes a matter of slashing aeronautical research, skimping on a veterans' hospital, denying aid to farmers, and so forth—then it is not so easy to carry out. Even where government agencies overlap—where the same function is performed by two or more agencies—the reform is still difficult; for it must mean that some people lose their jobs—and those people have votes! The result: Our legislators are forced to talk one way and act another, to content themselves with occasional outbursts of penny wisdom mixed with dollar foolishness.

Every student of public administration and history knows that, if our government expenditures are too high, it is not primarily because of personal corruption or technical incompetence on the part of civil servants and legislators.

As far as standards of intelligence, training, and personal financial account-ability are concerned, the present federal government ranks far better than that of earlier times or for that matter than most of those at the state and local levels.

Nor is it enough to blame the cost of government on "pork-barrel" spending. Some government money *is* spent on dubious projects; but desirable though removal of this pork may be, it would not go to the root of the matter. The real trouble goes much deeper. It lies within ourselves as citizens. We want government economy, and at the same time we want the governmental services that cost money!

To put the matter in a more sophisticated way: Government expenditure is a way of utilizing national output so as to meet human wants and needs. When national income rises, people want more and better schooling and other forms of government services, just as they want to spend more on personal clothing, housing, and recreation. Our social conscience and humanitarian standards have completely changed, so that today we all insist upon providing certain minimum standards of existence for those who are unable to provide for themselves.

From 1947 to 1949, Herbert Hoover and a bipartisan committee of 11 public-spirited citizens made an intensive study of the organization of the executive branch of the government. Three hundred experts were utilized to discover how the government could be made more efficient. In 1949 they published hundreds of pages of recommended reorganizations of the government, and accounting and procedural reforms. Just how much money these would save cannot be stated with exactitude, but some have estimated that 3 billion dollars might be saved if wastes were eliminated. A number of the recommended changes have been made; others are pending in 1951.

THE CHANGING FUNCTIONS OF GOVERNMENT

In the last 20 years, the Democrats have been in power. The country has witnessed the New Deal, a wartime economy, and a postwar Fair Deal defense economy. How serious a departure from the capitalistic system has all this been? This question can be tackled by considering government activity under four headings.

1. As we have already noted, there has been a great increase in the amount of government *control*. Nevertheless, much of this body of regulation can hardly be dignified by the title of "planning," and despite its bulk we are still a long way from a planned state.

2. As we have also seen, the increase in government expenditure means that as a nation we are consuming more of our national product *collectively*

rather than individually through private money purchases. Rather than pay to ride on the public roads as we do to ride on railroads, we pay for such valuable services by taxes.

But note that such collectively consumed goods and services are still *largely produced by free private enterprise.* The government may pay for a hospital or a typewriter, but each of these items is produced by free private enterprise. And so it is with most government expenditure on productive goods. This is hardly what the socialists mean by socialism—"government ownership and operation of factories, etc."[1]

3. Next we must analyze the third kind of government activity, direct government production. We find that throughout recent decades there has been but little expansion in this direction. Historically, our government has performed certain direct economic production functions, and not others. The post office and parcel post have long been a function of government, while private management has operated our telegraph service and railway express. Airports, but not railway terminal facilities, are usually governmentally owned. Governments now often provide water, gas, and electric utilities, but not telephone service. The reasons for drawing the line at any one place rather than another are partly historical, partly arbitrary, and to some degree changing.

The courts have held that, in the special case of "public utilities affected with public interest" there is limited possibility of effective competition between many independent producers; and it does not seem possible to decide which mode of operation would be the more successful except by a careful factual study which would transcend the field of economics.

Whatever the merits of the arguments on either side, it is important to realize that during the New Deal of the 1930's there was no vast expansion of government into such fields—except in one direction.[2] We did not nationalize our railroads as Sweden and many other countries have done, nor our coal industry, nor our banks, nor our radio broadcasting system, nor our insurance companies, nor our air lines. The New Deal differed in this important respect from the present 1951 Labor government in England, which has definite socialistic aspirations.

[1] See Chapter 35 which discusses certain differences between a socialized state and our own.

[2] The TVA (Tennessee Valley Authority) and other vast hydroelectric public-utility projects (Bonneville Dam in the Northwest, Hoover Dam in the Southwest, etc.) represent true cases where the government has taken over new active producing functions. It is noteworthy that the war plants built by the government are, almost without exception, being sold and leased to private industry or are being shut down. In the field of atomic energy, the government plays a dominant role; but even here it usually hires a private concern, such as General Electric or du Pont, to serve as its contracting agent.

Before leaving this third category, which involves the use of human and other resources directly by the government, we should recognize that there has been a substantial rise of the federal payroll and in the number of government employees. Many of the latter are in the Washington executive offices, in regional laboratories, in the armed services, and so forth. Even if they are not directly producing private goods and services in competition with private industry, such resources are being used by the government; and it behooves us all as citizens that they be used wisely and in the right amounts relative to the importance of our different national needs.

4. Finally, we turn to an activity of government which did expand tremendously in the 1930's and which will continue to loom large in the decades ahead, namely, government *welfare expenditures*, which transfer purchasing power to the needy or worthy without regard to their providing any service in return. Thus, payments are made to veterans, old people, blind and handicapped, orphans, and the unemployed. This fourth category of transfer expenditure deserves further detailed discussion. Indeed our modern governmental system is sometimes referred to as the "welfare state."

GOVERNMENT TRANSFER EXPENDITURES

A government check received by any such veteran or needy person differs economically from that received by a postal clerk or from that paid to a man who produces typewriters. It is important that we understand why, because our later discussion of national income will involve this same distinction between items that are "transfers" and items that we can truly count as parts of national production or income.

The payments to a postal clerk or typewriter producer are counted as parts of national income and output because they do cover services rendered, they do use up resources and production, and they do provide collective direct or indirect consumption to the citizens of the United States. Whether they are financed by taxes, by the sale of postage stamps, or by any other means, the government uses the dollars it collects to provide services for the public. Such dollars are as much part of national income as the dollars used by a railroad company to provide transportation services for its customers.

A blind widow's pension is something else again. Socially, it may be one of our most desirable expenditures, but nevertheless it is not part of national output or national income. Why? Because the widow does not render any services to the government or its citizens in exchange for the pension. She does not provide any labor, land, or capital. The pension increases her purchasing power. It permits her to live more adequately and to buy goods and services from other individuals. These goods and services that she buys are part of the national income and output; but they are attributable to the people and factories that have produced them, not to her.

Such transfer expenditures grew greatly as a result of World War II. Even earlier they grew, partly as a result of the depression, which made relief expenditures necessary, but also because new minimum standards of health, nutrition, and security have been set up by the collective conscience of the American people. Society now rules that children should not have rickets because of the bad luck or weakness of their parents, that poor people should not die at the age of thirty because of insufficient money for operations and needed care, that the old should be able to live out their years with some minimum of income.

Are such expenditures really anticapitalistic? We shall later see that "on the first round," these expenditures do not directly consume goods and services; but by swelling the purchasing power of their recipients, they do, "on the second round," create orders and jobs for free private enterprise. However, the thing to note is that the production induced by this process is both privately produced and privately consumed.

Unless these expenditures are financed by the printing of money or by government bond borrowing, larger taxes will have to be levied on the public, and it is for this reason that they are usually called "transfer expenditures." Often the more fortunate citizens are paying for the consumption of the less fortunate; and probably within reasonable limits, most people will feel that this is only as it should be.

Moreover to the extent that taxes come out of the income of the more well-to-do and thrifty and are used to make payments to the needy and ready-to-spend—to that extent the total of purchasing power is increased. In time of depression as we shall see, this may expand production and jobs. But in time of inflationary pressure, it may aggravate the upward spiral of prices and make shortages of goods worse.

THREE WAYS TO FINANCE EXPENDITURE

Where does the money come from to meet government expenditures? Primarily from three sources: (1) taxes,[1] (2) the issue of non-interest-bearing currency, and (3) interest-paying loans. Normally, taxes are the most important of these. During World War II borrowing was just as important, and during the Revolutionary War paper money was of greatest importance.

---

[1] Governments also receive some revenue from miscellaneous sources: sale of surplus equipment; sale of stamps, water, and gas; sale of public land; gifts from appreciative citizenry; etc.

Let us examine the precise differences among these three methods of finance. Suppose that the government has spent or is about to spend an extra billion dollars on some project that the American people and their legislative representatives deem necessary and desirable.

As a first alternative, the government can use its coercive powers and collect 1 billion dollars from its citizens in the form of one tax or another. Not all citizens would pay the same amount of taxes. Not all citizens would have received the same benefit from the government's expenditure. Some will have received more benefit than they have paid for. Others will have received less benefit than they have paid for, but Congress will have felt that they are better able to afford the tax burden than other groups in the community.

The tax has provided the money for government expenditure. But it has done something else in addition, something that is especially important at a time when there are no idle men or factories. Superficially, the government needs only dollars for its expenditure program. Actually, and much more important, it needs land, capital, and labor resources to carry out its project. Where are these resources to come from if there is full employment everywhere?

Here is where the taxes step in to perform another and much more important function than the mere provision of the necessary money. The individuals who are taxed find that their incomes are reduced. Because they cannot spend their receipted tax bills, they are no longer able to buy as much as previously of private consumption goods. These goods were being produced by land, labor, and capital. By contracting the production of such goods (or shifting goods directly to government use), we are releasing resources from the community's private consumption activities and shifting them to its collective governmental activities.

In a full-employment economy, scarcity and choice are all prevailing. The more resources the people consume collectively, the less there is left for them to consume individually, and vice versa. They must choose carefully between the worth to the community of (1) more and better hospitals, post offices, agricultural laboratories; and (2) greater disposable family incomes to be spent individually on more and better clothing, food, shelter, tobacco, and recreation.

FINANCING GOVERNMENT EXPENDITURE BY NEW MONEY

So much for the economic effects of tax finance under full employment. Let us examine the effects under the same conditions of full employment of the second method of financing our billion dollars of expenditure: printing new money. The government exercises its constitutional powers over the currency to print off one billion nice, new, crisp dollar bills. It finds that people are just as eager to work for these as for any other kind of money since they are all legal tender, interchangeable, and all the rest.

The American people have, therefore, succeeded in getting their billion-dollar collective project completed. The result has been completely painless, hasn't it? Why then ever levy taxes? Death may be inevitable but why must taxes be? The fallacy in these arguments applied to a full-employment economy should not be hard to isolate. And make no mistake about it, the arguments are then completely fallacious.

The government needs resources for its project—not primarily money. Where are the resources to come from in a full-employment world? Obviously only from the sacrifices of private individuals. By printing enough money, the government can outbid the present users of land, labor, and capital; it can suck resources into its own use. But in doing so, it will bid up wages, rents, and prices.

Now we see who really foots the bill. Because of the reduction in the supply of goods available for individuals' use, the cost of living will rise beyond the increase in people's money incomes. True, the government has not taken money away from them. But who can eat money or wear it on his back?

Such an increase in government expenditure in a full-employment world will necessarily cause some degree of inflation, and inflation is a mighty tax collector—albeit an indirect and often unobserved one. The hidden tax of higher prices tends to fall most heavily on the poor and on the relatively low-paid white-collar workers whose wages are sticky. There can be no doubt that inflation is a method of taxing, and a highly arbitrary and inequitable one.

FINANCING DEFICITS BY LOAN FINANCE OR BORROWING

We have now analyzed the difference between tax financing and new-money financing in a full-employment world. There remains the intermediate case of loan financing by the sale of government bonds. The government uses the services of land, labor, and capital as before. But it does not pay for these by giving people receipted tax bills as in the first mode of finance. Nor does it simply present them with currency that they can then spend as they please. Instead it gives them I.O.U.'s, payable with compound interest in 1, 5, or 25 years.

There is nothing compulsory about the process. People with savings are glad to subscribe for government bonds rather than hold their wealth all idle or in the form of private securities. Government bonds are an attractive investment because they can always be sold on the market or redeemed in case the need should arise. Equally important, there is never any possibility that the government—which has complete constitutional powers to issue new currency—

would ever be unable to pay off the holders of government bonds in full. A European might hesitate to hold our bonds under some circumstances because he could be sure only of being paid off in *dollars* and he would be most concerned about francs or pounds. But an American, whose concern will naturally be with dollars, can always rest easily even though his fortune is invested 99.9 per cent in government bonds, knowing that the *dollar value* of his principal is perfectly safe. As we shall later see, he cannot be so sure that 5 or 20 years from now the dollars that he gets back will purchase as many goods as they do now. Still, that is a risk which is not peculiar to government bonds; the same would be true of money in the bank; and if he were to buy railroad bonds, he would still run such a risk, along with the additional risk that the principal of his bonds might go into default when the day for collection arrives.

We shall learn in Part Two how the government can sell bonds to the banking system and thereby enable it to manufacture bank money, *i.e.*, bank deposits. For this and other reasons, the economic effects of financing a deficit by loans may be more nearly like those resulting from the issue of new money than like those resulting from taxation. Loan financing may not cause a significant curtailment of individual consumption with a subsequent release of resources for government use. At times of full employment, the result of such deficit financing is likely, therefore, to be inflationary. Prices have to be bid up by the government in order to win resources away from existing users.

If an excess of government expenditure over taxation increases inflationary pressure, then by reversing the process we should have a mechanism for *reducing* inflationary pressure. Actually this is what was done on a small scale in the postwar period, and should have been done even more intensively. Congress should have (1) cut down on government expenditure and (2) raised taxes in order to convert a deficit into a budgetary surplus. The resulting excess of tax revenue over government expenditure could have been used to retire or pay off part of the public debt; but in any case the heavy tax collections would have reduced the excessive spending of the public and helped to moderate the inflationary pressures. However, it is always easier for us American people and our politicians to vote increases in expenditure and decreases in taxes than the reverse.

WAR FINANCE

As an illustration of the importance of the above remarks, we need only recall that a large part of the costs of World War I were paid for by "inflation taxes" in the United States, Great Britain, France, and Germany.

In World War II, we had full employment and heavy new government expenditures. Only by reducing people's incomes through very heavy taxing, could the government have got the resources necessary to fit out and operate our costly military machine. Congress did vote some new taxes: on the incomes of both rich and poor, on the excess profits of corporations, on purchases of furs, cosmetics, liquors, tobacco, and so forth.

Nevertheless, it did not vote new taxes equal to the incredible costs of modern warfare. It was forced, therefore, to finance almost half of its war expenditures by the second method: by selling government bonds to cover its budgetary deficit. Only to the extent that people did cut down their consumption expenditures in order to buy savings bonds would such bond sales tend to have the same effects as taxes in releasing resources to the government without a bidding up of prices.

But chiefly, bonds were bought (1) by the banks out of "newly created bank money"—a process that will be described in Part Two, or (2) by individuals and insurance companies out of funds that they were already saving anyway. By and large, therefore, we had every right to expect a tremendous, cataclysmic inflation during the war.

Prices did gradually rise by about one-third, but not in the predicted explosive inflationary fashion. Why not? How did the government get its necessary resources without sending prices sky-high? The answer is to be found in the *direct controls* introduced by the government: resources were allocated by order from the civilian production to the war effort; prices were arbitrarily frozen; scarce goods were rationed according to social priorities rather than ability to pay.

THE POST-KOREAN DEFENSE PROGRAM

Since the Korean war of 1950, the United States has again found it necessary to draft men and to expand vastly our defense expenditure. These new expenditures may add 30 billion dollars of new annual spending to an economy that is already at full employment. The result will be inflationary price increases. Is there no way out? If we are really willing to increase taxes enough to cause a release of resources from civilian output to the defense effort, we might succeed in minimizing inflation.

But this probably means that we must raise 30 billion dollars of new tax revenue, or even more. It means that we must deliberately make ourselves so poor that we will not obtain the automobiles, houses, and television sets that compete with the defense effort for scarce materials and manpower. It means we must impoverish ourselves until our wives and dependents will feel they ought to get paying jobs and until we ourselves will feel the need to work Saturdays and overtime in order to make ends meet.

This is asking a lot of a democratic people. But what are the alternatives? They are (1) impoverishment by inflation, (2) direct controls on prices and wages with direct restrictions on consumption, or (3) weakening of the defense program itself.

FISCAL POLICY DURING BOOM AND DEPRESSION

Our conclusions concerning the different methods of finance can be summarized simply as they apply to a full-employment economy:

Any additional government expenditure which the people think necessary and desirable should be financed by at least as much additional taxes. The primary purposes of taxation are to spread the "real" costs of collective governmental activity fairly and equitably among individuals and to prevent inflation.

But the economic world as we have known it for the last century and a half is not a stable system in full-employment equilibrium. Occasionally it is running an inflationary fever; often, and for long periods, it is in the frozen torpor of unemployment and slump. Policies that are economically unsound in a full-employment world may be the height of wisdom in a period of deep and prolonged unemployment: levying taxes may be proper when we want people to release resources; in time of depression when we want to increase the number of both private and public jobs, increasing taxes may be disastrous. Similarly, policies that would wreck a normal world may be just what the doctor would order for an economy suffering from a runaway inflation.

No more than a warning to this effect need be sounded at this point. After the analysis of saving and investment in Part Two, the reader will be in a better position to understand the importance and the limitations of government fiscal policy. In Chapter 8, our discussion of public finance as it relates to the tax systems of the federal, state, and local governments will be continued. The expenditure of the states and localities and their coordination with the federal government and with each other are also examined.

SUMMARY

1. The economic role of government has been a steadily expanding one. Not only are more and more activities in our complex, interdependent society coming under direct regulation and control, but in addition an ever larger fraction of the nation's output is being devoted to collective governmental consumption. And an increasingly large part of the national income is being "transferred" by taxation and government welfare expenditure from the relatively rich to the relatively poor.

2. Since World War I, federal expenditure has far outstripped local and state expenditure. During the depression of the 1930's, expenditures on relief, public works, etc., lifted the federal budget to a level of almost 10 billion dollars. At best, our postwar budget will be more than triple prewar levels because of increased defense outlays, interest on the public debt, and aid to veterans. Should the postwar boom explode in a panic or peter out into a slump, federal expenditure on public works and development programs will certainly increase in magnitude, at the same time that welfare expenditure for the unemployed and needy will vastly expand.

3. Government expenditure is financed by three sources: taxes, interest-bearing loans, and issue of noninterest-bearing currency. In a full-employment world only the first method can be relied upon to secure an equitable distribution of the real costs of government. And in such a world, only the first will cause sufficient reduction in private individual consumption to release the necessary resources for governmental projects without inflation—that hidden tax collector. The proper fiscal policy for a period of unemployment and slump or for a period of inflation orgy will be discussed later in Part Two.

QUESTIONS FOR DISCUSSION

1. What are some things that the government does today that it didn't formerly do?

2. Between now and 1970, how would you expect the government's share in the national income to develop? Why? What factors would affect your answer?

3. How much does the increasing economic cost of government reflect decreasing efficiency? How would you go about making a scientific study of this question?

4. "The radical doctrines of three decades ago are the conservative doctrines of today." Is this ever true? Is it always true? Give favorable illustrations and exceptions.

5. "Government expenditure on goods and services represents collective consumption rather than individualistic consumption. but nevertheless it does represent consumption." Would you always agree? Give your own qualifications.

6. "If the postwar federal budget is to be brought anywhere near back to the prewar level, the veterans' program and national defense will have to be the main things reduced." Do you agree? Why or why not?

7. Compare the President's last budget message with Table 1. What are the principal differences?

8. What were some of the measures of the New Deal? Which have been abandoned, and which are still in effect?

9. Define and give examples of a transfer payment.

10. Contrast the effects of the three ways of financing government expenditure: (a) under full-employment conditions, and (b) under depressed conditions.

11. How was the war financed? How should it have been?

12. What should be current postwar tax policy?

Chapter 8: THE ECONOMIC ROLE

OF GOVERNMENT: FEDERAL

TAXATION AND LOCAL FINANCE

OUR discussion of public finance continues in this chapter with a survey of the federal tax system, followed by a brief examination of expenditure and taxation at the state and local levels. It concludes with a short discussion of the problems of coordinating the activities of different levels of government.

FEDERAL TAXATION

The great variety of present federal taxes is indicated by Table 1. Of these, the first two, personal income and death, are "equitable" in that they bear down "progressively" more on those people with higher incomes. Payroll and sales taxes (groups 4 and 5) are relatively "regressive" in that they take a larger fraction of the poor man's income than they do of the rich man's. The corporation tax is intermediate in its effects; on balance, it is probably progressive, since most dividend dollars go to people of more than median income. Although it is true that many poor widows and orphans own some shares of stock, still the total that they own is not a large fraction of all stock shares. But to the extent that corporations can pass the tax on to the consumer in higher prices, a tax on business profits fails to be progressive. Our federal tax system is immeasurably more progressive than it was 20 years ago or than are the tax systems of the states and localities today. A brief glance at the various taxes may be helpful.

Sales and Excise Taxes. In order of regressiveness, these would probably come first. So-called "liberals" usually oppose these taxes, while "conservatives" extol their virtues. As far as federal finance is concerned there has resulted a compromise: No general sales tax has been passed, but there are

169

taxes on cigarettes, liquors, amusements, cosmetics, and certain other commodities. A wartime world may necessitate new sales taxes.

Social Security, Payroll, and Employment Taxes. Most industries—with the exception of agriculture, nonprofit hospitals and schools, etc.—come under the Social Security Act. All employees are eligible to receive old-age retirement benefits of so much per month, depending upon their previous earnings and not upon any humiliating demonstration of poverty. To help pay for these benefits, the employee and employer in 1951 each contribute 1½ per cent of

TABLE 1. *Estimated Tax Receipts of Federal Government, Fiscal Year 1952 (In billions of dollars)*

1. Personal income taxes		$29
2. Death and gift taxes		1
3. Corporation income and excess-profit taxes		24
4. Employment or payroll taxes		5
5. Sales or excise taxes		11
	Tobacco and liquor	$5
	Mfg. and retail excises	3
	Customs duties	½
	Miscellaneous	2½
		$11
6. Other taxes and receipts		1
	Total tax collections	$71
Minus		
	Tax refunds	3
	Net total	$68

SOURCE: Author's January, 1951, rough revision of official Budget Bureau estimates to allow for new legislation in 1951 and income trends.

all wage income below $3,600 per year. The self-employed pay 2¼ per cent. No insurance company could possibly sell such liberal retirement and other benefits for so low a rate. Because Congress has abandoned the original actuarial-reserve plan in favor of a pay-as-you-go plan, it will later have to add a government contribution to that of the employer and employee as the age distribution of the population gradually shifts toward the older ages of retirement.

Taken by itself, the payroll tax is regressive in its impact upon the poor and middle classes. But combined with social security benefit payments, the degree of regressiveness is materially less.

Corporation Income Taxes. After a corporation has paid all its expenses and reckoned its annual income, it must pay part of its income to the federal government. In 1951 Congress passed a new law with the following features: A small corporation will pay 25 cents of each dollar of its net income in taxes; but when its earnings get above $25,000 per year, it will have to pay 47 cents of each extra dollar of earnings. For many years prior to 1950, corporations with incomes above $50,000 paid only a 38 per cent corporate tax rate on extra earnings rather than 47 per cent.

In both world wars, this and other countries had an excess-profits tax on corporations in addition to the above normal tax. The outlook in 1951 is for a stepped-up defense program and for new legislation which would tax almost 80 cents out of each dollar of excess corporate profits reckoned over and above a base defined in terms of preemergency earnings or in terms of a "normal" return on invested capital.[1]

Some people think that the peacetime tax rate is too high, that corporations are discouraged from venturing on worth-while, but risky, job-making investment projects. They argue that a small corporation would be able to grow more rapidly if it could plow back into the business what the government takes in taxes. Proponents of these views also say it is unfair "double taxation" for the government to tax corporate earnings and also to make the stockholders pay personal income taxes on the dividends received from corporations.

On the other side there are those who argue that corporations should be taxed heavily, with the bigger corporations taxed at progressively heavier rates. These people believe that, if the government must collect large sums of money and if further increases in the personal income tax are not feasible, then a tax on corporations is better than a sales tax or payroll tax. Moreover, they point out that corporations do not distribute all their earnings to the stockholders but save some to be plowed back in the business. The stockholder avoids personal income tax on these corporation savings, so that, according to this viewpoint, a corporation tax will at least partially remedy the situation. The problem is too complex for us even to attempt a final evaluation here.

THE PROGRESSIVE INCOME TAX

Before World War II, March 15 was an unhappy day, in which wails of anguish were heard throughout the land as people wrestled with their income tax blanks. They had then to pay taxes for the previous year's income, which often had already been spent.

Now things are better. All through the year every employer automatically withholds from each pay check most of what the employee will have to pay to the government. This puts us all on a pay-as-you-go basis, so that by the end of the year we are more or less all paid up even if our pay checks have all been spent.

[1] The economics of an excess-profits tax is discussed in Chapter 30 on profits.

Anyone with an annual income of under $5,000, and no appreciable non-withheld earnings, can at the end of the year simply send in to the government his withholding tax receipt. The government will compute his true tax, compare that with what he has paid, and refund or bill him for the difference. In this way the Bureau of Internal Revenue of the Treasury Department currently computes the tax bills for some 25 million people.

Anyone with an income higher than $5,000, or with income from property of more than $100, or with exceptional contributions to charity, must file a more elaborate income tax return. In fact, early in any year he must make a simple, rough estimate of his income for the rest of the year and how much will be withheld; each 3 months he makes a quarterly payment of the difference between what his tax will probably be and what will be withheld. Thus at the end of the year, he is just about paid up on a true pay-as-you-go basis. On the following March 15, a final reckoning with the government is made, and any difference between earlier provisional payments and the true amount of the tax is settled by a bill or a refund.

This is a tremendous improvement over the previous method of always paying this year for last year's income. In fact, the old method was tolerable only so long as just a few million relatively well-to-do citizens paid income taxes. Before the depression, few family men with incomes of less than $5,000 had to pay a personal income tax or even file a return, because of the very liberal exemptions of income. Now, exemptions have been drastically reduced so that the majority of all wage earners come under the income tax. A single person earning around $600 per year, or as little as $12 per week, will pay some tax. A wife will give a man an extra $600 of exempted income, and each dependent child will exempt an extra $600 of annual income from taxation. (These figures all refer to the 1951 rates, which will undoubtedly undergo modification in succeeding years.)

There is still some burning of the midnight oil around the Ides of March by those who are filling out income tax returns. However, many of those who are not permitted simply to send in their withholding receipt find their work much simplified by using the so-called "short form." This automatically allows a deduction of about 10 per cent for charitable gifts, medical and interest expenses, etc. All you have to do is fill in your name, your current marital status, consult a table, and write in your income tax.

The real grief comes only for those with enough varied income to require the long-form return. They must worry about the depreciation of their trucks, about their capital gains and losses on the sale of land or securities, about a self-financed trip to the medical convention, about tax-exempt interest from a state bond, etc.

However, even here the difficulties are commonly exaggerated. It is only a moderate intelligence test for any citizen to fill out his own tax form, with or without the aid of the many helpful pamphlets on the subject and with or without the aid of accountants and Bureau of Internal Revenue officials. Perhaps it should be a prerequisite for graduation from high school that the citizen be able to perform this important ritual.

Enough has been said about these details. The important thing is to know about how much a typical individual pays at different income levels, as shown by Table 2. Column (2) shows about how much people would have to pay in taxes for each of the incomes listed in Column (1). Note that the tax starts at a low figure for poor people and rises very rapidly in relation to income. Indeed, when your income climbs up into the millions, up to 86 per cent will go to the government.

TABLE 2. *Amount of Personal Income Tax to Be Paid at Different Income Levels by a Childless Couple, 1951*   .

Net income before exemptions	Personal income tax	Proportion of tax to income	Disposable income left after taxes
(1)	(2)	(3)	(4)
$ 1,000 (or below)	$ 0	0	$ 1,000 (or below)
3,000	360	12	2,640
5,000	760	15	4,240
10,000	1,900	19	8,100
20,000	4,900	24	15,100
50,000	19,500	39	30,500
200,000	143,000	72	57,000
1,000,000	860,000	86	140,000

Column (3) shows just how progressive the personal income tax is. A $10,000-a-year family is made to bear a relatively heavier burden than a $3,000-a-year man—19 rather than 12 per cent; and a millionaire is made to bear a still heavier relative burden. Column (4) shows the amount of disposable income left after taxes. Note that it always pays to get more income even if you are as rich as Doris Duke. The government always takes *less* than 91 cents out of each *extra* dollar. At incomes around $20,000 it begins to take more than half of each *extra* dollar.

The income tax achieves its purpose of sharing the cost of government more "equitably" in relation to income. It tends somewhat to reduce the inequality of disposable income. Thus, in Figure 1, the hypothetical effect of progressive taxes on the inequality of income is indicated in exaggerated form. Note how the area of inequality on the Lorenz diagram has been reduced; progressive taxation has shifted the solid line into the broken line, nearer to the 45° line of complete equality.

Often, doubts are raised as to whether high income taxes do not discourage effort and risk taking. This is not an easy question to answer since taxation will cause some people to work harder in order to make their million; many doctors, scientists, artists, and businessmen who enjoy their jobs and the sense of power or accomplishment that they bring, will work the same amount

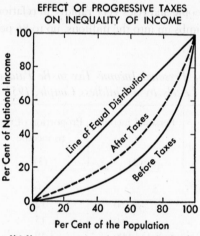

EFFECT OF PROGRESSIVE TAXES ON INEQUALITY OF INCOME

FIGURE 1. The heavy solid line represents the unequal distribution of income before taxes. The broken line shows how progressive taxes result in a more equal distribution of "disposable" income after taxes. The effect is exaggerated for emphasis.

for $30,000 as for $100,000; still others may prefer more leisure to work as a result of progressive taxes. The net result is hard to be dogmatic about. We must content ourselves with posing the problem and leave it for further discussion in Part Four.

The effects of progressive taxes on risky investment are easier to appraise. They are probably adverse. In part the government says to the taxpayer "Heads I win, tails you lose." For example, suppose a man earns $200,000 in 1 year and nothing in the next 3 years, while his brother earns $50,000 in each of the 4 years. Their average earnings before taxes over the period are the same, but the venturesome brother pays over the period $143,000 in taxes, leaving him with a total income after taxes of $57,000 (see Table 2). On the other hand, the steady brother pays a total of only $78,000 in taxes and is left with total income after taxes of $122,000 for the period. In this example, the progression in the tax system has penalized the venturesome brother to the tune of leaving him only half as well off as his conservative brother.

Opposing the unfavorable effect of progressive taxes on investment and jobs, there is an opposite effect. To the extent that dollars are taken from frugal wealthy people rather than from poor ready spenders, progressive taxes tend to keep purchasing power and jobs at a high level—at too high a level if inflation is threatening.

Thus no one can be sure whether the unfavorable effects of the personal income tax on investment offset the opposite effects in cutting down potentially excessive savings. In the last analysis, therefore, every voter must decide largely on ethical grounds whether he favors a more or less equalitarian society, greater or smaller rewards and incentives to individual initiative.

BRITISH REDISTRIBUTION OF INCOME

Other countries, such as the United Kingdom, have gone further toward redistributing income than the United States has cared to go. A recent study[1] shows that in 1949 about 41 per cent of Britain's privately produced income was collected in taxes. In 1938 this was only 24 per cent. About one-half of the 1949 taxes came from nonprogressive indirect taxes (particularly tobacco and liquor). About one-third came from steeply progressive direct taxes (chiefly on incomes). The remaining one-sixth of the taxes came from corporations.

Where did this money go? About half went for national defense, past wars, and general government. And half went for redistribution of income, largely in the form of (1) health and education; (2) old-age pensions, family allowances, and other personal transfer payments; (3) food and other subsidies to keep living costs down.

If we compare 1938 and 1949, we find that the working classes now consume about 73 per cent of total consumption as against only 63 per cent before World War II; needless to say their earnings have not gone up nearly so much. Who then has been squeezed? Curiously enough the wealthy classes (counting in their ownership of corporations) seem not to have suffered as extreme a relative drop in living standards as have the middle classes. This group—which corresponds roughly to that to which most American college students belong—has most felt the pinch.

And yet, this study shows that despite all talk about soaking the rich to help the poor, one must not lose sight of the facts that (1) the poor are actually soaking themselves to help themselves and (2) one type of poor man is being

[1] FINDLEY WEAVER, "Taxation and Redistribution in the United Kingdom," *Review of Economics and Statistics*, vol. XXXII, August, 1950, pp. 201–213.

soaked to help another. Thus, the working classes as a whole pay more in taxes than as a class they receive in benefits under the health, education, and pension programs. And the low-income man who happens not to drink or smoke, who lives in a government house and wears subsidized utility clothing is being very heavily subsidized by other members of the low-income group.

What are the effects of such a system on incentives and production? Who can say? Who can separate out the effect of one element in a complex social

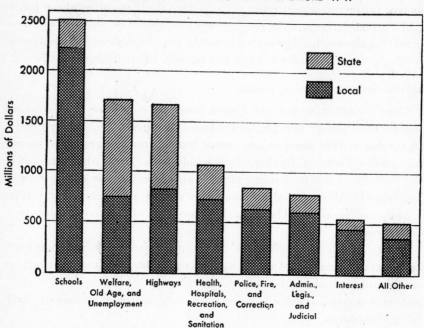

PURPOSES OF STATE AND LOCAL EXPENDITURE - 1941

FIGURE 2. SOURCE: Federal Reserve Board, *Postwar Economic Studies* No. 3.

and political situation? But this much is clear: Anyone who predicted on the basis of the above facts that total postwar production would necessarily be less than prewar would have misjudged the facts. According to Findley Weaver's report on the available data, total production in the postwar period grew far beyond that of the prewar.[1] Possibly if the tax load were judiciously lightened, it would grow even more rapidly.

STATE AND LOCAL EXPENDITURES

Let us now turn to public finance other than federal. Although quantitatively the federal government's multi-billion-dollar expenditures greatly exceed those of the states and localities, still these are very important in their own right.

[1] *Ibid.*, p 204.

To see what the states and localities spend their money on, turn to Figure 2. All these items are more or less self-explanatory. Note that expenditure on schools—mostly by localities—is the biggest single item by far. Table 3 shows state functions in more detail, for the year 1949.

TABLE 3. *Expenditures of States, 1949 (In billions)*

Total state expenditures.................................		$11.8
Total state expenditures exclusive of debt retirement.........		11.6
Current operations:		
Public welfare...........................	$1.3	
Highways...............................	0.5	
Schools.................................	0.8	
Bonus to veterans........................	0.5	
Hospitals, health, etc.....................	0.7	
Safety, control, correction.................	0.6	
National resources.......................	0.3	
Other...................................	0.3	
Total.................................		$5.0
Interest and trust funds.........................		$1.2
Capital outlay:		
Highways...............................	$1.3	
Schools.................................	0.2	
Other...................................	0.3	
Total.................................		$1.8
Aid paid to local governments:		
Highways...............................	0.6	
Public welfare...........................	0.6	
Schools.................................	1.7	
Other...................................	0.6	
Total.................................		$3.6

Source: Bureau of the Census, 1950.

STATE AND LOCAL TAXES

To see the main sources of funds to finance such expenditure, turn to Figure 3 and Table 4, which show the tax collections of state and local governments. In terms of the previous discussion of kinds of taxes, it must be admitted that, on the whole, the principal taxes of the states and localities are "regressive taxes." Let us discuss some of the more important ones.

Property Tax. It will be noted that the property tax still accounts for almost one-half of the total revenues of state and local finance and that the states have permitted the more needy localities to collect almost all property taxes, as Table 4 shows.

The property tax is levied primarily on real estate, land and buildings, but in some places also on personal property such as furniture and watches. Each locality sets an annual tax rate. Thus, in a large city $35 on each $1,000 of assessed valuation (3.5 per cent) may be the tax rate. This means that I must pay $350 of property taxes if my house has been assessed as being worth $10,000. However, in many places assessed valuations tend to be some fraction of true market value. Perhaps my house and all like it have a current market

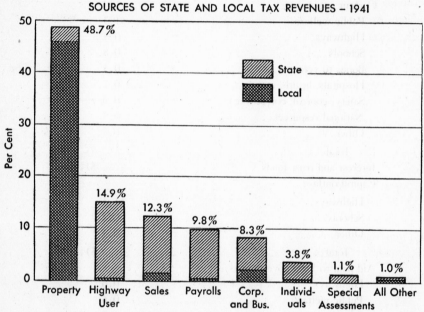

FIGURE 3. SOURCE: Federal Reserve Board, *Postwar Economic Studies* No. 3.

value of $15,000, but they may be assessed at about two-thirds that much. Really therefore, my true property tax rate is less than 3.5 per cent, nearer to 2.4 per cent.

The property tax is very inflexible. Rates and assessments tend to be changed only slowly. In bad times when real-estate values fall, the tax is very burdensome and gives rise to bankruptcy, mortgage foreclosures, and forced sales.

In colonial times, a man's total income and wealth may have been all connected with real estate; if so, then the effect of a tax on such property would have been roughly the same as a tax on income. Even then the property tax increased a rich man's taxes only in proportion to his total property—instead of increasing his taxes in greater proportion than income, as do modern progressive taxes. And today, when so much of wealth and income is divorced from real estate, many well-to-do people are able to avoid state and local taxes almost completely. Also, it is well known that small properties tend to be assessed relatively higher than large.

Highway User Taxes. As the name suggests, these revenues come from two primary sources: from a tax of so many pennies per gallon of gasoline and from license fees on automobiles, trucks, and drivers. In many states, more dollars are collected in this way than are spent on roads and bridges. The extra revenues are used for schools, old-age pensions, and other needs, just as in some colleges extra revenue from football games is used to buy track equipment or even Greek manuscripts.

TABLE 4. *Taxes and Revenues of State and Local Governments, 1948 (In billions)*

	State	Local	State and local
Taxes....................	$ 7.8	$6.6	$14.4
Property.................	0.3	5.8	6.1
Other...................	7.5	0.8	8.3
Aid from federal government.....	1.4	0.1	1.5
Aid from state government......		(3.2)	
Fees and miscellaneous........	0.8	1.2	2.0
Net total................	$10.0	$7.9	$17.9

SOURCE: *Economic Almanac for 1950* (National Industrial Conference Board, Inc., New York).

These highway taxes are usually justified on the grounds that the taxpayer is simply paying for the *benefit* of using the roads in much the same way as he pays for a railroad ticket or for his use of water and electricity.

Sales Taxes. In the past few years many states have begun to rely more and more on excises levied on tobacco, alcohol, and even on general sales. Most people—including many cigarette smokers and moderate drinkers—have a vague feeling that there is something immoral about tobacco and alcohol. They feel as though two birds are being killed with one stone when these articles are taxed; the state gets revenue and vice is made more expensive.

The same rationalization is not possible for, say, a 5 per cent tax on every-thing that a consumer buys whether it is a pair of shoes, a cake of soap, or a church candle. Rich and poor are taxed alike on each dollar spent; and since the poor are forced to spend a larger portion of their total dollars, it is easy to see that the sales tax is a regressive tax; *i.e.*, it takes a larger portion of low incomes than of high ones. Most reformers therefore regard it as an undesirable, inequitable tax which is only the child of necessity. Except as applied to clear-cut luxuries, they think it should be replaced by more progressive taxes, such as personal income or inheritance taxes.

Payroll and Business Taxes. States and localities often charge license fees for the privilege of acting as a corporation, running a tavern, and so forth. Some states tax the net income of a corporation as well, and collect miscellaneous other fees from business enterprises.

In addition, all states have been bribed by the federal government into collecting a wage tax equal to about 3 per cent of payrolls in occupations covered by social security. The proceeds are used to provide "unemployment compensation benefits or insurance" when workers become unemployed. Before the Federal Social Security Act was passed (1935), the few pioneering states, like Wisconsin and Ohio, which had unemployment insurance schemes were at a disadvantage. Industries would threaten, and occasionally more than threaten, to leave the state for neighboring places where there were no such unemployment compensation taxes and where an employer could wash his hands of a discharged worker. Naturally, even the states with good intentions tended to be dragged down to the level of those which were most irresponsible.

The Social Security Act changed all that. Instead of passing a federal act that many experts favored and many opposed, the national government accomplished the same thing by indirection. It passed a 3 per cent payroll tax on all states—but offered to rebate most of the proceeds to every state that set up a suitable unemployment compensation system. Every one of the 48 states suddenly discovered within its legislatures a burning enthusiasm for the unemployed worker, since now this cost the state nothing extra. The economics of social security as it concerns the individual and family will be discussed further in Chapter 10.

Personal Income and Inheritance Taxes. More than half the states imitate the federal government, but on a much smaller scale, by taxing individuals according to the size of their incomes. Such a method of taxation has already been discussed in connection with federal finance. A few important states, such as Illinois, do not rely at all on this relatively progressive tax; moreover, almost all those states that have an income tax could increase rates and collect more revenue from this source.

Inheritance taxes on individuals who inherit bequests of property upon death of a relative or friend are self-explanatory. They differ only in minor detail from estates taxes that are levied on the dead giver's estate and not on the receivers. Also, it will be obvious that gifts must be taxed, or else wealthy people would have every incentive to distribute before death all their wealth to their heirs, so as to escape taxation then.

Both the federal and the state governments share in estate and inheritance taxes. Once again, the federal government had to act to prevent states like Florida from advertising to old folks, "Come here to die and avoid all inheritance taxes." The federal government gives up part of its revenues to any state that passes such a tax law, by accepting a state tax receipt in part payment of a citizen's taxes. However, it goes only a small part of the whole way in this respect.

The inheritance and estates tax is called a progressive and democratic tax. The poor widow's inheritance usually pays no tax at all because of liberal exemptions, while the rich man's estate pays at a progressive rate. Social reformers attach great importance to death taxes for the purpose of preventing the development in this country of a permanent moneyed caste, living not on its effort and intelligence, but on its property inherited from one generation to the next. As of 1951, the Administration has argued that there are great loopholes in the present estates tax and has recommended a stiffening of rates.

There are other miscellaneous revenues which need hardly be described. Some localities sell natural gas and electricity. Some, especially in Nevada, tax slot machines and race-track betting. All collect some revenue from assessments on property owners who benefit from specific sewage and road improvements. A much more important revenue source, as we shall see in a moment, is the financial aid which the states receive from the federal government and which localities receive from the states.

Borrowing and Debt Repayment.   When all is counted in, it is still not true that the total of state and local expenditures equals the total of their revenues. The difference represents new borrowing or debt repayment. The wartime prosperity swelled state tax revenues (despite the rationing of gasoline). At the same time it became impossible to build new schools and highways and unnecessary to support so many needy people on relief.

As a result, in the war period most states were able to run a surplus and retire part of their previously accumulated debt. But since 1946 the states and localities have again been increasing their debts. Their costs have risen, and many school and highway projects deferred during World War II have finally been undertaken.

Between World War I and World War II, most state and local borrowing tended to behave perversely, so as to accentuate rather than damp down the business cycle. During the prosperous 1920's when the federal government was retiring part of its war debt, states and localities floated tremendous amounts of bonds, so as to build needed highways and schools at the high prices then prevailing. When the depression of the 1930's came, despite the publicity given to emergency borrowing of some cities, state and local governments on balance reduced their debts! They refused to build necessary public works even though costs were advantageous and jobs were desperately needed. Instead, they began to lean more and more on the federal government in this matter of public works as well as in connection with unemployment relief.

It is perhaps too much to ask the states and localities to take an active part in moderating the business cycle. But a minimum goal would be for them, if they cannot do good, at least to do no harm. If they are too weak to increase their outlay in depression, at least they should endeavor to withstand the temptation of increasing their expenditures in boom times. If they follow this advice, their dollars will go farther and the problem of unemployment will not be quite such a great and difficult one.

COORDINATING DIFFERENT LEVELS OF GOVERNMENT

Existing state and local boundaries do not reflect true economic entities. Gary, Indiana, is more truly a part of the Greater Chicago metropolitan region than it is of Indiana, and a similar relationship holds between Greenwich, Connecticut, and New York City. Relatively well-to-do people can commute from Wellesley, Massachusetts, to Boston in order to avoid having to share the high tax burden of keeping up Boston streets and aiding the Boston poor; and New Jersey suburbs beckon the wealthy New Yorker with the assurance that there is no income tax across the Hudson.[1] To avoid taxes, wealthy cosmopolitans even tried a few years ago to leave the United States for legal residences in Bermuda and elsewhere, until the war sent them scurrying home to the protecting arms of the Statue of Liberty.

What can be done about all these problems of coordinating different levels of government? The answer must be faced primarily in terms of political science rather than economics. In part we can and have set up new units of government cutting across existing boundaries: the Port of New York Authority, the Cook County Sanitary Commission, and so forth. All these fill a function. But sometimes the result is a patchwork of confusion. Thus, within the Greater Chicago area alone, there are literally *hundreds* of different units of government: three or four states, innumerable counties, townships, municipalities, and districts. Worse than that, any one citizen will be under the separate jurisdiction of a score of such overlapping agencies. It is not only that he does not know where to go when he gets a ticket for speeding; he is actually

---

[1] The city of Philadelphia collects a percentage tax on all wages earned by people working there, whether or not they live somewhere outside the city limits and commute.

paying taxes to the city of Chicago, to Cook County, to a School District, etc., etc.

From an economic point of view, some of the worst aspects of the existing situation are partially corrected by having the states make grants of money to the localities. In 1949, out of 11 billion dollars of state tax revenues, about one-third was shared with the localities—primarily for schools, highways, and public assistance (relief, old-age pensions, etc.). Only in this way can the poorer parts of each state maintain certain minimum standards of schooling, roads, and living. Only in this way can well-to-do suburbanites be prevented from running out completely upon their fair share of public responsibility.

Just as there are differences in financial need and income within a state, so are there tremendous differences in income and needs in different parts of the country. The South in particular has such a low economic income as to penalize seriously its citizens in the pursuit of an adequate education and standard of living. The logical step has been for the federal government, with its great taxing power all over the country, to share some of its revenues with the states —particularly since most modern economic problems (such as unemployment, good roads, etc.) are national in scope.

In 1949, the federal government made "grants-in-aid" to the states of $1\frac{3}{4}$ billion dollars, or of as much as one-sixth of their total tax revenues. These grants were primarily for highways, public welfare assistance, and education (vocational and agricultural training, etc.). Moreover, in the depressed years in the 1930's, the federal government made very large gifts to the states and localities in the form of hospitals, schools, and other public works constructed under the WPA (Works Progress Administration) and PWA (Public Works Administration).

To show how a typical grant-in-aid works, let us consider the federal old-age program under the Social Security Act. This consists of two parts: a contributory old-age pension plan run completely by the federal government, in which employees in most industries other than agriculture receive automatically—regardless of their needs—certain old-age benefits (pension, insurance, etc.) toward which they and their employers have helped to pay. This was discussed earlier in connection with the federal payroll tax. It has nothing to do with the states and will not be discussed further at this point.

However, there is a second part of the Social Security Act requiring the federal government to make "matching" grants-in-aid to the states to help them give assistance to the needy, aged, and handicapped. Thus, if New York State will vote $50 a month to its needy aged people, then the federal government will pay three-fourths of the first $20 and match the rest dollar for dollar (up to a total pension of $50 a month), thereby making the cost to the state only $20. Such a matching grant is easy to administer because of its automatic character. Also it obviously acts as an inducement to get the states to vote money for old-age assistance, since every dollar they provide does double duty, so to speak.

On the other hand, such a grant partially fails in its purpose of equalizing standards between rich and poor states. Thus, the state of Mississippi which cannot, or thinks it cannot, afford to vote pensions of much more than $20 per month, will receive only about $15 from the federal government. At the same time, wealthy New York is receiving $30 from the federal government. Once more we are up against a case of "to him who hath shall be given." It remains to be seen whether some future Congress will pass a remedying law in which grants-in-aid to the states will be based upon, and vary inversely with, the level of per capita state incomes.

The atomic bomb has perhaps taught us that ours is One World. We have yet to learn the full significance of the fact that this is One Country.

SUMMARY

1. About two-thirds of federal revenue comes from personal and corporation income taxes. The rest comes from so-called regressive taxes on payrolls and excises. The personal income tax is steeply progressive and tends to redistribute income between rich and poor. In Britain, this redistribution has gone considerably beyond that in the United States.

2. State and local expenditures have been rising in the postwar period: the principal items are education, highways, public welfare, and the ordinary police and safety functions of government.

3. The property tax is still the most important source of local revenue. Gasoline and sales taxes are important at the state level; gradually less regressive taxes are gaining in importance. In the postwar period, states and localities have reversed the wartime pattern. They have been spending more than they collect in taxation, thereby increasing their debts.

4. The problem of coordinating the federal, state, and local levels of government offers administrative difficulties. Increasingly the federal government gives grants of billions to the states, primarily for highways and matching grants-in-aid for social welfare. The states in turn are increasingly helping the localities in the fields of education, highways, and public assistance

QUESTIONS FOR DISCUSSION

1. Make a list of different kinds of taxes in order of their progressiveness. What is the importance of each at the (*a*) federal, (*b*) state, and (*c*) local level?

2. About how much would a single man pay in income tax at the present time if his total income was $2,000, $5,000, $20,000, or $1,000,000?

3. List different state and local expenditure categories in order of their quantitative importance. Compare Figure 2 and Table 3 for changes during the 1940's.

4. How do you think different government functions should be allocated among the three levels of government? How about revenues and grants-in-aid?

5. What has been your own state's postwar fiscal policy? Do you approve? Why?

6. Should a citizen in Massachusetts be taxed to help a citizen in Arkansas? To help a citizen in Vermont? In Massachusetts?

7. "Since people don't change their smoking habits as a result of taxation, and since the poor smoke, a tax on cigarettes is really no different from a tax on bread." Do you agree? What would you conclude ought to be done if the above statement were true?

8. "No country can continue to spend more than 25 per cent of its income on government." Discuss.

9. How should a defense program that runs into the tens of billions be financed in the 1950's?

Chapter 9: LABOR AND

INDUSTRIAL RELATIONS

AMERICA has become a "laboristic economy." This term, suggested by Sumner Slichter, Harvard's eminent authority on labor economics, no doubt has an element of exaggeration in it. Ours is still a "capitalistic economy," and it is also a "mixed economy" in which the role of government is exceedingly important. But no one can deny that the huge growth of labor unions since 1933 has made them seats of tremendous economic and political power. A John L. Lewis is not less important these days than a Henry Ford.

Unions are an important part of American life, and they are here to stay. By law and custom, free trade-unions are recognized as legitimate economic institutions in all modern democratic nations. In Hitler's Germany, Mussolini's Italy, and Stalin's Russia, labor unions as we know them were not permitted to exist.

PRESENT-DAY MEMBERSHIP

Some 15 million Americans belonged to a union in 1950. This means that about one-third of the nonagricultural working force is made up of union men. If we exclude white-collar workers, foremen, and executives, the proportion of union men would be still higher. And if we examine certain important industries—such as railway and water transportation, basic steel, automobiles, and printing—practically all eligible workers belong to unions.

Figure 1 shows the prodigious growth of union memberships since 1900: the slow, steady advance up to World War I, the upsurge during that war and immediately thereafter, and the rather sharp decline and slumping off during the 1920's. For the more recent period, Figure 1 shows the explosive acquisition of new members during the New Deal recovery years after the Great Depression, the continued rapid growth during World War II, and finally the leveling off of growth since the end of the war.

MEMBERSHIP IN AMERICAN LABOR UNIONS

FIGURE 1. SOURCE: Adapted from Florence Peterson, *American Labor Unions* (Harper, New York, 1945), and U.S. Department of Labor.

To what unions do workers belong? Figure 2 shows that about half, or 8 million belong to unions affiliated with the American Federation of Labor (AFL). The Congress of Industrial Organizations (CIO) has claim to almost 6 million members. In addition to the AFL and CIO, there are independent unions such as John L. Lewis' United Mine Workers (UMW), the great "big four" Railway Brotherhoods, etc.

Statistics of union memberships understate the influence of unions. Many nonunion people are covered by union agreements on wages, hours, and working conditions. If you took a solemn oath never to join a union or work under a union agreement, you would have to give up all hope of being a factory worker in many sectors of manufacturing industries. *In every single manufacturing industry*, at least 20 per cent of all wage earners came under union agreements in 1946—even if they were not actually union members. In 22 of the 53 manufacturing industries, no less than 80 to 100 per cent of wage earners worked under union agreements; in 13 industries, 60 to 79 per cent were under union agreement; in 13 more industries, 40 to 59 per cent of wage earners were under union agreements; and finally in only 5 industries were less than 40 per cent under such agreements. Outside of manufacturing industry, 80 to 100 per cent of all workers in construction, transportation, and mining were under union agreements. To avoid unions you must work for the government, go on a farm, or enter financial or service occupations.

NATIONAL AND LOCAL UNIONS

There are three important layers in the structure of American unions: (1) the *local* union, (2) the *national* union,[1] and the *federation* of national unions. To a union member, the *local* is by far the most important. He joins the local in his

[1] Many national unions have Canadian chapters and so are called international unions.

plant or town. He pays his dues to the local. Usually, the local union signs the collective bargaining agreement determining his wages and work conditions.

But the local is only one single chapter or lodge of the national union. Thus, a linotypist in Chicago belongs to the local union located there, but this is one

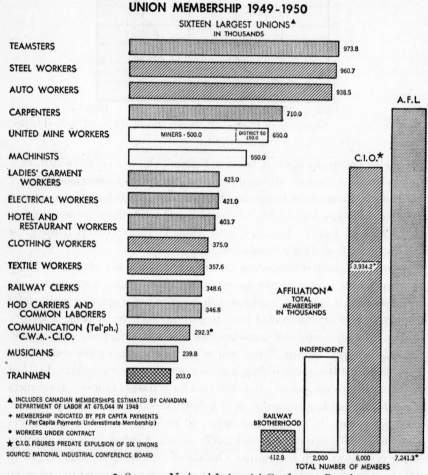

UNION MEMBERSHIP 1949-1950
SIXTEEN LARGEST UNIONS▲
IN THOUSANDS

TEAMSTERS	973.8
STEEL WORKERS	960.7
AUTO WORKERS	938.5
CARPENTERS	710.0
UNITED MINE WORKERS	MINERS - 500.0 DISTRICT 50 150.0 650.0
MACHINISTS	550.0
LADIES' GARMENT WORKERS	423.0
ELECTRICAL WORKERS	421.0
HOTEL AND RESTAURANT WORKERS	403.7
CLOTHING WORKERS	375.0
TEXTILE WORKERS	357.6
RAILWAY CLERKS	348.6
HOD CARRIERS AND COMMON LABORERS	346.8
COMMUNICATION (Tel'ph.) C.W.A.-C.I.O.	292.3•
MUSICIANS	239.8
TRAINMEN	203.0

A.F.L. 7,241.3+
C.I.O.* 3,934.2+

AFFILIATION▲
TOTAL MEMBERSHIP
IN THOUSANDS

INDEPENDENT

RAILWAY BROTHERHOOD 412.8

TOTAL NUMBER OF MEMBERS: 2,000 6,000

▲ INCLUDES CANADIAN MEMBERSHIPS ESTIMATED BY CANADIAN DEPARTMENT OF LABOR AT 675,044 IN 1948
+ MEMBERSHIP INDICATED BY PER CAPITA PAYMENTS (Per Capita Payments Underestimate Membership)
• WORKERS UNDER CONTRACT
★ C.I.O. FIGURES PREDATE EXPULSION OF SIX UNIONS
SOURCE: NATIONAL INDUSTRIAL CONFERENCE BOARD

FIGURE 2. SOURCE: National Industrial Conference Board.

of hundreds of local chapters of the International Typographical Union (AFL) whose headquarters is in Indianapolis. Generally, part of the local dues—one-half or less, usually—must go to the national union; the bylaws and practice of the local cannot transcend the broad policies laid down at the national level. The president and other officers of the local will probably be local workers; but the important office of business agent is a full-time job, the salary for which is often paid by the national union. The trend is increasing for the national unions to lend a hand in local-union collective bargaining.

Altogether there are over 200 autonomous national unions. As we have seen, half a dozen of these have over half a million members. But about 50 per cent of the national unions each have between 10,000 and 100,000 members, and 25 per cent of the national unions have less than 8,000 members.

The number of local union chapters or lodges is about 70,000. Some have as few as a dozen men. A few giant locals cover thousands of men. For example, the Ford local of the UAW(CIO) is the largest of all. It has no less than 65,000 members! The vast majority of locals fall in between in size, covering anywhere from 50 to 1,000 workers.

NATIONAL UNIONS AND THE FEDERATIONS

The AFL and CIO are loose federations made up primarily of national unions as members. The public thinks of these great federations as being the most important part of the labor movement. But they are not. They act as spokesmen for labor, but their own power is strictly limited. Thus Philip Murray wields more real power in his capacity as head of the Steel Workers Union than he does as president of the CIO. As a federation the AFL strongly disapproves of union discrimination against Negroes, but it has no power to act against those few of its member unions which have restrictive rules written into their constitutions. When the CIO in 1949 and 1950 expelled the United Electrical Workers (UE) and ten other allegedly left-wing unions held to have been communist-infiltrated, this was considered a precedent-breaking action.

In the last 20 years the federations have increased somewhat in importance and power, but they remain loose federations still. They are dependent upon the member national unions for financial support. Later when we survey the history of the American labor movement, we shall see that federalism has been a characteristic feature of its evolution. Like the Big Five nations on the Security Council of the United Nations, the national unions have insisted upon their "sovereignty" and right of veto and their right to "exclusive jurisdiction" over workers in their area.

Both the AFL and CIO have recently become very active in politics. The CIO'S Political Action Committee (PAC) often cooperates with the AFL's Labor's League for Political Education (LLPE) in supporting candidates favorable to labor. Though nominally nonpartisan, in fact they have usually supported Democratic candidates, but there are some notable exceptions. Moreover a number of labor leaders, such as John L. Lewis and William Hutcheson of the Carpenters' Union, have generally supported Republican presidential candidates.

Figure 3 gives organization charts for both the AFL and CIO. The state and city federations or industrial councils shown thereon lobby at these levels of government and cooperate in producing radio programs, parades, and election or strike solidarity. The charts also reveal that both AFL and CIO have a few local unions attached directly to them rather than to any national union. Usually, these locals are in new fields just in process of being organized or in

THE STRUCTURE OF AMERICAN UNIONS

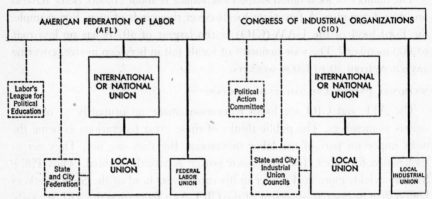

FIGURE 3. SOURCE: Adapted from Florence Peterson, *American Labor Unions* (Harper, New York, 1945).

fields that fall between jurisdiction and territories of the constituent national unions.

HOW DOES COLLECTIVE BARGAINING WORK?

In the following pages we shall trace the historical genesis of the present American labor movement. But first let us examine how collective bargaining is carried on.[1] Suppose you work in a factory that has just been organized. An AFL union has petitioned the National Labor Relations Board (NLRB) for an election to determine who shall be the exclusive bargaining agent in this plant. You mark a secret ballot in favor of the union; it wins more votes than, let us say, an existing so-called company union. A day is set for representatives of your union to meet with representatives of management around the bargaining table.

Seated at the table will probably be a vice-president in charge of industrial relations; with him will be attorneys from a law firm that specializes in the labor field. On the union side will be the local business agent of the union and a small committee of union officers, and handling the negotiations will be an expert from union headquarters. Probably he is neither a lawyer nor a professional economist, but the economic research staff of the union has helped him to prepare an extensive brief backing up the union's demands.

The union brief will analyze the company's profit position and published

[1] Chapter 28 includes a more analytical discussion of the collective bargaining process.

accounting records in great detail; it will present data showing that the president of the company receives $150,000 a year; etc. It will contain national figures on the changes in the cost of living and may even present local data to show that rents in that area have risen beyond the national average. The brief will also compare wages in that plant with those prevailing in other plants and other industries. It will bristle with theoretical arguments showing the necessity for higher wages to maintain workers' consumption and national full employment. The employer's brief will have carefully prepared rebuttals to each of these points. If this is an important industry, both union and management will be prepared with publicity releases to be given to the press at the proper time.

Hourly wage rates will not be the only issue in bargaining. In addition the union may be asking for a dues "checkoff" (whereby union dues are automatically deducted from the payroll of union members). The union may be bargaining for "maintenance of union membership," whereby union members cannot quit for the duration of the bargaining agreement; or it may be bargaining for other aspects of "union security." Pension and health-insurance demands may be discussed at the bargaining table. In many industries where piece rates prevail, the structure of rates will be an important subject for negotiation; the exact work load—how many looms each man will attend, etc.—may be discussed, and the general problem of how fast technological improvements shall be adopted will enter into the final contract. The seniority rights of workers and a grievance procedure for handling cases of discharge—these and many other problems will come into the collective bargaining.

Indeed, management has become greatly concerned over the inroads that organized labor has been trying to make into its prerogatives. Many employers feel that they can no longer run their business in the way that they feel is best. They find it difficult to hire whom they will, fire for just cause, determine work methods, decide on the order in which people will be laid off, etc. They feel that every new decision occasions a meeting of a new committee, and time that could better be spent on producing output must be devoted to labor relations. They feel that the worker acts as if he has a right to any job he has held for some time. Critics complain that a good many unions oppose incentive wage schemes, insist upon rigid seniority, discourage efficient work methods, and seriously limit the autonomy of management. A recent casebook on collective bargaining devotes more space to issues arising out of workers' rights in jobs than to any other single subject.[1]

But at last the contract, covering many pages of fine print, is signed. Everything is set down in black and white, including provisions for grievances that

[1] J. T. DUNLOP, *Collective Bargaining: Principles and Cases* (Irwin, Chicago, 1949).

arise during the life of the contract; often, too, there will be provisions for *arbitration* over issues that arise under it, with each side agreeing in advance to accept the decision of an impartial outside arbitrator. The usual life of a contract may be a year, with provisions made for reopening negotiations for a new contract under specified conditions.[1]

BRIEF HISTORY OF THE AMERICAN LABOR MOVEMENT

Although American labor was late in becoming organized, the beginnings go back well into post-Revolutionary War and pre-Civil War times. Local craft unions of highly skilled strategically placed workers (printers, etc.) were first to be formed; and periodically in boom times of employment or industrial unrest, these would combine in city and national federations for political and reform purposes. But not until the 1880's, when the American Federation of Labor was formed, did the American labor movement assume its characteristic present-day form.

The Knights of Labor.   In the post-Civil War decades of the last third of the nineteenth century, a "great upheaval" swept the land. Part of this populist revolt against the "big interests" was the formation of the Order of the Knights of Labor. At first this was a secret society to which all but "lawyers, bankers, gamblers or liquor dealers, and Pinkerton detectives" could join. Later, secrecy was dropped; and by 1886, the high-water mark, the Knights had some 700,000 members. The Knights represented an attempt to form *one great labor union* that would speak for all labor. But it was a heterogeneous collection whose members were craft unions of skilled workers, industrial unions of all workers in a given plant or industry, and mixed assemblies of anyone who cared to join.

The Knights were very interested in political reform and agitation. Some officials were more interested in "uplift" and radical political changes than in day-to-day increases in hourly wages. After a few unsuccessful strikes, the Knights declined in membership as rapidly as they had grown. America was obviously not susceptible to such a political labor movement, and the organization of the Knights of Labor was too loose to give it any staying power.[2]

---

[1] *Ibid.*, p. 74, lists the following main headings in collective bargaining agreements: (1) the rights of the management and union organizations, (2) compensation of employees, (3) the grievance procedure, (4) relative rights of different employees to particular jobs, and (5) the terms of the agreement.

[2] Again, around the time of World War I, the IWW (Industrial Workers of the World, or "Wobblies") was to attempt to organize the whole working class for the overthrow of capitalism, but it had limited success in its efforts to organize unskilled migratory workers, loggers, and metal mine workers. It had greater success in inducing panic in Wilson's At-

The American Federation of Labor. In 1881, and formally in 1886, the present-day labor movement took its form in the birth of the American Federation of Labor. For almost half a century, until his death in 1924, Samuel Gompers dominated this organization and gave the movement its characteristic pattern. Gompers himself was brought to this country as a child by immigrant parents. He was active in developing the Cigar Makers' Union and in founding the AFL as a rival organization to the Knights of Labor. Though early interested in socialistic uplift movements, he soon realized that no movement opposed to capitalism would flourish on American soil.

His main principles were simple:

1. He insisted on "business unionism" aiming at day-to-day higher wages and better work conditions. He forsook pie in the sky, instead asking for "more today than yesterday; more tomorrow than today." Labor was to achieve "more and still more" by gradualistic-evolutionary methods rather than revolutionary-uplift violence.

2. He committed the AFL to the principle of *federalism*, with each national union having autonomous sovereignty and "exclusive jurisdiction" over its craft specialty. This meant that the AFL would not tolerate "dual unionism"; Two unions could not try to organize the same workers; and even if they wanted to, a group of workers could not break away from a recognized national union.

3. Finally he insisted on *voluntarism*, with the government not to interfere with collective bargaining, either in favor of or against labor. In politics he favored "rewarding labor's friends, punishing labor's enemies"; but he would not commit labor to any one political party.

Thus, the AFL was a polar opposite of the Knights of Labor in almost every respect. As the Knights dwindled in importance, the AFL grew.

The Stagnant Twenties. Shortly after World War I, the AFL had about 5 million members and seemed to be riding high. But during the 1920's, the labor movement met with the most determined opposition from the National Association of Manufacturers (NAM) and other business groups. The "open shop" was declared to be the "American plan." Moreover, the 1920's was a "new era" of eternal prosperity. As John J. Raskob, General Motors executive and Democratic party bigwig said, anyone could easily get rich by saving $15 a week and investing it in stock-market parlays. (Raskob added that not only was it possible for people to become rich— it was their *duty* to become rich as well.) Also, the 1920's was one of those rare high-employment periods

---

torney General Palmer, who in 1920 threw suspected radicals in jail in defiance of civil liberties. But nothing came of the IWW, and it soon faded away into complete ineffectiveness.

when prices were not rising; so discontent over the cost of living was not operating to encourage unionization.

The AFL itself was rather stagnant. At Gompers' death, John L. Lewis and other strong men tried to get his job. As a result, William Green was elected as a compromise candidate and has been president ever since. Green had begun with the UMW and slowly—"funeral by funeral," as one labor textbook puts it—he worked his way up the bureaucratic ladder; gradually he became dependent for support upon the building trades and on the whole represented the viewpoint of the "craft unions," consisting of skilled workers of one occupation. His old boss, John L. Lewis, was associated on the other hand with the viewpoint of the "industrial unions," consisting of all the workers in a given industry or plant.

Recovery and the Formation of the CIO.   By the depths of the 1932 depression, the AFL had fallen to less than 3 million members. But with the recovery days, a new era for unionism was in the offing. The depression had soured the American public on many of the slogans of the 1920's and had excited class antagonisms. Moreover, even before the election of Franklin Roosevelt, the electorate and the courts began to modify their opposition toward union activities.

But within the AFL itself, the old insistence on the exclusive jurisdiction of national unions stood in the way of organization of the great mass-production industries. For example, before Judge Gary of U.S. Steel crushed the great 1919 steel strike, an unwieldy committee of some two-score craft unions was set up to conduct the strike. To this day the Carpenters and the Machinists unions have never been able to settle some of their differences.

Astute observers in 1933 saw the handwriting on the wall: industrial unions were to play an important part in the future. John L. Lewis of the UMW, the late Sidney Hillman of the Amalgamated Clothing Workers Union, and other leaders took matters in their own hands and in 1935 formed a committee to help organize the mass-production industries. For running counter to the exclusive jurisdiction principles of the AFL, they were later expelled from that organization, and so they formally organized the CIO, with Lewis as president. Helped by new government attitudes, legislation, and court decisions, a whirlwind campaign followed in which the important mass-production industries, such as automobiles, steel, rubber, and oil, were organized—despite the bitter opposition of the principal companies in these industries.

By this time the AFL had learned the important lesson of industrial unionism. It, too, began to organize on an industrial basis. It is fair to say that much of the strength of the AFL still resides in craft unions, but nonetheless it now has an important element of industrial unionization within its own organization. Since the founding of the CIO there has been considerable jurisdictional rivalry between it and the AFL. For example, each has rival textile unions organized on an industrial basis. A few CIO unions, such as David Dubinsky's Ladies Garment Workers' (ILGWU), have returned to the AFL.

Communists and Unions. For a long time the CIO was the more militant of the two great federations, and for a long time it was regarded as the more left wing.

Boring in by Communists has always been something of a problem for the union movement. For example, in the 1920's Dubinsky led a successful effort to oust the communist influence from his union. During the 1930's the Communists attempted to influence policy in many unions. They provided zealous labor organizers, and Lewis himself in his factional disputes with Philip Murray for a time tolerated their help. In the United Electrical Workers (until 1949 CIO), the National Maritime, and the longshoremen's unions, the struggles between the "Commies" and anti-Communists were especially severe; and in the International Fur and Leather Workers (CIO) the Communists did come into almost complete control.

The Communists, who usually comprised only a tiny percentage of membership, exercised an influence beyond their numbers because they acted as a unit, using Machiavellian tactics to achieve their goals. Those goals far transcended the day-to-day business unionism typical of American labor. Also as was shown dramatically on the day after Germany attacked Russia, the Communists followed the "Moscow party line" and suddenly ceased to attack Roosevelt as a "war monger" interested only in promoting an "imperialistic war." Instead they hailed Roosevelt as a great leader of the fight by democracies against fascism.

Again after World War II, when tension developed between this country and the Soviet Union, the Communists once more labeled the Democratic administration as the tool of the capitalistic interests. Up until that time, the labor movement had on the whole tolerated left-wing adherents as long as they stood also for the same things that the unions stood for. But since 1949 there has been a showdown. In addition to expelling the UEW and half a dozen other unions, the CIO in 1950 expelled Harry Bridges' West Coast longshoremen's union as a Communist-infiltrated union.

Except in a dozen unions the Communists have never attained any considerable power. And even in these unions, theirs has been almost entirely a minority influence resting on their cleverness in strategy and in identifying themselves with popular labor causes. Fortunately it is becoming increasingly easy to identify those who follow the Communist line and take their cue from the foreign policy of the Soviet Union. Only those who think that belonging to a trade-union is itself a treasonable act can rationally regard the American labor movement as being generally either revolutionary or subversive of our constitutional democratic system; but this political judgment is not to deny that many people, including the present author, have grave reservations concerning the *economic wisdom* of many of the policies pursued by labor unions.

The role of gangsterism in the union movement is quantitatively less important than communism. After the repeal of prohibition, corrupt gunmen did work their way into a few urban unions. Such union officials were as ready to sell out labor for a bribe as to fight in labor's interests. Labor has been fairly successful in cleaning its own house; in cities where there is effective law enforcement, the evil of labor gangsterism is well under control.

HOW DEMOCRATIC ARE UNIONS?

Earlier we encountered the problems involved in democratic control by stockholders of corporation management. A not dissimilar problem arises in connection with unions. It is true that union officials are elected to office, and all union members are given equal votes. But officers once elected often stay in power for a considerable time, and between annual conventions the union is usually run by a small executive board. A man like John L. Lewis is on the whole popular with his miners; but if a miner disagreed with the general policies laid down by Lewis, he would not get very far.

Like the average stockholder, but not to the same degree, the average union member does not participate very actively in policy formation. However, according to Sumner Slichter, who has made a study of this problem,

This does not mean the rank and file lack influence. Their influence is great, but influence is not participation. If democracy simply means strong rank and file influence, most unions are democratic. The typical situation in a union is similar to that found in most organizations, churches and clubs of all sorts. There is a minority which is sufficiently interested in the affairs of the organization to attend business meetings and to participate actively in discussing problems. In the case of unions this minority usually asks the officers to press for stiff demands—stiffer than employers would be willing to grant without a long fight, stiff enough to force many employers out of business. In order to avoid trouble, the great majority of the union would settle for much less than the active minority demand.

Quite naturally the professional leader feels on the spot. If he disappoints the active minority too deeply, his leadership will be challenged. If he gets the inactive majority into too much trouble, he may provoke revolt also. He compromises, as, of course, he must. Usually he is more interested in placating the active minority than the inactive majority because he knows that the support or opposition of the active members is more important than the support or opposition of the inactive members. The record shows that union officials lose their jobs, not for being too radical for the majority, but for being too conservative for the minority.[1]

OPPOSITION TO UNIONS BY AMERICAN EMPLOYERS

In its struggles for higher wages and recognition of unions,

American labor has employed clubs, shotguns, and dynamite. It is the hardest-hitting and most violent unionism in all the world. The European mind has real difficulty in understanding that blood will be shed for the trifling object of putting a few more cents per hour into the pay envelope, . . . that over a million workers will be on strike at the same time, causing a creeping paralysis to spread over the economy, *without these strikers being the advance guard of revolution.*[2]

To understand this pattern of violence, we must record the sad fact that of all the countries in the Western world, only in the United States have employers been militantly antiunion. Historically, American management fought unions tooth and nail. Only as recently as the late 1930's, companies like Ford Motors and Republic Steel were spending literally millions of dollars on private detectives in a losing fight against unionization. Bullets were flying on the picket lines and killing a dozen men as recently as Memorial Day, 1937, years after the law of the land gave unions the unmistakable right to organize.

It is to be hoped that this is all past history now. Certainly today all the automobile companies, big and little, are engaged in relatively peaceful collective bargaining; the same is true of both Big Steel and Little Steel. But to understand the pattern of American labor history, this unfortunate record of last-ditch employer opposition must be taken into account.

The chief weapons used by employers to combat unions have been (1) *discriminatory discharge* of union members, (2) the *blacklist*, (3) the *lockout*, (4) the "yellow-dog" contract, (5) the *labor spy*, (6) the *strikebreaker and armed guards*, and (7) the "company union."[3] In addition to these measures of employer self-help against unions, employers have used the courts to fight against unions.

To illustrate what these terms mean, imagine that I am a business executive

[1] S. H. SLICHTER, *The Challenge of Industrial Relations* (Cornell University Press, Ithaca, N.Y., 1947), p. 111.

[2] M. S. PITZELE, "Can American Labor Defeat the Communists?" *Atlantic Monthly*, March, 1947, p. 28, quoted in G. F. Bloom and H. R. Northrup, *Economics of Labor and Industrial Relations* (Blakiston, Philadelphia, 1950), p. 17. The second chapter of this text gives an excellent history of the American labor movement.

[3] *Violations of Free Speech and Rights of Labor*, Preliminary Report, Senate Report 46, 75th Congress, 15th Session (Government Printing Office, Washington, D.C., 1937). J. R. Commons' four-volume *History of American Labor* is a standard reference.

battling, back in the old days, against having my labor force unionized. I am not a cruel man; I am good to my family and I do not cheat my creditors; but to me war is war, and I feel it my duty to do battle in what I believe is a righteous cause. So, gory details omitted, here are some of the things that I might have been doing a score of years ago.

First, I ask the foremen which men are the ringleaders of the new union. Having learned their names, I fire them. More than that, I put their names on a blacklist so that all other employers are warned against hiring them. I help see to it that outside union organizers are tarred and feathered or run out of town on a rail; or at least they are warned to get out of town if they do not want to be arrested by the local constabulary for vagrancy and/or disturbing the peace. What influence I have is used to make sure that the local schools or churches are not made available to the union for their meetings and rallies.

Before the union can call a strike, I beat them to the punch and call a lockout. I close my plant until the men come to their senses and drop out of the union. Any new men I hire must sign a so-called yellow-dog contract promising never to join a union. If they go back on this contract, I take it to the courts for enforcement.

But in spite of my efforts, the union continues to make headway. So to protect myself against the union outsiders, I have to send away for outside help. There are a number of professional detective agencies who specialize in this kind of work; from them I can hire five men or five hundred. Of course, these men will not be liked by the violent union members, and so they must be armed in self-defense and in order to help protect private property from illegal violence. It may even be necessary to have some of them sworn in by the local sheriff as official deputies to help maintain order. I tell these professionals not to use violent methods, and I really mean it. But they are only human, and their own lives are in jeopardy; so it is only natural that they should do whatever seems necessary to protect themselves.

The unhappy day arrives when the union, losing all reason, calls a strike. I expect that only a few malcontents will walk out, but actually more than half the men get carried away by oratory and go out. They form a picket line outside the gates. They claim they are exercising their constitutional civil right of free speech, but their speech when they address my loyal employees reporting for work is hardly civil. "Scab" and "strikebreaker" are the politest of the words used. Even their women turn up in the picket line, shouting unladylike names such as "fink" and "goon" at my watchmen. Inevitably somebody gets carried away by the occasion and starts to throw stones at windows and at executives' cars. The crowd loses all reason and begins to tear down fences. In self-defense and to protect property from mob damage, some detective fires a shot. The next day the newspapers run headlines about labor massacres, and unfortunate public relations problems have been created.

In the end, I win the strike; the workers can hold out no longer. But faced with continued unrest and discontent after they have returned to work, I feel I must bow to the inevitable. If the men have to have a union, let them have one. But why must it be an uncooperative outside union rather than a reasonable one made up of men who have long been with the company and know its problems? So I encourage some of the born leaders among the men to form a "company union." I help pay for a barrel of beer for their initial get-together picnic; and to help the union treasury along, I let the boys sell soft drinks within the plant, the profits to go to the union treasury.

NEW PATTERN OF INDUSTRIAL RELATIONS

The business executive caricatured above is now extinct. He has been retired, and a new generation of management has taken over. Why? In the first place, the unions did succeed anyway in organizing most large plants during the 1930's; and it was simply not good business, in terms of the net earnings of the corporation concerned, to continue the expensive war against unions. In the second place, what finally brought the unions in successfully was not a superiority in arms and violence. The real change came about from the changed attitude of government. After 1930 the dice of government became loaded toward rather than against the union movement. Misguided though they might think the New Deal labor policies to be, business leaders knew they could not fight the United States government. We shall see in the next section just how this historical shift in the role of government came about.

Moreover, many business leaders began to understand the wisdom underlying the statement by Cyrus S. Ching, formerly vice-president of United States Rubber Company and subsequently head of federal Wage Stabilization:

Where we are dealing with organized labor, we are going to get about the type of leadership that we are ourselves.[1]

And they also recognize that there was at least a grain of realism in the statement by a labor leader:

Employers generally get the kind of labor relations they ask for. If the unions indulge in "excesses," then the employer as a rule has no one but himself to blame for it. For instance, if he engages the services of labor espionage agencies such as the Railway Audit, Pinkerton's or others, if he stocks up his plant with tear gas, hand grenades, submachine guns, blackjacks, rifles, and other implements of war, if he hires high-priced

[1] Cyrus S. Ching, "Problems in Collective Bargaining," *Journal of Business*, University of Chicago, January, 1938, Part 2, p. 40.

Wall Street lawyers to harass the union before the Labor Board and in the courts, if he distributes to his foremen anti-union literature and lets it be known to them that any harm they can do to the union would be forgiven by him, if he contributes to anti-labor organizations such as the notorious Johnstown Citizens' Committee, if he quibbles over words, if he refuses to consent to an election or to sign a contract when he knows the union has a majority, if after a contract has been forced from him he delays and hampers the settlements of grievances, if he continues to discriminate against union members, then labor will answer in kind and nine out of ten businessmen, viewing it from afar, will say, "Ah, another excess."[1]

So no observer of modern-day labor relations should get a false impression that all management has been antiunion. Violence makes the headlines while patient cooperation is unsensational and goes unnoticed. In countless industries there has been over the decades a successful pattern of peaceful and fruitful cooperation between labor and management. To highlight this fact, the National Planning Association has published some studies describing cases of successful labor relations.

Thus, the West Coast pulp and paper industry, whose leading member is the Crown Zellerbach Corporation, has had 14 years of healthy labor relationships. Only one strike occurred in the period, and that the result of a dispute between unions. The Dewey and Almy Chemical Company has a 9-year record of collective bargaining with its union, involving only one trifling work stoppage. The Nashua Gummed and Coated Paper Company has maintained relationships with no less than seven AFL unions for 15 years without a strike. And the Hickey-Freeman Company, a men's-clothing manufacturer, has dealt with unions for 29 years without a strike; for 18 years no grievance has ever gone as far as arbitration.

The Libbey-Owens-Ford Glass Company has had two long and costly strikes (in 15 years of union bargaining), one in 1936, the other in 1945. But the National Planning Association cited this as a case of *moving toward* a stable and constructive collective bargaining relationship: "Both the company and the union appear to be maturing—each acquiring a seasoned understanding of its respective objectives and each looking at the collective relationship in a practical and reasoned, rather than emotional, frame of mind."[2]

These are not cases in which peace has been maintained because the management or the union was soft. Hard bargaining on both sides is likely to accompany a good management-labor relationship. Each side has had a respect for the rights of the other. The two sides are not in love, but they are compatible.

[1] M. L. Cooke and P. Murray, *Organized Labor and Production* (Harper, New York, 1940), pp. 259–260.

[2] *Causes of Industrial Peace*, Case Studies 2 (National Planning Association, Washington, D.C., 1948).

ROLE OF GOVERNMENT AGAINST LABOR

When modern unions first began in Britain a century and a half ago, they were held to be illegal. The old common-law doctrines against monopolistic conspiracy in restraint of trade were used to put unionists in jail. Subsequently Parliament passed laws explicitly making union organization legal. In this country, too, by a century ago the courts recognized that it was not illegal conspiracy for men to organize in a union to raise their wages, provided they used legitimate *means* to achieve this legitimate end.

In 1890 the Sherman Antitrust Act was passed to make monopolistic restraints of trade illegal. It made no mention of labor unions. But in the next quarter of a century, the Sherman Act was used increasingly by the courts to curb the activities of unions. If a union struck for ends which in a judge's opinion were undesirable, he would rule against the union. And many of the traditional means used by unions were declared by judges to be illegal even if in pursuit of a legitimate end.

Criminal prosecutions against union men were not uncommon. Unions themselves, as well as their officers, were held liable for *damages: e.g.* in the important Danbury Hatters Case (1908) every member of the union, as well as the officers, was held personally responsible for the damages caused by a *boycott;* a settlement of one-quarter of a million dollars ruined the union. Moreover, often unions were harassed by expensive damage suits which they could not afford to fight even if they were pretty sure to win. In addition to restrictions on the boycott, the courts often ruled against picketing in the absence of a strike and picketing in numbers, even if there was no mass picketing of a violent nature. The judges recognized the validity of the yellow-dog contract and made free use of court *injunction* against labor.

Samuel Gompers, advocate as he was of labor's not taking an active role in politics, was forced into the political arena by what he felt was the stacking of the cards by government against the labor movement. In 1914, labor was successful in getting the Clayton Antitrust Act passed. Although hailed as "labor's Magna Carta" and designed to remove labor from prosecution under the Sherman Act, the Clayton Act did not mean the end of legislative and judicial opposition to the labor movement.

GOVERNMENT IN DEFENSE OF LABOR

But the tide was turning, and after 1930 the pendulum swung in support of unions and collective bargaining. In that year the Supreme Court upheld the constitutionality of the Railway Labor Act (1926) which accepted the basic premise of collective bargaining. In 1932 the Norris-La Guardia Act (1) explicitly ruled out federal enforcibility of the yellow-dog contract and (2) virtually wiped out injunctive interference by the courts in labor disputes, implicitly recognizing the validity of boycotting and group picketing in labor disputes.

Section 7 (a) of the *National Industrial Recovery Act*, 1933, (*NIRA*) actively encouraged collective bargaining. Finally the important National Labor Relations (Wagner) Act, 1935, was passed. It stated bluntly:

Employees shall have the right to self-organization, to form, join, or assist labor organizations, to bargain collectively through representatives of their own choosing, and to engage in concerted activities, for the purpose of collective bargaining or other mutual aid or protection [Sect. 7].

Moreover, it set up the National Labor Relations Board (NLRB) to make sure that employers do not engage in "unfair labor practices" against labor.[1] The NLRB also goes into plants and holds elections to see what organization is to be regarded as the collective bargaining representative of all the workers. It can, and does, issue "cease and desist orders" against employers, enforceable after appeal by the courts. The Wagner Act, like the later Taft-Hartley Act, applies only to industries in interstate commerce, but many states also passed "little Wagner Acts," and the Supreme Court in upholding the constitutionality of the Wagner Act, has interpreted interstate commerce broadly.

REFORM LEGISLATION

By 1940 the pendulum had swung still farther in favor of labor. The legislatures and the courts now recognized fully the right to collective bargaining, and heavy penalties were placed on the employer for his "unfair labor practices." But even this does not tell the full story. In the field of *protective* legislation, labor's tide was also running.

Back in the nineteenth century, when the first laws were passed regulating conditions of safety and health in factories, they were curiously enough passed by the Tory, or Conservative, party in England. The Whigs, or Liberals, who favored a policy of relative *laissez faire*, regarded such governmental fiats as interferences with natural rights and liberty; moreover, they argued that such interferences would do more harm than good, and under competition would gradually become unnecessary.

[1] The term "unfair labor practices" as used in the Wagner Act was a broad one referring to those activities of employers which interfere with employees' rights to self-organization. Examples of such employer practices are (1) firing men for joining a union, (2) refusing to hire men because they are sympathetic to unions, (3) threatening to close an establishment if employees join a union, (4) interfering with or dominating the administration of a union, or (5) refusing to bargain with the employees' designated representatives. In the Taft-Hartley Act, these provisions were generally retained and a set of "*union* unfair labor practices" was added.

In this country, early attempts to pass laws setting minimum wages and working conditions for women and limiting child labor were bitterly opposed. Many such laws were declared unconstitutional by the courts. But gradually protective legislation for women and minors became widespread. Just before World War I, Workmen's Compensation Acts providing benefits in case of injury were passed. But even as late as 1930 the AFL went on record in opposition to social security in general and minimum-wage laws for men.

The Franklin Roosevelt administration introduced a number of such "welfare-state" devices. The Social Security Act (1935) was passed, providing unemployment insurance or compensation, contributory old-age and other benefits, noncontributory old-age assistance, and assistance to handicapped groups. The Walsh-Healy Public Contracts Act (1936) provided that prevailing minimum standard wage rates, as prescribed by the Secretary of Labor, were to be paid on government contracts. In 1938, the federal government went all the way and passed the Fair Labor Standards Act. This set minimum wage rates for most privately employed nonagricultural workers engaged in interstate commerce (since 1949 at 75 cents per hour). Standards of 40 hours per week were set, with time and a half for hours in excess of this amount being mandatory in almost every case. Child labor in interstate commerce was finally barred. Many states, too, have minimum-wage and maximum-hours legislation.

TAFT-HARTLEY ACT

By the postwar period the pendulum had swung again. Franklin Roosevelt was dead. The New Deal had lost its steam and some of its public following. The electorate was fed up with strikes and rising prices. Labor was no longer considered the underdog. Among Congressmen there was a widespread feeling that the Wagner Act had been one-sided, that it favored labor and put all the penalties upon the employer. So in 1947 Congress passed the Labor-Management Relations (Taft-Hartley) Act.

This Act covers more than 20 pages of fine print. It has hundreds of detailed provisions which we need not try to understand. Primarily, its adherents aimed at a *two-edged* labor relations law that—unlike the Wagner Act—prescribes standards of conduct for unions as well as employers. The hand of the worker who does not want to join a union is also strengthened, as are rights of a member within the union as against the officers. Organized labor regards Taft-Hartley as a "slave labor act" and is bitterly opposed to it.

Some of the principal aims of the Taft-Hartley Act are briefly as follows:

1. *The closed shop is officially banned.* Employers do not have to hire union men. Even a union shop, where the employee must join the union within 30

days, is permitted only where a majority of all eligible workers (not all of those voting) insist upon this. State legislatures are given a free hand to impose stronger restrictions.

2. *Strikes in essential industries may be temporarily banned by injunction.* While earlier legislation had aimed mostly at injunctions secured by private parties, now the United States Attorney General can ask for an 80-day court injunction in situations that would "imperil the national health or safety." (The powers and duties of the NLRB to secure court injunctions against unfair labor practices are also expanded.)

3. *Unfair labor practices on the part of unions* are defined for the first time. Unions can be sued, among other things, for violation of a no-strike contract. Unions are now to be held responsible for acts of their agents. Their health and welfare funds are to be subject to strict supervision. Their exclusive right to handle grievances is curtailed. Their initiation fees cannot be unreasonable. They are forbidden to "featherbed" (*i.e.*, exact pay for services not performed). They must bargain collectively. Their right to an automatic checkoff of union dues is limited. Their right to discipline members for other activities than nonpayment of dues is restricted. Innumerable other restrictions on unions could also be listed. Employers, too, can be taken to court over violations of collective bargaining contracts.

4. *Unions are held strictly accountable.* They must file data giving names of officers, their pay, their manner of election, etc. Officers must swear that they are not Communists. Financial data for the union must be reported.

5. Political activity and financial contributions of unions to federal election and primary campaigns are forbidden. The free-speech rights of the employer are reaffirmed and strengthened.

6. *Secondary* boycotts and *jurisdictional* strikes are made illegal.

7. Supervisors ("foremen") are given no protection to bargain collectively; an employer bargains with them collectively only if he wishes to.

8. A 60-day strikeless period is provided, requiring that much advance notice if a collective bargaining contract is not to be renewed. The penalty on workers who strike during this period is loss of their Wagner Act rights. Arbitration is not to be compulsory, but new mediation and conciliation machinery—removed from the Department of Labor—has been provided for.

9. The NLRB is expanded in size from three to five members and given new responsibilities. It is also subject to new restrictions so that it becomes a quasi-judicial body. The General Counsel of the Board is given wide independent discretionary powers to prosecute cases.

After 4 years of operation and contrary to dire predictions of labor spokesmen, the Taft-Hartley Act has not vitally crippled the labor movement. Unions continue to bargain collectively; they continue to win NLRB elections as "exclusive bargaining agents." In certain trades, such as printing, the closed shop has legally been abolished, but all the operatives continue to be union men. The Communist affidavits have smoked out a few Communists, but a number of known Communists have blithely taken the required oath.

Management is still solidly in favor of Taft-Hartley, labor just as opposed. But the 4 years of the law's existence have *not* been particularly peaceful ones. As far as the right to strike in essential industries is concerned, President Truman has by-passed Taft-Hartley, relying primarily on "fact-finding boards" which put the collective bargainers on the spot; or in the case of the railroads, Truman has invoked World War I legal powers to take over the railroads nominally and have the laborers work for the government.

In such key industries, vital to the economic health and security of the nation, strikes are generally regarded by the public and the government as intolerable. The railways are a classic example of a field in which a work stoppage does untold harm to the community at large. Back in 1919 Governor Calvin Coolidge achieved fame when he quashed the Boston police strike with the statement, "There is no right to strike against the public safety, by anybody, anywhere, any time." To a degree, this same doctrine is applied today in many vital industries. In practice, as distinct from legal theory, the government does not permit strikes to continue in these vital areas.

POSTWAR LABOR PATTERNS

During World War II, the War Labor Board (WLB) set a general freeze on hourly wages. Payrolls rose sharply because of increased hours worked, but generally labor felt that its hourly wage rates did not keep up with the cost of living and productivity trends.

After the war ended, labor's pent-up frustrations exploded in widespread demand for a wage-rate increase; in order to keep the total weekly take-home pay from being reduced as hours of overtime work were cut out, a 30 per cent increase in wage rates was demanded. There followed a severe wave of strikes. In 1946 alone there were nation-wide strikes in coal, steel, meat-packing, and the railroad industries. Figure 4 tells the postwar work-stoppage story.

In the end, a national pattern of an 18½-cent-an-hour wage increase in a number of key industries was established and widely imitated. This was the so-called "first round" of wage increases, and it was followed by later rounds. Thus a new and somewhat disturbing postwar tendency developed: (1) wage bargains began to be made on a wider and wider scale; (2) there began to be a tendency for one great industry to imitate the pattern set by another key industry; (3) as each new round became widely imitated and began to raise costs and prices, it tended to be followed by another round.

Historically, our national productivity shows an average increase per year of something like 2 or 3 per cent. If money wages are to increase each year by an average of 10 per cent, what must be the result? There would certainly have to be an increase in costs and in the price level. Such an inflationary spiral might be self-perpetuating. Wages would chase prices and then push prices up

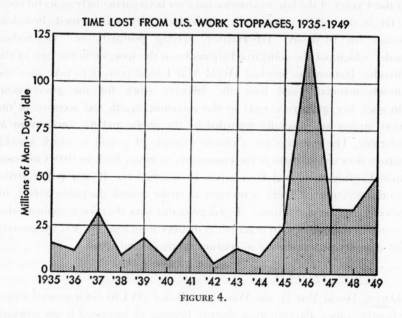

TIME LOST FROM U.S. WORK STOPPAGES, 1935-1949

FIGURE 4.

still further. It is this problem that worried people in the years 1945–1947; and, after a brief respite in 1948–1949, a renewed defense program once again in 1950–1951 raised the problem of inflation.

We shall study the general wage-price problem in later chapters. At this point a warning is in order: One must guard against exaggerating the universality of the postwar wage rounds; many industries and jobs did not share in the general increase. Also one must guard against assuming that the primary direction of causation was "Wage increases cause price rises" rather than "Price rises and inflationary money spending cause wage increases."[1]

---

[1] Many economists, by no means friendly to unions, believe the latter was true in the years after 1945. They think that the aftermath of World War II plus the cold war created a great excess of money-spending power; this pushed up prices of farm and factory products; and then wages followed. They think that without unions, prices and wages would still have risen. In my judgment there may be truth in both views of causation.

CONCLUSION

The primary aim of unions has been to improve wages and working conditions by collective bargaining. In the absence of collective bargaining, they insist that the individual worker—whose labor is regarded as perishable and whose family must live whether he works or not—is inferior in "bargaining power" to the more powerful employer—who is supposed to have greater financial "staying power" and who is suspected of using collusive monopoly power in his buying of labor.

Have unions really raised wages? Is collective bargaining consistent with the "laws of supply and demand"? What are some of the consequences on unemployment, price levels, and nonunionized labor if unions do succeed in their avowed purpose of raising wages?

All these questions cannot be answered until after we have studied the basic principles governing national income, its distribution, prices, and production. Their final discussion must therefore be reserved for Parts Two, Three, and Four of this book and most particularly Chapter 28.

SUMMARY

1. Labor unions have come to occupy an important role in the American economy, in terms of both membership and influence. Their present structure is in three layers: (a) local unions, (b) national unions, and (c) federations of unions (AFL and CIO), the first two being the most important.

2. Once a union has been recognized by an NLRB election as the exclusive bargaining agent of the workers, representatives of management and labor meet together to negotiate a contract fixing wage rates, conditions of work, productivity standards, degree of union recognition, seniority rights, grievance procedures, etc.[1]

3. By the 1880's, the typical American pattern of federated-non-political, gradualistic, business unionism had been established. Since 1933, the CIO and finally the AFL have modified the pattern in the direction of *industrial* unionization of mass-production industries rather than relying solely upon *craft unionization* of skilled workers.

4. Right up until the middle 1930's there was bitter opposition to unions. But finally the pendulum of government swung in support of collective bar-

[1] Chapter 28 deals in greater detail with the economics of wage determination under collective bargaining.

gaining, and since the Wagner Act (1935) most manufacturing industries have become unionized. The result has been less violence, but still vigorous collective bargaining between the opposing groups. By 1947 Congress felt that the Wagner Act was one-sided in favor of labor and passed the Taft-Hartley Act to define illegal collective bargaining practices on the part of unions.

5. A major postwar problem has been the relation of wage increases to the price level. If patterns are established of "successive rounds of general wage increases" that go far beyond the 2 or 3 per cent yearly increase in productivity, then the price level is almost sure to rise in an inflationary manner. A full-employment defense or peace economy brings this important economic problem to a crucial focus.

QUESTIONS FOR DISCUSSION

1. How extensive is union membership today? What were the main periods of union growth?

2. Describe the structure of America's organized labor. Describe the three layers of the union movement. Which are the largest unions in your own locality?

3. Historically American unions have followed the principles associated with Samuel Gompers. What are these? How have they been modified since 1933 and the rise of the CIO? How do you explain the fact that American labor has not been more active in politics along the lines of European socialistic movements?

4. Jot down half a dozen tactics used by labor and management when they are in bitter opposition. Give a short definition of all such terms as yellow-dog contract, scab, lockout, etc.

5. Give some contrasting examples of healthy and cooperative collective bargaining.

6. Describe the swing of the pendulum in the attitude of legislatures and courts toward organized labor before the Wagner Act and after. What has been the history of "protective reform legislation"?

7. Describe and discuss the important provisions of the Taft-Hartley Act.

8. Describe a real or imaginary plant in which collective bargaining is going on. What does this actually mean in terms of (a) a union member, (b) a nonunion member, (c) a union official, (d) business management? Describe a typical contract.

9. Describe the postwar pattern of wage and price behavior, bringing it up to the present moment.

Chapter 10: PERSONAL FINANCE

AND SOCIAL SECURITY

NOT everyone will come into first-hand contact with the workings of the gold standard or of federal reserve banking policy; but everyone will encounter, each day of his life, the problem of acquiring income, spending it upon consumption goods, and investing his savings so as to afford maximum protection against the vicissitudes of life.

BUDGETARY EXPENDITURE PATTERNS

No two families spend their money in exactly the same way, but statistics show that there is a predictable regularity—on the average—in the way people allocate their expenditures on such major items as food and clothing. Literally thousands of budgetary investigations have been made of the ways in which people at different levels of income spend their money; and there is remarkable agreement as to the general, qualitative pattern of behavior.[1]

Poor families must, of course, spend their incomes largely on the necessities of life: food, shelter, and in lesser degree, clothing. As income increases, expenditure on many food items goes up. People eat more and better. There is a shift away from the cheap, bulky carbohydrates to the more expensive meats and proteins, and to milk, fruit, and vegetables.

However, there are limits to the amount of extra money that people will spend on food when their incomes rise. Consequently, the percentage importance of food expenditure declines as income increases. (As a matter of fact, there are even a few cheap, but filling, items such as potatoes or oleomargarine whose consumption decreases absolutely with income. These are called "inferior goods.")

---

[1] These behavior patterns have sometimes been called "laws"—Engel's Laws, after the nineteenth-century Prussian statistician (not to be confused with the Engels of Marx and Engels) who first enunciated them clearly.

After one gets out of the very poorest income class, the proportion of income spent on shelter is pretty constant for a wide range. Before World War II, this was expressed in a familiar rule of thumb: One week's salary should cover one month's expenditure on rent and household utilities. To those unable to find an apartment in the postwar years, this must have seemed a quaint, outmoded rule. The other rule of thumb—that one should pay for a house no more than 2 years' income—has likewise become somewhat comical and obsolete in the 1950's.

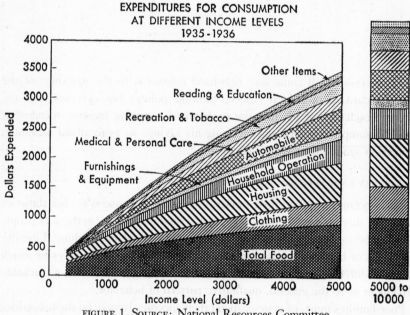

FIGURE 1. SOURCE: National Resources Committee.

Expenditure on clothing, recreation, medical care, and automobiles increases more than in proportion to income, until the very high incomes are reached. Of course, luxury items, almost by definition, increase in greater proportion than income; and in many ways, as we shall see in a moment, saving is the greatest luxury of all, particularly at very high incomes.

The above empirical generalizations are illustrated pictorially in Figures 1 and 2. Of course, prices have risen since the monumental study, *Consumers' Income in the United States, 1935–36* was made by the combined efforts of many government agencies (the National Resources Committee, the Bureau of Labor Statistics, the Bureau of Home Economics, and the WPA). However, further careful sampling surveys were made in the 1940's, and except for changes in relative prices and taxes, they represent a consistent corroborating picture.

One warning is needed. The average behavior of consumption expenditure does change fairly regularly with income. But averages do not tell all the story. Within the same income class there will be considerable spreading out around

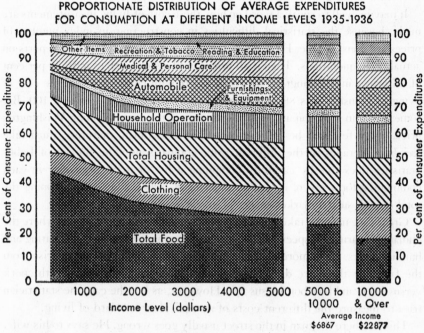

PROPORTIONATE DISTRIBUTION OF AVERAGE EXPENDITURES
FOR CONSUMPTION AT DIFFERENT INCOME LEVELS 1935-1936

FIGURE 2. SOURCE: National Resources Committee.

the average. The Joneses are heavy eaters and live in a crowded apartment; the Smiths with the same income pay much more for rent and forego driving a car.

REGIONAL DIFFERENCES IN THE COST OF LIVING

It should also be pointed out that prices and living conditions vary throughout the United States. House rents are cheaper in the country than in the city, and they used to be cheaper on the West Coast than in the East. The postwar period has lessened the regional differentials in the cost of living, primarily by raising prices in the previously cheaper places more than in the large Northern cities.

However, even before the war people were prone to exaggerate the differences in the cost of living between North and South and between different cities. According to careful studies by the Labor Department, the differences between the cost of living in large cities during the spring of 1945 were relatively minor. Expensive cities like Seattle or New York were only about 8 per cent above the average, and the least expensive cities like Kansas City or

Houston were about the same percentage below the average. While many Southern cities tended to have a low cost of living, some Northern cities had just as low or lower prices. On the other hand, Washington, which is fairly far south, was right up among the most expensive places.

It may be well to speak a word on how these cost-of-living measurements are made, because the statistical difficulties in constructing an index number of prices are considerable. First, a careful study must furnish accurate reports on actual price quotations. Then if all prices in Houston were exactly 88 per cent of all prices in Washington, we could assert with confidence that the cost of living in Houston was 88, as compared to Washington as a base of 100. But some prices in Houston are only 65 per cent of the corresponding Washington price, and a few will be 150 per cent. The statistician, therefore, must take *weighted* averages of the different price comparisons. The Bureau of Labor Statistics does this by carefully compiling a list of items necessary in each community for a given, *equivalent standard of living*, and then reckoning the total cost of such a market basket of goods.

Great care must be taken in doing this. For example, in the South, where the climate is warmer, a special allowance must be made in estimating heating and building costs. Even more difficult, and almost insoluble, problems arise from the fact that there are differences in taste between South and North: pork versus beef, and bourbon versus rye. However, as best he can, the statistician tries to measure the different costs of an equivalent standard of living.

This is where the man in the street usually goes wrong. He says to his wife, "I think I'll take that job teaching physics at Dixie Polytech. Of course, it only pays what we're now getting, but $3,500 there is like $5,500 here." It is true that people live on less in the South, but that is primarily because many of them live less well.

However, to the extent that we are worried about the problem of "keeping up with the Joneses," it is quite possible that a family in the South with $3,500 a year will feel happier than a comparable family in the North; because in the South there will be relatively fewer families with income in excess of that figure. This probably helps to explain why farmers, small-town people, and Negroes are more thrifty at any given level of income than white city dwellers. A Negro with $6,000 a year income in Columbus, Ohio, will be as near the top of the income pyramid of his group as is a white person on Park Avenue in New York City with a $40,000 income, and both may save about the same percentage of their income.

FAMILY DIFFERENCES IN THE COST OF LIVING

The same statistical budgetary data throw some light on the age-old question: "Can two live as cheaply as one?" According to the Bureau of Labor

Statistics, the answer is "no." Even if one works in the home, it costs a married couple about $10\frac{0}{7}0$ times what it costs a single person to live, on the average. This is still less, however, than it costs two to live singly.

Each child in the family inevitably adds to the cost of living. Thus, if it costs 70 to live alone and 100 to live with a wife, it will cost about 130 with one child, 160 with two, and so forth, for each additional child. (Of course, as the number of children increase, some "economies of scale and spreading the overhead" set in.) Studies of poor families with many children turn up a surprising fact: large families spend a smaller fraction of their income on housing than do small families. This is because they must spend so much for food just to keep alive.

Canada,[1] England, France, Sweden, and other governments have begun to give "family allowances" every month, the amount varying with the number of children in the family. This is done both for humanitarian reasons and to try to stimulate population growth. It is easy to see why the government, rather than private industry, must make these payments; for if corporations had to pay higher wages to men with large families, they might begin to alter their hiring policy in favor of ancient bachelors and against the heads of large families.

THE BACKWARD ART OF SPENDING MONEY

In spending their money, people act with regularity but not always with rationality. For example, people with incomes of around $3,000 per year are known to spend less upon medical care than modern science and prudence would seem to suggest is necessary. Furthermore, what people consider to be absolute necessities consist to a large degree not of physiological necessities, but of conventional social desirabilities. Almost for a joke a Middle Western economist once estimated how much it would cost to buy most cheaply a yearly diet with all the health ingredients (vitamins A, B, C, D, etc., iron, calcium, etc., etc.) recommended by the National Research Council. The cost per year (!) was $39 in 1939 and $57 in 1944. But of course the diet consisted of nothing so expensive as bread or potatoes, but rather of wheat flour, cabbage, lima beans, kidneys, and not much else. Most people would rather starve than eat such an unpalatable and monotonous diet, just as dogs who have been conditioned to eat fish alone will almost starve before they will touch delicious beefsteaks.

A corporation buying a great quantity of a commodity tests it carefully for quality and makes sure that it is bought from the cheapest source. Not so

[1] The Canadian government pays family allowances of $5 to $8 per month for each child, depending upon its age. After the fourth child, there is a slight reduction in these family-allowance payments.

the average consumer, who is an amateur when it comes to spending money. He pays 25 cents for 6 aspirin tablets when he could buy 100 equally good aspirin (monoaceticacidester of salicylic acid) tablets for 19 cents. Scarcely less money is spent on advertising the cigarettes he buys than is spent upon their tobacco content. The cost of the ingredients in a $2 lipstick is exactly the same as that in a 25-cent one, and time and time again disinterested laboratory testers have been unable to detect any differences between them at all. A can of Campbell's soup sells for 15 cents in a chain grocery store and next door at a little "independent" for 18 cents. A large glass of Coca-Cola contains less than twice the amount of a small one. Until forbidden to by law, coffee companies would sell their "first-grade" coffees under a different label at lower prices; and a well-known brand-name tire used to be sold at a considerable reduction in price by a big mail-order and department store under its own brand name.

The consumer's health as well as his pocketbook is at stake.[1] When Upton Sinclair published the novel, *The Jungle*, showing what conditions were like in the Chicago stockyards early in this century, many people stopped eating meat. Against the heavy opposition of business interests, Congress passed pure food and drug acts, but an American is still free to poison himself with hair dyes and to go to an early grave as a result of taking patent medicines and being his own doctor. The Federal Trade Commission prosecutes corporations indulging in extreme forms of misrepresentation in advertising, with the result that greater reliance is placed upon innuendo than upon direct statement. (For example, the label on a famous women's compound now says, "This preparation is recommended for those ailments to which it is adapted.")

A characteristic feature of our era is advertising. With our daily news and our Sunday pleasure rides, we are fed large doses of carefully selected descriptions of various products. A sizable amount of the nation's creative talent and a fraction of its paper and vacuum tubes are devoted to sales promotion. This has many economic advantages. Useful information can be brought to the public, mass-production markets are created, and as a by-product of advertising expense we have a free press, a choice of many radio and television programs, and thick magazines. On the other hand, much advertising is self-canceling and adds little to the consumer's valid information. And for each minute of symphony music, there is half an hour of "soap opera." The situation would be the more regrettable were it not for the apparent fact, surprising though it may seem, that many people seem to like advertising. They don't believe all they hear, but they can't help remembering it just the same.

[1] The interested reader may be referred to the somewhat partisan views expressed in Stuart Chase and F. J. Schlink, *Your Money's Worth* (Macmillan, New York, 1931); and A. Kallet and F. J. Schlink, *One Hundred Million Guinea Pigs* (Vanguard, New York, 1932).

INCOME PATTERNS OF SAVING AND CONSUMPTION

It is a matter of common observation that rich men save more than poor men, not only in absolute amounts but also in percentage amounts. The very poor are unable to save at all, but instead are dissaving each year; *i.e.*, they are spending more every year than they earn, the difference being covered by going into debt or using up previously accumulated savings. In 1944, the typical urban family with two children had to have $2,050 per year on the average in order to be able just to break even; in 1950 the same family had to have more than $3,100 to break even. Each dollar of income less than this amount sent the family into dissaving and debt, and each dollar of income above this amount went partially into saving.

Table 1 gives data on savings taken from a study of urban families in 1944, made by the Department of Labor. Column (2) shows the average amount of family saving (+) or dissaving (−) at each level of disposable income shown in Column (1). Consumption is just the other side of the saving picture and is shown in Column (3). The 1944 "break-even" point is at B, the entire $2,000 income being spent on consumption, with saving zero. At A, the $1,000 income,

TABLE 1. *Propensity of Urban Families to Save and Consume, 1944*

	Disposable income, after taxes (1)	Net saving (+) or dissaving (−) (2)	Consumption (3)
A	$1,000	− $180	$1,180
B	2,000	0	2,000
C	3,000	+ 300	2,700
D	4,000	+ 600	3,400
E	5,000	+1,000	4,000
F	6,000	+1,500	4,500
G	7,000	+2,000	5,000

SOURCE: Department of Labor Survey, with data for all families smoothed and rounded off.

the family spends $1,180 on consumption, the difference being financed out of dissaving or borrowing. Each extra $1,000 of family income is seen to be divided between extra consumption and extra saving. As we go from $1,000 to $2,000 of income, net (algebraic) saving increases by $180 and consumption increases by the rest of the $1,000 or by $820. (This $820 figure can also be derived and checked by taking the difference between the $1,180 spent by the poorest families on consumption and the $2,000 shown by Column (3) to be spent by the next poorest families on consumption.)

What happens to each new dollar of income as we go from $2,000 to $3,000 family income? A comparison of rows *B* and *C* in the table shows us that $700, or 70 cents of every new dollar, goes for extra consumption, and $300 or 30 cents of every new dollar goes for saving. We should be inclined to expect this from our knowledge of human behavior: as people get still richer, a larger fraction of every extra dollar begins to go for saving rather than consumption. The reader should verify that, in 1944, families appeared to put 50 per cent of all income over $5,000 into saving and only 50 per cent into consumption. Such a high degree of thriftiness cannot be normal and was due to the peculiar wartime conditions when goods were not available and when people were being urged to save.

Later when we come to the discussion in Part Two of how saving and investment determine the level of national income and employment, we shall see how crucially important are (1) the propensity-to-save schedule relating saving and income and its twin brother (2) the propensity-to-consume schedule relating consumption and income.

THE WARTIME ACCUMULATION OF SAVING

Let us investigate how people go about spending more than their income. They may of course spend out of previously hoarded cash. Or they may draw upon their balance at the bank, either from their checking or savings accounts. Or they may cash in a government saving bond. Or, if they are among the relatively few people with marketable bonds and stocks, they may request their broker to sell enough of their securities to finance a trip to California, a new automobile, or whatever ends of the family budget fail to meet.

As a result of the war, the American people have accumulated more savings than ever before in our history. During the half decade of war most families had abnormally high money incomes but were able to spend only at a normal rate on nondurable consumer goods, and at a very depressed rate on durable goods such as autos and radios. The difference between income and expenditure piled up in the form of war bonds, savings accounts, insurance policies, the paying off of previous debts, and finally in the holding of paper money and checking deposits. American individuals and businesses came out of the war with about 250 billion dollars ($\frac{1}{4}$ trillion!) of liquid savings—about 100 billion dollars, or 40 cents of every savings dollar, in government bonds; another 75 billion dollars, or 30 cents of every dollar, in the form of checking accounts; 25 billion dollars, or 10 cents of each dollar, in the form of paper currency; and finally about 50 billion dollars, or 20 cents of every dollar, in the form of savings accounts.

This total of liquid wealth represents a threefold increase as compared to the prewar, so that Americans on the average now have a nest egg equal to more than a year's income. This sum came into existence because of only one factor —the great wartime increase in the federal government's public debt. These assets in the hands of the public are just the other side of the social balance sheet which shows the government's liability. If the public debt is a completely bad thing, then these family savings are essentially a bad thing; if these family savings are a good thing, then the public debt cannot be as completely black as it is often painted.

In reality there is no such thing as the *average* family. The total of liquid assets is far from being divided equally among all families. A large family with many people working long hours in the shipyards might have been able to accumulate much saving during the war. So, too, might a speculator and a war profiteer; or a lieutenant commander in the Navy, who before the war made $2,200 a year and whose wife took a job and went to live with her family. On the other hand, a war worker with a large family who had to move to a new town and overpay on his automobile and house rent may have gone into debt during the war. Still other men and women may have squandered all they earned during the war—if not on silk shirts, then on night clubs and black-market nylons.

Fortunately, it is not necessary to rely on guesses concerning the distribution of war savings. At the request of the Federal Reserve Board, the Consumers' Survey Center at the University of Michigan makes careful statistical surveys of the distribution of savings. According to the *Federal Reserve Bulletin*, their surveys showed that in the late 1940's, a quarter of all families (or spending units) had no liquid savings at all: they had no savings accounts, no checking accounts, no government bonds. Half the families had less than $400 of savings. On the other hand, the 10 per cent of families with the highest savings averaged more than $10,000 of liquid assets apiece and had 60 per cent of the total liquid assets. Moreover, the statistics turned up one surprising result: Within any one income class, it appears that a small proportion of people tend to do most of the accumulating.

However, it still remains true as a broad generalization that the American people are better able to afford to make down payments on new houses and to buy new cars than ever before in history. Besides, as a result of the war, many people who succeeded in saving nothing at least got out of installment debt for the first time and could begin all over again.

HOW PEOPLE BORROW MONEY

Let us briefly explore the channels open to people who must borrow. Up until the last 15 years or so, poor people as a rule fell into the hands of unlicensed loan sharks, and they still do in some states which have not passed a uniform small-loan act. These loan sharks charge interest at anywhere from a low of 120 per cent per year to about 1,200 per cent per year! Not 12 per cent, 12 *hundred* per cent! It is not uncommon to hear of cases where a man borrowed $20 in 1929 because of illness, and then paid $2.25 every week until 1938, or $1,053 in all and at a rate of 600 per cent interest per year. The curse of the poor is their poverty. They go into debt because of a lack of money, and they cannot get out for the same reason. Moreover, the last thing that a loan shark wants is to have his loan paid back. He will occasionally use violence, but more often he blackmails his victim by threatening to tell his boss or wife. The borrower never realizes that legally he need only refuse to pay, and the loan shark will never dare bring the matter to court.

There is only one way to remedy this despicable situation. Paradoxically, it is by passing a small-loan act which *raises* the legal interest rate that can be charged to far above the 6 per cent maximum set by the old-time usury laws. For honest personal-finance companies cannot stay in business unless they can charge much higher rates than this on small loans. Such loans involve an element of risk and much costly red tape and supervision. A few states, primarily in the South and in the Rocky Mountain region, still have not adopted such sensible uniform small-loan legislation—primarily because of a campaign by the loan sharks of legislative bribing, blackmail, and demagogic appeal to protect the public against paying more than 6 per cent interest. The Russell Sage Foundation and other disinterested groups have made a study of this problem and their reports of the true facts are as incredible as any melodramatic novel.[1]

In the better regulated states, a person can borrow from a licensed personal finance company such a small sum as $250 and hope to pay it off in 12 installments at a cost of about 36 per cent interest per year, with no other fees. He can borrow from a Morris Plan or Industrial Bank for about 15 per cent per annum or less. If the company he works for has a credit union, he can probably borrow there at about 12 per cent per annum. If he is willing to put up some article of jewelry, he can borrow about three-fourths of its auction sale value at a better pawn shop, paying about 36 per cent per year interest.

If his local bank will make him a small personal loan, repayable in installments, he will probably pay around 10 per cent per year for it, unless he is known to be a very good risk. If he buys his automobile or furniture on installment credit from a reliable concern, he will probably pay something like 12

---

[1] The interested reader may be referred to Nos. 5 and 39 of the 25-cent Public Affairs Pamphlet Series, Public Affairs Committee, Inc., for an authoritative account of the loan-shark and consumer-credit problems. Almost all the subjects mentioned in this chapter are discussed interestingly and authoritatively in this series of pamphlets.

per cent interest per year. If he borrows by putting a mortgage on his house, he will pay 4, 5, or 6 per cent per year. If he has a life-insurance policy with a paid-up value, he can borrow on it from the insurance company at 5 or 6 per cent per year or from many banks at 4 per cent or less. If he has listed securities or government bonds, he can make a collateral loan on them at 4 per cent or less.

These charges vary from region to region and from institution to institution, being generally lowest in Northeastern large cities and being lowest for large short-term loans. Thus, a man in New York City can obtain a large-scale loan on his *marketable* government bonds at 1¾ per cent per year (per year not per month!) or less.

All the above interest rates are expressed in terms of the average *unpaid* balance. When a man is really paying 12 per cent per year on an installment loan, he probably thinks that he is only paying 6 per cent, or half as much. Let us see why. Suppose he is to pay $105 per month for 10 installments to pay off a $1,000 loan, the extra $5 being the monthly interest charge. Is he then paying an interest charge of $5 per month on a principal of $1,000—only ½ of 1 per cent per month? The answer is "no." He is really paying about 1 per cent per month or 12 per cent per year on his true *average unpaid balance*. The average amount of his indebtedness during the period is not $1,000 but only one-half that much, $500, because he is paying off the debt through the year. Interest of $5 per month on $500 is about 1 per cent per month or 12 per cent per year.

Few people realize this and are often swindled by unethical dealers. Moreover, some people will buy on installment credit, paying high rates of interest, at the same time that they have money in the bank earning only 1 per cent per year or war bonds earning only 3 or 4 per cent per year. They do this either out of ignorance or because they wish to make themselves save out of current income by having to make installment payments. Good advice for most people who must borrow or buy on installments is first to try a local bank or the credit union in the place they work.

The rise of consumer credit following World War II was tremendous. By September of 1950, it had grown to around 20 billion dollars (largely made up of installment credit and charge accounts), and wartime Regulation W was reenacted to help curb the volume of consumption expenditure. According to this regulation, a buyer had to make a down payment of one-third of the price of an automobile and pay the rest in not more than 15 months. Similar minimum down payments and amortization periods were prescribed for other items, such as house furnishings, and limits were also placed on unpaid charge accounts. Also, in an attempt to relieve the inflationary pressures created by the defense program, various limitations on Federal Housing Authority mortgage loans were instituted.

GOVERNMENT BONDS AS A FORM OF SAVING

Let us turn now to the more cheerful question of what people should do with their savings. A few idiots, timid souls, or criminals will hold their money in the form of small bills kept in their stockings or rolled up in the window curtains. More normal people will put some into the savings bank or postal savings (at the local post office) so as to earn 1 or 2 per cent per year. Still others will put a large part of their savings into United States savings bonds, Series E. These earn about 3 per cent interest per year and can be bought directly out of one's pay check under the payroll saving plan, or at any bank.

They are issued in multiples of $25 and are registered in the name of one or two co-owners, or one owner and a beneficiary. As they are nontransferable, they can be neither sold nor borrowed upon. Each $25 face-value bond costs $18.75, and its face value is paid in full at the end of 10 years. It is redeemable at any bank upon proper identification within 60 days after issue in accordance with the abridged scale of redemption values given in Table 2. These values are arranged so that the longer one holds the bonds the higher their yield; therefore, if a person has to cash in part of his bonds prior to maturity, he should always cash in his *newest* ones first.

TABLE 2. *Abridged Table of Redemption Values of Series E Bonds*

Issue price................... $18.75		Maturity value............... $25.00	
(Yield to maturity = 2.9 per cent per annum)*			
Value after 1 year............ $18.87		Value after 6 years.......... $21.00	
Value after 2 years............ 19.12		Value after 7 years.......... 22.00	
Value after 3 years............ 19.50		Value after 8 years.......... 23.00	
Value after 4 years............ 20.00		Value after 9 years.......... 24.00	
Value after 5 years............ 20.25		Value after 10 years.......... 25.00	

* $25 is to $18.75 as 4 is to 3. Any compound-interest table will tell us that 3 multiplied by $(1.03)^{10}$ is about 4, showing that the savings bonds yield just under 3 per cent interest.

A 3 per cent yield for a perfectly safe, instantly redeemable bond is a very great bargain. In fact, insurance companies and banks would gladly trade their $1\frac{1}{2}$, 2, and $2\frac{1}{2}$ per cent marketable bonds for Series E bonds were it not for the fact that the government rigidly limits the amount that any one person or institution can buy per year.[1] No patriotism is necessary to make a

[1] Series F is a 12-year bond similar to Series E but yielding only about $2\frac{1}{2}$ per cent; Series G is a nontransferable coupon bond yielding about the same percentage in yearly installments or coupons. In addition, there are marketable government bonds which mature after periods of time of 90 days, 1 year, or 20 years and more, and which bear interest yields of from 1 to $2\frac{1}{2}$ per cent.

wise person buy United States saving bonds from the government. If a government bond is not thought to be perfectly safe, then neither is paper money nor a bank account.

INVESTING IN SECURITIES

People with a great deal of savings will not put all their eggs in one basket, but aim at a diversified portfolio of securities such as the following $100,000 holdings of a New England widow:

Security Holdings

Government Bonds, Series E.................	$10,000
Government Bonds, Series G.................	10,000
Government Bonds, 2½% marketable..........	5,000
New York Central 4½% (due in 2013)........	5,000
Total bonds.............................	$30,000
U.S. Gypsum 7% preferred..................	$10,000
Marshall Field 4¼% preferred..............	10,000
Total preferred stock.....................	$20,000
American Tel. & Tel. common...............	$20,000
Firestone Tire common.....................	10,000
General Motors common....................	10,000
R. H. Macy & Co., common.................	5,000
Twentieth Century Fox common.............	5,000
Total common stock......................	$50,000

On such a portfolio of securities, she would in 1950 have received about $5,000 per year in total dividends and interest. If the widow is smart, she will seek reliable investment guidance. Private investors, universities, insurance companies, and even trust funds are turning more and more these days to common stocks. Their yield is higher, and they provide a better hedge against inflation. But they are not for amateurs. Increasingly, small investors are buying shares of investment trusts or mutual funds; these are not to be confused with investment banks—they are merely companies that invest people's savings in a diversified batch of common stocks.[1]

ECONOMICS OF HOME OWNERSHIP

The postwar period has witnessed a great building boom. During the depression and war years a backlog of needed housing built up. During and after the war, an unusually large number of marriages took place. With income and

[1] Benjamin Graham's *The Intelligent Investor* (Harper, New York, 1949) is a useful book to read on these subjects.

employment high, and in view of the difficulty in finding a rent-controlled house, many families wished to invest in home ownership. Except for shortages produced by defense needs, we could look forward to more than a million new dwellings being built annually. With labor and material costs high and in view of the limited technological advance in this backward industry, new and old homes tend to be priced since the war at almost double their prewar price.

Owning one's own home is not necessarily always a good investment, although it is usually an interesting hobby. Moreover, multiple dwellings of two, four, or more units often work out cheaper on a cost basis than the more popular single dwelling. Aside from the upkeep of a house, the most important costs are not the physical wearing out of the house but rather the deterioration and obsolescence of the neighborhood. From the personal viewpoint, there is also the problem that the family may suddenly have to move and sell at a loss, or that family size and needs may change with time. These risks would not be so great were it not for the risk of a depression in real-estate values as a result of business slump, overspeculation, or overexpansion of building. In decades of rising prices, the risks are less.

TABLE 3. *Monthly Cost to Own a $10,000 House*

1. Initial cash payments:

10% down payment (90% mortgage)	$1,000
Closing fees, commissions, etc.........................	200
Total cash payments	$1,200

2. Monthly cost (over 25 years) for

Interest (5%)	$ 23
Amortization (or paying back principal over 25 years)	30
Taxes (2½%)	21
Hazard insurance (0.2 of 1%)	2
Maintenance ($200 per annum)	17
Loss of interest on cash payments (3%)	3
Total monthly cost	$ 96

SOURCE: National Housing Agency, *Bulletin 2.*

A man making less than $4,000 a year cannot afford more than a $10,000 house (including cost of land).[1] Table 3 shows how much it will cost per month to carry the $10,000 house; of course a $5,000 or $15,000 house will be proportionately lower or higher.

[1] About 7 per cent of this $10,000 will usually go for unimproved land, and another 6 per cent for pipes and other improvements on the land. About 45 per cent will go for building materials (including delivery), and the remaining 42 per cent will go for labor and contractor's profits.

BUYING LIFE INSURANCE

Aside from government bonds, bank accounts, and homes, the only savings of most people are in the form of life insurance. This comes in three main forms: *group insurance* (provided, as the name implies, for a whole group of employees of institutions), so-called *industrial life insurance*, and finally so-called *ordinary life insurance*.

The first kind is gaining in popularity and usually represents an advantageous form of insurance, especially when the employer pays for part of it.

Just as the Holy Roman Empire was neither holy, nor Roman, nor an empire, so industrial insurance is not industrial and it is hardly insurance. It has nothing to do with industry but is used to refer to the few-hundred-dollar policies sold primarily to the very poor, usually for burial money. Generally, no health examination is required, and the agent calls at the house every week to collect the nickel or dime of insurance premium. Naturally a large part of this premium must go to the agent and to defray bookkeeping costs; so industrial insurance is not a very efficient form of insurance, especially when the great number of policy lapses by the poor are taken into consideration. The Temporary National Economic Committee of Congress severely criticized industrial insurance; the best that can be said about it is that—except for social security—it is the only insurance that poor people ever do take out.

The only insurance, then, that we need to consider is ordinary life insurance. This comes in a variety of different forms, the principal ones being (1) term insurance, (2) straight life and (3) endowment plan.

Term Insurance. Term insurance, which is not very popular in practice, is the easiest to understand. Let us say that 100,000 men of age 35 each sign up for $1,000 of insurance for a term of 1 year. Mortality statistics show that a definite percentage of them will die within the year, say 1 per cent, or 1,000 men. The company will have to pay out to widows and beneficiaries, therefore, 1,000 × $1,000 or 1 million dollars. It must charge each thirty-five-year-old man, therefore, slightly more than $10 as his insurance premium. The next year it begins all over again, but of course as the men get older the cost of the insurance will gradually rise. Under term insurance, each year stands on its own legs, so to speak, and there is no need for the company to accumulate large saving reserves. In fact, anyone who buys term insurance is doing no saving for the future at all. On the other hand, while he is young and with a growing family, he is getting the maximum possible insurance protection in case of death.[1]

[1] Servicemen in World War II were sold 8-year term life insurance at favorable rates. This can be and, because of the favorable rates and disability provisions, should eventually be converted into either ordinary, 20-payment, 30-payment, or endowment life insurance.

Straight Life Insurance.   Under straight life insurance, all the men who join at the age of 35 agree to pay a *constant* yearly premium until they die; this premium is naturally higher for people who join at 35 than for those joining at 34 or 30. This constant premium is set so that at first they are overpaying, on the average, for their insurance; *i.e.*, the company will begin by paying out to the whole group of thirty-five-year-olds less than it collects, the difference being invested at interest in a so-called "insurance reserve" which consists of stocks, bonds, and mortgages. Late in life, the steady constant premium is less than

RENEWABLE TERM LIFE INSURANCE

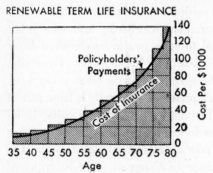

STRAIGHT LIFE

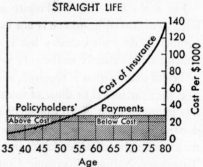

FIGURE 3*a*. Insurance premiums always just cover each period's actuarial costs, with no savings reserves piling up. SOURCE: *Public Affairs Pamphlet*, No. 62.

FIGURE 3*b*. Constant premiums at first exceed current actuarial costs, the difference being invested at compound interest in an actuarial reserve. Later, when the reverse is true, this reserve is used up. SOURCE: *Public Affairs Pamphlet*, No. 62.

the true insurance cost for the group, the difference coming out of the previously accumulated reserve. By the time everyone in the group is 100 and dead, all the reserve will have been used up.

Figure 3 illustrates the difference between renewable-term and straight life insurance for a man who joins at 35 and lives to be 80.

Endowment Plan.   Finally, an endowment plan policy provides a still larger element of saving than of insurance coverage. Under a 20-year endowment policy, the thirty-five-year-old man agrees to pay in a high constant premium for 20 years, after which time, at the age of 55, he will receive the whole face value of the policy even though he has not died. Thus endowment insurance is a combination of saving and insurance. Provided that it is not allowed to lapse prior to the end of the 20-year period, endowment insurance is a good thing for anyone who wants to make himself save regularly. However, under it, he will not receive any higher rate of return than he could get for himself by doing what the insurance company primarily does anyway, *i.e.*, by investing his savings regularly in government bonds.

For more details the student may be referred to the readable pamphlet "How to Buy Life Insurance"[1] or to his local agent. He will find that in practice each company's policy differs slightly in some provision from that of other companies, so that he will hardly know how to decide which is the best buy. The problem is complicated further by the fact that most "mutual" companies deliberately err on the side of overconservatism and overcharge their policyholders; then at the end of the year they pay back part of the overcharge in so-called "dividends." Still, according to the experts, policies of the various companies differ considerably in their true net cost, so that a little study of the problem and shopping around are worth while. Furthermore, in states like Massachusetts or New York, there are definite cost advantages to buying Savings Bank Life Insurance at an accredited bank. However, because life insurance is mostly "sold to people and not bought," the majority of the people will continue to pay slightly more buying from commercial companies.

SOCIAL SECURITY AND HEALTH

In 1937, the Social Security Act went into effect to help protect the American people against economic want resulting from old age or unemployment. Despite dire warnings at the time, the system has worked very well, and now both the Republican and the Democratic parties are pledged to its support.

The system works simply and consists of three parts: (1) contributory old-age retirement and survivors' benefits insurance, (2) unemployment compensation insurance, and (3) old-age assistance and public welfare. Under the first two plans, people, as a matter of right, automatically receive benefit payments when retired through old age or when unemployed. They do not have to go through a "needs test" to reveal whether they have any money of their own.

Social security taxes are levied against payrolls as described in Chapter 8, so that each person may be thought of as partially paying for his own benefits. However, social insurance or social security differs from private insurance in that a person may receive in benefits more than he is actuarially or mathematically entitled to on the basis of his payments, the difference being made up out of government taxes. A generation from now, when a larger fraction of the population will be above the retirement age, the contribution of the government will have to be considerably increased. Moreover, the system is now placed on a pay-as-you-go basis, so that no actuarial reserves need pile up.

Under the unemployment compensation plans, set up by the states at the instigation of the federal government, payments are made into an unemployment reserve fund every week that a worker is employed. If he should be laid

[1] *Public Affairs Pamphlet*, 62.

off, then by meeting certain requirements—such as being willing to accept any suitable job offered him by the Public Employment Exchange Office and having worked a minimum number of weeks in the period preceding his unemployment—he automatically receives a weekly unemployment compensation check whose magnitude depends upon his previous earnings and contributions. There is no humiliating "needs" test, nor are benefit payments set so high as to encourage people to remain idle. During prosperity, the unemployment reserve fund grows; during depression, when it is most needed, it is used to help support people and maintain general purchasing power.

The old-age assistance and public welfare part of the Social Security Act consists of grants-in-aid by the federal government to be used by the states to support the needy aged, blind, widowed and orphaned, physically and mentally handicapped, who themselves could not possibly contribute to their own support. The poorer states receive larger relative grants than do the richer.

GROWTH OF SOCIAL SECURITY: THE 1950 ACT

Not only is the social security system here to stay, but it is growing and being extended. Huge punch-card machines in Baltimore have made the administrative aspects of the program insignificant. Society today believes increasingly in the philosophy that the worst personal and social misfortunes result from contingencies over which the single individual has little control. In 1932 people walked the street without work; in 1929 and 1951 the same people had prosperous jobs; the answer is not wholly in them. Already annuities for widows and dependent children have been added to the social security benefits.

In 1950 Congress greatly extended the scope of Social Security. About 10 million new people began to be covered, and benefit payments were considerably increased. Farm labor, domestic help, and the self-employed were for the first time brought into the system, and employees of nonprofit organizations became eligible to join voluntarily.

The rate of tax payments continues to be $1\frac{1}{2}$ per cent paid by employer and $1\frac{1}{2}$ per cent by employee, but now this is applied on the first $3,600 of annual wages; the former figure was $3,000. Tax rates on employer and employee are each to rise by $\frac{1}{2}$ per cent in 1954, 1960, and 1965, and by $\frac{1}{4}$ per cent in 1970; so after 1970 each will pay $3\frac{1}{4}$ per cent. (The self-employed began in 1950 paying at a rate of $2\frac{1}{4}$ per cent.) This pattern of rates aims to put the program on a pay-as-you-go rather than actuarial-reserve basis.

Benefit payments were raised so that their new range is $15 to $150 per month rather than $10 to $85. As before, retirement payments are made to qualified individuals over sixty-five, to their wives or widows if over sixty-five, and to the widow of any insured person if over sixty-five or with children under eighteen. In addition, a lump-sum payment is paid when a worker dies, and there are a few miscellaneous benefit possibilities to parents and widowers. The exact formula for figuring benefits is quite complicated, but its general nature is as follows: A worker's own benefit depends primarily upon his average monthly wage and is more generously reckoned on the first $100 of monthly wages; for each extra year that he has been covered there is a slight further increase in his primary benefits. After his benefit has been reckoned, his wife will receive, after age sixty-five, an extra 50 per cent of his benefits; his widow will receive, after sixty-five, an extra 75 per cent; his surviving dependent children will receive a certain fraction too. All told, no family can receive more than $150 or 80 per cent of the worker's average monthly wage.

No one need know the details of the Act. Upon applying, he can learn from the nearest government office what he is entitled to. Suffice it to say that a private insurance company would have to charge tens of thousands of dollars for such generous annuities and privileges.

It is one of the great advantages of a pay-as-you-go social security system that it rests on the general tax capacity of the nation; if hyperinflation wiped out all private insurance and savings, social security could nonetheless start all over again, none the poorer. It is possible that in the next generation payments for sickness and disability and a comprehensive public health and hospital program will have been introduced. But this is still very controversial. In 1931, many medical associations strongly disapproved and fought against the systems of private health and hospitalization insurance such as Blue Cross or Blue Shield. Today they are among the strongest supporters of these systems.

Other countries, such as Britain and Scandinavia, have gone much further in the direction of a so-called welfare state than has the United States. Thus, in Britain a program of "cradle to grave" social security provides aid to a child's family at his birth and family allowances while he is a minor, gives him virtually feeless medical and dental care all his life, and helps provide him with income when unemployed, ill, or retired. After he is dead, the State helps to defray his funeral expenses and support his survivors. Such programs have a great appeal to the electorate and were introduced even before the Labor government came into power. These programs are, of course, not costless, and the electorate must democratically decide how far it is worth while to push them in terms of their true costs.

SUMMARY

1. The patterns of family expenditure on different consumption items, such as food, clothing, shelter, and saving, are fairly regular and predictable after we make allowances for family size and regional differences in the cost of living.

2. The important propensity-to-consume and propensity-to-save schedules show how people spend on consumption more than their incomes at low incomes, the difference representing algebraically negative saving or dissaving. As income increases beyond the break-even point, some fraction of each new dollar of disposable income (after taxes) goes into consumption and the rest goes into saving.

3. There are various ways in which a family can borrow, each involving widely differing rates of interest. Similarly, the ways in which a family can invest its savings include bank accounts, government bonds, owning one's own home, marketable stocks and bonds, and the purchase of one of the different forms of life insurance.

4. There are important differences between private and social insurance. Our social security program now provides the majority of our citizens, for the first time, a measure of protection against old age, unemployment, and physical handicaps. The program is still an expanding one.

QUESTIONS FOR DISCUSSION

1. Make up a budget for yourself or your family. What if your income were cut by 30 per cent or increased by that amount?

2. About what fraction of each extra dollar is consumed at the different income levels? Fill in a new column in Table 1.

3. Make certain assumptions about your own earnings and expenditure over the next 30 years. Draw up an investment program for yourself.

4. Which investments would you buy if you thought that inflation was ahead? Which if you thought that the outlook was for deflation?

5. Recently, life-insurance companies began to draw up their policies assuming only a 2½ per cent interest yield on their investments instead of 3 and 3½ per cent as previously. What effect would this have on life-insurance premiums? Of the three kinds of ordinary life insurance described in the text, which would have the greatest and least increases in premium rates?

6. "I want to buy an annuity which will do more than pay me a given dollar income until I die. To hedge against inflation, I want one which will pay me a given *real* income every year. More than that, I know that technological progress will give everyone increased real incomes in the years ahead, so that two decades from now everyone with my present real income will be surpassed by most of the population. What I really want is an annuity which guarantees that I will always remain at the same relative position in the income pyramid." Why can no private insurance company sell such an annuity policy? Could the government's social security program cover this man's need? Why would inflation, which might wipe out private insurance, leave social security protection undiminished?

7. The statement, "Only the very rich and the very poor receive adequate medical care," is only half true. Which half? Does the fact that there are three times as many doctors per capita in California as in South Carolina and five times as many dentists per capita in Oregon as in Mississippi prove that there are too many doctors and dentists on the West Coast?

8. Britain under state health spends about 4 per cent of her income on medical services. We spend over 5 per cent. The technical level of health care is generally believed better here than there. Can you conclude from these facts that we should or should not expand social security in this direction?

Chapter 11: NATIONAL INCOME

THE whole of our discussion of Part One leads up to and can be summarized by the important concepts of national income or net national product. Most simply, these are the final sum total of all labor and property incomes earned in producing the national output.

Only in the last decade or so have we had any adequate statistical data on these important concepts; only in the most advanced countries of the world are there yet readily available yearly data on changes in this all-important magnitude. Here in the United States we are fortunate in having national income estimates from the Department of Commerce (a branch of the federal government) and from the National Bureau of Economic Research (a non-profit scientific institute). Their estimates are in very good quantitative agreement so long as they claim to be using the same definitions, so we may have considerable confidence in national income statistics.[1]

By means of statistics of national income, we can chart the movements of a country from depression to prosperity, its steady long-term rate of economic growth and development, and finally its material standard of living in comparison with other nations. How then is national income defined and measured?

TWO VIEWS: MONEY INCOME OR MONEY OUTPUT

There are two different ways of looking at national income. Being essentially two aspects of the same thing, they each will have to add up to the same thing.

Approaching the problem from the first direction, we may say (1) that national income is the sum total of *income earned* by owners of the various productive factors: wages of workers, plus net interest on capital loans and securities, plus net rents and royalties, plus corporate profits, plus net income of unincorporated enterprises.

[1] The standard reference is to S. Kuznets, *National Income and Its Composition, 1919–1938* (National Bureau of Economic Research, Inc., New York, 1941), Vols. I and II. See also *Survey of Current Business* of the Department of Commerce, particularly the July, 1947, Supplement; and the July *National Income* issue of each subsequent year. In the United Kingdom a yearly *White Paper* gives data on national income. The United Nations attempts to report national incomes for all countries with available data.

Looked at from the other direction, we may say (2) that national income gives the total *net value of all goods and services produced* in a given year.

In the simplest case, we can imagine a circular flow of dollars going from business to the public in return for productive services of labor and property; this is just matched by a flow of consumption dollars going from the public to business to pay for the purchase of real consumption goods and services.

It does not matter—so long as there is a perfect circular flow—whether we measure the flow of national income in the upper loop where it appears in the form of people's *earned incomes* or we measure it in the lower loop as the *value of goods and services.* Either answer will be the same. (When we come to introduce saving

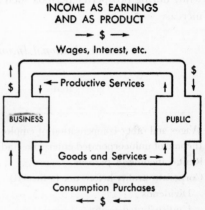

FIGURE 1. Two views of national income.

and investment and the government into the picture, the diagram will have to be made a little more complicated, but the two different ways of looking at national income will still be valid.)

FIRST VIEW OF NATIONAL INCOME: COST AND EARNINGS OF FACTORS
OF PRODUCTION

To arrive at estimates of the total flow of income accruing to the public we must carefully collect data (from company and government reports, tax returns, etc.) on (1) wages, salaries, and supplements earned by all employees; (2) net income of unincorporated business, meaning by this the net returns to farmers, doctors, partners, single proprietors, etc.; (3) net interest, received from private bonds, mortgages, and other loans; (4) net rents of persons, including estimates for self-occupied homes; (5) net corporate earnings, whether (*a*) distributed to the common and preferred stockholders as dividends, or (*b*) plowed back into (the surplus of) the corporation, as undistributed corporate profits, or (*c*) payable to the government in corporate income taxes. Table 1 shows these data for 1949.

It is rather remarkable how nearly constant are the proportions of the various categories of income over long periods of time, between both good years and bad. The size of the total social pie may wax and wane, but total wages seem always to add up to about two-thirds of the total.

The proportions of the remainder do not remain perfectly constant. Interest and rent payments tend to be relatively fixed charges on business enterprises· They do not at first decline so much in deep depression as the other items, with the result that corporate profits must show a greater relative decline. In fact during depressions profits may become negative for many firms and industries, while during prosperity periods such as 1941–1951 corporation profits greatly increase.

TABLE 1. *National Income Earned by Factors, 1949*

Items	Billions of dollars	Percentage
Wages and other compensation of employees...........	$140.6	65
Income of unincorporated enterprises (adjusted)........	34.4	16
Rental income of persons.....................	7.3	3
Corporate profits before tax (adjusted)........	29.8	14
Dividends............................ $ 7.8		
Undistributed profits.................. 9.2		
Corporate profits tax.................. 10.6		
Inventory valuation adjustment......... +2.2		
$29.8		
Net interest..................................	4.7	2
National income................................	$216.8	100

TRANSFER PAYMENTS

Not every sum of money that an individual receives in any period can be counted as personal income or as part of the national income. If I sell an old painting for $1,000, I am simply exchanging one kind of asset for another and so is the purchaser. But if I am a painter who produces one picture a month and thereby earns $12,000 a year, then all this (over and above my expenses for materials) will be counted as national income.

This is just another illustration of a transfer payment such as we met in the discussion of public finance in Chapter 7. There we pointed out why relief payments and pensions to disabled veterans or to the aged should not be counted in the national income.

The decisive test as to whether a given item should be counted in national income is as follows: *Does it represent a cost payment to a factor of production for a current contribution toward production?* This does not mean that the contribution to production by the income recipient must be rendered personally. Rent paid to him for the use of land that he has provided or interest on his capital—all these you must count (even if the charge seems to you exorbitant or undeserved) as long as they enter into the cost of production of some commodity.

The reader might amuse himself by trying to decide whether the following money transactions ought or ought not to enter into national income: (1) an inheritance of a million dollars, (2) a yearly gift of $1,000 from a rich aunt to avoid inheritance tax when she dies, (3) a student's monthly allowance from his father or from the Veterans' Administration, (4) the sale of an old house, either at its original cost or at a price that represents a nice tidy "capital gain," (5) relief allowances to needy families, (6) interest received on government bonds, (7) interest on a railroad bond, (8) wages of a dog catcher, (9) the earnings of a housemaid, (10) the value of the housekeeping services of a wife, (11) sales of vegetables from a farmer's garden, (12) the value of vegetables from a farmer's garden consumed by the family, (13) the estimated net rental value of the house I own and live in, (14) the income of an advertising salesman, (15) the income of a brewer, (16) the income of a monopolist. Some of these questions are very easy; some are very difficult borderline cases.[1]

REAL VERSUS MONEY INCOME

While national income is expressed in money terms, its importance depends upon what each dollar will buy. If inflation raised all prices and wages tenfold but left everything else unchanged, national income would appear ten times as large; but now each dollar would have only the same *real significance* as the old dime. If our money incomes all increase tenfold but we have to pay ten times as much for all goods, who would be so foolish as to think we are better off?

To take an actual example: From 1939 to 1949 national income almost exactly tripled, growing from 72 billion to 216 billion dollars. Part of this increase was really a fiction, being the result of the increase in prices over this decade.

Table 2 shows how we can allow for the fact that the price level rose by about $\frac{2}{3}$ (or $\frac{40}{60}$) between 1939 and 1949. To compute the change in *real* national income (expressed in dollars of constant purchasing power) as distinct from *money* national income (expressed in changing current prices), we must "deflate" the money figures by dividing them through by an index of the cost of living (or price level). In the end we find 1939 real national income was 120 billion dollars if expressed in constant 1949 prices rather than 72 billion

[1] Those excluded from national income are 1 to 6 and 10. The first six are transfer payments. A wife's housework services are not included simply because it is hard to find a market-price yardstick or any other to evaluate them. In all logic, they should be included, and national income should be increased by one-fifth or more. Items 14, 15, and 16 must be included. Item 6, interest on government bonds, since 1947 has been listed as a transfer payment rather than as part of national income; this is a debatable procedure.

TABLE 2. *Deflating of Money Income to Compute Real National Income*

Year	Money national income in current dollars (billions) (1)	Price index, 1949 as base (2)	Real national income in 1949 prices (billions) (3)
1949	$216	100	$216 \times {}^{100}\!/_{100} = \$216$
1939	$ 72	60	$ 72 \times {}^{100}\!/_{60} = \$120$

dollars expressed in the then current 1939 prices. Therefore, *real* national income had not quite doubled rather than having tripled.[1] Figure 2 summarizes the different movements of real and money income since 1929.

COMPARISON OF MONEY AND REAL
NATIONAL INCOME, U.S., 1929-1950

FIGURE 2. SOURCE: Department of Commerce.

SECOND VIEW OF NATIONAL INCOME: NET NATIONAL PRODUCT

In deflating national income to get a measure of what people's earnings will buy, we are getting away from the earnings approach. We are turning to the second way of looking at national income—as the net value of all goods and services produced in the year. Let us explore this further.

[1] Suppose that money national income is given in Column (1) and an index number of the cost of living (with 1949 prices = 100) in Column (2). Then Column (3) gives *real* national income, derived by dividing Column (1) by Column (2) and multiplying by 100.

For the year 1929, the reader can write in Column (1) = $87, Column (2) = 72 and can calculate Column (3), verifying that 1929 and 1939 had almost identical real incomes. If he likes, he can make the comparison using 1939 prices as a base.

The primary purpose of our economic activity is to get us consumption goods and services. A little thought will make it clear that the rendering of services must be included along with the production of tangible commodities. The pay of an opera singer or shoeshine boy enters into national income or net national product; the service each renders is as important in net national product as is the manufacture of a camera or for that matter a phonograph record. In fact, it will be clear to the reader upon reflection that material objects are useful in the last analysis only because of the services (or utilities) that they render.

But how can we add *diverse* goods and services to form a meaningful total? What is the meaning of 2 apples plus 3 oranges? At least two methods may be suggested of reducing the million and one different goods produced every year to a common denominator. The first method would apply some sort of psychological or welfare yardstick based on satisfactions enjoyed by people as a result of consuming different goods. It would not be theoretically inconceivable that someone might dream up a definition of "psychological utility" or "psychic income" whereby oranges and apples could be combined. The result would be somewhat arbitrary and might depend a great deal on how we weight different individuals' tastes; for example, a vegetarian and a cannibal might differ sharply in their estimate of people's psychic income.

For this and other reasons, economists prefer to use a second kind of yardstick or common denominator—namely, *money value or market price*. True, we cannot add apples and oranges by themselves. But once we know their relative prices—say apples 4 cents apiece and oranges 5 cents—then we can speak of the total value of 2 apples and 3 oranges as being 23 cents. Market price provides us with the factor that makes it possible to measure output in a common dimension.

To be sure, this is not a perfect solution. The total of money value is only a rough index of social welfare. Some of the best things in life cannot be measured in money. The Department of Commerce cannot always get hold of accurate estimates of the value of such items as a farmer's home-grown tomatoes, or of owner-occupied homes. But they do their best. Perfectly accurate market prices are hard even to define for such ambiguous services as a doctor's appointment. And finally, to cut the list short, we still have the earlier mentioned problem of deflating our resulting money total for fictitious, paper changes in the price level. (The reader should think up further difficulties and pitfalls.)

FINAL GOODS VERSUS DOUBLE COUNTING OF INTERMEDIATE GOODS

Even after we have brushed aside some of the worries of a perfectionist, we must still face the problem of deciding what goods are to be included in net national product. There is always the danger of double counting. It would be wrong, for example, to count bread in the net national product and also at the same time to count in the flour that went into that bread, or to triple count by also counting in the wheat.

To avoid this pitfall, the words *"net* value of goods and services" were inserted into our definition. We must first be sure that each included item truly represents a *final* good or service. Thus, a 10-cent loaf of bread was made from wheat which sold for 2 cents, from flour worth 3 cents, and baked dough worth 5 cents; finally wrapped, it was sold to the ultimate customer for 10 cents. Its contribution to the national product is not $2 + 3 + 5 + 10$ cents. That would involve considerable double counting. Why? Because the flour, dough, etc., are not *final* products. Only the 10-cent bread is a final product; the 20-cent total includes intermediate products.

If we insist upon decomposing the 10 cents of final product represented by the bread into the contributions of the different stages of production, we can always do so by concentrating on the so-called "value added" at each stage of production. This is nothing but a return to our first way of looking at net national product—from the standpoint of costs of production paid out at each stage as earned incomes to the owners of factors of production (wages, interest, etc.). Our final product equals the sum of value added at each stage of production:

TABLE 3. *Final Product, Value Added, and Intermediate Product*

Stage of production of a loaf of bread	Sales value, cents (1)	Cost of material, cents (2)	Value added, cents (3)
On the farm........................	2	— 0	= 2
At the mill and by transport.............	3	— 2	= 1
At the bakery.......................	5	— 3	= 2
By wholesaler and retail distributors......	10	— 5	= 5
Total value of final product...........	20	— 10	= 10, sum of value added

The reader can verify that there is no double counting. Why? Because in calculating the value added at each stage, we first carefully subtract all the costs of materials and intermediate products not produced in that stage but bought from other business firms. [The numbers in Table 3 show that *every intermediate product* appears both in Column (1) and *with opposite sign* in Column (2); hence it is canceled out.]

The value added at each stage can be broken down into wages, salaries, interest, and rents and into all the other components that we have already discussed in connection with the first way of looking at national income. So again we see that the two methods are perfectly equivalent and self-checking.[1]

SOME MINOR DIFFICULTIES

Usually there is no great difficulty in avoiding double counting; we concentrate on value added and omit all the intermediate goods that one business firm buys from another. It is easy to see that coal used in a baker's oven is not itself to be counted as part of national product if we have already counted in the full value of final bread consumption. It is also equally obvious that the coal burned in a home and yielding a final utility to consumers is part of national income or product. And very clearly, the ovens and plows used up in making a finished loaf of bread are to be counted (once but not twice!) in the value of national product.

Occasionally we are confronted with more difficult decisions. Should the traveling-expense account of a salesman be counted in as income? No. Like the coal in the baker's oven, this is a necessary expense of producing final goods and has already been counted in the value of final output. On the other hand, it is equally obvious that, when a firm provides housing for one of its workers, his wages are really increased by the rental value of this house and such an item has to be treated as a final good. Between these two clear cases, there are more difficult ones to classify. For example, suppose a salesman takes a client to an enjoyable baseball game or night club. Ought not we to consider this expense-account item at least in part as an addition to the salesman's pleasurable consumption and to his wage income? In practice, the income statistician arbitrarily treats any such items as intermediate rather than final products.

Conversely, a philosophical case can be made out for treating a good deal of man's consumption expenditure as really a necessary business expense; for example, a carpenter's overalls or his carfare to work. The practical national income statistician insists upon counting these as final consumption rather than as intermediate goods because, as soon as he begins to make one exception, he

---

[1] A failure to understand the relation between final product, value added, and intermediate goods lies at the basis of the mysterious "Type A and Type B payments" invented by a retired British engineer, Major Douglas, the founder of the Social Credit movement. This political party, which advocates the printing of new money, has followers in Canada, England, Australia, and California; and it has actually come into power in one of the western Canadian provinces. But it has there been forced to abandon its unorthodox economic program.

must make another—and pretty soon there might be no national income left, because all the food we eat would be counted as a necessary expense to keep up our working efficiency, and so forth.

THE THREE COMPONENTS OF NET NATIONAL PRODUCT

Excluding intermediate goods, what are the different kinds of product we are left with? As Figure 3 shows, there are three kinds of product contained in the total of net national product (NNP): (1) personal *consumption*

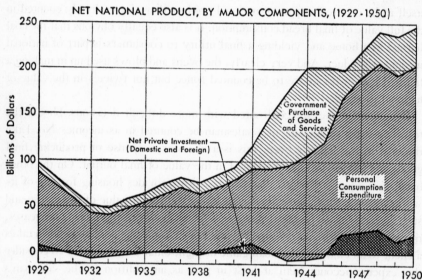

FIGURE 3. The topmost curve gives the level of NNP. Note that for several years, net private investment was actually negative, so that the NNP total was less than the sum of government purchases and consumption expenditure. SOURCE: Department of Commerce; 1950 figures are estimated from *Economic Report of the President*, July, 1950.

expenditure on goods and services; (2) net *private investment*, both domestic and foreign; (3) *government purchases* of goods and services.

The first of these we have already spoken of. Consumption expenditure means the purchase of clothing, corn flakes, concert performances, and all the thousands of goods and services which carry a price tag in the market and on which we spend our money.

The other two categories, net investment and government purchases, offer a few perplexities that require notice. Therefore, let us devote a few pages to each, beginning with the problems raised for the national income statistician by government.

Treatment of Taxes. If there were no government, we could calculate the net national product either by evaluating final products or by evaluating the total earnings of the factors of production. But taxes are a new element of costs that every firm must pay in addition to what it must pay to the factors of production. Should we include or exclude taxes in our final total?

Our earlier bread example gives us the answer. A loaf of bread that sells for 11 cents—the sum of 10 cents of factor costs and 1 cent of indirect taxes—does after all sell for 11 cents. Therefore, if we do want to measure the flow of output at actual *market* prices, we *must* include all indirect taxes. Also, it is not our concern that the laborers and capitalists who earn their incomes producing the bread have part of that income taken away from them in direct taxation. To whomever these incomes go, they have already been included in the price of the bread. *Thus, all taxes—direct and indirect—are included in net national product.*

But what has this done to our original way of looking at national income? Very clearly, once the government enters the picture to collect taxes, the factors of production no longer have at their disposal a total of earnings equal to the value of product. Their *disposable income* (left out of the earnings distributed to them after they have paid all their taxes and received all their unearned transfers) will certainly be less than net national product. In 1949, for example, disposable income was 187 billion dollars, or exactly 50 billion dollars less than the 237 billion of net national product.

Now that the government has created a discrepancy between our two ways of looking at income, to which of these two figures shall we give the name national income? The safest way would be always to present the two measures: net national product and disposable income. But newspaper men and the man on the street have become accustomed to the name "national income," and they want the Department of Commerce or the United Nations to give them a single figure. So the statisticians have agreed on a logically arbitrary compromise. Since 1947 they have agreed to include in national income certain taxes and to exclude certain other taxes. All personal taxes (such as income, payroll, and property taxes) are included in the national income concept; and since 1947, corporate income taxes have also been included. Excluded are the remaining indirect business taxes (such as sales taxes, customs, business property taxes, etc.). The resulting national income figure, therefore, falls short of net national product by the amount of such indirect business taxes. In 1949, these amounted to about 20 billion dollars. The resulting national income figure, on the other hand, was in 1949 30 billion dollars more than disposable income.

What are we to think of this compromise definition of national income that is part way between the earnings and value-of-product approaches? In my judgment, it has no particular logic behind it. On the other hand, as long as the measurers of national income stick to any one definition, it does not matter much exactly what they include or exclude. From the year-to-year changes in their statistics, we can get a pretty good notion of how the aggregate of the economy's activity is changing, and that is all we really want.[1]

Treatment of Government Expenditure. Omitting government transfer payments, the national income statistician includes all government purchases of goods and services in NNP. He evaluates each typewriter the government buys at its cost to the government; he evaluates the services of each judge and civil servant at their cost to the government.

After you think about it, you begin to wonder whether all the goods and services bought by government are really *final* products rather than intermediate products of the type we earlier regarded as double counting. When the government spends money on a road, is that an expenditure on final product or on intermediate product? Obviously, if the sole purpose of the road were to give people pleasure rides, we should have to consider it all a part of net national product. But to the extent that the money is spent in order for commercial trucks to ride on the road, many economists would argue that this is an intermediate product. Just as we refuse to double-count the coal burned up in baking an 11-cent loaf of bread, and just as we refuse to double-count the railroad expense incurred in bringing the bread to market by rail, economists argue that we should not double-count the public road expense necessary for trucks to bring the 11-cent loaf of bread to market.

This example shows the nature of our second difficulty raised by government: How much of government expenditure on goods and services should be regarded, not as final product, but as intermediate product and ought therefore to be excluded from the total of net national product? In practice, the national income statistician throws up his hands and declares that he is quite incapable of making an estimate on such a question. Rather than make a personal judgment, he arbitrarily decides to include in NNP *all* government purchases of goods and services at their money cost to the government, warning his readers that there may be double counting involved.

INVESTMENT OR CAPITAL FORMATION

Now let us again put government to one side and examine the third component of NNP: net private investment or capital formation. To arrive at the true net product of a country, we must, in addition to the flow of final con-

---

[1] Figure 5 shows how the different concepts all change together.

sumers' goods and services, take account also of capital formation: the net additions to our stock of (1) buildings, (2) equipment, and (3) inventories.

If our economy were not growing, the stock of capital would be constant. As any building or machine wore out, it would be replaced. In such a stationary society, consumption and net product would be identical; replacement and capital consumption would be identical.

But most economies are normally growing, so that consumption is less than net product. By how much? Net product exceeds consumption by the *value of net capital formation*, *i.e.*, by the value of net private investment.[1] Thus a farm pioneer out West at first had little in consumption goods to show for his efforts. But the improvements in land and buildings—all these had to be included in net national product.

In the unusual case of a great depression or a decadent society, consumption might actually exceed net production. Has the statistician gone crazy? Can we really consume what has not been produced? The key to the paradox lies in careful use of the word *net*. To illustrate the case of an economy that is disinvesting, consider a farmer. He begins in the spring with 10 bushels of seed corn; he ends up in the fall harvesting 110 bushels. Has he produced 110 bushels *net*? No. And if he were to eat or drink 110 bushels of corn, he would be consuming more than his true net product.

We see, therefore, that consumption will exceed net product to the extent that capital formation is negative, *i.e.*, to the extent that we have net *dis*investment rather than positive net investment. This is crystal-clear in the case of a community with huge stores of finished goods: canned foods, ready-to-wear clothing, etc. But actually, in modern nations the inventories of ready-to-consume finished goods are very small. Egypt may have lived for seven years on its stores, but we would starve in a few months. The important fact is this: A country can consume more than its net product by "eating up" its physical capital goods. Since nourishing soup cannot be made by boiling a dynamo or a hammer, how then are such capital goods actually eaten?

They are consumed in the sense that workers and other factors of production ordinarily engaged in their *replacement and maintenance* are diverted to the production of digestible consumer's goods. In a modern economy, such a

---

[1] We must always be careful to exclude from real capital formation "capital gains or losses" resulting from the marking up or marking down of prices. Suppose last year my inventory of wheat was 100 bushels worth $2 per bushel and this year I have 110 bushels at $3 per bushel. Then the value of my inventory has gone up by $130, or ($330 − $200). But the value of my increase in real physical capital is much less than this, being not more than $30. All financial windfalls, acts of God, and nonrecurring capital gains are excluded from the reckoning of income; this is the meaning of the adjustments indicated in many of the following tables.

process can go on for some time, and it is a more important source of enhanced consumption than is the actual using up of inventories of finished goods.

During World War II, it was deliberate national policy to enhance our striking power at the enemy (*i.e.*, to increase current military consumption) by preventing nonessential civilian capital goods from being replaced as rapidly as they were used up. Our houses and automobiles grew older and lacked paint so that the diverted resources could be poured into the war effort.

All this is summarized in Figure 4. Figure 4*a* illustrates a growing economy. The whole of the pie represents the total of net national product or income.

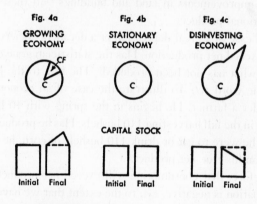

CAPITAL FORMATION AND INCOME

| Fig. 4a | Fig. 4b | Fig. 4c |
| GROWING ECONOMY | STATIONARY ECONOMY | DISINVESTING ECONOMY |

CAPITAL STOCK

| Initial   Final | Initial   Final | Initial   Final |

C = Consumption
CF = Capital Formation
Income = Algebraic Sum of Consumption and Capital Formation

FIGURES 4*a*, 4*b*, 4*c*.

The lower left-hand rectangle represents the initial stock of capital at the beginning of the year, and next to it is the final amount of capital at the end of the period. Note that the amount of product not consumed (the wedge of the pie saved) is equal to the increment in the stock of capital as shown by the little triangle.

Figure 4*b* illustrates the stationary case where consumption equals production and capital is just maintained intact. Figure 4*c* represents the case of retrogression when consumption exceeds net production. (Can you explain why?)

GROSS VERSUS NET INVESTMENT

Now we know how to calculate net national product: To public and private consumption goods and services we add net investment. Just how can the statisticians calculate this net investment figure? To do this they must first calculate how many *new buildings are constructed*, how much *new producers' durable equipment is built*, and how much *real inventories of goods have increased*.

Such a figure can be fairly easily estimated from available statistical data. But such a figure does not take account of the buildings and capital equipment currently being consumed and which must be *replaced* before we can truly speak of positive net investment. You cannot expect the gross total of births to give you the net growth of a human population; gross births *minus* deaths gives the correct net figure. Similarly, the total of all capital goods produced without any allowance being made for capital depreciation deserves the name of *gross* rather than *net* investment.

Gross investment involves double counting. An inflated NNP would result if you were to add the value of ovens used up in baking bread on top of the final loaves of bread; this would be as bad as to double-count the coal used up in baking bread along with the final product. Only the new ovens and bakeries in excess of capital consumption or depreciation allowances in the bakery industry deserve to be called net investment, and only the resulting figure for net investment can be added to consumption expenditure to get NNP.

Nonetheless the Department of Commerce statisticians often find it easier to estimate gross investment than to estimate net investment. This is because of the difficulty of getting reliable capital consumption estimates from the total of business accounting records. Each business concern can only make a guess at depreciation, and often different firms use quite different methods.

The task of estimating allowance for capital consumption or depreciation is difficult, but it must somehow be done. Table 4 shows how net private investment compares with gross private investment. Note the interesting case of 1932 in which net private investment was negative. Can you explain why?

TABLE 4. *Gross and Net Investment (In billions of dollars)*

	1929	1932	1949
1. New construction..............................	$ 7.8	$ 1.7	$17.3
2. Producers' durable equipment...................	6.4	1.8	19.5
3. Change in business inventories..................	1.6	−2.6	−3.7
4. Gross private domestic investment..............	$15.8	$ 0.9	$33.1
5. Allowances for depreciation or capital consumption (also = discrepancy between GNP and NNP)....	−8.8	−7.6	−18.8
6. Net private domestic investment.................	$ 7.0	$−6.7	$14.3
7. Net foreign investment........................	0.8	0.2	0.4
8. Net private investment.........................	$ 7.8	$−6.5	$14.7

GNP VERSUS NNP

Gross national product (GNP) is a name often met in official statistics. It represents the sum of (1) consumption purchases of goods and services, (2) government purchases of goods and services, and (3) gross private investment (foreign and domestic). GNP differs from NNP (net national product) in one way only: While NNP has *net* private investment in it, GNP has *gross* private

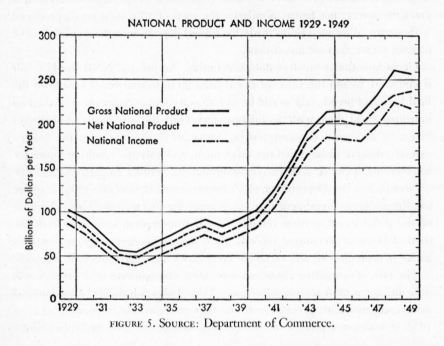

NATIONAL PRODUCT AND INCOME 1929-1949

FIGURE 5. SOURCE: Department of Commerce.

investment in it. The discrepancy between GNP and NNP is shown in row 5 of Table 4; it rarely exceeds 10 per cent. We have seen that the discrepancy represents double counting because of the failure to remove from the gross figures an allowance for capital consumed or depreciated.

Why do the statisticians knowingly double-count and present such a GNP figure? We have already seen the answer: Because of the difficulty of correctly estimating or allowing for capital consumption, the GNP figure is easier to get accurate estimates for. Recognizing this fact, nevertheless in this book we shall be primarily interested in net national product, without double counting and without omissions. Figure 5 shows the relative magnitude of GNP, NNP, and so-called national income. The tables in the statistical appendix to this chapter show further relations between the officially reported concepts.

INTERNATIONAL ASPECTS OF INCOME: NET FOREIGN INVESTMENT

Only one last concept needs to be explained. How does foreign trade enter into national income accounting? How did we arrive at Table 4's net foreign investment part of our investment total?

From the beginning we agree to mean by United States national income the income or product accruing to all "permanent residents" of the United States. This includes American citizens temporarily abroad and also unnaturalized immigrants who live permanently in the United States.

Note that, if an Englishman owns an acre of land in this country, his income therefrom is to be included in the United Kingdom national income and not in the United States national income. Similarly, if Americans receive dividends from British companies, this is part of the American income and not part of the British. Scotch whisky, even if drunk by an American, forms part of the United Kingdom NNP; our exports to the United Kingdom form part of the United States NNP.

The previous paragraph shows that it is a considerable task to allow for international aspects of income. We must take account of exports, imports, dividends paid in and out of a country, etc. As we shall see in Part Five's discussion of international finance, a balance of international payments between the United States and the rest of the world can be drawn up of all such items. There is no need at this point of our national income discussion to anticipate all the details of Part Five's discussion. We are interested only in the bare logic of the task of finding out the magnitude of net foreign investment, which must be combined with net private domestic investment to give us the third or investment component of NNP. (Turn back to Table 4.)

To get our net foreign investment we must calculate the surplus of all the goods and services we provide to foreigners over what they provide to us. Thus calculate A, the total of our exports to them (automobiles, shipping, etc.) plus our earnings from factors of production we own abroad (dividends and interest payable to us). Also calculate B, the total of what we import from them and must pay them for their ownership of productive factors located in this country. If A exceeds B, foreigners must be going into our debt; the surplus of A over B represents our net foreign investment. But note that B might exceed A in some years. What then? We are then buying more abroad than we are earning abroad, going into debt for the difference. Now our net foreign investment is negative, representing net foreign disinvestment for us.[1]

[1] Warning to the reader: Our government's Marshall Plan aid to foreigners is included in government purchases and not in net foreign investment. On the other hand, when the government's Export-Import Bank makes a loan to a foreign government, that is included in net foreign investment.

TABLE 5. *National Income and Product, 1949 (In billions of current dollars)*

Wages and other employee supplements	$140.6		Personal consumption expenditure			$178.8
Income of unincorporated enterprises (adjusted)	34.4		Government purchases of goods and services			43.3
Rent income of persons	7.3		Net foreign investment			.4
Corporate profits before taxes (adjusted)	29.8		Net private domestic investment			14.3
Dividends	$7.8		Equals Gross private domestic invest-			
Undistributed profits	9.2		ment		$33.1	
Corporate profits taxes	10.6		Minus Depreciation and capital con-			
	$27.6		sumption allowance		18.8	
Inventory valuation adjustment*	+2.2				$14.3	
	$29.8					
Net interest	4.7		Net National Product (at market prices)			$236.8
	$216.8		Depreciation			18.8
National Income	$216.8					$255.6
Indirect business taxes and adjustments†	20.0		Gross National Product (at market prices)			$255.6
	$236.8					
Net National Product	$236.8					
Depreciation or capital consumption allowances	18.8					
	$255.6					
Gross National Product	$255.6					

* Because prices fell in 1949, money profits were lowered; we therefore add an inventory valuation adjustment to raise the unadjusted figure of 27.6 billion dollars to the adjusted figure of 29.8 billion dollars.

† Includes business transfers, net government subsidies, and statistical discrepancy.

Table 5 brings together all the threads of our discussion of national income. It shows how we have modified the simple circular flow diagram of Figure 1 in order to take account of government taxes and expenditures, net and gross investment, and foreign investment.

The left-hand side of Table 5 shows how NNP can be built up from the earnings approach. The right-hand side shows how it can be built up from the flow-of-product approach. Table 5 also shows the relations between GNP, NNP, and national income. The reader may be referred to the Appendix Tables 6 to 8 for the behavior since 1929 of these important magnitudes.

SUMMARY

1. National income may first be looked at from the standpoint of the costs of output payable as earnings to the factors of production. It is thus equal to the sum: wages and supplements to employees + net income of unincorporated enterprise + net interest and rents + net corporate profits.

2. Or we may look at net national product as a flow of goods and services evaluated and made comparable by the use of market prices. Hence, NNP can be split into consumption expenditure on goods and services + government expenditure on goods and services + net private investment (domestic and foreign).

3. To eliminate fictitious changes in the price level, money income must be deflated by some index of changing prices. This gives a measure of real income, measured in terms of dollars of constant purchasing power.

4. Pure transfer items and windfall capital gains must be excluded from national income. Also, we must be careful not to double-count intermediate along with final product. Instead, we must concentrate on the value-added approach which cancels out at every stage all purchases of intermediate goods by one firm from another.

5. All indirect business taxes must be included in NNP if goods are to be evaluated at their market prices and cost to government. But indirect business taxes are not included in national income, since this concept is to represent factor earnings (before personal and corporate income taxes).

6. The problem of indirect business taxes should not be confused with the thornier problem of what part of government expenditure on goods and services is to be treated as intermediate services rendered to business rather than as

final product. The statistician refuses to judge this question. Instead, he warns his readers that all goods and services purchased by government have been arbitrarily included in the NNP figures.

7. Net product is correctly reached only after we have taken account of net capital formation or net investment. Consumption will fall short of net national product if resources are being used to build up the community's stock of capital goods.

8. Gross national product includes gross rather than net investment. Gross investment has not had subtracted from it any allowance for capital depreciation. Therefore, GNP involves some deliberate double counting in comparison with NNP. Because of the difficulty of evaluating capital consumption or depreciation, GNP is often used instead of—or along with—NNP.

9. International trade introduces one new problem of definition. National income is defined as income accruing to all permanent residents of a country. To arrive at this, we calculate from the international balance of payments the algebraic excess of our export sales and factor earnings over our imports and factor payments to foreign countries; thus we finally arrive at a figure for net foreign investment (+ or −). This is added algebraically into net investment and NNP.

There are many philosophical problems of defining national income. Once a definition has been agreed upon, the statistical estimates do not differ by a great deal, and the resulting data give a pretty good picture of changes over time. Therefore, the analysis of business cycles and unemployment, as discussed in Part Two, is enormously aided by the improvements in the national income data of the past decades.

QUESTIONS FOR DISCUSSION

1. Make a list of items that are easy to classify as being included in or excluded from national income. Make a list of difficult items.

2. Give some examples showing that money is not always a good measuring rod of well-being.

3. The 1932 depression decrease in money incomes exceeded the decrease in real incomes. How would you allow for this? Be specific.

4. List the items on a business statement of profit and loss as shown in the Appendix to Chapter 6. Which are part of value added? Of NNP? Of GNP?

5. Discuss the meaning of national income and disposable income as shown in Table 9. How are they related to NNP?

6. Why is it hard to classify government expenditure into final or intermediate product? Give examples such as a policeman, a postman, a government chemist, a judge, etc.

7. Discuss the changes in investment between 1929, 1932, and 1949. Are these changes important? Why?

8. Summarize some of the definitional problems raised by international trade.

9. What are some of the problems raised by capital formation?

10. From the data in the Appendix, try to reconstruct for 1948 a table exactly like Table 5. Do the same for 1950 or a later year using the *Federal Reserve Bulletin* or the *Survey of Current Business* for source material.

STATISTICAL APPENDIX TO CHAPTER 11

The following tables give basic data on the various national income concepts just as they appear in the official publications. In terms of our earlier discussion they should be more or less self-explanatory. Table 10 gives the available basic data on the working force, employment, and unemployment.

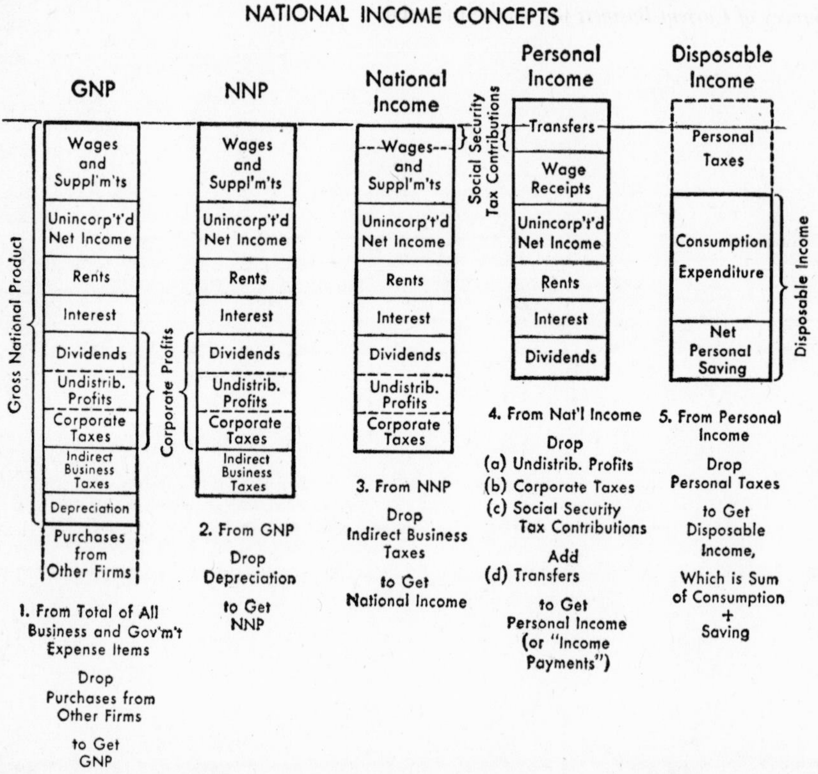

NATIONAL INCOME CONCEPTS

FIGURE 6. This summarizes the relationships between gross national product, net national product, national income, personal income, and disposable income. SOURCE: Department of Commerce revised concepts, adapted from Richard Ruggles, *An Introduction to National Income and Income Analysis* (McGraw-Hill, New York, 1949), a valuable reference.

Table 9 contains one new concept not earlier mentioned: personal income. It is analytically less important, but unlike NNP and the others, this figure is available on a monthly basis shortly after each month is over. Personal income differs from national income in that it does include transfer payments received by people from the government; on the other hand, it does not include the undistributed profits of corporations, or corporate profits taxes. The accompanying figure shows how personal income and the other four concepts are related. It illustrates the important items causing them to differ from one another. Table 9 lists some further, but minor, differences; these are unimportant in an introductory analysis.

TABLE 6. *Various Income Concepts, 1929–1950 (In billions of dollars)*

Period	Gross national product	Net national product	National income	Personal income	Disposable income	Net saving as per cent of disposable income
1929	103.8	95.0	87.4	85.1	82.5	4.5
1930	90.9	82.1	75.0	76.2	73.7	3.9
1931	75.9	67.6	58.9	64.8	63.0	2.9
1932	58.3	50.7	41.7	49.3	47.8	−2.9
1933	55.8	48.5	39.6	46.6	45.2	−2.7
1934	64.9	57.7	48.6	53.2	51.6	−0.4
1935	72.2	64.8	56.8	59.9	58.0	3.1
1936	82.5	74.8	64.7	68.4	66.1	5.4
1937	90.2	82.2	73.6	74.0	71.1	5.5
1938	84.7	76.7	67.4	68.3	65.5	1.5
1939	91.3	83.2	72.5	72.6	70.2	3.8
1940	101.4	93.0	81.3	78.3	75.7	4.9
1941	126.4	117.1	103.8	95.3	92.0	10.7
1942	161.6	151.6	137.1	122.7	116.7	21.9
1943	194.3	183.7	169.7	150.3	132.4	22.8
1944	213.7	201.8	183.8	165.9	147.0	24.1
1945	215.2	202.8	182.7	171.9	151.1	18.5
1946	211.1	198.9	180.3	177.7	158.9	7.6
1947	233.3	218.4	198.7	191.0	169.5	2.3
1948	259.1	241.7	223.5	209.5	188.4	5.8
1949	255.6	236.8	216.8	206.1	187.4	4.6
1950	278.8	257.9	236.2	222.4	202.1	5.6

SOURCE: Department of Commerce. Figures in 1950 are estimates from *Economic Report of the President*, January 1951.

TABLE 7. *National Income by Distributive Shares (Annual totals in billions of dollars)*

	1929	1933	1939	1941	1946	1947	1948	1949	1950* 1st quarter	1950* 2d quarter
National income.........	87.4	39.6	72.5	103.8	180.3	198.7	223.5	216.8	217.2	†
Compensation of employees...........	50.8	29.3	47.8	64.3	117.1	128.0	140.2	140.6	142.3	147.6
Wages and salaries ...	*50.2*	*28.8*	*45.7*	*61.7*	*111.2*	*122.1*	*134.4*	*134.2*	*135.2*	*140.2*
Private..........	45.2	23.7	37.5	51.5	90.6	104.8	115.7	113.7	114.3	119.2
Military.........	0.3	0.3	0.4	1.9	8.0	4.1	4.0	4.3	4.5	4.5
Government civilian	4.6	4.9	7.8	8.3	12.7	13.2	14.7	16.1	16.4	16.5
Supplements to wages and salaries.......	0.6	0.5	2.1	2.6	5.9	5.9	5.8	6.4	7.1	7.4
Proprietors' and rental income...........	19.7	7.2	14.7	20.8	42.0	42.4	47.3	41.7	41.5	41.3
Business and professional...........	8.3	2.9	6.8	9.6	20.6	19.8	22.1	21.0	21.4	22.3
Farm..............	5.7	2.3	4.5	6.9	14.8	15.6	17.7	13.4	12.8	11.8
Rental income of persons.............	5.8	2.0	3.5	4.3	6.6	7.1	7.5	7.3	7.3	7.2
Corporate profits and inventory valuation adjustment..	10.3	−2.0	5.8	14.6	18.3	24.7	31.8	29.8	28.4	†
Corporate profits before tax..............	*9.8*	*0.2*	*6.5*	*17.2*	*23.5*	*30.5*	*33.9*	*27.6*	*29.2*	†
Corporate profits tax liability.....	1.4	0.5	1.5	7.8	9.6	11.9	13.0	10.6	11.4	†
Corporate profits after tax.......	8.4	−0.4	5.0	9.4	13.9	18.5	20.9	17.0	17.8	†
Inventory valuation adjustment.......	0.5	−2.1	−0.7	−2.6	−5.2	−5.8	−2.0	2.2	−0.7	−2.3
Net interest...........	6.5	5.0	4.2	4.1	2.9	3.5	4.1	4.7	5.0	5.0

* Quarterly figures for 1950 are seasonally adjusted annual rates.
† Not available.
SOURCE: Department of Commerce.

TABLE 8. *Gross National Product or Expenditure (Annual totals in billions of dollars)*

	1929	1933	1939	1941	1946	1947	1948	1949	1950* 1st quarter	1950* 2d quarter
Gross national product	**103.8**	**55.8**	**91.3**	**126.4**	**211.1**	**233.3**	**259.1**	**255.6**	**262.5**	**269.9**
Personal consumption expenditures	**78.8**	**46.3**	**67.5**	**82.3**	**146.9**	**165.6**	**177.4**	**178.8**	**182.4**	**184.5**
Durable goods	9.4	3.5	6.7	9.8	16.6	21.4	22.9	23.8	26.9	26.7
Nondurable goods	37.7	22.3	35.3	44.0	85.8	95.1	100.9	98.5	97.5	99.0
Services	31.7	20.6	25.5	28.5	44.5	49.1	53.7	56.4	58.0	58.8
Gross private domestic investment	**15.8**	**1.3**	**9.9**	**18.3**	**28.7**	**30.2**	**43.1**	**33.0**	**40.5**	**45.9**
New construction	7.8	1.1	4.9	6.8	10.3	13.9	17.7	17.3	19.9	20.9
Producers' durable equipment	6.4	1.8	4.6	7.7	12.3	17.1	19.9	19.5	19.3	21.6
Change in business inventories	1.6	−1.6	0.4	3.9	6.1	−0.8	5.5	−3.7	1.3	3.4
Net foreign investment	**0.8**	**0.2**	**0.9**	**1.1**	**4.6**	**8.9**	**1.9**	**0.4**	**−1.9**	**−2.0**
Government purchases of goods and services	**8.5**	**8.0**	**13.1**	**24.7**	**30.9**	**28.6**	**36.6**	**43.3**	**41.4**	**41.4**
Federal	*1.3*	*2.0*	*5.2*	*16.9*	*20.9*	*15.8*	*21.0*	*25.3*	*22.5*	*22.6*
War	} 1.3	2.0	1.3	13.8	21.2	} 17.1	21.5	25.7	22.8	22.8
Nonwar			3.9	3.2	2.5					
Less: Government sales					2.7	1.3	0.5	0.4	0.3	0.2
State and local	7.2	5.9	7.9	7.8	10.0	12.8	15.6	18.0	18.9	18.8

* Quarterly figures for 1950 are seasonally adjusted annual rates.
SOURCE: Department of Commerce.

TABLE 9. *Relation of Gross National Product, National Income, Personal Income, and Saving (Annual totals in billions of dollars)*

	1929	1933	1939	1941	1946	1947	1948	1949	1950* 1st quarter	1950* 2d quarter
Gross national product..	103.8	55.8	91.3	126.4	211.1	233.3	259.1	255.6	262.5	269.9
Less: Capital consumption allowances...........	8.8	7.2	8.1	9.3	12.2	14.8	17.4	18.8	19.7	20.4
Indirect business tax and related liabilities.............	7.0	7.1	9.4	11.3	17.3	18.7	20.4	21.3	21.7	22.7
Business transfer payments...........	0.6	0.7	0.5	0.5	0.6	0.7	0.7	0.7	0.7	0.7
Statistical discrepancy	−0.1	1.2	1.4	1.6	1.7	0.3	−2.9	−1.9	3.4	†
Plus: Subsidies less current surplus of government enterprises...........	−0.1		0.5	0.1	0.9	−0.1	0.0	0.1	0.2	0.5
Equals: National income.	87.4	39.6	72.5	103.8	180.3	198.7	223.5	216.8	217.2	†
Less: Corporate profits and inventory valuation adjustment.............	10.3	−2.0	5.8	14.6	18.3	24.7	31.8	29.9	28.4	†
Contributions for social insurance.....	0.2	0.3	2.1	2.8	6.0	5.7	5.2	5.7	6.7	6.9
Excess of wage accruals over disbursements...........	0.0	0.0	0.0	0.0	0.0	0.0	0.0	0.0	0.0	0.0
Plus: Government transfer ments...............	0.9	1.5	2.5	2.6	10.9	11.1	10.6	11.6	20.9	14.7
Net interest paid by government.......	1.0	1.2	1.2	1.3	4.4	4.4	4.5	4.7	4.7	4.7
Dividends...........	5.8	2.1	3.8	4.5	5.8	6.6	7.5	7.8	8.1	8.1
Business transfer payments...........	0.6	0.7	0.5	0.5	0.6	0.7	0.7	0.7	0.7	0.7
Equals: Personal income.	85.1	46.6	72.6	95.3	177.7	191.0	209.5	206.1	216.4	214.7
Less: *Personal tax and related payments*..............	2.6	1.5	2.4	3.3	18.8	21.5	21.2	18.7	18.7	19.2
Federal.............	1.3	0.5	1.2	2.0	17.2	19.6	19.0	16.2	16.1	16.6
State and local......	1.4	1.0	1.2	1.3	1.6	1.9	2.2	2.5	2.6	2.6
Equals: Disposable personal income..........	82.5	45.2	70.2	92.0	158.9	169.5	188.4	187.4	197.7	195.5
Less: Personal consumption expenditures......	78.8	46.3	67.5	82.3	146.9	165.6	177.4	178.8	182.4	184.5
Equals: Personal saving..	3.7	−1.2	2.7	9.8	12.0	3.9	10.9	8.6	15.3	11.0

* Quarterly figures for 1950 are seasonally adjusted annual rates.

† Not available.

NOTE: NNP can be calculated as the difference between the first two lines.

SOURCE: Department of Commerce.

TABLE 10. *Labor Force, Employment, and Unemployment, 1929–1950*

Period	Total labor force (including armed forces)*	Armed forces*	Civilian labor force					Unemployment as percent of total civilian labor force
			Total civilian labor force	Employment†			Unemployment	
				Total	Agricultural	Non-agricultural		
	Thousands of persons, 14 years of age and over							
Monthly average:								
1929	49,440	260	49,180	47,630	10,450	37,180	1,550	3.2
1930	50,080	260	49,820	45,480	10,340	35,140	4,340	8.7
1931	50,680	260	50,420	42,400	10,290	32,110	8,020	15.9
1932	51,250	250	51,000	38,940	10,170	28,770	12,060	23.6
1933	51,840	250	51,590	38,760	10,090	28,670	12,830	24.9
1934	52,490	260	52,230	40,890	9,900	30,990	11,340	21.7
1935	53,140	270	52,870	42,260	10,110	32,150	10,610	20.1
1936	53,740	300	53,440	44,410	10,000	34,410	9,030	16.9
1937	54,320	320	54,000	46,300	9,820	36,480	7,700	14.3
1938	54,950	340	54,610	44,220	9,690	34,530	10,390	19.0
1939	55,600	370	55,230	45,750	9,610	36,140	9,480	17.2
1940	56,030	390	55,640	47,520	9,540	37,980	8,120	14.6
1941	57,380	1,470	55,910	50,350	9,100	41,250	5,560	9.9
1942	60,230	3,820	56,410	53,750	9,250	44,500	2,660	4.7
1943	64,410	8,870	55,540	54,470	9,080	45,390	1,070	1.9
1944	65,890	11,260	54,630	53,960	8,950	45,010	670	1.2
1945	65,140	11,280	53,860	52,820	8,580	44,240	1,040	1.9
1946	60,820	3,300	57,520	55,250	8,320	46,930	2,270	3.9
1947	61,608	1,440	60,168	58,027	8,266	49,761	2,142	3.6
1948	62,748	1,306	61,442	59,378	7,973	51,405	2,064	3.4
1949	63,571	1,466	62,105	58,710	8,026	50,684	3,395	5.5
1949—First half	62,732	1,483	61,249	58,060	7,940	50,120	3,189	5.2
Second half	64,411	1,450	62,960	59,359	8,112	51,247	3,602	5.7
1950—First half	63,776	1,347	62,429	58,555	7,233	51,322	3,874	6.2

* Data for 1940–1950 exclude about 150,000 members of the armed forces who were outside the continental United States in 1940 and who were therefore not enumerated in the 1940 census. This figure is deducted by the Census Bureau from its current estimates for comparability with 1940 data.

† Includes part-time workers and those who had jobs but were not at work for such reasons as vacation, illness, bad weather, temporary layoff, and industrial disputes.

NOTE. Labor force data are based on a survey made during the week which includes the 8th of the month.

Detail will not necessarily add to totals because of rounding.

SOURCES: Department of Labor (1929–1939), Department of Commerce (1940–1950), President's Report, July, 1950.

PART TWO

Determination of

National Income and

Its Fluctuations

PART TWO

Determination of

National Income and

Its Fluctuations

Chapter 12: SAVING,

CONSUMPTION, AND INVESTMENT

IN PART ONE the groundwork was laid for an understanding of the concept of national income. Now we can go beyond the anatomy of the problem to see what causes national income to rise, to fall, to be what it is at any time rather than something larger or smaller. This chapter provides an introduction to what is called the "modern theory of income analysis." The principal stress is upon the *level of total spending as determined by the interplay of the monetary forces of saving and investment.*

Although much of this analysis is due to an English economist, John Maynard Keynes (later made Lord Keynes, Baron of Tilton, before his death in 1946), today its broad fundamentals are increasingly accepted by economists of all schools of thought, including, it is important to notice, many writers who do not share Keynes's particular policy viewpoints and who differ on technical details of analysis.[1]

The income analysis here described is itself neutral: it can be used as well to defend private enterprise as to limit it, as well to attack as to defend government fiscal intervention. When business organizations such as the United States Chamber of Commerce, the Committee for Economic Development, or the National City Bank use the terminology of saving and investment, it is absurd to think that this implies that they are "Keynesian" in the sense of belonging to that narrow band of zealots associated with some of the policy programs that Keynes himself espoused during the Great Depression.

---

[1] Keynes himself was a many-sided genius who won eminence in the field of mathematics and philosophy and in the literary field. In addition he found time to run a large insurance company, to advise the British Treasury, to serve on the governing board of the Bank of England, to edit a world-famous economic journal, and to sponsor the ballet and the drama. He was also an economist who knew how to make money, both for himself and for King's College, Cambridge. His 1936 book. *The General Theory of Employment, Interest, and Money* created one of the greatest stirs in economic thinking of the century and is likely to live longer than his other works as a classic.

In recent years 90 per cent of American economists have stopped being "Keynesian economists" or "anti-Keynesian economists." Instead they have worked toward a synthesis of whatever is valuable in older economics and in modern theories of income determination. The result might be called neo-classical economics and is accepted in its broad outlines by all but about 5 per cent of extreme left-wing and right-wing writers.

THE CLEAVAGE BETWEEN SAVING AND INVESTMENT

The most important single fact about saving and investment is that in our industrial society they are largely done by different people and for different reasons.

This was not always so; even today, when a farmer devotes his time to drain-ing a field instead of to planting and harvesting a crop, he is saving and at the same time investing. He is saving because he is abstaining from present con-sumption in order to provide for larger consumption in the future, the amount of his saving being measured by the difference between his net real income and his consumption. But he is also investing; *i.e.*, he is undertaking net capital for-mation, improving the productive capacity of his land and equipment.

Not only are saving and investment the same things for a primitive farmer, but his reasons for undertaking them are the same. He abstains from present consumption (saves) only because there is a possibility or need to drain the field (to invest). If there were no investment opportunity, it would never occur to him to save; nor would there be any way for him to save should he be so foolish as to wish to.

In our modern economy, net capital formation or investment is carried on by business enterprises, especially corporations. When a corporation or a small business has great investment opportunities, its owners will be tempted to plow back much of its earnings into the business. To an important degree, therefore, business saving depends directly upon business investment.

Nevertheless, saving is also done by an entirely different group: by indi-viduals, by families, by households. An individual may wish to save for a great variety of reasons: because he wishes to provide for his old age or for a future expenditure (a vacation or an automobile). Or he may feel insecure and wish to guard against a rainy day. Or he may wish to leave an estate to his children or to his children's children. Or he may be an eighty-year-old miser with no heirs who enjoys the act of accumulating for its own sake. Or he may already have signed himself up to a savings program because an insurance salesman bought him a drink. Or he may desire the power that greater wealth brings. Or thrift may simply be a habit, a conditioned reflex whose origin he himself does not know. And so forth.

Whatever the individual's motivation to save, it has little directly to do with investment or investment opportunities. This truth is obscured by the fact that in everyday language "investment" does not always have the same meaning as in economic discussions. We have defined "net investment" or capital formation to be the net increase in the community's real capital (equipment, buildings, inventories, etc.). But the man on the street speaks of "investing" when he buys a piece of land, an old security, or any title to property. For economists these are clearly *transfer* items. What one man is investing, some one else is disinvesting. There is net investment only when new real capital is created.

In short, even if there are no real investment opportunities that seem profitable, an individual will often still wish to save. He can always buy an existing security or asset. If necessary, he can accumulate, or try to accumulate, cash.

THE VARIABILITY OF INVESTMENT

Thus, we are left with our proposition that *saving and investing are done by different individuals and for largely independent reasons*. Net capital formation (with the exception of housing, automobiles, and other "consumers' durables") takes place largely in business enterprise. Its amount is highly variable from year to year and decade to decade. This capricious, volatile behavior is understandable when we come to realize that investment opportunities depend on *new* discoveries, *new* products, *new* territories and frontiers, *new* resources, *new* population, *higher* production and income. Note the emphasis on new and on higher. Investment depends on the *dynamic* and relatively unpredictable elements of *growth* in the system, on elements outside the economic system itself: technology, politics, optimistic and pessimistic expectations, governmental tax and expenditure, legislative policies, etc.

This extreme variability of investment is the next important fact to be emphasized. We shall see that an industrial system such as our own can do many wonderful things. It can mobilize men, equipment and know-how to respond to any given demand for goods and services. Over time it can improve upon its own response.

But there is one thing it cannot do. It cannot guarantee that there will be just exactly the required amount of investment to ensure full employment: not too little so as to cause unemployment, nor too much so as to cause inflation. As far as total investment or money-spending power is concerned, the system is without any thermostat. For decades there may be too much investment, leading to periods of chronic inflation. For other years or decades, there may be too little investment, leading to deflation, losses, excess capacity, unemployment, and destitution.

Nor is there any "invisible hand" guaranteeing that the good years will equal the bad, or that our scientists will discover at just the right time precisely sufficient new products and processes to keep the system on an even keel. From the 1850's to the 1870's railroads were built all over the world. In the next two decades nothing quite took their place. The automobile and public utilities produced a similar revolution in the 1920's. In the 1930's plastics, air conditioning, radio, television, etc., were of trifling importance as contributing to total net investment.

Scientific progress was going on in the 1930's. Our wartime production shows that clearly. But some scientific discoveries can have a harmful effect on employment and purchasing power, both in the long run and in the short run, but especially in the latter. Again, there is no automatic principle of compensation which guarantees that technological change will produce a *sufficiently* favorable effect on purchasing power, or even any favorable effect.

In the 1950's we live in a peace that is no peace. Our government finds it necessary to spend tens of billions on national defense. At the same time private investment and consumption are booming and (as of 1951) we are already at full employment. The result is predictable: a tendency toward inflationary price rises.

Then this is one of our most important economic lessons. As far as total investment is concerned, the system is in the lap of the gods. We may be lucky or unlucky, and the only thing we can say about luck is that it is going to change. Fortunately, things need not be left to luck. We shall see that perfectly sensible public and private policies can be followed which will greatly enhance the stability and productive growth of our economic system. They cannot be expected to wipe out business fluctuations 100 per cent. This would not be the goal even if it could be achieved. But they can attempt to reduce the amplitude of wild fluctuations in prices, employment, and production—as the following chapters discuss. The next chapter will show how investment and saving determine the equilibrium level of national income. First, we must understand the important graphical relations relating consumption, saving, and income.

THE PROPENSITY-TO-CONSUME SCHEDULE

Income is the single most important determinant of consumption and saving. Poor families must spend much of their income on the necessities of life—food, shelter, and, in lesser degree, clothing. By and large, rich men can, and do, save more than poor men, not only more absolutely, but a larger percentage of their income.

In Chapter 10, we saw how people with different sized budgets spend their incomes on the various consumption items and on saving. Turn to Table 1, where the 1944 family data given in Table 1 of Chapter 10 have been re-arranged. For the moment disregard Columns (3) to (5) of this table and concentrate on consumption expenditure at each level of income.

TABLE 1. *Propensity to Consume and to Save, Urban Families, 1944*

Disposable income (after taxes)	Consumption expenditure	Marginal propensity to consume (MPC)	Net saving	Marginal propensity to save MPS = 1 − MPC
			(4) = (1) − (2)	
(1)	(2)	(3)		(5)
A. $1,000	$1,180		−$180	
		$\frac{820}{1,000} = 0.82$		0.18
B. 2,000	2,000		0	
		$\frac{700}{1,000} = 0.7$		0.3
C. 3,000	2,700		300	
		$\frac{700}{1,000} = 0.7$		0.3
D. 4,000	3,400		600	
		$\frac{600}{1,000} = 0.6$		0.4
E. 5,000	4,000		1,000	
		$\frac{500}{1,000} = 0.5$		0.5
F. 6,000	4,500		1,500	
		$\frac{500}{1,000} = 0.5$		0.5
G. 7,000	5,000		2,000	

SOURCE: Table 1, Chapter 10.

This same relation can be shown even more vividly in diagrammatic form. In Figure 1, the total of consumption expenditure in Column (2) is plotted against family disposable income of Column 1; through the resulting circles, *A, B, C, D, E, F,* and *G,* a smooth curve has been drawn. This is called the consumption schedule, or propensity-to-consume schedule, or often simply the propensity to consume. The consumption schedule is a basic, important concept whose general properties we must study.

It will help you to understand these properties if first you look at the light, 45° line also shown in Figure 1. Inasmuch as the vertical axis of consumption has been drawn to the same scale as the horizontal axis of income, any point lying on the 45° helping line has the following simple property: Its indicated consumption expenditure—measured by the vertical distance of the point from the horizontal axis—is exactly equal to 100 per cent of its indicated level of disposable income—measured by the horizontal distance of the point from the vertical axis. The reader should use his eye to verify that any point *not* on the 45° line cannot possibly be equidistant from the two axes.

The 45° line will tell us right away, therefore, whether consumption spending is equal to or greater or less than the level of income. The point on the consumption schedule where it intersects the 45° line tells us the level of disposable income at which families just break even. This break-even point is at *B*; here, consumption expenditure is exactly equal to disposable income; the family is borrowing nothing and on balance saving nothing. Similarly, *anywhere else* on the propensity-to-consume curve, the family cannot be just breaking even. To the right of point *B*, the curve lies below the 45° line; the arrows in Figure 1 show that the vertical distance (consumption expenditure) is less than the horizontal distance (disposable income). If the family is not spending all its income, then it must be saving the remainder. The 45° line tells us more than that; it enables us to find *how much* the family is saving. Net saving is measured by the distance from the propensity-to-consume curve up to the 45° line, as shown by the appropriate arrows.

Similarly, to the left of point *B*, our 45° helping line tells us that the family is for the moment somehow spending more than the income it receives. The excess of consumption over income is its "net dissaving" and is measured by the vertical distance between the two curves.

To review: When the propensity-to-consume schedule lies above the 45° line, the family is dissaving. Where the two curves meet, the family is just breaking even. Where the propensity to consume lies below the 45° line, the family is performing net positive saving. And the amount of dissaving or saving is always measured by the distance between the two curves.

This means that we can easily derive from the consumption schedule in Figure 1 a new schedule: the propensity to save. Graphically, this is shown in Figure 2. Again we show disposable income on the horizontal axis; vertically we now show what the family *does not* spend, its net saving—whether negative or positive in amount. This propensity-to-save curve comes directly from Figure 1. It is simply the distance between the 45° line and the propensity-to-consume schedule. At a point such as *A* in Figure 1, the fact that the family's savings were negative was indicated by the propensity-to-consume schedule lying above the helping line. Figure 2 shows this fact directly, and similarly for the positive savings that begin when family income pushes past point B.

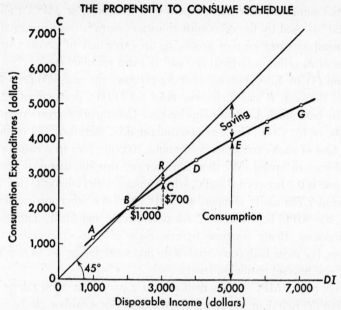

FIGURE 1. This shows how consumption depends on family income; the steepness of the consumption schedule depends on the MPC. SOURCE: Table 1.

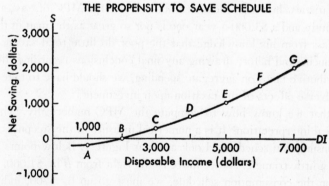

FIGURE 2. This shows how some fraction of every extra dollar of family income goes into saving. SOURCE: Table 1 and Figure 1.

The reader should check with the saving column of Table 1 to verify the correctness of the drawing.

THE MARGINAL PROPENSITY TO CONSUME

In the next chapter, we shall be attaching much importance to the *extra* amount that will be spent on consumption if people are given an *extra* dollar of income. Economists are so interested in this concept that they have given it a special name: the marginal propensity to consume, or MPC. (The word "marginal" is used by the economist to mean "extra"; thus, marginal cost is later defined as extra cost of producing an extra unit of product, marginal utility as extra utility, marginal revenue as extra revenue, etc.)

Column (3) of Table 1 shows how we compute the marginal propensity to consume. Between B and C, income rises by $1,000, going from $2,000 to $3,000. By how much does consumption rise? Consumption grows from $2,000 to $2,700, or by $700. The extra consumption is, therefore, 0.7 of the extra income. Out of each extra dollar of income, 70 cents goes to consumption and 30 cents goes to saving. We therefore can say that the marginal propensity to consume is 0.7 between B and C, which agrees with Column (3) of Table 1.

The reader can easily compute the MPC between other income levels. In Table 1, the MPC begins at 0.82 for poor people and finally falls to 0.5 at higher incomes. Being wartime figures, these give an exaggerated view of thriftiness, but most budgetary studies do find some falling off of the MPC as incomes rise beyond minimum levels.

If a rich man's MPC is less than that of a poor man, then taking dollars away from the rich man and giving them to his poor neighbor can be expected to raise the total level of consumption expenditure and to decrease the average level of thriftiness. But an important warning is in order: Careful study of budget statistics show that the difference between the MPC of, say, a $7,000-a-year family and a $3,000-a-year one is not so great as the man in the street might guess from his knowledge that the poor do little total saving and the rich do much. And before drawing any final conclusions regarding the effects of redistributive taxes on aggregate spending, we should have to take account of any adverse effects of the taxation upon investment.

Now that we know how to compute the MPC numerically, what is its geometrical interpretation? It is a numerical measure of the steepness of slope of the consumption schedule.[1] Look again at Figure 1. Below points B and C is drawn a little triangle. As we move to the right from B by $1,000, in order to stay on the consumption schedule, we must go up by $700, indicating a numerical slope of $700/$1,000, or 0.7. Now we can understand why most family consumption schedules have a slight convex curvature (viewed from above).

[1] By the numerical slope of the line XY, we always mean the numerical ratio of the length ZY to the length XZ.

THE MARGINAL PROPENSITY TO SAVE

Along with the marginal propensity to consume goes a Siamese-twin concept, the marginal propensity *to save*, or MPS. This is defined as the fraction of each extra dollar that goes to saving instead of to consumption. Why are MPC and MPS joined like Siamese twins? Since each extra dollar of income must be divided between extra consumption and extra saving, it is obvious that, if MPC is 0.7, then MPS must be 0.3. (What would MPS be if MPC were 0.6? Or 0.99?) A comparison of Columns (3) and (5) of Table 1 confirms our common-sense feeling that at any income level, MPC and MPS must always add up to exactly 1, no more and no less.

You can also verify from Figure 2 that the numerical steepness of slope of the propensity-to-save schedule is the geometrical expression of MPS. This shows that the savings schedule will always have the opposite curvature to that of the consumption schedule: as MPC falls, MPS must rise. And since every extra dollar must be divide up between extra consumption and extra saving, it follows that neither the consumption nor the savings schedule can *anywhere* have a slope as steep as the 45° line, which by definition has a slope of 1. (Remember that we are here discussing *marginal* propensities. At point *A*, for example, the family is spending more than its income; but that does not alter the fact that, at *A*, its *marginal* propensity to consume out of *extra* income is less than 1.)

THE COMMUNITY'S OVER-ALL CONSUMPTION SCHEDULE

So far we have been talking about the consumption patterns shown by families of different incomes. To study what determines national income, we are interested in a slightly different propensity-to-consume schedule. We are

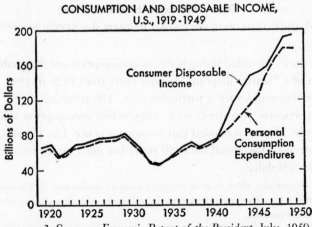

CONSUMPTION AND DISPOSABLE INCOME, U.S., 1919-1949

FIGURE 3. SOURCE: *Economic Report of the President*, July, 1950.

interested in how the total of *all* consumption spending in the United States changes as the total of our national income rises. Aggregate income is not the only factor determining aggregate consumption, but common sense and statistical experience tell us that it is one of the most important factors. Note in Figure 3 how closely consumption follows yearly disposable income; the only exceptional period is that of the war when goods were scarce and rationed and people were urged to save.

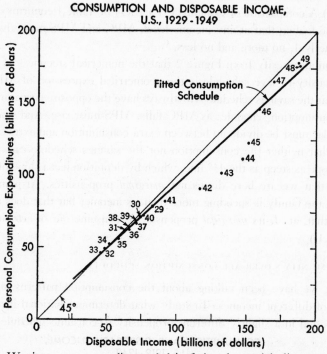

FIGURE 4. Wartime years were disregarded in fitting the straight-line propensity to consume.

Figure 4 shows the relationship between consumption and disposable income in the form of a "scatter diagram" for the years from 1929 to 1949. Each dot indicates the magnitudes for a particular year. The resulting scatter of points shows no particular curvature, so a straight-line consumption schedule has been drawn in. We are reminded that economics is not, like physics, an exact science; note how the actual data fall near, but not exactly on, the "fitted" consumption schedule.[1]

[1] So that no reader may think there is any great accuracy in this line, let the author explain that he has fitted it by stretching a black thread through the peacetime data at what appeared to be a reasonable position.

QUALIFICATIONS

We are now prepared for the theory of income determination. We have the crucially important consumption and saving schedules that will be used in the next chapter. But a few final warnings are in order.

The national consumption schedule must be in some sense an aggregation of the family schedules. Yet even if we knew that the family schedules were perfectly reliable, we should still have to know something about the distribution of income before we could get the national schedule. Thus, if the Lorenz curve of income distribution were to shift toward greater inequality, we should expect the national saving schedule to shift upward and the national consumption schedule to shift downward. (Why?)

Aside from the distribution of income, there is a second factor that must be taken into account in any attempt to relate the family and national patterns. Suppose my income were to go from $5,000 a year to $40,000 a year. Would I spend and save my money in the same way that the budget studies showed $40,000-a-year people spend their money? Not necessarily. Especially at the beginning, I would be *nouveau riche* and have different patterns of behavior.

A third reason why it is difficult to go from the family to the national consumption schedule is suggested by the expression "keeping up with the Joneses." Fifty years ago if your family had $2,000 worth of purchasing power, you would have been well-to-do and far above the break-even point of zero saving. But by 1944 many people had incomes above that level. Because man is a social animal, what he regards as necessary comforts of life depends on what he sees others consuming. So today with $2,000 of income, you would be desperately poor and unable to make ends meet. This fact that one man's consumption depends upon the incomes and consumption of others means that we cannot expect the final national pattern to be the simple sum of the separate family patterns. It also means that we must expect the consumption schedule to be shifting upward as living standards rise with each passing year and decade.

A number of other important qualifications will occur to the reader. The national consumption schedule will shift every time that prices change and total population grows. Statisticians sometimes try to allow for this by working with per capita consumption and per capita income, expressed in real terms by means of a deflating price index of the sort discussed in the last chapter.

We can think of still other reasons why the propensity-to-consume schedule might shift around. Thus, at the end of World War II, many economists made a famous wrong prediction. They neglected the fact that people came out of the war with greatly increased amounts of past liquid savings; for this and other reasons, the consumption schedule turned out to be at a higher level than many pessimistic predictions had indicated.

Again we are reminded that no social science can have great exactitude. We shall have to use tools, like the propensity-to-consume curve—or later in Part Three, curves of supply and demand—which we know are subject to error and which tend to shift through time rather than remain stable.

SUMMARY

1. Income is one of the most important determinants of consumption and saving. The propensity to consume is the schedule relating consumption and income. Because any dollar of income is either saved or consumed, the propensity-to-save schedule is the other side of the propensity-to-consume picture.

2. The consumption schedule rises with income. Below some break-even point people consume more than their income. The break-even point is depicted graphically at the point where the consumption schedule intersects a helping 45° line. To the right of the break-even point, net saving is positive and can be read from Figure 1 by measuring the vertical distance that the consumption schedule lies below the 45° line.

3. The saving schedule is almost the mirror image or Siamese twin of the consumption schedule. It, too, rises with income but usually at a much slower rate. Its indicated break-even point must, of course, be at the same income level as in Figure 1, but graphically this is recognized in Figure 2 as the point where the saving schedule intersects the horizontal axis and passes from being negative to being positive.

4. The marginal propensities to consume and to save, MPC and MPS, represent the fractions of each extra dollar of income that are, respectively, consumed and saved. Their sum is unity: MPC + MPS = 1. Geometrically they are shown by the numerical steepness of the slope of the consumption and saving schedules. Typically, there is an empirical tendency for the MPC to decline as people become richer and for the MPS to rise; this means that the consumption schedule has a slight convex curvature while the saving schedule has an opposite and equal concave curvature. It also means that redistributing incomes from higher to lower incomes has a slight tendency to increase the total spent on consumption out of any given income.

5. (a) If we knew the distribution of income for each level of disposable income, (b) if families always stuck to the same consumption-income patterns,

(*c*) if we could forget the fact that one man's consumption is influenced by the income levels of his neighbors, and (*d*) if price levels, population, corporate saving, and taxes could be neglected, then we could aggregate the family consumption schedules to get the national propensity-to-consume schedule. The statistical data suggest that total consumption expenditure follows rather closely the changes in total disposable income. But in using the propensity-to-consume concept in the next chapter's discussion of income determination, we must beware of forming an exaggerated notion of the accuracy and empirical stability of such a theoretical concept.

QUESTIONS FOR DISCUSSION

1. What are some of the reasons why people save? What are some of the forms in which they keep their savings?

2. Exactly how in Table 1 were the MPC and MPS computed? Illustrate between *A* and *B*. Is marginal a good name for extra? Explain why MPC + MPS = 1.

3. I spend all my income on consumption. Draw my consumption and saving schedules.

4. Do you think the break-even point is the same in New York and in Mississippi? What do you think is the current break-even point in your community? List a number of ways a person can incur negative net saving for a while.

5. "Along the consumption schedule, income always changes more than does consumption." Why? Show that this is even more true for movements along the saving schedule.

6. What factors must be taken into consideration if we want to aggregate family budgetary propensity-to-consume schedules to arrive at a national propensity-to-consume schedule? What would happen to the amount consumed out of 200 billion dollars of national income if the degree of inequality of income were increased? To the amount saved? What if total taxes out of the 200 billion dollars were to increase? If people were to have more government bonds and bank deposits, how would that affect saving out of 200 billion dollars of national income?

Chapter 13: THE THEORY OF

INCOME DETERMINATION

ALL modern economists are agreed that the important factor in causing income and employment to fluctuate is investment. The preceding chapter has given us the tools to show how an increase in investment will generate an increase in money income that is even bigger than itself. Whether we are to

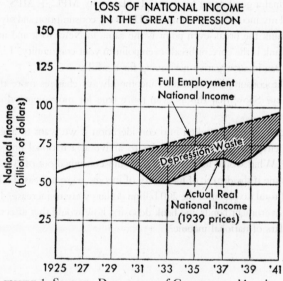

**LOSS OF NATIONAL INCOME
IN THE GREAT DEPRESSION**

FIGURE 1. SOURCE: Department of Commerce, old series.

face a situation of inflationary bidding up of prices or shall live in a frigid state of mass unemployment depends, we shall see, upon the level of investment.

There is no need to emphasize the importance of the problem of income determination. For the last 10 years, nations everywhere have been plagued by problems connected with too high general money demand, shortages, and price increases. But memories are short, and there is danger that we shall forget the tremendous costs that were associated with the mass unemployment of the prewar great depression. Figure 1 reminds us that the cost of that depression—as measured in terms of the value of production wasted through unemployment of men and machines—ran to around 300 billion dollars. It is scarcely an exaggeration to say that the economic costs of that depression were of the same general magnitude as the costs of all the economic resources which had to be used up in World War II itself.

A. DETERMINATION OF THE EQUILIBRIUM LEVEL OF INCOME

Figures 2a and 2b give a simplified picture of the propensity-to-consume and propensity-to-save schedules for the community. As discussed in the preceding chapter, they are drawn up on the basis of our knowledge of the thriftiness of different families, the distribution of incomes between families, and so forth. At the beginning, we shall make the further simplifying assumptions that there are no taxes or undistributed corporate profits to worry about; hence, we do not have to worry about any distinction between national income and disposable income. Also, we shall initially neglect any changes in the price level.

HOW INCOME IS DETERMINED AT THE LEVEL WHERE SAVING AND INVESTMENT SCHEDULES INTERSECT

We have seen that saving and investment are dependent on quite different factors: that saving tends to depend in a "passive" way upon income while volatile investment depends upon "autonomous" factors of dynamic growth. For simplicity, let us first suppose that investment opportunities are such that net investment would be exactly 10 billion dollars per year regardless of the level of national income. This means that, if we were to draw a schedule of investment against national income, it would have to be a *horizontal* line, always the same distance above the horizontal axis. In Figure 3, this simplified investment schedule is labeled *II* to distinguish it from the *SS* saving schedule.

The saving and investment schedules intersect at a level of national income equal to the distance *OM*. This intersection of the *saving and investment schedules is the equilibrium toward which income will gravitate.* Under our assumed conditions, no other level of income can perpetuate itself. The remaining pages of Section A of this chapter are devoted to the single task of

THE CONSUMPTION AND SAVING SCHEDULES

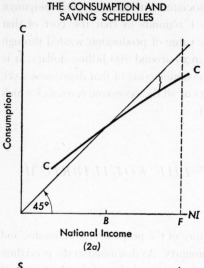

FIGURES 2a and 2b. The propensity-to-consume and propensity-to-save schedules for the community. The vertical distances shown by brackets are equal.

explaining this important truth.

Let us see why the equilibrium income must eventually be at E, the point of intersection between the investment and saving schedules. First, suppose income were higher than the intersection point. Then investment spending would be *less* than what people would want to save; total spending on consumption plus investment would then add up to less than the cost of national output; businessmen would be unable to sell enough to justify their current level of output. So they would contract their production and lay workers off. Only by the time national income had dropped back to the equilibrium level would people have such small incomes as to be finally *willing to save exactly what businessmen are willing to invest.* Income would not thereafter have to fall any further; no additional men would have to join the ranks of the unemployed.

Similarly, it can be shown that income will not permanently remain below the equilibrium level where the saving that people want to do is matched by

HOW SAVING AND INVESTMENT DETERMINE INCOME

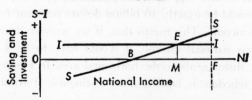

FIGURE 3. The level of income is determined by the intersection of II with SS.

continuing profitable investment opportunities. For example, suppose income were temporarily so small that businesses wanted to invest *more* than people were willing to save. Then total spending on consumption and investment would be "tending" to exceed the costs of national income earned by factors for producing the national product. Profits would be buoyant; so entrepreneurs would be hiring more men and causing national income to rise. How far would income tend to rise? Up to the equilibrium intersection point, at which saving and investment would be just in balance and income would have a tendency neither to rise nor fall.

INCOME DETERMINATION BY CONSUMPTION AND INVESTMENT

There is a second way of showing how income is determined, other than by the intersection of the saving and investment schedules. The final result is exactly the same, but our understanding and confidence in the theory of income determination will be increased if we work through this second approach. This second approach is called the consumption-plus-investment rather than the saving-investment approach. It concentrates on the question: Is the total spending—on consumption plus investment—as large as the total costs of national output? If it is less, production will drop; if more, production will rise; if total spending exactly equals all costs of output (including "normal profits"), then an equilibrium level of national income and employment can persist. To see this graphically, we must

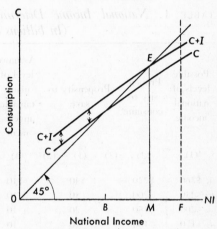

HOW CONSUMPTION AND INVESTMENT
DETERMINE INCOME

FIGURE 4. This is an alternative to Figure 3. Adding investment to consumption gives the same result as saving-and-investment analysis.

add the investment schedule on top of the consumption schedule. The resulting equilibrium level of income shown in Figure 4 will be at the intersection of the 45° line with this new $C + I$ schedule.

Why does this intersection determine the equilibrium level of national income? Because along the 45° line, the level of national income as recorded on the horizontal axis is exactly equal to the sum of the vertical distances representing the amount of consumption plus investment expenditure that people are willing to make. This shows that at E, and only at E, businesses are getting back just enough to justify their continuing that level of national product.

Needless to say, this must give us exactly the same income as will the intersection of saving and investment. The reader should compare Figures 3 and

4 and satisfy himself that it is not an accident for these two different kinds of intersection to give exactly the same level of national income.

The two methods of showing national income determination are really identical, each being a different aspect of the same thing. Some people like to speak of income as determined by consumption plus investment expenditure; others like to state income determination in terms of saving and investment.

ARITHMETICAL DEMONSTRATION OF INCOME DETERMINATION: A THIRD RESTATE-
MENT

A thoughtful reader may still not be satisfied with his comprehension of *why* the equilibrium level of income will have to be at the intersection of the saving and investment schedules. What forces push income to that level and no other?

TABLE 1. *National Income Determination by Saving and Investment*
(In billions of dollars)

Possible levels of national income	Propensity to consume	Propensity to save	Assumed level of maintainable investment	Paid out by businesses	Received back by businesses, C + I	Resulting tendency of of income
(1)	(2)	(3) = (1) − (2)	(4)	(5) = (1)	(6) = (2) + (4)	(7)
a. $260	$220	$40	$10	$260 >	$230	↓Contraction
b. 230	200	30	10	230 >	210	↓Contraction
c. 200	180	20	10	200 >	190	↓Contraction
d. 170	160	10	10	170 =	170	↕Equilibrium
e. 140	140	0	10	140 <	150	↑Expansion
f. 110	120	−10	10	110 <	130	↑Expansion

An arithmetic example may help to clinch his grasp of this important matter. In Table 1, an especially simple pattern of the propensity to save against national income has been recorded. The break-even level of income where the nation is too poor to do any net saving on balance is assumed to be 140 billion dollars. Each change of national income of 30 billion dollars is assumed to lead to a 10-billion-dollar change in saving and a 20-billion-dollar change in consumption; in other words, MPC is assumed to be constant and exactly equal to $\frac{2}{3}$ with MPS = $\frac{1}{3}$. For this reason, the saving propensity schedule, SS, in Figure 5 takes on the especially simple form of a perfectly straight line.

What shall we assume about investment? For simplicity, let us suppose again that the only level of investment that can be maintained indefinitely is exactly 10 billion dollars, as shown in Column (4) of Table 1.

Now, Columns (5) and (6) are the crucial ones. Column (5) shows how much money business firms are *paying out* in costs of production to wage earners, interest-, rent-, and profit-receivers. This is nothing but national income of Column (1) copied once again into Column (5), because our repeated discussions of Chapter 11 showed that total cost payments represent one way of looking at income.

DEMONSTRATION THAT INCOME MOVES TOWARD EQUILIBRIUM

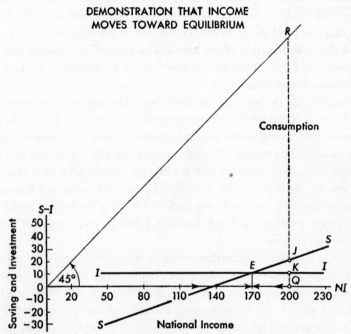

FIGURE 5. The converging arrows show how income moves to the equilibrium intersection. SOURCE: Table 1.

Column (6), on the other hand, shows what business firms would be *getting back* in the form of consumption sales plus investment (or net increase in their assets as shown on their consolidated balance sheets).

When business firms as a whole are paying out more than they get back, they will then contract their operations and national income will tend to fall. When they are getting back more than they are paying out, they will increase their production, and national income will rise. Only when the level of scheduled saving is exactly equal to scheduled investment will business firms continue to be in aggregative equilibrium. Their sales will then be just enough to justify continuing their current level of aggregate output, so national income will neither expand nor contract.

This same story is shown in Figure 5. National income can be read in either of two ways: on the horizontal axis, or (from the nature of a 45° line) as the equivalent vertical distance from that axis up to the helping 45° line. The line *SS* represents the saving schedule; the line *II* represents the scheduled level of investment that can be maintained over time. Consumption can also be seen on the figure. Since income not saved is consumed, consumption is always the vertical distance between the saving schedule and the 45° line.

Now we can use Figure 5 to confirm what has just been shown by the arithmetic of Table 1. No level of income can long persist if it is higher than the equilibrium level given by the saving and investment intersection at 170 billion dollars. To the right of the intersection point *E*, the *amount paid out* by businesses would exceed the *amount received back* by businesses in the form of consumption plus investment.

Graphically this is shown by the following: The amount continuously paid out by business is the whole distance up to the 45° line, *e.g.*, from *Q* to *R*; but the amount that would continuously be received back by business would be only the sum of investment *QK* and consumption *JR*. There is a gap of *JK*. Businesses face a real dilemma. For a while they could keep their prices high and let unsold goods pile up on their shelves, but that would not represent an equilibrium situation and could not persist. Or for a while they could lower prices on their goods and sell at below cost, but that, too, would not represent an equilibrium situation.

Thus, it is completely clear that income cannot permanently be maintained higher than the equilibrium level—*where the amount of saving that people want to do is matched by the amount of investment businessmen are willing to maintain.* A persistent gap of the *JK* type must, through attempts to cut down losses and excessive inventories, result in a contraction of employment and national income back toward the equilibrium point at which there is no gap. Therefore, the arrow near *Q* points leftward back toward the equilibrium level.

The reader should go through a similar argument to show why income will tend to rise from any place to the left of the equilibrium-intersection level. Indicate on the diagram the relation between what business pays out and what it receives back. Show that there will be a favorable gap: Businesses will either be selling so much as to be depleting inventories on their shelves, or they will be temporarily raising their prices and earning extra profits. In either case, they will be tempted to expand their employment and production. Draw in the required arrow to show the resulting expansion of income back toward the equilibrium level.

THE SIMPLE THEORY OF INCOME DETERMINATION RESTATED

Figure 6 pulls together in a simplified way the main elements of income determination. Without saving and investment, there would be a circular flow of income between business and the public: business pays out (in the upper pipe) wages, interest, rents, and profits to the public in return for the services of labor and property; and in the lower pipe the public pays consumption funds to business in return for goods and services.

To be realistic, we must recognize that the public will wish to save some of its income, as shown in the spigot at Z. Therefore, business firms cannot expect their consumption sales to be as large as the total of wages, interest, rents, and profits.

HOW INVESTMENT DETERMINES INCOME

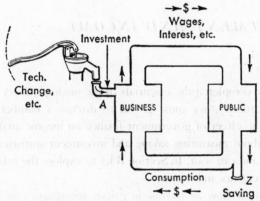

FIGURE 6. Technological change, population growth, and other dynamic factors keep the investment pump handle going. Income rises and falls with changes in investment, its equilibrium level, at any time, being realized only when intended saving at Z matches intended investment at A.

Some monetary cranks think that this saving necessarily means unemployment and depression. Such a view is simply incorrect. If there happen to be profitable investment opportunities, business firms will be paying out wages, interest, and other costs in part for new investment goods rather than 100 per cent for consumption goods. Hence, to continue to be happy, business needs to receive back in consumption sales only *part* of the total income paid out to the public—only that part which involves the cost of current consumption goods. The saving of the public will do no harm to national income so long as it is not greater than what business can profitably invest.

In Figure 6, investment is shown being pumped into the income stream at A. The handle of the pump is being moved by (1) technological invention, (2) population growth, and (3) other dynamic factors. When the investment pump is going at a rapid pace, national income is high and reaches its equilibrium rate when the saving at Z just balances the investment at A.[1]

[1] Similar, but more complicated, hydraulic models have actually been built in England to

This demonstrates that the pessimistic monetary cranks who think that saving is always disastrous are plain wrong. But there is also a second school of monetary cranks: they go to the opposite extreme and insist that saving and investment can never cause income to be too high or too low. They make the fatal error of rigidly connecting up the pipe at Z with the pipe at A. Roomfuls of books have been written on this subject, but it is only in the last few decades that economists have learned how to separate out the truth and falsity of both extreme viewpoints. The next 100 pages deal with this important question, in its relation to income, banking and business cycle policy.

B. *INVESTMENT AND INCOME*

THE "MULTIPLIER"

We have now completed the essentials of the modern theory of income determination. Naturally, we must go on to discuss a number of important qualifications: the effect of government finance on income analysis, and how you would go about measuring saving and investment statistically. But these are refinements and can wait. In Section B let us explore the relations between investment movements and income.

Let us first show how *an increase in private investment will cause income to expand*, and a *decrease in investment will cause it to contract*. This is not a very surprising result. After all, we have learned that investment is one part of net national product; when one of the parts increases in value, we should naturally expect the whole to increase in value.

That is only part of the study. Our theory of income determination gives us a much more striking result. Modern income analysis shows that an increase in net investment will increase national income by a multiplied amount—by an amount greater than itself! Investment dollars are high-powered, double-duty dollars, so to speak.

This amplified effect of investment on income is called the "multiplier" doctrine; the word "multiplier" itself is used for *the numerical coefficient showing how great an increase in income results from each increase in investment.* Some examples will make this terminology clear. If an increase of investment of 5 billion dollars causes an increase of income of 15 billion dollars, then the multiplier is 3. If the increase in income were 20 billion dollars, then the multi-

---

illustrate to students at the London School of Economics and Leeds University the nature of income determination. A.W. PHILLIPS, "Mechanical Models in Economic Dynamics," *Economica*, August, 1950, pp. 283–305.

plier would be 4. The multiplier is the number by which the change in investment must be amplified (or multiplied) in order to get the resulting change in income.

No proof has yet been presented to show that the multiplier will be greater than 1. But using ordinary common sense, we can begin to see why, when I hire unemployed resources to build a $1,000 garage, there will be a secondary expansion of national income and production, over and above my primary investment. My carpenters and lumber producers will get an extra $1,000 of income. But that is not the end of the story. If they all have a marginal propensity to consume of $\frac{2}{3}$, they will now spend $666.67 on new consumption goods. The producers of these goods will now have an extra income of $666.67. If their MPC is also $\frac{2}{3}$, they in turn will spend $444.44, or $\frac{2}{3}$ of $666.67 (or $\frac{2}{3}$ of $\frac{2}{3}$ of $1,000). So the process will go on, with each new round of spending being $\frac{2}{3}$ of the previous round.

Thus a whole endless chain of secondary consumption respending is set up by my primary $1,000 of investment spending. But it is a dwindling chain, and it all adds up to a finite amount. Either by grade-school arithmetic or high-school geometric progression,[1] we get

$$
\left.
\begin{array}{c}
\$1,000.00 \\
+ \\
666.67 \\
+ \\
444.44 \\
+ \\
295.29 \\
+ \\
197.53 \\
+ \\
\cdots
\end{array}
\right\}
=
\left\{
\begin{array}{c}
1 \times \$1,000 \\
+ \\
\frac{2}{3} \times \$1,000 \\
+ \\
\left(\frac{2}{3}\right)^2 \times \$1,000 \\
+ \\
\left(\frac{2}{3}\right)^3 \times \$1,000 \\
+ \\
\left(\frac{2}{3}\right)^4 \times \$1,000 \\
+ \\
\cdots
\end{array}
\right.
$$

$$
\begin{array}{c}
\$2,999.9999 \\
\text{or} \\
\$3,000
\end{array}
\qquad
\frac{1}{1 - \frac{2}{3}} \times \$1,000 \text{ or } 3 \times \$1,000
$$

[1] The formula for an infinite geometric progression is:

$$
1 + r + r^2 + r^3 + \ldots + r^n + \ldots = \frac{1}{1 - r},
$$

as long as r is less than 1 in absolute value.

This shows that, with an MPC of $\frac{2}{3}$, the multiplier must be 3, consisting of the 1 of primary investment plus 2 extra of secondary consumption responding.

The same arithmetic would give a multiplier of 4 if the MPC were $\frac{3}{4}$. (Hint: What does $1 + \frac{3}{4} + (\frac{3}{4})^2 + (\frac{3}{4})^3 + \cdots$ finally add up to?) If the MPC were $\frac{1}{2}$, the multiplier would be 2. The size of the multiplier seems to depend upon how large the MPC is. Or it can be expressed in terms of the twin concept, the MPS. If the MPS were $\frac{1}{4}$, the MPC would be $\frac{3}{4}$, and the multiplier would be 4. If the MPS were $\frac{1}{3}$, the multiplier would be 3. If the MPS were $1/X$, the multiplier would be X.

By this time the reader will guess that the multiplier is always the upside-down or "reciprocal" of the marginal propensity to save. Our general multiplier formula is always

$$\text{Change in income} = \frac{1}{\text{MPS}} \times \text{change in investment}$$

$$= \frac{1}{1 - \text{MPC}} \times \text{change in investment}$$

In other words, the greater the extra consumption spending, the greater the multiplier. The greater the "leakage" into extra saving at each round of spending, the smaller the final multiplier.

GRAPHICAL PICTURE OF THE MULTIPLIER

Up to this point, we have discussed the multiplier in terms of common sense and arithmetic. Will our saving-investment analysis of income give us

MULTIPLIER EFFECTS OF INVESTMENT ON INCOME

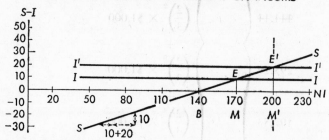

FIGURE 7. Investment has a primary expansionary effect on income; in addition, because of consumption responding, it has a secondary effect as well.

the same result? The answer must, of course, be "yes." Suppose the MPS is $\frac{1}{3}$ and now a new series of inventions comes along and gives rise to an extra 10 billion dollars of continuing investment opportunities, over and above our previous 10 billion dollars. Then the increase in investment should raise national income from 170 billion to 200 billion dollars if the multiplier is correctly given by our previous analysis.

Figure 7 confirms this result. Our old investment schedule *II* is shifted upward by 10 billion dollars to the new level *I'I'*. The new intersection point is *E'*. Lo and behold, the increase in income is exactly three times as much as the increase in investment. This is because a MPS of only ⅓ means a relatively flat *SS* saving schedule. As the dotted arrows show, the horizontal income distance is always three times as great as the "primary" vertical saving-investment distance, the discrepancy being equal to the secondary "consumption responding."

In short, income must rise enough to bring out a volume of voluntary saving equal to the new investment. With a MPS of ⅓, income has to rise by how much in order to bring out 10 billion dollars of new saving?[1] By exactly 30 billion dollars.

INDUCED INVESTMENT AND THE PARADOX OF THRIFT

Until now we have always treated net investment as an autonomous element, absolutely independent of national income. All our investment schedules have been drawn as horizontal lines, their level being always the same regardless of income. This simplification can now be relaxed.

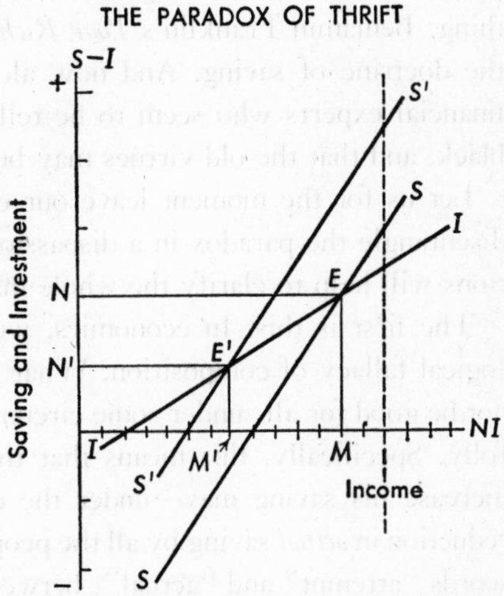

Any practical businessman will tell you that he is more likely to add to his plant or equipment if his sales are high relative to his plant capacity. In the short run (before businessmen have had time to adjust their capital stock to a changed plateau of income), it is reasonable for us to draw the *I-I* schedule in Figure 8 as a rising curve. *An increase in national income may induce a higher level of net investment.*

As before, the equilibrium level of (maintainable) national income is given by the intersection of the investment and saving schedules; or in

THE PARADOX OF THRIFT

FIGURE 8. The investment schedule is now a rising one because of investment induced by income changes. An increase in the desire to save (from *SS* to *S'S'*) results in less realized saving and investment because income is lowered.

the first instance by the point *E* in Figure 8. So long as the *SS* curve always cuts the *I-I* curve from below, busi-

[1] Table 1 will also verify this answer. In Column (4), we now have 20 billion dollars instead of 10 billion dollars of investment. The new equilibrium level of income now shifts to the *c* row (200 billion dollars income) from the old equilibrium level in the *d* row (170 billion dollars).

nessmen's action will always bring the economic system back to the equilibrium level.[1]

Induced investment means that anything increasing national income is likely to be good for the capital-goods industries; anything hurting national income is likely to be bad for those industries. This throws a new spotlight on the age-old question of thrift versus consumption. It shows that an increased desire to consume—which is another way of looking at a decreased desire to save—is likely to boost business sales and increase investment. An increase in thriftiness, on the other hand, is likely to reduce inflationary pressure in times of booming incomes; but in time of depression, it is likely to make the depression worse and reduce the amount of actual net capital formation in the community. *High consumption and high investment then go hand in hand rather than being competing.*

This surprising result is sometimes called the "paradox of thrift." It is a paradox because in kindergarten we are all taught that thrift is *always* a good thing. Benjamin Franklin's *Poor Richard's Almanac* never tired of preaching the doctrine of saving. And now along comes a new generation of alleged financial experts who seem to be telling us that black is white and white is black, and that the old virtues may be modern sins.

Let us for the moment leave our cherished beliefs to the side, and try to disentangle the paradox in a dispassionate, scientific manner. Two considerations will help to clarify the whole matter.

The first is this. In economics, we must always be on guard against the logical fallacy of composition. What is good for each person separately need not be good for all; under some circumstances, private prudence may be social folly. Specifically, this means that the *attempt* of each and every person to increase his saving may—under the conditions to be described—result in a reduction in *actual* saving by all the people in the community. Note the italicized words "attempt" and "actual"; between them there may be a world of difference if people find themselves thrown out of jobs and with lowered incomes.

The second clue to the paradox of thrift lies in the question of whether or not national income is at a depression level. If we were at full employment, then obviously the more of our national product that we devoted to current consumption, the less would be available for capital formation. If output could be assumed to be always at its maximum, then the old-fashioned doctrine of thrift

[1] If the two curves crossed in the opposite way, we should have unstable equilibrium, and the economy would rush away—in either direction—from the intersection neighborhood. A physical analogy may be suggestive: An egg on its side is in stable equilibrium; when given a slight disturbance, it returns to equilibrium. An egg on its tip is in unstable equilibrium; a light touch and it topples. Note to the reader: In Figure 8 the vertical scale has been enlarged so that the eye can clearly see the effect of induced investment.

would be absolutely correct—correct, be it noted, from both the individual and the social standpoints. In primitive agricultural communities, such as the American colonies of Franklin's day, there was truth in Franklin's prescription. The same was true during World Wars I and II, and it becomes true during periods of inflation and boom: if people will become more thrifty, then less consumption will mean more investment.

But according to the statistical records, full employment and inflationary conditions have occurred only occasionally in our recent history. Much of the time there was some wastage of resources, some unemployment, some insufficiency of demand, investment, and purchasing power. When this is the case, everything goes into reverse. What once was a social virtue may then become a social vice. What is true for the individual—that extra thriftiness means increased saving and wealth—may then become completely untrue for the community as a whole.

Under conditions of unemployment, the *attempt to save* may result in *less*, not more, saving. The individual who saves cuts down on his consumption. He passes on less purchasing power than before. Therefore, someone else's income is reduced. For one man's outgo is another man's income. If one individual succeeds in saving more, it is because someone else is forced to dissave. If one individual succeeds in hoarding more money, someone else must do without. If all individuals try to hoard, they cannot all succeed in doing so, but they can force down the velocity of circulation of money—and national income.

Thus, when there is unemployment, consumption and investment are complementary, not competitive. What helps one helps the other. The attempt to cut down on consumption (to save) only results in a reduction of income until everyone feels poor enough no longer to try to save more than can be invested. Moreover, at lower levels of income, less and not more capital goods will be needed. Therefore, *investment will actually be less*.

Let us clinch our common-sense understanding of this paradox by turning to the income analysis chart of Figure 8. An increase in thriftiness or the desire to save will shift the SS curve upward to S'S'. Note that the new intersection, E', is now at a lower level of income. Because of induced *dis*investment, the drop in income will also mean smaller investment. Thus both income and investment have actually decreased. The attempt to save more in depression times has resulted in less actual saving!

If true, this is an important lesson. Never again can people be urged in time of depression to tighten their belts, to save more in order to restore prosperity. The result will be just the reverse—a worsening of the vicious deflationary spiral.

What becomes of the argument that wealthy people are needed to provide saving, that inequality of the distribution of income is needed to push up the saving schedule? We see it then go into reverse. An economic lobbyist to the capital goods industries would, if he has their selfish interests at heart, advocate less thriftiness in depressed times, so that the consumption schedule will be pushed upward, and so that attempts to save—which then really lead only to decreases in income—will be discouraged. For only then will investment and sales of heavy capital goods flourish.[1]

THE DEFLATIONARY GAP

The multiplier is a two-edged sword. It will cut for you or against you. It will amplify new investment as we have seen. But it will also amplify downward any decrease in investment. Thus, if investment opportunities drop by 10 billion dollars in our earlier examples, then national income will have to fall by three times as much—by 30 billion dollars. If net investment drops away to zero, income will have to fall down to the break-even point where the community is made poor enough to stop all net savings.

This shows that there may be nothing particularly good about what we have called the equilibrium level of national income. If investment is low, the equilibrium level of income will involve much unemployment and wastage of national resources. The only level of national income that we are entitled to regard as a desirable goal is that near to full employment. But we shall end up at such a level of high employment only if investment opportunities happen to be as large as full-employment saving.

Unless this full-employment saving is "offset" by private investment (or by governmental policies), the nation cannot continue to enjoy full employment. There is then said to be a "deflationary gap," the size of this gap being measured by the deficiency of investment compared with full-employment saving.

We can picture the deflationary gap in Figure 3 as the vertical distance between the saving and investment schedules at the full-employment level of income, F. Or, as in Figure 9, we can picture the deflationary gap on a consumption-plus-investment graph. (For the present, ignore completely the top line in Figure 9, labeled $C' + I'$; this refers to a different situation we are to discuss later.) Suppose that 250 billion dollars represents the full-employment

---

[1] We have seen that this line of argument does not apply in conditions of full employment. It also requires some slight modifications to allow for the fact that thriftiness, by lowering income, may also lower interest rates and promote investment, or it may depress wages and prices and thereby increase the real purchasing power of people's money holdings enough to destroy their initial thriftiness. In the author's opinion, these qualifications are rather unimportant in time of depression.

income. Suppose that, at this income, the scheduled total of $C + I$ adds up only to 245 billion dollars, as shown at G. This leaves a 5-billion-dollar deflationary gap between G and F. Since we obviously cannot then remain at full employment, what will happen? Will income drop by only 5 billion dollars? Clearly not. It must drop by some greater multiple of the original deflationary gap. If each dollar of reduced income results in a cut of $\$\frac{2}{3}$ in consumption spending, income will have to fall until it has dropped three times as much as the original deflationary gap. (See Figure 9's point E.)

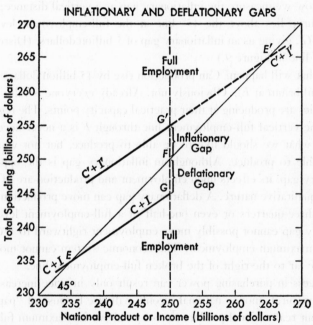

INFLATIONARY AND DEFLATIONARY GAPS

FIGURE 9. Between G and F, we have a deflationary gap because of the 5-billion-dollar deficiency of $C + I$. From F to G' we have an equal inflationary gap because of excessive $C' + I'$ over what can be produced at full employment. (Warning: The deflationary and inflationary gaps are two different, although comparable, situations.)

What can be done about this? If we continue to leave the government out of the picture, we must have either an increase in investment or an increase in consumption. By how much must the level of investment or of the consumption schedule shift upward if full employment is to be restored? By the full 15 billion dollars of needed income? Surely not. Because of the multiplier, to wipe out a deflationary gap, the $C + I$ schedule need shift upward only by the amount of the gap itself, and not by any multiple of the gap.

Before turning to the inflationary gap, let us note one thing our graph has taught us. Earlier, we saw that investment dollars are high-powered dollars which have multiple effects on income. Now we realize that upward shifts in the consumption schedule have the same high-powered effects on income. It is the aggregate of $C + I$ that determines aggregate spending.

THE PROCESS OF PRICE INFLATION

Instead of a deflationary gap, we may have an inflationary gap. If investment tends to be greater than full-employment saving, then more goods will be demanded of business than it can produce and prices will begin to rise. Figure 9 shows how we measure the inflationary gap as a vertical distance: The new $C' + I'$ curve lies above the 45° line at the full-employment level by the distance FG', giving us an inflationary gap of 5 billion dollars. (Disregard now the $C + I$ line in Figure 9.)

Now what will happen? Can production rise by 15 billion dollars to give us a new equilibrium at E'? Obviously not. Already everyone is fully employed and factories are producing at their practical capacity points. The region to the right of the vertical full-employment line through F is a never-never land. It shows us what we should like to be able to produce, but not what we are actually able to produce. Although an inflationary gap is the opposite of a deflationary gap, its effects upon employment and production are of a slightly different qualitative nature. A deflationary gap can move production leftward, down to three-quarters or even one-half of a full-employment level. But an inflationary gap cannot possibly move employment rightward to 150 per cent of full or maximum employment. The economic system cannot move in real terms very far to the right of the broken full-employment line.

The excess in purchasing power can result only in price increases and an inflationary spiral; money national income will rise because of "paper" price changes, but real national product cannot go above its maximum full-employment level. Unfortunately, the upward movement of prices will continue for as long as there is an inflationary gap,[1] *i.e.*, until we are lucky enough for investment or consumption demand to fall off, or smart enough as a nation to adopt corrective policies that will wipe out the inflationary gap.

Far from being "depression economics," modern income analysis has many of its most important applications in connection with the process of inflation and what can be done about it. During and after World War II, the concept

---

[1] The process does not end with higher prices. The new higher price level will not equilibrate total supply and demand once and for all. On the contrary, since the higher prices received by businesses become in turn somebody's income—that of worker or property owner—demand again shifts upward and prices must continue to rise. Attempts of labor to secure higher wages as compensation for the soaring cost of living may only cause the inflationary spiral to zoom at a dizzier speed.

of the inflationary gap was indispensable in indicating the quantitative magnitude of taxation needed to keep decontrolled prices from rising; and without understanding the rudiments of income analysis, we shall not be able in the years ahead to follow the important economic issues discussed in Congress and the public press.[1]

C. FISCAL POLICY IN INCOME DETERMINATION

When there is a large inflationary or deflationary gap, the government is called upon to do something about the price rise or the widespread unemployment. Tax and government expenditure policies will change the equilibrium level of income. So we must explicitly introduce government fiscal policy into the picture to see exactly how income determination is affected.

It will simplify our task if in the beginning we analyze the effects of government expenditure with taxes held constant. With taxes in the picture, no longer can we ignore the distinction between disposable income, national income, and net national product. From now on all our charts will carry NNP, or net national product, on their axes. This is because we are interested in the total of employment and product, whether of a private or public nature.

In Chapter 11 we learned that net national product consists of three, rather than two, parts; namely,

$$\text{NNP} = \text{consumption expenditure} + \text{private net investment} + \text{government expenditure on goods and services}$$
$$= C + I + G$$

Therefore, on our 45°-line diagram in Figure 10, we must superimpose upon the consumption schedule not only private investment but also government expenditure G. This is because public road building is financially no different from private railroad building and collective consumption expenditure involved

---

[1] The post-Korean defense program is an example. With American and European governments spending more on arms, many people have advocated closing the resulting inflationary gap of n billion dollars by means of increased output. This is all to the good; it will probably help if the full-employment line in Figure 9 shifts rightward. But will an increase in product equal to the inflationary gap of n billion dollars be sufficient to "close the gap"? Examination of E' in Figure 9 shows that output will have to rise *by a multiple of the gap* if it is to be closed in this way alone.

in maintaining a free public library has the same effect upon jobs as private consumption expenditure for movies or rental libraries.

We end up with the $C + I + G$ schedule showing the amount of total spending forthcoming at each level of NNP. We now must go to the inter-section with the 45° line to read off the equilibrium level of national prod-uct. At this equilibrium NNP level, the total amount the nation wants to spend on all goods is just equal in value to their full costs of produc-tion.

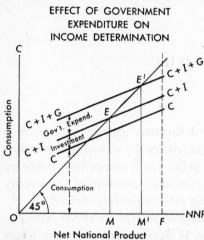

EFFECT OF GOVERNMENT EXPENDITURE ON INCOME DETERMINATION

FIGURE 10. An increase in government expenditure, with no increase in taxes, has multiplier effects on income just like private investment. On top of the con-sumption schedule, we must add the other two components of net national product, namely, private investment, I, and govern-ment expenditure on goods and services, G.

Figure 10 shows that government expenditure, taken by itself and dis-regarding taxes, has a multiplier effect upon income just like that of private investment. The reason is, of course, that a chain of consumption respend-ing is set into motion by the road builders, librarians, and other people who receive primary income from the government.[1]

TAXATION AND EQUILIBRIUM INCOME

Now let us turn to the depressing effects of taxes on the equilibrium NNP level. Without graphs, our com-mon sense tells us what must happen when the government (1) takes away more money from us in taxes while (2) at the same time holding its expenditure constant. Extra taxes will mean we have lower real disposable incomes, and lower disposable incomes mean we shall cut down on our consumption spending. Obviously, if investment and govern-

---

[1] Our saving-investment diagram will give the same answer as the 45°-line diagram. The increase in government expenditure means an equivalent increase in the government deficit if taxes have not been increased. Net saving must always equal private investment + govern-ment deficit. Therefore, we add the deficit on top of the II curve and get our new greater equilibrium level of national income at the intersection with the SS curve. In more advanced discussions, we could employ Figure 10 to show how induced investment or government ex-penditure (i.e., induced by a changed level of income) will enter into the multiplier. The final change in income resulting from a unit upward shift in the $C + I + G$ schedule will always turn out to be $1 \div (1 - K)$ where K is the slope of the $C + I + G$ schedule and might be called the "marginal propensity to spend."

ment expenditure remain the same, a reduction in consumption spending will then reduce net national product and employment; or if we already were having an inflationary gap, the new taxes will help close the gap and wipe out excessive inflationary price increases.

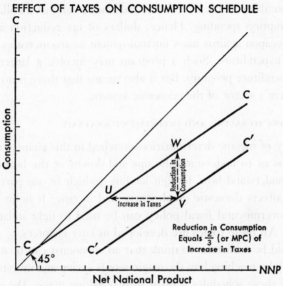

EFFECT OF TAXES ON CONSUMPTION SCHEDULE

FIGURE 11. Taxes shift CC downward to $C'C'$. Because part of the extra dollars go to saving, the cut in consumption WV is less than the new taxes UV.

Our graphs confirm this reasoning: $I + G$ is unchanged, and the increase in taxes will shift the consumption schedule downward; so in all, the $C + I + G$ schedule will shift downward, and its new intersection with the crucial 45° line must definitely be at a lower equilibrium level of net national product.

Figure 11 shows how tax receipts shift the CC schedule downward.[1] Suppose people have an MPC of about ⅔; new taxes of 15 billion dollars now causes their disposable income to fall 15 billion dollars below NNP. Will consumption fall by 15 billion? No. With an MPC of ⅔, consumption will fall by only 10 billion dollars; personal saving will fall the remaining 5 billion.

Now we know something that common sense did not immediately tell us. To offset a 10-billion-dollar upward shift in $I + G$, we must increase tax collections by more than 10 billion dollars. This means that (1) when increased government defense spending is added onto a full-employment economy with a balanced budget, then (2) taxes will probably have to be increased by

[1] The shift of CC in Figure 11 can be regarded either as a fall or as a movement to the right. The rightward movement equals the full amount of the tax. Why? Because we must subtract the full tax from the NNP at V to get its associated disposable income and consumption, as shown at U.

more than enough to balance the budget if we are really determined to avoid an inflationary gap.

We can easily reverse the above analysis to explain why tax reductions help to fight a bad depression. Each dollar of tax reduction leads to an increase in people's disposable income by a dollar and leads to almost a dollar increase in initial consumption spending. Hence, dollars of tax reduction are almost as powerful a weapon against mass unemployment as are increases in dollars of government expenditure. Such a program may involve a larger deficit than would an expenditure program. But it also means that there is no expansion of the government's sector of the economic system.

QUALIFICATIONS TO SAVING AND INVESTMENT ANALYSIS

The theory of income determination sketched in this chapter is a powerful tool.[1] It helps us to understand the ups and downs of the business cycle. It helps us to understand how foreign lending (which is one part of total net investment) affects domestic employment and income. It helps us to understand how governmental fiscal policy can be used to fight inflation and unemployment. All these topics are developed in later chapters.

But it would be a mistake to think that an economist can be made out of a parrot, simply by teaching him the magic words saving and investment. Behind the scenes of these schedules a great deal is taking place. We shall see that interest rates may go up, causing the investment schedule to shift downward. Or an increase in the public's holding of government bonds and other wealth may shift the consumption schedule upward. Or rising living standards (resulting from advertising and the invention of new products) may shift the consumption schedule up just as it has in the past.

In short, it is an oversimplification to regard investment as always an autonomous factor, and consumption always a passive factor depending upon income. True, this is a fruitful oversimplification. But as we have already seen, some of net investment may be "induced" by income changes in the short run. Likewise, consumption will sometimes shift autonomously even though income has remained constant. And, as the reader can verify by experimenting with the saving-investment and the 45°-line diagrams, such shifts in the consumption or saving schedules have multiplier effects upon national income— just like the multiplier effects of changes in investment.

---

[1] Corporate saving can be handled graphically in much the same way as taxes, but this may be left to more advanced discussions.

SUMMARY

A. INCOME DETERMINATION

1. The motives that make people save are quite different from those that make businesses invest. Net investment tends to depend on such autonomous elements as new population, new territory, new inventions, new tastes, and other growth elements; consumption and saving tend to behave along passive schedules plotted against national income.

2. People's wishes to save and the willingness of businesses to invest are brought into line with each other by means of changes in national income. The equilibrium level of national income must be at the intersection of the saving and investment schedules; or what is exactly the same thing, at the intersection of the consumption plus investment schedule with the 45° line of total income.

3. If incomes were to be temporarily above the equilibrium level, business would find itself unable to sell all it is producing at prices that fully cover all costs of production. For a short time inventories might pile up or sales at a loss might take place, but eventually employment and production would be cut back toward the equilibrium level. The only plateau of income that can be maintained is at the income level where families will voluntarily continue to save exactly as much as business will voluntarily continue to invest.

4. To sum up the matter most simply: Investment calls the tune; investment causes income to rise or fall until voluntary saving has adjusted itself to the level of maintainable investment.[1] The simplest sequence is:

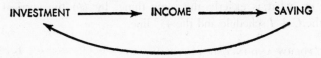

INVESTMENT ⟶ INCOME ⟶ SAVING

B. INVESTMENT AND INCOME

5. Investment has a multiplier effect on income. When investment changes, there is an equal primary change in national income. But as these primary

---

[1] The equality of the saving that people are willing to maintain with the investment that business firms are willing to maintain is the equilibrium condition that permits national income to remain steady. This equality should not be confused with the definitional identity of measured saving and investment at *every* income level. Such a confusion would be like the century-old fallacy that says, "Supply and demand cannot possibly determine competitive market price, because after all, the amount bought must necessarily be identically equal to the amount sold" (see Part Three). For the readers who are interested, the Appendix to this chapter gives further explanation of the equality of saving and investment.

income receivers in the capital goods industries get more earned income, they set into motion a whole chain of additional secondary consumption spending. If people always spend about $\frac{2}{3}$ of each extra dollar of income upon consumption, the total of the multiplier chain will be

$$1 + \frac{2}{3} + (\frac{2}{3})^2 + \cdots = \frac{1}{1 - \frac{2}{3}} = 3$$

The multiplier works backward or forward, amplifying either increases or decreases in investment. The multiplier is numerically equal to the reciprocal of the MPS; this is because it always takes more than a dollar's change in income to bring forth a dollar's change in saving.

6. The *attempt* to save more is quite different from the achievement of increased saving for society as a whole. The paradox of thrift shows how an increase in thriftiness may reduce already depressed income and, through induced effects on investment, actually result in less net investment. Only when employment always remains full are consumption and investment competing; only then are private virtues always social virtues.

The moral is not for each individual to squander his money during a depression, trying to be patriotic. Instead, through proper national policies, we must recreate a high-employment environment in which private virtues are no longer social follies.

7. In short, we must avoid both inflationary and deflationary gaps, so that full-employment saving and investment just match without inflation. We measure the size of the deflationary or inflationary gap as the vertical discrepancy at full-employment income between (a) the saving and investment schedules or, what is exactly the same thing, by (b) the vertical distance between the $C + I$ schedule and the 45° line.

C. FISCAL POLICY AND INCOME DETERMINATION

8. An increase in government expenditure—taken by itself with taxes and investment unchanged—has expansionary effects on national product much like those of net investment. The schedule of $C + I + G$ shifts upward to a higher equilibrium intersection with the 45° line.

9. An increase in taxes—taken by itself with investment and government expenditure unchanged—depresses the equilibrium level of national product. The schedule of consumption plotted against NNP is shifted downward by taxes; but since extra dollars go partly into saving, the dollar drop in consumption will not be quite so great as the dollars of new taxes. Therefore, to combat an inflationary or deflationary gap, we may require an even larger change in taxation.

10. The art of economics consists of recognizing both the core of truth in the simple theory of income determination and also its needed qualifications. In later chapters we shall see how interest rates and other factors may cause shifts in the schedules that determine levels of national income.

We must leave to Chapter 19 the analysis of government surpluses, deficits, debt, and fiscal policy. To the intervening chapters we must turn for an analysis of money and prices, banking policy and interest, and the wild dance of the business cycle.

QUESTIONS FOR DISCUSSION

1. The saving and investment diagram and the 45° -line (or consumption + investment) diagram are two different ways of showing how national income is determined. Describe each. Show that they are equivalent. As an aid to understanding, which do you prefer?

2. Reconstruct Table 1 assuming that net investment is equal to (a) 20 billion dollars, (b) 40 billion dollars. What is the resulting difference in national income? Is this greater or smaller than the change in investment? Why?

3. Describe in a few paragraphs (a) the common sense, (b) the arithmetic, and (c) the geometry of the multiplier. What are the multipliers if MPC = 0.9? 0.8? 0.5?

4. "While no one *attempts* to save with any thought of investment outlets, yet the amount that all succeed in saving is brought into alignment with investment by the movements of national income. But the alignment is performed on a cruel Procrustean bed with income and employment being lopped off if the desire to save is excessive in comparison with available investment or with an inflationary straining of demand if investment is excessive." Do you agree? Is the final *equality* of saving and investment described here the same thing as the *identity* of measured saving and measured investment? (Hint: See the Appendix.)

5. In Figure 3, how would you measure the deflationary gap? In Figures 4 and 5? in Table 1? How would you change the figures to show an inflationary gap?

6. Give arguments for and against thriftiness. Distinguish carefully (a) between the individual and the community viewpoint and (b) between different states of business activity.

7. Describe briefly the effects upon income of (a) government expenditure, (b) taxes, (c) our sale of less goods and services to foreigners than we buy from them.

8. Suppose that there is an increase in corporate saving—corporations pay out less money in dividends. Do you think this would have the same effect on the consumption schedule as an increase in taxes? Why?

9. What do you regard as some of the limitations of the saving and investment analysis of national income?

10. Use the tools of this chapter to discuss the problems raised by a greatly expanded defense program.

11. "The problem of technological unemployment is why a displaced worker does not get a new job. Technological improvements (a) keep pushing the producible full-employment income rightward, (b) both create and destroy investment opportunities, and (c) create new products and consumption standards that raise the propensity to consume. Depending upon how we weigh these different effects, we may arrive at the conclusion that technological change increases unemployment or at the opposite conclusion." Discuss and analyze. Without the theory of income determination, how would you begin to analyze the problem of technological unemployment?

APPENDIX TO CHAPTER 13
THE TWO KINDS OF EQUALITY OF
SAVING AND INVESTMENT[1]

Not so many years ago when income analysis was new, people used to get confused over the problem of the equality of saving and investment. Our graphs have enabled us to get rid of all confusion, to recognize that there are two very different senses in which saving can be said to be equal to investment.

1. *The identity of measured saving and investment.* National income is determined by the interplay of saving and investment. This should not be misunderstood to imply that during a depression a statistician can measure saving, then measure investment, and expect to find that the former is statistically greater than the latter.

The discussion of national income in Chapter 11 reveals that—leaving government finance aside—the total of saving of any period is defined in such a way that it must be exactly equal to the total of net investment of that period. Saving is the difference between total income and total consumption; or in terms of the pie diagram of Figure 4 in Chapter 11, saving equals ◁. Net investment or net capital formation was the difference between the capital stock at the end and the beginning of the period; or to ⌐ minus ☐. By the very definition of national income or of net national product (which consists of consumption plus net investment), measurable saving and measurable investment are simply two different names for the same thing: namely, net income minus consumption.[2]

2. *The equilibrium equality of scheduled saving and investment.* This *identity* of measurable saving and measurable investment at every income level is not the same thing as the *equality* of the *scheduled* amounts of saving and investment which takes place only at the equilibrium level of income. If income is temporarily pulled away for some reason from the longer-run equilibrium level, then the amount of investment that businesses will be willing to maintain will not be equal to the saving that people will want to continue to make. Despite the superficial identity of measured saving and investment, national income will not be able to remain away from the equilibrium level indefinitely—be-

---

[1] This can be skipped by beginning students.

[2] This identity has an exact analogue: the amount bought must be identically equal to the amount sold in any transaction involving the exchange of goods for money.

cause in the next period, dissatisfied savers or investors will act so as to set in motion a return toward equilibrium.

Two examples, out of many possible ones, may be presented to illustrate how national income may temporarily be away from the equilibrium level with scheduled investment and saving unequal—but, of course, with measured investment and saving being always defined so as to come out equal at every instant of time.

In the first example, suppose that every family suddenly decides to have a higher propensity to consume and hence a lower propensity to save. This should finally lead to a higher equilibrium level of national income. But not necessarily all at once. On the first day of the new era, they will troop to the stores and increase their consumption purchases (by, let us say, 1 million dollars) out of their as yet unchanged incomes. Merchants had no reason to foresee this development; therefore they will find their inventory of goods reduced by 1 million dollars. National income has not risen to the new equilibrium level: indeed, it has not yet risen at all. This is because the reduction of consumers' *intended* saving was temporarily matched by an *unintentional* reduction in business inventory investment. But—and this is the crux of the matter— businessmen will not continue indefinitely to deplete their inventories. In subsequent periods when they increase their production orders, national income will rise to its equilibrium level, where everyone is content to maintain the *status quo*.

In our second example, suppose that businesses begin to take advantage of new investment opportunities. They borrow money from banks or spend their idle cash balances to give construction jobs to workers. According to our equilibrium analysis, secondary consumption respending should have a multiplier effect upon income beyond the original primary effect. But this respending process may take time to work itself out. There may be a short period of delay between the moment when people receive new income and the time when they are able to spend it. In the short run, therefore, the economic system may fall short of the equilibrium level because the new investment has been temporarily offset by increased saving: not yet having time to spend their higher incomes, people are temporarily forced *below* their consumption schedule and *above* their saving schedule. When national income finally ceases growing and settles down, then people will be back on their SS schedule and income will be at the new equilibrium intersection.

What this section says can be boiled down to the following:

The equality of the saving and investment that people are willing to continue to make holds only at the equilibrium level of income. But the definitional identity of measured saving and investment holds all the time—even when income is away from the equilibrium level and is in process of being pushed, by people's dissatisfaction with their actual realized saving and investment, back toward equilibrium.[1]

[1] After the reader has mastered the supply and demand analysis of Part Three, he will encounter an exactly parallel problem: The measured amount of a commodity sold will in every period equal the measured amount bought, but there is a second, entirely different kind of equality of supply and demand at the equilibrium market price where schedules cross.

Chapter 14: PRICES AND MONEY

OUR previous analysis showed that the interplay of saving and investment determines the level of total spending. In turn, the level of total spending crucially affects the behavior of prices generally. Total spending affects prices in two related ways, via direct demand and via cost: (1) When extra dollars of demand collide with an inexpansible supply of goods, prices are directly bid up; (2) when jobs are very plentiful, workers ask for and receive higher wages, thus sending up money costs of production and putting upward pressure on prices.

In this chapter we are first interested in some of the broad effects of these price changes: the effects of inflation, deflation, and the goals of long-term price behavior. Second, we are interested in the question: What does the total stock of money consist of in a modern economy? This in turn provides an introduction to the basic problems of the next few chapters, namely: How can changes in banking policy cause changes in the interest rate, the total stock of money and debt, and other financial assets? And how do all such monetary changes impinge on the basic schedules of saving and investment so as to affect production, employment, and prices?

INFLATION, DEFLATION, AND REDISTRIBUTION OF INCOME BETWEEN ECONOMIC CLASSES

By inflation we mean a period of generally rising prices. By deflation we mean a period in which most prices are falling. The root cause of inflation and deflation is a change in total money *spending* relative to the flow of goods offered for sale. If the total flow of purchasing power coming on to the market is not matched by a sufficient flow of goods, prices will tend to rise. On the other hand, when total spending declines, prices and the real flow of production tend to be depressed.

Neither in inflation nor in deflation do all prices move in the same direction or in exactly the same proportion. As a result of changes in *relative* prices and in total spending, the two processes of inflation and deflation cause definite and characteristic changes in (1) the distribution of income between economic classes and (2) total output.

Inflation tends to favor debtors and profit receivers at the expense of creditors and fixed-income receivers, while the effects of deflation are the opposite. Suppose a creditor lends $1,000 today and is paid back one year from now. If in the meantime prices have doubled, then the debtor will be paying back only about one-half as much real purchasing power as was given to him.

If prices were to increase a trillion-fold, as they did in the German inflation of 1920–1923, then the wealth of creditors would be completely wiped out. This actually happened to German university endowments and life-insurance assets. After World War II an American who earned 4 per cent yearly on a mortgage found that he was not even holding his own as far as the *real purchasing power* of the dollar was concerned. United States government savings bonds bought for $75 in 1941 paid off $100 in 1951. But one one hundred 1951 dollars had a lower purchasing power than did seventy-five 1941 dollars. During and after World War I, American prices were still more inadequately controlled, with the result that white-collar workers like teachers, postmen, and book-keepers found their relatively fixed incomes inadequate to maintain living standards in the face of the rising cost of living. Widows living on fixed pensions, on life-insurance annuities, or on bond interest found themselves in the same difficult straits because the postwar dollar would buy less than a prewar 50-cent piece.

On the other hand, anyone who invests his money in real estate, in common stocks, or in sacks of flour makes a great money profit during inflation. The volume of business sales shoots up. Prices rise between the time that the businessmen buy and sell their merchandise. Fixed or overhead costs remain the same. Other costs rise but not so rapidly as prices. For all these reasons profits increase—often faster than does the cost of living. In such periods of great inflation, every reckless fool can become a great financier. Some workers in highly organized occupations may, by militant collective bargaining, be able to keep up with the high cost of living, but many find their real wages shrinking.

In time of deflation, the shoe is on the other foot. Creditors and fixed-income receivers tend to gain at the expense of debtors and profit receivers. If prices fall between the time that a creditor lends money and is repaid, then he gets back more purchasing power than he lent. Between the time that a merchant buys and sells goods, he will have to take a loss.

The schoolteacher who keeps her job and whose pay is not cut too deeply finds that her real income has increased. The widow who withstood the temptation to buy common stock during the boom and instead put all her money into gilt-edge government bonds finds herself better off. At the same time the government finds that the real burden of its public debt has gone up relative to tax collections and national income. A hoarder who earns no money interest on his mattress cache finds that the real value of his wealth is increasing every day as prices fall. If prices fall at the rate of 10 per cent per year, he is being rewarded for his antisocial act of hoarding at a 10 per cent rate of interest in real terms, while the businessman who is foolish enough to give someone a job will probably find that he cannot even get back his original outlay, much less earn a profit.

EFFECTS OF CHANGING PRICES ON OUTPUT AND EMPLOYMENT

An increase in prices is usually associated with an increase in employment. In mild inflation the wheels of industry are well lubricated and total output goes up. Private investment is brisk, and jobs plentiful. Thus a little inflation is usually to be preferred to a little deflation. The losses to fixed-income groups are usually less than the gains to the rest of the community. Even workers with relatively fixed wages are often better off because of improved employment opportunities and greater take-home pay; and a rise in interest rates on new securities may partly make up any losses to creditors.

In deflation, on the other hand, the growing unemployment of labor and capital causes the total of the community's well-being to be less, so that those few who gain receive much less benefit than those who lose. As a matter of fact, in deep depression, almost everyone—including the creditor who is left with uncollectible debts—is likely to suffer.

The above remarks show conclusively why an increase in consumption or investment spending is a good thing in times of unemployment, even if there is some upward pressure on prices. When the economic system is suffering from acute deflation, it makes little sense to criticize public or private spending on the ground that this might be inflationary. Actually most of the increased spending will then go to increase production and create jobs. But the same reasoning shows that once full employment and full plant capacity have been reached any further increases in spending must necessarily be completely wasted in "paper" price increases.

GALLOPING INFLATION

If price increases could be held down to, say, less than 5 per cent per year, such a mild steady inflation need not cause too great concern. But if each increase in prices becomes the signal for an increase in wages and costs, which again sends prices up still further, we may be in the midst of a malignant, galloping, hyperinflation. Nothing good is to be said for a rapid rise of prices such as took place in Germany in 1920–1923 and more recently in China and

Hungary. Production and even the social order are then disorganized. The total wealth of large groups of the population is wiped out as money becomes worthless. Debtors ruthlessly pursue creditors in order to pay off their obligations in valueless money. Speculators profiteer. Housewives rush to spend their husbands' pay checks before prices rise still further, but in doing so only bid prices up even faster.

As a Southerner said during the Confederate inflation,

We used to go to the stores with money in our pockets and come back with food in our baskets. Now we go with money in baskets and return with food in our pockets. Everything is scarce except money! Prices are chaotic and production disorganized, A meal which used to cost the same amount as an opera ticket now costs twenty times as much. Business is often at a standstill because no one knows how much to charge. As a result, everybody tends to hoard "things" and to try to get rid of the "bad" paper money, which drives the "good" metal money out of circulation. A partial return to barter—with all its inconveniences—is the result.

Fortunately, there are few, if any, cases of hyperinflation except during war or in the backwash of war and revolution. There are some economists, however, who fear that our system is becoming jittery with a tendency to go into an explosive price rise whenever full employment comes into view. If workers, farmers, and businessmen become aware that their welfare depends as much on what their money can buy as upon their money earnings, perhaps this awareness may cause them in the future to moderate their demands for higher prices and money wages. This would tend to have a favorable result: for then all increases in purchasing power would go to create increases in employment and real output, rather than simply to dissipate themselves in higher prices.

If workers, farmers, and businessmen do not learn this lesson, our economic system may be in for a bad time. In that case, whenever there is enough purchasing power to bring the system near to full employment, there will tend to result a vicious upward spiral of prices and wages. Even more ominous is the possibility that prices may begin to shoot up *long before* full employment is reached.[1] As a result full employment may never be reached.

Such behavior would not alarm those who believe in direct control by government of prices and wages, *i.e.*, in a permanent OPA. But those who value freedom of enterprise and dislike unnecessary authoritative government controls, would be much disturbed by what this would imply for efficiency and freedom.[2]

[1] This is what happened in the short-lived 1936–1937 boom, which was followed by the sharp, but brief, 1938 recession.

[2] The dilemma of a price-wage policy for full employment is discussed again at the end of Chapter 19 on fiscal policy.

PAST BEHAVIOR OF PRICES

Figure 1 shows the historical ups and downs of wholesale prices.[1] Each war is clearly marked by a peak. At first glance there seem to be no general upward or downward trends. But look carefully at the chart to see what has happened

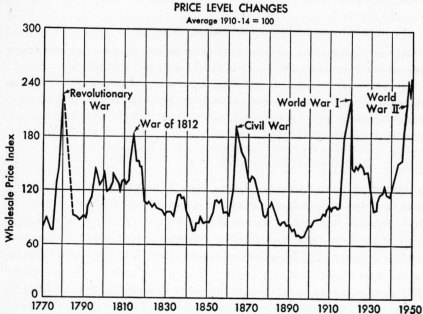

PRICE LEVEL CHANGES
Average 1910-14 = 100

FIGURE 1. SOURCE: Leonard P. Ayres, *Our National Debt after Great Wars*, Committee on Public Debt Policy.

in the twentieth century. The trend of prices has been generally upward; the value of the dollar—as measured by its purchasing power, by what it can buy—has been cut in half since pre-World War I.

As an omen for the future, note one terribly significant fact: After World War II there was no decline in prices at all comparable to what followed previous wars. Wages and prices have become sticky as far as downward movements are concerned; also government has become quick to act to stem any depression that is beginning to get under way. If prices rise in good times

[1] There are many statistical and theoretical problems in computing an average index number of prices. Not only is it difficult to get accurate price quotations for all commodities, but there is also the question of how to weight the different prices. The cost of living for a rich man may change differently from that for a poor man, just as the cost of living of a vegetarian may change differently from that of a steak addict. In view of these difficulties, it is surprising how much alike are the changes of different kinds of index numbers. See Chapter 10 for our earlier discussion of index numbers.

and do not fall much in bad times, what is the long-term outlook for prices? The question answers itself.

Ideally, we all want a progressive full-employment economy in which the excesses of the business cycle are moderated. We want to control the "mad dance of the dollar" as the business cycle passes from boom to crisis and slump. But as far as the long-run trend of prices is concerned, there are three possible programs espoused by different economists:

1. *Prices—on the average—are to be stable.* As output increases over time owing to population increase and technological progress, the total of spending rises. Money wages and real wages also rise as a result of increases in productivity over time.

2. *Prices are to be gently rising.* Because full-employment output is also increasing with productivity and growth, total spending rises even faster than prices. Money wages also rise rapidly; but the increase in real wages is not quite so great, because of the upward trend in the cost of living.

3. *Prices are to be falling steadily.* The total of money wages and property income remains almost constant. But the increase in output resulting from improved technological productivity is passed on to all consumers in lower prices. Real wages rise even though money wages may remain constant. Such a fall in prices need not depress business activity unduly, provided that it results from previous reductions in cost.

All three solutions are tolerable if unemployment is kept at a low figure. But economic history and analysis suggest that high employment is least likely to be maintained under the third possibility, and the real burden of the public debt would be heaviest. Most of the vigorous periods of healthy capitalist development have been during periods of stable or gently rising prices. Capitalism, itself, developed during the centuries when Spanish New World gold was raising prices—not because anyone planned it that way, but simply because our monetary system used to consist of precious metals, and Columbus accidentally discovered the New World. The life expectancy of free private enterprise may well be lowered if there are to be deflation and falling prices in the decades ahead.

Suppose we do agree that there is nothing alarming in a gently rising trend of prices. Can such a gentle rise remain gentle? Or will it more likely snowball into a rapid rate of increase, thereby creating grave problems for fixed-income groups and older people who had hoped to retire on their savings? Those who believe "it can't happen here" need only look to the historical experience of a country like Brazil; there prices have steadily risen for more than a century!

If you lived in Brazil, how would you feel about holding idle cash as its purchasing power melted away?

IMPORTANCE OF MONEY[1]

The behavior of prices is intimately related to the balance of saving and investment expenditure. We have already seen, and we shall later see further, that direct operation on the flow of government expenditure and the flow of taxation can alter the equilibrium flow of income. The supply of money and of liquid assets such as government bonds can also have effects upon the level of the investment and saving schedules. The government, through the federal reserve system, has a responsibility to use monetary policy to help curb inflation and fight depressions.

The next three chapters deal with monetary and banking policy. The rest of this chapter provides an introductory survey of the money supply of a modern community.

THE THREE KINDS OF MONEY: SMALL COINS, PAPER CURRENCY, AND BANK DEPOSITS

Let us list the main categories of money with which we all have daily contact: small change, paper currency, and bank-deposit money.

First, there is small change: copper pennies, nickel five-cent pieces, silver dimes, quarters, half dollars, and (in the Far West) silver dollars. These all constitute our so-called "fractional currency." In total they do not add up to very much—in fact, to much less than one-twentieth of the community's cash. Because the metal in all these coins is worth far less than their face value, they are termed "token money." Obviously, these coins are valued far beyond their metallic worth only because they can be readily converted into other kinds of money—20 nickels to the dollar, etc. They are not forced upon anybody; their quantity is limited by the public's demand for them to buy cigarettes, newspapers, and so forth.

Far more important is the second kind of money: "folding money" or paper currency. Most of us know little more about a one-dollar or five-dollar bill than that each is inscribed with the picture of some American statesman, that each contains the signature of one or another government official, and— most important of all—each bears a number showing its face value.

If you look at a one-dollar bill more closely, you will find that it contains the words "Silver Certificate." This means that the United States Treasury is

[1] Part C of Chapter 3 gave an introductory description of the superiority of money over barter in facilitating exchange and division of labor; the reader may turn to those pages for a discussion of the functioning of money as a unit of account and a medium of exchange.

holding on deposit a silver dollar for you to claim if you wish. But as has been already mentioned, a silver dollar contains considerably less than a dollar's worth of silver. Obviously, if you really want silver, you will do much better to buy it on the open market with your paper dollar, rather than go to the Treasury. Anyone who knows much about American politics and history realizes that some paper currency is called "silver" certificates only because a few Western senators from mining states have been able to persuade Congress to give silver mining a continuing subsidy by buying up quantities of silver for monetary use. Otherwise, silver has absolutely no monetary significance; many foreign countries are abandoning it even for small coins, and silver is beginning to lose its hold on the Orient.

If you examine a ten-dollar bill or some other paper bill, you will probably find that it says "Federal Reserve Note."[1] Like the dollar bill, this announces itself as "legal tender for all debts, public and private," but it contains the further, and nonsensical, statement that it "is redeemable in *lawful money* at the United States Treasury or at any Federal Reserve Bank." The words "lawful money" have been italicized, *because there is no such thing* other than "legal tender" bills under discussion, namely, federal reserve notes, silver certificates, etc. In other words, your old wrinkled ten-dollar bill is redeemable into a crisp new bill, into two fives, or into ten ones if you prefer. But that is all.[2] Today, all American money is essentially "fiat" money. It is money because the government decrees that it is money and because the public accepts that decree.

Back before 1933, when the present college generation was just beginning to have birthdays, it was not uncommon for good little boys and girls to be presented on anniversaries with five- or ten-dollar gold pieces. And gold certificates were often seen in circulation. These certificates were warehouse receipts promising the bearer redemption in gold upon application to the United States Treasury. But in 1933, when Congress raised the buying prices of gold from about $21 to $35 an ounce, all gold—except that tied up in wedding rings and dental fillings—was called in. This was done so that holders or hoarders of gold could not make a 67 per cent profit as a result of the devaluation of the dollar. At the same time, all gold certificates—ten-dollar bills (or larger),

[1] Two-dollar bills, considered to be bad luck in most parts of the country other than New England, are so-called United States Notes—remnants of the greenbacks used to finance the Civil War. Occasionally you may run into a bill that says "Federal Reserve Bank Note" or even a "National Bank Note" containing the name of some near-by national bank. These are being gradually retired from circulation.

[2] A Cleveland businessman recently wrote to the Treasury asking for some "lawful money" in return for a ten-dollar bill. He received two polite letters in reply, and no satisfaction at all.

printed in green on one side and goldish orange on the other—were called in. Congress ruled that these certificates were not to be exchanged for gold upon being called in, but simply for ordinary paper dollars. A few absent-minded people still have not turned in their gold certificates, but once these are brought to a bank, they will be retired from circulation forever and replaced by other bills.[1]

From the standpoint of understanding the nature of money, it is a good thing that these gold certificates no longer exist. The modern student need not be misled, as were earlier generations of students, by some mystical belief that "gold backing" is what gives money its value. Certainly gold has little or nothing to do with the problem. Every expert knows that the popular conception that money has more value if it is exchangeable into gold exactly reverses the true relation. If it were not that gold has some monetary uses, its value as a metal would be much less than it is today. We should have cheaper inlays and wedding rings, and South African miners would be poorer than they are. We shall later see that, when a government requires itself to hold some fraction of gold reserves against its paper money, the gold affects prices only through its ability to *limit or to expand the volume of paper money and total spending*. This was overlooked by foolish European chancellors of the exchequer who, after World War I, tried to stop inflation by accumulating new gold reserves through the purchase of gold on the open market with newly printed money. Of course, the effect was just the opposite. Later they had to reverse the process and use their gold to buy up and burn outstanding paper money.

WHY CHECKING DEPOSITS ARE CONSIDERED TO BE MONEY

There is also a third category of what economists call money, in addition to metallic small change and paper currency. This is so-called "bank money"—made up of bank deposits subject to checking on demand. If I have $1,000 in my checking account at the Cambridge Trust Company, that deposit can be regarded as money because I can pay for purchases with checks drawn upon it. The deposit is like any other medium of exchange and, being payable on demand, it serves as a "standard of value" or "unit of account" in the same sense as $1,000 worth of silver quarters, *i.e.*, both the deposit and the quarters are convertible into standard money or cash at fixed terms, dollar for dollar.

Possessing the essential properties of money, bank demand deposits might just as well be counted as money. And they are.[2]

---

[1] The courts also upheld a statute that invalidated contracts calling for payment in gold; only payment in terms of dollars was permitted. Otherwise, creditors would have made a 67 per cent profit on the revaluation and debtors would have lost 67 per cent. As we shall see in Chapter 17, the 12 Federal Reserve Banks hold special-type gold certificates.

[2] My balance on deposit in the bank is usually considered to be money—not the checks

Actually, as was noted in the discussion of money in Chapter 3, bank money is quantitatively more important than currency because most transactions are consummated by check. The convenience of checks for mailing, for paying the exact sum of money due, for providing a receipt in the form of the canceled check voucher, for protecting against loss when stolen or misplaced (while unendorsed or, for that matter, endorsed)—all these advantages are obvious and explain the widespread use of bank money.

Table 1 illustrates the quantitative importance of the three kinds of money in 1950.

TABLE 1. *Total Quantity of United States Money in Circulation and "Near-money" (In billions of dollars)*

	March, 1939		June, 1950	
1. Small change (outside of banks):				
Minor coins......................	$0.2		$ 0.4	
Silver coins......................	0.4		1.1	
		$ 0.6		$ 1.5
2. Paper currency (outside of banks):				
Federal reserve notes...............	$4.3		$22.7	
Silver certificates and U.S. notes.......	1.6		2.5	
Other currency (largely in process of being retired).....................	0.3		0.4	
		$ 6.2		$ 25.6
3. Bank money				
Demand deposits of all banks (adjusted to exclude government deposits, etc.)	26.1		85.4	
Total money......................		$32.9		$112.5
4. "Near-money" (estimated):				
Time or savings deposits (includes mutual savings banks, postal savings, and savings and loan agencies).............	$30 0		$ 69.0	
U.S. government bonds held by individuals and businesses (excluding banks, insurance companies, etc.).....	12.0		85.0	
Total "near-money"...............	$42.0		$154.0	

SOURCE: *Federal Reserve Bulletins.*

that I write. These represent only the spending or transfer of money; the money itself, quantitatively, is the deposit.

LIQUID WEALTH OR "NEAR-MONEY"

Along with the total of money, Table 1 also shows the total of "near-money." What is meant by this concept? Different economists define the term differently. I shall include in near-money the total of savings deposits which any person could quickly cash in and the total of government bonds which anyone could present for redemption or sell for cash in the open market.

These liquid-wealth items have many of the properties of money. True, I do not pay my monthly expenses directly with government bonds, and so I hesitate to call such an item money. Nonetheless, the fact that I have such an easily cashable asset means that my current spending habits are probably affected in much the same way as they would be if I owned a bank deposit instead of the government bonds. Similarly, if I have $10,000 on demand deposit and my brother has $5,000 on time deposit and $5,000 on demand deposit, will our saving and consumption schedules be very different ones? At equal incomes, is my brother likely to save a much larger percentage of his income than I am?

No dogmatic answers can be given to these questions. But this much is clear: Government bonds and savings accounts have many of the same effects as do currency and demand deposits, and hence economists often call such liquid assets "near-money."

CONCLUSION

Part of the favorable postwar balance between saving and investment is explained by the tremendous wartime growth, shown in Table 1, of our total liquid wealth. How were 60 billion dollars of demand deposits created during the last decade? The next chapter shows how our banking system can create deposits. The following two chapters then go on to examine the effects of changing monetary and debt conditions on the level of national income and prices.

SUMMARY

1. When prices change in periods of inflation or deflation, they do not all change in exactly the same degree. Instead of being neutral, such price changes have definite real effects on the economic system.

2. In times of inflation, debtors and profit receivers benefit at the expense of creditors and fixed-income groups. Deflation has opposite effects upon the distribution of income between economic classes.

3. Aside from causing transfers between economic groups, deflation acts

to reduce the total of national production and employment. Until it becomes excessive, inflation tends to expand employment and output, because the lag of costs behind prices stimulates industrial expansion.

4. Desirable long-term goals are stable prices or slowly rising prices, with money wages rising even more rapidly as the growth of productivity makes higher real wages possible. Realistically, we must recognize that there is a serious long-term problem of keeping prices from showing a too strong upward trend.

5. There are three kinds of modern money: small token coins (or small change), fiat paper currency issued by the government and its federal reserve system, and demand bank deposits subject to check. Being convertible into each other at par, all these have the same value unit for unit, independently of the trifling paper, ink, and metal costs involved in each.

6. "Near-money" is defined as those liquid assets which a person can easily and quickly convert into cash and which therefore have many of the same effects on the propensity to consume as does money itself. According to this definition, savings accounts and government bonds are near-money.

7. As a result of World War II, the money supply has more than tripled; the same is true of the total of near-money. The following chapters are concerned with the causes and effects of such monetary changes.

QUESTIONS FOR DISCUSSION

1. If you were sure of inflation ahead, what are some of the things you might do to protect yourself against it?

2. List some of the dramatic happenings that go with galloping hyperinflation.

3. "A depression is really a great time of opportunity, for him who will recognize it." Comment.

4. Explain the following carefully: inflation, prosperity, deflation, depression, hyperinflation, technological cost-price reduction.

5. Sometimes wages or loan contracts are expressed in terms of a sliding scale rather than in terms of fixed money. How would you use an index of the cost of living to protect workers against a change in real wages due to price-level changes? How would you do the same thing with respect to an I.O.U.?

6. Take inventory of the different kinds of money in the pockets of the class members. Make up a table. What about checking deposits?

7. Why are checks used as often as they are? Why not more often? Trace the history of a check that you send to your broker when you buy one share of A.T. & T. stock at $175 per share. Suppose that your broker is 1,000 miles away.

8. Twenty-five years from now when national income may be 400 billion dollars,

what do you think our money supply will look like? What about the value of a dollar, or the price level?

9. A man spends half his income on one loaf of bread, half on one dozen hyacinths. The price of bread doubles, while the price of hyacinths halves. Compute an index of the cost of living: (a) using the "before" situation as 100, (b) using the "after" situation as 100. Why is there a difference? If so, which—if either—is right?

10. Explain what is meant by "near-money" and why the concept got its name.

11. Two identical twins have identical incomes and wealth. One has half of his wealth in cash and half in liquid government bonds. The other has nine-tenths in cash and one-tenth in bonds. Will their propensities to consume be significantly different?

Chapter 15: FUNDAMENTALS OF

THE BANKING SYSTEM AND

DEPOSIT CREATION

THE outstanding importance of bank deposits as part of the community's money supply has already been discussed. This chapter continues the discussion in two distinct parts. In the first, we must examine briefly the important facts and functionings of the modern banking system, showing how the present-day commercial bank gradually began to keep only "fractional cash reserves" against its deposits; in the second part, an attempt is made to describe simply and clearly how the banking system "manufactures" bank deposits.

A. *NATURE AND FUNCTIONING OF THE MODERN BANKING SYSTEM*

THE PRESENT STATUS OF BANKING

Today there are about 14,000 banks in the United States that accept checking deposits. Only about a third of these banks are national banks, the rest being under state supervision. All national banks are automatically members of the federal reserve system, and in addition most of the larger state institutions are federal reserve members. Although this still leaves more than half of all the banks not members of the federal reserve system, they are sufficiently small in size so that their deposits are only about one-fifth of the total.[1] Moreover,

---

[1] Many of these state banks that are not full-fledged members nevertheless do belong to the federal reserve clearinghouse system and are able to use this service in handling checks on other banks.

since 1933 almost all commercial banks, state or national, have had their deposits insured by the FDIC (Federal Deposit Insurance Corporation). Initially, the FDIC insured each deposit up to the sum of $5,000; in 1950, the limit was raised from $5,000 to $10,000.

Unlike England or Canada where a few large banks with hundreds of branches are dominant, the United States has tended to rely upon many independent, relatively small, localized units.[1] Until fairly recently, almost anyone could open a bank with relatively limited capital. It is not surprising, therefore, that the American history of bank failures and losses to depositors has been a grievous one. Indeed, only about one-half the banks in existence in 1915 are still solvent; even in prosperous 1929, long before the great depression, no less than 659 banks with estimated total deposits of 200 million dollars failed. Since the FDIC, things have changed; today a bank failure is a great rarity.

The primary economic function of commercial banks is to receive demand deposits and to honor checks drawn upon them. Another important function is to lend money to local merchants, farmers, and industrialists. Banks also perform a variety of other functions in competition with other financial institutions. Thus, they usually accept savings or time deposits—theoretically withdrawable only after 30 days' notice—but in fact usually withdrawn (by their owners) on demand. In taking on such a function, the commercial banks are, in parts of the country like New England, competing with the so-called "mutual savings banks" which accept only time deposits; almost anywhere in the country they are competing with cooperative building and loan societies and postal savings. In selling money orders or travelers' checks, the banks are competing with the post office and with Western Union. In handling "trusts" and estates, they overlap with investment counselors, executors, and other fiduciaries.

Furthermore, even in lending money to individuals and businessmen, the banks are competing with finance companies, and with so-called "factors," who provide corporations with working capital. In buying bonds, mortgages, and other securities, the banks are in competition with insurance companies and other investors.[2]

The commercial banks are by no means, therefore, our only financial institutions. But, by definition, they are the only organizations able to provide

[1] In California, the Bank of America has numerous branches all over the state, just as the Chase National Bank has branches all over New York City, and just as a few holding companies control many banks in Minnesota and Wisconsin. But by and large, the old American distrust of "big finance" has caused legislatures to restrict multiple-branch banking.

[2] Massachusetts and New York State savings banks actually sell life insurance, and at such low rates and favorable terms as to compete seriously with commercial insurance companies.

"bank money," *i.e.*, checkable demand deposits which can be conveniently used as a medium of exchange. Therein lies their primary importance and chief economic interest. For, except with respect to this unique function, the modern American commercial bank seemed at the war's end to be gradually becoming hardly more than a holder of government bonds—an indirect agency by means of which business and the public indirectly hold the great public debt.[1]

Since V-E and V-J days, bank loans have had a considerable increase, largely to help business, farmers, and the public to finance the large volume of postwar activity, carried on at high postwar price levels. Interestingly enough, in recent years commercial banks have begun increasingly to make "term loans" of more than a year's duration, thus refuting the belief of those theorists who believe that banks should provide only short-term, 90-day seasonal credit.

CREATION OF THE FEDERAL RESERVE SYSTEM

In 1913, the Federal Reserve Act was passed by Congress and signed by President Wilson. The panic of 1907, with its more than usual epidemic of bank failures, was the straw that broke the camel's back: the country was fed up once and for all with the anarchy of unstable private banking. After half a dozen years' agitation and discussion by both the Republican and Democratic parties, the federal reserve system was formed—in face of the opposition of the large banks and of bankers' associations.

The country was divided into 12 federal reserve districts, each with its own Federal Reserve Bank. The initial capital of each bank was subscribed by the commercial bank members of the federal reserve system; and so *nominally* they are each corporations owned by the "Member Banks." All are coordinated by the 7-member Board of Governors of the federal reserve system in Washington.[2]

When the system was first established, numerous petty "checks and balances" were written into the law, largely on the basis of a number of now obsolete theories about money and because of the then prevailing fear of centralized banking authority. It was another example of what is so common in our history: the desire of the American people to go swimming without going near the water. We wanted, we desperately needed a Central Bank;

[1] In 1950, bank holdings of government securities were about double their loans and about four times their agricultural or industrial loans. This is a marked contrast to the 1920's, when loans dominated.

[2] There is also a 12-man Federal Open Market Committee, consisting of 5 representatives of the 12 districts as well as the 7-man Board of Governors. In addition a Federal Advisory Council, consisting of a representative selected by each of the 12 banks, can make suggestions but is without legal powers.

yet we were afraid of the concept. Therefore, a compromise bill was passed—dividing the country up into 12 separate districts; providing for six directors of each bank to be appointed by the vote of the Member Banks and three to be appointed by the Board of Governors; requiring three of the local six directors to be bankers and the other three to represent business, industry, and agriculture, respectively; providing 14-year terms for governors; limiting the 12 Reserve Banks to certain special types of loans, and preventing them from buying bonds directly from the government; etc.

Today none of these restrictions is of primary importance. Again and again Congress has modified the original act whenever one of these restrictions stood in the way of the needs of the time. Let us examine, therefore, the effective realities and present status of the federal reserve system.

It consists of a Board of Governors with wide powers who usually work very closely with the President and the Treasury, and who have in effect 12 branch offices throughout the land. Although the Member Banks nominally own the Reserve Banks, in fact no profits over 6 per cent of the original capital may be paid out to Member Banks; and almost all excess earnings are paid into the United States Treasury. Although the Reserve Banks have been enormously profitable, the public interest and not profit is their goal; and many of their most important activities are deliberately adopted in the full knowledge that they will involve losses.[1]

The detailed functionings of the Federal Reserve Banks are reserved for discussion in the next chapter. Here it is only necessary to know that they are banks for bankers and for the government. Most of the federal taxes and expenditures pass through the Reserve Banks. The Member Banks hold their cash reserves on deposit in the nearest Reserve Bank, and look to it for help in time of crisis and for leadership at all times.

BANKING AS A BUSINESS

The ordinary commercial bank is a relatively simple and unexciting business concern. Banking is a business much like any other business. A bank provides certain services for its customers and in return receives payments from them in one form or another. If possible, it tries to earn a capital yield for its stockholders or owners.

A bank's balance sheet shows certain assets, certain liabilities, and certain capital ownership. Except for minor rearrangements, the bank's published

[1] That the details of ownership of a Central Bank are not vital is indicated by the history of the Bank of England. For two and a half centuries prior to its being nationalized by the present Labor government, it was a private corporation; but for the latter part of that period it acted (except for a few slips) pretty much the same as it would have if officially part of the government.

balance sheet looks, on the whole, much like the balance sheet of any other business, and rather simpler than most.

The only peculiar feature about the consolidated balance sheet of all national banks shown in Table 1 is the fact that such a large portion of the banks' liabilities are payable on demand; *i.e.*, they are deposits subject to checking. This fact is intriguing to the economist because he chooses to call such demand liabilities money; but to the banker it is a familiar condition which has long since been taken for granted. He knows full well that, although it would be possible for every depositor suddenly to decide to withdraw all his money from

TABLE 1. *Consolidated Balance Sheet of All National Banks, June 30, 1949*
(In billions of dollars)

Assets		Liabilities and Net Worth	
Cash and balances with Reserve Banks and other banks	$20.5	Capital accounts	$ 5.8
Loans and discounts	22.6	Demand deposits	58.4
U.S. government obligations	35.6	Time deposits	20.1
Other securities	5.5	Other liabilities	0.8
Other assets	0.9		
Total	$85.1	Total	$85.1

SOURCE: United States Treasury.

the bank on the same day, nevertheless the probability of this happening is infinitely remote. Each day as some people are withdrawing their money, others are normally making deposits that tend to cancel the withdrawals. As a matter of fact, in our growing economy the new deposits more than offset the widthdrawals.

This, however, need not be strictly true at any one moment, in any one day, or in any one week. By chance alone the amount of withdrawals might exceed deposits for some period of time, just as a coin may land with heads turned up rather than tails for a consecutive number of tosses. For this reason, the banker keeps a little cash handy in his cash vaults and a "reserve deposit" at the near-by Federal Reserve Bank. *Normally the till money in the bank's own vaults and its reserves at the Reserve Bank need be only a small fraction of the bank's total deposits;* and the same mathematical law of large numbers which makes life insurance possible assures the banker that the larger his bank and the more numerous his independent depositors, the smaller need this fraction be.

HOW BANKS DEVELOPED OUT OF GOLDSMITH ESTABLISHMENTS

All these facts are so much taken for granted by every modern banker that he is hardly aware of them. But it was not always so. Commercial banking is usually assumed to have begun with the ancient goldsmiths who developed the practice of storing people's gold and valuables for safekeeping. At first such establishments were simply like parcel checkrooms or warehouses. The depositor left his gold for safekeeping, was given a receipt, later presented that receipt, paid a small fee for safekeeping, and got back his gold.

Quite obviously, however, money is wanted only for what it will buy, not for its own sake. Money has an anonymous quality, so that one dollar is just as good as another, and one piece of pure gold as good as another. The goldsmiths soon found it more convenient *not* to have to tag the gold belonging to any one individual so as to be able to give to him upon request exactly the same piece of gold that he had left. Instead, the customer was quite willing to accept a receipt for an amount of gold or money *of a given value*, even though it was not the identical particle of matter that he had actually left.

This is important. Therein lies a significant difference between today's bank and a checkroom or warehouse. If I check my bag at Grand Central Station and later see someone walking down the street with that same suitcase, there is nothing for me to do but call my lawyer and sue the railroad company. If I mark my initials on a $10 bill, deposit it in my bank account, and later notice it in the hands of a stranger, I have no grievance against the bank management. They have agreed only to pay me on demand any old $10 of legal tender.

But let us return to the goldsmith establishments which are supposed to typify the first embryonic commercial banks. What would balance sheets of a typical establishment look like? Perhaps like Table 2.

TABLE 2. *Balance Sheet of Early Bank*

Assets		Liabilities and Net Worth	
Cash.....................	$1,000,000	Capital and surplus........	$ 50,000
Loans and investments......	50,000	Demand deposit liability....	1,000,000
Total..................	$1,050,000	Total..................	$1,050,000

We have assumed that the company has long since dropped its activities as a smith and is principally occupied with storing people's money for safekeeping. Over past time, 1 million dollars has been deposited in its vaults, and this whole sum it holds as a cash asset. To balance this asset, there is a current deposit liability of the same amount. Actually such a business need have no other assets (except the negligible value of its office space and vaults). But there is no reason why its owners should not have—on the side, so to speak—subscribed $50,000 of capital to be lent out at interest or to buy securities such as stocks or bonds. On the asset side this amount is shown under the heading Loans and Investments; this is balanced on the right-hand side by a similar sum in the Capital account.

At this primitive stage, the bank would be of no particular interest to the economist. The investment and capital items have nothing to do with the bank's deposits; if all the loans and investments should go sour and become worthless, the loss would fall completely on the stockholders who have agreed to take that risk in the hope of making a profit. Every depositor could still be paid off in full out of the 100 per cent cash reserves held by the bank. The bank would still cover its overhead and clerical expenses by making its customers pay storage charges. (These charges would presumably vary with the length of time the customer left his money for safekeeping, the average amount of his money that required safekeeping, and the number of times the turnover of his account made it necessary for a clerk to wait on him and keep records.)

The economist would have little interest in such a bank's operations. The bank money[1]—the demand deposits created jointly by the bank's willingness to accept a demand obligation and the customer's willingness to hold a deposit—would just offset the amount of ordinary money (currency or coin) placed in the bank's safe and withdrawn from active circulation. The whole process would be of no more interest than if the public decided to convert some of its dollar bills into an equivalent amount of quarters and dimes. In fancy language, we would say that the banking system is having a *neutral* effect on spending and prices since it is neither adding to nor subtracting from the total of ("active") money.

Before leaving this simple first stage of banking, we must point out that there is a substantial group of economic experts who today advocate as a thoroughgoing reform of our banking system the return to a system of 100 per cent cash reserves against all demand deposits. This, they say, is the only safe system of banking, in which depositors can really all get their money out of the bank any time they all want it together. It is the only honest system of banking, in which the banks are not "creating" new money for their own profit, and in so doing usurping the constitutional monetary prerogatives of the government. Finally, it is the only system of banking in which the banking system is neutral, neither creating money in time of boom and thereby adding to inflation, nor contracting the money supply in times of panic and depression and thereby adding to deflation, bankruptcy, and unemployment.

We cannot appraise the value of this reform until we have examined the nature of modern banks operating with only fractional legal reserve ratios.

MODERN FRACTIONAL RESERVE BANKING

Let us return to our early goldsmith-banker to see how modern banks gradually evolved. If he were an alert fellow, he would soon notice that, al-

[1] The economist would consider the demand deposit as money just as soon as the custom grew up for depositors to pay for the goods they bought by giving the storekeeper a little note to the bank saying, "Mr. Goldsmith, pay to the order of Sears, Roebuck $2.99, (signed) John Q. Doe." In other words, as soon as the use of checks became customary.

though his deposits are payable on demand, they are not all withdrawn together. He would soon learn that, although 100 per cent reserves are necessary if the bank is to be liquidated and all depositors to be paid off in full, they are not at all necessary if his bank is a "going concern." New deposits tend to balance withdrawals. Only a little till money, perhaps less than 2 per cent, will ever be needed in the form of vault cash.[1]

At first he probably thought this discovery too good to be true. Then perhaps he recalled the story of a rival bank in which a dishonest clerk ran off with 95 per cent of the bank's cash reserve—and the fact was never discovered for 50 years. No one ever had occasion to go to the back rooms of the vault because all withdrawals were financed by recently deposited money held in the front vaults!

We can imagine our intelligent banker—at first cautiously—beginning to acquire bonds and other earning assets with some of the cash entrusted to his care. Everything works out all right; depositors are still paid off on demand, and the bank has made some extra earnings. Gradually the banker no longer feels it necessary to conceal from his depositors what he is doing. If a depositor complains, the banker retorts, "Your money is safe. If you don't like my way of doing business, you are at liberty to withdraw your funds. Besides, haven't you noticed that the new method of fractional cash reserves has enabled me to lower my service charges to you? Also, it has enabled me to give a helping hand to our local businessmen who need more capital to buy new tools, buildings, and inventories. Such capital formation benefits consumers because they get better goods for lower prices. It also creates jobs for workers."

Little wonder, therefore, that all banks should have begun to invest most of the money deposited with them in earning assets and to keep only fractional cash reserves against deposits. Indeed, as long as business confidence remains high, and provided the managers of the bank are judicious in their choice of loans and investments, *there is no reason why the bank should keep much more than 2 per cent cash reserves against deposits.*

What if the banker makes a mistake in his investments? Since nobody's judgment is perfect and since all investments involve some element of speculative risk, this is certainly a possibility that must be reckoned with. To lessen

[1] If the bank could pay off its depositors with one of its own checks (or as in former times with one of its paper bank notes), it might not have to keep any till money at all! By judiciously limiting the rate at which it was making investments, the bank could ensure that the checks it received from other banks plus the cash deposited in it were just matched by its outpayments. An occasional, temporary outward drain of funds could be met by permitting the bank to pay by check what it owed to other banks for the few hours or days until some part of its asset portfolio was able to be liquidated or until it contracted its operations so as to get in a surplus of inpayments over outpayments.

the possibility of extreme losses, the banker can try to diversify his investments as much as possible, so as not to put all his eggs in one basket. More than that, a conservative bank will have a considerable amount of capital put up by the stockholders. For example, capital stock may have been issued equal to 10 per cent of demand deposits. Then, even if all the bank's assets are in earning investments rather than in nonearning cash, the depositors are protected against all capital losses that do not exceed 10 per cent of the bank's investment portfolio. In ordinary times, this would be quite sufficient so long as the bank confines its activities to gilt-edge bonds, well-investigated mortgages, and conservative business loans.

There is only one last requirement that the bank would have to meet if we are to give it an A+ in deportment. The management must watch the general trend in the growth of its deposits to make sure that the city in which it is located is not becoming a "ghost town" and that the bank is not losing deposits steadily over a long period of time. If this were the case, the bank's investment portfolio would have to be arranged so that it consisted of securities and loans that could be gradually liquidated over time and converted into cash to meet depositors' withdrawals.

Even if the bank is not a declining business, prudent managers must still protect themselves against a temporary surge of withdrawals. To hold cash against such a contingency would be costly, since cash earns no yield. They will usually decide, therefore, to hold in their portfolios as secondary reserves some securities that always have a ready market and can be liquidated at short notice. Government bonds serve this purpose admirably. Short-term bonds (called notes, bills, or certificates) vary little in value and can be liquidated simply by not buying new ones as the old ones come due every 90 days or 12 months. But even long-term government bonds, with 30 years of life before they mature, can serve as secondary reserves in normal times, because they can always be transferred to some other buyer at some quoted market price.[1] The important thing in this connection is not the *date of maturity* of the bond or loan, but rather how "shiftable" the asset is to some other investment institution. Thus, a 90-day loan to a local merchant, which is nonshiftable, is intrinsically less appropriate as secondary reserves than a 90-year gilt-edge bond traded on an organized securities exchange.

LEGAL RESERVE REQUIREMENTS

The above precepts of sound banking practice are quite simple and understandable. They are a little harder to carry out in practice than to state in

---

[1] There is a saying that "You can sell government bonds even on Sunday."

principle; but the same is true of most sage prescriptions concerning sound investing and wise living.

If we compare a "going and growing" bank with any corporation, the sur_ prising thing is not how little cash reserves the banks keep, but that they keep any at all (in excess of till-money requirements). *As long as financial skies are sunny, the same logic that compels the abandonment of a system of 100 per cent reserves argues in favor of negligible reserves!*

TABLE 3. *Legal Reserve Rates for Federal Reserve Member Banks, February, 1951**

	Reserve rates against demand deposits, per cent	Reserve rates against time deposits, per cent
Central Reserve City Banks (New York and Chicago)	24	6
Reserve City Banks (large and medium cities)	20	6
Other Member Banks (small town or country)	14	6

* Before 1936, reserve requirements were for a long time at 13, 10, and 7 per cent against demand deposits and 3 per cent against time deposits. Subsequently, Congress gave the Federal Reserve Board authority to raise these rates, at its discretion, up to double these figures, or to 26, 20, 14, and 6 per cent, respectively. Every few years, the reserve rates have been changed in order to stabilize business activity, as Chapter 17 will discuss.

Yet, if we turn to the facts, we find that a modern prudent bank is expected— and required by law!—to keep a substantial portion of its assets in nonearning cash. These "legal reserves" are in addition to the till money in the bank's vaults and are kept on deposit with the local Federal Reserve Bank. They are never to be used up so long as the bank is solvent. At the present time commercial Member Banks belonging to the federal reserve system are, on the average, legally required to keep in the form of nonearning cash reserves deposited with the Federal Reserve Bank a little less than 20 per cent of their demand deposits.[1] More precisely, Table 3 gives the present-day legal reserve requirements of all member banks of the federal reserve system.

[1] English banks are required by force of custom rather than law to keep about 8 to 10 per cent cash reserves, and, if possible, another 20 per cent in the secondary form of short-term government and private "bills" (highly endorsed, secured, and negotiable, short-term promissory notes).

If, as has just been argued, reserves seem to be largely unnecessary, why are there such legal requirements? And why, in all logic, should the so-called "time" or "saving" deposits of banks require only a 6 per cent reserve ratio? Although these are theoretically withdrawable only on 30 days' notice, are not they in fact paid on personal demand? Surely no bank that can be solvent in 30 days can really be bankrupt today? Moreover, why are there lower reserve rates required for savings deposits, which above all embody the savings of the poor and whose safety is of paramount importance?

PARADOXES OF FRACTIONAL RESERVE BANKING

A partial answer to our paradox arises from the fundamental fact that *fractional reserve banking* is essentially an unstable, "fair-weather" business. As long as all depositors do not want to withdraw all their deposits at one and the same time, they are free to have their money on demand. But as soon as they all care to exercise this right simultaneously, no one can have his money! A single bank can weather a bank run by shifting its assets on to some other financial institution and thereby converting them into cash. But in time of financial panic, all banks together cannot meet a general run by liquidating their portfolios. There is then no one—except the government and Federal Reserve Banks—to whom their earning assets can be shifted; no way to keep even the strongest and most conservative bank from becoming bankrupt.

This perverse situation is made all the worse because of a similar perversity on the part of depositors. As long as they know they can have their money from the bank, the depositors do not want it. As soon as they know (or suspect) that they cannot withdraw their money, they insist on having it! But when all act upon this fear or suspicion, they unwittingly transform it from an unfounded rumor into actual reality.

This is borne out by the history of private banking. Both here and in England it is a history of periodic crisis, panic, and bankruptcy.[1] When the foul storm blows, all banks are bowled over, and, afterward only the strongest institutions are able to get back on their feet. The weaker ones are gone forever and with them part of the depositors' money.

It is against such financial contingencies that the custom of requiring legal reserves against deposits grew up. *As a result, modern private banking is an uneasy compromise of elements which are unnecessary if the sun is shining and insufficient if it is not.* In time of financial panic, no purely private banking system with less than 100 per cent cash reserves will do, certainly not one with 10 or 20 per cent reserves—as the bank crisis of 1933 shows. In normal times when

[1] Some 8,000 banks with more than 5 billion dollars of deposits became insolvent in 1930–1933.

money can be safely invested at a profit, there is no good reason for requiring nonearning cash reserves of anywhere near the legal amounts.

Actually legal reserve requirements can conceivably cause more banks to fail than otherwise. Because banks had little excess reserves prior to the crisis of the early 1930's, the first drain of deposits caused some banks to fall below their legal reserve ratios. Thus, technically, they became insolvent and were shut down, thus intensifying the panic. Some of the closed banks might possibly have been able to weather the crisis if they had not been declared insolvent. After all, most insurance companies, whose assets declined in market value and marketability along with bank assets in the years following 1929, were able to weather the storm just because their policy contracts did not require them to *appear* to be able to liquidate all their liabilities at an instant's notice. Except for loans on policies, they were largely able to meet all demands for cash from the new business coming in.

Even a bank with cash reserves far in excess of legal requirements can be in a very bad condition if the true value of its earning assets has fallen far enough below their cost. The extra cash reserve may enable it to put up a bold, false front and best a psychological bank run. (For this purpose the best strategy is always to maintain a cheerful countenance and to pay out money gladly and freely to all comers in the hope that this will allay their doubts and fears and end the panic.) But still from a long-run standpoint, the bank may be completely insolvent.

Making the bank hold extra dollars of cash is a very indirect and somewhat ineffective way of protecting depositors from suffering when banks incur losses on their earning assets. All that can be said for this method is that each dollar held in cash is at least safe from loss. Sound principles of bank management and bank regulation imply infinitely more—and possibly less—than this.

MAKING BANKS SAFE

Perhaps this is a rather gloomy picture. Certainly if one reviews the history of private, small-scale nineteenth-century banking, there is plenty of gloom to be found in it. However, the above remarks are not still fully applicable because today we no longer have a purely *private* banking system. All countries have long recognized that banking is one of those activities "affected with public interest" and in need of government control. They have created Central Banks, like the federal reserve system and the Bank of England, to correct the intrinsic instability of laissez-faire banking. All the monetary and fiscal powers of the government's Treasury Department are used to keep financial panics from developing and to stem them when they do. In addition, through bank examinations and by enforceable rules, the freedom of behavior of bank management is narrowly limited.

The successive steps taken by government to modify the instability of laissez-faire banking can be briefly described:

1. *Regulation of Bank Formation and Activity.* For decades, either the state or federal authorities have set down the conditions under which banks could be formed—the minimum amount of capital they must have, etc. Bank examiners periodically scrutinize the composition of bank assets and pass on the bank's solvency, always keeping in mind that an ounce of prevention is worth a pound of cure.

2. *Formation of Federal Reserve System.* The next great forward step was the establishment of central banks, whose primary function is to stand as a rock of Gibraltar in time of panic, to be ready to use the full monetary powers of the government to stem collapse of the banking system. The other subsidiary, but important, functions of a central bank will be discussed later.

3. *Government Insurance of Bank Deposits.* One of the most important government bank reforms is also one of the most recent. Following the bank crisis of 1933, the FDIC was set up to insure the safety of all bank deposits originally up to $5,000, but since 1950 up to $10,000, per deposit.[1] All banks which are members of the federal reserve system *must* belong, and most state banks also do belong. In return for a yearly payment by the banks, which varies with their total deposits, all their customers are completely protected against any loss (up to $10,000) even if the bank should go bankrupt.

The importance of this measure can hardly be exaggerated. It would be absolutely wrong to say that bank bankruptcy is no longer a danger. But, certainly, there need never again be universal bank runs. From now on banks will be closed up by bank examiners and government authorities, and not by the panicky behavior of depositors whose fears bring on the very contingency they are most afraid of. A single bank need no longer fear that its reputation, like that of a good woman, is compromised simply by being accused, regardless of the truth of the charge.

How is government action able to bring about this important change, without which our system of small unit banking would remain perilously unsafe? First, by relying on the comforting basic principle underlying all insurance; *i.e.*, by being able to average out and cancel off large-scale probabilities. Second,

---

[1] In 1950, there were about 104 million depositors in FDIC-insured banks; the $10,000 limit insured more than 98 per cent of all dollars on deposit. On a $\frac{1}{12}$ of 1 per cent annual premium charged on all deposits, the FDIC has accumulated more than a billion dollars of surplus.

and most important in view of our many earlier warnings that depressions cannot be insured against by ordinary actuarial methods, is the fact that the government can (and must!) use its *boundless emergency monetary powers* to avert collapse whenever a real financial crisis should arise.

B. *THE CREATION OF BANK DEPOSITS*

CAN BANKS REALLY CREATE MONEY?

We now turn to one of the most interesting aspects of money and credit, the process called "multiple expansion of bank deposits." This is little understood. Most people have heard that in some mysterious manner banks are able to create money out of thin air, but too few really understand how the process works.

Actually, there is nothing magical or incomprehensible about the creation of bank deposits. At every step of the way, any intelligent person can follow what is happening to the banks' accounts. The true explanation of deposit creation is simple. What is difficult to grasp are the false explanations still in wide circulation.

According to these false explanations, the managers of an ordinary bank are able, by some use of their fountain pens, to lend several dollars for each dollar left on deposit with them. No wonder practical bankers see red when such behavior is attributed to them. They only wish they could do so! As every banker well knows, he cannot invest money that he does not have; and any money that he does invest in buying a security or making a loan will soon leave his bank.

Bankers, therefore, often go to the opposite extreme. Because each small bank is limited in the way it can "create money," they sometimes argue that the whole banking system cannot create money. "After all," they say, "we can invest only what is left with us. We don't create anything. We only put the community's savings to work." Bankers who argue in this way are quite wrong. They have become enmeshed in our old friend, the fallacy of composition: what is true for each is not true for all. The banking system as a whole can do what each small bank cannot do!

Our answer then to the question of this section is in the affirmative. Yes, the banking system and the public do, between them, create about $5 of bank deposits for every dollar taken out of circulation and left in the banks. Let us see how.

HOW DEPOSITS ARE CREATED

We begin with a brand-new deposit of $1,000 which is brought to a bank. Now, if banks were to keep 100 per cent cash reserve balances, like the old goldsmiths, they could not create any extra money out of a new deposit of $1,000 left with them. The depositor would be simply giving up $1,000 of currency for a $1,000 checking deposit whenever he brought his money to the bank.

The change in the bank's balance sheet, as far as the new demand deposit is concerned, would be as shown in Table 4a.

TABLE 4a. *Original Bank in Initial Position*

Assets		Liabilities	
Cash reserve balances	+$1,000	Deposits	+$1,000
Total	+$1,000	Total	+$1,000

The bank has not created this deposit *alone*. The customer had to be willing to make the deposit. Once he took the initiative, the bank was also willing to accept a checking account from the customer. Together the bank and the public have "created" $1,000 of bank money or deposit. But there is no multiple expansion, no 5 for 1 or anything else. So long as the banks keep 100 per cent reserves, the growth of bank money is just offset by the decline of currency in circulation.

Suppose now that the bank does not have to keep 100 per cent reserves. Suppose that the law requires it to keep only 20 per cent legal reserves. (It can always keep larger reserves if it wishes to; but if there are many outstanding, relatively safe, interest-yielding government bonds or numerous profitable lending opportunities, the bank will not find it profitable to keep much more reserves than the law requires.)

What can the bank now do? Can it expand its loans and investments by $4,000 so that the change in its balance sheet looks as shown in Table 4b?

TABLE 4b. *Impossible Situation for Single Small Bank*

Assets		Liabilities	
Cash reserve balances	+$1,000	Deposits	+$5,000
Loans and investments	+ 4,000		
Total	+$5,000	Total	+$5,000

The answer is definitely "no." Why not? Total assets equal total liabilities. Cash reserves meet the legal requirement of being 20 per cent of total deposits.

True enough. But how does the bank pay for the investments or earning assets that it buys? Like everyone else it writes out a check to the man who sells the bond or signs the promissory note. If all such people would promise not to cash the bank's check—or what is the same thing, to hold all such money frozen on deposit in the bank—then, of course, the bank could buy all it wants to without losing any cash.

In fact, no one will borrow money at 6 per cent just to hold it all in the bank. The borrower spends the money on labor, on materials, or perhaps on an automobile. The money will very soon, therefore, have to be paid out of the bank. And if the bank is only one of many banks serving that city, county, state, and country, only a fraction of the sums withdrawn will ever come back to the original bank in another customer's deposit.

This loss of cash by a bank expanding its investments is even more clearly seen if the bank buys a bond rather than makes a local loan. The man who sells to a New England bank a United States government bond through a New York brokerage house may himself live in Columbus, Ohio. He puts the check that he receives in his own bank. This Columbus bank, of course, presents the check—through the federal reserve clearing system—to the New England bank for payment. The New England bank loses cash, or what is the same thing, loses part of its legal reserve deposit at the (Boston) Federal Reserve Bank. (Go back and read this paragraph over again until you are sure you can follow the various steps.)

A bank cannot eat its cake and have it too. The New England bank cannot buy a bond and keep its cash at the same time. Table 4b gives, therefore, a completely false picture of what an individual bank can do. Does this mean that Table 4a tells the end of the story? Must the bank, therefore, behave like the 100 per cent reserve goldsmith bankers? Of course not. Although the bank cannot jack its deposits up to five times its cash reserve, it certainly can *reduce its cash down* to one-fifth of its deposits. Nothing is easier. For, as we have just seen, all it has to do is buy $800 worth of earning assets—bonds, loans, or mortgages. In a day or so it will lose practically all this cash as its checks come back for payment. Now its balance sheet will be as shown in Table 4c.

TABLE 4c. *Original Bank in Final Position*

Assets		Liabilities	
Cash reserve balances	+$ 200	Deposits	+$1,000
Loans and investments	+ 800		
Total	+$1,000	Total	+$1,000

As far as this first bank is concerned, we are through. Its legal reserves are just enought to match its deposits. There is nothing more it can do until the public decides to bring in some more money on deposit.

But the banking system as a whole cannot yet settle down. The people who sold the bonds or borrowed from the bank will presumably deposit the proceeds in some other bank or will pay them out to someone else who will make such a deposit. Our original bank has thus lost $800 to some other banks in the system. If we lump these other banks all together and call them "second-generation banks," their balance sheets now appear as shown in Table 4d.

TABLE 4d. *Second-generation Banks in Initial Position*

Assets		Liabilities	
Cash reserve balances.........	+$800	Deposits....................	+$800
Total...................	+$800	Total...................	+$800

Of course, these banks are scattered all over the country. (Our original bank might even constitute a small part of the second generation as a few of its checks fell into the hands of its own depositors.) To these banks the dollars deposited are just like any other dollars, *just like our original deposit;* these banks don't know and don't care, that they are second in a chain of deposits. They do know, and they do care, that they are now holding too much non-earning cash. Only one-fifth of $800, or $160, is legally needed against $800 deposits. Therefore, they can, and will, use the other four-fifths to buy $640 worth of loans and investments; so that in a few days, their balance sheet will have reached equilibrium as shown in Table 4e.

TABLE 4e. *Final Position of Second-generation Banks*

Assets		Liabilities	
Cash reserve balances.........	+$160	Deposits....................	+$800
Loans and investments.........	+ 640		
Total...................	+$800	Total...................	+$800

So much for the second-generation banks. Thus far, the original $1,000 taken out of hand-to-hand circulation and put into the banking system has given rise to $1,000 (first-generation deposits) plus $800 (second-generation deposits). The total of money has increased. And the end is not yet in sight.

For the $640 spent by the second-generation banks in acquiring loans and investments will go to a new set of banks called the "third-generation banks." The reader should by now be able to fill in their balance sheets as they look

TABLE 4f. *Initial Position of Third-generation Banks*

Assets		Liabilities	
Cash reserve balances.........	+....	Deposits....................	+....
Loans and investments.........	....		
Total...................	+....	Total...................	+$640

initially (see Table 4*f*). Clearly the third-generation banks will at first have *excess* cash *reserves* of an amount equal to four-fifths of $640, or $512. After this sum has been spent on loans and investments—and only then—the third-generation banks will reach equilibrium with the balance sheet as shown in Table 4*g*.

TABLE 4*g*. *Final Equilibrium of Third-generation Banks*

Assets		Liabilities	
Cash reserve balances	+$128	Deposits	+$640
Loans and investments	+ 512		
Total	+$640	Total	+$640

The total of bank deposit money is now $1,000 plus $800 plus $640, or $2,440. This is already almost 2½ to 1 expansion. But a fourth generation of banks will clearly end up with four-fifths of $640 in deposits, or $512; and the fifth generation will get four-fifths of $512, or $409.60; and the sixth generation four-fifths of $409.60; and so on; until finally by the twenty-fifth round, we shall have got all but $1 of the total sum of the infinitely many series of generations.

What will be the final sum: $1,000 + $800 + $640 + $512 + $409.60 + · · · ? If we patiently do out the sum by arithmetic, we shall find that it gets

TABLE 4*h*. *Multiple Expansion of Bank Deposits through the Banking System*

	New deposits	New loans and invest- ments	Cash reserve balances
Original banks	$1,000.00	$ 800.00	$ 200.00
2d-generation banks	800.00	640.00	160.00
3d-generation banks	640.00	512.00	128.00
4th-generation banks	512.00	409.60	102.40
5th-generation banks	409.60	327.68	81.92
6th-generation banks	327.68	262.14*	65.54*
7th-generation banks	262.14*	209.72*	52.42*
8th-generation banks	209.72*	167.77*	41.95*
9th-generation banks	167.77*	134.22*	33.55*
10th-generation banks	134.22*	107.37*	26.85*
Sum of first 10 generation banks	$4,463.13*	$3,570.50*	$ 892.63*
Sum of remaining generation banks	536.87*	429.50*	107.37*
Total for banking system as a whole	$5,000.00	$4,000.00	$1,000.00

* Rounded off to two decimal places.

to \$4999.999 . . . and "finally" to \$5,000. Table 4*h* shows the complete effects of the chain of deposit creation.

We can also get the same answer in two other ways—by common sense and by elementary algebra.[1]

Common sense tells us that the process of deposit creation can come to an end only when no bank *anywhere in the system* has cash reserves in excess of the 20 per cent reserve ratio to deposits. In all our previous examples no cash has ever leaked out of the banking system, but has simply gone out, as a result of security purchases, from one set of banks into another set of banks' vaults. Everyone will be at equilibrium only when a consolidated balance sheet for all the banks together—for the first, the second, and the hundredth generation— would look as shown in Table 4*i*. For if deposits were less than \$5,000, the 20 per cent ratio would not yet be reached and equilibrium would not yet have been achieved.

TABLE 4*i*. *Consolidated Balance Sheet Showing Final Position of All Banks Together*

Assets		Liabilities	
Cash reserve balances	+\$1,000	Deposits	+\$5,000
Loans and investments	+\$4,000		
Total	+\$5,000	Total	+\$5,000

If the reader will compare Table 4*i* with Table 4*b* previously marked *impossible*, he will see that the whole banking system can do what no one bank can do by itself. Bank money has been created 5 for 1—and all the while each bank has invested and lent only a fraction of what it has received as deposits!

Who creates the multiple expansion of deposits? Three parties do so jointly: the public by always keeping its money in the bank on deposit; the banks by keeping only a fraction of their deposits in the form of cash; the public and private borrowers who make it possible for the banks to find earning assets to buy with their excess cash. There is also a fourth party, the Central Bank, which by its activities makes it possible for new reserves to come to the banking system, as the next chapters will show.

There is nothing paradoxical in the fact that total bank deposits are several times as great as the amount of paper cash in existence anywhere; the same is true of the total of government bonds and real-estate values. Deposits are something that banks *owe* their customers; cash is *left* in a bank, but it does not

[1] This can be proved by algebra as follows:

$$\$1,000 + \$800 + \$640 + \cdots = \$1,000[1 + \tfrac{4}{5} + (\tfrac{4}{5})^2 + (\tfrac{4}{5})^3 + \cdots]$$
$$= \$1,000 \left(\frac{1}{1 - \tfrac{4}{5}} \right) = \$1,000\ (5)$$
$$= \$5,000$$

remain in that bank. Throughout its lifetime a dollar may have been *left* in many banks, just as it may be used over a long period of time to buy hundreds of dollars of merchandise. The one thing to keep firmly in mind is that bank deposits are one of the three forms of modern money, and quantitatively the most important.

Before leaving this section, the reader should test his knowledge of credit creation by tracing through in detail what happens when a nervous widow permanently *withdraws* $1,000 from a single bank and hides it in her attic. (1) The bank loses $1,000 of cash and $1,000 of deposits. But it previously held only 20 per cent cash reserves or $200 against her deposit. Clearly it must have given up to her some of its legally necessary cash reserves held against its other demand deposits. Show that its total reserves are now below the legal minimum. (2) Therefore, it must sell $800 worth of investments or call in that many loans. The first-generation bank will be in equilibrium only when its balance sheet finally looks as shown in Table 5*a*.

TABLE 5*a*. *Equilibrium Position of Original Bank Losing a Deposit*

Assets		Liabilities	
Cash reserve balances	−$ 200	Deposits	−$1,000
Loans and investments	− 800		
Total	−$1,000	Total	−$1,000

But in selling its securities, our original bank has drained $800 from a second generation of banks; and they in turn by liquidating securities, drain reserves from a third generation. And so it goes—until the widow's withdrawal of $1,000 has produced a chain "killing off" $5,000 worth of deposits throughout the whole system and $4,000 of bank-earning assets. The student should trace through each stage: Table 5*b*, Table 5*c*, . . . , etc.

The reader should also be able to show how an initial deposit of $1,000 can result in $10,000 of bank deposits if banks keep only 10 per cent reserve ratios, as they used to until 1936.

A "MONOPOLY BANK"

In all of the above processes, it was assumed that no cash leaked out of the banking system into someone's mattress or into permanent hand-to-hand circulation. The banking system was then in the enviable position of finding that its checks were always deposited somewhere within itself.

This being so, it is easy to see that a single "monopoly bank" (with many branches), serving the whole nation, would be able to do at once what we have said each small bank cannot do. Its balance sheet could quickly go to the condition shown in Table 4*b* or 4*i*. It could write checks freely to pay for securities or loans, knowing that the people to whom they are paid would always deposit their proceeds back in the one and only monopoly bank. In countries like England, where there is a "big 5" group of branch banks, or like Canada where there are a few large banks, or in states like California where there are a few great multiple-branch banks—in such cases a bank may be able to lend out more than its legal excess reserves, knowing that part of the money will come back to itself in later "generations." However, these so-called "derivative" or "self-returning" deposits are not important for the United States, and calling attention to them often only confuses the beginning student.

SIMULTANEOUS EXPANSION OR CONTRACTION BY ALL BANKS

In the previous section we have seen how the banking system can reach the limits of its expansion through many successive rounds or generations. If we allow half a week for checks to clear at each stage and for decisions to be made, then 5 to 8 weeks would be required for the process to have substantially worked itself out through more than a dozen rounds.

As a practical matter, it is usually not necessary to follow the chain of each dollar deposited through its successive rounds. For example, a decrease in hoarding by the public will affect almost all the banks at the same time. They will all receive some new deposits at pretty much the same time. They will all have excess reserves in the first instance, and so they will all together begin to buy securities or make loans.

When a single small bank, all by itself, writes checks to acquire securities, these checks go to other banks and it loses cash. But when all are writing checks simultaneously and in balance, there will tend to be a cancellation of new checks deposited in each bank against those paid out. No one bank need lose cash reserves. Consequently, without going through the successive generations of the previous section, all banks together can simply and blithely expand their loans and investments—so long as they do not jeopardize their reserve position —until deposits are finally brought into a 5:1 relation to cash. When this state has been reached, the banking system has reached the limit of its ability to create money.

The reader should work through the similar process by which all banks simultaneously contract money 5:1 for each dollar of reserve withdrawn from the banking system, and also he should show how a monopoly bank would contract.

THREE QUALIFICATIONS

Finally, three qualifications must be made. We have shown that $1,000 taken out of hand-to-hand circulation and put into a bank can result in an increase of $5,000 of bank deposits. This assumed that all the new money remained somewhere in the banking system, in one bank or another at every stage of the process, and that all banks were able to keep "loaned up" with no "excess reserves."

1. *Leakage into Hand-to-hand Circulation.*   It is quite possible, however, and even likely, that somewhere along the chain of deposit expansion some individual who receives a check will not leave the proceeds in a bank, but will withdraw it into circulation or into hoarding outside the banking system. As a matter of fact, in boom times when bank deposits are expanding, there is usually at the same time an increased need for pennies, dimes, and paper currency to transact the increased volume of petty transactions.

The effects of such withdrawals on our analysis are simple. When $1,000 stayed in the banking system, $5,000 of new deposits were created. If $200 were to leak out into circulation outside the banks, and only $800 of new reserves were to remain in the banking system, then the new deposits created would be $4,000 ($800 × 5). The banking system can always amplify in a 5:1 ratio whatever amount of new reserves is permanently left with it.

2. *Leakage into Bank Vault Cash.*   Similar to the leakage of cash into circulation outside the banks is the fact that banks will have to keep some of their new cash in the form of till money, or vault cash. This is in addition to their legally required 20 per cent reserves left on deposit with the local Federal Reserve Bank. Such cash cannot be counted as part of the bank's 20 per cent legal reserve because all legal reserves must be on deposit with the Federal Reserve Bank in the bank's district. In 1951, something like 2 per cent of their deposits were kept by banks as till money. An increase of such vault cash acts rather like a leakage of cash into hand-to-hand circulation. Instead of having new deposits equal to 5 × $1,000, we have them equal to about 5 × ($1,000 − $100) or $4,500. This is because $100—more or less 2 per cent of $5,000—is the amount of vault cash which the bank cannot use as its legal reserve.[1]

3. *Possible Excess Reserves.*   Our description of multiple deposit creation has proceeded on the assumption that the commercial banks stick fairly closely to their legal reserve ratios. Of course there is no reason why a bank cannot choose to keep more than the legally required amount of reserves. Thus, suppose the original bank receiving a new $1,000 deposit had been satisfied to hold $800 of it in excess reserves. Then the whole process would have ended right there, with no multiple expansion of deposits. Or if banks were always to keep 5 per cent excess reserves, in addition to the 20 per cent legal

---

[1] Another way of expressing this relation, and one that is slightly more exact, is as follows: The new $1,000 will give rise not to

$$\$1,000 \times \frac{1}{0.20} \text{ but to } \$1,000 \times \frac{1}{(0.20 + 0.02)}$$

This gives $4,545.45 of new deposits.

requirement, we should have a chain of expansion of deposits of the form $[1 + \frac{3}{4} + (\frac{3}{4})^2 + \cdot \cdot \cdot]$ rather than $[1 + \frac{4}{5} + (\frac{4}{5})^2 + \cdot \cdot \cdot]$, with only a 4:1 rather than a 5:1 expansion of deposits.

Hence there is nothing automatic about deposit creation. Four factors are necessary: The banks must somehow receive new reserves; they must be willing to make loans or buy securities; someone must be willing to borrow or to sell securities; and finally, the public must choose to leave its money on deposit with the banks. We shall return to the problem of excess and legal reserves in Chapter 17.

SUMMARY

A. THE MODERN BANKING SYSTEM

1. The American banking system consists primarily of relatively small-scale unit banks, chartered by the national government or by the states. Although less than half are members of the federal reserve system, their deposits include four-fifths of the total of all deposits.

2. The functions of commercial banks are numerous and overlap with those of such other financial institutions as mutual savings banks, cooperative building and loan societies, finance companies, trusteeships, and insurance companies. But in their function of collecting and honoring bank checks, the commercial banks perform a unique and important economic role. Their demand deposits constitute the single most important component of our money supply or medium of exchange.

3. The federal reserve system consists primarily of (a) Member Banks, (b) the 12 Federal Reserve Banks spread over the country, (c) the Board of Governors of the federal reserve system in Washington.

Although nominally corporations owned by the member banks, the Federal Reserve Banks are, in fact, almost branches of the federal government, possessing wide powers and being concerned with the public interest rather than with bank profits. In practice, their activities are not independent of Treasury and Administration policy. It is the primary responsibility of the Reserve Banks to use their powers in time of panic so as to prevent a collapse of the banking system and at all times to contribute toward full employment with stable prices.

4. Modern banks gradually evolved from the old goldsmith establishments in which money and valuables were stored. The practice finally became general of holding far less than 100 per cent reserves against deposits, the rest being invested in securities and loans for an interest yield.

5. The resulting laissez-faire fractional reserve system would be a fair-weather system with great instability, were it not for government control and assistance. If depositors all try to withdraw their money, they can ruin the banking system despite the existence of legal reserves. On the other hand, when financial skies are clear, cash reserves far less than the legal requirements will enable a bank to meet all calls upon it.

6. Without government regulation and examination, without the federal reserve system, and without the guaranteeing of bank deposits by the FDIC, our system of small unit banking would be intolerable. Indeed, a few economists think that a return to a 100 per cent reserve banking system is desirable and necessary, not only for safety, but also to prevent banks from creating bank deposits.

B. THE CREATION OF BANK DEPOSITS

7. Bank demand deposits serve as a medium of exchange and a store of value; they are considered, therefore, to be money.

8. If banks kept 100 per cent cash reserves against all deposits, there would be no creation of money when currency was taken out of circulation and deposited in the banking system. There would be only a 1:1 exchange of one kind of money for another kind of money.

9. Modern banks do not keep 100 per cent cash reserves against deposits. In 1951 large-city members of the federal reserve system are required to keep, on deposit with the regional Federal Reserve Bank, legal reserves equal to 24 or 20 per cent of demand deposits; small-town Member Banks need keep only 14 per cent.

10. Consequently, the banking system as a whole—together with public or private borrowers and the depositing public—does create deposit money almost 5:1 for each new dollar taken out of circulation and left on deposit somewhere in the system.

11. Each small bank is limited in its ability to create deposits. It cannot lend or invest more than it has received from depositors; it can lend only about four-fifths as much. Its deposits are five times its cash only because it spends away cash every time it buys earning assets, only because its cash decreases and not because its deposits increase.

12. But the system as a whole can do what each small bank cannot do. This can be seen if we examine a monopoly bank in a closed community. The checks written by such a bank always come back to it; therefore the only restriction upon its ability to expand its investments and deposits (its assets *and* its liabilities in double-entry bookkeeping) is the requirement that it keep one-fifth cash reserve ratios against deposits. When deposits have expanded

until they are five times the increase of reserves, the monopoly bank is "loaned up" and can create no further deposits until given more cash reserves.

13. In present-day America, there is no monopoly bank. Nevertheless, the same 5 : 1 expansion of bank deposits takes place. The first individual bank receiving a new $1,000 of deposits spends four-fifths of its newly acquired cash on loans and investments. This gives a second group of banks four-fifths of $1,000 in new deposits. They, in turn, keep one-fifth in cash and spend the other four-fifths for new earning assets; this causes them to lose cash to a third set of banks, whose deposits have gone up by four-fifths of four-fifths of $1,000. Obviously, if we follow through the successive groups of banks in the dwindling, never-ending chain, we find for the system as a whole that new deposits created are

$$\$1,000 + \$800 + \$640 + \$512 + \cdots$$
$$= \$1,000 \times \left[1 + \frac{4}{5} + \left(\frac{4}{5}\right)^2 + \left(\frac{4}{5}\right)^3 + \cdots \right]$$
$$= \$1,000 \left(\frac{1}{1 - \frac{4}{5}}\right) = \$1,000 \left(\frac{1}{\frac{1}{5}}\right) = \$5,000$$

Only when every one of the thousand dollars of new reserves supports $5 of deposits somewhere in the system, will the limits to deposit expansion be reached. Then the system is loaned up; it can create no new deposits until it is given more reserves.

14. In practice, it is not necessary to wait for the successive rounds in the chain of $1,000, $800, $640, etc., to work themselves out. Usually, many banks tend to get new reserves at about the same time. If they all expand their loans and investments pretty much in balance, their outpayments will tend to cancel each other. Consequently, they will not lose cash. And so, all together can rather quickly expand their earning assets and deposits to the 5 : 1 limit.

15. As a minor qualification to the above discussion, we must admit that there will be some leakage of the new cash reserves of the banking system into circulation outside the banks. Therefore, instead of 5 × $1,000 of new deposits created as in the previous examples, we may have 5 × something less than $1,000—the difference being what is withdrawn out of the system. It is still correct to say that the new deposits created will be 5 times whatever is the amount of the new legal reserves left with the banks.

A second minor qualification must take account of the need of banks to use a little of their new reserves for vault cash or till money. Recently this has been about 2 per cent of deposits. This reduces our true ratio of expansion from about 5/1 to about 4.5/1, or more exactly 1/(0.20 + 0.02).

A third and more important qualification results from the fact that a bank may keep *excess reserves* in addition to legally required reserves.

In this chapter we have seen how bank deposits are kept at about five times the legal reserves of the banking system. In Chapter 17, we shall learn how the Federal Reserve Banks cause bank reserves to go up when an expansion of the total money supply is desired. When a contraction of the quantity of money is in order, the Federal Reserve authorities pull the brakes. Instead of pumping new reserves into the banking system, they kill off some of the reserves. We shall see that in so doing they are able to reduce the quantity of money, not 1 for 1, but, as we have shown, almost 5 for 1. Chapter 16, the next chapter, explains why economists think that monetary policy has important effects on interest rates, investment, and income.

QUESTIONS FOR DISCUSSION

1. Describe the banking setup in your area. Make a list of the services rendered by banks. Who else renders such services? Examine the balance sheets of local banks. What is the meaning of the different items? Can you find out how local checks are cleared?

2. Suppose that all banks kept 100 per cent reserves. How different would they be?

3. Assume a 10 per cent reserve ratio. Trace through the process of multiple bank expansion, duplicating Tables 4*a* through 4*i*. Reverse the process.

4. Do bankers create deposits? Who does? If a banker receives a new deposit and new reserves, is he always able to find borrowers? What can he do to increase his loans beyond lowering his interest charges? Can he always expand his holdings of government securities? How does he go about it?

5. How would you invest a bank's money? Give a typical portfolio of investments.

6. Comment on the following 1939 statement of the Board of Governors of the federal reserve system: "The federal reserve system can see to it that banks have enough reserves to make money available to commerce, industry, and agriculture at low rates; but it cannot make the people borrow, and it cannot make the public spend the deposits that result when the banks do make loans and investments."

7. How would your answer to Question 3 be changed if banks always kept 2 per cent of their deposits in the form of vault cash?

8. In Table 1 of Chapter 14, demand deposits showed about a 60-billion-dollar increase in the recent war decade. About how much of an increase in legal reserves and in loans and investments would this involve? (Hint: Use a 20 per cent reserve rate.)

Chapter 16: MONEY, INTEREST,

AND INCOME

IN THE last two chapters we have seen what the supply of money and near-money looks like. We have seen how bank deposits, the most important of the three forms of money, can be manufactured by the banking system in a 5 to 1 fashion out of any new reserves provided to the banks.

In this chapter we ask: Why is the supply of money important? How does it affect total consumption and investment spending? How does it affect prices? What are the crucial relations between money and interest rates and investment?

After these questions have been discussed, we shall be ready to tackle the important problem of the next chapter: Exactly what can a Central Bank, like the Bank of England or the 12 Federal Reserve Banks, do to help stabilize employment and prices through the weapons of monetary policy?

HOW MONEY AFFECTS SAVING AND INVESTMENT OR TOTAL SPENDING

To put matters most simply, an increase in the amount of *money* tends to depress the rate of *interest*; and a reduction in the interest rate tends to increase the flow of *investment* spending, thereby raising *income*, consumption, and production or prices. The key words have been italicized: money, interest, investment, and income.

The next chapter will explain the detailed mechanics by which the Federal Reserve Banks, the Treasury, and the commercial banks manage to increase and decrease the total supply of money. Let us here skip all the details and concentrate on fundamentals. For this purpose let us imagine that we are dealing with a primitive Central Banker. Essentially he is a state-licensed counterfeiter whom the state has given the right to print money under certain circumstances. (Actually this is the historical way that many Central Banks, such as the Bank of England, did begin.) The money he prints is indistinguishable from all the other money in circulation, and for simplicity suppose him not to perform the banking function of holding the deposits of any person or bank. What are the conditions under which he might print and pay out money?

First, you could conceivably imagine him to print money in order to hire labor and to make purchases of goods and services. This would certainly have upward influences on the level of income for all the reasons discussed in connection with saving and investment. But no state would give a Central Banker the right to print money for such a purpose. It would be the Treasurer and not the Central Banker who would make such direct purchases, and such an activity we should more likely wish to call a fiscal-policy operation rather than simply an act of monetary policy. We may leave fiscal policy to Chapter 19. Here we wish to provide an introduction to the problems of Central Banking policy of the type to be discussed in detail in the next chapter.

Second, the Central Banker might print money in order to buy up government bonds. This would be well within his charter, which requires him always to acquire an asset when he issues his beautifully printed currency or I. O. U.'s. Suppose he does buy 1 billion dollars of government bonds in the open market? Surely, the effect of this so-called "open-market purchase" will be to bid up the price of government bonds. Such an increase in bond prices is exactly equivalent to a reduction in the interest yield of government bonds. Why? Because if a bond continues to pay $3 per year and rises in price from $100 to something above $100, then certainly its annual interest yield has fallen to below 3 per cent. Or let us put the same thing in a different way. If people who used to have their wealth in the form of government bonds now have lots of excess cash, they will be looking around for places to invest their money. This means that interest rates to borrowers will be low.

Instead of buying bonds, the primitive Central Banker might print new money and lend it out at interest. As a new lender of money, he will tend to compete down the existing market rate of interest, reinforcing the effect of the open-market purchase of government bonds.

Essentially, the above represents the basic fact about Central Banking. The Central Banker issues new liabilities in order to expand his "loans and investments," thereby tending to depress interest rates, to increase investment, and to increase income.

If he wants to contract income spending, he does the reverse: He sells bonds on the open market and calls in his loans; with the decline in the total of his loans and investments, there is a decline in his outstanding liabilities of currency as a result of the money paid back to him and received by him for the sale of bonds. This money he can now burn. The effect of these contractionary operations has been to raise interest rates, contract investment, and reduce income. In contrast to an "easy or cheap-money policy" this is called a "tight-money policy."

LOWER INTEREST RATES REINFORCED BY MORE LIBERAL CREDIT RATIONING

"Easy money" or "cheap money" is the name given by economists to a condition of low interest rates and readily available credit. There is one important aspect of the increase in the money supply that should not be neglected but is often overlooked. You may read in the newspapers or in brokers' records that interest rates on such and such a security or loan have fallen by so much. But that is far from the whole story. Even if a lender should make little or no change in the rate of interest that he advertises to his customers, there may probably still be the following important effect of "easy money."

Borrowers who previously would have been considered to be just a little too risky will now be granted loans. This is because the lender now has plenty of money on hand begging for investment opportunities; the lender will now be rationing out credit much more liberally than would be the case if the money market were very tight and interest rates were tending to rise. The plentiful supply of money will also tend to bid up the prices of common stocks. It will be easier now to find buyers for new issues of common stocks. And business firms generally will find it somewhat easier to raise equity capital as well as to raise loan capital.

Whenever in what follows I speak of a lowering of interest rates, I shall also have in mind the equally important relaxation of the rationing of credit and general increase in the availability of equity and loan capital to business.

MONETARY EXPANSION MERELY A CHANGE OF THE FORM OF ASSETS HELD BY THE COMMUNITY?

At this point you may be puzzled. You may wonder whether a Central Banker who deals only in such used assets as bonds can have any appreciable effects on the flow of spending at all like those of a Treasurer who is engaged in direct fiscal policy. You may ask: Has much been accomplished by monetary policy?

To answer this question let us suppose that the Central Banker has issued 1 billion dollars of new money in order to buy government bonds that people used to own.

How has the combined balance sheet changed for everybody in the community other than the Central Banker? Table 1 shows that people generally now have 1 billion dollars more of new currency. But to get this they sold 1 billion dollars of government bonds. As an offset against the 1-billion-dollar increase in new money, there is a 1-billion-dollar decrease in the total of a money substitute, namely, government bonds.

TABLE 1. *Change in Community's Balance Sheet from a One-billion-dollar Monetary Expansion (In billions)*

Change in Assets		Change in Liabilities and Net Worth	
Money................................	+1		
Government bonds (or near-money)	−1		
Total change..................	0	Total change....................	0

Has there been any immediate increase in the community's wealth as a result of the monetary expansion? No. At first appearance there seems to have been merely a change in the form in which people are holding their assets.

If this were all that monetary policy involved, it would not be very important. What our table does not show is the general easing of interest rates and the increased availability of credit to would-be investors. It does not show the upward shift in the earlier chapters' investment-income schedule resulting from the lowered rate of interest. It does not show the primary and secondary increases in income resulting from the increased flow of investment. It does not show the increased stock of buildings, equipment, and inventories that will later result from the cumulation of a high rate of investment.

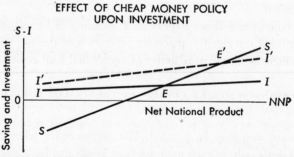

EFFECT OF CHEAP MONEY POLICY
UPON INVESTMENT

FIGURE 1. Cheap money shifts the investment schedule upward from *II*, thereby raising income from *E* to *E'*.

Figure 1 shows how low interest rates and increased cheapness and availability of money have shifted the investment schedule *II* upward to *I'I'*. This will, of course, raise the equilibrium level of income flow. Unemployment will tend to decline; or if already there are substantially full employment and full utilization of plant capacity, then prices will tend to rise.

You may wonder whether the reduced rate of interest will have any appreciable effects on the saving schedule. Will people be less thrifty at lower interest rates, thereby shifting the *SS* schedule downward and further accentuating the increase in income and spending? As Part Four[1] later discusses in detail, the factual evidence suggests that the propensity to consume and save is not affected very much by variations of the interest rate alone. If interest rates fall from 5 per cent to 3 per cent, will I save more or less out of a given income? Either answer is possible, depending upon the person. The weight of evidence seems to be in favor of the conclusion that personal consumption and saving are not appreciably affected on balance by changes in the rate of interest alone.

QUALIFICATIONS TO MONETARY POLICY

In actual practice monetary policy is not always so powerful as this discussion may suggest. Usually it is regarded as at best a supplement to other stabilization policies, such as fiscal policy. There are three limits to the potency of monetary policy:

1. Changes in the amount of money may have very *weak effects on the rate of interest* if rates are already very low and if people are quite indifferent between holding bonds and holding money. People merely give up near-money in exchange for the counterfeiter's money, and the prices of bonds hardly change at all. Banks and other lenders already have plenty of excess cash to lend out to good borrowers; so the Central Banker's willingness to make new loans hardly changes the competitive situation with respect to availability of credit.

2. Even if there are some changes in the rate of interest, the rate of *investment spending may turn out to be relatively little affected by changes in interest rates*. The prospects for investment may depend much more on the depressed state of business (overcapacity of plants, falling price level for inventories) than upon minor changes of 1 or 2 per cent in the interest rate. Businessmen may already find themselves with funds for which there is no real investment outlook; instead they may be repaying their loans as their real assets are allowed to wear out and go unreplaced.

3. Finally, the Central Banker may *be unwilling to push monetary policy very far*. He may claim that changes in the prices of bonds will have unsettling effects on the banking system and on people's confidence. He may be afraid that higher interest rates will increase the earnings of the banks at the expense of the taxpayer who must foot the bill for interest on the public debt. Or the Central Bank's big brother, the Treasury, may not let him change interest rates very much, arguing that the advantages gained by way of induced changes in total spending are of minor importance in comparison with the financial damage done to the taxpayer and to stability in the money market. Whether

[1] See the Appendix to Chapter 29.

all the above arguments are true or false, the result may be limited willingness of the Central Bank to push monetary policy very far.

Cases in point are the postwar behavior of the Bank of England, the Federal Reserve Banks, and the chief Central Banks of Western Europe and the British Commonwealth. With the exception of Belgium and Italy, in no country have the authorities slammed on the monetary brakes really hard.

SUMMARY

1. The essence of monetary policy can be expressed in the single sentence: An increase in the total supply of *money* tends to decrease the rate of *interest*, thereby raising *investment* and *income*.

2. A primitive Central Bank that can print money and use it to buy government bonds or make loans illustrates how such an easy-money policy is brought about: The prices of bonds are bid up by the open-market operation and their interest yields fall; the new source from which businessmen can borrow also eases the interest rates they must pay. In addition to the actual change in interest rates, there is a no less important improvement in the availability of credit. Lenders are less choosy in rationing out credit to marginal borrowers.

3. A tight-money policy is simply the reverse of the above. The Central Banker reduces his total of loans and investments on the asset side of his balance sheet. And to match this, his liabilities of outstanding currency are reduced. To the extent that the public has sold government bonds to the Central Bank, the public's balance sheet will show an increase in money matched by an opposite decrease of near-money.

But not shown on the balance sheet will be the lessened availability of credit to would-be investors and the increase in interest rates. With credit harder to get, the investment schedule will shift downward and its equilibrium intersection with the saving schedule will be at a lower level of income.

4. In practice, monetary policy may not have such strong effects on income for any one of three reasons or for a combination of the three. (*a*) Central Banking operations may have little effect on the rate of interest; especially is this likely to be true when the rate of interest is already near zero and people are indifferent between holding money and near-money. (*b*) Conditions may be such that the position of the investment schedule is relatively independent of the rate of interest and of credit conditions. Firms may already have plenty of funds, and their investment plans may depend more upon the state of their

expectations and degree of excess capacity than upon the ease of borrowing. (c) Economists generally have a higher opinion of the potency of monetary policy to curb a boom than they do of its power to cure a slump. But if there is a large public debt outstanding, the Central Banker may be unwilling or not be permitted to tighten money for fear of the effect on the stability of bond prices. So again monetary policy may, in fact, turn out to have done little good.

The reader may turn to the Appendix if he wishes to understand the relationship between the analysis presented in these last chapters and other ways that economists sometimes use to analyze the same facts: the "Quantity Theory of Money," and the related notion of liquidity-demand for money. However, any reader may, if he wishes, skip the Appendix and turn to the following chapters on Central Banking and fiscal policy.

QUESTIONS FOR DISCUSSION

1. Describe the activity of Central Banking reduced down to simplest terms.

2. Draw up the balance sheet for such a Central Banker after he had been in business for a while. What are his liabilities? His assets?

3. Give definitions of easy money, tight money, open-market purchase or sale, loans and investments as applied to a bank, availability of credit.

4. Suppose you are a businessman. How would monetary policy affect you?

5. Draw up a balance sheet showing the effect on the public of an open-market operation designed to tighten credit.

6. Show the same thing that Figure 1 shows, but use a 45°-line diagram to show income determination.

7. What if E in Figure 1 were already at the point of full employment? What would a cheap-money policy then do?

8. Appraise the three reasons why sole reliance cannot always be placed on monetary policy. Is the last one a criticism of monetary policy or of the people in charge? Which do you think most important?

APPENDIX TO CHAPTER 16
THE "QUANTITY THEORY" AND THE
LIQUIDITY DEMAND FOR MONEY

This chapter showed the steps by which changing the quantity of money may affect money spending and prices. The discussion will be continued in Chapter 17, showing in more detail how a Central Bank such as the federal reserve system functions in changing the quantity of money.

Years ago, many economists omitted some of the detailed steps described in Chapter 16. Instead they shortened the argument: they relied on a particularly simplified theory called the "quantity theory of money," or what might more exactly be called "the theory that the level of money spending and of prices *is directly proportional* to the quantity of money in existence."

Few, if any, economists hold rigidly to the quantity theory today. But it still has much popular appeal; and in analyzing its limitations—*e.g.*, in the "liquidity preference" discussion at the close of this Appendix—our understanding of Central Bank operations will be furthered, and we shall be better equipped for Chapter 17's discussion of the federal reserve system.

THE QUANTITY THEORY OF MONEY

In its simplest form, the argument goes something like the following:

As long as any commodity is scarce, its value will be high. If you increase the supply of wheat, its price will fall. Money is no exception. Even though the paper in a particular nation's money is worthless, fiat money will have value as long as (1) people are accustomed to using the money in question in making their exchanges and (2) as long as the total supply of money is kept *limited in amount*. Of course, if the printing presses spit out billions and billions of units of money, then prices will rise indefinitely high and money will become worthless.

But money differs from wheat and other commodities in an important respect: Money is useful only for what it will buy. The demand for money, therefore, has a very special form: *Double the value of money or halve the price level and you will exactly halve the amount of money which people will wish to hold*. Why? Because if everything now costs only one-half as much, people's cash requirements will be only half as great. In fact, when the prices of absolutely everything change in exactly the same proportion, money is the *only* commodity whose demand is changed—because as far as all *real* magnitudes are concerned, nothing has changed.

Consequently, these theorists arrive at the important conclusion: Other things being equal, *the price level is directly proportional to the amount of money in existence; conversely, the amount of money that people will hold is directly proportional to the price level.* If the total amount of all kinds of money is M and the price level is P, then according to the simplified quantity theory,

$$M = kP \quad \text{or} \quad P = \frac{1}{k} M$$

where k is a factor of proportionality which remains constant if "other things are equal."[1]

In bare essentials, this is the quantity theory. How valid is it? How useful? As stated, it is obviously a highly simplified theory, and most economists today would say it is a highly *over*simplified theory. The "other things" do not always—or often—remain equal in real life, and so the simple quantity theory breaks down. At the very least, in these days when near-money is so important, M should have added to it some allowance for the size of time deposits and for government bonds held by the public.

The fact, however, that the quantity theory is a simplification of the truth and does not always hold with great precision should not be used to damn it utterly. If at least it indicates the general direction of economic behavior, that would be a great deal to be said in its favor.

Unfortunately, even this limited claim cannot always be made for the quantity theory. Its weaknesses have been particularly apparent in connection with attempts to interpret economic events of the past 20 years. Some of the reasons for this we shall see presently.

But first, mention should be made of some of its more valid applications. In times of great inflation when the printing presses are pouring out floods of paper money, the general direction of causation is so simple that even a simplified theory can throw much light on the facts. During the hyperinflations characteristic of some wars or periods of postwar breakdown, the quantity theory could aid in the interpretation of economic events. The recent Chinese and Hungarian inflations provide such examples; and so does the 1920–1923 German inflation. Still earlier examples occur in American history during the Revolutionary War and at the time when the Southern Confederacy was forced to issue tremendous amounts of paper money.[2]

---

[1] For example, if k is equal to 5, then M is always five times the price level. Doubling prices would exactly double M. If k were 0.7, the same thing would be true. The important thing is that k remain a constant. Then prices and money will be proportional.

[2] Even in such times, the painstaking observer will be left with the feeling that the quantity theory does not get down to the fundamental reasons why money is being created at

The simple quantity theory may also have a limited validity in interpreting some of the historical long swings in the price level: the rise in prices following the Spanish discovery of New World gold, the rise in prices after the Californian and Australian gold discoveries of the middle of the nineteenth century, and the rise in prices around the turn of the century as a result of South African and Alaskan gold production.

The truth of the quantity theory of prices depends upon two propositions, neither of which is universally valid: (1) *Prices* must be proportional to *total spending* and (2) *total spending* must be proportional to the amount of *total money* in existence. It would then follow that prices are proportional to the total quantity of money. If either or both (1) and (2) fail to be true, the quantity theory fails as a correct explanation of prices.[1]

INADEQUACIES OF THE QUANTITY THEORY: (1) PRICES NOT PROP RTIONAL TO TOTAL SPENDING

That prices are not always proportional to total spending is clearly seen if we examine an upswing of business activity from a time of deep depression. If the output of goods increases along with the total of spending, *i.e.*, so long as there is still unemployment of labor and factories, there is no need for prices to increase much. In fact, economies of mass production may permit prices to fall as demand increases. Only if we were to make the highly unrealistic assumption of full employment and constant total output—only then would an increase in the total of spending always send prices up proportionately. But if, on the contrary, total output should double, then spending could double without having *any* effect on prices!

In most cycles of business activity, the truth lies somewhere in between: An increase from depression levels in total spending causes a considerable increase in output and a less than proportionate increase in average prices; during a recession of business, the drop in spending results in a drop in output and employment with less than a proportionate fall in prices.

One further example shows how unjustified is the assumption that output will always remain constant in such a way as to keep total spending and prices in direct proportion to each other. Suppose that trade-unions succeed in getting fantastic wage increases, so that competitive costs and prices both double.

the rate it is being created. The true direction of causation is by no means in the one-way direction from M to P.

[1] There is a third serious drawback to the quantity theory which cannot be discussed in an elementary treatment of the subject. Even if it were valid, the quantity theory would be of limited usefulness to the extent that the quantity theorists have no theory—except an inadequate and superficial one—of what determines changes in the quantity of money.

The author does not assert that this must *necessarily* cause a reduction in employment and production. But certainly no one—least of all a believer in the quantity theory—will deny that there might follow, under some assumptions about banking policy, a cut in production as a result of such a vast increase in prices. It follows in such a case that total spending will less than double when prices double.

INADEQUACIES OF THE QUANTITY THEORY: (2) TOTAL SPENDING NOT PROPORTIONAL TO THE STOCK OF MONEY

The quantity of money is a stock. Like any asset, it exists at an instant of time. An instantaneous "still photo," or balance sheet, would record its amount. Total spending, excluding all "transfer" transactions, is the sum of the values of all output, *e.g.*, the price of oranges times the number of oranges produced plus the price of apples times the number of apples produced, and so forth for all goods and services. Total spending represents a *flow of income over time*, a rate of dollars per day, per month, or per year. Dimensionally speaking, spending bears the same relationship to the stock of money that a flow of water through a lake bears to the lake itself.

We saw in Chapter 3 that the interest rate relates the capital value of an asset and its flow of income. What is the factor relating the flow of income spending to the stock of money? It is easy to give a name to this factor; but, as we shall see, it is not very helpful to do so. In fact, scientists must constantly guard against a universal human weakness which makes us impute life and importance into a concept just because it has received a name and has been called to our attention.

The factor relating the volume of spending per unit time to the total stock of money is the *income velocity of circulation of money*. The total stock of money in the United States during 1950 was about 110 billion dollars. (This includes coins, paper currency outside the banks, and checking deposits.) The total volume of spending on final products (including net capital formation) was, of course, equal to net national product or to about 260 billion dollars. Consequently, we can say that the average income velocity of money was about 2.4 per year or about 0.2 per month. This means that, although some coins, bills, and deposits were used many times during that year, other units of money were not used even once.[1]

---

[1] Of course, most transactions are not for final goods and services, but rather are transfers; *e.g.*, when a baker pays a miller for flour, when an investor buys a stock or shares or real estate, etc. According to recent statistics of bank debits (checking transactions), urban bank deposits turn over some 18 times a year outside of New York City and 24 times a year in New York City. This velocity of circulation for all transaction purposes must be contrasted with the 2.2 income velocity rate of turnover against final goods and services.

We may summarize the definition of the average income velocity of circulation of money, V, as follows:

$$\text{Average income velocity per year} = \frac{\text{rate of income spending per year}}{\text{total volume of money}}$$

or in symbols:

$$V = \frac{p_1 q_1 + p_2 q_2 + \cdots}{M} = \frac{\text{sum pq}}{M} = \frac{PQ}{M}$$

where M = total volume of all money

$p_1 q_1$ = amount spent on the first good or service (*e.g.*, oranges)

$p_2 q_2$ = amount spent on second good or service (*e.g.*, apples)

P = average price level of output

Q = total quantity of output per unit time

Note that this equation is simply a definition of the velocity of circulation of money—nothing more and nothing less.

So much for the definition of the velocity of money. What good does it do us to have introduced the concept? The older economists, who were good quantity theorists through thick and thin, thought it did lots of good. Today, those of their ranks who are still alive are not so sure; and the new generation of economists tends to believe that the concept of velocity is of limited usefulness and that in most circumstances of boom and depression, it may do more harm than good.

It puts off answering a question by asking another question. Thus, one of the reasons given for the Great Depression of the 1930's was the reduced velocity of circulation of money. But why was velocity reduced? To know that is already to know the answer to the riddle of the slump. Similarly, those who thought recovery could be ensured by increasing the quantity of money were disappointed by the unexpected decline in the velocity of the new money.

This takes us back to the heading of the present section; or to the fact that the quantity theory is invalidated by the failure of total spending to be proportional to the quantity of money. In terms of our new concept, this concept may be explained as follows: *the velocity of circulation of money is not even approximately constant.* It changes in boom and depression in a way that cannot be predicted except from fundamental factors such as savings and investment, trade-union policy, technological innovations, the total quantity of money, the composition of that quantity of money, the way that money came into existence, the amount of near-money, and finally—to bring the list to an end—the movement and structure of interest rates and security prices.[1]

[1] If correct, these statements illustrate the relative sterility of the so-called "quantity equation of exchange," according to which

ACTIVE AND INACTIVE MONEY

One bitter lesson we have learned since 1929: There is no inherent tendency for money to be spent for goods at a constant velocity. If my current income is low, and if my expectations are pessimistic concerning real investment projects, then I may hold large sums of cash from 1930 to 1940 without at all increasing my spending. Call this hoarding if you like; but if interest rates are low, and if I am pessimistic concerning the future values of securities and real estate, then to hold cash is the most sensible speculation that I can make.

There are many ways that we might split up the demand for money. One convenient breakdown is to split money up into two parts. (1) There is a *transaction demand for money* to facilitate our ordinary purchases of goods and services. (2) There is what I might call a *liquidity demand for money*, in order to hold part of our wealth in a form whose cash value is safe and which will be readily available against unforeseen contingencies.[1]

Now we can see why the quantity theorists went wrong in believing in the constancy of V: They forgot about the second liquidity demand for money and concentrated only on the first transaction demand. If the transaction demand were the only one, then the total of M might indeed tend to be in fairly close proportion to the level of total money spending. We could then speak of all money as "active money" with a fairly constant and quite large velocity of circulation. If the experience of the decades before 1929 could be trusted, then active money could be expected to have a velocity of at least three or four times per year. A good deal less money would today be needed in the community to finance national incomes of the present magnitude. What

$$MV = PQ \qquad \text{or} \qquad P = \frac{V}{Q} M$$

This is a truism based, as we have just seen, on the definition of V, and it should not be confused with the quantity theory, which had the merit of attempting to set up an explanatory hypothesis to fit facts. If, as the older writers thought, V were a constant, or if the movements of Q were such as to offset the movements of V, thereby leaving V/Q a constant, then the equation of exchange might be a useful truism. But if, as has been argued. V is a catchall which is as hard to understand as the business cycle itself, then the equation of exchange is a blind alley or possibly a red herring. Instead of setting out the important questions in a useful way, it diverts attention from the really interesting and important problems. The better economists of a generation ago often used their common sense to arrive at correct judgments of how spending and prices would behave; then later they translated these judgments into the language of V and other variables in the equation of exchange.

[1] Often the demand for money is broken up into three components, but in this discussion the author found it convenient to lump into the liquidity demand for money all those elements which do not depend directly upon the level of money income (the so-called "speculative motive" and part at least of the so-called "precautionary motive").

would happen to the present excess money if it all had to be active? Supposedly it would all have to be spent for consumption, thereby bidding up the prices of goods and services. Prices would have to rise to an equilibrium level just high enough to keep all the money in existence circulating "actively."

For a quarter of a century any such simple concept of all money as being active money has been false to the facts. Thus, in the depression the transaction demand declined with the decline in incomes; people were very much on edge and increased their precautionary balances; more important, with interest rates so low, people had little inducement to buy securities rather than to hold

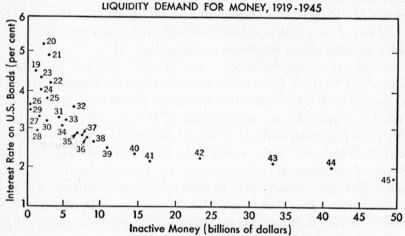

LIQUIDITY DEMAND FOR MONEY, 1919-1945

FIGURE 2. SOURCE: James Tobin, "Monetary Velocity and Monetary Policy—A Rejoinder," *The Review of Economics and Statistics*, November, 1948, p. 315.

nonearning cash. They were apprehensive concerning the future losses they might experience in buying securities, and so they increased their holdings of money.

In short, the facts force us to split money up into at least two categories: active (transactions) money, which depends primarily on the flow of income, and inactive (liquidity) money, which depends very much on the lowness of interest rates and the uncertainty of the future. Even this is an oversimplified picture, since the shifts in the demand for inactive money (for precautionary and speculative reasons) can be very rapid and unpredictable. But at least it helps us recognize the more extreme shortcomings of an oversimplified monetary approach.

Figure 2 shows one calculation of the way that the total of inactive money has increased with the lowness of interest rates. On the basis of past experience concerning the minimum amount of money needed for transaction purposes, we can make rough estimates of the amount of active money needed at any time to take care of transactions. Subtracting the calculated total of active money from the total of all money, we arrive at the total of inactive money. Note how small were the inactive hoards of money people held during the 1920's, when interest rates were high and people were optimistic. Contrast this to the tremendous increase in inactive money during the 1930's.

MONEY AND THE DETERMINATION OF INTEREST RATES

This discussion gives us one clue to the determination of the interest rate, or the structure of interest rates. From one point of view, interest can be thought of as the "price of money." (More precisely, it is the price of the *use* of money.)

The late Lord Keynes showed how a large supply of money will—other things being equal—tend to depress interest rates. Suppose gold mines or printing presses or the banking system have created a large amount of money some time in the past. This money has to be held by someone. If more money is given to people than they find convenient or necessary for their level of income and expenditure, what will they do? The simple quantity theory thought that they would spend it on consumers' goods. But this would pass the money on to someone else; and he, also being unwilling to hold the "hot brick," will spend it on consumers' goods. In the end, the prices of consumers' goods will be bid so high that people will finally need all the existing money just for transaction purposes. So argued the quantity theorists.

Keynes argued that people's consumption spending depends primarily on their income and total wealth, and only secondarily upon the composition of their wealth between cash and less liquid assets. Therefore, if the amount of total M tends to be too large, people and banks will try to use the excess to buy securities—not consumers' goods. This will gradually raise the price of stocks and bonds, or what is the same thing, reduce interest rates.

How long will this process go on? At first, one might be tempted to say until all the extra money is used up. But this would be wrong, since the money cannot be used up in this way. For every buyer of a bond, there is a seller and the money appears in his pockets. The only true end to the process is as follows:

An increase in total money tends—other things being equal—to lower the rate of interest, until finally the yield of stocks and bonds is so low that they have ceased any longer to be attractive alternatives to the holding of cash. *At a low enough rate of interest, people will finally develop a strong enough liquidity motive for holding all the existing amount of money.*

This is an important clue to the determination of interest. It is often called the liquidity-preference theory of interest. Later, Chapter 29 will show that it is only one clue among a number. The "net productivity of capital goods" will also be shown to have a vital bearing on interest—particularly on the long-run rate of interest of any economic system that maintains full employment at stable prices. We must not forget the qualifying expression, "other things being equal." Other things do not remain perfectly equal: people's expectations about the future profitability of noncash assets may change, which can affect interest, even though M does not change.

HISTORY OF INTEREST RATES FROM 1932 TO WORLD WAR II

The above analysis is often called the "theory of liquidity preference." It explains not only why people will hold idle money, but also why they will put so much of their money into short-term securities as to bid up their prices and bid down their interest yields almost to zero.

This is exactly what happened all through the 1930's. Remembering interest rates of 6 per cent, investors regarded rates of 3 or 4 per cent as only temporary. Therefore, they feared capital losses if they bought long-term securities. Instead they held cash, or bought short-term government bonds whose capital values are almost perfectly fixed because their maturity date is so near. The strong demand for such liquid short-term securities caused their prices to rise and their yield to go down to a fraction of a fraction of 1 per cent per annum.

Gradually as time passed and the long-expected return to high interest rates failed to materialize, banks and insurance companies found that they had been passing up 3 and 4 per cent on long-term securities because of their unfounded fears. Very slowly they began to buy long-term securities, thus bidding up their prices and bidding down their yields. But the process was remarkably slow.

Two distinct factors help to explain this slowness in the decline of long-term rates: first, the fact that investors still kept fearing each year a future decline in capital values and an increase in interest rates, even though events had proved their last year's expectations to be wrong on this point.

Second, the federal government was spending more than it taxed in those years, and borrowing the difference. The new supply of bonds coming on the market helped to keep security prices down and to keep interest yields up. Next to the 50-billion-dollar yearly deficits of World War II, the 3- or 4-billion-dollar annual deficits of the New Deal days may seem trifling; but they loomed larger in those days, and they did provide an important outlet for bank and insurance-company funds. Without this relatively safe investment outlet, the tremendous inflow of gold into this country during the 1930's would undoubtedly have depressed interest rates even more than it did.[1]

The history of the decade prior to our entrance into the war is one of slowly falling long-term rates of interest, with short-term rates down almost to zero, and with many financial institutions holding unprecedented amounts of idle cash. The next chapter will bring the story up to date.

SUMMARY TO APPENDIX

1. In its simplest and most interesting form, the quantity theory says that prices tend to be proportional to the quantity of money.

2. This is regarded as an oversimplification because its two implicit assumptions are not factually true: (a) There is very far from a direct proportionate relationship between prices and total spending; the total of output is an important variable rather than a constant. (b) There is very far from a directly proportionate relationship between the flow of total spending and the stock of total money. The velocity of circulation of money is an important variable and not a constant. The velocity varies with changes in interest rates, expectations, saving and investment schedules, and other economic variables.

3. At the least we must split the total demand for money into two components: the active-money *transaction demand* that is largely dependent upon the level of money income; and the more volatile inactive-money *liquidity demand* that depends upon the lowness of interest rates, people's expectations concerning the future prices of assets other than money, and the precautions they feel are necessary against contingencies.

[1] Interest-rate theory is one of the most difficult parts of economics, and an elementary treatment can only hope to raise the important issues. Later, in Chapter 29, the role of real factors in determining the rate of interest is synthesized with the role played by money. For those interested in refinements of economic theory, it can be said that recent discussions have greatly reduced the area of disagreement between the various differing theories. In particular it has become recognized that (1) if all wages and prices can fall flexibly downward, (2) if the total of money and near-money does not at the same time shrink as much as prices do, and (3) if too perverse expectations are not generated by the fall*ing* of prices— if all these conditions are realized—then the real value of money and near-money may finally be raised enough to shift the saving schedule downward far enough to wipe out the deflationary gap and restore full employment. However, few economists have recommended such a deflationary process as the best way of getting money to be "active"; it is usually thought better to follow alternative expansionary monetary and fiscal policies. A. C. Pigou, long professor of economics at Cambridge University, has helped clarify these theoretical issues.

4. We can if we wish describe the process by which monetary policy produces a lower interest rate in terms of the liquidity-preference theory of interest. An increase in the stock of M will result in a new equilibrium level of interest rates that is just low enough to induce people to be willing to hold all the new M. The history of the last 20 years provides a good illustration of this theory. But this does not mean that the same facts cannot be described in other terms or that the interest rate is not crucially affected by such real factors as the "net productivity of capital." (See Chapter 29 for further discussion.)

QUESTIONS FOR DISCUSSION

1. Defend and criticize the quantity theory. If it is not 100 per cent right, is it worthless?

2. What is meant by M, V, P, and Q? How are they related? Is this a useful relation in your opinion?

3. Define active money, inactive money, and what are the same things, transaction demand and liquidity demand. Give examples.

4. What was the history of interest rates during the 1930's? Explain.

Chapter 17: FEDERAL

RESERVE AND CENTRAL BANK

MONETARY POLICY

ALTHOUGH nominally a corporation owned by its Member Banks, the Federal Reserve Banks are in fact, as we have seen, equivalent to a branch of the government. Like the Bank of England or the Bank of France, they constitute a Central Bank—a bank for bankers. Instead of seeking profits, the Federal Reserve Banks have for their sole purpose the promotion of the public interest.

The Federal Reserve Banks, together with the United States Treasury, provide us with our supply of currency. Almost more important, the Reserve Banks are *the ultimate creators of the reserves of the Member Banks;* and as we have seen in the previous chapters, each $1 change in bank reserves may have a fivefold effect upon the volume of bank money or demand deposits.

CONTROLLING THE BUSINESS CYCLE BY CONTROLLING THE QUANTITY OF MONEY

The activities of the Reserve Banks (1) in connection with the clearings of checks and (2) as fiscal agent for the United States Treasury are important; but they are of a routine character and have already been briefly discussed. Here we shall be concerned with the vital function of the Federal Reserve Banks *as creator and controller of the community's supply of money, and as a vital factor determining the level of interest yields on government and private securities.*

Left to itself, our economic system is subject to alternate spells of boom and slump, prosperity and depression, inflation and deflation. Associated with boom times are upswings in the community's total stock of cash and deposit money; and associated with years of depression is a reduction in the total quantity of money.

Our earlier discussion of saving and investment has taught us that the primary cause of fluctuation in business activity is the fluctuation in *public and private investment*. Older economists did not realize this. They tended to attach primary causal importance to fluctuations in M, the total quantity of money. According to them, when M goes up—either because mines are spitting out gold, or because governments are printing new money, or because banks are expanding their investments and deposits, or for all these reasons—then prices rise and there will be a boom. When limits to the further creation of new money have been reached, prices can no longer rise, and the system will probably go into a downward spiral of depression and deflation. Loans will be called in or paid off, banks will go bankrupt, the total of M will decrease, and depression will stalk the land. A favorable upturn can come only when M stops decreasing and begins to rise. Then we are off on another complete cycle.

This is an oversimplified version of the monetary theory of the business cycle, but not an unfair account of its essential beliefs. Since believers in this theory diagnosed the causes of the boom in terms of fluctuations in M, their prescription of monetary stabilization to cure the system of its business-cycle jitters followed very logically.[1] The primary duty of the Federal Reserve Board authorities, according to this theory, should be (1) to increase M in bad times, (2) to decrease M in good times when business activity is too high, or in short (3) to stabilize the cyclical fluctuations in the supply of money. According to the quantity theory, this would stabilize prices.

Today, after our experiences in two world wars, after the relatively prosperous decade of the 1920's and the relatively depressed decade of the 1930's, we no longer hold out high hopes for effectively maintaining full employment and high production by means of federal reserve monetary policy alone. To see why this should be so, we must first analyze the exact steps by which the Reserve Banks are able to influence and control the supply of money.

BRIEF PREVIEW OF HOW THE RESERVE BANKS CAN AFFECT THE MONEY SUPPLY

To state the matter most briefly, the 12 Reserve Banks can act much like the primitive Central Banker of the last chapter. Like him they can expand the amount of outstanding money M. They do this as he did, by acquiring assets: loans and investments and also one new asset not previously mentioned —gold certificates. At the same time as the Reserve Banks assets go up, their liabilities must rise by an equal amount. Like the counterfeiter, they can print currency, namely, the federal reserve notes paid out to people while acquiring

---

[1] Some of the more cautious members of this school admitted that the origin of the cycle might be nonmonetary. But they still believed that monetary measures can offset other destabilizing influences.

loans, investments, and gold certificates. But unlike the primitive Central Banker, who did not hold deposits, the 12 Reserve Banks can expand their liabilities by writing checks that entitle commercial Member Banks to a deposit in the Reserve Banks; and as long as the Member Bank keeps this money on deposit at the Reserve Bank, then only a small part of the increase in the liabilities of the Reserve Banks need take the form of new currency issued.

To contract the supply of money, the Reserve Banks must do just the reverse. They must give up security loans, investments, or gold certificates and take back an equivalent amount of their federal reserve notes or deposit liabilities. The effects of such a contraction do not end here.

Such a contraction will reduce the currency in the hands of the public and the banks and reduce the deposits held by the Member Banks with the 12 Reserve Banks. We have seen that these deposits constitute the "reserve balances" of the Member Banks; and if these fall $1 below the legal require- ment of 20 per cent of commercial bank demand deposits, *then the Member Banks as a whole must contract demand deposits by* $5. Thus, changes in the deposit liabilities of the 12 Reserve Banks may have a 5 : 1 leverage on the total supply of money—upward or downward.

This briefly is the essence of Central Bank control of the supply of money. Let us examine the process in greater detail.

THE FEDERAL RESERVE BANKS' BALANCE SHEET

The role of the Federal Reserve Banks can best be understood from an examination of their combined balance sheet. Table 1 indicates the principal

TABLE 1. *Combined Balance Sheet of Twelve Federal Reserve Banks, June 30, 1949 (In billions of dollars)*

Assets		Liabilities and Net Worth	
Gold certificates and other cash...	$23.2	Capital accounts	$ 0.9
U.S. government securities	18.0	Federal reserve notes	22.8
Loans and acceptances	0.3	Deposits:	
Miscellaneous other assets (pri-		Member Bank reserves	16.4
marily "uncollected items")..	3.0	U.S. Treasury...............	0.5
		Foreign and other...........	1.4
		Miscellaneous liabilities.........	2.5
Total.....................	$44.5	Total.....................	$44.5

assets and liabilities of the 12 Reserve Banks. In appearance, it is not unlike the balance sheet of any ordinary bank. It contains on the asset side cash, loans, and securities and on the liability side capital accounts, deposit obligations, and a new large item, federal reserve notes outstanding.

Any Central Bank has a crucial influence on the supply of money because of the character of its two main liabilities. The first of these liabilities is the paper money which it has issued: in this country federal reserve notes (and in Britain, Bank of England notes). These federal reserve notes are held either by the public directly or as vault cash by the commercial banks.[1]

The second main liability of the Reserve Banks consists of the sums of money which the Member Banks hold on deposit with them and which constitute the reserves of the Member Banks. These balances are vitally important, because when they increase by $1, demand bank deposits can increase by $5; when they decrease by $1, bank demand deposits may shrink by $5; and without a change in the total of Member Bank reserves, bank deposits cannot increase.[2]

GOLD CERTIFICATES

How do these Reserve Bank liabilities, which constitute such an important part of the nation's money supply, come into existence? Since assets and liabilities must always balance, we need only inquire how the Reserve Bank's assets come into existence. The assets are of two main kinds, gold certificates and the total of government securities and loans.

The gold certificates come into existence more or less independently of any policy decisions on the part of the Reserve Bank authorities. So long as a country makes a practice of being on the gold standard, the process is fairly straightforward and automatic. Our government agrees to buy all gold brought to it at $35 an ounce. Since 1933, no American residents have been permitted to hold monetary gold. Today a gold-mining company will sell its newly produced gold in small part to jewelers and dentists, but in the larger part to the United States Treasury. The same will happen to any gold that is imported into the United States from abroad, whether to pay for our export of goods or to buy some of our long- or short-term capital securities.

In either case, we may suppose that the gold is sold to the United States Treasury in return for a check drawn upon the government's deposit account at the Federal Reserve Bank. The gold seller might cash this check and take

---

[1] A century ago, before checking deposits had acquired their present dominant importance, these paper units of money were the most important part of a nation's money supply. Formerly, private banks could and did issue bank notes, or paper money. These liabilities, payable on demand, circulated and provided an important part of the community's money supply, just as they still do in Scotland and some other countries. But the growth of checking accounts and the difficulties of public control of private note issue have caused most countries to restrict the issue of new currency to the Central Bank and Treasury.

[2] This assumes that the banks do not hold considerable "excess reserves" above their legal requirements.

the proceeds in federal reserve notes or other paper currency. More likely, he will deposit the government check in his own bank account. His bank will deposit the check in its account at the Federal Reserve Bank. The total of Member Bank balances is thereby swelled by as much as the reduction in the government deposit balance. The total of Reserve Bank assets and liabilities is still unchanged.

But unless the United States Treasury is deliberately trying to "sterilize" the gold inflow (as it has done on a few occasions in the past to fight inflation), it will not let the process end there. It will wish to replenish its depleted deposit account at the Reserve Banks. To do this, it will issue gold certificates against its newly acquired gold, and put these certificates into the Reserve Bank in exchange for a deposit as large as it was originally holding.

At the end of the whole process, the Reserve Bank has an increase in its assets (gold certificates) and an increase in its liabilities over the previous situation (new Member Bank reserve deposits). The Member Banks have increased assets (new reserve balances) and also increased deposit liabilities. The public—importers or gold miners—has less gold and more bank deposits. The government has the same amount of deposits as before; but now it has more gold in its vaults at Fort Knox, Kentucky, against which it has issued new gold certificates.

This completes the discussion of how gold certificates come into being. In addition, the Reserve Banks hold a few silver certificates and coins that have been deposited with it in the past, but these are not important enough to discuss.

"RESERVE BANK CREDIT"

The part of our money supply that has arisen from Reserve Bank acquisition of gold certificates is the passive part. Its magnitude depends upon the happenstance of gold discoveries, on withdrawals of gold in and out of the industrial uses of gold, and on gold flows in and out of the United States. If this were the whole story, our money supply would be a very haphazard quantity, having little to do with our economic needs and leading in some periods toward inflationary expansion and in other periods toward deflation and monetary stringency.

Fortunately, a Central Bank can adopt policies that deliberately cause its assets other than gold certificates to expand or contract; in this way it can cause its total liabilities to grow when the community needs more money and to contract when less money is called for. Therefore, the really important assets on its balance sheet are these other assets. These earning assets today consist primarily of government securities; formerly loans (or rediscounts) were important, but for the last 15 years they have been negligible (see Table 1).

This total of investment and loans is often called the amount of "Reserve Bank Credit." By causing Reserve Bank Credit to grow, the Reserve authorities are able to expand the total of demand deposits and of federal reserve notes in circulation. By engineering a contraction of Reserve Bank Credit, the authorities can cause our money supply to shrink.

FEDERAL RESERVE "OPEN-MARKET" OPERATIONS

Let us follow the process of deliberately expanding Reserve Bank Credit and the money supply. By far the most important way of doing this is through what is called an "open-market purchase." The 12 Reserve Banks could buy a bushel of wheat, a man's services for a year, or anything else, and the mechanics of the process would be the same. But, exactly like the primitive Central Banker of the last chapter, actually, they almost always confine their open-market purchases and sales to government securities: long-term or short-term government bonds, especially short terms of a year or less maturity.[1]

The Reserve Bank goes to the market and buys, let us say, a million dollars' worth of government bonds. It pays its check to the sellers, who may be private individuals or a bank. If the sellers want to cash this check in for currency, the Federal Reserve Bank will present them with federal reserve notes; the community's money supply has gone up by 1 million dollars, and availability of credit has been that much increased.

It is more likely that the sellers will wish to hold most of their proceeds in the form of a deposit. If the seller was a bank, it will then simply deposit the check (that it received for the bonds) in its account at the Federal Reserve Bank. If the seller was a private individual, the same thing will happen, but with one intermediate step. The private seller will deposit the Reserve Bank's check in his own account. His bank will then deposit the check in its account at the Reserve Bank.

In either case, the open-market purchase of 1 million dollars has resulted in an equivalent expansion of the Reserve Bank's assets (investments) and in its deposit liabilities.

But this is hardly more than a beginning. The commercial Member Banks will now have at least four-fifths of 1 million dollars of *excess reserves*. (This is because of the 20 per cent legal reserve ratio required against deposits.) Therefore, the commercial banks will have an incentive to go out and acquire

[1] Formerly the Treasury did not sell government bonds directly to the Federal Reserve Banks. This was because of a belief that the government is not to be trusted. But since the Federal Reserve Banks could buy bonds from the market on the day after the government had issued them, the emptiness of this curb was clearly revealed. For the last few years even this pretense was dropped, and some government obligations were sold directly to the Reserve Banks; in the postwar period, refundings are handled directly with the government.

new earning assets (loans and investments). On the basis of the discussion in Chapter 15 the reader will realize that the whole process can give rise to a chain of multiple deposit creation—which need come to an end only when the commercial banks as a whole have experienced a 5-million-dollar expansion in bank deposits.

TABLE 2a. *Effect of a Million-dollar Open-market Purchase on Federal Reserve Bank's Balance Sheet*

Assets		Liabilities	
Investments.............	+$1 million	(Legal) Reserve deposits..	+$1 million
Total.................	+$1 million	Total.................	+$1 million

Tables 2a and 2b summarize the possible 5:1 leverage on the money supply resulting from Federal Reserve Bank open-market purchases. After this has caused a 5:1 expansion of Member Bank deposits, the final effect on Member Banks' balance sheets is as shown in Table 2b.

TABLE 2b. *Final Effect on Member Banks of a Million-dollar Open-market Purchase*

Assets		Liabilities	
Legal reserves...........	+$1 million	Deposits................	+$5 million
Loans and investments.....	+$4 million		
Total.................	+$5 million	Total.................	+$5 million

As will be discussed again in a moment, we must qualify this discussion to take account of the possibility that there may actually result less than the maximum 5:1 expansion possible. Before worrying about this, the reader should clinch his understanding of the mechanism of open-market operations by working through the details of the reverse operation: Let the Reserve Bank engage in an open-market sale of 1 million dollars of government securities in order to engineer a multiple contraction of the money supply. Show how this kills off 1 million dollars of reserves and 5 million dollars of deposits.

LOAN AND REDISCOUNT POLICY

If the Reserve Banks acquire some other asset than government bonds—for example, a loan—the mechanical expansionary effects are exactly the same; and if they contract their loans, then the contractionary effect is just like that of an open-market sale. Originally, the founders of the federal reserve system thought that the loan operations of the Reserve Banks would be by far their most powerful weapon. But when we glance back at the Combined Balance

Sheet of the Reserve Banks (Table 1), we see how wrong these expectations have turned out to be. The total of loans and acceptances is of absolutely negligible quantitative importance and has been for a long time.

When the original Federal Reserve Act was passed in 1913, the experts all attached great importance to providing short-term working capital for industry, trade, and agriculture. The commercial banks were to be encouraged to make 90-day loans to businessmen and farmers on the basis of crops, inventories, and shipments of goods. To make sure that the banks always had money for these worthy purposes, the Federal Reserve Bank stood ready to "rediscount" all such advances: *i.e.*, the Member Bank could take the customer's I.O.U., endorse it, and then turn it over to the Federal Reserve Bank, which would advance the face value of the note minus a published interest charge—known as the "rediscount rate." (This rediscount rate was normally below the interest rate charged by banks on their loans.)

In other words, the commercial bank would get a check from the Federal Reserve Bank, or what is the same thing, its legal reserve deposit would be increased. This increase in reserve balances of the banking system enables that system—but not the single bank in question—to expand total deposits five times as much, and total loans and investments four times as much. Thus, by rediscounting one customer's I.O.U. out of every five, the banks could theoretically create any amount of new loans and deposits—so long as the Federal Reserve Banks continue to expand their rediscounts.

Some of the founders of the federal reserve system thought that this process would work automatically and well. The Reserve authorities would not need to exercise any intelligence or make any decisions. So long as the banks confined themselves to "bona fide, short-term, self-liquidating working capital loans meeting the legitimate needs of trade," the system would take care of itself. But the short-lived inflation of 1919–1920 after World War I put an end to this simple notion. It showed plainly that such a theory implied an expansion of M during inflationary boom times, just when there was already too much spending; and a contraction of M in depression when borrowers were few but spending was desperately needed.

After this period of disillusionment, there grew up in the 1920's the theory that the rediscount rate might be a powerful weapon of monetary control. By raising the rediscount rate, the Reserve authorities were supposed to be able to engineer a contraction of the money supply and to tighten interest rates all along the line. By lowering the rediscount rate, they were supposed to be able to increase capital availability and lower interest rates.

In view of the infinitesimal use of rediscounting, this cannot now be regarded as an important weapon of monetary control. The real importance of the Reserve Bank's lending powers probably lies in the firm support that it can always give to our banking system in time of financial crisis.

Since 1933, the Federal Reserve Act has been drastically amended. The Reserve Banks can lend to almost anybody, not just to banks. Also, they can lend to banks and can issue notes, not only against short-term industrial and agricultural promissory notes, but also against government bonds put up by the banks as collateral, or in some cases, against *any* agreed-upon collateral. Since 1933, despite the reduction of the rediscount rate, banks have preferred to borrow on government bonds rather than on customers' promissory notes, which have been profitable but scarce. Most often, today, when banks need more cash, they simply sell some of their government bonds on the open market, or occasionally some of their highest grade promissory notes known as "bankers' acceptances."[1] As a matter of form, the Reserve Banks raise the rediscount rate when their open-market operations are raising interest rates. In 1951, the rediscount rate was raised to $1\frac{3}{4}$ per cent in line with a general upward movement in short-term interest rates.

In addition to rediscounts, the Reserve Banks can lend directly to private industry, but this they rarely do. Primarily, they leave this function to the commercial banks, to the Home Owners' Loan Corporation, to the RFC, and the various farm credit agencies. Also, the Reserve Banks stand ready to buy up all bankers' acceptances at some published interest rate. Thus, the market rather than the Reserve Banks takes the initiative in determining how many acceptances the Reserve Banks will hold; but the Reserve Banks by changing the interest rate that they charge for holding acceptances, relative to market rates of interest, can indirectly influence the level of their assets held in the form of acceptances.

CHANGING RESERVE REQUIREMENTS AS A WEAPON OF MONETARY CONTROL

In addition to selling off its earning assets—bonds or loans—and thereby reducing the Reserve Bank Credit basis underlying the legal reserves of the banking system, the Reserve authorities and Congress can engineer a contraction of the supply of money in one other important way. If Congress gave them the power, they might raise the legal reserve requirements of the Member Banks from present levels to some higher levels, say 40:40:40.[2] Banks would

[1] For our purpose bankers' acceptances may be considered simply to be highly negotiable promissory notes, well secured by merchandise and by the endorsement of a reliable bank. Acceptances usually run for 90 days or short periods and have a very low rate of interest yield. Quantitatively they are of minor importance today.

[2] In 1947 when inflation seemed in prospect, the Reserve Board asked Congress for the power to raise reserve requirements, at any future date that it desired, beyond the present limits permitted it, namely, beyond 26:20:14.

then find that their legal reserves were inadequate in comparison with their deposits. They would have to sell many of their securities to the public—probably at some loss. The public would use up its bank accounts buying the bonds, and the process would come to an end only when about one-half of all deposits had been destroyed. Then and only then would the banks find that their old unchanged dollar reserves were large enough in relation to their deposits to meet the new legal requirements. The depressed price of bonds would be equivalent to higher interest rates or "tight money."

It would make for great confusion if the legal reserve ratios of banks were constantly being changed. Consequently, this weapon would probably be used only at infrequent intervals. Moreover, such an extreme increase of reserve requirements as that mentioned above would take place only at a time when banks already had large excess reserves over and above their legal requirements. Fearing a possible inflationary expansion of bank deposits at some future date, the Reserve authorities might then decide to convert the potentially "hot" excess reserves into relatively stable legal reserves by raising legal reserve ratios. This is exactly what was done in 1936–1937, when reserve ratios were raised in a number of steps from 13:10:7 to 26:20:14.

THE PROBLEM OF "EXCESS RESERVES"

During the Great Depression, there was a great decrease of bank deposits, of at least a third. How was this brought about? Was it because gold left our shores, thereby causing gold certificates to disappear from the Reserve Banks, and at the same time causing a reduction in reserve deposits and a 5:1 or 10:1 contraction of bank deposits? The answer is "no." Gold was coming into this country during much of the period.

Was it because of open-market operations of the Reserve Banks? Were they perhaps selling government bonds to the public and to the Member Banks, and thereby destroying Member Bank reserves and causing a multiple destruction of deposits? The answer is again "no." Throughout most of the early 1930's, the Reserve Banks were buying government bonds on the open market in an attempt to increase bank reserves and lower interest rates. (They also tried, but with little success, to get commercial banks to expand their loans and discounts.)

How then can we explain the great decline in bank deposits? The answer lies partially in the fact that the banks began to keep a much higher proportion of reserves to deposits than they had formerly: They preferred to keep higher reserves than they were *legally* required to keep. Banks were fearful of making loans during the depression, and they did not even find government bonds too attractive.[1]

[1] In other words, all the discussion in the Appendix to Chapter 16 of why people hold idle, nonyielding money applies with full force to the behavior of bankers during the 1930's.

Now we have seen that the Federal Reserve authorities can kill off M by raising legal reserve ratios from say 10 to 20 per cent, or from 20 to 30 per cent. The Member Bankers can by themselves do the same thing without any laws being passed at all. Suppose they suddenly decide to hold 30 per cent reserves against deposits even though only 20 per cent are legally required, the extra 10 per cent constituting what is called "excess reserves?" Then bank deposits will have to be greatly contracted.

The Federal Reserve Board was disturbed at the destruction of bank deposits during the depression as a result of bankers holding excess reserves. But more than that, they were disturbed because excess reserves act as a buffer which protects the Member Banks against control by the Federal Reserve Banks. If the Member Banks have excess reserves, then open-market sales of government bonds by the Reserve Banks will not necessarily force the Member Banks into a multiple contraction of demand deposits.

The open-market sales kill off some Member Bank reserves. True enough. But the banks have more than enough reserves already and need not call in a single loan or sell to the public a single security. Consequently, there is no 5:1 change in demand deposits, nor even a 2:1, or 1:1. The Member Banks have simply traded some of their excess reserves for old government bonds.

The existence of excess reserves helps to explain why monetary policy by a Central Bank may be relatively ineffective in contracting deposits and curtailing inflation. It also explains why the Central Bank is relatively powerless to initiate an expansion from depressed conditions. Open-market purchases may serve only to increase the amount of excess reserves, with the process ending there.

SUMMARY OF RESERVE BANKS' CONTROL OVER MONEY

This is a good place to outline the Reserve authorities' power over the money supply. First, there is a part of our money supply which arises passively from gold production and gold imports, regardless of the direct volition of the Reserve authorities.

This can be countered or supplemented, however, by deliberate Central Bank policies. If the Reserve authorities wish to contract the money supply and tighten interest rates, they may take the following steps:

1. Most important is the *open-market operation*. By selling government securities, they can reduce federal reserve notes and Member Bank reserves, and through the latter engineer as much as a fivefold contraction of demand deposits.

2. Next in importance to open-market operations is a policy of *raising reserve requirements*.

3. Less important is *loan policy:* raising the rediscount rate, raising the discount or interest rate on acceptances, etc.

4. They may also try to use *moral suasion,* putting public and private pressure on the banks to contract their operations.

5. Finally, the Board of Governors has the power to *raise margin requirements* for stock-market purchasing, if necessary up to 100 per cent. During World War II and since 1950 it also exercised direct control over the terms of installment and charge-account purchasing, specifying minimum down payments and maximum periods of payment. Control of the terms of mortgage borrowing for new houses is a further highly important *direct selective control over credit.*

The reader may work out the various steps to be followed if an expansion, rather than a contraction, of the money supply is desired.

THE PYRAMID OF CREDIT

Figure 1 summarizes the relation between the commercial or Member Banks and the public; between the banks and the Federal Reserve Banks; and between the Reserve Banks and the Treasury. At the bottom of the pyramid is a relatively small amount of gold held by the United States Treasury, about 24 billion dollars' worth in late 1950. A little of this is held as nominal "backing" against the relatively minor amount of coins and paper money issued by the Treasury, and a little is held by the Exchange Equalization Fund for use in connection with the United States quota in the International Monetary Fund. But by far the largest part is matched by gold certificates in the coffers of the Federal Reserve Banks—some 23 billion dollars in all.

Moving up the pyramid from the Treasury to the Federal Reserve Banks, we find their total liabilities and total assets to be over 40 billion dollars, so that Reserve Bank cash reserves are more than half of their total liabilities. Just as the commercial banks have a legal minimum reserve ratio against deposit liabilities, so the Federal Reserve Banks have a legal minimum reserve ratio of required cash to be held against their deposits and currency liabilities. In 1950, 25 per cent was the legal ratio; until World War II, the ratios were 35 and 40 per cent, respectively.

However, the Federal Reserve Banks' legal reserve ratio does *not* have the significance of the Member Banks' legal ratios. The Member Banks *in fact* operate near their legal ratios much of the time; to the extent that they do so, they must react mechanically and lose their autonomy of action. They are not free, at any given time, to increase their earning assets and their customers' deposits. But it is the essence of Central Banking to pursue deliberate, discretionary policies in the public interest. This can be done only if the Reserve authorities resist the temptation to earn profits by always buying earning assets right up to their legal reserve limit. The Reserve Banks are therefore normally operating at far higher reserve ratios than are required. In fact, when their actual reserve ratio approaches the legal ratio, an impairment of their

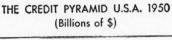

THE CREDIT PYRAMID U.S.A. 1950
(Billions of $)

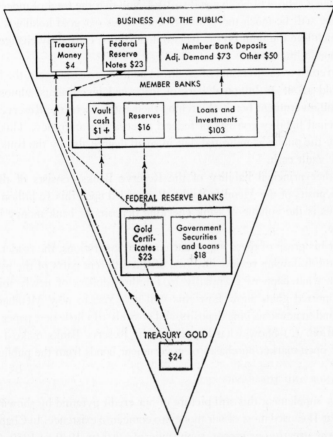

FIGURE 1. This shows how our money supply adds up to several times the gold base underlying the federal reserve system. SOURCE: Data from *Federal Reserve Bulletin*.

power and freedom is in sight. At such times Congress very properly passes a new law lowering their legal ratio.

Theoretically, you would think that each new dollar of gold at the base of the pyramid could expand ultimate bank deposits not simply by $5:1$ ($1 \div \frac{1}{5}$), but by $20:1 = 5 \times 4 = 1 \div (\frac{1}{5} \times \frac{1}{4})$. Why? Because each dollar of gold in the Reserve Banks can theoretically expand the legal reserve deposits of the Member Banks 4 times; and each dollar of Member Bank reserves can further expand ordinary bank demand deposits 5 times, or 20:1 in all.

Actually, the Reserve authorities do not mechanically expand 4:1 for each extra dollar of cash received by them. Therefore, 5:1 is more realistic for the system as a whole than 20:1. Before the present generation of college students hold their twenty-fifth reunion, it is not at all impossible that the Federal Reserve legal ratio will be changed to 10:1, and that the total of money in the community will be much more than twenty times our gold holdings. A legal limit, which like the limit on the federal debt can be constantly changed, is no real economic limitation.[1]

Let us return to the pyramid of credit. In addition to cash assets, the Reserve Banks hold about 28 billion dollars of loans and investments, almost all in short-term government bonds. Matching their total assets, the Reserve Banks' first principal liability consists of federal reserve note currency. This is held largely by the public as indicated, but in small degree also by the banks as till money or vault cash.

The other principal liability of the Reserve Banks consists of the legal reserve deposits of the Member Banks. Pyramided upon this 16 billion dollars of reserves is the volume of bank checking deposits or bank money held by the public.

To test his grasp of these important financial institutions, the reader should perform the following review in terms of the different parts of the pyramid: (1) Show what happens eventually to 1 billion dollars of newly mined or newly imported gold. Show how this will give rise to new Member Bank reserves and to new checking deposits, and possibly to a little new paper money in circulation. (2) Show what happens if the Reserve Banks make 1 billion dollars of open-market purchases of government bonds from the public.

WAR FINANCE AND THE BANKS

We may supplement this still picture of our credit pyramid by showing how World War II caused most of our money to come into existence. In Chapter 14, we saw how greatly our money supply increased from 1939 to 1950: from a total of 33 to 112 billion dollars. Most of this took the form of demand deposits and federal reserve notes. Now we are in a position to explain how this all came about.

During World War II, the government found it necessary to spend more than half the gross national product on guns, ships, men, and so forth. At first this

[1] Today this is taken for granted. But one of the contributing reasons for the severity of the 1920–1921 price collapse was the failure of anyone to think of this easy solution to the Federal Reserve Bank's shortage of legal reserves.

resulted in increased output and reduced unemployment. Finally output reached its peak. Congress was unwilling to raise taxes sufficiently to get people to stop consuming the resources necessary for the war effort. Patriotic exhortations to save more were also not strong enough. Therefore, price controls, rationing, and deliberate making of goods unavailable had to step in to cut down on private consumption and increase private saving.

We financed the war by a huge excess of government expenditure over taxes. Corresponding to this huge deficit, direct controls forced an abnormally high rate of saving on people. They were free to save their extra income in whatever form they liked: payroll war bonds, life insurance, savings accounts, paper currency, demand deposits, etc. People chose to put about half their savings in government bonds; another portion went indirectly into government bonds via insurance companies and savings banks; the rest they chose to hold in the form of currency or demand deposits. In fact, because so many men were away from home, because of black markets, because of the great increase in incomes of the poor—for all these reasons there was an astonishingly large increase in the amount of paper currency, largely federal reserve notes, that people wished to hold.

To all this, the government raised no objections; it urged thrift and war bonds on people, but let them do finally as they liked. Regardless of the form in which the public chose to hold its wealth, the same gigantic deficit had to be covered by loan financing. *The Treasury simply sold to the banking system whatever bonds the public would not take.* To the extent that people chose to hold demand deposits, bonds were sold to the commercial banks. To make sure that these banks did not run out of legal reserves, the Treasury sold about 20 per cent of all bonds to the 12 Reserve Banks—thereby expanding Reserve Bank Credit and Member Bank reserves. In addition, of course, some further bonds had to be sold to the Reserve Banks so as to enable them to issue the required amount of federal reserve notes.

Figure 2 is a well-known chart which appears monthly in the *Federal Reserve Bulletin*. It shows conclusively that the increase in our money supply from 1939 to 1950 had nothing to do with gold, but followed from the expansion of Reserve Bank Credit, made necessary by our unwillingness to finance the war by taxation.

In this way, interest rates were kept at a low level, and money proved no bottleneck to the successful prosecution of the war. Unlike past wars, the Treasury was able to make this one a "2 per cent war."[1]

---

[1] The process described in the preceding paragraph is sometimes described as "monetization of the public debt." Reversing the process in the postwar period, or "demonetizing the public debt," would take place if the public decided to use its demand deposits and cur-

THE INADEQUACIES OF MONETARY CONTROL OF THE BUSINESS CYCLE

Today few economists regard federal reserve monetary policy as a panacea for controlling the business cycle. Purely monetary factors are considered to be as much symptoms as causes, albeit often symptoms with aggravating effects that should not be completely neglected.

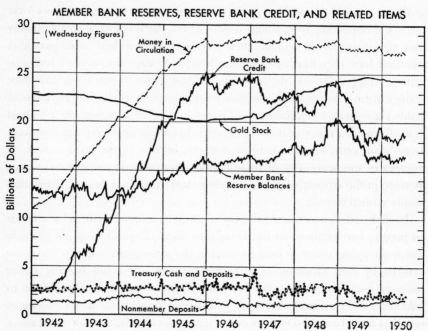

MEMBER BANK RESERVES, RESERVE BANK CREDIT, AND RELATED ITEMS

FIGURE 2. This shows how our money supply was expanded as a result of government bond sales to Member Banks and to the 12 Reserve Banks. SOURCE: *Federal Reserve Bulletin.*

By increasing the volume of their government securities and loans and by lowering Member Bank legal reserve requirements, the Reserve Banks can encourage an increase in the supply of money and bank deposits. They can encourage but, without taking drastic action, they cannot *compel.* For in the middle of a deep depression just when we most want Reserve policy to be effective, the Member Banks are likely to be timid about buying new investments or making loans. If the Reserve authorities buy government bonds in

---

rency to take over the government bonds held by the banking system. The total of liquid wealth (salable and redeemable government bonds plus money) would remain exactly the same. Unless one believes in a simple quantity theory of money and prices, it is hard to see how this, by itself, would be any less (or more) inflationary.

the open market and thereby swell bank reserves, the banks will not put these funds to work but will simply hold reserves. Result: no 5 for 1, "no nothing," simply a substitution on the bank's balance sheet of idle cash for old government bonds. If banks and the public are quite indifferent between gilt-edged bonds—whose yields are already very low—and idle cash, then the Reserve authorities may not even succeed in bidding up the price of old government bonds; or what is the same thing, in bidding down the interest rate.

Even if the authorities should succeed in forcing down short-term interest rates, they may find it impossible to convince investors that long-term rates will stay low. If by superhuman efforts, they do get interest rates down on high-grade gilt-edged government and private securities, the interest rates charged on more risky new investments financed by mortgage or commercial loans or stock-market flotations may remain sticky. In other words, *an expansionary monetary policy may not lower effective interest rates very much but may simply spend itself in making everybody more liquid.*

What if interest rates are finally lowered? A number of questionnaire studies of businessmen's behavior suggest that the level of the interest rate is not an important factor in their investment decisions. Particularly in deep depression when there is widespread excess capacity, *investment is likely to be inelastic with respect to the interest rate.* The same is also likely to apply to people's decisions on how much of their incomes to spend on consumption.

In terms of the quantity theory of money, we may say that the velocity of circulation of money does not remain constant. "You can lead a horse to water, but you can't make him drink." You can force money on the system in exchange for government bonds, its close money substitute; but you cannot make the money circulate against new goods and new jobs. You can get some interest rates down, but not all to the same degree. You can tempt businessmen with cheap rates of borrowing, but you cannot make them borrow and spend on new investment goods.[1]

The Reserve authorities may be a little more successful in putting on the brakes of monetary contraction. If interest rates are raised and the availability of credit reduced, investment spending may be reduced. But it is not at all clear that changes of a few per cent in the interest-rate structure will have a quantitatively important effect on total spending. But even this is not certain. Much investment is today relatively independent of the short-term capital market and of banking rates of interest. Moreover, if the authorities rely simply on over-all quantitative control as they did in 1929, they may find it necessary, in order to choke off a speculative stock-market boom, to raise rates of interest

---

[1] The banking authorities—unlike the fiscal authorities—deal only in secondhand assets, in transfer items. They are powerless to act directly on people's incomes and on production!

so high for "legitimate" industrial borrowers as to create a depression. It is not good medical practice to put a tourniquet around the patient's neck in order to check a little bleeding at the ear. Recent legislation has relied partially on the greater use of specific qualitative controls: changing "margin" requirements on brokers' loans, charging special RFC rates for investment activities to be encouraged, placing special curbs and limitations on installment selling and other consumer credit, etc. But, in part, the answer must be found outside of monetary policy.

PUBLIC DEBT MANAGEMENT AND POSTWAR MONETARY CONTROL

The effectiveness of monetary controls has been weakened in recent years by the fact that there is some quarter of a trillion dollars of government debt outstanding. The Treasury has been very concerned lest an increase in interest rates should depress the prices of old government bonds and raise the interest charges on new borrowing. The Federal Reserve has felt an obligation to help its big brother the Treasury and also an obligation to help government bond prices from crashing as they did after World War I. It has supported the prices of government bonds by buying them whenever their prices tended to fall below par. As long as it performs this function for its big brother, the Reserve Board realizes that it is severely limited in the degree to which it can put on the monetary brakes to fight postwar inflation.

Let us see why a policy of supporting government bond prices makes a deflationary monetary policy difficult. First, suppose that the Reserve Board does drastically raise reserve requirements. Will this choke off bank loans? If banks now found themselves short of reserves, it might tend to do so. But will banks be very short of reserves if they are able to get any needed amount of new reserves by selling government bonds to the Reserve Banks? Raising reserve requirements may still have some slight restrictive effect on credit, but the effect will not be nearly so great as it would be if the Reserve Banks were to let the prices of bonds fall and their interest yields rise.

Or consider the second weapon of Central Banking for contracting credit, namely, open-market sales of bonds. Such sales will depress bond prices. Indeed what other essential purpose have they but to raise interest rates and tighten credit generally? If your big brother asks you to support bond prices by buying them whenever necessary, then obviously you are not free to sell bonds and depress their prices. Except for moral suasion, direct controls, or the unimportant discount rate, there is nothing the Reserve Banks can do unless Congress gives them new powers.

From 1946 to 1948, the Reserve Banks did put mild deflationary pressure on the money market by raising short-term rates from the wartime levels of a fraction of 1 per cent up to about 1½ per cent on bonds of not more than a year's duration. They let long-term government bonds fall in price down to par value of 100. Beyond this they have not dared to go.

In the summer of 1950, after the Korean war again raised the serious specter of inflation, the Reserve Board got into a small fight with the Treasury. For the first time, it broke away from the influence of its big brother; it refused to help keep the short-term rate down to as low a figure as the Secretary of the Treasury wished. The Reserve Banks in effect permitted the short-term interest rate in the market to remain higher than the new interest rate set by the Treasury. As a result, the market did *not* buy the newly issued bonds. Who did?

The Reserve Banks themselves bought the new bonds. You may think that this was just what big brother wanted. But when you remember that the Reserve Banks send all their excess profits to the Treasury anyway, you will realize that, *as much as the Treasury saved on nominally lower interest rates, it lost in profits to be received from the Reserve Banks.* It is like taking out your boss to a big dinner and then putting the bill on the expense account he allows you.

It is not important to understand the details of the above situation. What is important is to realize that stable bond prices and low interest rates for Treasury borrowings are major obstacles to monetary contraction. It will be interesting to see whether the Reserve Banks will break away from Treasury influence if inflation persists in the years ahead.

SUMMARY

1. In Chapter 15 it was shown that demand deposits of the commercial banking system can fluctuate in a 5:1 amplification of changes in bank reserves. In this chapter, it is shown that the Federal Reserve Banks—or any Central Bank—are able to control and influence the direction and quantity of bank reserves. These Member Bank reserves (together with outstanding paper federal reserve notes) constitute the principal liabilities of the Reserve Banks. By understanding the process by which Federal Reserve Bank assets come into existence, we have the key to the behavior of these liabilities.

2. The first principal asset of the Reserve Banks consists of gold certificates. For a country on the gold standard, whose Treasury agrees to buy and sell all gold brought to it, the process by which these gold certificates change in amount is more or less automatic; it depends primarily upon gold mining and the importing or exporting of gold. Each dollar of new gold adds about a dollar

to gold certificates and to Member Bank reserves and indirectly makes possible several dollars in multiplied commercial bank demand deposits.

3. Far from automatic, however, is the process by which the Reserve authorities increase the volume of federal reserve credit by expanding their holdings of *earning assets:* primarily short-term government securities, but also longer term bonds and a few loans, acceptances, or rediscounts. When the total of these earning assets—often called Reserve Bank Credit—expands, then Member Bank reserves are increased, interest rates are eased, and demand deposits may rise fivefold. When the total of Reserve Bank Credit contracts, then bank reserves and deposits must shrink and interest rates tend to rise. These changes are supposed to induce the desired changes in investment and consumption spending.

4. During the 1920's, the Federal Reserve authorities used to be able to control the volume of their earning assets to some degree by means of the rediscount rate, the raising of which decreased its loans and put upward pressure on market interest rates in general. But in recent years the volume of Federal Reserve loans of all kinds has diminished to a mere trickle, so that primary reliance must be placed upon open-market purchases and sales of government securities. When the Reserve Banks buy securities on the open market, they depress interest rates and increase bank reserves, thereby paving the way for an expansion of bank deposits and investment expenditure. When they sell, the opposite tends to happen.

5. However, in the 1930's, the Member Banks often tended to hold excess reserves. So the power of the Reserve authorities to engineer a contraction or expansion of the total money supply was seriously limited. Moreover, interest rates have often tended to be sticky, and investment spending to be unresponsive to changes in the interest rate.

6. To some degree, the power of Congress and the Reserve Board to raise or lower legal reserve requirements helps to plug up these loopholes to monetary control, but only in part. Other supplementary methods of affecting business conditions involve the use of moral suasion to persuade the banks to expand or contract their credit operations, the regulation of margin requirements for buying securities, and the direct selective controls on installment selling, consumers' credit, and mortgage loans.

7. War and postwar finance provide a convenient exercise illustrating the principles of modern central banking. Partly as a result of the need of the Treasury and the banking system to keep up government bond prices and keep down interest rates, and partly as a result of the demonstrated weaknesses of monetary control policies from 1929 to 1941, the trend of modern thinking seems to be away from central banking money and interest rate policy and toward the fiscal policies discussed in Chapter 19.

QUESTIONS FOR DISCUSSION

1. In what federal reserve district is your locality? Where is the nearest branch? Can you open up an account there? Why not? Have you ever seen the *Monthly Newsletter* for your reserve district?

2. There is an excellent little descriptive book on the federal reserve system called *The Federal Reserve System, Its Purposes and Functions*. If you are interested, look up in it the details of how your check to someone in another part of the country is cleared.

3. Try to interpret the various items on the latest combined balance sheet of the Reserve Banks.

4. You find an ounce of gold in a cave. Describe the steps in the process set up by your selling it to the Treasury.

5. You buy $1,000 in gold from the Treasury to ship to South America. Describe all the effects on the banking system and the supply of American money.

6. "Gold movements affected prices only because we followed the practice of using them as a barometer, signalling us to expand or contract the total of money supply. Of course, the gold standard was a stupid system. But it was wiser to tie ourselves to such an imperfect system than to trust corrupt legislatures whose tendency is always to print inflationary paper money." Discuss.

7. Trace through the effects of a 1-billion-dollar open-market sale.

8. Trace the effects of a doubling of reserve requirements.

9. List the weapons of monetary control of the Reserve authorities. How powerful are they (*a*) to control M, (*b*) to control interest rates, (*c*) to control prices, (*d*) to control employment and unemployment? Justify your answer.

10. How would postwar debt retirement out of a surplus of taxes affect the banking system? Trace the steps.

11. Discuss once again the statement of the Reserve Board given in Question 6 of Chapter 15.

12. Comment on the following 1939 Reserve Board pronouncements:

"[The Board] recognizes the importance of making every effort to achieve the underlying objective, which, broadly speaking, is the fullest practicable utilization of the country's human and material resources . . . stability in production and employment is a more satisfactory objective of public policy than price stability alone."

" . . . experience has shown the prices do not depend primarily on the volume or the cost of money."

" . . . that the Board's control over the volume of money is not and cannot be made complete."

" . . . and that steady average prices, even if obtainable by official action, would not assure lasting prosperity."

" . . . the powers over [the supply and cost of money] possessed by the Treasury now outweigh those of the [Federal Reserve] System."

Chapter 18: THE BUSINESS CYCLE

WE have now examined the economic forces operating to determine the level of national income—the balance of saving and investment; and how money, banks, and central bank finance affect this balance. We must turn in this chapter to the problem of how and why the level of national income fluctuates. We may leave to Chapter 19 on fiscal policy the question of what can be done to keep national income relatively stable and employment relatively high.

PROSPERITY AND DEPRESSION

Business conditions never stand still. Prosperity is followed by a panic or a crash. National income, employment, and production fall. Prices and profits decline and men are thrown out of work. Eventually the bottom is reached, and revival begins. The recovery may be slow or fast. It may be incomplete, or it may be so strong as to lead to a new boom. The new prosperity may represent a long, sustained plateau of brisk demand, plentiful jobs, buoyant prices, and increased living standards. Or it may represent a quick, inflationary flaring up of prices and speculation, to be followed by another disastrous slump.

Such in brief is the so-called "business cycle" that has characterized the industrialized nations of the world for the last century and a half at least, ever since an elaborate, interdependent, *money economy* began to replace a relatively self-sufficient, precommercial society.

No two business cycles are quite the same; yet they all have much in common. They are not identical twins, but they are recognizable as belonging to the same family. No exact formula, such as might apply to the motions of the moon or of a simple pendulum, can be used to predict the timing of future (or past) business cycles. Rather do they resemble, in their rough appearance and irregularities, the fluctuations of disease epidemics, the vagaries of the weather, or the variations in a child's temperature.

To democratic nations, the business cycle presents a challenge—almost an ultimatum. Either we learn to control depressions and inflationary booms better than we did before World War II, or the political structure of our society will hang in jeopardy. For the ups and downs in business do not cancel out. At the top of the boom—if we are lucky!—there may be relatively favorable job opportunities for all who wish to work. Throughout the rest of the business cycle, men's lives are being wasted, and the progress of our economic society falls short of our true economic possibilities. If, as before the war, America marks time for another decade, the collectivized nations of the world, who need have no fear of the business cycle as we know it, will forge that much nearer or beyond us. Worse than that, peace-loving people who do not pretend to know very much advanced economics will begin to wonder why it is that during two World Wars individuals were freed for the first time from the insecurity of losing their jobs and livelihoods.

From these introductory remarks, it will be clear that the business cycle is simply one further aspect of the economic problem of achieving and maintaining high levels of jobs and production, and a healthy progressive economy.

MEASURING AND FORECASTING THE BUSINESS CYCLE

Figure 1 shows how the economic system has been plagued with the business cycle throughout our history as a nation, although never with so sustained and

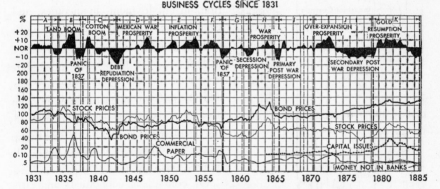

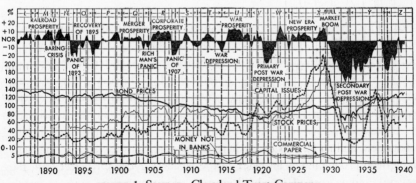

FIGURE 1. SOURCE: Cleveland Trust Company.

costly a slump as in the post-1929 great depression. The same pattern of cyclical fluctuations is repeated in England, Germany, and other foreign nations with surprisingly few variations. But it is a strange fact that the United States, supposedly one of the youngest and most vigorous of nations, tends always to have greater average amounts of unemployment and greater variation in unemployment than any other country. Not only was this true in 1933, when our percentage of unemployment surpassed even that of Germany, but it appears to have been the case for almost as far back as we have any records or indications.

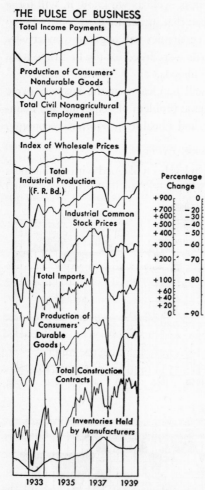

THE PULSE OF BUSINESS

Total Income Payments

Production of Consumers' Nondurable Goods

Total Civil Nonagricultural Employment

Index of Wholesale Prices

Total Industrial Production (F. R. Bd.)

Industrial Common Stock Prices

Total Imports

Production of Consumers' Durable Goods

Total Construction Contracts

Inventories Held by Manufacturers

Percentage Change

+900	0
+700	−20
+600	−30
+500	−40
+400	−50
+300	−60
+200	−70
+100	−80
+60	
+40	
+20	
0	−90

1933   1935   1937   1939

FIGURE 2. Note the common pattern of the business cycle. SOURCE: National Bureau of Economic Research.

Figure 2 shows a number of diverse recent economic "time series," presented next to each other for comparison. Note the all-pervasive common pulse of the business cycle: in production, in employment, in incomes, and even in such particular series as stock-market prices and imports. Moreover, if data had been included on such non-economic matters as marriages, births, and malnutrition, we should also be able to see in them the heavy hand of the business cycle. Even political party elections follow the business cycle; in depressions, the ins go out.

Of course, as economists and citizens, we are primarily interested in the fluctuations in total jobs, total production, and total (real) national income. But for many countries and for many earlier decades, such data are very hard to come by. Moreover, certain specialists are often interested in various secondary series: in stock prices, in wholesale prices, in profits, in steel production, and so forth. Often, therefore, statisticians use such a time series as pig-iron production as an index of the business cycle. Or better still, they may take some sort of weighted average of many series—such as freight-car loadings, electric-power production, or bank clearings (value of checks cashed)—and combine them into a barometer of the business cycle. Figure 1 illustrated such an index of business activity.

Many grown men, who should perhaps know better, ruin their eyesight peering at charts like those shown in Figure 2, in the hope of finding a magic forecaster which always moves up or down a few months *before* business conditions, and by its movements signals the coming trend of events. Alas, they might almost as well consult a fortuneteller. For example, in 1937 the stock market began to turn down early in the year as though in anticipation of the sharp mid-year recession of 1937–1938. But if we go back to 1929, we find that the stock market continued to climb until late in October, whereas business conditions—we now know!—began to turn down some months earlier. Many brave souls have been led to believe in one system or another for "calling the turns" of the cycle, but usually the next boom or depression kills off their hopes and—it may be added—their clients.

Let us for the moment, therefore, stick to the facts and statistics. Later we shall attempt to devise hypotheses and explanatory theories to account for the broad factual patterns, but not for the month-to-month happenings.

STATISTICAL CORRECTION FOR SEASONAL VARIATION AND FOR TRENDS

First, of course, we must remove from our statistical data irrelevant, disturbing factors such as seasonal patterns, and also certain so-called long-term "trends." If Sears Roebuck's sales go up from November to December, 1937, we cannot conclude from this that the 1937 recession is over. Retail trade goes up every Christmas, just as New Hampshire hotels tend to be crowded in summer. The statistician attempts to remove the "seasonal influence" by carefully studying previous yearly patterns. If he finds that every December tends to involve about 150 per cent as much business as the average month of the year, and every January only 90 per cent, then he will take the actual raw monthly data and divide all the December figures by 1.5 and all the January figures by 0.9, and so forth, for each month. After this has been done, the statistician will end up with a time series of monthly department-store sales which have been "seasonally adjusted." These will show what we expected all along, that business was really still declining throughout all the last months of 1937, because December's increase of business over November's was less than the seasonal normal.

A similar problem arises when we examine the fluctuations over time of such a rapidly growing time series as electric-power consumption. Electric-power production did not decline much in the depression. But the depression is to be seen in that series, nevertheless. It rears its ugly head in the form of a *slowing down of the rate of growth* of the time series as compared to its normal or long-term "secular trend." If we draw a smooth trend line or curve, either by eye or by some statistical formula, through the *electric-power production* chart, we shall discover the business cycle in the twistings of the data above and below the trend line. If we measure the vertical deviations up and down from the trend line and plot them on a separate diagram, we shall get a pretty clear picture of the business cycle.[1] Let us take a look at it.

THE FOUR PHASES OF THE CYCLE

Early writers on the business cycle, possessing little quantitative information, tended to attach disproportionate attention to *panics* and *crises* such as the collapse of the South Sea Bubble in 1720, the panic of 1837, the Jay Cooke panic of 1873, the Cleveland panic of 1893, the "rich man's panic" of 1907, and of course, the superduper stock-market crash of "black Tuesday," Oct. 29, 1929. Later writers began soon to speak of two phases of business: prosperity and depression, or boom and slump—with peaks and troughs marking the turning points in between.

Today, it is recognized that not every period of improving business need necessarily take us all the way to full employment. For example, throughout the decade of the 1930's there was a measure of recovery from the 1932–1933 trough levels, but we could by no means speak of the period as being one of true prosperity. The prevailing fashion, therefore, is to follow the terminology of the late Wesley C. Mitchell, long-time director of the nonprofit National Bureau of Economic Research and assiduous student of business cycles.[2]

The cycle is broken up by Mitchell and many other economists into four phases, the two most important ones being called the periods of "expansion" and "contraction." The expansion phase comes to an end and goes into the contraction phase at the so-called upper turning point (peak) called "recession." Similarly, the contraction phase gives way to that of expansion at the lower turning point (trough) or "revival." Thus, the four phases keep repeating themselves in the oversimplified picture as shown in Figure 3. Note that the emphasis now is not so much on *high* or *low* business activity, but on the dynamic aspects of *rising* or *falling* business activity.

---

[1] The reader may be referred to any standard textbook on statistics for these technical procedures. Let it be said, however, that cautious judgment must be exercised in using the mechanical tools of statistics. A beginner, who is carelessly "eliminating a trend," may throw out the baby along with the bath water if he is not careful, or at least distort the true appearance of the infant.

[2] W. C. MITCHELL, *Business Cycles: The Problem and Its Setting* (National Bureau of Economic Research, Inc., New York, 1927).

Each phase of the cycle passes into the next. Each phase is characterized by different economic conditions,[1] and each requires special explanatory principles. But let us continue a little while more with the facts before attempting analysis and theorizing.

How long are the usual economic cycles? This depends upon how many minor cycles you wish to count. Most observers have no trouble in agreeing on the major cycles, which run somewhere around 8 to 10 years in length. Everyone agrees that the late 1920's represent a period of prosperity and the

FOUR PHASES OF THE CYCLE

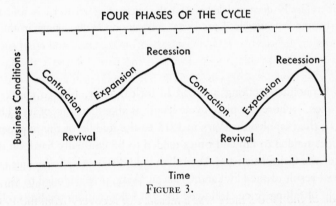

Time
FIGURE 3.

early 1930's one of depression, and similarly with the past major business cycles. But not all economists attach much importance to the shorter minor cycles which are often to be seen in economic charts. In 1924 and 1927, there were small dips in business activity. Shall we call the 1920's, therefore, three different (minor) cycles or one major prosperity period? From late 1948 to early summer of 1949, the United States suffered a mild recession. Shall that count as a cycle?

In an elementary introduction of this type, it is perhaps best to stick primarily to major business cycles. For our purposes we may accept Professor Alvin H. Hansen's brief summary:[2]

The American experience indicates that the major business cycle has had an average duration of a little over eight years. Thus, from 1795 to 1937 there were seventeen cycles of an average duration of 8.35 years. . . .

Since one to two minor peaks regularly occur between the major peaks, it is clear that the minor cycle is something less than half the duration of the major cycle. In

[1] For example, during expansion, we find that employment, production, prices, money, wages, interest rates, and profits are usually rising, while the reverse is true during contraction.

[2] ALVIN H. HANSEN, *Fiscal Policy and Business Cycles* (Norton, New York, 1941), pp. 18–19, 20, 23–24.

the one hundred and thirty-year period 1807 to 1937 there were thirty-seven minor cycles with an average duration of 3.51 years.

. . . it appears that the building cycle averages somewhere between seventeen and eighteen years in length, or almost precisely twice the length of the major business cycle. . . .

. . . American experience indicates that with a high degree of regularity every other major business boom coincides roughly with a boom in building construction, while the succeeding major cycle recovery is forced to buck up against a building slump. . . .

. . . the depressions which have fallen in the interval of the construction down-swing are typically deep and long. And the succeeding recovery is held back and retarded by the unfavorable depressional influence from the slump in the building industry.

LONG WAVES?

Some economists, taking a broad historical view, like to speak of very "long waves," whose complete cycle length is about half a century. Thus from the end of the Napoleonic Wars in 1815 to the middle of the nineteenth century, prices tended to fall and times tended to be unusually hard, on the average. After the Californian and Australian gold discoveries following 1850, and as a partial result of the Civil and Crimean Wars, prices tended to rise. A new long cycle of falling prices followed the 1873 depression, tending to last until the 1890's when there was a great increase in gold production following the South African and Alaskan discoveries and improvements in gold refining McKinley and the Republican party swam to prosperity and power on the crest of the new long wave.

Whether these long waves are simply historical accidents due to chance gold discoveries, political wars, and chance inventions, it is still too soon to say.[1]

A FIRST CLUE TO THE BUSINESS CYCLE: CAPITAL FORMATION

Professor Hansen's emphasis on construction gives us our first clues as to the causation of the business cycle. Certain economic variables always show greater fluctuations than others in the business cycle. Thus, if we were to plot pig-iron production and anthracite-coal consumption side by side, we should hardly see the business cycle in the latter, whereas in the pig-iron series there would be little else to see but the business cycle. Why? Because anthracite is used largely for heating people's houses, and in both good and bad times most people are going to manage to keep reasonably warm. Pig iron, on the other hand, is one of the principal ingredients of capital and durable goods of all kinds: of plant equipment and durable machinery, of industrial and residen-

---

[1] The interested reader may be referred to J. A. Schumpeter, *Business Cycles* (McGraw-Hill, New York, 1939), Chaps. 6, 7.

tial construction, of automobiles, washing machines, and other durable consumers' goods.

By their nature, such durable goods are subject to violently erratic patterns of demand. In bad times their new purchase can be indefinitely postponed; in a good year, everyone may suddenly decide to stock up on a 10-year supply of the services of such durable goods. *Our first clue to the nature of the business cycle lies then in the fact that it is the durable or capital goods sector of the economy which shows by far the greatest cyclical fluctuations.*[1]

If the reader will turn back a few pages to Figure 2, he will see the contrast between capital and nondurable goods fluctuations clearly brought out. The last few time series all represent various categories of durable or capital-goods formation. Note how wide their swings all are, as compared to those of the second time series which represents nondurable consumers' goods. Except for a few short, choppy surface disturbances in this latter series, it will be seen to follow the general flow of income in a rather passive fashion. Consumption movements seem the effect rather than cause of the business cycle, while there is good reason to believe that the movements of durable goods represent key causes in a more fundamental sense.

It is comforting to find that our statistical analysis supports and confirms the emphasis in previous chapters on the crucial importance of the capital investment process.

A FEW THEORIES OF THE BUSINESS CYCLE

An industrious student could easily compile a list of separate theories of the business cycle which would run into the dozens.[2] Each theory seems to be

[1] Lord Beveridge in his *Full Employment in a Free Society* (Norton, New York, 1945) made a careful calculation of the degree of variability of the capital-goods industries in Great Britain ever since 1785 and found it to be twice as great as for other industries. Some economists and statisticians also think that they can detect a tendency for *construction* and other capital-goods series to "lead" general business activity by some interval at both the upturn and the downturn of business, but this is less certain.

[2] We may just mention a few of the better known theories: (1) the *monetary* theory, which attributes the cycle to the expansion and contraction of bank credit (Hawtrey, *et al.*); (2) the *innovation* theory, which attributes the cycle to the clustering of important inventions such as the railroad (Schumpeter, Hansen, *et al.*); (3) the *psychological* theory, which treats the cycle as a case of people's infecting each other with pessimistic and optimistic expectations (Pigou, Bagehot, *et al.*); (4) the *underconsumption* theory, which claims that too much income goes to wealthy or thrifty people compared to what can be invested (Hobson, Foster and Catchings, *et al.*); (5) the *overinvestment* theory, which claims that too much rather than too little investment causes recessions (Hayek, Mises, *et al.*); (6) the *sunspot-weather-crop* theories (Jevons, Moore). The interested reader should consult G. Haberler, *Prosperity and Depression* (League of Nations, Geneva, 1944, 3d ed.) or some other business-cycles text for further information on this subject.

quite different; but when we examine them closely and throw out those which obviously contradict the facts or the rules of logic, or which just appear to be conveying an explanation when really they are not saying anything at all— when we do all this, we are left with a relatively few different explanations. Most of them differ from each other only in emphasis. One man believes the cycle to be primarily the result of fluctuations in total net investment, while another prefers to attribute the cycle to fluctuations in the rate of technological inventions and innovations, which act on business *through* net investment. A third man says that the root of the cycle is to be found in the fact that the creation of deposit money by our banking system causes investment spending to expand and contract so as to create boom and bust.

These sound like three different theories, and in most advanced textbooks they might be given the names of three different writers, but from our standpoint they are but three different aspects of the same process. (This does not mean that there is perfect agreement among all theories of the cycle or that there are not some important differences in emphasis between different writers.)

To classify the different theories, we may first divide them into the two categories of primarily external and primarily internal theories. The external theories find the root cause of the business cycle in the fluctuations of something *outside* the economic system—in sunspot cycles, in wars, revolutions, and political events, in gold discoveries, in rates of growth of population and migrations, in discoveries of new lands and resources, and finally in scientific and technological discoveries and innovations.

The internal theories look for mechanisms *within* the economic system itself which will give rise to self-generating business cycles, so that every expansion will breed recession and contraction, and every contraction will in turn breed revival and expansion, in an irregular, repeating, never-ending chain.

If you believe in the sunspot theory of the business cycle, then the distinction between external and internal is a fairly easy one to draw; although even here, when you come to explain how and why disturbances on the surface of the sun give rise to the business cycle, you begin to get involved in the internal nature of the economic system. But at least no one can seriously argue that the direction of causation is in doubt, or that the economic system causes the sunspots to fluctuate, instead of vice versa. However, when it comes to such other external factors as wars and politics, or even births and gold discoveries, there is always some doubt as to whether the economic system does not at least react back on the so-called "external" factors, making the distinction between external and internal not such a hard and fast one. Still, no one will deny that any such "feedback" effects take us outside the traditional boundaries of economics, and this is the justification for maintaining the distinction between external and internal theories.

Few professional economists today put much stock in these physical theories. Not infrequently an amateur economist, often a scientist in some other field, will argue that sunspots, which have an average periodicity of some 11 to 13 years, have important effects upon the weather. This affects crops. Good crops cause low incomes and bad business. Or else it is the other way round, and good crops are supposed to mean prosperity. The sunspot theorists cannot always make up their minds just which. In other versions, it is said that sunspots affect the intensity of solar radiation. Everyone knows that vitamin D depends on sunshine, and that people near the North Pole become despondent during the long winter nights. Hence, sunspots affect business by affecting pessimism, optimism, or health in general. One ingenious writer, dropping sunspots because they did not give an 8-year cycle, set forth the belief that whenever the planet Venus came between the sun and the earth, this caused magnetic absorptions and an 8-year business cycle.

Unfortunately, the field of economics has not the classic simplicity of physics or mathematics. In those fields a crank who thinks he can square the circle or build a perpetual-motion machine can be shown up, if not to his own satisfaction, at least to that of every competent observer. In economics, it is not quite so easy to demonstrate that sunspot theories of the cycle are all moonshine, especially if their proponents are willing to spend a lifetime manipulating statistics until they produce agreement. This sad fact is important not because we find it difficult to disprove the sunspot theory—no one really cares much today about sunspot theories—but rather because our cockiness about what we think are better and truer theories must always be subject to liberal reservations in view of the complexity of economic observations and data which makes it difficult to disprove a bad theory or verify a good one.

As against the crude external sunspot theory, we may describe a simple example of a possible crude internal theory. If machinery and other durable goods all had the same length of life, say 8 or 10 years, then we might try to explain a business cycle of the same length by this fact. If once a boom got started—never mind how—then there would be a bunching of new capital goods all of the same age. A few years later before these goods had worn out, there would be little need for replacement. This would cause a depression.

But after 8 or 10 years all the capital equipment would suddenly wear out and would all have to be replaced, giving rise to an inflationary boom. This in turn would give rise to another complete cycle, with a new cycle of depression and boom every decade. Thus, as a result of self-generating "replacement waves," we might have a purely internal business-cycle theory.

Actually, not all equipment has the same length of life; and not even all identical automobiles produced on the same day are in need of being replaced at the same time. Therefore, any bunching of equipment expenditures will tend over time to spread itself out, at most giving rise to weaker and weaker replacement peaks. Twenty-five years after the Civil War one might have observed a deficit of births because of that conflict. But another generation later and the dip would be hardly noticeable, while today it is just as if there had never been that particular violent disturbance of population. Replacement waves, therefore, are like a plucked violin string. They tend to dampen down and die away unless there is a new disturbance.

The laws of physics guarantee that friction will lessen any purely autonomous physical fluctuations. In social science, there is no law like that of the conservation of energy preventing the creation of purchasing power. Therefore, a much better example than replacement waves of a self-generating cycle would be the case where people became alternately optimistic and pessimistic, each stage leading as inevitably into the next just as the manic stage of an insane person leads eventually to the depressive stage. We cannot rule out such an internal theory. But neither can we be satisfied with it as it stands, for it does not explain a great deal.

COMBINING EXTERNAL AND INTERNAL ELEMENTS INTO A SYNTHESIS

Everyone has observed how a window or a tuning fork may be brought into pronounced vibration when a certain note is sounded. Is this vibration externally or internally caused? The answer is both. The sounded note is certainly an external cause. But the window or tuning fork responds according to its own internal nature, coming into strong resonance not with any sounded note but only with one of a certain definite pitch. It takes the right kind of trumpets to bring down the walls of Jericho.

Likewise we may look upon the business cycle as not unlike a toy rocking horse which is subjected to occasional outside pushes. The pushes need not be regular; great technical inventions never are. But just as the horse rocks with a frequency and amplitude that depend partly upon its internal nature (its size and weight), so too will the economic system according to its *internal* nature respond to fluctuations in external factors. Both external and internal factors are important, then, in explaining the business cycle.

Most economists today believe in a synthesis or combination of external and internal theories. In explaining the major cycles, they place crucial emphasis on fluctuations in *investment* or *capital* goods. Primary causes of these capricious and volatile investment fluctuations are to be found in such external factors as (1) technological innovation and (2) dynamic growth of population and of territory. With these external factors, we must combine the internal factors that cause any initial change in investment to be amplified in a cumulative, multiplied fashion—as people who are given work in the capital-goods industries respend part of their new income on consumption goods and as an air of optimism begins to pervade the business community, causing firms to go to the banks and the securities market for new credit accommodation.

Also, it is necessary to point out that the general business situation definitely reacts back on investment. If high consumption sales make businessmen optimistic, they are more likely to embark upon venturesome investment programs. Inventions or scientific discoveries may occur independently of the business cycle, but their economic introduction will most certainly depend on business conditions. When national income moved to a new postwar plateau some 50 per cent higher than prewar, it was reasonable to expect that a considerable volume of capital formation (new machines, added inventories, construction) would be induced. Therefore, especially in the short run, investment may be in part an *effect* as well as a cause of the level of income.

In the longer run, no matter how high a plateau of income is maintained, the stock of capital goods will become adjusted at a higher level and new net investment will drop off to zero unless there is (1) a growth of income, (2) a continuing improvement of technology, or (3) a never-ending reduction in interest rates. The first of these processes, showing how investment demand may be induced by *growth* of sales and income, has been given a rather high-sounding name—the "acceleration principle." Almost all writers bring it in as one strand in their final business-cycle theories. Let us examine how this internal cyclical mechanism works itself out and interacts with other factors.

THE ACCELERATION PRINCIPLE

According to this law, society's needed stock of capital, whether inventory or equipment, depends primarily upon the level of income or production. Additions to the stock of capital, or what we customarily call *net* investment, will take place only when income is growing. As a result, a prosperity period may come to an end—not simply because consumption sales have gone down—but simply because sales have *leveled off* at a high level or have continued to grow but at a lower rate than previously.

A simplified arithmetical example will make this clear. Imagine a typical textile-manufacturing firm whose stock of capital equipment is always kept equal to about ten times the value of its yearly sales of cloth.[1] Thus, when its sales have remained at 6 million dollars per year for some time, its balance sheet will show 60 million dollars of capital equipment, consisting of perhaps 20 machines of different ages with one wearing out each year and being replaced. Because replacement just balances depreciation, there is no *net* investment or saving being done by the corporation. *Gross* investment is taking place at the rate of 3 million dollars per year, representing the yearly replacement of one machine. (The other 3 million dollars of sales may be assumed to go for wages and dividends.)

TABLE 1. *Illustration of the Acceleration Principle (In millions of dollars)*

Time	Yearly sales	Stock of capital	Net investment N.I.	Gross investment, G. I. (N.I. + replacement)
First phase				
First year	$ 6	$ 60	$ 0	1 machine at $3 = $3
Second year	6	60	0	1 machine at $3 = $3
Third year	6	60	0	1 machine at $3 = $3
Second phase				
Fourth year	$ 9	$ 90	$30	(1 + 10) machines at $3 = $33
Fifth year	12	120	30	(1 + 10) machines at $3 = $33
Sixth year	15	150	30	(1 + 10) machines at $3 = $33
Third phase				
Seventh year.	$15	$150	$ 0	1 machine at $3 = $3
Fourth phase (to be filled in by reader)				
Eighth year	$14.7	—	−$3	

Now let us suppose that, in the fourth year, sales rise by 50 per cent—from 6 to 9 million dollars. Then the number of machines must also rise by 50 per cent, or from 20 to 30 machines. In the fourth year, 11 machines must be bought, 10 new ones in addition to the replacement of the worn-out one.

[1] We are ignoring any possible change in interest rates or degree of utilization of capacity in order to keep our discussion simple. This could be remedied. Also the reader may wish to include inventory change as well as equipment change in the analysis.

Sales have gone up by 50 per cent. How much has machine production gone up? By 1,000 per cent! It is this accelerated effect of a change in consumption on investment levels that gives the acceleration principle its name.

If sales continue to rise in both the fifth and the sixth years by 3 million dollars, then we shall continue to have 11 new machines ordered in every year. This is shown in Table 1.

So far, the acceleration principle has given us no trouble. On the contrary, it has given us a tremendous increase in investment spending as a result of a moderate increase in consumption sales. But now we are riding a tiger. Consumption has to keep increasing in order for investment to stand still! If consumption should stop growing at so rapid a rate—if it should level off in the seventh year even at the high level of 15 million dollars per year—then net investment will fall away to zero, and gross investment will fall back to 1 machine (see the table). In other words, a drop of zero per cent in sales has resulted in a 90 per cent drop in gross investment and a 100 per cent drop in net investment!

The Lord giveth and the Lord taketh away. The acceleration principle is a two-edged sword. If sales should drop below 15 million dollars, gross investment would drop away to nothing; in fact, the firm would want to disinvest by selling off some of its machinery on the used-equipment market. It is now clear that a depression can set in just because consumption has stopped growing so rapidly, even if it has not dropped off absolutely, but only leveled off at a high level.

Needless to say, the curtailment of production in the machine-producing industries will cause them to shut down, will curtail their income and spending on food and clothing, and lead to still further "multiplier" changes in spending. This might ultimately cause textile sales to stop growing altogether, or even to decline. This will cause a further accelerated drop in net investment. Thus, we may be in a vicious circle whereby the acceleration principle and the multiplier interact so as to produce a cumulative deflationary (or inflationary) spiral.

It is easy to see that in the acceleration principle we have a powerful factor making for economic instability. We have all heard of situations where people have to keep running in order to stand still. In the economic world, matters may be still worse: the system may have to keep running at an ever-faster pace just in order to stand still.

If business sales go up and down, the acceleration principle intensifies their fluctuation. It induces net investment on the upswing but causes about the same amount of net *disinvestment* on the downswing. In the long run, if the system is growing because of population increase or higher real incomes, then the acceleration principle works primarily as a stimulating factor: growing national income causes extensive growth of capital, which in turn means that investment demand will be brisk and unemployment relatively low.

SUMMARY

1. The business cycle is a pulse common to almost all sectors of economic life and to all capitalistic countries. Movements in national income, unemployment, production, prices, and profits are not so regular and predictable as the orbits of the planets or the oscillations of a pendulum, and there is no magical method of forecasting the turns of business activity.

2. However, the four phases of expansion-recession-contraction-revival can be separated out for analysis and can be distinguished from seasonal fluctuations or long-term trends. The resulting pattern of 8- to 10-year major cycles, shorter minor cycles, and longer construction cycles has been carefully described by economists, statisticians, and historians.

3. When it comes to theories to explain the cycle, our first clue is to be found in the greater amplitude of fluctuations of investment or durable capital-goods formation. Although most economists agree on this fact, they differ in their emphasis upon external or internal factors. Increasingly the experts are tending toward a synthesis of external and internal factors, where on the one hand importance is attached to fluctuations in inventions, in population and territorial growth, in gold discoveries and political warfare. On the other hand, economists stress also the way that these external changes in investment opportunities are modified by the multiplier reactions of the economic system, the credit practices of banks, waves of optimism and pessimism, replacement cycles, the acceleration principle which brings in dynamic rates of change as well as levels, and still other feedback effects of income upon investment.

We must now turn to the problem of what can be done to moderate the wild contortions of the cycle, not only to calm it down, but to do so at a level of high employment and long-term growing income. This is the challenge to fiscal policy.

QUESTIONS FOR DISCUSSION

1. What is meant by the business cycle? What are some of the steps that you would follow to measure it?

2. Describe the history of business cycles in this country.

3. Describe the different phases of the cycle.

4. Which theory or theories of the cycle do you like best? Why?

5. Write a two-page explanation of the acceleration principle.

6. In what phase of the cycle are we now?

7. Why is it important to be able to forecast the future of business activity? Illustrate with examples of typical businesses. How could you go about forecasting? How much confidence would you have in the result?

Chapter 19 FISCAL POLICY

AND FULL EMPLOYMENT

WITHOUT INFLATION

WE have seen in earlier chapters that the behavior of saving and investment determines the level of national income and employment. We have seen that private investment often fluctuates widely from year to year. History shows how painful and wasteful the business cycle has been in the past; today everyone is in agreement that, unless we succeed in laying the ghost of instability in the future, American free enterprise will be in jeopardy.

What prescription follows from our economic diagnosis? No single answer can be given; there is no single cure-all for the economic ills of society. Business, labor, and agriculture must all attempt to pursue price and wage policies aimed at maintaining a stable, high-employment economy. The federal reserve system can also do a little, by way of interest and monetary policy, to prevent an aggravation of the business cycle. But, if all these measures have been tried and they still do not succeed in avoiding the perils of heavy unemployment or extreme inflation, then there is still the public weapon of fiscal policy. This is not to say that fiscal policy, alone, is a cure-all, but it is an important part of any economic program.

The reader is warned that the subject matter of this chapter is still in a controversial stage. While stress has been placed on limitations as well as on advantages of different fiscal policies, it is idle to believe that, in the present inadequate state of our scientific economic knowledge, economists are in agreement as to the importance of the pros and cons. No reader should form his opinions upon the basis of a hasty reading of some superficially persuasive argument.

A. *SHORT-RUN AND LONG-RUN FISCAL POLICY*

By a positive fiscal policy, we mean the process of shaping public *taxation* and public *expenditure* so as (1) to help dampen down the swings of the business cycle and (2) to contribute toward the maintenance of a progressive, high-employment economy free from excessive inflation or deflation.

The war years have shown fiscal policy to be a very powerful weapon. Indeed, some would argue that it is like the atomic bomb, too powerful a weapon to let men and governments play with; that it would be better if fiscal policy were never used. However, it is absolutely certain that, just as no nation will sit idly by and let smallpox decimate the population, so too in every country fiscal policy always comes into play whever depressions gain headway. There is no choice then but to attempt to lead fiscal policy along economically sound rather than destructive channels. Every government always has a fiscal policy whether it realizes it or not. The real issue is whether this shall be a constructive one or an unconscious, bumbling one.

COUNTERCYCLICAL COMPENSATION VERSUS LONG-RANGE FISCAL POLICY

There are two main programs of fiscal policy. The first is the least controversial and involves nothing more than the attempt to dampen down the amplitude of the business cycle. This is called a purely "countercyclical compensatory," or "anticyclical" fiscal policy. It involves a budget that is balanced over the business cycle. The second and more controversial part of fiscal policy involves long-range action designed to lift the average level of purchasing power and employment throughout the business cycle as a whole; or, if the long-range situation is inflationary, it involves continued action designed to reduce the average level of purchasing power over the whole cycle.

COUNTERCYCLICAL COMPENSATORY POLICY

When private investment shoots up too high, it seems natural to ask that the government should try to compensate by curtailing public investment and expenditure and increasing its tax collections. On the other hand, when private investment and consumption go off into a slump, the government is then to compensate by stepping up its previously postponed expenditures and by reducing its tax collections. According to the countercyclical view, the government budget need not be in balance in each and every month or year; on the contrary, during inflationary times, the budget should show a surplus of tax receipts over expenditures so that the public debt can be reduced. But when bad times come, then the budget should show a deficit of taxes over expenditures, with the public debt returning to its previous level. Only over the whole business cycle need the budget be in balance.

In a nutshell, that is all there is to countercyclical compensatory fiscal policy. Stated in this way, it is seen to be a rather conservative doctrine—too conservative, some of the present generation of economists would be inclined to argue.

TYPES OF COUNTERCYCLICAL POLICY

Public Works.   This principle of countercyclical finance with respect to public works was introduced into the American system by Herbert Hoover, while he was Secretary of Commerce to Republican President Coolidge. Hoover argued, and rightly, that inasmuch as the government finds it necessary to build a certain amount of roads, hospitals, schools, post offices, etc., then surely it would be better if these projects were intelligently planned so as not all to fall at a time when private construction is booming and manpower is scarce. Instead, they should be postponed until the time when private industry releases materials and men.

In consequence, there will result a relative stabilization of total business activity, since the peak of construction will be cut down and since the depression trough of construction will be at least partly filled in. Not only will jobs be created when needed most, but more than that, the government will be getting its necessary public works at lower prices and through efficient production. All this is so obviously sensible that no one was surprised when in 1931 Hoover and a Democratic Congress passed a law requiring the federal government to set up a "permanent shelf of public-works projects" with long-range plans and blueprints always at hand, drawn up in such a way as to permit the anticyclical timing of public works.

Figure 1*b* contrasts the stabilizing effect of countercyclical finance to Figure 1*a*, which shows how national income would fluctuate if the budget were balanced in each and every month or year. In Figure 1*b*, fiscal policy acts so as to balance the budget over the cycle, but during the boom there is a surplus that is just canceled by the later depression deficit. Note how this has helped to reduce the fluctuations in national income: from the old pattern *ABCDE* to the less violent pattern *AbCdE*.

Note, too, that the government's activity is just *opposite* in phase to the private cycle, so that it can compensate and dampen down the cycle. The shaded areas show how, as a result, the boom is reduced and how the depression is mitigated. The aim is to "chop off the hills to fill in the valleys." Note, too, that the effect on income has been a multiple of the surplus or deficit; this is because the familiar multiplier is at work both in boom and in depression.

The private economy is often like a machine without an effective steering wheel or governor. Compensatory fiscal policy tries to introduce such a governor or thermostatic control device. As shown in the figure, compensatory policy tries to reduce the amplitude of the cycle; it does not necessarily hope to

HOW COUNTER-CYCLICAL FISCAL POLICY WORKS

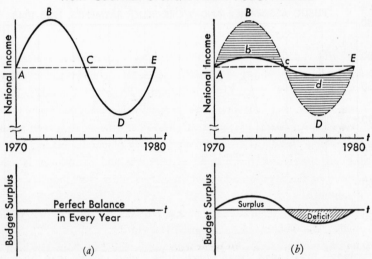

FIGURE 1. In the right-hand diagrams, the government is helping to moderate the amplitude of the business cycle by balancing the budget over the cycle rather than in every year. Note the depression budgetary deficit matched by boomtime surplus.

wipe out altogether every bit of fluctuation. Moreover, everyone recognizes that it is very difficult to time our public works exactly as we should want them. We cannot simply throw a switch when we want more purchasing power and reverse the dial when we want less. Time is required to get a project under way, especially if it is a big one. Once under way, it would be difficult and expensive to abandon it. Because of these technical difficulties of starting and stopping public works and because we need time to discover whether we are really in a boom or a depression, our ambition must be less pretentious than that of creating 100 per cent stability of national income.

Welfare and Other Expenditures.   Fortunately, these difficulties are not insurmountable. Fortunately, too, public-works planning is only one of a number of anticyclical devices. Even without any planning at all, government expenditures on relief and unemployment automatically rise when people get thrown out of work, and automatically tend to fall when jobs again become plentiful.

In country after country all over the world the Great Depression caused budgets to become automatically unbalanced, in part because of an automatic increase in expenditures. Our own 48 states tend to build up in good times an Unemployment Compensation Reserve Fund, less being paid out in benefits to the unemployed than is being collected in payroll taxes. During bad times, the reverse is true: payments to unemployed workers exceed tax collections, and purchasing power is partly maintained by spending out of the accumulated reserve funds.

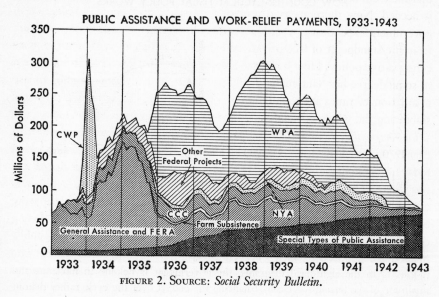

FIGURE 2. SOURCE: *Social Security Bulletin*.

During the depressed 1930's, the WPA provided work relief on public projects (schools, swimming pools, road building, writers' and drama projects, etc.). The PWA provided funds for privately contracted federal and state projects. Home relief was provided for the unemployed and needy. Not all these projects were ideal; some were hastily improvised and unwisely administered. But they did patch up a potentially revolutionary situation and provide for basic human needs, at the same time contributing (with multiplier effects as well) to purchasing power and employment. Figure 2 shows a breakdown of emergency expenditure during the 1930's.

Automatic Changes in Tax Receipts. In addition to public-works expenditure and welfare expenditure, countercyclical compensatory fiscal policy can also rely on cyclically timed tax policies. We have already seen in the earlier chapters on public finance (Chapters 7 and 8) that our federal tax system has important income elements in it, so that tax collections tend to vary strongly with national income. Even without Congress or the state legislatures changing any laws, it turns out that governmental tax collections tend to rise automatically when national income rises and to fall off when national income falls off[1]; and because of the progressive elements in our tax structure, our relative tax collections vary even more sharply than income itself.

A century ago, writers thought that stability of tax revenue was a good thing, and they would have looked with disapproval on the present-day tendency for tax receipts to rise and fall with national income. Today, most believe that the truth is just the reverse. To dampen down a boom, a budgetary surplus is needed. Now there are two ways to produce a surplus: by a reduction in government expenditure, yes; but also by an increase in tax receipts. Indeed, from the standpoint of free private enterprise, tax changes represent the more conservative policy. How lucky we are, therefore, that our present tax system to some degree has "automatic flexibility," with its collections tending to rise in inflationary times and to fall in times of depression. This is a powerful factor stabilizing the whole economy and moderating the business cycle.

Countercyclical Tax-rate Changes. Even this is not all. Congress can also change tax rates. Back before World War I (and still in a few quarters even today), people thought it obviously desirable to balance the budget *in each and every year.* Therefore, they tried to raise tax rates whenever the public was experiencing falling incomes, and to reduce tax rates when incomes were becoming inflated. Once again, the pendulum of expert opinion has swung completely around; today, all but the most conservative students of public finance are opposed to such "perverse flexibility" of tax rates. Those who believe in a countercyclical compensatory fiscal policy argue that the time to reduce tax rates is in depression, when over-all purchasing power is too low; and the time to step up tax rates is during boom times.

Thus taxes as well as expenditures are important for a countercyclical compensatory policy.

LIMITATIONS ON COUNTERCYCLICAL COMPENSATORY POLICY

We have already mentioned (1) some of the difficulties in planning large public-works projects so that they can be quickly got under way or curtailed, and also (2) some of the forecasting difficulties in deciding just exactly when the time has come to step on the gas rather than the brakes. In addition to these two, there are still other limitations on a perfectly effective countercyclical policy.

Effects on Private Investment. A third limitation has to do with changes in private investment. For example, some would argue that government expendi-

[1] For each 10 billion dollars of change in national income, the collections of our 1951–1952 tax system change by more than $3\frac{1}{2}$ billion dollars.

ture or deficits may not really add much to purchasing power during depressions. If private investment could be assumed constant, then public expenditures would of course have favorable primary effects upon income and employment; more than that, the consumption respending of successive portions of income would give rise to the familiar multiplier chain of favorable secondary effects. But what if private investment is frightened off by government expenditure or by the deficit?

This is certainly a possibility. Businessmen may say, "With that man in the White House spending recklessly, we're going to abandon even the little private investment we had planned." Or a private utility company may curtail investment because it fears the threat of public hydroelectric projects. Or when the government spending gives people money to buy in retail stores, the effect in time of deep depression may simply be to permit the merchant to work down his inventory of surplus merchandise; if he does not reorder production goods, the public expenditure has been just about neutralized by induced private *dis*investment (in inventory) and the multiplier chain is stopped dead in its tracks.

On the other hand, there may be favorable effects on private investment which are just the opposite to these unfavorable repercussions of government finance. When current production is at a low ebb and there is excess plant capacity, no prudent businessman feels like undertaking new capital formation. If the government is able to boost retail sales and the production of consumption goods, then businessmen will have the financial ability and at least some motive to renew equipment and build new plant. (An example of this was provided by the discussion in Chapter 18 of the acceleration principle relating induced investment to the upward change in sales.)

Where there are two such opposing tendencies—favorable and unfavorable effects upon private investment—facts rather than arguments must be our guide. Although economics does not permit us to make controlled experiments to settle the point conclusively, the bulk of the statistical data that have come to the attention of this writer suggests that private investment tends to move on the whole sympathetically with the level of national income. The cash register calls the tune, and in a free-enterprise society, rightly so.

This does not mean that we can neglect unfavorable psychological reactions to deficit financing. But these adverse reactions are of much greater importance in connection with long-range deficit financing than with the purely countercyclical case where the budget is balanced over the cycle. We may profitably defer this topic to later sections.

Fiscal Perversity of Local Finance.   A fourth limitation on compensatory finance arises from the behavior of state and local governments. Unlike the federal government, they have a tendency toward a perverse cyclical pattern—borrowing for hospitals and schools in good times and reducing their debts in bad times. This serves to aggravate rather than dampen down the business cycle.

However, it would be unfair to criticize them too harshly for this. The credit of the federal government actually improves in bad times; also it has the constitutional powers to issue currency and to use the Central Bank to float its loans if Congress deems this necessary. The states and localities, on the other hand, are subject to greater credit difficulties when it comes to borrowing —although in recent years federal grants-in-aid have been an important source of finance for local public works. Also, states and localities are often hamstrung by constitutional limitations upon their depression borrowing.

On the whole, it is probably too much to expect the states and localities to pursue a militant anticyclical spending policy. But at the very least, we can set for them the goal of being neutral with respect to the cycle rather than aggravating it by buying new fire engines and war monuments during inflation and cutting all services to the bone during depression. Also, it is to be hoped that local governments will avoid *perverse cyclical flexibility* with respect to tax rates, such as introducing deflationary, regressive sales taxes during depression times and cutting income tax rates during prosperity.

The "Pump-priming" Confusion.   In addition to the above four criticisms, a number of other limitations upon countercyclical compensatory fiscal policy could be listed. But only one last criticism will be mentioned here. Many people are disappointed to find that *after the government curtails its depression spending, the national income may again fall back to a low level.* Really this is not a criticism of compensatory policy, but rather a case of confusing it with what is popularly called government "pump priming."

When the New Deal was still very new, many people thought that, if the government would only spend a little money, the economy would be lifted from the doldrums and would carry on forever after on its own steam. If only you pour a little water into the pump to prime it, it will repay you with an endless stream of water.

Actually, countercyclical compensatory fiscal policy is as different from pump priming as a gasoline engine is from a perpetual-motion machine. Stop feeding gas and the motor stops; stop eating and you will waste away. So with compensatory finance: public spending may have powerful secondary effects; still, like private investment itself, its effects cease soon after it ceases. In economics, there are few magical ways of getting something for nothing.[1]

[1] One way of getting a pump-priming situation would be to consider a system where a dollar of expenditure did not create a multiplier chain of $3 = 1 + \frac{2}{3} + (\frac{2}{3})^2 + \cdots$,

So much for the limitations to countercyclical fiscal policy. In conclusion, we may simply note that few people would object in theory to its precepts. What they do occasionally object to is the tendency or danger that what starts out as an innocent-looking countercyclical fiscal policy may turn into a policy of long-range spending. For example, consider the period 1933 to 1938 as a complete cycle. Certainly 1936 and 1937 were in retrospect its best years, and according to the purely countercyclical view should have been years of budgetary surplus. But at the time, with almost 10 million unemployed, putting on the fiscal brakes hardly seemed rational or "political."

LONG-RUN FISCAL POLICY

Let us turn, therefore, to the longer run problem. If we could always be sure of 5 lean years of private investment too small to maintain high employment, followed by 5 fat years in which investments were too large to permit high employment at stable prices, then countercyclical finance might be perfect. But what if we move into a postwar era where the years of high boom tend always to *outnumber* those of depression? Then, in such a period of "secular exhilaration," many would argue that the government should not balance the budget over each business cycle. Instead, it should average a "budgetary surplus" (of taxes over expenditure) throughout most of each business cycle and over a long period of years.

This is clearly something quite different from a countercyclical policy aimed at smoothing out fluctuations; it is a policy of *continuous long-run surplus financing* aimed at reducing the average level of purchasing power and inflation.

On the other hand, suppose that the level and fluctuations in private investment were such as to give us a pattern of national income like that shown in Figure 3. Although our manpower, resources, and know-how are such as to make it possible for the American economy to produce the indicated *potential* pattern of real product, suppose that the balance of saving and investment tends to give the *actual* pattern shown by *ABCDEFG*. The reader can draw in a third line showing what would be the pattern of income if only a countercyclical smoothing-out policy were pursued. Obviously, there would still be a wastage of resources and product most of the time, even if the contortions of the business cycle were partly ironed out.

Many modern writers would argue for a *long-run policy of full compensation* in such a case. According to them, it would not necessarily be desirable to pull

---

but rather created a chain of the form: infinity $= 1 + 1 + 1 + 1 + \cdots + 1 + \cdots$. Without any "saving leakages," the pump would give you any amount of water in return for the original amount used for priming.

the brakes at A, or at C, or at G. Only at E would a strongly contracting spending policy be called for.

According to this new school of fiscal theorists, fiscal policy ought—in such a period of "secular stagnation"—to be expansionary much if not most of the time. Over the business cycle as a whole, the budget might not be in balance, because the lean years would be outnumbering the good ones. As national income grows, so too might the public debt. All this is still controversial, and the reader is warned that many eminent economists are opposed to any policy of continuous deficits.[1]

PATTERN OF CHRONIC STAGNATION

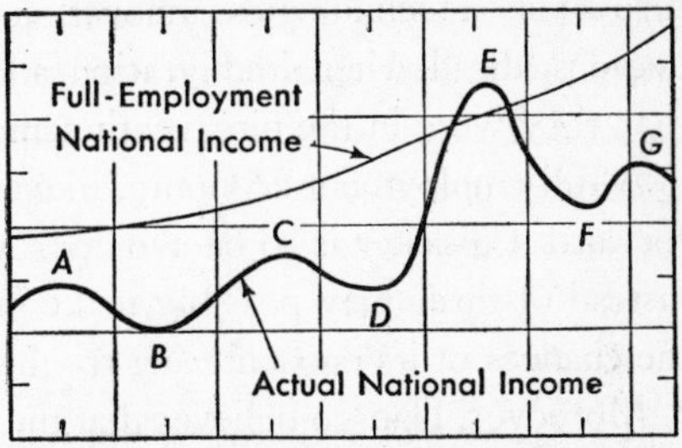

FIGURE 3. Hypothetical data to illustrate case where simple countercyclical finance is held inadequate to achieve stable high employment.

Long-run surplus financing and long-run deficit financing both differ from a purely countercyclical policy. Which will be appropriate depends upon the happenstance of the long-run balance of saving and investment. Let us first turn to the more pessimistic view of stagnant investment opportunities relative to full-employment saving.

SECULAR STAGNATION?

Such a view is often called "secular stagnation." It is associated with the name of Professor Alvin H. Hansen of Harvard University. According to Hansen, dynamic investment is the mainspring of economic fluctuations. As investment shifts to high gear, total demand is high and jobs are plentiful; when the capricious factors making for investment happen to be unfavorable for a long time, the economic system may go through years or decades of considerable unemployment.

So far, almost all economists would agree with Hansen. But a number would get off the band wagon when he goes on to express his opinion that there are a number of long-run factors in the American situation which make it possible or even probable that investment will be a lagging factor relative to full-employment saving. He thinks that a relatively "mature economy" like the United States is especially susceptible to stagnant investment and unemployment. Some of his reasons are as follows:

Investment Prospects. In the past the principal determinants of investment have been these dynamic—not static!—elements: *rapid population growth, dis-*

[1] See the lengthy study, *The American Industrial Enterprise System* (National Association of Manufacturers, New York, 1946), Vol. II, Chap. 18.

covery and settlement of new territory, and *technological innovation*. The geographical frontier is long since gone. Even before World War I the first two of these investment determinants were beginning to slow down. After World War I, and particularly in the decade of the 1930's, almost the full brunt was thrown upon technological innovation. This will be even more noticeable in the decades ahead when immigration and birth rates are sure to be much less than they were in the nineteenth century.

A full-employment economy, like an airplane, cannot stand still; it must go forward if disaster is to be avoided. An airplane traveling on only one engine instead of three may possibly make out all right, but as a betting proposition the chances of its encountering trouble are increased.

Moreover, Hansen believes that the third dynamic factor behind investment, technological innovation, will go on at a more brilliant pace than ever before in our history, but may to a considerable extent take the form of inventions that *lessen rather than increase the amount of needed investment*. Thus the invention of the airliner may make possible the development of Siberia without billions and billions of dollars of investment in public roads and railroads. The invention of wireless radio or of the multiple-message cable all economize on the tremendous amount of investment needed in capital installations. Atomic energy may minimize the need in many parts of the world for costly hydroelectric reclamation projects. Science gives and takes as far as investment is concerned, and Hansen thinks there may continue to be—what he believes to have been true of the 1930's—a preponderance of "capital-saving invention."

Personal and Corporate Saving Prospects. Hansen's views with respect to the future of saving round out his theory. He believes that people tend to divide their extra income between consumption and saving. Our incredibly creative scientists and engineers can be expected to increase our full-employment real incomes at a rapid rate. Probably, real wages and productivity will continue to grow at the compound-interest rate of 2 to 3 per cent per year, or even faster than in the past.

If people's tastes and standards of consumption remained the same, this vast increase in income would probably mean an even greater proportionate increase in saving. Fortunately for the prospects of avoiding mass unemployment, people's consumption standards do not remain constant. Their needs and desires are constantly expanding, because of new products invented, because of advertising, because of social custom and imitation.

Throughout all our history the consumption-income schedule has been shifting upward; the propensity-to-save schedule has been shifting downward. We now have pretty good statistical records going back more than half a century. These show, rather than an increase in the ratio of saving to income, a remarkable constancy of the proportion which the American people have saved out of past full-employment incomes. Hansen sees no reason why the same should not continue to be true in the years ahead. If rising living standards keep pace with rising productivity, then the percentage of personal saving that has to be offset by investment need not get worse—especially if progressive tax and expenditure policies help to maintain a high consumption economy, and if bold and vigorous attacks on unemployment are effective in forestalling any tendency for people to get frightened into oversaving and to fall behind in their acquiring of higher living standards.

Personal savings are only part of the picture. Increasingly, corporate saving is growing in importance, and here Hansen is less optimistic. It is sound business management for corporations to make full accounting allowances for depreciation and obsolescence; it is sound practice to withhold part of dividends and plow back earnings into a growing business. Hansen thinks that these business savings may be more than enough to finance replacement of capital equipment and new capital formation. And to the extent that corporate investment is completely financed by additional net (or gross) corporate saving, to that extent such investment is not available to offset personal saving and cannot add very much to jobs and purchasing power.

Hansen, who is by nature a confirmed optimist, hopes that the maintenance of continued full employment will cause businessmen to be contented with low unit profits on a high volume of production and with moderate rates of profit and saving.

Some of Hansen's followers are less guarded than he is. Also, there is a sizable body of conservative opinion which is much more pessimistic than he is, in that they agree with him as to the pattern of future and past facts but disagree as to the basic cause of stagnation. They are inclined to attribute the failure of investment in the pre- and postwar periods to the interference of government with business and to reform legislation. With nations all over the world moving increasingly toward a planned state, and with the American electorate showing an unwillingness to turn the hour hand back toward *laissez faire*, holders of this view naturally tend to be rather despondent.

Before turning to criticisms of the Hansen stagnation thesis, let us beware of one of its common misunderstandings. It is not the growth of our productive potentialities that is believed likely to be stagnant. As Figure 3 clearly shows, the secular stagnationists believe that our scientists will be more productive than ever—inventing glass neckties and causing 1 man-hour to do the work previously required of 2. As we have seen, Hansen believes that productivity and full-employment production may grow at a compound interest rate, doubling at every generation. The only thing that he thinks is likely to stagnate—if nothing is done about it—is our ability to keep everybody employed so as to realize our potentialities; or to put the matter differently, the level of investment relative to full-employment saving may stagnate in a wealthy, mature economy.

The 6 years since 1945 have proved to be quite the reverse of any gloomy expectations concerning the stagnation of a mature economy. And as long as the present tense international situation prevails, there seems to be small reason to fear that there will be too little dollar spending in the United States. It is ironical that the Russians accept it as an inevitable fact that the postwar capitalistic system must experience a tremendous crisis and collapse. Yet every military move they make has the quite opposite effect of ensuring that the capitalist countries will pursue such extensive military expenditures as to make any depression impossible!

STAGNATION A BOGEY?

By no means are all, or most, economists prepared to regard the stagnation theory as proved or even probable. But surprisingly little vigorous and detailed opposition appeared in print until the Machinery and Allied Products Institute, a federation of trade associations in the industrial equipment field, published a full-size volume entitled *The Bogey of Economic Maturity*. This was prepared by George Terborgh, an able economist, and constitutes the fullest reference source for anyone interested in the arguments against the stagnation viewpoint. Without going into details, some of his viewpoints can be briefly mentioned here.

Terborgh believes that the stagnation and mature-economy thesis is a bogey without sound factual or theoretical basis. It is a child of the pessimistic depression period. Prior to 1929, there was little or no evidence of senility of the American economy; and just as one swallow does not make a summer, so one depression, even a great one, cannot establish a presumption toward stagnation. Terborgh also believes that the income analysis along saving and investment lines is in itself neutral and establishes no presumption in favor of stagnation. Of course, misuse of the analysis may seem to favor stagnation; *e.g.*, at any time in the past century it would have been difficult to name the industries that would provide us with investment, so that a simple-minded calculator of savings might at any time have come to pessimistic and incorrect conclusions.

Turning to specific facts, Terborgh admits that population growth provides an important quantitative source for investment; but this does not prove that investment would fail to go elsewhere if there were no population growth. Moreover, when population growth slows down, the elderly, retired portion of the population grows in relative importance. Therefore, the slowing down of population growth reduces saving at the same time when it may have diminishing tendencies on investment. Finally, and this is perhaps most important of all, the percentage decline in population has been going on for a century. Why, then, did stagnation not develop years and years ago?

So too with the disappearing frontier. The geographical frontier disappeared in the 1890's. Why no stagnation at that time? Why should new people on new land lead to more investment than new people on old settled land?

Turning to the third source of investment, technological innovation, Terborgh questions the vital importance of a few great and dramatic industries.

The important thing is the total flow of technological development, not its degree of concentration. Given an abundance of rising industries like aviation, mechanical refrigeration, air-conditioning, radio, television, rayon, plastics, quick-freezing, prefabricated housing, light metals, powdered metals, high-octane gasoline, gas turbines, jet propulsion, spun glass, cotton pickers, combined harvesters, electronics—to name only a few at random—the total volume of direct and induced investment can be tremendous. . . . There is . . . no evidence of an increasing proportion of capital-saving innovation.[1]

Terborgh also disbelieves in the bogey of an increase in self-financed business investment. His studies lead him to believe that the great depression of the 1930's must be explained in other terms, and that the immediate outlook is a relatively favorable one:

If . . . we suffer from a chronic insufficiency of *consumption and investment combined*, it will not be, in our judgment, because investment opportunity in a physical and technological sense is persistently inadequate to absorb our unconsumed income; but rather because of political and economic policies that discourage investment justified, under more favorable policies, by these physical factors.[2]

The task of cyclical stabilization is difficult enough without the distraction of stagnationist soothsaying. Even if we renounce the fatuous perfectionism of "sixty million guaranteed jobs," aspiring rather to the more modest immediate goal of relative stability, the task is still difficult. It is not, however, impossible. To its accomplishment, haunted no longer by the demons of economic maturity, we can proceed with courage and resolution.[2]

We shall not attempt here to weigh the relative merits of the stagnation viewpoint. Economic analysis must be prepared to understand the policies called for by stagnation; it must be no less prepared to meet the opposite situation of long-range inflationary conditions. In the author's personal judg-

[1] GEORGE TERBORGH, *The Bogey of Economic Maturity* (Machinery and Allied Products Institute, Chicago, 1945), pp. 89, 96.

[2] *Ibid.*, pp. 213, 226.

ment, the outlook for the next few years is inflationary enough so that secular exhilaration rather than secular stagnation may be our most important worry.

SECULAR EXHILARATION, LONG-RUN SURPLUS FINANCING, AND DEBT RETIREMENT

Suppose that private investment demand and the propensity to consume should be so buoyant that the schedules of saving and investment tend to intersect at an income higher than we have the manpower to produce. There would then be a tendency toward "overfull employment." There would be more than a tendency toward inflation, there would be actual inflation. The dollar shrinks in value as prices soar. People want to buy more goods than can be produced; prices are bid up and for the moment may seem to discourage excessive purchases. But the higher prices do not permanently equate supply and demand. The higher prices constitute someone's income—a farmer's, a businessman's, or a worker's. Again demand is excessive, again prices rise, and we have the familiar case of an inflationary spiral which cannot burn itself out so long as the savings and investment schedules fail to intersect at full employment.[1]

There is one thing to do. The government must cut its expenditures in order to reduce purchasing power; it must increase its tax collections so as to produce a surplus. It is not enough to do this for a day or a year; it must continue to run a surplus for as long as total demand remains excessive.

What does this mean for the early 1950's? Suppose that government defense expenditures go up by tens of billions of dollars, employment is already full, and the federal budget just in balance. Suppose that we want to use direct controls as little as possible and we are not very optimistic that much will actually be accomplished by federal reserve monetary policy. Then nondefense government expenditure will have to be cut wherever possible. And new taxes will have to be levied in order to get people to give up to the defense effort resources that were previously being used for civilian production. How much new taxes will be required to cause a reduction in private spending of 10 billion dollars? Because people have a marginal propensity to consume of less than 1, we shall have to reduce their disposable incomes by more than 10 billion dollars to cause a 10-billion-dollar cut in their spending. Thus, if fiscal policy alone is to avoid inflation, we shall probably have to increase taxes enough to run a budgetary surplus. Whether we shall get so large an increase in taxes is doubtful and remains to be seen.[2]

---

[1] See the earlier discussion of inflation in Chapters 13 and 14.

[2] The Appendix discusses some of the current problems of fiscal policy of the early 1950's.

B. *THE PUBLIC DEBT AND POSTWAR FISCAL POLICY*

Let us now turn to the problems raised by a new and startling fact: As a result of World War II the public debt of the federal government is one-quarter of a trillion dollars! What are the real problems created by such a debt? Are there any false problems associated with it? What are the important noneconomic factors that must be reckoned with in any discussion of this vital political issue?

THE PUBLIC DEBT AND ITS LIMITATIONS

In appraising the burdens involved in a public debt, we must carefully avoid the unscientific practice of making up our minds in advance that whatever is true of one small merchant's debt is also necessarily true of the government's debt. Prejudging the problem in this way might come perilously close to the logical fallacy of composition; and, instead of permitting us to isolate the true—all too real!—burdens of the public debt, might only confuse the issue.

External versus Internal Debt.   A large *external* public debt, owed to people outside of the United States, would be a real burden and limitation upon the American economy. This is because as a nation we should be forced to ship valuable goods and services abroad to meet the interest charges on the external debt and possibly to amortize some of its principal. If 10 per cent of the national income had to go abroad in this way, the burden would be—if not an intolerable one—nevertheless a weighty one. The American people would have to work harder and longer, and they would have to do without.

There are also burdens involved in an internally held public debt like our present one, *but the burdens of an internal debt are qualitatively and quantitatively different from those of an external debt.* This is the first and most important lesson to be grasped, without which nobody can go far in understanding the economics of the public debt. The interest on an internal debt is paid by Americans to Americans; there is no *direct* loss of goods and services. When interest on the debt is paid out of taxation, there is no *direct* loss of disposable income; Paul receives what Peter loses, and sometimes—but only sometimes—Paul and Peter are one and the same person.

Borrowing and Shifting Economic Burdens through Time.   Still another confusion between an external and internal debt is involved in the often-met statement: "When we borrow rather than tax in order to fight a war, then the true economic burden is really being shifted to the future generations who will have to pay interest and principal on the debt." As applied to an external debt, this shift of burden through time might be true. It is unmistakably false in reference to an internal debt. Why?

To fight a war now, we must hurl present-day munitions at the enemy; not dollar bills and not future goods and services. If we borrow munitions from some neutral country and pledge our children and grandchildren to repay them in goods and services, then it may truly be said that external borrowing permits a shift of economic burden between present and future generations.

But suppose there is no outside nation to lend us goods. Suppose civilian capital formation has already been cut down to the bone, but still our government needs more resources for the war effort. Suppose Congress is not willing to vote taxes large enough to permit the government to balance its swollen budget or stringent enough to reduce people's spending to where they will release resources for the war effort and stop bidding up prices. The government will then be running a deficit and will build up a huge debt. (It may also have to pass price-control and rationing laws, but that need not concern us here.)

Can it then be truthfully said that "internal borrowing shifts the war burden to future generations while taxing places it on the present generation"? A thousand times no! The present generation must still give up resources to produce the munitions hurled at the enemy. In the future, some of our grandchildren will be giving up goods and services to other grandchildren. That is the nub of the matter. The only way in which we can impose a direct burden on the future nation as a whole is by incurring an external debt or by passing along less capital equipment to our posterity.

This explains why the British are a great deal more worried about their small external debt than they are over their vastly greater internal debt; the former directly impoverishes the British Isles. Fortunately, the United States has come out of the most costly war in all history with little impairment of capital equipment and external debt.

"We All Owe It to Ourselves." If an internal debt is simultaneously owed and owned by Americans, why do some people think that the wartime creation of 250 billion dollars of government bonds makes the public more wealthy and more ready to spend? If we draw up a consolidated balance sheet for the nation as a whole, we see that the (internal) debt represents a kind of fictitious financial wealth, which cancels out as a liability and asset.

However, purely financial assets do have important effects. Anybody owning government bonds includes them when drawing up his periodic balance sheet, along with his other assets. But he is a very rare man indeed if he also includes as a present liability the amount of *future* taxes which he may have to pay to finance government interest payments or debt retirement. He does not even have a way of estimating his share of these taxes. The result is that the internal debt, which as a liability should exactly cancel out itself as an asset, tends instead to be counted by people primarily as an asset. Given a nest egg of bonds which they can either sell or cash in, people *feel* richer and more secure and therefore tend to have a higher propensity to consume out of current income.

Debt Management and Monetary Policy. The existence of a large outstanding public debt may also have an influence on the interest rate and on its use to fight the business cycle. Some writers fear that channeling investment funds into the purchase of government bonds will raise the rate of interest to private borrowers. Alexander Hamilton, the spokesman of the conservative Federalist party, had just the opposite opinion. He felt that, rightly managed and in the right amounts, a public debt would be "a national blessing" because it would provide a secure gilt-edge asset that would give businessmen an income and enable them to trade for smaller profits.

As was shown in Chapter 17 on Central Banking, the federal reserve authorities have strong powers to regulate rates of interest on government bonds. Therefore, any undue upward or downward pressure of the debt upon interest rates can be offset by open-market purchases and sale of government securities. But, and this is an ironic paradox, the existence of the vast public debt, while it enhances their power, at the same times serves to inhibit the exercise of effective monetary and interest policy by the Federal Reserve Banks.

It will be recalled that monetary policy is supposed to act so as to raise interest rates and tighten credit conditions when over-all demand threatens to be inflationary. But with large amounts of bonds in the hands of banks and the public, the governmental authorities have a strong incentive toward keeping up the selling price of government bonds—in order to keep interest charges on the debt low and prevent financial embarrassment of financial institutions holding government bonds. If government bonds cannot fall in price, then interest rates cannot be tightened; people and banks are always able to convert their bonds into the cash they need for consumption or investment spending. A large debt, therefore, tends to discourage the use of monetary policy to control the business cycle and serves to throw an even larger burden on fiscal policy.[1]

The True Indirect Burden of Interest Charges. When taxes are used to pay interest charges on the public debt, then money goes from one pocket into

[1] The effects upon consumption of the large outstanding amount of government bond assets may make matters worse. Consumption becomes less responsive to disposable income and may become more changeable. Fiscal policy then has more work to do and has less leverage to do it. Chapter 17 discussed the difficulties for Central Banking policy created by the Treasury's insistence on stable bond prices.

another. No direct burden like that of an external debt is involved. But it would be wrong to jump to the hasty conclusion that no burden of any kind is involved. There is an indirect burden which may be very important.

In the first place, although money merely goes out from one pocket and into another, the trousers in question may be worn by different people. The present national debt is very widely held, so that almost every individual has some share, either through outright holdings or through bank deposits and insurance policies. Nevertheless, the statistical evidence suggests that the people who receive bond interest are *on the average* not in the lower income brackets. Thus interest on the public debt constitutes a regressive (Robin Hood in reverse) element in our fiscal system. "Soaking the poor to pay the rich" tends to reduce purchasing power and runs counter to many modern notions of equity. Nevertheless, it is a necessary evil if past commitments with respect to the public debt are to be scrupulously honored, as they must be.

However, with our present public debt this transfer from one income class to another is probably not its single most important indirect burden. More important, *transferring tax money from Peter to pay bond interest to the same Peter will involve a heavy indirect burden on the economy!* This is because taxation always has some distorting effects on people's economic behavior. Centuries ago houses were taxed on their windows, with the result that people built dark houses, even though the government still collected the same revenue by simply raising rates on the few remaining windows. Similarly, taxing people's income may cause them to work too little, or in many cases too hard, in their attempt to maintain the same standard of living. Perhaps of even more importance, high corporation or personal income taxes will often have adverse effects upon people's willingness to venture their capital on risky enterprises. The result: less technological progress and fewer jobs.

At this point, the reader may protest that this is all nonsense and that there is no net tax burden involved in an internal transfer since it is being assumed that we all own bonds in proportion to our share of taxes, and in effect are only paying to ourselves. This reasoning is quite mistaken. *Taxes on each individual matched by exactly equal interest payments to him do not cancel out!*

This is so because what is true of all is not true for each individual. Suppose for simplicity that all Americans earn $4,500 a year in wages. Suppose that each owns $25,000 in government bonds, which at 2 per cent bring in a yield of $500 per year. To pay this interest the government, let us say, adds 10 per cent (in addition to existing taxes) on total income of $5,000 ($4,500 + $500). Previously it just paid me to work an extra bit of overtime to earn the last dollar of my $5,000. But now the government takes another dime out of that dollar. I (and every American like me) may now feel that it does not pay to work such long hours. By cutting out, say, one-third of my working hours, my income is now only $3,500. The tax has distorted national effort and production.

The unconvinced reader will say at this point: "What if everybody else cuts his hours as you do? Then the extra tax rate will have to be raised from 10 per cent to almost 15 per cent if the total of bond interest is to be covered." True enough. But this only proves the point. The final situation may end up with even a greater distortion of effort and risk taking, and with an even higher tax rate. This all happens because, although the nation cannot avoid raising taxes equal to the interest payment, each individual knows that he can affect his taxes by varying his effort, with his own small interest payments going on anyway, regardless of what he as a single small person does.

The above example is oversimplified and undoubtedly exaggerates the harmful effects of internal transfers. Also, different kinds of taxes differ in their harmful effects, but in any case with our taxes already so high, any further burden due to interest on the public debt is just that much more harmful.

Moreover, we have neglected the beneficial effects of interest payments to banks, universities, widows, and other *rentiers*. If there were no public debt or if interest rates were to fall substantially, then (1) charitable institutions would have to be supported by public and private current contributions more than by interest on perpetual endowments, (2) social security and annuities would have to take the place of *rentier* interest, and (3) service charges by banks would have to be increasingly relied upon instead of government bond interest.

THE QUANTITATIVE PROBLEM OF THE DEBT

We may summarize the above section on the economics of a public debt as follows: (1) Our internal debt does not involve the direct burden of an external debt or the same possibility of shifting real burdens between generations. (2) Although we all owe it to ourselves, people tend to treat bonds as a safe liquid asset which increases their willingness to consume out of current income. The huge volume of outstanding debt hampers an anticyclical interest rate policy because the authorities are loath to see bond prices fluctuate. (3) An internal debt involves an important *indirect* burden whenever new taxes have to be raised to meet interest payments. This would be true even if the typical person was taxed by as much as his own interest payments, but it is further aggravated by the fact that interest receivers appear to be somewhat more wealthy than average taxpayers.

To assess the importance of the public debt, we must turn to the facts. Do interest payments on it swallow up most of the national income? How does the total of all interest payments, public and private, compare with past years and with the experience of other countries? What about foreseeable future trends?

In Chapter 7 (Figure 1) the historic growth of our national debt was pictured.[1]

To see how the present quarter of a trillion dollar debt compares with the past and some other countries, Table 1 has been drawn up. It shows for selected times and places the size of national debts and their relationship to size of national income and interest payments. Thus, in 1950 our national debt of 257 billion dollars represented about one year of national income, and its interest payments represented less than 3 per cent of national income. Note that England, in 1818, 1923, and 1946 had an internal debt estimated at more than twice national income, and her interest on the debt as a percentage of national income far exceeded anything that we need look forward to. Yet, the century before World War I was England's greatest century—greatest in power and material progress. Nevertheless, as the table shows, her national debt was not substantially reduced; but with the steady growth of her national income, the debt and its interest charges shrank to almost nothing in relative quantitative magnitude.

In view of these statistics and careful qualitative analysis, the reader must form his own judgment as to whether the national debt constitutes as yet a problem of the first magnitude in comparison with the problems of national defence, the atomic bomb, unemployment, or inflation. Whether productivity will continue to rise in the future, whether labor and management can learn to bargain collectively without strikes and inflation—all these are not less important than the debt itself.

Yet there is a tremendous amount of emotion involved in people's attitudes toward the debt, and this we must not dismiss lightly. Like sex or religion, the

[1] By mid-1950, the total federal debt had climbed back to the early 1947 level of about 257 billion dollars. But note the following interesting shifts in its composition:

	1947	1950
Commercial and mutual savings banks.................	$84	$76
Federal Reserve Banks............................	24	18
Insurance companies.............................	25	20
Individuals....	64	67
Corporations and miscellaneous.....................	23	30
Federal, state, and local governments.................	37	46

In 1947, about 51 billion dollars of the total was in the form of familiar United States savings bonds; by 1950, this figure had dropped to 50 billion.

public debt is a subject that we all love to discuss. Many people used to predict the end of the world when the debt reached one-hundredth, one-tenth, and one-fifth of its present level; each year when the dire disaster had not appeared, they renewed their predictions for the following years.

In dispassionately analyzing the growth of the debt, one error we must avoid: *we must not forget that the real national product of the United States is an ever-growing thing.*

TABLE 1. *National Debt and Interest Charges Relative to National Income*

Year	National debt	Interest charges on national debt	National income	Size of debt in years of national income	Interest charges as a per cent of national income
				$(5) =$	$(6) \div 100 =$
(1)	(2)	(3)	(4)	$(2) \div (4)$	$(3) \div (4)$
United States:	(Billions)	(Billions)	(Billions)		
1950*	$257	$5.7	$236	1.1	2.4
1939	34.9	0.97	68.5	0.5	1.4
1932	18.2	0.64	46.7	0.4	1.4
1929	15.1	0.67	79.5	0.2	0.8
1920	23.5	1.06	68.4	0.3	1.5
1916	1.2	0.02	38.7	0.0+	0.0+
1868	2.6	0.13	6.8	0.4	2.0
Britain:	(Millions)	(Millions)	(Millions)		
1946*	£24,500	£500	£8,000	3.1	6.2+
1923	7,700	271	2,300	2.0+	7.1
1913	656	17	2,30	0.3	0.7
1818	840	31	400	2.1	7.7

* Estimated.

SOURCE: *Economic Almanac*, Department of Commerce, U.S. Treasury; *Colwyn Report* Statistical Abstract of United Kingdom. Data rounded off.

Population increase has slowed down some, but for a long time our numbers will continue to grow. As to productivity, there is absolutely no indication that man-hour efficiency and new techniques have begun to slacken off. Upon this, stagnationists and exhilarationists both agree. What seemed like a big debt in 1790 would be nothing today. What our children will come to regard as a big debt, our great grandchildren may consider relatively unimportant.

This explains why England and France, in the crucially formative years of the capitalistic system and Industrial Revolution, were able to go on—not only decade after decade but almost century after century—with their budgets in balance less than half the time. This same factor of growth explains why in the United States, where real national production doubles every generation or so, the public debt might increase by 250 billion dollars in 25 years without its relative percentage burden growing.

This would give the wildest believer in government spending an average deficit of some 10 billion dollars per year before he would have to turn to such even more unorthodox financial expedients as printing money or selling interest-free bonds to the Federal Reserve Banks. Moreover, before turning to such expedients, he would still have open to him the now familiar process of keeping down interest rates on government bonds by a conventional easy-money banking policy.

Could a nation fanatically addicted to deficit spending pursue such a policy for the rest of our lives and beyond? Study of the mechanics of banking and income determination suggests that the barrier to this would not be financial. The barrier would have to be political. And the effects of such a policy depend crucially upon whether it impinges on an economy that is already inflationary or deflationary. If the electorate and Congress learn the half truth that expenditure is expansionary while forgetting the fact that unpleasant taxes may be necessary to curb undue expansion, then in the present author's opinion, the long-term outlook may be in the direction of rising prices.

USEFUL VERSUS WASTEFUL FISCAL POLICY

Those who believe in an active fiscal policy set up a perfectionist goal: the maintenance of total effective demand at a level high enough to prevent the wastes of mass unemployment, and low enough so as not to lead to a level of inflationary total spending in excess of total producible goods.

Or, to put the matter in technical terms, they argue that fiscal policy should shape taxes and expenditure, quantitatively and qualitatively, so that the economy's saving and investment schedules will intersect neither to the right nor to the left of the region of high (or full) employment. Many equally competent economists insist that there are other goals of equal or greater importance and that great harm can result from too avid a search for perfection.

It cannot be repeated too often that building pyramids or digging holes and filling them up is indefensible. True, in comparison with a policy of doing nothing about a deep depression, such boondoggling might seem in some ways preferable, because of the favorable respending effects of those who receive government expenditures. But such a policy is surely only the lesser of two evils. Properly planned useful public works have just as favorable secondary effects, and in addition they fill important human needs.

Nor is it necessary or always desirable to fight a depression with useful public works. If the American people feel that private consumption should have a higher social priority, tax reduction or transfer expenditure should be relied upon. The extra income available from the conquest of unemployment will then be going for privately produced and purchased goods.

Which of the alternatives of government expenditure or tax reduction should be followed if private investment and consumption are lacking? The answer cannot be given simply in terms of financial orthodoxy: the size of the deficit. It must be given in terms of what the American people consider to be the pressing postwar social priorities.

If 10 billion dollars of resources were to be released from investment purposes, the American people would wish to use part of this for extra food, extra clothes, extra leisure, etc. This suggests tax reduction (or increase in transfer expenditure). But the American people may also want to spend part of their newly available income on education, on public health, on urban redevelopment projects, on roads, etc. This suggests some use of government expenditure in depressed times.

The one way that the American people should not want to spend their income is upon involuntary unemployment. There should never be any need to indulge in wasteful or inefficient government expenditure; the government should always get something useful for the resources it uses up. If collective consumption projects have a lower social priority than private consumption, then the proper fiscal policy is one of tax reduction and transfer expenditure.

A FUNDAMENTAL DIFFICULTY WITH FULL EMPLOYMENT

One last and important set of qualifications must be made before completing the discussion of fiscal policy and, indeed, of the whole problem of national income determination. In a rough way, we know what is meant by full or high employment; but only in a rough way.

Of course, full employment does not mean that every man, woman, and child should be out at work every hour of a 24-hour day. It does not mean that I can hold out for a job as pitcher with the New York Yankees, or as a $100-a-day carpenter. But it does mean that reasonably efficient workers, willing to work at the currently prevailing ("fair") wage rates, need not find themselves unemployable as a result of too little general demand. Women who want to do so can work in the home, youths can go to school if they prefer to, and the aged or unwell can retire from the labor force; but none of these are to be forced to do so because of job shortages.

The real difficulty with full employment lies not in its rough definition but in the fact that *wages and prices may begin to soar while there is still considerable unemployment and excess capacity*. An increase in private investment spending or in government spending may be prevented from effectuating full employment, its favorable dollar effects being wasted by a paper rise in prices.

If businessmen and trade-unions react perversely to an increased demand, fiscal policy cannot be relied upon to achieve and maintain full employment. Some pessimists have argued that there is nothing to do but hope for a large enough "army of the unemployed" to keep laborers from making unreasonable wage demands; thus, a reserve army of 10 million jobless hanging around factory gates might keep wages from rising and labor from becoming obstreperous. Still others might see no escape from the dilemma other than to have some degree of inflation most of the time.

Still other writers would then advocate the use of direct price and wage controls to keep prices from spiraling upward at high employment levels. In the present writer's personal opinion, efficient peacetime, nonemergency, over-all price controls would involve a degree of planning incompatible with past, and probably present, philosophical beliefs of the great majority of the American people. For, as we shall see in Parts Three and Four, the problem of setting appropriate social prices is a tremendously complex one—so complex that the whole nature of our economic system would have to be different, once we had decided not to rely upon market forces.

It is hardly too much to say that this price-wage question is the biggest unsolved economic problem of our time: *Can business, labor, and agriculture learn to act in such a way as to avoid inflation whenever private or public spending brings us anywhere near to full employment?* A wage and price policy for full employment—that is America's greatest problem and challenge.

THE EMPLOYMENT ACT OF 1946

Obviously no one has a crystal ball to read the future, particularly the distant future. The case for and against secular stagnation cannot be definitely assessed. But fortunately—and this requires great emphasis—it is not necessary for Congress or the experts to be able to see a decade or more into the future in order to pursue correct economic policies currently.

In the momentous Employment Act of 1946, both political parties in Congress affirmed the responsibility of the government, and of private enterprise, to fight mass unemployment and inflation. This law provided for a Council of Economic Advisers which each year is to keep Congress and the President informed as to the state of "employment, production, and purchasing power"; also a Joint Congressional Committee is set up whose duty it is to study and evaluate the recommendations contained in the President's Annual Economic Report.

By itself, fiscal policy is not enough to create a healthy state of stable high employment with rising productivity and efficient use of economic resources in production. In fact, the remaining chapters of this book are concerned with the proper relations of prices and different branches of production in a world where the problem of over-all effective demand is nonexistent. If ever the curse of general inflation or deflation has been banished, there will rise to the top of our national policy agenda—and properly so—the true and abiding universal economic problems which every economic society has had to face since the Garden of Eden.

SUMMARY

A. SHORT-RUN AND LONG-RUN FISCAL POLICY

1. Fiscal policies with respect to government spending and taxing fall into two categories: the less controversial problem of countercyclical compensatory spending aimed simply at ironing out the worst swings of the business cycle but not at altering the average level of spending over the whole cycle; and long-run fiscal policy aimed at raising or lowering the average level of income so as to maintain high employment without inflation.

2. Four aspects of a countercyclical policy involve (*a*) careful planning of public-works projects; (*b*) proper timing of welfare and other government spending; (*c*) quasi-automatic changes in tax collections brought about by income changes even with no alterations in tax rates; (*d*) quantitative (and qualitative) changes in tax rates so as to increase tax receipts in prosperity and decrease them in bad times.

The reader should be acquainted with the difficulties of countercyclical finance, and appreciate the difference between it and the special theory of pump priming.

3. We go beyond the realm of countercyclical finance when we argue for a long-run policy of tax surplus and debt retirement if there should turn out to be a postwar era of excessive total demand, *i.e.*, an era of secular exhilaration.

4. If, instead of there being too much demand, there should turn out to be unemployment and too little "offsets to saving," the same reasoning would advocate a long-run increase in the average level of government spending, or decrease in tax collections. It would not insist upon the budget's necessarily

being balanced over the cycle, arguing that the public debt will grow with the growth of the whole economy.

B. DEBT AND POSTWAR POLICY

5. The reader should understand the economic effects of an internal debt: (*a*) the difference between the direct burden of an external and internal debt, and the ability of a country to shift burdens through time in the two cases; (*b*) the effect of the public debt on people's financial wealth and consumption habits; (*c*) the difficulties created by the debt for a countercyclical interest rate policy because of the desire of government authorities to stabilize bond prices; (*d*) the important indirect burden of collecting taxes to pay interest on a debt, even if we all owe it to ourselves.

It is important, also, to know roughly what the size of the postwar federal debt is in relation to national income and interest charges, in order to assess the present, both in terms of the past and in terms of the future. The growth of the debt must be appraised in terms of the growth of the economy as a whole.

6. A full (or high) employment program has as its goal a level of total spending which is neither too little nor too great—so that the saving and investment schedules intersect in the region of full employment. The Employment Act of 1946 represents an important innovation in our national government, affirming responsibility of the government for employment opportunities and setting up executive and congressional machinery for policy action.

7. Our economy is still confronted with the dilemma that any approach to full employment—whether brought about publicly or privately—may be followed by wage increases and price rises even before unemployment disappears or idle capacity comes into use. A wage-price policy for full employment provides a fundamental challenge to our mixed system of private enterprise and public responsibility.

QUESTIONS FOR DISCUSSION

1. "No nation can avoid having a fiscal policy. With the government such an important part of the present-day economy, it is almost impossible even to define a 'neutral fiscal policy.' It is even harder to give rational reasons for preferring such a policy to an active fiscal program aimed at preventing inflation and deflation." Subject this statement to critical examination, possibly bringing in some noneconomic considerations.

2. Draw up a list of new college buildings and projects that might be made part

of a planned countercyclical program. What would some of the difficulties and disadvantages be in carrying this out?

3. What phase of the business cycle are you now in? What taxation policies would seem appropriate? What expenditure policies?

4. Qualitatively, how would you vary the relative importance of different kinds of taxes (such as income tax rates and exemptions, sales tax rates, or property taxes) so as to compensate for unemployment or inflation?

5. From the early 1870's to the middle 1890's, depressions were deep and prolonged, booms were short-lived and relatively anemic, the price level was declining. What long-run fiscal policy do you think should have been followed in that quarter of a century? Would your answer be the same for the following 20 years leading up to World War I, a period of rising prices and comparative prosperity?

6. Comment on the following quotation from the English historian of the last century, Lord Macaulay:

"At every stage in the growth of that debt the nation has set up the same cry of anguish and despair. At every stage in the growth of that debt it has been seriously asserted by wise men that bankruptcy and ruin were at hand. Yet still the debt went on growing; and still bankruptcy and ruin were as remote as ever. . . .

"The prophets of evil were under a double delusion. They erroneously imagined that there was an exact analogy between the case of an individual who is in debt to another individual and the case of a society which is in debt to a part of itself. . . . They made no allowance for the effect produced by the incessant progress of every experimental science, and by the incessant efforts of every man to get on in life. They saw that the debt grew; and they forgot that other things grew as well as the debt."

7. Professor A. P. Lerner has set down the following (abbreviated) principles of "Functional Finance." Criticize:

"There are effective instruments in the hands of the government for maintaining full employment and preventing inflation, but their use is hindered by strong prejudices. The instruments are not available until it is recognized that the size of the national debt is relatively unimportant, that the interest on the debt is not a burden on the nation, and that the nation cannot be made "bankrupt" by internally held debt. Every debit has a corresponding credit. Only external debt is like individual debt and impoverishes the nation. The purpose of taxation is never to raise money but to leave less in the hands of the taxpayer. . . . There is no room for the *principle* of balancing the budget . . . ."

8. "Say what you will, graft keeps money in circulation and gets things done." What do you say?

9. The Council of Economic Advisers to the President, in its first report under the Employment Act of 1946, questions that "we can always create full employment by pumping enough purchasing power into the system," and the doctrine that we have only to "turn the faucet off and cause a contraction." According to the Council Report, " . . . we cannot assume that deficiency of demand in one particular area or of one

particular character can be made up just by adding purchasing power in general, for instance through tax relief. . . . If labor is pricing itself out of jobs or manufacturers and farmers are pricing themselves out of a market, or capital is pricing itself out of investment, the basic remedy is the correction of these specific situations, not the injection of some aggregate purchasing power in a dose measured in size to offset an estimated future total of unemployment."

With how much of this would you agree? Why?

10. Write a two-page summary of the description of the growth of the public debt in the Appendix to this chapter. Do the same for its retirement.

APPENDIX TO CHAPTER 19
CURRENT FISCAL POLICY

Since the Korean war of 1950, the defense programs of the United States and Western Europe have been sharply increased. The emphasis must shift therefore from debt retirement such as took place in the late 1940's back toward the wartime pattern of budgetary deficits and growing debt. Ideally, the defense program should be put on a full pay-as-you-go basis. Indeed if inflation is to be avoided by fiscal policy alone, taxes should increase by more than the increase in expenditure, so that there will be a budgetary surplus. Since this is less likely to happen, let us begin our brief discussion with the case of growing debt, concluding with the mechanics of debt retirement and surplus financing.

DEFICIT FINANCING AND THE BANKS

For definiteness, suppose that the defense program grows so much that, even with new taxes and retrenchments in ordinary civilian government expenditure, there is still a cash deficit for the government of 5 billion dollars per year. Over the next few years, therefore, the debt will grow from 260 billion to 265 billion to 270 billion dollars, and so forth. Of course, all this is hypothetical and in no sense a forecast.

How will this deficit be financed? People will be urged to buy government bonds. It is especially important that they be urged to cut down on their consumption in order to buy government bonds, and not simply be urged to put their savings into government bonds. If I draw my money out of a bank and buy bonds, I am not helping the defense effort; but if I sign up for a payroll bond-purchase plan and in consequence cut down on my spending, then I am helping to release resources to the war effort.

Let us suppose that the public does purchase more savings bonds than it cashes in. Still, there is no reason to expect that, even if interest rates were "sweetened"—i.e., raised—a little bit, net private bond purchases will fully equal the deficit. Even the indirect purchases of bonds by individuals, through financial intermediaries such as insurance companies or mutual saving banks, would probably not be sufficient to finance fully a large deficit.[1]

[1] Often the proposal is made that the government issue a bond guaranteeing to its buyer a constant purchasing power, being paid off in greater or lesser dollars depending upon movements in the cost of living. The Treasury is not likely to issue such a bond for a variety of reasons; so it is rather academic to discuss such a case even though it does raise some interesting questions. Would purchasers of these bonds be cutting down on their consumption or be simply changing the form in which they hold their savings? After there were tremendous

What will the government then do? Undoubtedly it will have to sell bonds to the commercial banks and to the Federal Reserve Banks. If reserve ratios are kept at about the present average levels, somewhere around 20 per cent, the Treasury will probably sell about four bonds to the commercial banks for each bond it sells to the Federal Reserve. For each 1 billion dollars of bonds bought by the Reserve Banks to finance the deficit, there is made available to the Member Banks a 1-billion-dollar increase in their reserves. In turn such an increase in reserves makes possible a 5-billion-dollar increase in their demand deposits, as we have seen. What will the banks hold against this 5 billion dollars of deposits? They will hold 20 per cent in reserves, *i.e.*, 1 billion dollars; and they will hold the other 80 per cent in government bonds, *i.e.*, 4 billion dollars.

To summarize: As the debt grows, the total of money and near-money will grow. To the extent that individuals and nonbanking institutions do buy the bonds, the commercial banks and Reserve Banks will not have to buy them. To the extent that the banks do have to buy new government bonds, the total supply of money will grow.[1]

WHAT LEVEL OF INTEREST RATES?

A big question in all this is the structure of interest rates that will prevail in the years ahead. It is entirely up to the Treasury and the Reserve Banks as to what interest rates shall prevail. They can keep interest rates low or they can keep them high, provided they are willing to face the consequences of their behavior—in terms of the amount of bonds to be bought by the Reserve Banks, the total of interest charges to be borne by the Treasury, and the resulting inflationary gap.

There are at least two possibilities. (1) They may freeze the present pattern of interest rates as was done during World War II, with short-term rates between 1 and 2 per cent and with long-term rates between 2 and 3 per cent. Or (2) they may boldly push short-term rates up further.[2] The big question

---

quantities of such bonds outstanding, would the problem of controlling subsequent inflation become even more formidable? (Suppose from 1941 to 1945 such bonds had been issued. What would the price increase in 1946 to 1949 have been?) If the cost of living were to fall, would people be good sports and accept lower payments or would there be a public uproar?

[1] An expansion of currency in circulation can also be expected under the above circumstances. Part of the bonds bought by the Federal Reserve Banks will be offset by an increase in federal reserve notes outstanding.

[2] And will the level of long-term bonds finally be permitted to rise, causing existing 2½ per cent bonds to fall below par? Or will the authorities fear that falling bond prices tend to discourage further bond purchases, and will they for this reason continue to support the prices of long-terms even if this means that the Reserve Banks have to buy many long-terms?

is whether by itself this will much tighten the availability of credit to private borrowers, whether it will accomplish even as little as might be accomplished by oratorical campaigns urging bankers to hold down their loans to borrowers, particularly to speculative borrowers. Will it have even a fraction of the contracting effect that direct selective controls on consumer credit and home building will have? These are vitally important questions that the future must answer.

SURPLUS FINANCING AND DEBT RETIREMENT[1]

About the recent past we can be more definite. In postwar years like the fiscal years 1947 to 1949, the government was able to run a budgetary cash surplus. To help reduce inflationary pressure, tax collections were kept in excess of cash expenditures. This fiscal policy operation tended to have direct contractionary effects on disposable income and spending. What is to be done with surplus money collected by fiscal policy in this way? The Treasury has two choices: (1) It can remove its surplus tax collections out of the banking system into its deposit with the Reserve Banks and use that deposit to retire some of the bonds held by the Reserve Banks, or (2) it can buy bonds from the public and the commercial banks.

The first policy means that the public is losing cash and the commercial banks are losing reserves. They will have to contract their deposits in a $5:1$ ratio. The availability of credit would be sharply reduced, and interest rates would tighten up. Undoubtedly the banks would try to sell bonds to the Reserve Banks to replenish their reserves. And if the Reserve Banks maintain the prices of government bonds by buying them up, then this first choice of policy open to the Treasury has been negated: The debt held by the Reserve Banks has not been reduced.

So let us look at the second choice: that of using the surplus to retire government bonds held by the commercial banks and, to a very minor degree, bonds held by nonbank investors. People pay billions of dollars of taxes—taxes that go into the government surplus instead of being spent for the purchase of goods and services by government. So people's bank deposits are depleted, and those of the Treasury are swelled. If the Treasury buys bonds from the public, the public gets its deposits back and has ended up with less near-money, *i.e.*, less government bonds. To some degree this will ease interest rates as the public uses part of its cash to restore the old balance between its earning and nonearning assets.[2]

If the Treasury uses 5-billion-dollar surplus tax collections to buy bonds held

---

[1] The remainder of this Appendix is difficult and can be skipped at a first reading.

[2] See Chapter 29 in Part Four for a further discussion of interest rates and assets.

by the banks, then what? The public's deposits are down by 5 billion dollars. The government ends up with no deposit and only with its own old bonds, which it proceeds to burn. The banks have lost 5 billion dollars of deposits that they used to owe to the public; they have also lost, on the asset side of their balance sheet, 5 billion dollars of government bonds. Their reserves are unchanged.

But note this important fact: Because of the 5-billion-dollar decline in their deposits, unchanged reserves means that they now have 4 billion dollars of excess reserves, which they will be anxious to lend out. This will tend to lower interest rates and to lead to easy money. So now we can sum up: (1) To the extent that the Treasury uses its fiscal surplus to buy back bonds from the Reserve Banks, it puts contractionary pressure on bank reserves and the availability of credit. Such a monetary policy reinforces fiscal policy. (2) To the extent that it buys back bonds from the public and commercial banks, it creates excess cash reserves and tends to increase the cheapness and availability of credit. Such a monetary policy of debt management tends to work against the contractionary fiscal policy.

What was actually done during the years of surplus 1947–1949? Both monetary policies were followed: Bonds were retired from the banks, and at the same time bonds were retired from the Federal Reserve Banks. Except for some pressure to tighten short-term interest rates upward, not much was done to fight inflation by federal reserve policy during this period. Business could always borrow from the banks at fairly cheap rates, and interest rates on home mortgages were also relatively low, especially for veterans and for those who could qualify for FHA-guaranteed loans.[1]

The same postwar dilemma of what to do about the prices of government bonds has to be faced whether or not there is a budgetary surplus. This is the crucial problem raised for monetary policy by the existence of the large public debt.

---

[1] A few facts on the period 1947–1950 may help. The total debt held outside of governments fell by about 9 billion dollars. The Reserve Banks, the ordinary banks, and the insurance companies reduced their holdings by about 8, 6, and 5 billion dollars, respectively. Individuals and corporations (especially corporation pension funds!) increased their holdings by 3 and 7 billion dollars, respectively. During this same period, we were selling so much abroad that gold was flowing in to swell bank reserves, enabling the banks to increase their total loans by about 50 per cent, or by roughly 15 billion dollars, despite the reduction in federal reserve credit.

PART THREE

The Composition

and Pricing

of National Output

Chapter 20: DETERMINATION OF

PRICE BY SUPPLY AND DEMAND

PART ONE gave us the factual background and basic concepts leading up to national income. Part Two analyzed the monetary mechanism whereby saving and investment determine the level and movement of national income. It also showed how monetary and fiscal policy can influence the course of spending, employment, production, and price levels.

Here in Part Three we begin the no less important discussion of the principles governing the individual pricing of the different kinds of output. We investigate the forces determining what the composition of national income shall be in terms of particular goods and services. Earlier, in Chapter 3, a telescopic picture was presented of how supply and demand determine What, How, and For Whom goods shall be produced in an economy. Now we put a microscope to bear upon a typical single market to see just how supply and demand work themselves out in detail.

Then later in Part Four, we shall be able to bring the same tools to bear on the problem of the distribution of national income between the owners of labor and property. We shall see how supply and demand have to be modified to explain the pricing of productive services (wages, interest, land rents, etc.). This will complete our over-all view of the three problems of What, How, and For Whom. Supply and demand do not tell all the story. But they tell an important part of it.

THE DEMAND SCHEDULE

Let us begin with demand. Everyone has observed that the higher the price charged for an article, the less of it will be sold. And the lower its price, the more units people will buy. Thus there exists at any one time a definite relation between the price of a good such as wheat and the quantity demanded of that good. The following hypothetical table relating *price* and *quantity demanded* is an example of what economists call a "demand schedule." At any price, such as $5 per bushel, there is a definite quantity of wheat that will be bought by all the consumers in the market—in this case 9 (million) bushels per month. At a lower price, such as $4, the quantity bought is even greater, being 10 (million) units. From Table 1 we can determine the *quantity bought at any price*, by comparing Column (2) with Column (1).

TABLE 1. *Demand Schedule Showing Relationship between Price and Quantity of Wheat Sold*

	Price of wheat per bu. P (1)	Quantity demanded, million bu. per month Q (2)	Value of sales, millions of dollars per month price × quantity (3) = (1) × (2)
A	$ 5	9	$45
B	4	10	—
C	3	12	—
D	2	15	—
E	1	20	$20

The total number of dollars of revenue received for the sale of wheat is equal to the number of bushels sold times the price per bushel. Thus if the price is $5 and the quantity sold 9 (million) bushels, then the total revenue received from the sale of wheat is 45 million dollars. The reader can easily fill in the missing blanks in the total revenue column (3) of Table 1.

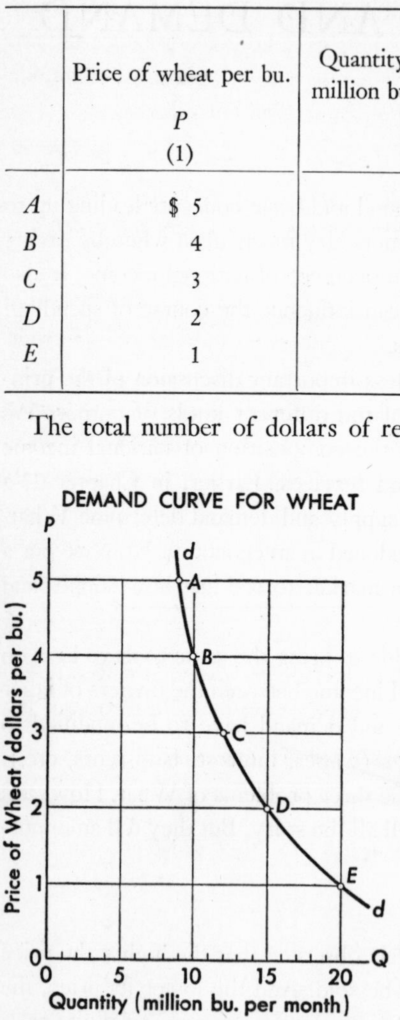

THE DEMAND CURVE

The same numerical data of Table 1 can be given a more graphic interpretation. On the vertical scale in Figure 1 we represent the various prices of wheat, measured in dollars per bushel. On the horizontal scale, we measure the quantity of wheat (in terms of bushels) that will be bought.

Just as a city corner is located as soon as you know its street and avenue, so is

DEMAND CURVE FOR WHEAT

FIGURE 1. This shows how much wheat would be bought at each and every possible price.

a ship's position located as soon as you know its latitude and longitude.

Similarly, to plot a point on this diagram, we must have two coordinate numbers, a price and a quantity. For our first point *A*, corresponding to $5 and 9 million bushels, we move upward 5 units and then over to the right 9 units. A circle marks the spot *A*. To get the next circle, at *B*, we go up only 4 units and over to the right 10 units. The last circle is shown by *E*. Through the circles we draw a smooth curve, marked *dd*.

This picturization of the demand schedule is called the "demand curve." Note how quantity and price are inversely related. The curve slopes downward, going from northwest to southeast. This may be given a name: the *law of diminishing demand*, as price rises. This law is true of almost all commodities: wheat, electric razors, cotton, ethyl gasoline, and corn flakes.

> *The law of diminishing demand: If the price of a good is cut, more of it will be demanded. To say the same thing in another way, if a greater quantity of a good is thrown on the market, it can be sold only at a lower price.*

A number of obvious reasons can be given for the prevalence of the law of diminishing demand: (1) At lower prices the consumer's dollar goes further. He can *afford* to buy more. (2) At lower prices, he will *want* to buy more. Cheap wheat means that people will want to get their calories by *substituting* bread for potatoes and white bread for rye bread. (3) Secondary uses of wheat such as for grain alcohol in producing synthetic rubber will be possible only at sufficiently low prices. Each reduction in price will tend to bring in some new buyers and some new uses by old buyers, until finally the price is zero and wheat is used with the lavishness of a free good.

ELASTIC AND INELASTIC DEMANDS

Different goods vary in the *degree* to which their use expands with a reduction in price. In fact, wheat was not a very good example to illustrate our law

TABLE 2. *Demand Schedule for Automobiles*

	Price per automobile *P* (1)	Quantity demanded per year, thousands *Q* (2)	Value of sales, or total revenue per year $R = P \times Q$ (3) = (1) × (2)
A	$2,500	10	$25,000
B	2,000	60	120,000
C	1,500	120	180,000
D	1,000	200	200,000
E	500	300	150,000

of diminishing demand, because its demand is rather "inelastic." The demand for automobiles, at least in the good old days of the Model T Ford, would have been a better example because it represents an "elastic" demand. A relatively large increase in quantity of automobiles sold resulted from small cuts in their price. This is illustrated in Table 2.

Now let us plot the demand curves for automobiles and for wheat upon the same chart, by a careful juxtaposition of scales (Figure 2). Immediately we see their difference. The two curves have the point *C* in common, and at this point the automobile curve is much flatter. On it, the quantity demanded is very *elastic* with respect to price changes. Contrariwise, the wheat curve is steep because its demand is rather *inelastic* at *C*.

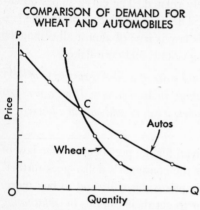

COMPARISON OF DEMAND FOR
WHEAT AND AUTOMOBILES

FIGURE 2. This shows how the response of automobile sales to price changes is more "elastic" than is the response of wheat sales, which is relatively "inelastic."

ELASTICITY OF DEMAND DEPENDS ON TOTAL REVENUE

Now how shall we decide whether the demand curve is (1) *elastic* at a given point on it, (2) *inelastic* at that point, or (3) a *borderline* case between being elastic and being inelastic? The crucial test will be given to us by the behavior of total dollar revenue, shown already in Column (3) of our previous tables.

If total revenue goes up when we cut price, then demand is said to be elastic. If total revenue goes down when we cut price, then demand is said to be inelastic. If total revenue remains the same, then we are in the borderline case between elasticity and inelasticity. In a moment we shall give the name unitary elasticity to this borderline case.

Turn back to Table 1 and look at Column (3). Notice that, every time we cut the price of wheat, the total revenue received from its sale goes down. Hence, the wheat demand curve is inelastic at all the points shown.

Contrast this with the automobile data of Table 2. As we cut the price of an automobile from $2,500 to $2,000, what happens to total revenue? Dollar revenue actually rises. Why? Because the quantity sold increases by a much larger percentage than the price falls. Therefore, between *A* and *B*, the automobile demand curve is certainly elastic. The same is true between *B* and *C* and between *C* and *D*.

But note what happens when the price of automobiles falls below D. Total revenue ceases to rise. The automobile demand curve has become inelastic between D and E. Clearly, somewhere around D, it has passed from being elastic to inelastic. Somewhere around D we can expect to find the borderline case of unitary elasticity, with total revenue remaining unchanged as price is cut.

If one wishes only to know simply whether demand is elastic, inelastic, or unitary, a simple test can be applied. Calculate the ratio: total revenue at lower price ÷ total revenue at higher price. If this ratio is greater than 1, demand is elastic; if it is less than 1, demand is inelastic; if it is exactly equal to 1, we have the borderline case of unitary elasticity of demand.

TABLE 3. *Demand Curve for Movie Seats, as an Illustration of Unitary Elasticity of Demand*

	Price per ticket P (1)	Quantity demanded per week, total revenue ÷ price Q (2) = (3) ÷ (1)	Total revenue, or value of sales R (3)
A	$1.00	3,600	$3,600
B	0.80	_____	3,600
C	0.60	_____	3,600
D	0.40	_____	3,600
E	0.20	18,000	3,600

A demand schedule for movies is shown in Table 3. It is drawn up on the assumption that total revenue is the same at every price; hence it is a case of unitary elasticity. The reader can calculate what must be the missing Q's in Column (2). He can also superimpose on Figure 2 the resulting unitary-elasticity demand curve for movies, noting that it is very steep at high P's and very flat at low P's.

NUMERICAL COEFFICIENT OF ELASTICITY

By now we shall have begun to see what the behavior of total revenue and elasticity depends upon. It depends upon whether the percentage change in quantity is greater or less than the percentage reduction in price. If the percentage change in quantity is *greater* than the percentage change in price, then total revenue will *rise* and we can say that the demand is here *elastic*. If the percentage change in Q is *less* than the percentage change in P, then demand is inelastic.

What if the two percentage changes are exactly equal? Then the loss in P is just matched by the gain in Q. Total revenue, which is $P \times Q$, remains unchanged. This is the borderline case of unitary elasticity. An example would be the case where whenever I exactly halve my price, there always results an exactly compensating doubling of my sales.

If we wish to have an exact numerical measure of elasticity, the following formula defines a convenient coefficient:

Elasticity coefficient = percentage increase in quantity

$$\div \text{ percentage cut in price} = \frac{\% \text{ change in } Q}{\% \text{ change in } P}$$

Three cases are possible: (1) The elasticity coefficient may be greater than 1; (2) it may be less than 1; or finally, (3) it may be exactly 1.

Where the elasticity coefficient is greater than 1, the demand is elastic (like the automobile example). Where the coefficient is less than 1, the demand is inelastic (like the wheat example). Where the elasticity coefficient is exactly 1, we have the case of "unitary elasticity": The changes in Q have just balanced the changes in P as far as total revenue is concerned (as in the movie case).

The important thing is to realize *how total dollar revenue changes*. For, as we shall see again and again, this is what all producers are interested in, not in P or Q alone. Memorizing formulas is not important, and the detailed way of measuring the elasticity coefficient between two points on a demand curve may be relegated to a footnote.[1]

Two warnings should be given. Beginning students of economics often associate elasticity with geometrical flatness of the demand curve, and they associate inelasticity with geometrical steepness. This involves a slight oversimplification. True enough, a perfectly vertical curve does have zero elasticity, and a perfectly horizontal curve does have infinite elasticity. Nonetheless, our

---

[1] Let us calculate the coefficient of elasticity between two points on a demand curve, *e.g.*, between A and B in Table 1 or Figure 1. P drops from \$5 to \$4. How big a percentage drop is this absolute drop of \$1? Is it $\frac{1}{5}$, *i.e.*, 20 per cent? Or is it $\frac{1}{4}$, *i.e.*, 25 per cent? The difference is not terribly important, but people used to argue themselves blue in the face over which is correct. Let us always use the following compromise rule for computing percentage changes: We divide the absolute change in P by the *average* of the higher and lower P. Thus a cut from \$5 to \$4 represents a percentage change of $1/4.5$, or about 22 per cent. Now what percentage change does the increase in Q from 9 to 10 units represent? By our rule, this is $1/9.5$, or about 14 per cent. Our final coefficient of elasticity tells us we must take the ratio of these percentage changes, giving us about $14\frac{4}{22}$, which is certainly less than 1, as we should have expected from this known case of inelastic demand.

Or the reader can use this formula to verify that the demand for automobiles turns inelastic between D and E. He can also verify that, if a halving of P means a doubling of Q, the above formula gives an elasticity coefficient of exactly 1.00, as it should.

earlier movie data from Table 3 warn us that, even though elasticity remains the same along a curve, its steepness will change.

Or consider the example of a demand curve which is a straight line. Its slope or steepness is everywhere the same. Is its elasticity everywhere the same? Definitely not, as calculation of its total revenue will show. As we go from its highest price downward, its revenue rises, which means elasticity is greater than 1. At the halfway point its elasticity is exactly 1 because there total revenue turns out to be at its maximum. At still lower prices, its demand becomes inelastic. These properties of a straight-line demand curve are proven in more advanced texts. Or the reader may verify them by referring to Table 1 and Figure 1*b* of Chapter 24, which illustrate just such a demand situation.

Where has the beginning student gone wrong? He has forgotten that elasticity depends on *percentage* changes; it does not depend on *absolute* changes as does geometrical steepness of the curve.

This same example teaches us a second truth: *Elasticity is usually different at each different part of a commodity's demand curve.* Earlier, the author spoke loosely of the demand for wheat being inelastic and the demand for autos being elastic. But actually, we saw that, at low enough prices, the demand for automobiles turned inelastic. Similarly, had the wheat curve been extended to much higher prices, it would have finally become elastic as it approached the vertical axis.

What then do we mean when we say that a commodity has inelastic demand? What we really mean is the following: At the price levels for the commodity *that have generally been prevailing in the market*, its demand is inelastic. That is all such a statement can mean.

ELASTICITY IN PERFECT AND IMPERFECT COMPETITION

A few illustrations show the importance of the concept of elasticity. If a monopolist should gain control of a very necessary commodity much desired in some circumstances, like penicillin, he can take advantage of its inelasticity of demand and make great profits by jacking up his price. On the other hand, in a highly competitive trade, where patents and consumers' good will are not important, demand for any one firm's output will be very elastic. Why? Because at the slightest raising of price, buyers will go elsewhere and substitute the output of other firms. Thus one small wheat farmer has such a negligible effect upon the price at the Chicago Board of Trade, that the demand for his wheat is infinitely elastic. He can sell 100, 200, 300, or 1,000 bushels of wheat without affecting the price. But at the very slightest increase in price over that of the market, he loses *all* his sales. His demand curve is therefore very flat as in Figure 3.

In the first chapter we learned that it is a fallacy to think that what is true for each is also true for all together. Here we have an instance as applied to farmers. Although the demand for each competitive farmer's wheat is very elastic, we already know that the demand for all wheat is very inelastic. The difference results from the great disparity of the horizontal scale of Figure 3 and the scale of Figure 1. Farmer Brown's piddling few carloads will not move us 1/1,000 inch along the industry's demand curve. Price on the diagram, Figure 1, will be imperceptibly changed. No wonder that Brown thinks *his* demand is elastic. What if all the millions of Browns, Smiths, and O'Malleys bring a few carloads to market? Then we move a substantial distance along the whole industry's inelastic wheat-demand curve.

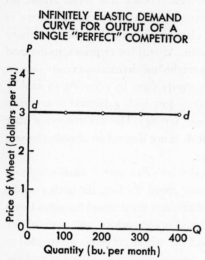

INFINITELY ELASTIC DEMAND CURVE FOR OUTPUT OF A SINGLE "PERFECT" COMPETITOR

FIGURE 3. The perfectly competitive individual seller is such a small part of the total market that he can sell all he wishes without depressing the prevailing price. Under imperfect competition, a firm's demand curve slopes downward.

In fact, when all farmers are lucky enough to have a large crop, their total revenue actually goes down. Does this mean that farmers pray for drought and bugs? Not necessarily. The more calculating ones pray for bugs on everyone else's field, but none on their own. But since that cannot be expected to happen often, the next best thing is for everyone to have bugs.

Now we begin to understand what we shall study in detail in a moment: (1) why farmers wish to restrict crop production to raise their incomes and (2) why they cannot rely on each individual farmer to do his part in restricting, unless government force or bribery is employed.

THE SUPPLY SCHEDULE

Enough has now been said of demand. Let us now turn briefly to the sellers' side or to the supply schedule. The demand schedule related prices and the amounts consumers wish to buy. *By the supply schedule, we naturally mean the relation between prices and the amounts that producers are willing to produce and sell.* Table 4 illustrates the supply schedule for wheat.

Unlike the demand curve, the supply curve in Figure 4 for wheat rises upward and to the right, from southwest to northeast. At a higher price of wheat, farmers will take acreage out of corn cultivation and put it into wheat. Also

TABLE 4. *Supply Schedule for Wheat*

	Each possible price per bu.	Quantity that sellers will supply, million bu. per month
A	$5	18
B	4	16
C	3	12
D	2	7
E	1	0

SUPPLY CURVE FOR WHEAT

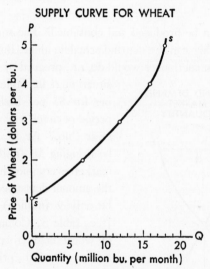

FIGURE 4. This shows how much wheat will be produced at each and every possible price.

they can afford the cost of more fertilizer, more machinery, and poorer land. All these factors increase output with higher prices.

EQUILIBRIUM OF SUPPLY AND DEMAND

For the moment let us say no more about what determines the supply curve. We take it as given. Let us now combine our analysis of demand and supply to see how competitive market price is determined. This is done in Table 5.

So far we have been considering all prices as possible. We have said, "If price is such and such, sales will be such and such; if price is so and so, sales will be so and so; etc." But to just which level will price *actually* go? And

TABLE 5. *Supply and Demand Schedules for Wheat*

	Possible prices per bu.	Quantity demanded, million bu. per month	Quantity supplied, million bu. per month	Pressure on price
	(1)	(2)	(3)	(4)
A	$5	9	18	↓ Falling
B	4	10	16	↓ Falling
C*	3*	12*	12*	↕ Neutral*
D	2	15	7	↑ Rising
E	1	20	0	↑ Rising

* The equilibrium price and output.

how much will then be produced and consumed? The supply schedule alone cannot tell us. Neither can the demand schedule alone. But both together can.

Let us do what an auctioneer would do, *i.e.*, proceed by trial and error. Can

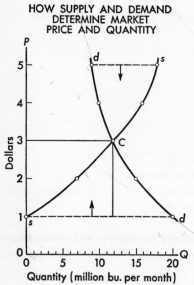

HOW SUPPLY AND DEMAND DETERMINE MARKET PRICE AND QUANTITY

FIGURE 5. The "equilibrium" price is at the intersection of the two curves, where the price is such as to make the amounts demanded and supplied exactly equal.

situation *A* in Table 5, with wheat selling for $5 per bushel prevail for any period of time? The answer is a loud and clear "no." At $5, the producers will be bringing 18 (million) bushels to the market every month [Column (3)]. But the amount demanded by consumers will be only 9 (million) bushels per month [see Table 5, Column (2)]. As stocks of wheat begin to pile up, competitive sellers will cut the price just a little. Thus as Column (4) shows, price will tend to fall. But it will not fall indefinitely down to zero.

To see this, let us try the point *E* with price equal to only $1 per bushel. Can that price persist? Again, obviously not. For a comparison of Columns (2) and (3) shows that consumption will exceed production *at that price*. Storehouses will begin to be emptied; disappointed demanders who cannot get wheat will tend to bid the price up. This upward pressure on price is indicated in Column (4) by the rising arrow.

We could go on to try out other prices, but by now the answer is obvious. *The only equilibrium price, i.e., the only price that can last—is that at which the amounts supplied and demanded are equal.* Only at C, with a price of $3, will the amount demanded, 12 (million) bushels per month, exactly equal the amount supplied. Price is at equilibrium, just as an olive at the bottom of a cocktail glass is at equilibrium, because there is no tendency for it to rise or fall. Of course, this stationary price may not be reached at once. There may have to be an initial period of trial and error, of oscillation around the right level before price finally settles down and supply balances demand.

Figure 5 shows the same result in pictorial form. The supply and demand curves are superimposed on the same diagram. They cross at one intersection point. This point C represents the equilibrium price and quantity.

At a higher price, the dotted line shows the *excess* of supply over demand. The arrow points downward to show the direction in which price will move because of the competition of *sellers*. At a price lower than equilibrium price, $3, the dotted line shows that demand overmatches supply. Consequently the eager bidding of *buyers* requires us to point the arrow indicator upward to show the pressure that they are exerting on price. Only at the point C will there be a balancing of forces and a stationary maintainable price.

This gives the essence of the doctrine of supply and demand. All that is left to do is point out some of the cases to which it can be applied and some to which it cannot.

SUMMARY

1. By the demand schedule we mean a table showing the different quantities of a good that can be sold at each different price. The same relationship plotted on a diagram is the demand curve.

2. With few exceptions, the higher the price, the lower will be the quantity sold, and vice versa. Almost all commodities are subject to this "law of diminishing demand," but in different degrees.

3. Elasticity of demand depends on what happens to total revenue as price is cut. Demand is elastic, inelastic, or unitary, depending upon whether a reduction in price increases, decreases, or does not change total revenue. The numerical coefficient of elasticity of demand is defined as the percentage increase in quantity divided by the percentage cut in price.

4. A perfect competitor is defined as a seller too small to have an appreciable effect on the price of the good he sells. His demand curve is, by definition,

horizontal and of infinite elasticity. An imperfect competitor is one who has some degree of monopolistic control over the price of his goods. His demand curve is of less than infinite elasticity of demand and slopes downward.

5. The supply curve or schedule represents the relationship between the prices and the quantities of a good that producers will be willing to sell. Usually, but not always, the supply curve rises upward and to the right, the higher prices calling forth larger supplies.

6. Market equilibrium can take place only at a price where the quantities supplied and demanded are identical. At any price higher than the equilibrium intersection of the supply and demand curves, the quantity supplied will exceed the quantity demanded; a downward pressure on price will result as some sellers begin to undermine the going price. Similarly, the reader should be able to show why any price lower than the equilibrium price will meet irresistible upward pressure.

QUESTIONS FOR DISCUSSION

1. List a number of factors that might increase the demand for wheat. Do the same for the supply of wheat.

2. Which of the following do you think has the most inelastic demand: perfume, salt, penicillin, cigarettes, ice cream, chocolate ice cream, Sealtest chocolate ice cream? Try to give reasons for your answer.

3. Comment on the following: "How can price be determined by the equality of supply and demand? After all, the 'amount bought' must be the same in every transaction as the 'amount sold.' How then could they be different at every price but the unique equilibrium price?"

4. Kidneys and livers used to sell for about the same price per pound until science discovered the great nutritive value of liver for building red corpuscles. Just what did this discovery do to their relative prices, and how did this come about?

5. What would a cheap mechanical cotton picker do to the price of cotton? To the wages of farm laborers?

6. Spell out the arguments which show that price must settle down at the equilibrium intersection of supply and demand. Imagine that price is at first too high. Then too low.

Chapter 21: SUPPLY AND DEMAND (CONTINUED): AGRICULTURAL AID AND OTHER APPLICATIONS

OTHER things being equal, as economists are fond of saying, there is a unique schedule of supply or demand at any instant of time. But other things will not remain equal. The demand for cotton is declining over the years because of reductions in the price of rayon. The supply schedule of gasoline is increasing because technological progress permits more to be produced at the same cost. As costs and tastes change, as incomes vary, as the prices of rival products (coffee in relation to tea) or cooperating products (sugar in relation to tea) change, our schedules will shift. What will be the effects on consumption, production, and price?

All beginners in the field of economics must beware of a common error. They must take care not to confuse an increase in *demand*—by which is meant a shift of the whole curve to the right and upward, as more is bought at each and every price—with an increase in the *quantity demanded* as a result of moving to a lower price *on the same demand curve*. By "demand" is meant the whole demand curve; by "supply" is meant the whole supply curve; by an "increase" in demand or supply is meant a shift of the whole curve in question to the right. To indicate a single point on a demand curve, we speak of the "quantity bought" or the "quantity demanded" *at a particular price*. A movement *along* the same curve is "a change in the quantity demanded as a result of a price change." It does not represent any change in the demand schedule. The need for this warning will appear in a moment.

SHIFTS IN SUPPLY: A TAX EXAMPLE

We can illustrate the case of a shift in the entire curve by referring back to Table 5 and Figure 5 at the close of the last chapter, which portrayed hypothetical supply and demand schedules for wheat. These resulted in an equilibrium price of $3 per bushel.

Let us now introduce a new factor which will disturb this equilibrium. In particular, let us assume that the government imposes a sales tax on wheat. On each and every sale, the producer is required to pay a tax of $1 per bushel of wheat. What is the final effect or "incidence" of the tax? Does its burden fall completely on the producer who must in the first instance pay it? Or may it be shifted in part on to consumers? The answer can be derived only by the use of our supply and demand curves.

EFFECT OF UNIT TAX ON
COMPETITIVE PRICE AND OUTPUT

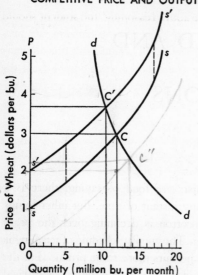

FIGURE 1. A unit tax shifts the supply curve upward by just the amount of the tax and gives rise to a new equilibrium price and quantity.

There is no reason for the demand curve of the consumers to have changed at all. At $3 consumers will still be willing to buy only 12 (million) bushels per month; they neither know nor care that the producers must pay a tax.

But the whole supply curve is shifted leftward and upward: leftward because at each market price the producers will now supply less as a result of the tax, upward because to get the producers to bring any given quantity to market, say 12 (million) units, we must give them a higher market price than before—$4 rather than $3, or higher by the $1 tax.

The student should be able to fill in a new supply column, resembling the Column (3) in Chapter 20's Table 5, but with each price raised by $1. In Figure 1, the demand curve dd is unchanged, but the supply curve ss has been shifted everywhere up by $1 to a new parallel supply curve s's'.

Where will the new equilibrium price be? The answer is found at the intersection of the new demand and supply curves, or at C' where s's' and dd meet. Because supply has decreased, the price is higher. Also the amount bought and the amount sold are less. If we read the graph carefully, we find that the new equilibrium price has risen from $3 to about $3⅔. The new equilibrium output, at which purchases and sales are in equilibrium, has fallen from 12 (million) to about 10.6 (million) bushels.

Who pays the tax? Well, the wheat farmers do in part because now they receive only $2⅔ ($3⅔ − $1) rather than $3. But the consumer also shares in the burden, because the price received by the producer has not fallen by as much as the tax. To the consumer, the wheat now costs $2⅔ plus the $1 tax, or $3⅔ all told. Because the consumers need wheat so badly, they pay ⅔ of the tax, and the producers pay ⅓ of the tax. As a final burden, the community is poorer because it is consuming less wheat.

As a check upon his understanding of the above reasoning, the student should consider the case of an opposite shift in supply. Let the government pay producers a subsidy of $1 per bushel of wheat instead of taxing them this amount. Draw the new curve $s''s''$. Where is C'', its intersection with dd? What is the new price? The new quantity? How much of the benefit goes to the producer? How much to the consumer?

SHIFTS IN DEMAND

The student can now probably guess how a change in demand is to be treated. The curve dd shifts rightward or leftward to a new curve $d'd'$. Where this intersects the old supply curve ss, we have the new price and quantity. He should also be able to handle the case where *both* curves shift simultaneously.

At the end of this chapter, in the Appendix, there are a number of examples to be worked out by the reader. They are designed to do more than test his understanding of the above analysis: They provide an introduction to a number of important economic situations and principles.

A COMMON FALLACY

By now the student has mastered supply and demand. Or has he? He knows that a tax will have the effect of raising the price that the consumer will have to pay. Or does he know this? What about the following argument of a kind often seen in the press and heard from the platform:

The effect of a tax on a commodity might seem at first sight to be an advance in price to the consumer. But an advance in price will diminish the demand. And a reduced demand will send the price down again. It is not certain, therefore, after all, that the tax will really raise the price.[1]

---

[1] Taken from a quotation in H. D. Henderson, *Supply and Demand* (Cambridge, London, 1922), p. 27. The quotation could have been made even more fantastic as follows: "Price goes up and demand falls. This sends price down which makes demand rise. This makes price go up. But the higher price makes demand fall . . . . " And so we have a perpetual oscillation in price, up and down, down and up. The student should spot the error.

Well, what about it? Will the tax raise the price or not? According to the editor's written word and the Senator's oratory, the answer is "no." Obviously, we have here an example of the treachery of words. One of the four sentences in the quotation is false because the word "demand" is being used in the wrong sense. The student has already been warned against confusing a movement *along* an unchanged curve from a *shift* in the curve.

Actually, the correct answer would be more or less as follows:

A tax will raise the price to the consumer and will lower the price received by the producer, the difference going to the government. At the higher price a smaller quantity will be bought by consumers. This is as it should be because producers are also supplying a smaller quantity at the lower price which they receive. Thus the amounts bought and sold are in balance where the new supply and demand schedules intersect, and there will be no further change in price.

IS THE LAW OF SUPPLY AND DEMAND IMMUTABLE?

Competitive price and quantity are determined by supply and demand. But do not prices depend on other factors such as the amount of gold production or whether there is a war going on? Actually, price does depend on many such factors. However, they are not *in addition* to supply and demand but are included in the numerous forces which determine or *act through* supply and demand. Thus if new gold production gives everyone higher incomes, it will shift demand curves and raise prices. But it is still true that competitive price is determined by supply and demand.

At this point a thoughtful reader should be moved to voice protest. Nothing much has been said about price as being determined by cost of production. Shouldn't this be listed as a third factor in addition to supply and demand? Again our answer is the same. *Competitive price is affected by cost of production only to the extent that the latter affects supply.* If God sends manna from heaven without cost but in limited supply, then its price will not be zero but will be given by the intersection of the demand and supply curves. On the other hand, if it would cost $50,000 to print the national anthem on the head of a pin, but there is no demand for such a commodity, it simply will not be produced and would not command $50,000 if it were produced. (What the market price of something nonexistent should be called I leave to the pleasure and imagination of the reader.)

This doesn't mean that cost of production is unimportant for price determination. Under competition it is especially important. But its importance shows itself *through its effects upon supply.* Businessmen do not produce for their health. If they cannot get a price high enough to cover their past costs, then they will not like it. Nevertheless, under competition once the crop is in, so to speak, there is not much they can do about it. But they will not continue *in the future* to supply goods at prices that fail to cover the *extra* costs incurred to produce these goods. Thus supply depends intimately on cost, especially on "extra costs," and so too must price.

Moreover, to say that price equals cost does not in itself tell us which is the cause of which. In many cases where an industry uses a productive factor highly specialized to itself (*e.g.*, baseball players, opera singers, vineyard land), *price determines cost rather than vice versa.* Grain land is dear because the price of grain is high. Apartment buildings sell for little because rents are low. This type of relationship was overlooked by the Massachusetts dairy farmers who petitioned during World War II for a higher milk price "because the price of cows is high." If their request had been granted, they would soon have observed the price of cows chasing the milk price upward.[1]

These examples show us that supply and demand are not ultimate explanations of price. They are simply useful catch-all categories for analyzing and describing the multitude of forces, causes, and factors impinging on price. Rather than being final answers, supply and demand simply represent initial questions. Our work is not over but just begun.

This should help to debunk the tendency of neophytes who have just mastered the elements of market price determination to utter sagely, "You can't repeal the law of supply and demand. King Canute could not command the ocean tide to retreat from his throne on the seashore. No more can the government get around or interfere with the workings of supply and demand."

It would be better never to have learned any economics than to be left with this misleading half-baked untruth. Of course the government can affect price. It can do so by affecting supply or demand, or both. At the end of this chapter we shall examine how government programs for restricting farm production are able to raise price and income by cutting down on supply. Similar programs by government cartels have been pursued all over the world: Brazil has burned coffee to raise its price; Britain during the 1920's pursued the "Stevenson policy" of artificially controlling the price of rubber; sugar is still under international control.

These governments have not violated the law of supply and demand. They have worked through the law of supply and demand. The state has no secret economic weapons or tricks. What is true for the state is also true for individuals. Anyone can affect the price of wheat so long as he has money to throw on the market or wheat to hold off it. Rockefeller, Ford, and Astor could band

---

[1] Where a factor of production is inelastic in supply, as in all these cases, its cost is "price-determined" rather than "price-determining" and its return is called an "economic rent." See Case 3 in the Appendix to this chapter and also Part Four.

together to create an easy-money policy if they wished to badly enough. All they would have to do would be to offer to supply enough funds to everyone at a low rate of interest. With this new supply on the market, the rate of interest would have to fall.

Every trade-union influences wages, or tries to, by directly or indirectly affecting the supply of labor. Anyone with a somewhat distinctive commodity may try by advertising to increase the demand for his product, and by restricting supply to raise price above his extra costs of production. It should be remembered however that, as soon as individual producers become important enough to affect the price of the things they sell, then they cease to be perfect competitors in the strict sense, and their behavior must be analyzed in terms of a blend of monopoly and competition, *i.e.*, in terms of monopolistic or imperfect competition as described in Chapter 25.

PRICES FIXED BY LAW

There is one important interference with supply and demand whose effects we must analyze. The government sometimes sets a maximum price by law, or a minimum wage. During the war ceilings were placed on items in the cost of living. A floor of 75 cents is placed on hourly wages of most factory workers. These interferences by law are quite different from government actions, previously described, which work through supply and demand.

Consider, say, the market for sugar, which has ordinary curves of supply and demand such as we have repeatedly met in this chapter. Suppose that the government through an Office of Price Stabilization (OPS) establishes an order prohibiting sugar from rising above 7 cents a pound (retail). Now because of prosperity or bad crops, let demand be so high and supply so small that the equilibrium price would have been 20 cents a pound if the government had not intervened. This high price would have contributed to profiteering in that industry, it would have represented a rather heavy "tax" on the poor who could least afford it, and it would only have added fuel to an inflationary spiral in the cost of living, with all sorts of inflationary reactions on workers' wage demands, and so forth.

Therefore, the government through Congress and the OPS decides to hold the line on prices. It passes a law putting a maximum price on sugar at the old level of 7 cents a pound. The line *MN* represents the legal price ceiling. Now what will happen?

At the legal ceiling price supply and demand do not match. Consumers want thousands of pounds of sugar in excess of what producers are willing to supply. This is shown by the gap between *M* and *N*. This gap is so large that there will not long be enough on grocers' shelves or in the warehouses to make up the difference. Somebody will have to be drinking bitter coffee. If it were not for the maximum price law, that somebody would gladly bid the price up to 8 or 9 cents or more, rather than do without sugar. As in our earlier discussion (Chapter 20, Figure 5), we could show this by putting an upward pointing arrow perpendicular to MN. The arrow would not stop pointing upward until price had been bid up to the equilibrium level of 20 cents.

It is against the law for the consumer to bid a higher price. Even if she should be so unpatriotic, the seller could not legally take the higher price. There follows a period of frustration and shortage—a sort of game of musical chairs in which somebody is left holding the empty bag when the orchestra stops playing. The inadequate supply of sugar must somehow be rationed. At first, this may be done by "first come, first served" with or without limited sales to each customer. Lines form and women have to spend much of their time on expeditions foraging for food. But this is no solution since somebody must be left at the end of the line when the sugar is gone.

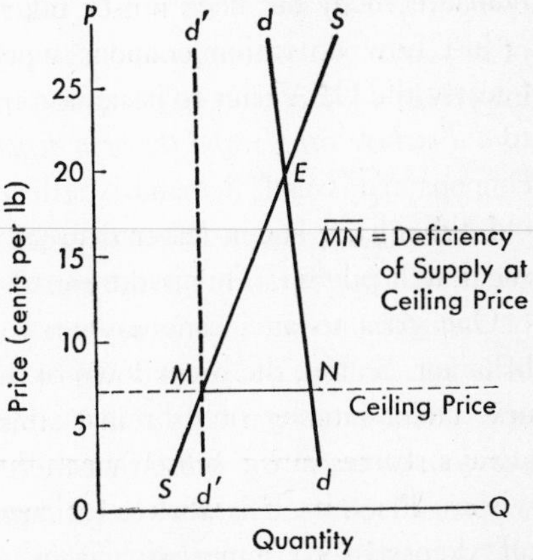

The price mechanism is stymied and blocked. Nonmonetary considerations must determine who will be the lucky buyers and who the unlucky ones: the accident of being in the store when the sugar is unveiled, the warmth of the smile that the customer flashes on the grocer, her previous standing at the store in question, and the amount of other things that the customer is willing to buy.

ECONOMIC EFFECTS OF
A MAXIMUM PRICE CEILING
ON SUGAR

$\overline{MN}$ = Deficiency of Supply at Ceiling Price

FIGURE 2. Without a legal price ceiling, price would rise to E. At the artificial ceiling price, supply and demand do not balance and some method of rationing, formal or informal, is needed to allocate the short supply and bring the effective demand down to $d'd'$.

Nobody is very happy, least of all the harassed grocer. Were it not for the community's elementary sense of fair play, the situation would soon become intolerable. Patriotism is more effective in motivating people to brief acts of intense heroism than to putting up day after day with an uncomfortable situation. So it is no wonder that black markets occasionally develop. The really surprising thing is how infrequently they do occur.

If for political or social reasons market price is not to be permitted to rise high enough to bring demand down to the level of supply, the only solution under these circumstances lies in outright coupon or point rationing.

Once this is adopted most people heave a sigh of relief, because now sellers need not turn people away and buyers can count upon getting their fair quota of the limited supplies. Of course there are always a few women and soapbox orators, who are longer on intuition than brains and who blame their troubles on the mechanism of rationing itself rather than on the shortage. "If only the government could print more coupon points," they sigh. As if that would help rather than hurt the situation! Such people are like the ignorant ancient kings who used to slay the messengers bringing them bad news. They add spice to the human comedy but need not be taken seriously.

Just how do ration coupons work out in terms of supply and demand? Clearly the OPA tries to issue just enough of them to lower the demand curve to $d'd'$ *where supply and the new demand balance at the ceiling price*. If too many coupons are issued, demand is still too far to the right and we encounter the old difficulties, but in lesser degree. If too few coupons are issued, stocks of sugar will pile up. This is the signal for liberalizing the sugar ration.

One goes to an insane asylum to learn to appreciate the normal human behavior. So too, the breakdown of the price mechanism during war gives us a new understanding of its remarkable efficiency in normal times. Goods are always scarce, in the sense that there is never enough to give everyone all he wishes. Price itself is always rationing scarce supplies: rising so as to choke off excessive consumption and in order to expand production; falling to encourage consumption, discourage production, and work off excess inventories. During World War II the price mechanism had to be supplemented by direct controls and rationing, because—as we saw in the analysis of inflation in Part Two—when everything is "short" relative to demand and full-employment capacity, reliance on the price mechanism is inequitable and gives rise to an endless inflationary spiral with grave economic consequences. The 1951 general price-wage freeze provides a laboratory case showing what happens when fiat replaces free markets.

ECONOMICS OF AGRICULTURAL AID PROGRAMS

Let us close this chapter with a discussion of what is probably the most important present-day application of competitive supply and demand theory: the area of agriculture.

Back in Chapter 5 we saw that the four main types of direct farm-aid programs work as follows: (1) Government marketing agreements aim to lower the supply of a farm crop and thereby raise its market price. (2) Storage programs guarantee the farmers a fixed price; by loan or outright purchase, the government takes off the market whatever amount of a crop consumers are unwilling to buy at the stated parity price. (3) A new program, associated with the name of Charles Brannan, President Truman's Secretary of Agriculture, would aim at paying the farmer a high price; but especially in the case of perishable crops, the government would sell back to the market all that it has bought from the farmer. The consumer would end up paying a lower price than the farmer receives, with the government footing the bill for the difference. (4) Finally there are direct outright gifts and subsidies to farm families.

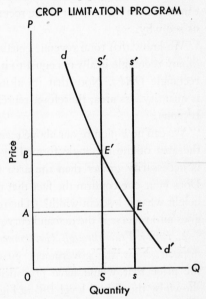

CROP LIMITATION PROGRAM

The last of these need not have any direct connection with market supply and demand, and so it will not be discussed here. But our supply and demand curves well illustrate the other three programs.

1. *Crop Restriction Programs.* Figure 3 shows how the crop agreements actually work. Before the government steps in, the supply and demand curves are given by $s's$ and dd'. The equilibrium price would be at E. In return for certain financial inducements, the farmers vote to limit their acreage of the crop in question. Let us suppose, even though many of the facts of the 1930's suggest that this is not a true supposition, that the program does succeed in limiting the supply produced of the farm crop. What has the result been?

FIGURE 3. The government marketing agreement reduces supply from $s's$ to $S'S$, thereby raising price. Provided demand is inelastic, total farm income (measured by the E' and E rectangular areas) is increased.

The new supply curve is shown by $S'S$. It intersects the demand curve at the new higher equilibrium price shown by E'. The consumer is paying a higher price and consuming a smaller quantity. The farmer is receiving a higher price. But he is selling a smaller output. Is he better or worse off?

The answer depends primarily upon the elasticity of demand. If the demand curve for agriculture is inelastic, as many authorities believe, then a cut in output will raise price so much that the total revenue collected will actually increase. Disregarding any change in farm costs, and it is the notorious stickiness of such costs that explains the fact that our supply curves have been drawn so steeply inelastic, we can formulate the following conclusion:

If the demand for farm products is inelastic rather than elastic, then a program of crop reduction will result in higher total revenue to the farmer.

Before leaving this first and simplest case, let us note that we can read off total revenue from a demand-curve diagram: Total revenue at a point like E can be shown by the area of the rectangle that E forms with the two axes. Let us see why.

We know that total revenue equals $P \times Q$. But also remember that the area of any rectangle is always equal to its altitude times its base. Now look at the rectangle OAEs. Note that its altitude OA is price. Note that its base Os is quantity. Its area, therefore, represents price times quantity, or total dollar revenue.

We can now picture our above result. Because the demand curve is inelastic, the area of the rectangle formed by means of the new equilibrium point E' is necessarily *greater* than the area formed by the old equilibrium point E. Does your eye confirm the fact that the new rectangle more than makes up in height what it loses in width? (The reader can show how this whole argument goes into reverse if the demand curve is elastic.)

2. *Parity Price through Government Purchase.* This case is a little more difficult. Now the government guarantees the farmer a price higher than the price that would have prevailed in the market. This "price floor" is shown by the dotted level BB' in Figure 4. At so high a price, consumers will not buy all the crop supplied. Consumers will be on the demand curve at the point C. But farmers are supplying the full amount shown by the point F. If nothing is done by the government, price must fall to E, which is below the parity price.

So what does the government have to do? By outright purchase or through some kind of loan red tape, it must acquire the unsold portion between C and F, marked with a bracket. This either will go into storage or will have to be left to rot. What then has the final result been?

The government has increased the price received by the farmer from E to F, as shown by the vertical bracket. But unlike the previous case, the farmers can now sell as much as they want to; so the increased price is clear gravy to them, representing a clear increase in their incomes. The consumers are now paying a higher price and buying less; to them Case 2 is just as bad as Case 1. Who then is footing the bill for the extra income now received by the farmers in comparison with the previous case? Obviously, the government: The Treasury is having to shell out an amount of dollars equal to the part of the crop they must buy times the full market price. (In terms of area, the

Treasury's expense is shown by the shaded area *CFsS*. Can you explain why?)
Of course if the demand curve *dd'* were in later years to shift upward so

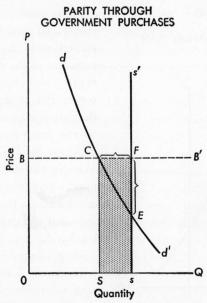

**PARITY THROUGH
GOVERNMENT PURCHASES**

FIGURE 4. The government raises price to the parity level by buying for storage what-ever part of the supply consumers will not buy. The cost to the government is shown by the shaded rectangular area.

that it intersected the supply curve at *F* or above, then the Treasury would not have to do anything to ensure parity. Indeed, it might in such a prosperous year exactly reverse the above procedure; instead of buying part to add to storage, it might take food out of storage and sell it. The interested reader can draw a new curve *DD'*, showing how this reverse process works. (Hint: Now the Treasury collects revenue instead of incurring costs.)

3. *Brannan's Plan for a Producer-Consumer Price Differential.* This is the most complicated case of all. The so-called Brannan plan involves a mixture of all the above programs, but for simplicity let us neglect the matter of crop restriction and concentrate only on its most striking feature. According to this plan, the farmer is to be guaranteed the same parity as in Case 2. But instead of leaving the food to rot in storage, it is to be sold to the public for current consumption at whatever market price it will bring. How is the farmer to receive the parity price if market price proves to be below that figure? The Department of Agriculture simply writes him a check for the difference. In effect, then, it is much as though the government had bought the crop at the

parity price—as in Case 2—but had then sold it on the open market for whatever price it would bring. Figure 5 illustrates the essence of the result.

Every bit produced, as shown by the ss' supply curve, will now go to the consumer. Consumption will end up at the original point E; the "law of

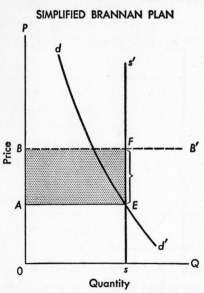

SIMPLIFIED BRANNAN PLAN

FIGURE 5. The government pays the difference between the price received by producers (shown at F) and the lower price paid by consumers (shown at E). The cost to the government is given by the shaded area; it will exceed the cost under Case 2 provided demand is inelastic.

supply and demand" tells us that, for consumers to buy the full crop, price must fall to the point where the demand curve intersects the supply curve. But producers are promised the parity price for their entire crop. So the price they are to receive is indicated by F (just as in Case 2). Who pays the difference? The government—by sending each primary producer a check, the amount of which is indicated in Figure 5 by the vertical bracket EF.

How much does all this cost the government? The answer is apparent once we realize that the government must pay the difference between the producers' and consumers' price *on each and every unit produced!* (In terms of area, the expense to the government is the shaded rectangular area $ABFE$. Here in Case 3 the shaded rectangle goes all the way leftward to the price axis, whereas back in Case 2 the shaded rectangle of government expense went all the way downward to the quantity axis.)

An important question is the following: Will the Brannan plan of Case 3 cost the Treasury more or less than would Case 2's plan of having the government withhold from the consumers part of the crop? The answer to this complicated question turns out to depend upon our old friend elasticity of demand and upon nothing else.

Look at the problem this way: Under either plan the producers are equally well off, being at F in both cases and receiving the same total income. Remember, too, that under either plan the producers' revenue can come from only two sources: the total revenue paid by the consumers plus the government's contribution. Hence, to answer the question, "Which plan costs the government the most dollars?" we need only answer the much simpler question,

"Which plan collects the greater total revenue from consumers: the plan where the consumers pay a high price and buy little; or the plan where consumers pay a low price and buy much?"

However, this is nothing but the question we have met again and again in connection with the definition of elasticity. A point high up on the demand curve like E' will collect more total revenue than a point low down like E provided the demand is inelastic in that interval. If demand were elastic, then the reverse would be true.

So now we can answer the question of relative cost as follows: The Brannan plan of making food available to consumers will currently cost the Treasury more money than will a purchase-for-storage-or-destruction program provided the demand curve is inelastic. If it is elastic, the reverse will be true.

In closing do not forget that a plan which makes food available to consumers may be considered by some citizens the preferable program, even if it costs the Treasury more money.

SUMMARY

1. The apparatus of supply and demand enables us to analyze the effects of shifts in either curve or in both simultaneously. Beginners must avoid the pitfall of confusing the expression "an increase in demand" (*i.e.*, an outward shift of the whole demand curve) with "an increase in quantity demanded" as a result of a reduction in price, *i.e.*, a movement down along an unchanged curve.

2. A thousand forces affect price. But in a free competitive market they do so only by acting through supply and demand. For example, cost of production affects competitive price only through affecting supply; otherwise not at all.

3. Although the government usually affects price by operating on either supply or demand, occasionally it passes laws that interfere with the workings of competitive markets. Under such circumstances, supply and demand need not be equal; some producer or consumer may wish to sell or buy more than he is able to do at the legal price. Unless the discrepancies are parceled out by legislation (rationing, etc.), disorder and black markets may result.

4. Government programs to limit crops, to guarantee a parity price by government purchase and storage, and to raise the price to the producer while keeping it low to the consumer are all understandable in terms of diagrams of supply and demand. The final effect of the different programs, in terms of the burdens imposed on consumer and government, differ. The nature of the differences depends intimately upon the concept of elasticity of demand.

QUESTIONS FOR DISCUSSION

1. Examine the diagram below, which shows demand and supply curves for wheat for different years, and then fill in the table alongside showing the price of wheat for each of the four years.

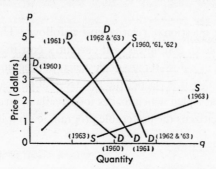

Year	Price
1960	
1961	
1962	
1963	

2. Show that, when demand is very inelastic, a sales tax will fall mostly on consumers. If demand is elastic, show the reverse. What if supply were very elastic, as in the case of a completely horizontal ss curve? What if supply were completely inelastic?

3. A ship arrives in port with an exceptionally large cargo of fish that will not keep. Use the market demand curve to show what determines the short-run equilibrium price. What if the fish could be stored? What common-sense modifications would you have to make in your conclusions?

4. Suppose that over the long run it costs $10,000 a trip to pay for a fishing ship's expenses. Suppose that each trip averages 50,000 pounds of fish. What will the long-run equilibrium price of fish be? Explain in terms of supply and demand. (Hint: Draw in a long-run horizontal supply curve at the proper level.)

5. Give some reasons why limiting a farmer's acreage for a particular crop might not reduce the total supply much. How will it affect the supply of nonlimited crops? The demand for fertilizer?

6. Suppose that demands for agricultural products are all elastic. Modify the conclusions reached in the text for the three aid programs. What if the demand for the crop in question had exactly unitary elasticity?

7. In Figure 3, label the intersection of *AE* and *SE'* with the letter *R*. Then show that *REsS* is greater in area than *RABE'* if demand is elastic. Give a detailed interpretation in terms of total revenue to justify your answer. What if demand were inelastic between *E'* and *E*?

8. What is an increased demand for cowhides likely to do to the price of beef? (Hint: Ranchers now receive more for a live cow.)

9. If the demand for automobiles is elastic, why would not Henry Ford cut the price of his car indefinitely?

APPENDIX TO CHAPTER 21
CASES ON SUPPLY AND DEMAND

PROPOSITION 1.   (a) *As a general rule an increase in demand, supply being constant, will raise price.* (b) *Probably also, but less certainly, it will increase the quantity bought and sold.* A decrease in demand has opposite effects.

PROPOSITION 2.   *An increase in supply, demand being constant, will almost certainly lower price and increase the quantity bought and sold.* The effects of a decrease in supply are just the opposite.

These two important propositions summarize the qualitative effects of shifts in supply and demand. But the exact quantitative degree of change in price and quantity depends upon the specific shapes of the curves in each instance. A number of cases may be distinguished.

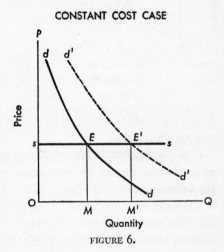

CONSTANT COST CASE

FIGURE 6.

CASE 1. *Constant Cost.*   Imagine a manufactured item, like razor blades, whose production can be easily expanded by merely duplicating machinery, plant space, factories, and labor. To produce 100,000 blades per day simply requires us to do the same thing as when we were manufacturing 1,000 per day, except on a hundredfold scale. In this case the supply curve, *ss*, in Figure 6, is a horizontal line at the constant level of unit costs. An increase in demand will shift the new intersection point, *E'*, to the right, increasing quantity but leaving price unchanged.

What will be the effects of a sales tax of, say, 5 cents per blade, on output and price paid by the consumer? Fill in the diagram.

CASE 2. *Increasing Costs and Diminishing Returns.*   Suppose that an industry like wine-grape growing requires a certain kind of soil and location (sunny hillsides, etc.). Such sites are limited in number. The annual output of wine can be increased to some extent by adding more labor and fertilizer to each acre of land and by bidding away more hill sites from other uses. But as we saw in Chapter 2, the law of diminishing returns will begin to operate if variable factors of production, like labor and fertilizer, are added to fixed amounts of a factor like land. Why is that? Because each new variable addition of labor and fertilizer has a *smaller proportion* of land to work with. By the same token, each fixed unit of land has more labor and fertilizer cooperating with it. Therefore land's productivity and earnings are higher. The result: getting extra amounts of wine sends total costs up more than proportionately. Therefore, the cost per unit of wine is rising. The supply curve travels upward from southwest to northeast because at *lower* market prices, *less* will be supplied. At higher prices, *more* will be supplied.

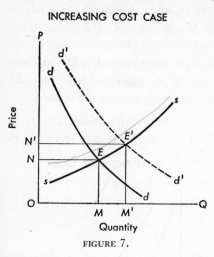

INCREASING COST CASE

FIGURE 7.

Figure 7 shows the supply curve *ss*. What will be the effect on price of an increase in demand? On quantity?

Show by means of a diagram that a tax of 5 cents per ounce of wine will raise price to the consumer by less than a similar tax on razor blades did. Why? What will be the effect on the price received by the producer? If the original demand curves for wine and razors are similar, show that the fall in the output of razors will be *greater* than that of wine. Why?

CASE 3. *Completely Inelastic Supply and Economic Rent.* Some commodities or productive factors are completely fixed in amount, regardless of price, as the following examples show.

There is only one Mona Lisa painting. Nature's original endowment of the "natural and indestructible" qualities of land can also often be taken as fixed in amount. Raising the price offered for land cannot create more than four corners at State and Madison in Chicago. High-paid artists and businessmen who love their work would continue to work at their jobs even if their salaries fell tremendously. Once a bridge is built, it must earn "what the traffic will bear" regardless of its past sunk costs. Numerous other examples could be given.

In all of them the supply curve goes straight up and down, at least in the relevant region. Look at Figure 8. A higher price cannot elicit an increase in supply; nor is the higher price necessary to bring out the existing supply, for even at lower prices the same amount will still be forthcoming. Because it is price-determined rather than price-determining, the return to the factor of production is known as a *pure economic rent or surplus*, which need not be paid to call out the required supply.

If now demand shifts upward, the whole effect is to raise price. Quantity is unchanged. Moreover, the increase in price exactly equals the upward shift in demand.

Likewise if a tax is placed upon the commodity, its whole effect is to reduce the price received by the supplier by exactly the amount of the tax. The tax is shifted completely to the supplier, who absorbs it all out of his economic rent or surplus. The consumer buys exactly as much of the good or service as before and at no extra cost.

CASE 4. *A Backward Rising Supply Curve.* Early explorers into new lands often noted that, when they raised the wages of natives, they received less labor rather than more. If wages were doubled, instead of working 6 days a week for their minimum of subsistence, the natives might go fishing for 3 days. The same has been observed among so-called "modern civilized people." As improved technology raises real wages, people feel that they ought to take part of their higher earnings in the form of more leisure and less work. This partly explains why over the decades the average factory working week has dropped from 84 to 40 hours, and why the wives, children, and aged parents of workers do not have to find jobs in such great numbers in order to help make ends meet.[1]

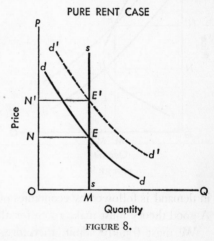

PURE RENT CASE

FIGURE 8.

To a lesser degree the same effect has been observed with respect to the supply of savings. Some people, it is true, will save more money if the interest rate is raised. Others are indifferent to the rate of interest; they save money automatically, depending upon their life-insurance commitments, habits, and incomes. But others—and these are the ones of significance in this connection— are trying to put by some certain sum of money for a "rainy day," for their old age, for a trip to Europe, or for their children's college education. If the rate of interest earned on their savings goes up, they no longer need save so much to meet these goals. Likewise, at a lower rate of interest their supply of savings goes up because more is necessary to meet the same goals. Thus, if such people are numerically important, we again have a backward-bending supply curve of savings just as we did for labor in the previous paragraph. In Part Four we shall discuss a number of such cases.

[1] An attempt to measure this statistically is to be found in Paul H. Douglas, *Theory of Wages* (Macmillan, New York, 1934).

Figure 9 indicates the supply curve of labor in this case. At first it rises as higher wages coax out more labor, but beyond the point T higher wages induce more leisure and less work. An increase in demand does increase the price of labor in agreement with Proposition 1 (a). But note how lucky we were to have added the words "but less certainly" in 1 (b)! For the increase in demand has *decreased* rather than increased the quantity of labor.

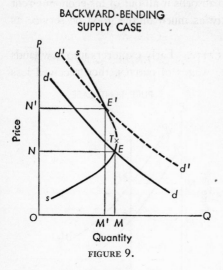

BACKWARD-BENDING
SUPPLY CASE

FIGURE 9.

A partial verification of such a possibility is found in the fact that a decrease in demand for farm products during a depression often causes farmers to work harder in order to restore their incomes. The result: More rather than less is produced in response to a decrease in demand.

CASE 5. *A Possible Exception: Decreasing Cost.* Heretofore our examples have agreed with Proposition 1 (a), that an increase in demand raises price. But what about the often observed case where an increase in demand is followed by economies of mass production and decreasing costs? A good theory must make room for all the facts.

We must frankly admit, therefore, that our first proposition may break down and have exceptions. Of course, we can try to save face a little by pointing out that many of the most important reductions in cost following an increase in demand really represent *permanent downward shifts* in the supply curve rather than movements down a fixed-supply curve.

Let us illustrate this by the case where the government increases its demand for radar sets. The first few sets built must be constructed in the laboratory by experimental methods. They are tailor-made, custom-built, and very expensive per unit. But the know-how gained in the process makes possible the further production of sets for very much less per unit. Even if demand were to go back again to its previous level, price would not return to its previous higher level. In traveling along the arrow EE' marked with a question mark, we are not moving reversibly along the supply curve. Instead, the supply curve has shifted irreversibly downward from ss to $s's'$, so that, even when demand is back again at dd, the price is now lower at E'' than it was originally.

The case discussed really does not come under the heading of Proposition 1, but falls under the heading of Proposition 2 dealing with shifts in supply. The final result agrees with the latter's conclusion that an increase in supply will lower price and increase quantity. (Compare E and E''.) But the present case is still an unusual one because the shift of supply has been induced by a shift in demand.

From the standpoint of economic history, there is tremendous importance in such cases of reduced cost over time as a result of technological progress partly induced by the expansion of a mass market. Goods are constantly being improved in quality and cheapened in price. The fact that the economist's static-supply curves do not throw much illumination on this phenomenon should not be used to belittle its tremendous significance.

What about the case of genuine *reversible* economies of large-scale production—cases where going back to small-scale production does again send costs up? The alert modern economist will not deny its importance. But he will point out that in a competitive industry each firm will have *already* expanded its output to where the *extra* cost of producing a unit of output has begun to turn up. This is

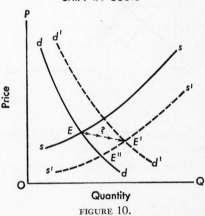

CASE OF HISTORICAL DOWNWARD
SHIFT IN COSTS

FIGURE 10.

so because each competitive producer will have no fear of spoiling his own market and will have had every incentive to expand his production through and beyond the decreasing cost stage.

The observant critic will not yet be satisfied. Suppose that an industry's demand is so small that one or a few firms working at efficient large-scale production can satisfy all demands. With decreasing costs the firm or firms will expand production and drive other competitors out, since each loss of their markets sends competitors' costs up still farther and lessens their power to compete. "Isn't all this possible?" the critic will ask. The honest economist will answer, "Not only possible, but likely in many industries. Modern technology makes perfect competition of numerous producers out of the question in many lines of activity. In such cases, and they may be the rule rather than the exception, we must replace the analysis of this chapter by the more general analysis of *imperfect or monopolistic competition*."[1] This is discussed in detail in Chapters 24 and 25.

[1] There remains one possibility discussed in advanced economic textbooks. If an increased demand for an industry's product causes each firm's cost curve to *shift downward* (a)

CASE 6. *Shifts in Supply.* All of the above discussion, with the exception of part of Case 5, dealt with a shift in demand and no shift in supply. To analyze Proposition 2, we must now shift supply, keeping demand constant. This is done in Figure 11.

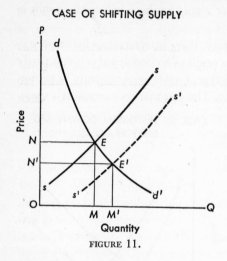

CASE OF SHIFTING SUPPLY

FIGURE 11.

If the law of diminishing demand is valid, then increased supply must send us *down* the demand curve, decreasing price and increasing quantity. The student may verify, by drawing diagrams or by comparing automobiles and wheat, the following quantitative corollaries of Proposition 2:

a. *An increase in supply will decrease price most when demand is inelastic, and decrease price least when demand is relatively elastic.*

b. *An increase in supply will increase quantity least when demand is inelastic, most when demand is elastic.*

What are the common-sense reasons for these corollaries? Illustrate with automobiles and wheat.

THREE EXCEPTIONS

In concluding, three rather unimportant exceptions to the universal law of diminishing demand will be briefly mentioned.

First, items such as diamonds, women's hats, and other goods that are valued not for their intrinsic qualities so much as for their "snob appeal" and expensiveness may fall off in demand if their price is cut. Chic New York shops sometimes take advantage of this fact and find that they do better in moving a slow-selling item if they raise its price.[1] Customers think, "It really must be good if it costs so much," as if it were universally true that "You only get what you pay for." A penetrating early twentieth-century writer, Thor-

---

because cheaper and better trained labor becomes available, (b) because better information centers and markets are created, (c) because productivity of factors in one firm is enhanced by expanded production elsewhere, or (d) because raw materials produced at decreasing costs by other quasi-monopolized industries become cheaper, then this industry may have a truly reversible, competitive, supply curve which is downward sloping. Alfred Marshall, the great English economist of the turn of the century, called this a case of *"external economies"* of production, *i.e.*, economies external to each firm in an industry.

[1] Similarly, a Boston night club found it paid to advertise itself as the "most expensive place in town."

stein Veblen,[1] coined the phrase "conspicuous consumption" for the phenomena where things are valued because their price tag shows all over them.

There is a second exception to the law of diminishing consumption, which is important especially in the short run. When the price of steel or a share of common stock is first lowered, buyers may not think to themselves, "Ah, this is now cheap. I will buy." Instead they may think, "Aha! Price is falling and will probably fall still more. I'll cut down on my orders and wait until the price falls farther." The same effect (in reverse) is often observed when prices begin to rise: buyers rush to purchase in anticipation of still higher prices. The result: in the short run the amounts demanded may rise rather than fall with increases in price.[2]

The third exception is rather unimportant in practice, but interesting as a curiosity. Certain items, like potatoes, are bought in great quantity by poor people simply because they are cheap and filling. In nineteenth-century Ireland, the peasants were so poor that a good deal of their income was spent in this way. Only in good times did they have a little money to spend on meat, bread, and perhaps a few lace curtains. Now what would happen if the price of potatoes should rise? To the despairing housewife this would be just like a cut in her man's income. The family now becomes so poor that, paradoxically, they have to give up all meat and luxuries and fill up even more than before on potatoes. Consequently, the higher the price, the more may potatoes be demanded!

The student may try his hand at finding still other exceptions. But he must not commit the cardinal error of confusing a shift in demand with a movement along the curve. He will receive harsh treatment at the bar of justice if he offers, as a fourth exception, the fact that in prosperity price goes up and so does the quantity demanded. Why?

[1] T. VEBLEN, *The Theory of the Leisure Class* (Macmillan, New York, 1899).

[2] This is a dynamic effect hinging not on high or low levels of price but on "the rate of change of price." The destabilizing effects of this are shown in connection with the discussion of stock-market speculation in Chapter 22.

Chapter 22: THE DYNAMICS

OF SPECULATION AND RISK

IN a well-organized competitive market, there tends to be at any one time and place a single prevailing price. This is because of the action of professional speculators or *arbitragers* who keep their ear to the market and, as soon as they learn of any price differences, buy at the cheaper price and sell at the dearer price, thereby making a profit for themselves—at the same time tending to equalize the price.[1]

Two markets at a considerable distance from each other may tend to have different prices. Wheat in Chicago may sell for a few cents more per hundred than in Kansas City, because of the shipping, insurance, and interest charges involved in transportation. But if ever the price in Chicago should rise by more than the few cents of shipping costs, speculators will buy in Kansas City and ship to Chicago, thereby bringing the price up in Kansas City and down in Chicago to the normal differential charge.[2]

SPECULATION AND PRICE BEHAVIOR OVER TIME

In an ideal competitive market there tends to be a definite pattern of prices *over time* just as there is over space. But the difficulties of predicting the future make this pattern a less perfect one, so that we have an equilibrium that is constantly being disturbed but is always in the process of reforming itself—not unlike the surface of the ocean.

Let us consider the simplest case of a grain that is harvested at one period of

---

[1] On the floor of the Chicago Board of Trade, the important market for grain, some half a hundred important "pit scalpers," or dealers, are said to make all their profits on price changes within each day, closing out all their transactions every night and sleeping peacefully until the next day.

[2] Wheat in Chicago can fall down to the Kansas City price, but then no grain will be flowing between the two cities. Commodities always follow a "reverse law of gravity"—they always flow *up* a rising price hill, whose gradient depends on transport cost.

the year. This crop must be made to last all the year if privation is to be avoided. Since no one passes a law regulating the storage of grain, how is this desirable state of affairs brought about? The answer is through the attempts of speculators to make a profit. A well-informed speculator who is a specialist in this grain realizes that, if all of the grain is thrown on the market in the autumn, it will fetch a very low price because of the glutting of the market. On the other hand, some months later with almost no grain coming on the market, the price will tend to skyrocket upward.

This is what would tend to happen were it not for the action of speculators. They realize that by (1) purchasing some of the autumn crop while it is cheap, (2) withholding it in storage, and (3) selling it later when the price has risen, they can make a profit. This they do. But in doing so, they increase the autumn demand for grain and raise its autumn price; and they increase the spring supply of grain and lower its price at that time. At the same time that they are equalizing the price over the year, they are equalizing the supply coming on the market in each month— which is as it should be. Moreover, if there is brisk competition among speculators, none will make an excessive profit over the costs that he incurs (including of course the wages necessary to keep him in this line of activity). Actually the speculator himself

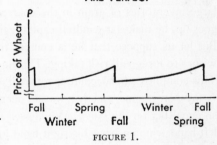

IDEAL PATTERN OF SEASONAL PRICES
WHEN SPECULATORS' FORECASTS
ARE PERFECT

FIGURE 1.

may never touch a grain of wheat or a bale of cotton, nor need he know anything about storage, warehouses, or delivery. He merely buys and sells bits of paper, but the effect is exactly as described above.

Now there is one and only one monthly price pattern which will result in neither profits nor losses. A little thought will show that it will not be a pattern of constant prices, but rather one with lowest prices in the autumn and then gradually rising prices until the peak is reached just before the new wheat comes in. The price must rise from month to month to compensate for the storage and interest costs of carrying the crop in storage, in exactly the same way that the price must rise over space from one mile to the next to compensate for the cost of transportation. Figure 1 shows the behavior of prices over an ideal yearly cycle. The increase in price from month to month is not constant, because of the accelerated growth of compound interest on the money tied up in the stored crop.

Not all fluctuations in activity can be so accurately forecast as the seasonal harvesting of a crop. No one can predict with confidence next year's weather or whether a depression will develop in the near future. But to the extent that speculators can form any accurate guesses today about the future *scarcity* of a commodity, they will tend to buy it now for *future* delivery, thereby causing (1) a withdrawal of present supply, (2) an increase of present price, (3) an increase in amount stored, (4) an increase in future supply, (5) a reduction in future price, or in all a relative stabilization of price and consumption over time. The reader should trace through the opposite process by which speculators stabilize prices when they correctly foresee an exceptionally large future crop and a low future price: how they then begin to "sell short"[1] for future delivery, tending to depress current prices, increase present consumption, decrease carry-over of stocks, and so forth.

Aside from their possible influence toward stabilizing prices, speculators have another important function. By being willing to take risks on their own shoulders, they enable others to avoid risk. For example, a miller must carry large inventories of grain in the course of his business. If the price of grain goes up, he makes a windfall capital gain; if down, he makes a windfall loss. But let us suppose that he is content to earn his living by milling flour and wishes to forego all risk taking. This he can do by a process called "hedging." This complicated procedure is rather like a man who bets on Army to win the Army-Navy game, and then washes out this transaction, or covers it, by placing an equal bet on the Navy. Whichever side wins, he comes out the same, his left hand winning what his right hand loses.[2]

To the extent that speculators forecast accurately, they provide a definite social service. To the extent that they forecast badly, they tend to aggravate

---

[1] There is really nothing mysterious about selling short. I simply put in an order to my broker in which I agree, in return for a certain price *now*, to deliver *at some later date* (usually but not always exactly specified) an amount of grain. Usually at the time of putting in the order, I do not have on hand the grain. But I legally fulfill my contract by later "covering"; *i.e.*, buying the grain and making delivery. If I later have to pay a higher price in covering than I now receive when selling short, then I make a loss. But if I have guessed right and prices do fall in the intervening period, then I "buy in" for less than I have received and make a profit. Selling short in the stock market works out similarly, except that I am free to cover and make future delivery of the stock at any time I please. In the meantime, the man who has bought the stock receives his stock shares. How? As a result of the fact that my broker, obligingly, lends me the stock certificates to make delivery. Later when I cover, I buy in the stock and turn over the certificates to my obliging broker.

[2] Likewise the miller, in quoting his present price for flour, will do so only after having bought a "future contract" for delivery of wheat to replace his used-up inventory of grain. If the price of wheat should go up a month from now, then the miller will have made a loss by selling his flour too cheap. But the gain he makes on his future purchase just cancels out his loss, and so he is "hedged" against risk.

the variability of prices. Were it not for the detailed statistical information provided by the Department of Agriculture and private agencies, the traders of the Chicago Board of Trade would find themselves at the mercy of every idle rumor, hope, and fear. For speculation is essentially a mass contagion, like the inexplicable dancing crazes that swept medieval villages, the Dutch tulip mania that sent the price of a single bulb higher than that of a house, the South Sea Bubble in which companies sold stock at fabulous prices for enterprises which would "later be revealed."

THE GREAT STOCK-MARKET CRASH

This was illustrated more recently in the United States during the fabulous stock market boom of the "roaring twenties." Housewives, Pullman porters, college students between classes—all bought and sold common and preferred stocks. Most purchases in this wild "bull" market were "on margin"; *i.e.*, the buyer of $10,000 worth of stocks had to put up only $2,500 or less in cash, borrowing the difference by pledging his newly bought stocks. What matter that he had to pay his broker 5, 6, or 7 per cent per year on his borrowing when in one day Auburn Motors or Bethlehem Steel might jump 10 per cent in value!

The most wonderful thing about a bull market is that it creates its own hopes. If people buy because they think stocks will rise, their act of buying sends up the price of stocks. This causes them to buy still further, and sends the dizzy dance off on another round. And unlike a game of cards or dice, no one loses what the winners gain. Everybody gets a prize! Of course, the prizes are all on paper and would disappear if everyone tried to cash them in. But why should anyone wish to sell such lucrative securities?

When the whole world is mad, 'tis folly to be sane. Suppose one were so wise or so naïve as to believe that the public-utilities holding companies were paper pyramids on cardboard foundations; or that Florida dream real-estate developments were midway between pine thicket and swamp; or that private foreign loans to South America and Europe were being frittered away in roads to nowhere or on public swimming pools? What could such a social misfit do? He would soon learn the first rule of property values: "A thing is worth what people *think* it is worth." Unfortunately, to be successful this has to be applied in connection with the second rule, which is as hard to follow in practice as belling the cat or catching birds by putting salt on their tails: "Don't be the sucker left holding the bag."

When the black October crash of 1929 came, everyone was caught, the big-league professionals and the piddling amateurs—Andrew Mellon, John D. Rockefeller, the engineer in the White House, and the economics professor from Yale. The bottom fell out of the market. Brokers had to sell out the "margin" accounts of investors who could no longer pony up extra funds to cover the depleted value of their collateral,[1] sending the market down still further. Even those who did not buy on margin lost one-third of their capital by the end of the year, and five-sixths by 1932.

The bull market was over and the bear market had taken its place. And, as the former had lived on its dreams, so the latter was consumed by its own nightmares. Billions of dollars of security values were wiped out every month, taking with them not only the capital of gamblers out for speculative gains, but also the widow's mite supposedly invested for steady income. A "blue chip" stock like United States Steel fell from a 1929 high of 261 to a 1932 low of 21 while less respectable securities dropped off the Board completely. Even though President Hoover and his administration were friendly toward business, in vain did they try to restore confidence by predicting that "prosperity is just around the corner" and "stocks are excellent buys at their present levels."

Finally, after the great banking crisis of 1933 and the NRA, the stock market began to follow general business recovery. Figure 2 shows the movements of stock market values over the whole period. Although stocks were bullish in 1936–1937 and again during World War II, they have never at any time returned to anything like the peak levels of 1929.

To the age-old question, does the market follow business activity or business activity the market, no simple answer can be given. It is reasonably clear that business activity, national income, and corporate earnings determine stock prices and not vice versa; and also that the psychological effects of market movements no longer have primary importance, but are in the nature of a grim national side show. But still the market can occasionally *anticipate* changes in national income and total purchasing power. It then appears to be leading them when really it is following what it thinks they will be later.

There are no simply stated foolproof rules for making money out of the stock market. Anyone who can accurately predict the future course of business activity will prosper, but there is no such person. At least four main classes of investors and speculators can be distinguished:

1. The group who simply buy and hold. If the national economy has a long-time upward trend, they fare reasonably well over the long run. They might do even better if they would follow the statistical advice of investment services as to how to switch to companies of more favorable growth prospects.

[1] Frederick Lewis Allen's amusing and interesting chronicle of the 1920's, *Only Yesterday*, gives a detailed account of the role of the stock-market boom in American life.

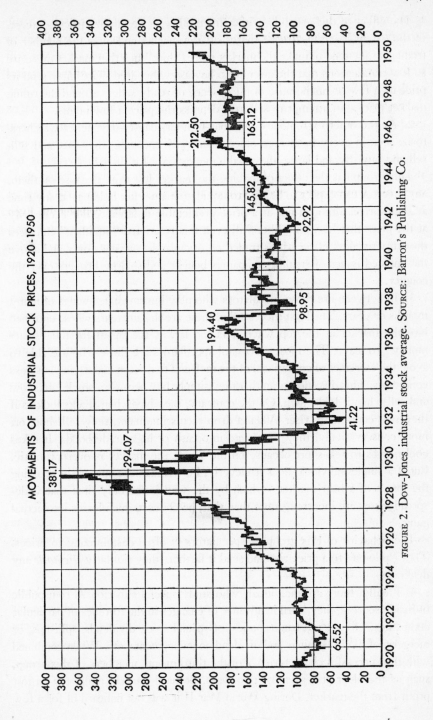

MOVEMENTS OF INDUSTRIAL STOCK PRICES, 1920-1950

FIGURE 2. Dow-Jones industrial stock average. SOURCE: Barron's Publishing Co.

The effect of this group is neither to stabilize or destabilize prices; except, to the extent that they freeze shares off the market and limit the number of tradings, they tend to make the market more "thin." In a thin market there are so few transactions that the attempt to buy a few hundred shares may send its price up a few points because of the absence of ready sellers around the ruling market price. An attempt to sell may depress the price a few points.

2. At the other extreme are the hour-to-hour, day-to-day ticker watchers, to be seen in every brokerage office. Generally speaking, they buy and sell, sell and buy. By and large, they make money only for their brokers.

This group has the effect of making the market less thin. Because of them, any investor can expect to be able to liquidate his market holdings at any time at some price, although not at a price predictable in advance nor necessarily at the price that he would like. Still even this restricted "liquidity" enhances the attractiveness of securities traded on organized exchanges over and above the unlisted issues of smaller companies bought and sold by brokers over the counter.

3. In between are those speculators who play intermediate swings of many months or years. The least successful of these are the amateurs whose entrance into the market at the top when it is too late is the signal for the "smart money" to leave. The most successful speculators are those who are able to avoid the extremes of enthusiasm of the mob and to discern underlying business conditions. This does not mean that they simply buy because a stock looks low and sell when it looks high. On the contrary, they buy when stocks look as if they will continue to rise. When a drop seems imminent, they sell short or, more conservatively, they simply go into cash or high-grade bonds. It takes cool nerves to sell short because on the whole the market is overoptimistic. But if a single individual does it cleverly, he will achieve success in avoiding the losses of a bear market—which by the way is the only time that widespread losses are incurred; more than that, he converts such losses into actual gains.

The behavior of this group of speculators is often destabilizing to prices. They "pile on" to a price rise and send it farther; they similarly *accentuate* any decline.

4. Finally, there are individuals who study special situations. From public or inside sources, they learn in advance of changes in the fortunes of particular companies: of rumored bankruptcies, of special stock dividends, split-ups, or mergers, of likely earnings and dividend announcements, etc. When combined with the successful characteristics of the third group, members of this group, such as the elder statesman of two wars, Bernard Baruch, make the largest profit from the market. During World War II it was not unheard of for a few

alert operators to run \$1,000 up to \$1,000,000 at the same time keeping profits in the form of less heavily taxed capital gains.

But the investor must take to heart Baruch's caution:

If you are ready to give up everything else—to study the whole history and background of the market and all the principal companies whose stocks are on the board as carefully as a medical student studies anatomy—If you can do all that, and, in addition, you have the cool nerves of a great gambler, the sixth sense of a kind of clairvoyant, and the courage of a lion, you have a ghost of a chance.

GAMBLING AND DIMINISHING UTILITY

The defenders of speculation resent the charge that it represents simply another form of gambling, like betting on the horse races or buying a lottery ticket. They emphasize that an uncertain world necessarily involves risk and that someone must bear risks. They claim that the knowledge and the venturesomeness of the speculator are chained to a socially useful purpose, thereby reducing fluctuations and risks to others. We have seen that this is not always the case and that speculation may be destabilizing; but certainly no one can deny all validity to the above claims.

Why is gambling considered such a bad thing? Part of the reason, perhaps the most important part, lies in the field of morals, ethics, and religion; upon these the economist is not qualified to pass exact judgment. There is, however, a substantial economic case to be made against gambling.

First, it involves simply *sterile transfers of money* between individuals, creating no new value.[1] While creating no value, gambling does nevertheless absorb time and resources. When pursued beyond the limits of recreation, where the main purpose after all is to "kill" time, gambling subtracts from the national income.

The second economic disadvantage of gambling is the fact that it tends to promote *inequality* and *instability of incomes*. People who sit down to the gaming table with the same amount of money go away with widely different amounts. A gambler (and his family) must expect to be on the top of the world one day, and when luck changes—which is the only predictable thing about it —he may almost starve.

But why is inequality of income over time and between persons considered such a bad thing? One answer is to be found in the widely held belief that the

---

[1] Actually in all professional gambling arrangements, the participants lose out on balance. The leakage comes from the fact that the odds are always rigged in favor of the "house" so that even an "honest" house will win in the long run. Moderate gambling among friends may be considered as a form of consumption or recreation activity whose cost to the group as a whole is zero.

gain in well-being achieved by an *extra* $1,000 of income is not so great as the loss in well-being of foregoing $1,000 of income. Therefore, a bet at fair odds involves an economic loss: the money you stand to win balances the money you may lose, but the satisfaction you stand to win is less than the satisfaction you stand to lose.

Similarly, if it can be assumed that individuals are all "roughly the same" and are ethically comparable, then the dollars gained by the rich do not create so much welfare as the dollars lost by the poor. This has been used not only as a criticism of gambling, but as a positive argument in favor of "progressive" taxation aimed at lowering the inequality of the distribution of income.[1]

Just as the law of diminishing returns was seen to underlie the Malthusian theory of population, so is the "law of diminishing (marginal or extra) utility" used by many economists to condemn professional gambling. According to this law, as money income increases, each new dollar adds something to well-being, but less and less. In the same way, each extra unit of any good that can be bought with money contributes less and less satisfaction or utility. When we get as much of a food as we wish (*e.g.*, water), it becomes a "free good" because still further units add nothing new to our utility.

As an example of this law, consider the utility or satisfaction to be derived from consuming more or less sugar per week. The accompanying hypothetical table shows how many units of utility are associated with an individual's consumption of different amounts of sugar per week.

TABLE 1. *Utility Schedule of Sugar*

Pounds of sugar per week	Amount of total utility	Extra utility due to last lb.
0	0	
1	4	4
2	7	3
3	9	2
4	10	1
5	10	0

The first part of Figure 3 shows how *total utility* grows with the amount of sugar consumed; the second, how much *extra utility* is added with each new

[1] Economists used to think that they could scientifically prove the desirability of income redistribution by this type of argument. Today it is widely realized that such an argument is based on implicit ethical judgments concerning the deserts of different people and that an issue like this one must be decided on a-scientific ethical grounds. The issue of incentives must also enter in forming any decision on policy.

pound of sugar consumption. The first set of blocks is increasing, but the law of diminishing utility causes the second set to be decreasing; *i.e.*, the steps go downhill. Note that the sum of all the blocks in the second diagram is equal to the last pillar of blocks in the first diagram. This corresponds to the fact that total utility is the sum of the extra utility added by each of the units.

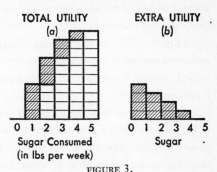

FIGURE 3.

ECONOMICS OF INSURANCE

We are now in a position to see why insurance, which appears to be just another form of gambling, actually has exactly opposite effects. For the same reasons that gambling is bad, insurance is economically advantageous.

In buying fire insurance on his house, the owner seems to be betting with the insurance company that his house will burn down. If it does not, and the odds are heavily in favor of its not burning, the owner forfeits the small premium charge. If it does burn down, the company loses the bet and must reimburse the owner to the tune of the face value of the policy agreed upon. (For the obvious reason of removing temptation from hard-up home owners who like fire engines, the face value of the policy tends to be something less than the money value of the property insured.)

What is true of fire insurance is equally true of life, accident, automobile, or any other kind of insurance. Actually the famous Lloyd's of London, which is not a corporation but simply a place for insurance brokers to come together, will insure a ball team against rain, dancers against infantile paralysis, a hotel keeper against a damage suit from the widow of a man killed in a fight with another man who bought a drink in the hotel's cocktail lounge, and will write numerous other bizarre policies. But by the common law, Lloyd's cannot bet $10,000 with me that it will not snow on Christmas, since I do not have an "insurable interest" of that amount. But a ski resort owner, who stands to lose that much if it does not snow, would have such an insurable interest and could buy such a policy. Economic theory shows what the difference is between these two cases.

Insurance is the opposite of gambling because what is unpredictable and subject to chance *for the individual* is highly predictable and uniform *in the mass*. Whether John C. Smith, age twenty and in good health, will live for 30 more years is a matter of chance, but the famous *law of large numbers* guarantees that out of 100,000-odd twenty-year-olds in good health only a definite proportion will still be alive at the end of such a period of time. The life-insurance company can easily set a life policy premium rate at which it will never lose money. Certainly therefore, the company is not gambling. What about the buyer of life insurance, is he gambling? Actually it is not hard to 'show the reverse to be true: the man who does not insure his house is doing the gambling. He is risking the whole value of his house against the small premium saved. If his house does not burn down in any year, he has won his bet; if it does, as occasionally must happen, he loses his bet and incurs a tremendous penalty.

At this point, a sporting man will say, "So what? Of course, a man gambles when he doesn't buy insurance. But the odds on such a bet are not unfavorable. In fact, they are favorable, because we know that the insurance company is not in business for its health. It must keep records, it must support insurance salesmen, and so forth.   All this costs money and must be 'loaded' on to the insurance premium, detracting from the perfect mathematical odds of the buyer and making the odds for the nonbuyer a little better."

To which a rational man will reply, "When I am among friends, I don't mind a small game of chance for relaxation even at slightly unfavorable odds. But when a big bet is involved, even if the odds are favorable, then I pass. I insure my house because I hardly miss the premium each year, and if it should burn down without being covered, I would feel the loss an awful lot. When I insure, my living standards over time and income are always the same, come what may. When I don't, I may be up for a while, but I risk going way down."

Obviously, although it has been left unsaid, the law of diminishing utility—which makes the satisfaction from wins less important than the privation from losses—is one way of justifying the above reasoning. *This law of diminishing utility tells us that a steady income, equitably divided among individuals instead of arbitrarily apportioned between the lucky or unlucky people whose house did or did not burn down, is economically advantageous.*[1] Also, when a family chooses to buy hospital and medical insurance, there is also the belief that this will be a relatively painless way of making itself "save against a rainy day." This self-imposed compulsory saving feature is another beneficial characteristic of insurance.

WHAT CAN BE INSURED

Undoubtedly then, insurance is a highly important way of spreading risks. Why then can we not insure ourselves against all the risks of life? The answer

---

[1] As will be seen in connection with the discussion of consumer behavior in the next chapter, not all economists are willing to make assumptions about "utility." There, such an attitude will make no difference; here, it might.

lies in the indisputable fact that certain definite mathematical conditions are necessary before sufficiently exact actuarial probabilities can be determined. What are these?

First, we must have a *large number of events*. Only then will there be possible a pooling of risks and a "cancellation of averages." The bank at Monte Carlo knows there is safety in numbers. The lucky streak of an Arabian prince will be canceled by the losings of a fake Ukrainian countess or else by her next night's losings. Once in a blue moon someone may "break the bank" but in a few more lunar cycles the "house" will more than break even.

But large numbers are not enough. No prudent fire-insurance company would confine itself to the island of Manhattan even though there are thousands of buildings there. *The uncertain events must be relatively independent.* Each throw of the dice, each chance of loss by fire, should stand relatively by itself. Obviously, a great fire like that of Chicago in 1871 or in San Francisco after the earthquake, would subject all the buildings in the same locality to the same risk. The company would be making a bet on one event, not on thousands of independent events. Instead, it must diversify its risks. Private companies cannot, without government aid, bear the risks of atom-bomb insurance. And it is not possible to buy unemployment insurance from a private company. Depressions are great plagues which hit all sections and all classes at one and the same time, with a probability that cannot be computed in advance with any precision. Therefore only the government, whose business it is to take losses, can take the responsibility of providing unemployment compensation benefit payments. As we have seen in our earlier discussions of Social Security, the government usually does make its benefit payments increase with the size of the worker's or his employer's contribution into the Unemployment Compensation Reserve Fund; nevertheless, the government does not follow the actuarial principles appropriate to private insurance. The lowest paid workers usually stand to receive more benefits than they are called upon to pay for. This is in accord with the fundamental principles of social security or social insurance, which always place a deservedly large emphasis upon the human needs of the recipients.

An ever larger number of life's uncertainties are being banished by insurance. In addition to life, automobile, accident, fire and theft, employee bonding, and other traditional forms of insurance, we are beginning to see the great growth of private old-age annuities, hospital insurance (*e.g.*, Blue Cross), medical insurance (*e.g.*, White Cross, Blue Shield), and so forth. In addition, as we have seen, the possibility of hedging permits those of us who wish to be safe to throw part of the risks of life upon speculators who wish to take risks.

But there still remain, and probably always will, numerous risks of personal and business life. No one can insure the success of a new beauty shop, a new mousetrap, or a hopeful opera singer. Without error there cannot be trial; and without trial, there cannot be progress.

SUMMARY

1. The intelligent profit-seeking action of speculators and *arbitragers* tends to create certain definite equilibrium patterns of price over space and time. To the extent that speculators moderate price and consumption instability, they are performing a socially useful purpose. To the extent that they provide a market and permit others to hedge against risk, they are performing a further socially useful function.

2. But to the extent that speculators pile on to price changes and cause great fluctuations in stock prices, commodities, and foreign exchange rates, their function is a harmful one.

3. The economic principle of diminishing (marginal) utility is one way of showing why gambling is economically unsound and insurance sound. There are, of course, necessarily fundamental and important differences between private and social insurance or social security.

QUESTIONS FOR DISCUSSION

1. If the complete shipping costs per bushel of wheat between Kansas City and Chicago are exactly 2 cents, then only one of the following statements is true:

   a. Wheat must sell for 2 cents more in Chicago than in Kansas City.

   b. Wheat must sell for 2 cents more in Kansas City than in Chicago.

   c. Wheat in Chicago can continue to sell for more than 2 cents above the Kansas City price.

   d. Chicago and Kansas City wheat can never sell for the same price, or for within 1 cent of each other.

   e. If wheat is flowing between the two cities, the difference in price will tend to be neither more, nor less, than 2 cents; if wheat is not flowing between them, the price difference can be anything less than 2 cents.

Which is true?

2. Pretend that you are engaging in some stock or commodity transactions. Start out with $10,000 and follow the newspapers to see how you make out.

3. "I can't afford to sell my United States Steel stock today (1930) because if I do I'll take such a great loss over what I paid for it in 1929." Was this good reasoning?

4. Should doctors' services be made subject to private insurance principles?

5. "I love the thrill of gambling, of risking all on the turn of a card. What do I care for odds or economic principles?" Can economic science pass judgment on whether such a person should gamble or not?

6. Can you reverse the reasoning concerning the desirability of gambling so that it will apply to two individuals with increasing rather than decreasing marginal utility of income?

7. List some important differences between private insurance and social security. Are they rivals?

Chapter 23: THE THEORY OF

CONSUMPTION AND DEMAND

IN A competitive market, price is determined by the schedules of supply and demand. In later discussion, we shall investigate what is behind the market supply schedule in a competitive market. This will bring us to the study of costs, which no reader of economics would ever find it profitable to skip. But in this chapter, we may briefly digress in order to analyze what is going on behind the market demand curve for consumer goods.

Why is it a digression to study the theories underlying the way people make their consumption decisions? It is a digression because for most purposes we might just as well accept the market demand as an observable fact. Many economists feel that not a great deal is gained by trying to go behind this observable fact. Therefore, many readers may prefer simply to skip a chapter like the present one.

SUMMING INDIVIDUAL DEMANDS TO GET MARKET DEMAND

The market demand curve for a good like beef is arrived at by summing up the amounts of beef that will be demanded by each consumer. Each consumer has a demand curve that can be plotted against the price of beef. It generally slopes downward and to the right, dropping from northeast to southwest. If all consumers were alike in their demands and there were 1 million consumers, then we could think of the market demand curve as a millionfold enlargement of each consumer's demand curve.

But people are not all exactly alike. Some have high incomes; some have low. Some greatly desire beef, while others prefer pork or vegetables. What must we do to the demand schedules or curves of each consumer to arrive at the total market demand curve? All that we have to do is to calculate the sum total of what each and every consumer will consume at any given price; we then plot that total amount as a point on the market demand curve; or if we like, we may set the total down in a table like those first seen in Chapter 20. In any case, we sum individual demands at each price and end up finally with the market demand curve.

THEORY OF CONSUMER'S CHOICE

But suppose we want to go behind the individual's demand curve. Why do you buy 100 pounds of beef a year when the price if $1 per pound and only 25 pounds when the price rises to $2 a pound? Why does a reduction in the price of pork cause you to cut down on your beef purchases? Why might an increase in the price of sauce to put on your beef cause you to cut down a little bit on your beef purchases? Why does an increase in your income cause you to increase your purchase of beef and reduce your purchase of oleomargarine?

A rather fancy theory was developed in the nineteenth century to explain the way a consumer arrives at decisions on what to buy. To begin with, the consumer starts out with a certain amount of income that he—or perhaps we should say "she"—can spend. In addition, he is confronted with a whole array of market prices for all the things he can buy. These prices are quoted to him, and ordinarily they are beyond his power to alter.

Immediately the problem of choice becomes apparent. If goods were free, or if his income were great enough so that he could buy every last thing that suits his fancy, this would not be so. But as things are, the more he buys of one good, the less he can buy of others. Therefore, the advantages of any good must be balanced against the advantages of all the rest. In performing this calculation of comparing goods, it is not enough for him simply to balance the advantage of different goods on an equal basis. A steak may be preferred to a can of Spam, but if the steak costs ten times as much, he may decide to buy the Spam. In other words, it is extra satisfaction secured *per unit of money expended* that matters to him. The satisfaction to be derived from different goods is not to be equal if their prices are different; but their extra satisfactions must end up *proportional* to the respective prices of the goods.

The theory being described assumes that the consumer has rather definite opinions about his own (family's) preferences as between different amounts of goods. If a psychologist quizzed him about them, he could probably answer many of the questions. But not necessarily all. Many of these opinions are on the subconscious level because he has become accustomed through repeated experience to make decisions almost automatically. As a matter of fact, most people like to keep deliberate decision making down to as low a level as possible.[1]

---

[1] Some daring economists assume that the consumer experiences a definite quantitative amount of satisfaction or anticipated pleasure when confronted with a given batch of goods. This definite psychological quantity or sensation is given the name "utility." If a first batch

In any case, the consumer, possessed of a given income and set of prices of goods, is thereby confronted with a wide range of final batches of goods. Automatically or unconsciously, he can appraise and compare them and finally pick out the best combination, or what is called the "equilibrium combination."

How shall we characterize this equilibrium position? Obviously, it is one from which the consumer will not care to depart. He will be unwilling to give up buying something of one item in order to substitute something of another. Why? Because he has already made his choice of the best combination, and any other combination is inferior.

Or to put the matter another way. He buys more and more units of all commodities until the last little units of each of them yield him satisfactions that are proportional to their respective prices. When the last 10-cent pound of beans yields twice as much satisfaction as does the last 5-cent pound of sugar, then he stops, knowing that he has arrived at the equilibrium point. Notice that the critical satisfactions to be compared concern not the total quantity of each commodity consumed but only the *last* or "marginal" increments. *At this point the extra utility per last cent or nickel is the same in all uses*; this is a necessary condition for equilibrium.

Why? Because if it were not—if the last penny spent on sugar yielded *less* satisfaction than that spent on beans—it would pay him to switch a penny from sugar buying to the purchase of some more beans. When it no longer pays to switch purchases, because the satisfaction per penny from beans has finally fallen to the level of that from sugar, then he has reached the equilibrium position and will stop.[1] This shows us, by the way, that the equilibrium posi-

---

of goods and services, *A*, registers a higher utility score than a second batch, *B*, and they cost the same, then he will buy *A* and not *B*.

More cautious writers prefer to be agnostic on the question of utility as a magnitude. All they assume is that the consumer can compare *A* and *B* and know which he prefers. Whether this is done by giving each some numerical score, these writers do not claim to know; nor do they care since the "facts" of consumer's behavior are the same in either case.

[1] The cautious economists mentioned in the previous footnote, who do not believe in utility as a numerical quantity, would not object to the use of the word "satisfaction" in the above paragraph. This is because the numerical level of this term is not used, but only *comparative* or *relative* levels of utility. Still, the purists in this group would prefer to reformulate the condition of equilibrium so as to avoid all possibility of misunderstanding. They would say, *for the consumer to be in equilibrium, the relative prices (or costs) of each good must be just matched by the rates at which he is just willing to substitute them (in small amounts) for each other; or when relative prices equal relative extra utilities.*

Of course this adds up to exactly the same thing as the other formulation. For example, if the cost ratio of beans to sugar did not match the consumer's relative utility or substitution

tion in this field, as in other parts of economic life, is usually approached only after a period of trial and error.

HEART OF THE THEORY RESTATED

The few pages above summarize all that there is to the theory of consumer's behavior. The discussion could be amplified by numerous diagrams and tables, but that is not really necessary. The beginning student of economics need keep firmly in mind only the following three sets of propositions:

1. A consumer with only a finite income, confronted with (nonzero) prices, cannot buy as much as he wants of everything. He must choose and balance, and in doing so must take relative prices into consideration.

2. The consumer is supposed to have a fairly definite set of preferences so that he knows whether a given situation is better, worse, or indifferent as compared to another situation.

3. The consumer is able, therefore, to select out of all possible situations available to him because of (1) the one which is "best" as determined by (2). This is the *equilibrium situation*, characterized by the condition that no further substitution between goods is desirable, because already expenditure has been allocated among goods until *the last penny spent on each commodity gives the same addition of satisfaction as does the last penny spent on every other commodity.*

PRICE AND INCOME CHANGES IN DEMAND

This theory explains how the amount demanded of each good is determined, once the consumer is given a set of prices and income. Thus it also explains why the amount demanded of a good will change when its price changes, or for that matter when income changes or *the price of some other good* changes.

The first of these three changes, involving the variation in quantity demanded of a good as its own price is raised or lowered, is nothing other than our old friend the demand curve. The second, which relates variations in demand to income changes, is of the greatest importance both in comparing the behavior of rich and poor and in connection with the effects of ups and downs in national income and employment. The wealth of factual material on this subject has earlier been discussed in terms of family budget behavior, and the propensity to save or consume.

CROSS RELATIONS OF DEMAND

Let us begin by discussing the third case in which the amount demanded of one good changes when the price of another good changes. This rather interest-

---

ratio (as determined by his preferences), it would pay him to substitute one for the other. When would he stop? Only at the equilibrium point where price ratios and substitution ratios are equal.

ing case of cross interrelationship can be disposed of briefly because its results are in line with general experience. Thus everyone knows that raising the price of tea will decrease the amount demanded of tea. It will also affect the amounts demanded of other commodities. For example, a higher price for tea will lower the demand for a commodity like sugar; *i.e.*, it will shift the whole demand schedule of sugar downward. But it will also increase the amount demanded of coffee. Probably it will have little or no effect on the demand for salt.

We say, therefore, that tea and coffee are *rival*, or *competing*, products, or *substitutes*. Tea and sugar, on the other hand, are *cooperating*, or *complementary* commodities, or *complements*. The in-between pair of tea and salt are said to represent *independent* commodities. The reader will of course be able to classify such pairs as beef and pork, turkey and cranberry sauce, automobiles and gasoline, trucks and railroad freight, oil and coal.

RESPONSE OF QUANTITY TO OWN PRICE

So much for crisscross relationships between goods. Returning now to the relationships between a commodity and its own price, we are in a position to understand why the law of *diminishing demand* probably holds true, or why more will be bought at a lower price.

In the first place, being able to buy a good at a lower price is just like having an increase in your (real) income, particularly if you have been buying a great deal of the commodity. With a higher real income you can afford to buy more of this good, and of every good. And unless the commodity is of the so-called "inferior" variety like oleomargarine or potatoes, you will ordinarily choose to buy something more of it once your real income has been increased. (This is sometimes called an "income effect.")

The second factor explaining diminishing consumption is equally obvious. If the price of wheat goes down while other prices do not, then wheat has become relatively cheaper. It pays therefore to *substitute* some wheat for other goods in order to maintain one's standard of living most cheaply. Thus wheat becomes a relatively cheaper source of calories than before, and more of it will be bought and less of potatoes. Similarly, a cheapening of movies relative to stage plays may cause the consumer to seek more of his amusement in the cheaper direction. The consumer is doing here only what every businessman does when cheapening the price of one productive factor causes him to adjust his production methods so as to substitute the cheap input for other kinds of inputs; by this process of substitution, he is able to produce the same output at lower total cost. (This second reason for expanding demand at lower price is sometimes called a "substitution effect.")

Of course, the quantitative importance of each of these effects varies with the good in question and with the consumer. Under some circumstances the resulting demand curve is very *elastic:* *e.g.,* where the consumer has been spending a good deal on the commodity and where ready substitutes are available; for example, a drunkard's demand for Scotch whisky. But if the commodity is like salt, which involves only a small fraction of the consumer's budget, which is not easily replaceable by other items, and which is necessary in small amounts to complement more important items, then demand will be *inelastic.*

All this agrees with common-sense notions about economics: that *scarcity* or *rarity* is what gives value to a good in exchange.

Some economists try to "prove" the validity of this generalization by analogy with a fundamental psychological generalization called the Weber-Fechner Law. According to this law, a man who can just perceive a difference in light intensity between a 10- and a 15-watt light bulb will not be able to perceive a difference between a 20-watt bulb and a 25-watt bulb, even though the arithmetic difference in intensity is the same. But he will be able to tell the difference between 20 watts and 30 watts or between 200 watts and 300 watts—because the percentage difference in intensity is what is important. This same effect, a diminution in ability to perceive and recognize minimum differences in stimuli, is claimed by the psychologist to hold with respect to perception of sounds, weights (placed on or in one's hand), and so forth.

The connection of these phenomena with the diminution in desire of an economic consumer for additional units of a commodity is, to say the least, rather far-fetched. The relation is, at best, suggestive rather than conclusive. The validity of the economic law of diminishing consumption must stand or fall on the basis of the economic behavior of consumers. If it should fail, the economist's duty is to modify his theory so as to be consistent with the observable facts.

CONSUMER BEHAVIOR AND THE DEMAND CURVE

Let us now show what the preceding sections mean in terms of our old friend the demand curve. This curve is, of course, simply the graphical picture of the response of quantity bought of a good to the change in its *own* price. But quantity bought may change also as a result of changes in the *prices of other goods* or as a result of a change in the consumer's *income.* The demand curve is drawn on the assumption that these other things *do not* change. But what if they do? Then the whole demand curve will *shift* to the right or to the left.

Figure 1 illustrates such changes. Given a certain income and established prices for all other goods, then we can draw the consumer's demand for beef. If the price is *AB*, then he will buy the quantity *OB*. Suppose now that his income rises. Even though the price of beef is unchanged, he will in all probability buy more beef than before; hence the demand curve must have shifted to the right—say to $D'D'$, with A' indicating his new total purchase of beef. If his income should fall, then we may expect a reduction in quantity bought—there *must* be a reduction if income falls far enough. This we illustrate by $D''D''$ and by A''.

We can also use Figure 1 to illustrate the effect of changed prices of other goods. A fall in the price of pork may well cause our consumer to buy less beef; the demand curve shifts to, say, $D''D''$. But what if the price of beef sauce were to fall? The change may be small or nonexistent. But if there is any change, it will be in the direction of *increased* beef purchases. Why this difference in response? Because pork is a rival, a substitute product for beef; beef sauce is a cooperating, a complementary commodity with respect to beef.

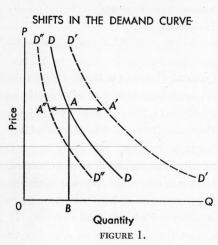

SHIFTS IN THE DEMAND CURVE

Quantity

FIGURE 1.

The important point is that, with such changes, the whole demand curve will shift. In shifting, it may change its shape; the $D'D'$ curve in Figure 1, for example, has less bend in it than DD. But such points are unimportant in an introductory survey; the Appendix to this chapter gives a more rigorous treatment of the background of consumer behavior.

THE PARADOX OF VALUE

The preceding theories help to explain a famous question that troubled Adam Smith whose book, *The Wealth of Nations* (1776), marks the beginning of modern economics. He asked, "How is it that water, which is so very useful that life is impossible without it, has such a low price—while diamonds, which are quite unnecessary, have such a high price?"

Today even a beginning student can give a correct answer to this problem. "That's simply explained," he will write on an examination. "The supply and demand curves for water are such that they intersect at a very low price, while the supply and demand curves for diamonds are such that they intersect at a high price." This is not an incorrect answer. Adam Smith could not have given it because supply and demand curves as descriptive tools had not yet been invented and were not to be for 75 years or more.

A modern economic neophyte might also attempt to dispose of a similar fundamental question asked by the medieval churchmen: "Is not interest on money unfair usury? Why should there be an interest rate charged for the use of money or capital so long as the principal of the loan is repaid in full?"

After he had read an economic textbook, the student might reply. "Whether or not there is to be a rate of interest is not a philosophical question to be settled by considering the origin of the word in the Latin language; or even by considering what Aristotle had to say about it. No," he will continue, "the problem simply boils down to the question whether the supply schedule of the money or capital funds available for investment intersects the demand schedule at a positive rate of interest. If it does—and throughout history it has—then there will be a rate of interest."

Once again, this is not an incorrect argument. But both of these answers are of the sort that would earn a pass rather than high honors on a final examination. For after he had mastered the lingo, old Adam Smith would naturally ask the question, "But *why* do supply and demand for water intersect at such a low price?"

The answer is by now easy to phrase. It consists of two parts. (1) Diamonds are very scarce; the cost of getting extra ones is high. And water is relatively abundant; the cost of more water in most parts of the world is low.

These propositions would have seemed reasonable to even the classical economists of more than a century ago, who would probably have let it go at that, and would not have known how to reconcile these facts about cost with the equally valid fact that the world's water is more *useful* than the world's supply of diamonds. (In fact, Adam Smith never did quite resolve the paradox. He was content simply to point out that the "value in use" of a good—its total contribution to economic welfare—is not the same thing as its "value in exchange"—the total money value or revenue for which it will sell.)

But today, we should add to the cost considerations of (1) the following: (2) the total usefulness of water does not determine its price or demand.

Only the relative usefulness and cost of the *last* little bit of water determine its price. Why? Because people are free to buy or not buy that last little bit. If water is priced higher than its last extra usefulness, then that last unit cannot be sold. Therefore, the price must fall until it reaches exactly the level of usefulness of the last little bit, no more and no less. Moreover, because every unit of water is exactly like any other unit and because there is only one price in a competitive market, *every unit must sell for what the last least useful unit sells for.* (As one student put the matter: The theory of economic value is easy to understand if you just remember that the tail wags the dog.)

Now we know that the more there is of a commodity, the less becomes the relative desirability of its last little unit—even though its total usefulness always grows as we get more of the commodity. Therefore, it is obvious why a large amount of water has a low price. Or even why air is actually a free good despite its vast usefulness. The later units pull down the market value of all units.

This completes the brief excursion behind the supply and demand curves necessary to explain Smith's paradox of value.

CONSUMER'S SURPLUS

This discussion emphasizes that the accounting system which records the "total economic value" or revenue of a good (price × quantity) differs from that necessary to record "total welfare." The total economic value of air is zero; its contribution to welfare, very great.[1] Similarly, if we increase the quantity produced of a commodity like wheat whose demand is inelastic, we obviously increase the community's welfare, even though we destroy some economic value.

Thus, there is always a gap between total welfare and total economic value. This gap is in the nature of a *surplus*, which the consumer gets because he always "receives more than he pays for."

Nor does he benefit at the expense of the seller. In a swap, one party does not lose what the other gains. Unlike energy which cannot be created or destroyed, the well-being of all participants is increased by trade.

It is not hard to see how this surplus arises. Each unit of a good that the consumer buys costs him only as much as the last unit is worth. But by our fundamental law, the *earlier* units are worth *more* to him than the last. Therefore, he enjoys a surplus on each of these earlier units. When trade stops benefiting him and giving him a surplus, he stops buying.

As final clinching evidence that the consumer always receives a surplus, we may cite the fact that a ruthless seller could present the consumer with an ultimatum: "Either you pay me an extra amount of money for the whole block of the good that you are consuming, or you must go without all the units, from first to last. Take it or leave it!" The consumer would certainly be willing to pay an extra amount rather than do without the good altogether.

Many ingenious ways have been suggested for measuring this consumer's surplus, but they are of no particular significance. The important thing is to see how lucky the citizens of modern efficient communities really are. The *privilege of being able to buy a vast array of goods at low prices cannot be overestimated.*

This is a humbling thought. If ever a person becomes arrogantly proud of *his* economic productivity and *his* level of real earnings, let him pause and reflect. If he were transported with all his skills and energies intact to a primitive

[1] Or, as Smith would say, its value in use is very great; its value in exchange, negligible.

desert island, how much would his money earnings buy? Indeed, without capital machinery, without rich resources, without other labor, and above all without the technological knowledge which each generation inherits from society's past, how much could *he* produce? It is only too clear that all of us are reaping the benefits of an economic world we never made.

This basic fact is well stated in the following quotation:

The organizer of industry who thinks that he has "made" himself and his business has found a whole social system ready to his hand in skilled workers, machinery, a market, peace and order—a vast apparatus and a pervasive atmosphere, the joint creation of millions of men and scores of generations. Take away the whole social factor and we have not Robinson Crusoe, with his salvage from the wreck and his acquired knowledge, but the naked savage living on roots, berries, and vermin.[1]

SUMMARY

1. A consumer with a given money income, confronted by finite prices, is limited in what he can buy and so must choose and substitute. To the extent that he is acting rationally, he will consciously or unconsciously substitute one good for another until he has reached the highest level of satisfaction. At this equilibrium point, the last penny spent on each kind of good will yield exactly the same extra satisfaction.

2. The equilibrium amount demanded of any good will change when either income, its own price, or the price of some other good changes. The last change introduces the notion of competing, independent, or complementary goods.

3. The downward response of a good when its price rises—or the relation between scarcity of a good and its price—is the basic economic law of diminishing demand. Together with the important recognition that it is the cost and desirability of the last unit of an article, this law helps to explain Adam Smith's famous paradox of value concerning water and diamonds.

4. Consumer's surplus is a reflection of the fact that the total economic welfare of any good is greater than its total monetary value. This is because all units of a good, being interchangeable, sell for as little as the last is worth. Consequently, the consumer is receiving a surplus on all previous units.

[1] L. T. HOBHOUSE, *The Elements of Social Justice* (Holt, New York, 1922), pp. 162–163.

QUESTIONS FOR DISCUSSION

1. "I don't know much about art, but I do know what I like." Is this a correct statement? Do people know what they like in the way of consumption goods? Do they usually like "what is good for them"?

2. Why is it nonsensical to say:

   a. In equilibrium, the satisfaction from the last 5 cents' worth of peas must equal the satisfaction from the last 4 cents' worth of sugar?

   b. In equilibrium, the satisfactions derived from all commodities must be equal?

   c. In equilibrium, the last little bits of satisfaction derived from all commodities must be equal?

   b. In equilibrium, the satisfactions derived from the dollars spent on all commodities must be the same?

   Write out a correct fifth statement.

3. Why would your correct condition of equilibrium have to be modified in its application to goods, like automobiles, which are not infinitely divisible like sugar or gasoline? (Hint: Would it be possible to shift 1 penny or $1 from the purchase of automobiles to the purchase of sugar or fountain pens?)

4. Why do farmers work hard when their efforts produce only large crops, low prices, and lower farm incomes? Would anyone benefit from the process?

5. How much would you be willing to pay rather than give up all movies completely? How much do you spend per year on movies?

6. "You only get what you pay for." Is this true?

7. Oscar Wilde said, "What is a cynic? A man who knows the price of everything, and the value of nothing." Could not the same be said of an economist who confined his attention to accounting and statistical dollar data?

8. How would you go about measuring your own utility? With an X-ray machine or a yardstick or a Geiger counter or a smile recorder or a blood-pressure instrument or a cash register or a record of your gambling on the races or records of your budget behavior in buying food and clothing? Or do you think it impossible?

9. "At a price of 10 cents I would buy one orange; at 8 cents apiece, two oranges; at 3 cents apiece, three oranges. What is the most I would be willing to pay for three oranges if a dealer told me that I had to buy three or none at all?" (Hint: If the daily allowance that I can spend is small, I shall certainly not be willing to pay 10 + 8 + 3 cents for the three; *e.g.*, that would be impossible if my daily allowance is 20 cents. This poses the riddle of how to measure consumers' surplus in terms of money. Unfortunately, there is no simple answer to the above simple question.)

APPENDIX TO CHAPTER 23
GEOMETRICAL ANALYSIS OF
CONSUMER EQUILIBRIUM

It is often instructive to show graphically, and without using the language of numerical utility, exactly what the consumer's equilibrium position looks like.

THE INDIFFERENCE CURVE

We start out by considering a consumer with a given money income, all of which he spends on consumption. He buys only two commodities, say food and clothing, at definite quoted prices. The consumer is supposed to be able to tell us whether (1) he prefers a given combination or batch of the two goods, say 3 units of food and 2 of clothing, to some second combination or batch, say 2 units of food and 3 of clothing or (2) he is "indifferent" as between the two combinations or (3) he actually prefers the second batch of goods to the first one.

Let us suppose that actually these two batches are equally good in the eyes of our consumer—that he is indifferent as to which of the two he receives. Let us go on to list in Table 1 some of the other combinations of goods between which the individual in question is likewise just indifferent.

TABLE 1. *Indifference Table Showing Equally Desirable Combinations of Goods*

	A	B	C	D
Food................	1	2	3	4
Clothing............	6	3	2	1½

Figure 2 shows these combinations diagrammatically. We measure units of clothing upon one axis and units of food upon the other. Each of our four combinations or batches, A, B, C, D, is represented by a single point. But these four are by no means the only combinations that would leave our consumer just indifferent as between them. Another batch, such as 1½ units of food and 4 of clothing, might be ranked as just equal to any of A, B, C, or D above, and there are many others. The curved line of Figure 2, linking up the four points, is an "indifference curve." *Every* point thereon represents a different combination of the two goods; and the indifference curve is so drawn that, if our consumer were given his choice of any point on it, he would not know which one to choose. All would be equally desirable to him, and he would be indifferent as to which batch he received.

It should be noted that this indifference curve is of concave curvature viewed from above. As we move downward and to the right along the curve—a movement which implies increasing the quantity of food and reducing that of clothing—the slope of the curve becomes flatter. The curve is so drawn because this illustrates a property which seems most often to hold true in real life and which we may call the law of substitution:

> *Law of substitution: The scarcer a good, the greater its relative substitution value; the extra utility of the good that has become scarce rises relative to the extra utility of the good that has become plentiful.*

For example, the consumer who is at position *A* in Table 1 is willing to give up 3 units of clothing in order to get a second unit of food. At *A*, he would

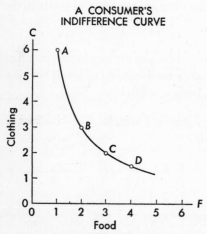

A CONSUMER'S
INDIFFERENCE CURVE

FIGURE 2. Each point on the curve represents some combination of food units and clothing units. Each and any point would be equally satisfactory to the given consumer. The points *A, B, C, D* are those of Table 1.

swap 3 of his 6 clothing units in exchange for 1 extra food unit. But when he has moved to *B*, he would sacrifice only *one* of his remaining clothing supply in order to obtain a third food unit—a one-for-one swap. And for a fourth unit of food, he would yield only ½ unit from his dwindling supply of clothing.

If we join the points *A* and *B* of Figure 2, we find that the slope of the resulting line (neglecting its sign) has a value of 3. Join *B* and *C*, and the slope is 1; join *C* and *D*, and the slope is ½. These figures—3, 1, ½—are simply the "swapping terms" that we noted just above.

But to move from *A* to *B* is to move a considerable distance along the curve. What of the swapping terms for smaller movements? If the consumer is at *A* and we consider a movement to the intermediate position (not shown in Table 1) of 1½ food and 4 clothing, the swapping ratio would be 4. And it is clear that, as the movement along the curve grows smaller, the closer the swapping terms come to the actual slope of the indifference curve.[1]

So the slope of the indifference curve is the measure of the terms on which—for very small changes—the consumer would be willing to exchange a little of his supply of one good in return for a little more of the other. And an indifference curve which is concave in the manner of Figure 2 conforms to the law of substitution earlier noted. As the consumer's supply of food increases—and his supply of clothing dwindles—the less and less favorable will be the terms on which he could be persuaded to take a little more food in exchange for a little less clothing. The precise shape and slope of an indifference curve will, of course, vary from one consumer to the next; but for this introductory discussion, it seems reasonable to assume that the general concave shape of the curve in Figure 1 is typical.

THE INDIFFERENCE MAP

Table 1 is but one of an infinite number of possible tables. We could have started out with a still higher level of satisfaction or indifference and listed some of the different combinations that belonged to it in the mind of our consumer. One such table might have begun with 2 food and 7 clothing; another with 3 food and 7 clothing. Each table could be portrayed graphically; each has its corresponding curve. Figure 3 shows four such curves; that of Figure 2 is now labeled U_3. This figure is analogous to a geographical contour map. A person who walks along the path indicated by a particular height contour on such a map will find that he is neither climbing nor descending; similarly the consumer who moves from one position to another along a single indifference curve enjoys neither increasing nor decreasing satisfaction from the change in the flow of goods that he is receiv-

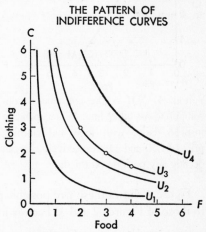

THE PATTERN OF
INDIFFERENCE CURVES

FIGURE 3. The curves labeled U_1, U_2, U_3, and U_4 represent indifference curves, or contour lines of equal utility or satisfaction. U_3 is the curve of Figure 2.

[1] By the slope of the indifference curve, we mean this: To find the slope of the curve at, say, the point B, take a ruler and place it so that it is just tangent to the curve at B—it touches the curve, but does not cross it either above or below B. Mark the points at which the ruler's edge crosses the two axes. The slope is the ratio of the distance cut off on the vertical axis to the distance cut off on the horizontal axis. At B, for example, the slope is 6/4, or 1½.

ing. Of course, only a few of the possible indifference curves or equal-utility lines are shown in Figure 3.

Note that, as we increase both goods and hence move in a northeasterly direction across this "map," we are crossing successive indifference curves; we are reaching higher and higher levels of satisfaction. Unless the consumer is satiated, he would be enjoying increasing satisfaction from receiving increased quantities of *both* goods. Hence curve U_3 stands for a higher level of satisfaction than U_2; U_4, for a higher level of satisfaction than U_3 and so forth.

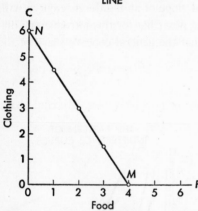

FIGURE 4. *NM* is the consumer's consumption-possibility line. When spending just $6 daily, with food and clothing prices $1.50 and $1, respectively, he can occupy any position on this line.

THE CONSUMPTION-POSSIBILITY LINE

Now let us set the consumer's indifference map aside for a moment and consider his fixed income. He has, say, $6 per day to spend, and he is confronted with fixed prices for food and clothing—say $1.50 for food, $1 for clothing. It is clear that he could spend his money on any one of a variety of alternative combinations of food and clothing. At one extreme, he could buy 4 food units and no clothing; at the other, 6 clothing units and no food. Table 2 illustrates some of the possible ways in which his $6 could be allocated.

Figure 4 shows these five possible positions on a diagram with axes similar to those of Figures 2 and 3. Each is indicated by a small circle, and it will be

TABLE 2. *Alternative Expenditure Patterns with Given Income and Prices*

| Food............. | 4 | 3 | 2 | 1 | 0 |
| Clothing.......... | 0 | $1\frac{1}{2}$ | 3 | $4\frac{1}{2}$ | 6 |

noted that they all lie on a straight line, which is labeled *NM*. Moreover, any other attainable point, such as $3\frac{1}{3}$ food units and 1 clothing unit, would lie upon *NM*.[1] *NM* sums up all possible positions that our consumer could occupy, in spending his $6 income.

[1] This is so because if we designate quantities of food and clothing bought as F and C, respectively, total expenditure on food must be $\$1\frac{1}{2}F$ and total expenditure on clothing, $\$1C$. If daily expenditure is $6, the following equation must hold: $\$6 = \$1\frac{1}{2}F + \$1C$. This is a simple linear equation—the equation of the line *NM*.

The slope of *NM* (neglecting its sign) is ⅔, which is the ratio of food price to clothing price; and the common sense of this line is clear enough. Given these prices, every time our consumer gives up 1½ clothing units (thereby dropping down 1½ vertical units on the diagram), he can gain 1 unit of food (*i.e.*, move east 1 horizontal unit). Or what is the same thing, he can exchange 3 clothing units for 2 food units. We can call *NM* the consumer's "consumption-possibility" line.

THE EQUILIBRIUM POSITION

Now we are ready to put our two parts together. The axes of Figure 4 were the same as those of Figures 2 and 3. We can superimpose the consumption-possibility line *NM* upon the consumer's indifference map, as in Figure 5. He is free to move anywhere along *NM*.

Positions to the right and upward of *NM* are barred to him unless he spends more than $6 daily, and positions to the left and below *NM* are unimportant, since we assume that he will want to spend the full $6. Where will the consumer move? Obviously to that point which yields the greatest satisfaction; or, in other words, to the highest available indifference curve, which in this case must be at point *B*. At *B*, the consumption-possibility line just touches—but does not cross[1]—the indifference curve U_3; this is the highest curve he can reach.

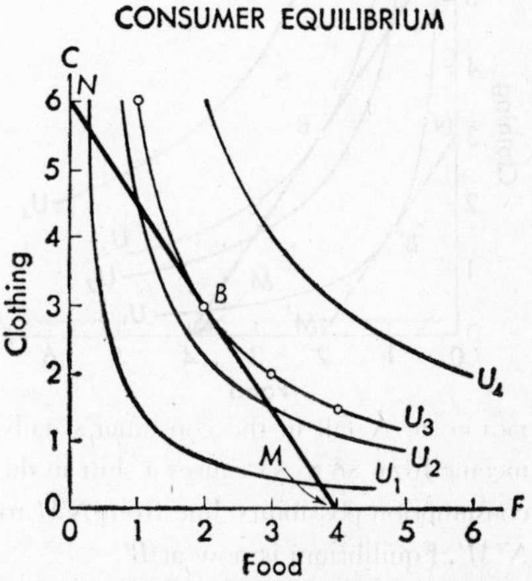

Geometrically, the consumer is at equilibrium where the slope of his con-

CONSUMER EQUILIBRIUM

FIGURE 5. This is a combination of Figures 3 and 4. Equilibrium is at the point of tangency *B*, where the consumption-possibility line reaches the highest attainable level of satisfaction or utility.

sumption-possibility line is exactly equal to the slope of his indifference curve. And as we have already noted, the slope of the consumption-possibility line is the ratio of food price to clothing price. We may say, then, that equilibrium is attained when the consumer's *substitution ratio* is just equal to the ratio of food price to clothing price.[2]

[1] At any point other than *B* on *NM*, *NM* is crossing indifference curves. And as long as the consumer can keep crossing indifference curves, he can keep moving to higher ones.

[2] The substitution ratio, or slope of the indifference curve, can be shown to be nothing but the ratio of the extra utility of food to that of clothing. So our tangency condition is just another way of stating that a good's price and its extra utility must be proportional, in equilibrium.

CHANGES IN INCOME AND PRICE

Our understanding of the process will be furthered by considering the effects of (1) a change in money income and (2) a change in the price of one of the two goods.

1. Assume first that the consumer's daily income is halved, the two prices remaining unchanged. We could prepare another table, similar to Table 2, showing the consumption possibilities that are now open to him. Plotting these

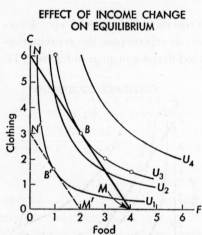

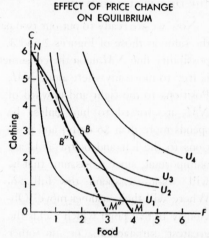

FIGURE 6. A fall in the consumer's daily income from $6 to $3 causes a shift in the consumption-possibility line from NM to N'M'. Equilibrium is now at B'.

FIGURE 7. A rise in the price of food from $1.50 to $2 causes the consumption-possibility line to rotate from NM to NM''. Equilibrium is now at B''.

points on a diagram such as Figure 6, we should find that the new consumption-possibility line occupies the position N'M' in Figure 6. The line has made a parallel shift, in the southwesterly direction.[1] The consumer is now free to move only along this line. Again he will move to the highest attainable indifference curve, or to the point B'. A similar tangency condition for equilibrium again applies.

2. Now let us return our consumer to his previous daily income of $6, but now assume that the price of food rises from $1.50 to $2. Again we must examine the change in the consumption-possibility line. This time, we shall find that it has pivoted on the point N and is now NM'',[2] as in Figure 7. The common sense of such a shift is clear. Since the price of clothing is unchanged, the point N is just as available as it was before. But since the price of food has

[1] The equation of the consumption-possibility line is now $3 = $1½F + $1C.

[2] The equation of the consumption-possibility line is now $6 = $2F + $1C.

risen, point M, which meant 4 food units had been purchasable, is no longer attainable. With food costing $2 per unit, only 3 units can now be bought with a daily income of $6. So the new consumption-possibility line must still pass through N, but it must pivot around N and pass through M'', which is nearer to the origin than the old point M. (The new line has a slope of 2/1. Why?) Equilibrium is now at B''; we have a new tangency situation in that equilibrium.

To clinch his understanding, the reader should work out the cases of (1) an increase in income and (2) a fall in the price of clothing or food.

SUMMARY TO APPENDIX

1. If a consumer has a fixed money income, all of which he spends, and is confronted with market prices of two goods, the consumption-possibility line upon which he is free to move is a straight line. The steepness of the line's slope depends on the ratio of the two market prices; how far out from the origin it lies depends on the size of his income.

2. The consumer will move along this consumption-possibility line until he reaches the highest indifference curve attainable. At this point, the consumption-possibility line will touch, but not cross, an indifference curve. Hence equilibrium is at the point of tangency, where the *slope of the consumption-possibility line* (the ratio of the two prices) exactly equals the *slope of the indifference curve* (the substitution ratio or relative-extra-utility ratio of the two goods).

3. A fall in income will move the consumption-possibility line inward, usually causing less of both goods to be bought. A change in the price of one good alone will, other things being equal, cause the consumption-possibility line to pivot so as to change its slope. In any case, whatever change has occurred, a new equilibrium point of highest satisfaction will be reached. It will be identified by a new point of tangency, where extra utilities are again proportional to market prices.

QUESTIONS FOR DISCUSSION

1. Explain why an indifference curve can be drawn through every and any point on an indifference map. Can you explain why two indifference curves could never cross?

2. Can you explain the following: If the extra utility of food is very great relative to the extra utility of clothing, the indifference curve (using the axes as drawn in this Appendix) will be very steep? If the opposite holds, explain why the indifference curve will be flat.

3. If the consumer is at a point on his consumption-possibility line where it crosses an indifference curve, explain why he cannot have reached equilibrium. Which way would he move?

4. Suppose that the indifference curves were all convex instead of being concave. Show that the consumer would then want to move until he is consuming only one of the two goods. (Hint: A point of tangency, in such a case, would represent the *worst* possible way to spend one's money—a position of minimum rather than maximum satisfaction.)

Chapter 24: EQUILIBRIUM OF

THE FIRM: COST AND REVENUE

IN THE last chapter we went behind the demand curve to see what consumer decisions were in its background. Now we wish to examine the decisions that every business firm must make. We must study the principles that underlie the rational behavior of a producer interested in maximizing his profits.

But the time has now come to drop the assumption that competition is perfect. In this chapter we wish to develop principles of behavior that are valid for imperfect as well as for perfect competitors. In the Appendix to this chapter, the very special case of a perfect competitor is analyzed to show some of the forces that lie behind the supply curves of earlier chapters. In the next chapter, our principles are used to throw light on several important patterns of imperfect competition.

IMPERFECT OR MONOPOLISTIC COMPETITION

In these days when "perfect" competition exists only in a few lines of agriculture, we cannot be content to understand perfectly competitive industries alone but must examine the behavior of firms who have some monopoly power and are able to affect the selling prices of their products. Such firms may be very large, very profitable, and in possession of patents or special advantages which effectively exclude other firms from producing the same products. In this case, they may be called a "monopoly." The Bell Telephone System, or the prewar Aluminum Company of America may perhaps qualify for this title.

More often a firm has *some* control over price, but only to a limited extent. It has certain peculiar advantages of know-how, location, trade-marks, and reputation; at the same time it has rivals of which the same is true. We may say, therefore, that the firm has some monopoly powers but is also subject to some competition. We do not have perfect competition, nor do we have complete monopoly. Instead we have imperfect competition, a blending of competition and monopoly; or, in short, what may be termed *monopolistic competition.*[1]

One may construct a line, whose one extremity represents "pure" or perfect competition and whose other end represents complete monopoly.

Pure or Perfect Competition	Monopolistic or Imperfect Competition	Complete Monopoly
1. Includes a few agricultural industries	1. Includes most firms and industries	1. Rare
2. No control over price by firm	2. Some control over prices (depending on similarity of substitute products and upon the number, location, etc., of rivals)	2. Considerable control over price except as limited by government regulation or fear of public opinion, and by fears that substitute products will come into use
3. Production of identical products by many firms	3. Sellers of identical products are few at best, though there may be many sellers of somewhat similar products	3. Only one seller in the industry
4. Usually an organized market exchange or auction	4. Advertising rivalry	4. "Institutional" and public-relations advertising

Most of modern life falls under the heading of monopolistic competition; for example, barber shops, the radio and electrical industry, steel, automobiles, retail stores, etc. Exclusive monopolies, like public utilities or telephones, are usually regulated by the government; and even they must take account of the potential competition of alternative products—oil for gas, or cables for telephones. This shows how relatively unimportant complete monopolies are.

The student may easily apply two simple tests to convince himself of how unimportant pure or perfect competition is today:

1. How many firms find it *un*necessary to spend money on advertising, salesmen, and marketing? Obviously, very few except for farmers who produce a homogeneous crop.

2. How many firms are unwilling to take on new business at the prevailing price? Obviously, in normal times, only those same farmers mentioned above

---

[1] The interested reader should consult E. H. Chamberlin, *Theory of Monopolistic Competition* (Harvard University Press, Cambridge, Mass., 1946) especially Chaps. 1 and 4.

are unwilling to do so—unwilling because they have already taken to the market all the production that they wish to with no fear of depressing the price. The vast majority of firms normally welcome new buyers.

Both of these answers are incompatible with really perfect competition. The analysis to follow must clearly be general enough to apply to all cases—not just to perfect competition—if it is to throw light on the economic world as it really is, and not as we might wish it to be.

THE FIRM'S DEMAND UNDER PERFECT AND MONOPOLISTIC COMPETITION

For simplicity, let us consider a single firm which produces only a single commodity. It is in business to make as much money as possible. Ideally it

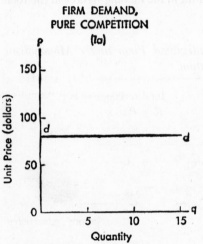

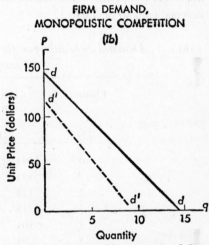

FIGURE 1a. This shows infinitely elastic demand for product of firm under "pure" or "perfect" competition.

FIGURE 1b. Demand for product of firm under "monopolistic" competition. The broken line $d'd'$ shows a fall in the demand schedule as a result of a cut in rivals' prices.

would like to charge a very high price and to sell a very large quantity of output. But it knows, or it will soon learn from experience, that these are not independent variables: it cannot set its price very high and at the same time succeed in selling a great deal; to sell a large quantity it must lower its price; and to get a high price, it must keep its commodity scarce.

In other words, the firm is subject to a demand curve, such as was described in Chapter 20 on Supply and Demand; only there we always referred to the demand curve for the industry, whereas now we are speaking of the demand curve for the individual firm. If the firm is in a perfectly competitive field, its demand curve will be very flat, with practically infinite elasticity. If the firm is a complete monopoly, it will be able to raise prices without unduly decreasing sales; and the action of other firms will not be able to shift its curve downward and to the left. Usually, most modern business firms find themselves somewhere in between these conditions, *i.e.*, under monopolistic competition. Their demand curve will have some downward tilt, and it will be shifted downward by the action of rival firms. Two of these three cases are shown in Figure 1.

PRICE, QUANTITY, AND TOTAL REVENUE

Since imperfect competition includes perfect competition as one very special instance, we may concentrate upon the more general case. Table 1 represents the original demand schedule for the firm under monopolistic or imperfect competition. The reader should fill in the missing figures in the total revenue column of Table 1.

TABLE 1. *Demand Schedule for the Individual Firm under Monopolistic Competition*

Quantity q (1)	Price P (2)	Total revenue $R = P \times q$ (3)
0	$144 or more	$ 0
1	134	—
2	124	248
3	114	—
4	104	—
5	94	—
6	84	504
*7	*74	*518
8	64	512
9	54	—
10	44	—

* Equilibrium point of maximum profit, in zero-cost case.

Clearly, the firm will not charge the highest possible price of $134. Why not? Because then it does not maximize its profits. It is then collecting the highest possible (average) revenue per unit, but it is selling only one unit, and collecting only $134 of total revenue.

How much will the firm produce, and at what price? This question cannot be answered until we know something about its costs of production. For the moment, let us neglect all costs. Clearly, the best quantity for the firm is then around 7 units, and the best price is around $74. This answer is derived from an examination of the total revenue column, $R = P \times q$, where the point of highest total revenue is starred. Price is not at a maximum; neither is quantity. But *total* revenue is being maximized.

TOTAL AND MARGINAL COSTS

It is now simple to introduce costs into the picture. Just as the firm had to make a guess at its demand curve, so it must try to estimate the approximate dollar expense that will be incurred in producing different outputs. Although the accounting difficulties in arriving at such a total cost curve are very great and may involve considerable guesswork, the firm's accounting and production departments must endeavor to determine which costs are *fixed*, independently of changes in output, and which are *variable costs* changing with output. Table 2 is an example of such an estimate for a certain firm.

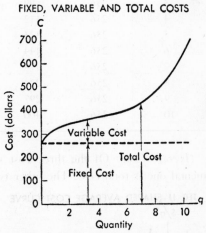

FIXED, VARIABLE AND TOTAL COSTS

Fixed Costs. Column (1) indicates the different levels of production per unit time, going from 0 up to 10 units. Column (2) indicates that the firm's fixed costs per time period are $256 even if it produces nothing. By definition, fixed costs are fixed; they remain at $256 at all levels of output. They result from past commitments, from costs that are already "sunk," overhead expenses, etc.

FIGURE 2. The horizontal broken line shows the level of fixed cost as given in Table 2. The solid line shows total cost if measured from the q axis, variable cost if measured from the dotted line of fixed cost.

Variable Costs. Column (3) lists the estimated amounts of total variable costs per unit time at different levels of production. By definition, variable costs are zero when no output is being produced. But they change with quantity, q. At first as output increases, variable costs seem to grow quite rapidly. But as output increases further, *economies of mass production* come into play and variable costs do not seem to be increasing proportionately with output. Later on, however, as diminishing returns set in, variable costs begin to shoot up more rapidly than output.

Total Cost. This is given in Column (4). It is nothing but the sum of fixed and variable costs. It must begin, therefore, even with zero production, at $256 and increase from there on like variable costs. Figure 2 illustrates the three different cost categories pictorially.

TABLE 2. *Fixed, Variable, and Total Costs of Individual Firm*

Quantity q	Fixed cost FC	Variable cost VC	Total cost $TC = FC + VC$	Average cost per unit $AC = TC \div q$	Marginal cost per unit MC
(1)	(2)	(3)	(4)	(5)	(6)
0	$256	$ 0	$256	Infinity	
1	256	64	320	$320	$ 64
2	256	84	340	170	20
3	256	99	355	118.33	15
4	256	112	368	92	13
5	256	125	381	76.20	13
6	256	144	400	66.67	19
7	256	175	431	61.57	31
8	256	224	480	60	49
9	256	297	553	61.44	73
10	256	400	656	65.60	103

Average Cost. Of the three cost schedules discussed, clearly the fundamental one is total cost. The other two are refinements which can easily be calculated from it. Sometimes, however, accountants find it convenient to make still other cost calculations. Thus, in Column (5) of Table 2, there is listed *average or unit cost* of production. This is easily derived by dividing total cost by the number of units of output in order to get the average cost per unit. (Too much importance should not be attached to average costs because, after all, it is *total* dollar profit and costs that interest any firm.)

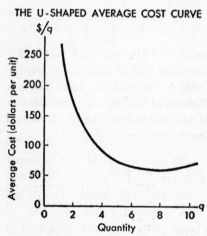

THE U-SHAPED AVERAGE COST CURVE

$/q

Average Cost (dollars per unit)

250
200
150
100
50
0

0   2   4   6   8   10   q

Quantity

FIGURE 3. The average cost curve is computed by dividing total cost by the number of units of production, as given in Table 2.

Average costs are very high at first because the large fixed costs are saddled on to so few units. In fact, when output is zero, costs per unit have to be infinite. If only one unit were produced, average costs would be $320. But as more units are produced, the $256 of fixed cost is spread over more and more units. This explains the early rapid decline of average costs in Table 2 and in Figure 3.

After the overhead has been spread thin over many units, fixed costs can no longer have much influence on average costs. Variable costs become important, and as average variable costs begin to rise because of limitations of plant space and management difficulties, average costs finally begin to turn up. Thus, in Table 2, Column (5), and in Figure 3, average costs are at their lowest at 8 units, where they are only $60 per unit. Expanding output beyond this point causes average costs to rise. Thus, the average curve is U-shaped: falling at first because of spreading the overhead and economies of mass production, but ultimately rising because of diminishing returns.

Marginal Cost. The businessman must decide how much to produce so as to make the greatest profits. He will be more interested, therefore, in the *extra* costs of changing output rather than in over-all average costs.

Column (6) of Table 2 lists the difference in total costs for each extra unit of output. Such extra costs are important enough in economic theory to rate a new and distinctive name: *marginal cost.* Thus, the marginal cost in going from the fifth unit to the sixth unit is derived from Column (4) by subtracting the total cost of 5 units from the total cost of 6 units. This gives $400 − $381, or $19. (What is the marginal cost in going from the eighth to the ninth unit? Why?)

MARGINAL REVENUE AND PRICE

In a similar way, we define *marginal revenue* as the extra revenue resulting from selling an *extra* unit of goods. Marginal revenue would be derived from the total revenue column of Table 1. This is indicated in Table 3, which repeats Table 1 but has one new column for marginal revenue.

At first, the reader may wonder why there is any difference between price, Column (2), and marginal revenue, Column (4). In going from 2 to 3 units of output, why isn't marginal revenue equal to the price at which the third unit is sold? Why isn't it, therefore, $114 instead of the indicated figure of $94?

True, the third unit is sold for $114. But to get it sold, we had to cut the price on the previous 2 units by $10 each (from $124 to $114). This loss on the previous units must be charged up against the third unit in reckoning marginal revenue; thus, the marginal revenue is $114 − (2 × $10), or $94. Generally speaking, marginal revenue is less than the price, as indicated by the fundamental formula:[1]

[1] The interested reader might check the relationship between price and marginal revenue in Table 3 at some one or more points, by calculating the loss in revenue resulting from the price reduction necessary to get the last unit sold.

Marginal revenue of nth unit = difference in total revenue in going from (n − 1) to n units = price of nth unit − loss in revenue on previous units resulting from price reduction

Only under perfect competition, where the sale of extra units will never depress price at all, is the second loss-in-revenue term zero. Only then will price and marginal revenue be identical. This explains why a competitive firm need never advertise in order to increase its sales at the existing price, and why it has all the business it wants at the prevailing price.

TABLE 3. *Marginal Revenue and Price*

Quantity q (1)	Price p (2)	Total revenue $R = p \times q$ (3)	Marginal revenue MR (4)
0	$144 or higher	$ 0	
1	134	134	$134
2	124	248	114
3	114	342	94
4	104	416	74
5	94	470	54
6	84	504	34
*7	*74	*518	14
8	64	512	*
9	54	486	− 6
10	44	440	−26
			−46

* Point of unitary elasticity and zero marginal revenue.

If elasticity of demand as defined in Chapter 20 falls to less than unity, so that the percentage decrease in price always exceeds the percentage rise in quantity sold, any increase in output will actually *lower* total revenue. In other words, marginal revenue will become negative. Why? Because the second term in our formula—the loss on previous units—will outbalance the first term—the price received on the last unit. From the standpoint of personal profit, the firm would do better under such conditions to burn up extra output rather than let it "spoil the market."

MAXIMIZING PROFITS

We may now bring all our relevant facts together in a supertable, Table 4. Total profit is, of course, the column of greatest interest in this table.

What quantity will maximize total profits, and what price? The simplest way to solve this problem is to compute Column (5), total profit, which is simply the difference between total revenue and total cost. Running our eyes down this column tells us that the optimal quantity is 6 units, with a price of $84 per unit. No other situation will give us as much profit as the $104 which that situation brings in.

Another way of arriving at the same result is to compare marginal revenue, Column (6), and marginal cost, Column (7). So long as a step toward extra output gives us more marginal revenue than marginal cost, we continue to produce more output. But whenever marginal cost exceeds marginal revenue, we contract output. Where is equilibrium? *Where marginal cost and marginal*

TABLE 4. *Summary Table Showing Revenue, Cost, and Profit Data for the Firm*

Quantity q	Price p	Total revenue $R = p \times q$	Total cost $TC = FC + VC$	Profit Pro $(5) = (4) - (3)$	Marginal revenue MR	Marginal cost MC	Marginal profit $MR - MC = MPro$ $(8) = (6) - (7)$
(1)	(2)	(3)	(4)		(6)	(7)	
0	$144 or higher	$ 0	$256	−$256			
					$134	$ 64	+$ 70
1	134	134	320	− 186			
					114	20	+ 94
2	124	248	340	− 92			
					94	15	+ 79
3	114	342	355	− 13			
					74	13	+ 61
4	104	416	368	+ 48			
					54	13	+ 41
5	94	470	381	+ 89			
					34	19	+ 15
*6	*84	504	400	+*104			*
					14	31	− 17
7	74	518	431	+ 87			
					− 6	49	− 55
8	64	512	480	+ 32			
					−26	73	− 99
9	54	486	553	− 67			
					−46	103	− 149
10	44	440	656	− 216			

* Optimum or Best-Profit point.

revenue are in balance. Again we are led to the optimal situation of maximum profits.

This second way of finding the optimum point by comparing marginal cost and revenue is neither better nor worse than the first method of simply examining total profits. They are really exactly the same thing, as is shown by Column (8), labeled "marginal profit." This is the difference between marginal revenue and marginal cost; or what is the same thing, the *extra* profit from each additional unit of output. So long as marginal profit is positive, we keep expanding quantity. When marginal profit is negative, we contract output. We are at the optimal equilibrium point when marginal costs cancel out marginal revenue; or what is the same thing, where marginal profit passes from + to − as shown by the star in Column (8).

GRAPHICAL DEPICTION OF FIRM'S OPTIMUM POSITION

The three curves of Figure 4 illustrate this same procedure. *Total revenue* is a hill whose slope is rising as long as demand is elastic, and falling after the demand has become inelastic. *Total costs* are rising, because you usually can't get extra output for nothing. *Total profit* is the difference between total revenue and cost. It is shown in two places on the diagram: directly by the lowest curve, and also as the vertical distance between the two upper curves. At small outputs, total cost exceeds total revenue and the firm cannot break even; again at very large outputs, price is so low and costs so high that it is again "in the red." Somewhere in between is the optimum point of maximum profit.

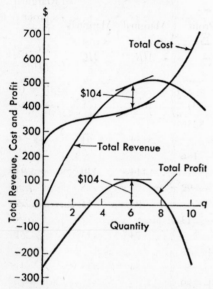

GRAPHICAL DETERMINATION OF OUTPUT WHICH GIVES THE GREATEST TOTAL PROFIT

FIGURE 4. The *total profit* curve represents the difference between the *total revenue* and the *total cost* curves. Total profit is at a maximum when that difference is greatest, *i.e.*, where the slopes of the total cost and revenue curves are parallel and equal.

This optimum quantity is clearly 6 units. This is where total profit is at a maximum. This is where the vertical difference between the two upper curves is greatest.[1]

[1] The optimum price cannot be immediately indicated on this diagram. However, knowing

It is also the quantity at which the slopes of the total revenue curve and the total cost curve are exactly parallel; and where the slope of the total profit curve is zero and horizontal. At any smaller outputs, such as 4 units, the two slopes are widening out; therefore, the vertical distance between the two curves is increasing and the firm will expand its output.

At any output larger than the optimum, the two slopes are narrowing; by moving backward, we can increase the vertical distance between revenue and cost. Only at the optimum point, where the slopes are exactly parallel, will it pay to move neither to the right nor to the left. This is the firm's equilibrium position of maximum profits.

These respective slopes of the total cost and total revenue curves are nothing but our recent acquaintances, marginal cost and marginal revenue. In Figure 5, the same determination of best output is shown in a new way. The MC and MR curves are plotted for each output (either from the data of Table 4 or by reading off the numerical slopes from Figure 4). Where the MC curve exactly intersects the

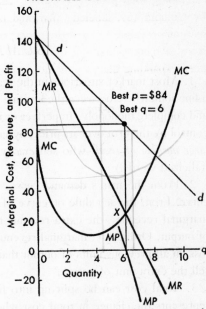

ALTERNATIVE GRAPHICAL
DETERMINATION OF MOST
PROFITABLE OUTPUT AND PRICE

FIGURE 5. The most profitable output is found at the intersection of the marginal revenue and marginal cost curves where marginal profit is zero; the price to be charged for the best output is found by going up to the demand curve.

MR curve, at 6 units, is our most profitable output; at this same output, the curve of marginal profit, $MPro = MR - MC$, passes from plus to minus and crosses the horizontal axis. Now that we know the best quantity is 6 units, we can run up to the demand curve and find our best price (or average revenue) of $84 per unit.

We are once again led back by the geometry to our fundamental rule: profits are at a maximum when

Marginal cost = marginal revenue

the quantity to be 6, we can easily determine the price, $84, by consulting the table; or by running up to the demand curve of Figures 1*b* or 5 at a *q* of 6 units, we can read off price.

The next chapter examines the applicability of these maximizing principles to various realistic industrial situations. The reader interested in how they apply to the interesting but rather unrealistic case of perfect competition is referred to the Appendix to this chapter.

SUMMARY

1. Most market situations in the real world can be thought of as falling on a line somewhere between the limiting extremes of pure or perfect competition and complete monopoly. Imperfect or monopolistic competition involves some control by the firm over its price, by virtue of the fact that there are not *a very large number of rivals* who sell *exactly the same product* as it does. (Note the italicized words.)

2. From the firm's demand curve, we can easily derive its total revenue curve. From the schedule or curve of total revenue we can easily derive its marginal revenue—the extra revenue resulting from the sale of an extra unit of output. Ordinarily, marginal revenue will fall short of price because of the loss on all previous units of output that will result when we drop our price to sell the extra unit of output.

3. Total cost can be split up into fixed and variable costs. Marginal cost represents the change in total cost when we produce an extra unit of output. It is not the same thing as average cost per unit, which is the ratio of total cost to total output. Because of "spreading the overhead" and any economies of scale, the average cost curve at first falls, later rising in a U-shaped fashion as the firm's production begins to near "capacity."

4. A firm will find its maximum profit position where the last little unit it sells brings in extra revenue just equal to its extra cost. This same result can be shown graphically by the equality of the slopes of the total revenue and total cost curves. In any case, *marginal revenue = marginal cost* must hold at the equilibrium position of maximum profit.

QUESTIONS FOR DISCUSSION

1. Describe the distinguishing features of perfect and imperfect competition.

2. What does it mean to say that a corporation charges "what the traffic will bear?"

3. How would you divide these various elements of cost as between fixed and variable costs: payrolls, power and light, taxes, depreciation, executives' salaries, raw materials, etc.?

4. Carefully define marginal revenue. Likewise marginal cost.

5. What is the numerical value of marginal revenue when the demand curve is of unitary elasticity, as in Table 3 of Chapter 20? Why?

6. What would average and marginal cost look like if fixed costs were $100, average variable costs were constant at $10 per unit (total variable costs increasing proportionally with output)? Plot marginal cost, average (total) cost, average variable cost, and average fixed cost on the same diagram.

7. "A lump-sum tax on a firm will have no effect on its best output and price as long as the firm stays in business. Similarly, a 10 per cent tax on a firm's profits will not change its best price or output." Why are these statements true, at least in the short run? Could the same be said of a tax on sales or on each unit of goods produced? Why not?

APPENDIX TO CHAPTER 24
COST IN RELATION TO
COMPETITIVE SUPPLY

There is nothing mysterious about the above relations of profit maximization. They simply represent common sense and elementary arithmetic. There is no reason why they should not apply to the competitive wheat farmer as well as to a firm employed in an imperfectly competitive field.

However, one special feature is present in the case of the perfect competitor. At his optimum position, marginal revenue must, of course, equal marginal cost. But as we earlier learned, the pure competitor can sell all he wishes at a given price. Let us repeat this important characteristic of pure or perfect competition. The market price is given to each small, competitive seller. Marginal revenue and price then turn out to be identical, there being no loss on previous units to be subtracted from the price received from the extra unit sold.

We may combine the above statements, therefore, and say that a perfect competitor, who has no fear of spoiling the market, will always produce up to the point where marginal costs begin to exceed price; or as his equilibrium condition, we have

•   **Marginal cost = price**

Now we can predict how much the firm will supply at different prices. If we retain our previous costs, we may read from Figure 6 on page 510 the supply schedule for the firm in terms of price. Thus, if the price is $100, it will pay to produce 9 units but not 10. This is because the $100 horizontal price line in Figure 6 intersects the steps of marginal cost at 9 units. Or referring back to the cost data of Column (6) of Table 2, we see that it pays to produce every additional unit up to the tenth, because that one costs $103 extra and brings in only an additional $100.

This assumes that *fractions* of a unit cannot be produced and sold. Why should we rule out fractions? Of course, a farmer cannot sell one-third of an egg, but he certainly can sell one-third of a carload of eggs. Even if single eggs represent our units of measurement, he can sell eggs at the rate of 1 every 3 hours, which is one-third of an egg per hour. The smooth curve in Fig. 6 shows marginal costs when our units are made indefinitely divisible. It, rather than the irregular steps, enables us to determine the exact quantity response of the firm to different prices.[1]

[1] The careful reader will already have noted that we used continuously divisible units

Thus, when the market price at which the firm can sell is $100 per unit, production will be pushed to the point marked *A*, or to about 9.4 units. Only at that quantity does marginal cost equal price. Only there are its profits at a maximum when price is $100.

As the price drops to $80, the firm will supply only the units shown at point *B*, or about 8.9 units. This is because the dotted marginal cost curve intersects the $80 price line at that output.

Suppose the price were only $70. What would the firm supply? The $70 price line is seen to intersect the dotted *MC* curve twice: once at around 8.4 units and again at around 0.2 unit. Our formula, price = *MC*, is ambiguous. It gives too many answers. Which is the right one?

There is only one final test. We must compute total profit and see where it is larger. The answer is quite obvious. The larger output is the correct one. For if the firm produces only around 1 unit, its revenue is $70 × 1, its cost in Table 2 = $320, and its profits are around −$250. But if it produces about 8 units, its profits are about ($70 × 8) − $480 or about $80. The best output, therefore, is at *C*, not at *C′*.

It is not difficult to patch up our price = *MC* rule so that it will not let us down again and make us recompute profit. When price or marginal revenue

---

whenever we identified marginal cost with the geometrical slope of the total cost curve. Actually, we have been using two slightly different concepts of marginal cost, as the accompanying diagram makes clear.

THE RELATION BETWEEN SLOPE AND MARGINAL COST

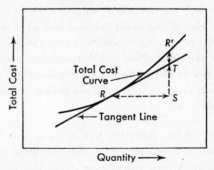

Two slightly different versions of marginal cost are shown on this diagram. The distance from *R* to *S* represents one extra unit of output. The distance from *S* to *R′* represents the resulting increase in total cost, which is the first and simplest definition of marginal cost. The second definition is given by the slope of the total cost curve at the point *R*, or what is the same thing numerically, by the distance from *S* to *T*. In the limit as the size of the extra units becomes small, the discrepancy between the two definitions—or *TR′*—becomes relatively negligible.

equals marginal cost, we can only be sure that profit is standing still. But whether it is leveling off "at the top of the hill of profits," or "at the bottom of the valley," our formula does not tell us. We must, therefore, add to the

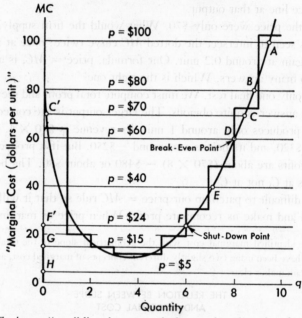

USE OF MARGINAL COST CURVE TO
DETERMINE SUPPLY RESPONSE OF
FIRM TO VARYING PRICES

FIGURE 6. The heavy "step" line shows marginal cost when the units of production are indivisible. The heavy curved line shows marginal cost when the units are infinitely divisible. Given a market price, as represented by each horizontal line above, a firm will produce up to the point of its intersection with that part of the marginal cost curve which is rising. Thus at a price of $40 a firm would produce about 7.1 units. At any price below $24, the firm will prefer to shut down and produce nothing rather than fail to recover even its variable costs.

$MR = MC$ requirement the condition that *marginal cost must be shooting up more rapidly than marginal revenue*. At C this condition was met; at C' the opposite condition held. A little calculation shows that this fact makes C' the worst rather than the best place to be. It pays to move to either the right or the left of that point, because profits are there at a minimum.

DECREASING COSTS AND THE BREAKDOWN OF PERFECT COMPETITION

From now on our rule under perfect competition must take the form

Price = marginal cost, and marginal cost must be rising

Alternatively, we can say that the supply curve of the firm consists of only that part of the U-shaped marginal cost curve (in Figure 6) which is rising. For, if marginal cost is falling, the firm has every reason to expand its output further, since each new step brings it the same extra revenue but lower extra cost.

This second part of our rule is not just a theoretical refinement. It shows us how and why competition tends to break down! Technology of a given industry often becomes more and more complicated so that efficient production is possible only on a gigantic scale. Until this scale is reached, average and marginal costs tend to fall. Competitive firms tend, therefore, to expand their output. A period of cutthroat or ruinous competition may follow in which all firms have heavy losses. Finally, those few firms which have the most resources or which enjoyed the earliest start will drive the others out of the field, leaving us no longer with perfect competition but with monopolistic competition.

Although other facts than cost were also involved, this seems to be what happened in the automobile industry. Out of a 100-odd American car manufacturers, only a half-dozen of any significance are left. And of these, the "big three," General Motors, Chrysler, and Ford are of predominant importance. The same thing is likely to happen to the "flivver airplane" industry in the next few decades. It does not happen to wheat farming, because each farmer's marginal cost curve turns up long before he becomes sufficiently important to affect the market price. If an invention were discovered which made a million-acre farm the most efficient size, agriculture would cease to be as perfectly competitive as it is.

MINIMIZING LOSSES AND DECIDING WHEN TO SHUT DOWN

Let us return to the supply curve of our hypothetical firm. If price drops to $60, the firm will produce 8 units and will just break even. (This includes wages of managers, and a normal return on invested capital.)

What if price drops down to below $60, the level of lowest average cost? Suppose that times are so hard that the market price is only $40. If the firm produces about 7.1 units, as indicated by the point E where $P = MC$, its total revenue will be around $280 ($40 × 7) while its total costs will be about $431 (see Table 2). The firm is "in the red," producing at a loss of some $140 to $150. Our formula of marginal cost and price seems to have led us to ruin.

But has it? If the firm chooses to shut down completely rather than run at a loss, its revenue will be zero and its fixed costs will still be $256. Obviously, its loss would then be $256, an even greater sum than when it is producing 7.1 units. In other words, equating marginal costs to marginal revenue is optimal even when profits are negative, because in that way losses are kept to a minimum. A perfectly rational businessman will disregard his fixed costs entirely in deciding whether to accept some extra business, for he knows that fixed costs will go on anyway and, therefore, must "cancel out of any decision." As long as he receives total revenue in excess of his variable costs, so that he has something above his out-of-pocket costs, he will be better off to accept the extra business.

What happens if price continues to decrease, down below even $24? At that figure, if the firm produces 6 units, its total revenue will be $144 and its variable cost will be $144. It will be just indifferent between producing or shutting down completely, because in either case it will lose $256.

At any price below $24, say at $15, the firm will not even recover its variable costs. Obviously, therefore, it will choose to shut down. Our marginal cost and price formula is no longer relevant.[1]

We may summarize by saying that any costs that are strictly fixed should be treated as bygones if necessary. "There is no use crying about spilt milk." To make the best of the situation, we minimize our losses by equating marginal cost to price—and marginal cost is unaffected by fixed costs.[2] It is better to earn something above our variable costs which can be applied toward our fixed cost commitments, than to have to pay out fixed costs while receiving nothing.

The above analysis refers to the short run. In the long run our fixed commitments finally expire. Contracts terminate. Buildings wear out, and the decision arises as to whether they should be replaced or contracts renewed. In deciding this question, no costs are (as yet) fixed. In the long run, therefore, the firm is not forced to produce at a loss. It will still produce that output at which marginal cost equals price; but firms will enter or leave the industry until price is just equal to average cost.

Therefore, when there is "free entry," our long-run equilibrium condition for a perfectly competitive firm can be written as

$$\text{Marginal cost} = \text{price} = \text{average cost}[3]$$

[1] It tells us that producing 5 units is better than producing 4 or 6. But all are worse than producing 0 units.

[2] In Column (3) of Table 2, the same fixed costs are in the total cost figures for both the tenth and the ninth unit. Therefore, they cancel out of all marginal cost computations. Why?

[3] This point, where $P = MC = AC$, will be at the bottom of the U-shaped average cost curve. Two different reasons for this can be given. First, if the typical firm were producing at any average cost bigger than the minimum, somebody else—under free entry—could come in and make a profit by selling at the existing price. The second reason is more technical: as long as marginal cost is below average cost, the production of a new unit must pull the average down. Similarly, it can be shown that where the marginal cost curve lies above the average cost curve, the average cost curve must be rising. It follows, therefore, that

FIRM AND INDUSTRY

Now that we have the short-run supply response of the competitive firm, we are able to show exactly how the industry's total supply curve is formed. Figure 7 shows the picture of a typical small firm side by side with that of the whole industry. Note the great difference in scale of quantity along the firm's hori-

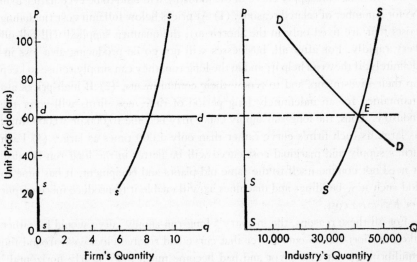

ADDING THE SUPPLY CURVES OF COMPETITIVE FIRMS
TO GET THE SUPPLY CURVE OF THE INDUSTRY

FIGURE 7. The supply curve of the individual firm *ss* consists of two parts, corresponding to the price ranges at which the firm will operate and at which it will shut down. This curve is summed horizontally 5,000 times to get the industry supply curve *SS* assuming that all 5,000 firms are alike. The demand curve for the firm is *dd*, a horizontal straight line, since the output of one firm has a negligible effect on price. Geometrically, *dd* is the same as a very small segment of *DD* around the point *E*, the segment being stretched out to the scale of the firm diagram.

zontal axis as compared to the industry. The picture of the firm can be thought of as representing a thousandfold magnification of a little vertical strip around the equilibrium point of the industry. The industry demand curve *DD* is so stretched horizontally that it appears perfectly flat on the firm's diagram, or as *dd*.

However, the *firm's* supply curve is not flat, but is as indicated. Also, the

---

at the intersection of the marginal and the average cost curves. the average curve must be just standing still, at its minimum value.

The reader should be warned against attaching optimal significance to this minimum *AC* point. The competitive firm is forced there by free entry against its will.

industry's supply curve is nothing but the *sum* of the amounts that all the firms will produce at each of the prices. If all the firms were exactly alike and if there were 5,000 firms in the industry, then the industry supply curve *SS* would be a 5,000-fold exaggeration of the *ss* curve of each firm.[1] It would appear infinitely flatter than the firm's supply curve, were it not for the great change of horizontal scale.

This completes the story of the short-run supply conditions of a competitive firm. The long-run supply curve of the industry will tend to be even flatter than *SS* for a number of related reasons: (1) At prices below full unit cost (including costs that are fixed only in the short run), the quantity supplied will fall off very rapidly. For after all, businesses will not go on producing at a loss indefinitely, if they can help it; and in the long run, they can simply refuse to keep up their investments and to renew their commitments. (2) If high prices are maintained for an indefinitely long period of time, new firms will enter the industry. Thus, the long-run supply curve may become 10,000 or 50,000 times as large as each firm's curve rather than only 5,000 times as large. (3) Each firm's supply and marginal cost curve will be flatter in the long run because it need not confine itself to the same old plants and equipment. It has time to add such new buildings and machines as will enable it to produce more output for less *extra* cost.

For all these reasons, the industry's long-run supply curve would be rather like the short-run *SS* curve after that curve had rotated clockwise around the equilibrium point as a pivot and had become much more nearly horizontal.[2] The student should draw in such a curve and label it *S'S'*.

The history of agriculture in each past war illustrates how supply is more elastic in the long than in the short run. When food prices fly skyward, output does not at first respond very much. But repeated years of prosperity finally send production greatly upward. After the boom has passed, years and years of painfully low prices may be necessary before downward agricultural readjustments are made.

---

[1] If the enterprises are not all alike, and not even two farms in the same county ever are, the industry's supply curve is still the resultant of adding (horizontally) the supply responses of all the individual firms.

[2] In the Appendix to Chapter 21 on Supply and Demand, Cases 1, 2, and 3 illustrated the different degrees of flatness that an industry's supply curve might show.

SUMMARY TO APPENDIX

1. For a perfect competitor marginal revenue and price are exactly the same thing, there being no loss on previous units for him to worry about. The maximum condition, marginal revenue equals marginal cost, can for the perfect competitor be rewritten: Price equals marginal cost. It always pays him to expand his output up to the point where the cost of the last unit begins to exceed the market price of the good.

2. It must follow then that the supply curve of the firm is its marginal cost curve, provided that the curve is rising and provided that the price has not fallen so low that he finds it better to shut down completely rather than fail to recover even his variable costs.

3. If price and marginal cost are in excess of the firm's average cost, it will be making a positive profit. If price and marginal cost are below the firm's average cost, it will be making a loss; if this continues for a long time, it will prefer eventually to go out of business rather than reinvest its money in replacing its worn-out plant. If new competitive firms can come into the industry and produce at the same cost as the given firm, any positive profits (in excess of a "normal return" on capital and labor invested) will in the long-run equilibrium be competed away. In this final equilibrium price and marginal cost will both be equal to minimum average cost.

4. The sum of all the firms' short-run supply curves gives the industry's supply curve. In the long run, when the number of firms in the industry can change, the industry's supply curve will become flatter and more elastic.

5. If production of a given commodity is subject to decreasing marginal costs, then a few firms will expand to dominate the market and perfect competition will be impossible.

QUESTIONS FOR DISCUSSION

1. Explain in common-sense terms why you as a perfect competitor would make $MC = P$.

2. How does total revenue look to a perfect competitor? Make a drawing of total cost and revenue, showing the maximum profit point.

3. When would you decide to shut down a plant?

4. Why is a falling *MC* curve never a supply curve? (Hint: Show that competition would then become "cutthroat" or "ruinous.")

5. "If there is free competitive entry of new firms, price must fall to the level of minimum average costs." Show why *P* cannot in the long run be lower or higher than this equilibrium level.

6. How is the supply curve of the industry related to firm's cost: in the short run and in the long run?

Chapter 25: PATTERNS OF

IMPERFECT COMPETITION

THE LAST chapter has now paved the way for a bird's-eye view of the actual market structure of modern-day industry. How do firms go about setting their prices? What is the role of the theoretical tools used in the last chapter to analyze profit maximization? What are some of the important patterns of imperfect competition? Finally, what dilemmas for public antitrust policy do they raise?

DO FIRMS MAXIMIZE PROFITS?

To what degree do businessmen actually try to maximize their profits? To what extent do they succeed if they do try to do so? These are not easy questions to give any precise answer to. Certainly this much is true: If a firm is absolutely reckless in calculating its costs and revenues, then the Darwinian law of the survival of the fittest will probably eliminate it from the economic scene.

Therefore, those firms which actually do manage to survive cannot be completely oblivious to the maximization of profits. But that does not necessarily mean that every firm is seeking desperately to squeeze out the last little ounce of profit from every transaction. As soon as it becomes of any considerable size, it can afford to relax a little in its maximizing activities. Moreover, it is probably good business to take the long view and not concentrate on purely immediate gains. Many acts of altruism and apparent generosity can be amply defended in terms of public relations and the maximization of long-run profits.

Consider a firm that is maximizing its profits in a fairly sensible manner. Does that mean it is calculating elaborate geometrical curves of cost and revenue and from them deriving elaborate measures of marginal cost and revenue? Obviously not, as you will soon learn if you inquire about current business practices. Even if the firm itself is not approaching the problem with conscious awareness of the particular marginal tools of the theoretical economist, to the extent that it truly is making a pretty fair guess as to where its highest profits are realized, it will be making extra revenue and extra cost approximately equal. It does this without curves, just by feeling its way to the optimum by trial and error.

FULL-COST PRICING

One of the reasons why business is a fascinating activity is the fact that inexact guesses must be made on the basis of incomplete information. It is no small task for a large or small business to make an estimate of the shape of the demand curve for its products. A railroad can only guess whether a 20 per cent reduction in fares will bring it many more customers. A radio company has no exact way of judging the elasticity of demand for its many products.

Realistically speaking, we must recognize that modern business firms—even the largest—cannot accurately determine marginal revenue and marginal cost. They cannot determine their optimum price and output with nice exactitude. Yet the day's work must somehow get done. Prices must be set on their products. Here is where average cost or unit cost often plays an important role.

Put yourself in the position of the president of a company producing many products where prices are at its disposal. Your last year's sales are known to you, but your next period's sales can only be guessed even if you leave prices unchanged. Not knowing the extent or elasticity of demand for your products, you will be unable to determine marginal revenue. What will you do?

Probably, you will call in your accountants and sales managers. "Boys," you will say, "what will our volume of output approximately be if we stay on our toes and keep our share of the market?" In making their answers, the sales force will have to guess at the probable level of business activity, consumers' needs, etc.

After they have made their estimates, you will turn to the cost experts and probably ask for the unit cost of producing each product in question at those levels of output. There will be plenty of headaches in aiming at any sort of figure. For example, how shall the administrative and plant overhead costs be allocated between different products? Or if a given process simultaneously creates joint products like meat and hides, how shall the costs be allocated between them? Or if a building will last for many years, how much should be charged against current operations?

Headache or no headache, it is the duty of the accountants to come out with some sort of answer as to unit costs. Management must now decide by how much to mark up price over the cost figure. Depending upon its estimate of the consumers' reaction and the pricing policy of its competitors, the firm may perhaps decide on a 5, 10, or 30 per cent markup.

In bad times when price competition is particularly keen, businessmen may even set prices at less than "full costs" because of the realization that fixed expenses will go on whether or not production is at a low level. But price will never be set below unit *variable* costs unless the item in question is being used as a "loss leader" to attract other business now and in the future, or unless the firm is willing to incur temporary losses in order to crush a rival and drive him out of business completely.

BREAK-EVEN CHARTS

Businessmen often speak of their break-even points. You will hear them complain that postwar union wage demands have raised the level of their break-even points to a dangerous degree, so that, if there is any slackening of the peak full-employment levels of sales, then profits may soon turn into losses. What is meant by the concept of a "break-even point"?

Usually it means the following: In many industries, it turns out that variable costs increase pretty much in direct proportion to output. Double output and you double total variable costs; triple output and you triple total variable costs; no matter how you change output, as long as you stay within the limits of your plant's capacity, unit variable costs seem to be just about a constant. If this is a tolerable approximation to the truth, then your total cost curve has been simplified down to being a straight line.

Let us further suppose that you have already fixed upon the price you are going to charge. Probably you used some sort of markup rule to do so, but however you made your decision does not much matter. With your unit variable costs constant for each extra bit of output, and with your revenue from that bit of output constant, it is clear that your profits will grow with your sales. As a matter of fact, at small outputs you will not even be earning enough to cover your fixed costs; but as your sales increase, this loss will dwindle and you will reach a point where you just cover your fixed costs (in addition to variable costs for that output). Your sales have now reached the break-even point.[1]

Beyond this break-even point, your profits will begin to materialize. Anything you can do to increase your sales will be all to the good. Figure 1 gives a geometrical picture of a break-even point chart. *OR* shows how your revenue

[1] This should not be confused with the break-even point of consumption and income met in Part Two's discussion of saving. There is only a geometrical resemblance between the two concepts.

grows as you succeed in selling more goods at the same price. *FC* shows how your costs grow from the initial fixed-cost point *F* to the level of plant capacity *C*, where costs begin to shoot up rapidly. The break-even point is at *B*. If your sales fall below this level, you are incurring losses, whose magnitude is shown by the vertical broken lines between the two schedules. If your sales increase beyond the break-even point, your profits increase more and more, as

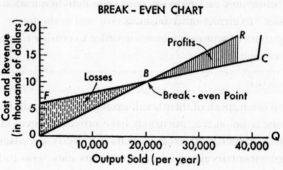

BREAK - EVEN CHART

FIGURE 1. This shows how profits grow as sales increase beyond the break-even point *B*.

measured by the vertical solid lines between the two schedules. By locating his position on a chart such as this one, the businessman is constantly stimulated to reconsider his price policy, his production methods, and his sales-promotion techniques.

Many investigators of actual business pricing policies have testified that corporations often do follow the above described practice of quoting prices on a "cost and markup" basis, hoping thereby not only to recover their "full cost outlays," but also to make a return on their investments. This theory is therefore realistic, but it is not very informative. It stops tantalizingly short of telling us *why* the average markup is 40 per cent in one industry and 5 per cent in another; or why, before the war, one large firm in the automobile industry was able to earn 30 per cent of the book value of its invested capital while another firm almost as large could earn only about ½ of 1 per cent on its capital.

There seems to be nothing to do about this unsatisfactory situation but try to specify a number of different competitive and monopolistic patterns characteristic of various important industrial situations. Four important patterns, intermingling monopoly and competition, are discussed in the remaining pages of this chapter.

ILLUSTRATIVE PATTERNS OF PRICE

1. *Chronically Overcrowded Sick Industries.* Many fields are characterized by an excessive number of firms. Most of these do a small volume of business

and remain in the industry only until they have lost their capital. Grocery stores, taverns, restaurants, night clubs, and gasoline stations are typical examples taken from retail trade. But much the same thing is true of the textile industry, the dress trade, and many other industries that require very little initial capital.

Why don't such unprofitable concerns leave the industry? The answer is that they do. But as fast as they leave, new firms enter the industry, leaving the total number unchanged or even growing.

Why do new firms enter the industry in the face of the fact that most existing firms are making losses? Apparently, partly out of ignorance and partly because "hope springs eternal." An old couple putting their lifetime savings of a few thousand dollars into a little retail grocery store do so in the belief that *their* venture will be different, theirs will succeed—and anyway, in the grocery business no one need starve. But alas, with no special business aptitude and with less than the minimum amount of capital necessary for efficient operation, they last in business only until their original capital has gone.

Or in the dress trade, a worker will often save his money in order to become his own boss. He knows that most concerns are not covering their costs, but he also has heard of a few lucky firms whose special "novelty styles" have become a smash hit and have yielded large monetary profits. Even though the odds are heavily weighted against the new entrant, he is willing to buy a ticket in the sweepstake of success.

These chronically overcrowded industries need not be what the economist has called "perfectly competitive"—although in the case of agriculture or "cotton gray goods," they may happen to be so. Too many firms in such a competitive industry is a bad thing, involving as it does wastes of resources and losses. But at least in such a competitive industry the consumer partly gains, through lower prices, what the producers are losing.

Unfortunately, in most chronically overcrowded sick industries market competition is quite imperfect. Being inefficient producers, the small concerns do not sell very cheaply. Instead of competing on a price basis, they tend to charge fairly high prices and simply to divide the business. The resulting economic situation under this form of monopolistic competition may be worse even than under complete monopoly: not only is price excessive, but in addition valuable resources are wasted because each firm has too much idle plant and manpower. The situation is triply bad: producers make losses, resources are wasted, and the prices charged the consumer are too high.

It is to be feared that the liberal credit terms to veterans under the G.I. Bill of Rights may accentuate this problem of injudicious investment by small businessmen into already sick occupations and industries. The only thing that can be said for such small businesses is that they make jobs. But the jobs they make are largely an illusion as far as pay is concerned, and represent boon-doggling of as reprehensible and unnecessary a kind as would public-works projects aimed at simply digging holes and filling them in again.

2. *The Case of Few Sellers of Identical Products.* At the other extreme are industries in which there are only two, three, or a few sellers, all producing almost exactly the same products. In such cases, there is always the temptation for each firm to try to undersell the others by the least little bit in the hope of getting a larger share of the total business.

This explains, for example, the railroad price wars of the past century. Customers shipping goods from Chicago to New York will always pick the route that offers even a few pennies of extra cheapness. Thus, each of the three or four trunk lines would intermittently undercut the existing rate schedules, until finally a disastrously low level of rates was reached. At the same time, for short hauls where shippers had no alternative, the railroads would jack up the rates—thus creating an anomalous, discriminatory pattern of charges. The Interstate Commerce Commission was established in 1887 to regulate railroad rates and earnings and prevent such unstable price conditions.

Even without government regulations, in industries characterized by heavy overhead costs and identical products, there usually grows up the realization that competition is ruinous. Formal or informal meetings are held, whose theme song is "We're all in it together." Each firm is taught the lesson that other firms will not stand idly by while it cuts its prices; rather they too will cut their prices, so that everyone will end up worse off.

Therefore, tacitly or explicitly, the firms try to agree on a price that maximizes the profits of all. Trade associations, keeping one eye on the Justice Department lawyers who enforce the Sherman Antitrust Act, may impose penalties on any chiseler in the industry who makes secret price concessions. Occasionally, as new conditions or firms upset the *status quo* in the industry, another price war may break out—to last until everyone has again learned his lesson and the morale of the industry is restored.

In finishing with this second pattern, we must note that the desire of corporations to earn a fair return on their past investments may be at variance with the well-being of the consumer. Too much plant capacity may have been built in the industry in the past; but that isn't justification for continuing high prices and scarce output. Competition, which the businessman regards as destructive, cutthroat, and ruinous may actually be the only way to get the redundant plant capacity into operation or to discourage its maintenance. (Having made the mistake of building the plants, society ought not to add the further error of failing to use them to best advantage.) Losses or subnormal profits is the free-enterprise way of discouraging excess capacity.

The steel and other metal industries are examples of this pattern of imperfect competition. They are naturally very fearful that the additional plant capacity built during the war may make maintenance of an "orderly" price structure difficult in the years following the immediate postwar period.

3. *Monopolies Maintained by Constant Research and Advertising.* Still another common industrial pattern is that of a firm that has considerable control over price by virtue of its technological efficiency, its patents, its trade-marks, and its slogans. Its "monopoly profits" are plowed back into further research and advertising, so it is always able to keep abreast or ahead of its rivals. General Motors, duPont, and General Electric are perhaps typical of such companies. In setting prices, a "reasonable" markup over computed unit costs is introduced. Long-run considerations such as the possibility of developing new mass markets keep the firm from "charging all that the traffic will bear" in the immediate future. Moreover, fears of new rivals and aroused public opinion often keep the corporation from being "hoggish" in setting prices.

Because research and advertising are expensive and their results cumulative, success tends to breed success, and profits tend to breed more profits. Therefore, small business cannot always effectively compete with such firms. While admitting the efficiency and progress of some of the monopolists described, critics go on to argue that society would be *still* better off if the full advantages of efficiency were passed on to consumers, or plowed back into research aimed at technological improvements and not simply at profits, if less advertising dollars were spent on "soap operas" and jingles, and if more research dollars went into fundamental science rather than into patentable gadgets. Obviously, this is a controversial subject, upon which each citizen must form his own final judgment.

4. *Publicly Regulated Monopolies.* As a last case, let us consider a "perfect" monopoly licensed by the state and under government regulation. Such public utilities include gas and light companies, telephone and communication services, railroads and public carriers, etc. Since it is obviously uneconomical to have two local sets of telephone wires, an exclusive franchise is given to a single company. (Why is not the same thing true of milk delivery?)

But having given the utility company a complete monopoly, the state steps in to protect the consumer by setting maximum rates. Usually this is done by public regulating commissions, which specify the maximum prices that can be charged for each kind of service.

In setting such prices it has long been customary to pick prices that will try to give the company a fair return on its capital. Rates such as 5, 6, or 7 per cent are often selected as representing a fair return.

Much more complex is the question of determining the *capital value* base of the company to which this "fair rate" is to be applied. Three measures of fair capital value have been suggested at one time or another: (1) *original cost* (minus depreciation), or the sum of all past prudent investments; (2) *current reproduction cost* (minus depreciation), or the cost of replacing the company's equipment at present prices, corrected for the age and condition of the property; and (3) *capitalized market value* of the public utility's securities or assets.

Of these methods, the third is universally recognized to be nonsensical. As was shown in the earlier discussion of interest and capital (Chapter 3)[1] and good will (Chapter 6), the market value of any income-earning property is given by capitalizing its annual return by the interest rate. For a regulating authority to use capitalized market value as a base for measuring capital would be tantamount to recognizing *any level of earning*, high or low, as fair. Once having been capitalized, excessively high earnings will appear as only moderate interest returns, and the same is true of excessively low earnings. The method of capitalized earnings begs the question that the authorities must answer!

The American courts have, therefore, vacillated between *original* cost and *reproduction* cost. So long as the general price level does not change, the two are not very different. But over a period of decades, when prices may greatly increase, reproduction cost will involve higher earnings and rates than original costs. In periods of declining prices, the reverse discrepancy is to be observed: the use of original cost leads to greater leniency to the nonspeculative investors in public-utility securities. But reproduction cost leads to a more flexible price structure and gives less weight to the dead hand of past costs.[2]

BRIEF HISTORY OF ANTITRUST POLICY

Around the turn of the century, America went through a period of widespread trust formation. Small companies were merged into large; big and small

[1] This matter is more fully discussed in Chapter 29.

[2] From the standpoint of the advanced discussions of "welfare economics," neither method is ideal. Writers in this field have set up a perfectionist formula which would involve pricing of public-utility services at not more than the extra or marginal costs of services. However, this is a radical doctrine which, as a practical matter, few economists would endorse. It could lead to excessive returns to the owners if demand was large in comparison with capacity. But more likely, it would lead to inadequate returns to original investors. Although the state could then, if it wished to, secure by a subsidy justice for investors without interfering with desirable output or price, this would represent a departure from present practice.

The great Federal power projects such as the TVA and Bonneville Dam are from one viewpoint partial approaches toward such a system of pricing. However, the fact that the government can raise capital in larger sums and at lower costs than private industry, and the fact that the same set of dams can simultaneously achieve the ends of national defense, navigation, flood control, and irrigation make any simple yardstick comparison between private and public operations impossible.

companies combined collusively to limit supply and raise price. Huge stock-market promotion schemes flourished.

The public was naturally growing concerned over the growth of monopoly. In 1890, the Sherman Antitrust Act was passed, making it illegal to monopolize trade or to conspire in restraint of trade. On paper, this Act represented a major advance over the previous common-law restrictions on monopolistic conspiracies. But it was adopted with little discussion, indeed without attracting much attention of a favorable or unfavorable nature; and beyond an antipathy toward "monopoly," there is no evidence that anyone had clear notions concerning which actions were to be regarded as legal or illegal.

In the early 1900's, the Republican administrations of Theodore Roosevelt and William Howard Taft witnessed the first surge of activity under the Sherman Act. Thus, the Supreme Court prevented Morgan and Harriman from using a holding company to bring about a merger of their Northern Pacific Railroad with Hill's Great Northern. Later, the Supreme Court ordered the American Tobacco Company and Standard Oil each to be broken up into a number of separate companies.

By the end of this first period, the Supreme Court had enunciated the "rule of reason": Only *unreasonable* restraints of trade (agreements, mergers, predation, and the like) were to come within the scope of the Sherman Act and to be considered illegal. The Clayton Antitrust Act (1914), in addition to seeking to exclude labor from antitrust action, tried to define illegal behavior more specifically, so that all matters would not have to be left to the subjective opinion of federal judges; but the problem of defining proper norms was left as vague as ever. The U.S. Steel case affords a good example of the state of affairs in the period which followed the burst of antitrust activity under Roosevelt and Taft. This case began before World War I, but the arguments persisted until it was finally settled in 1920, when the Court held that U.S. Steel was not a monopoly. Mere bigness was not of itself a crime if the corporation in question behaved with proper discretion.

During the 1920's, antitrust action languished somewhat. And with the coming of the depression in the early 1930's, people ceased to worry about price increases; pressure came from business—especially small business—for legislation to keep prices *up* rather than down. This culminated in the "NRA codes," established by industry committees under the National Industrial Recovery Act (1933). These codes blatantly and shamelessly provided for collusive action to keep prices from being cut by means of vigorous competition. The NRA was later declared unconstitutional, but from the mid-1930's there stemmed much federal and state legislation designed to restrict *competition*—not monopoly! Thus, under the Robinson-Patman Act, a businessman could not try to increase his sales by selling part of his product under a different brand name at a "below-cost" price. And the Miller-Tydings Act opened the way for all kinds of state laws requiring "resale price maintenance," *i.e.*, laws to prevent any store from selling brand-name merchandise at less than some established fair-cost level.

Since 1938, the government's Antitrust Division has taken a new lease on life. The number of its staff has now increased a hundredfold over the days of Teddy Roosevelt. Prosecutions and court cases have greatly increased in number. A businessman now looks over his shoulder before he dictates any letter that might appear damaging in an antitrust action. Thurman Arnold, prewar head of Antitrust, even attempted to tackle the building industry with its notoriously backward technology. Industries such as glass, cigarettes, cement and many others have all come under heavy attack.

DILEMMAS OF PUBLIC POLICY

We cannot enter upon the vast and important literature that has grown up around the legal technicalities and economic aspects of antitrust policy. The striking thing to the economist is the difficulty of defining any proper public policy. He feels that lawyers and the courts have concentrated on the letter of the law, without any means of defining its spirit with any precision. If a businessman should be caught with an indiscreet set of letters in his files, the Court throws the book at him. But if another company has consistently done the same thing in less overt fashion, it is immune from prosecution. The legal mind is not so much concerned with the height of prices, which it has no means of measuring, as it is with the methods by which prices are set. But the economist is still in a dilemma. Years ago, economists used to regard perfect competition as the ideal; any deviation from it was regarded as a "bad thing." Today, we realize that all the world is an exception to perfect competition. Were we to chop off the head of everyone who is an imperfect competitor, there would be few heads left. Where then shall we draw the line? How shall we define "reasonably effective" or "workable" competition? This is one of the most important problems facing economists today, and it calls for further careful study.[1]

---

[1] Paradoxically, for all its inconsistencies and indeterminacies, the American antitrust program seems, in the opinion of many specialists, on balance to have done a great deal of good. It seems to have served as a preventative of some of the grossly monopolistic practices that exist in the European countries lacking similar legislation.

SUMMARY

1. Few business firms are able to develop exact curves of cost and revenue. This does not mean that they are oblivious to profit maximization. In terms of trial and error, they may be doing a tolerably good job of keeping alive as a business entity and of achieving long-run optimum profits.

2. Under imperfect competition, a firm may have to make rough guesses in setting its price. Often it will use some kind of a markup over an estimate of unit cost. Break-even point charts may play an active role in the businessman's thinking about the pricing problem.

3. Nonetheless, it is market conditions that usually determine how much of a markup any firm can safely count on getting; so in a sense the problem is merely reposed. Only factual investigations of each situation can tell what the result is likely to be.

4. Chronically sick industries characterized by overentry, the case of few sellers of substantially identical commodities, quasi monopolies maintained by diligent research and new product development, and regulated public utilities represent only four out of a great many possible patterns.

5. Public policy with respect to the antitrust problem raises deep and important questions. Once economists realize that perfect competition is not a universally attainable norm, the problem of defining and attaining "effectively workable" competition becomes paramount.

QUESTIONS FOR DISCUSSION

1. Give examples of behavior by business firms suggesting that they do seek to maximize their profits. Give some apparent exceptions.

2. Suppose you ran a large electric company. How would you go about maximizing profits? How would you estimate elasticity of demand? Would reading an economic textbook be the way to learn how to be successful in this respect?

3. What is meant by full-cost pricing? Give examples of how this might work.

4. Explain the assumptions underlying a break-even chart. Is it just a special case of the last chapter's Figure 4? Where would your profits be greatest on such a chart? Are you free to move there of your own volition?

5. Describe the pattern of competition and monopoly in the automobile industry, the cigarette industry, the aluminum industry, the mousetrap industry, the women's dress trade, the retail grocery trade, the barbershop trade.

6. (a) A perfectly rational entrepreneur will disregard his fixed costs in setting price. (b) Heavy fixed or overhead costs often make for cutthroat or ruinous competition which leads to monopoly and the death of competition. Are these two statements consistent?

7. "The tragedy of monopolistic competition often has nothing to do with excessive profits. Rather there may be no profits at all, the high price being frittered away in small volume and inefficient production." Discuss.

8. "It is Utopian to try to break monopolies up into even a few effectively competing units, because the basic cause of monopoly is the law of decreasing cost with mass production and, in any case, a few competitors are not enough to duplicate the pricing patterns of perfect competition." Discuss both parts of this statement.

9. "The A and P Company is not bad just because it is big." Discuss.

PART FOUR

Distribution of Income:

The Pricing of

Productive Factors

Chapter 26: THEORY OF

PRODUCTION AND MARGINAL-

PRODUCTS

IN THE next few chapters of Part Four, we are primarily concerned with how factors of production get priced in the market place—with the determination of (1) *rents* of land and other resources, (2) *wages* of various kinds of labor, (3) *interest* rates on capital assets, and (4) *profits*. But first in this chapter, we must investigate how business firms combine the different factors of production in order to produce commodities most cheaply. The theory of *production* is an important part of the theory of distribution; for, at the same time that the problem of For Whom is being resolved, the problem of How factors of production are used to produce goods is also being resolved.

Distribution is treated here after the earlier discussion of the mechanism by which supply and demand determine What shall be produced and at what price. But in real life it is much like the question: Which came first, the chicken or the egg? You cannot fully analyze the demand for bread until you already know what people's incomes are; and you can't know how high people's wages will be bid, until you already know what the market for products is likely to be. In real life these problems of commodity and factor pricing are all resolved simultaneously from day to day, with mistakes always being made and always being in a process of continual correction.

THE TWO PROBLEMS OF PRODUCTION THEORY

Every businessman must solve two related problems: (1) He must learn how to produce each output as cheaply as possible, and (2) he must find which of all possible outputs is the most profitable one to aim at. The problem of the Best-Profit output has already been discussed in Chapter 24, and a brief review

531

is all we shall require. But before this review, let us turn to the first problem of the Least-Cost combination of factors of production.

DETERMINING THE LEAST-COST COMBINATION OF FACTORS

As president of a large company I call in my production engineers and cost accountants and I say to them: With present-day wages, rents, and machine costs, how shall we combine labor and land and machines if we want to produce 50,000 yards of cloth per month as cheaply as possible? How shall we best combine these same factor inputs if we want to step up production to 100,000 yards per month or down to 25,000 per month? How do our decisions change when market wages and other factor prices change?

To answer these questions the accountants must first learn the physical facts of life from the engineers: If we use x units of labor, y units of land, and z units of a certain kind of machinery, how much will our physical output of cloth be? Can we produce this same physical volume by using more machinery and less labor? If so, exactly how much machinery will be necessary to take the place of each man?

These are all detailed quantitative technical questions. Only after the cost accountants have the technological information well in hand can they start making their money cost calculations. Perhaps they will estimate that with labor at \$2.10 an hour and electric power at $\frac{1}{2}$ cent per kilowatt hour, it will be cheaper to use much machinery and few men to produce the target output of 50,000 yards per month. But if the price of labor fell to \$1 an hour, the opposite decision might lead to lower total cost of production. Then perhaps it would pay to use few machines and many men.

If the output to be aimed at is only 25,000 rather than 50,000, a new Least-Cost decision of how to use the factor inputs can, of course, be made. Occasionally, but by no means always, the cost accountants might decide that, to produce half as much output, we should now hire only half as much of each and every factor: half as much labor, half as many machines, etc. But very often it will be found that there is a new way to combine the factors which will represent the cheapest way to produce the new output; e.g., we may not be able to get rid of our machinery in depression time, so we may then end up using much machinery to produce each bolt of cloth; or if a great expansion of production is aimed at in a postwar boom, we may then decide that we can afford for the first time to use a huge automatic power loom.

In any case, for each different output—$q = 25,000$, $50,000$, $75,000$, etc.— the business firm should be able on the basis of technological engineering data and economic data on factor-prices to make up a neat table showing an estimate of the best total dollar-cost schedule, as in Table 1.

TABLE 1. *Least-Cost Data for Different Outputs**

	Output, yd. per month q	Total cost TC
A	25,000	$ 70,000
B	50,000	100,000
C	75,000	130,000
D	100,000	170,000

* Technology, wage rates, and other factor prices are assumed known.

In real life, of course, such a table could not be perfectly accurate but would have to represent a bold guess based on as much information as is at hand. Note that all the cost curves of the previous chapters involved just such cost data. Only now do we understand how the different cost figures were arrived at.

To summarize briefly: If a firm knows the technical facts of production and market prices for labor, machines, and other inputs, it can determine how much of these factors to hire in order to produce each and every different output of its finished commodities at least expense. For each output, there will be a best combination of the factors—a Least-Cost combination. In this way the firm's demands for the different inputs can be drawn up, and at the same time its Least-Cost curves (total, average, marginal, etc.) can be uniquely arrived at.

FACTOR-PRICES AND THE BEST-PROFIT LEVEL OF OUTPUT

Now we know how the accountants answer the first question put to them by the president of a company—that of finding the Least-Cost factor combination for each level of output. Let us turn to his second question: How much shall we produce and sell each year; how do we find the Best-Profit output?

Until this second question is answered, we really do not know what the final demand of the firm will be for each factor of production; we know only the *schedule* of the different amounts it *would* demand at all different outputs. This will not satisfy our personnel men or machine buyers; they want to know exactly how many men and machines to make contracts for. And that, too, is what interests a congressman worried about the unemployment situation.

Our earlier discussion of maximum net profit, or of marginal revenue equals marginal cost, has already provided us with the answer to this second question. Let us review briefly. We shall ask our market experts what the general shape of the demand curve for our product is like. They will make their best rough estimates, and from these we can compute the total revenue of each different output. Comparing total revenue with our calculated total cost, we shall always increase output as long as marginal revenue is greater than marginal cost, and stop increasing output only when $MR = MC$. Table 2 shows how the demand-revenue data can be combined with our cost data to determine the Best-Profit output at C, or 75,000 units of production per month.

TABLE 2. *Best-Profit Output*

	Output, yd. per month q	Price per yd.* p	Total revenue $p \times q$ TR	Total cost† TC	
A	25,000	$2.40	$ 60,000	$ 70,000	$MR > MC$
B	50,000	2.20	110,000	100,000	$MR > MC$
C	**75,000**	**2.00**	**150,000**	**130,000**	**MR = MC**
D	100,000	1.75	175,000	170,000	$MR < MC$

* From demand curve.
† From Table 1.

We have now seen how the firm makes its production decisions—how it finds all its Least-Cost factor combinations and its Best-Profit output. In the rest of this chapter, we shall see how the amount of each factor demanded will change when its price changes; that is, we shall study the demand curve for each factor of production.

DEMAND FOR FACTORS A DERIVED DEMAND

Why do people demand a finished good like a magazine or an overcoat? They do so because of the satisfaction which they hope to enjoy from its use. But when a businessman demands a factor input, why is that? Surely not for the direct satisfaction that he hopes to get from those inputs. He wants the productive factors because of the production and revenue that he hopes to secure from them.

Satisfactions are in the picture, but at one stage removed. The satisfactions that we consumers get from an overcoat help to determine how much a textile company can sell the coat for and how many coats it can sell. Therefore you would be right in insisting that consumer satisfactions do *ultimately* determine the firm's demand for inputs.

Still, the firm's demand for labor is *derived indirectly* from the consumer demand for its final product. That is why economists speak of the demand for productive factors as a "derived demand!" Effort involved in making coats is of no interest to society for its own sake; we pay men to sew because of the satisfaction to be gained from the finished product. Sometimes the derived demands go through many stages: Wool is wanted to spin yarn; yarn is wanted to weave cloth; cloth is wanted to make coats. All the previous demands are derived from the ultimate consumer demand for the satisfactions to be secured from the finished product.

DEMAND FOR FACTORS A JOINTLY INTERDEPENDENT DEMAND

Another peculiarity about the demand for inputs stems from this technological fact: Factors usually do not work alone. A shovel by itself is worthless to me if I wish a cellar; a man with his bare hands is equally worthless. Together the man and shovel can dig my cellar. In other words, the quantity of a good produced depends *jointly* upon all the available inputs.

We cannot say which is more important in producing a baby—a mother or a father. So, too, we cannot in most cases hope to demonstrate how much of the physical product has been *caused* by any one of the different factors *taken by itself*. The different factors *interact* with each other. Usually they reinforce each other's effectiveness, but sometimes they get in each other's way and compete rather than complement each other.

What are some of the consequences of this jointness or interdependence between the productivities of the different factor inputs? One obvious consequence is this: The amount of labor demanded will depend on its wage rate, but the labor demanded will also depend upon the price of machines. The same is true of the demand for machines. By raising miners' wages, John L. Lewis creates good business for power tools. *Thus, the demand for each input will depend upon the prices of all inputs, not on its own price alone. Cross* elasticities between different factors are as important as regular elasticities.

A FALSE PROBLEM OF CAUSATION

All this every businessman knows, and he has taken it into account in determining the Least-Cost combination of the factors appropriate for each level of production. But please make careful note: The president of a company never has to call in his experts and ask them, "How much of our product was physically caused by labor alone? How much by machine tools alone, etc.?" He would not fire any engineer or accountant who could not answer such a question. He would fire them only if they were wasteful in hiring factors or if they persisted in choosing a level of production that yielded lower profits than some other level. As long as the experts know how much the different inputs cost in the market place, they can always determine how much of the different factors it is best to hire. They do this by systematic trial and error; they never have to worry themselves about insoluble philosophical problems. Even if some newly hired accountant spent his lunch hour puzzling over the problem of how to separate the physical causation of joint product created by the separate factors, what would it matter? Any solution he came up with could be safely disregarded by all concerned. At one time some economists thought this philosophical problem of causation was important for distribution and production theory. It is not, and that is why the point must be strongly insisted on.

MARGINAL-PRODUCT AND DIMINISHING RETURNS

Production theory is treated in detail in the Appendix to this chapter. It is enough here to sketch briefly the important concept of marginal-product that lies behind the factor demand decisions of the firm.

Marginal cost, we know, means extra cost, and marginal revenue means extra revenue. So you would probably guess that marginal-product is just another name for extra product. And you would be right. But to emphasize that we are talking about physical output rather than dollars, we shall be careful to speak of *marginal-physical-product*.

Back in Chapter 2 we already encountered the law of diminishing returns and saw what its consequences were when a variable factor—such as labor— was added more and more to a fixed factor—such as land. Turning back to that chapter, you can translate that discussion into the new language of marginal-product. The result will read something like the following:

Definition: The marginal-physical-product of labor is the number of units of extra product that results when (1) we hold all other productive factors constant and (2) increase labor by 1 unit.

You can similarly write down the definition for the marginal-physical-product of any other productive factor (such as land, shovels, etc.)

The law of diminishing returns tells us that, as we add more and more of a variable factor to given fixed factors, the marginal-physical-product of the variable factor will ultimately decline, becoming lower and lower. (This is because the marginal-physical-product of any factor depends upon the amount of the *other* factors that it has to work with. Give an example.)

EQUALIZATION OF ALL MARGINAL-PHYSICAL-PRODUCTS-PER-DOLLAR

How can the president of a company make sure that his experts have really determined the Least-Cost combination of factor inputs needed to produce any given output? He can ask them, "How many dollars are you spending on hand labor, on skilled labor, on machines, on land, etc.?" He can ask them, "Why don't you hire a little more of land and substitute it for a little less of machines or of hand labor, etc.?"

They would have to reply as follows: "If we hire an extra unit of land, it will cost us, say, $100; the amount of extra product that it gives us—or its marginal-physical-product—will be perhaps 50 units of output. Thus for each extra dollar we spend on land, the *marginal-product-per-dollar* is $50\!\!/\!\!100$, or 0.5, per dollar."

Now suppose that one extra unit of skilled labor costs $4 per hour and the marginal-physical-product resulting from its use is more than 2 units. Then the marginal-product-per-dollar of skilled labor would be more than $2/4$, or more than 0.5, per dollar.

"Aha!" the president would cry out, "you fellows ought to realize that, when you take a dollar from land where its marginal-product-per-dollar is only 0.5 and transfer it to labor where its marginal-product-per-dollar is greater than 0.5, a net gain will result—a saving of expense.

"If, for any two factors A and B, you find

$$\frac{\text{Marg.-phys.-product of } A}{\text{Price of } A} \text{ greater than } \frac{\text{marg.-phys.-product of } B}{\text{price of } B}$$

then you should switch funds from the lower to the higher; you should substitute more of factor A for less of factor B. And keep doing this as long as you can. Of course as you add more and more of A, the law of diminishing returns will probably set in and (1) begin to reduce A's *marginal-product-per-dollar*; and also as you give up more and more of B, the same law of diminishing returns suggests (2) that B's *marginal-product-per-dollar* will begin to rise.

"At some point, perhaps at 0.8 per dollar, they will become equal. And only when they have become equal can you be sure you are at the Least-Cost equilibrium point."

This is good advice. And we can easily see that the same equality of marginal-product-per-dollar must hold for *every* pair of inputs, and for all inputs together there must be a common equality. All this can be summarized in the following first principle:

Marginal-product principle of Least-Cost: Factor substitution must take place until the marginal-physical-product-per-dollar has been equalized for every factor, or until

$$\frac{\text{Marg.-phys.-prod. of A}}{\text{Price of A}} = \frac{\text{marg.-phys.-prod. of B}}{\text{price of B}} = \cdots = \frac{\text{marg.-phys.-prod. of Z}}{\text{price of Z}}$$

Note that the marginal-physical-product of each factor is *proportional* to its price, but it is not *equal* to that price. Nor are marginal-physical-products of the different factors to be made equal to one another—unless factor-prices should all happen to be equal. There is no point in trying to equate a man's product with that of a bulldozer; but the product of an extra dollar spent on each of them should be the same.

The common sense of all this is fairly simple. A consumer maximizes his total satisfaction only when he spends his money on different goods until the marginal utility per dollar has become exactly equal in every use. An eager student will try to reallocate his study of different courses until the last hour spent on each can be estimated to yield the same contribution to his grade average or scholarly fame. A similar equalization rule holds for the substitutions that will minimize cost.

USING LESS OF A FACTOR AS ITS PRICE RISES: SUBSTITUTABILITY

From this fundamental condition of substitutability at Least-Cost equilibrium, an important result immediately follows. If the price of A goes up, that will lower its marginal-product-per-dollar[1] and thereby disturb the equilibrium equality. To restore the Least-Cost balance, we must clearly give up something of the expensive factor and substitute other factors for it. We may trust to the law of diminishing returns to bring up A's marginal-product-per-dollar and to bring down B's and C's marginal-product-per-dollar—until finally a new equilibrium is reached where all are again equal. But in the new equilibrium less of A will be used.

All this may be summarized in the second fundamental principle:

Substitutability Principle: Raising the price of one input relative to the prices of others will tend to reduce the amount of that input demanded, and it will tend to cause other inputs to be substituted for it in producing any given output.

HOW FACTOR PRICE INCREASES CHANGE BEST-PROFIT OUTPUT

Our marginal-product and substitutability principles have shown us how raising the price of an input such as labor will result in firms demanding less of that input. This "substitution-effect" is only part of the story; in addition there will be an "output-effect"—whose usual tendency is to cause even less of the input to be used. Let us see why.

With wages raised, costs of production must tend to be higher. And as long as the demand curve and marginal revenue are unchanged, the firm will now find it most profitable to cut down on its production to the point where the new

---

[1] Thus if we double the price of A, we initially halve the marginal-physical-product-per-dollar. Why? Because price of A appears in the *denominator* of the previous expression for marginal-physical-product-per-dollar.

marginal cost equals marginal revenue. To consumers, this cut in production must, of course, mean higher prices.

How does this output-effect influence the demand elasticity of the factor input whose price has been raised? This cut in production means a *further* drop in the amount of the factor demanded by the firm; *i.e.*, in addition to (1) the substitution-effect on the Least-Cost combination, the amount demanded of the factor is almost sure to go down further because of (2) the curtailment of the Best-Profit level of output.

This output-effect is also likely to curtail the demand for the other factors of production. Part of the extra demand for them as a result of substitution will be offset by the secondary cut in production. Indeed this output-effect on other factors may be greater than the favorable primary substitution-effect on those factors. That is why the sellers of rival machines may sometimes curse the attempt of a union to raise wages, namely, when high wages serve to price the industry out of its market.

All this we may summarize in a third principle:

> *Output-effect of Factor-price Changes: In addition to the reduction in demand for a factor resulting from the substitution-effect, there will usually be a further reduction in its demand because of the reduction in the firm's output resulting from the new balance between marginal revenue and the higher level of marginal cost.*

MARGINAL-REVENUE-PRODUCTS AND FACTOR PRICES

We have seen (1) that, at the Best-Profit output, $MR = MC$ and (2) that, at each and every output, the Least-Cost factor combination requires marginal-physical-products of all the factors to be *proportional* to their prices. This completes the theory of production. In this section we can put the above two facts together; we can go beyond the statement of *proportionality* to arrive at an *equality* that must hold between factor prices and marginal products.

We shall find that, when we have multiplied the marginal-physical-product of a factor by the amount of marginal revenue brought in by each unit of output sold, we define a new concept called "marginal-revenue-product." And now we can state more than a proportionality between factor prices and marginal products: We can state that *factor prices in final equilibrium must all exactly equal marginal-revenue-products.*

To understand what this means, put yourself in the shoes of a businessman trying to decide how many men to hire at a given market wage rate. In deciding whether to hire an extra man or not, you will, of course, want to know his marginal-*physical*-product—how much extra output you get when he is hired as compared with when he is not hired. But as a businessman interested in avoiding losses and in making profits, you are interested in the physical product only because you hope that product will bring you extra *dollars* of sales revenue. If elasticity of demand for your goods is rather low, so that each extra unit thrown on the market requires a great drop of price on all the units previously sold, what then? Clearly the marginal revenue will be very low, and sometimes even negative. In such cases, you will not be willing to add a man even though his marginal-physical-product is very great. This is because you are interested in the extra dollars he brings in; you will want to calculate an important new concept:

Definition: Marginal-revenue-product
= marginal-physical-product ✕ marginal revenue

If either of the right-hand magnitudes is very low, you will not be anxious to hire the extra man; for what you are interested in is their product as measured by the left-hand concept, marginal-revenue-product (measured in dollars and cents per input.) Only as long as each extra man's wage is *less* than his marginal-revenue-product will you continue to add men. When marginal-revenue-product of a man or of any other resource finally begins to drop below its competitively determined market wage or factor-price, there you will stop hiring more. There—and only there!—you will be in equilibrium.

This common-sense principle of balancing the advantages and disadvantages of any marginal decision can be summarized in our fourth principle, which summarizes all our previous principles.

Best-Profit Marginal Equivalence in Factor Hiring:

1. Each input will be hired up to the point where its marginal-revenue-product is finally equal to its ruling market price; thus in the final Best-Profit equilibrium position

Marginal-revenue-product of A = price of A
Marginal-revenue-product of B = price of B
Marginal-revenue-product of C = price of C

. . .
. . .
. . .

Marginal-revenue-product of Z = price of Z[1]

[1] This is simply another way of looking at the earlier conditions of Least-Cost and $MR = MC$. After all, it is marginal-physical-product that, together with factor prices, gives us *marginal cost*. And since marginal revenue is equated to marginal cost, it follows that there must be a very definite relation between factor prices and marginal-revenue-product, as the Appendix further shows.

2. When a factor's price goes up, less of that factor will be used—
until the equilibrium relation is restored.

TWO REALISTIC QUALIFICATIONS

1. *Monopoly-buying-power.* Note that the equilibrium relationship comes about by having marginal-revenue-product equate itself to the market wage or factor-price. It is not true that the market factor-price equates itself to the firm's marginal-revenue-product. Why not? Because we are implicitly assuming all along that any one firm is too small to have any appreciable effect on the going levels of wages and factor-prices.

If a firm became big enough to have an appreciable effect on the market price of the factors it buys, then the factor supply curve would not appear to it to be perfectly elastic and horizontal. Rather, it would rise as increased quantities of the factor were demanded. Such might be the case of one big factory in a small isolated town. Then the economist would say that the firm has "monopoly-buying-power"; and in all the above principles, he would have to introduce modifications that result from such monopoly-buying-power. For example, such a businessman would realize that the *extra cost* to him of hiring an extra worker is not the ruling market wage that he would then have to pay a typical worker. *It would be greater than market wages by the extra amount he would have to pay all his previous workers after he has bid up the wage in order to obtain the new man.* Therefore, in all our previous principles we would have to adjust all the market prices, price of *A*, price of *B*, etc., for this extra element of expense.[1]

2. *Discontinuity and Nonsubstitutability.* There is a second qualification that must sometimes be made. We have calculated the marginal-physical-product of any one input by (*a*) holding all the other inputs constant and then (*b*) increasing the input in question by 1 unit. The resulting increase in physical product was then measured, and that was identified as the factor's marginal-physical-product. Now in some technological processes the factor inputs work very intimately together, so that, when you increase only one of them, holding the others constant, you get *zero extra product* and, when you decrease one factor alone, you lose *the whole product* produced by both together; only when you change them both *in combination* do you seem to get a nice smooth curve of marginal-physical-product.

Certainly such discontinuities can sometimes happen, but perhaps they do not occur quite so often as some critics have claimed. Thus, critics often point out examples where one man is always using one shovel or where it seems to take a certain amount of gold to produce a watch band and no amount of labor

---

[1] Footnote 1, p. 601 of Chapter 28, shows how this monopoly-buying-power affects the economics of collective bargaining.

can substitute for this gold. But actually in any digging operation, extra shovels must usually be kept on hand; and if shovel prices were very high and wages were low, workers on different shifts might use the same implements so that the shovel requirements could be kept down to a minimum; also, we might in time change the size of the shovels or introduce bulldozers, thereby changing the proportions of the factors. Or in the above case of the gold watch band, there will almost certainly be some waste of metal in the form of shavings and dust; and if wages were low enough relative to the price of gold, it would pay us to hire more men to produce the same number of watch bands out of less gold—the labor being, in effect, a substitute for the use of more gold.

Numerous other arguments and examples could be given in reply to those who stress fixity of factor-proportions and discontinuities in substitutability and marginal-products. Nonetheless in some technical processes, there may not be continuous substitutability between the various inputs, and so the calculated marginal-physical-products may become very erratic and lumpy. It was once thought that this would spoil the economic theory of production. But that is fortunately not so.

If you own a business with this type of technology, you can still apply all the Least-Cost and Best-Profit principles outlined above—in fact, it will be easier for you to do so, inasmuch as your engineers can then rule out many factor combinations from the very beginning. If adding a man without adding other inputs will result in no extra product, then nobody but a fool would ever be tempted to do this. And if adding a combined dose of labor and machines gives rise to a big increase in revenue product—bigger even than the combined factor costs of the labor and machines—you will, of course, add such a combination. You will continue to add such combinations until finally the law of diminishing physical returns or the law of diminishing marginal revenue acts to bring the *combined* marginal-revenue-product down to the combined factor-cost.[1]

The only difference that technical discontinuities and lumpinesses make in our results is the following: In such cases, when the factor-price first changes, it may not pay the firm to change the way it combines that factor with other factors. Then after the factor-price has changed a lot, it may suddenly pay the firm to make a drastic rearrangement over to an entirely new and different combination of factors. Thus, such discontinuities have no other effect on our theory of production than to make it likely that the derived demand for a factor will show patches of inelastic demand (with little change in amount bought) coupled with occasional *huge discontinuities* of demand. Nonetheless the firm's

---

[1] Occasionally in advanced economic works, the words "marginal-*net*-product" are used instead of "marginal-product" to describe cases like the above.

demand curve for each factor is still well determined, just as it is in the nicely continuous case. Our same logic still applies.

SUMMARY

1. Distribution is concerned with the determination of different people's income or with the basic question of For Whom economic goods are to be produced. It studies the problem of how the different factors of production—land, labor, capital, entrepreneurship, and risk taking—are priced in the market place, or how supply and demand interact to determine all kinds of wages, rents, interest yields, profits, etc. (Needless to say this primary distribution of market-determined income is then modified by government taxes and expenditure programs to create ultimately the final actual pattern of individual and family income.)

2. To understand why the demand curves for the factors of production are what they are, we must investigate the theory of production and cost within a firm. This is because the demand for inputs is a *derived demand*—derived indirectly from the final demand by the consumer. The problem is complicated by the fact that the demand for factors is a *joint demand*—joint because the factors interact with each other in producing final product.

3. If he is given ruling market prices of all factors and is given engineering, technical information about the effects of factor changes on final product, the businessman can solve the two problems: (*a*) of substituting the different factors for each other so as to realize the Least-Cost combination—at which he has equalized the marginal-physical-product per dollar spent on every factor used—and (*b*) of finally determining which of all possible outputs is his Best-Profit position where $MR = MC$.

4. In consequence of these two principles, the business firm reacts to an increase in the market price of any factor by *substituting* other inputs for it in producing any given output. And in addition to this primary substitution-effect on demand, there is usually a further secondary reduction in demand because of an output-effect: It now becomes profitable for the firm to hire fewer factors, reducing its scale of output and charging the consumer a higher price—up to the point where MR again equals the new and higher MC.

5. An exactly equivalent way of looking at the production equilibrium is the following: We can go from the *proportionality* of marginal-*physical*-products and factor-prices to the *equality* of marginal-*revenue*-products with factor prices. Why must this hold in the Best-Profit equilibrium? Because any busi-

nessman with common sense will stop hiring any factor at the point where its market price has begun to exceed what its marginal-physical-product will bring in to his firm in actual dollars of marginal revenue.

6. A qualification is in order if the firm is a big enough part of the factor market to have an appreciable effect on the prices of factors it buys. In such a case of "monopoly-buying-power," the firm will have to reckon the cost of hiring an extra unit of input as something greater than the ruling market price of that factor—greater because the firm knows it will have to raise the wages of all previously hired units of that factor in order to keep them satisfied in relation to the newly hired unit. This thought will, of course, reduce the firm's willingness to expand its hiring.

7. We must slightly qualify our theory if there are technical discontinuities in the substitutability of different factors in production; but these cases of fixed-proportions will not spoil our theory of production. The firm will then work with various combinations of more than one factor and will find it easier rather than harder to make all its decisions. Its derived demands for the separate factors will still be perfectly well determined—although possibly inelastic and discontinuous in patches.

In the next few chapters we shall apply these principles of derived demand to show how supply and demand operate in the factor markets to determine rents, wages, and other factor-prices. An Appendix to this chapter gives a review of the theory of production for those interested in a more geometrical approach.

QUESTIONS FOR DISCUSSION

1. What are the four major categories of income? Is a category like wages of labor really something homogeneous, or can it in turn be broken down into wages of unskilled workers, wages of chemists, etc.? What about capital? Land?

2. What are the two major production problems a firm must solve? How would the responsibility be divided up between engineers, cost accountants, personnel people, etc.?

3. How would an increase in wages affect Table 1? How would it affect the amount demanded of labor needed to produce 75,000 units? The amount demanded of machines? Why would the demand for machines change even though its price has not changed?

4. Give a common-sense explanation of why $MR = MC$ at the Best-Profit output.

5. Give some examples to explain the concepts of "derived demand" and "joint demand."

6. Convince a skeptic of the truth of the rule that to reach a Least-Cost point you must equalize the marginal-productivity-per-dollar spent on every factor. Show this to be true even if we have not yet decided on the Best-Profit output.

7. Show that when a factor price rises there is (a) a substitution-effect and (b) an output-effect that tends further to reduce the demand for the factor.

8. Define marginal-revenue-product, distinguishing it from marginal-physical-product. Give a common-sense explanation to show that profits are not at a maximum unless each factor-price is exactly equal to its marginal-revenue-product. (The Appendix shows that this last condition is just another way of stating the combined conditions of Least Cost and Best Profit, i.e. just another way of stating the equality of MC and MR and the equality of the marginal-physical-product-per-dollar spent on each factor.)

9. A firm finds that the demand for its product has increased (the demand curve has shifted to the right). Explain the process that it should follow in order to reach a new equilibrium with respect to price, output, and quantities of factors hired.

10. Wheat can be grown with various combinations of land, machinery, labor and fertilizer? What information is necessary in order to decide what combination should be chosen? Explain the process by which the decision would be made.

11. Give an example of possible monopoly-buying-power. Show that in your example there would have to be a slight modification of the previously stated marginal conditions. Where a firm has monopoly-buying-power with respect to labor, do you think the firm would buy more labor, less labor, or the same amount of labor as it would buy in the absence of such monopoly-buying-power?

12. Give examples of discontinuities and lack of substitutability. Does this make the Least-Cost and Best-Profit questions more or less difficult?

APPENDIX TO CHAPTER 26
GRAPHICAL DEPICTION OF
PRODUCTION THEORY

THE "PRODUCTION FUNCTION" CONCEPT

Underlying economics is technology. As far as we are concerned, the technical expert has completed his job when he has handed on to the economist. accountant, or cost engineer the *physical relationship between output and various inputs*. This relationship is called the "production function." The production function tells us how much output we can hope to get if we have so much labor *and* so much capital *and* so much land, etc.

In the simplest case, where there are assumed to be only two inputs, labor L and capital C, and one output q, the production function is given by a two-way table as in Table 3. This looks very much like a baseball schedule or like

TABLE 3. *Production Function Relating the Amount of Output to Varying Combinations of Labor and Capital Inputs*

No. of units of capital	1	2	3	4	5	6
6	**346**	490	600	693	775	846
5	316	448	548	632	705	775
4	282	400	490	564	632	693
3	245	**346**	423	490	548	600
2	200	282	**346**	400	448	490
1	141	200	245	282	316	**346**
	1	2	3	4	5	6

No. of units of labor

a mileage chart giving the distance between different cities. Along the left-hand side are listed the varying amounts of capital, going from 1 unit up through 6. Along the bottom are listed the amounts of labor, going from 1 through 6. If we are interested in knowing exactly what output there will be when 5 units of capital and 2 units of labor are available, we count up 5 units of capital and then go over 2 units of labor. The answer is seen to be 448 units of product. Similarly, we find that 3 units of capital and 6 of labor will produce 600 units of output. Thus, for any combination of labor and capital, the production function tells us how much product we shall have (using, of course, the best methods as decided by the technical engineer).

THE LAW OF DIMINISHING RETURNS ONCE AGAIN

In Chapter 2 we met the law of diminishing returns, which told us that adding more and more of a variable factor (like labor) to a fixed factor (like capital) resulted eventually in smaller and smaller additions of product. This is very nicely illustrated by Table 3.

First recall that we have given the name "marginal-physical-product of labor" to the extra production resulting from *one* additional unit of labor. At any point in Table 3 the marginal-physical-product of labor can be derived by subtracting the given number (representing product at that point) from the number on its right lying in the same row. Thus, when there are 2 units of capital and 4 units of labor, the marginal-physical-product of an additional laborer is 48, or 448 — 400.

By the "marginal-physical-product of capital" we mean, of course, the extra product resulting from one additional unit of capital, labor being held constant. It involves a comparison of adjacent items in a given column. Thus, when there are 2 units of capital and 4 units of labor, the marginal-physical-product of capital is 90, or 490 — 400. The reader should be able to compute the marginal-physical-product of labor or capital at any point inside the table.

Having defined what we mean by the marginal-physical-product of an input, we are now in a position to restate the law of diminishing returns:

As we hold a fixed input constant and increase a variable input, the marginal-physical-product of the variable input will decline—at least after a point.

To illustrate this, hold capital constant in Table 3 by sticking to a given row —say that corresponding to capital equal to 2 units. Now let labor increase from 1 to 2 units, from 2 to 3 units, and so forth. What happens to product at each step?

As labor goes from 1 to 2 units, product increases from 200 to 282 units, or by 82 units. But the next dose of labor adds only 64 units, or 346 — 282. Diminishing returns have set in! Still further additions of a single unit of labor give us, respectively, only 54 extra units of output, 48 units, and finally only 42 units. The reader should check some other row to verify that the law of diminishing returns holds there too. He should also verify that the same law holds true when labor is held constant and capital is added in a number of steps. (Hint: Examine the changes in product in any *column*.)

At this point, it is well to recall the explanation given for diminishing returns. In Chapter 2, this was attributed to the fact that the fixed factor decreases *relative* to the variable factor. Each unit of the variable factor has less and less of the fixed factor to work with, and it is only natural that extra product should begin to fall off.

If this explanation is to hold water, there should be no diminishing returns when both factors are increased in proportion. When labor increases from 1 to 2 and capital *simultaneously* increases from 1 to 2, we should get the same increase in product as when both increase simultaneously from 2 to 3. This can be verified from Table 3.[1] In the first move we go from 141 to 282, and in the second move product increases from 282 to 423, an equal jump of 141 units.

Also, this explanation of diminishing returns in terms of the proportions of the inputs would lead us to expect that increasing capital will improve the marginal-physical-product of labor. Again this can be verified from our table: The fifth unit of labor adds 48 units of product when there are only 2 units of capital; but at 3 units of capital, a fifth unit of labor adds 58 units of product.

GRAPHS OF MARGINAL-PRODUCT AND DIMINISHING RETURNS

Figure 1 shows how total product varies when we increase labor, holding capital constant at 3 units. Each new unit of labor is adding less and less to total product.

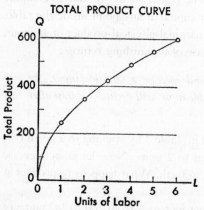

TOTAL PRODUCT CURVE

FIGURE 1. The total product obtained when varying amounts of labor are combined with 3 units of capital.

In Figures 2a and 2b, the amounts of marginal-physical-products are plotted, first in steps and then as a smoothed curve.

In Figure 2a, the area of the first slab gives total product, 245, resulting from the first unit of labor added to the 3 fixed units of capital. To get the total product resulting after 2 units of labor have been added, we must add the area of the first two slabs—which will turn out to be 346 units of output. The sum of the first three slabs will be 423 units. What total product will the sum of all six slabs equal?

Turn now to the smooth curve of Figure 2b. To get the total product corre-

---

[1] Not all production functions met with in real economic life would have these special properties of so-called "constant returns to scale."

sponding to 6 units of labor, we add together all the area up to $L = 6$. How would you get total product corresponding to any other value of L—such as $L = 1, 2, 4, 3\frac{1}{2}$?

The reader should be able to draw in on Figure 1 the curve of total product that results when we add different amounts of labor, but hold capital constant at

THE MARGINAL-PHYSICAL-PRODUCT OF LABOR

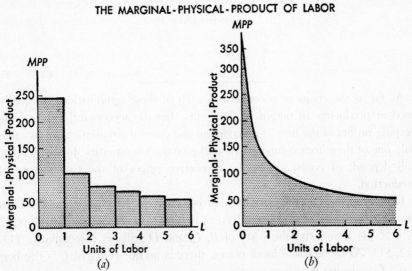

FIGURES 2a and 2b. The marginal-physical-product of labor when combined with 3 units of capital. As the steps of (a) are made continuously divisible, we get (b).

the higher level of 4 units. What is the reason for the implied shift in the marginal-physical-product curve of Figure 2b that this implies? The reader should be able to draw a similar figure showing how total product behaves when we vary capital and hold labor constant—say at 1 unit.

It could happen that the marginal-physical-product rose at first instead of falling; this would mean that diminishing returns began to set in only after some initial stage. The slabs in Figure 2b would first be rising and then falling. What kind of a wiggle would the curve in Figure 1 then have?

LEAST–COST COMBINATION FOR ANY GIVEN OUTPUT

The numerical production function shows that the engineer is not able to tell us definitely how any given output is to be produced. There is more than one way to kill a cat. And there is more than one way to produce any given output. Thus, the boldfaced numbers in Table 3 show that the output $q = 346$ can be produced in any one of the following ways:[1]

[1] The reader can and should make up a similar table for output equal to 490 units or to some other number.

TABLE 4. *Alternative Ways of Producing the Output q = 346*

	Labor L	Capital C
A	1	6
B	2	3
C	3	2
D	6	1

As far as the engineer is concerned, each of these combinations is equally good at producing an output of 346 units. But the accountant, interested in keeping profits of the firm at a maximum and costs at a minimum, knows that only one of these four combinations will give the lowest costs. Just which one will depend, of course, upon the respective prices of the two factors of production.

Let us suppose that the price of labor is $2 and the price of capital $3. Then the sum of the labor and capital costs in situation A will be $20 (1 × $2 + 6 × $3). Similarly, the costs of B, C, and D will be, respectively, $13, $12, $15. At these stated input prices, there is no question that C is the best way of producing the given output.

If either of the prices of the inputs changes, the equilibrium proportion of the inputs will always change so as to use *less* of the input that has gone up relatively most in price. Thus, if labor stays at $2 per unit but capital falls to $1 per unit, the new optimal combination will be B, where more capital is used and less labor and where total cost is only $7. The reader should verify this by computing the new total expense of all other combinations and seeing that they are higher.

Exactly the same sort of thing can be done for any other output; as soon as all input prices are known, we can experiment until we have found the Least-Cost input combination. (To clinch his understanding of the principles involved, the reader should work out the optimum production decision and cost for output equal to 490 units when price of labor is $2 and price of capital is $3.)

EQUAL-PRODUCT AND EQUAL-COST CONTOURS: GRAPH OF LEAST-COST POSITION

The common-sense numerical analysis of the way in which a firm will combine inputs to minimize costs can be made more vivid by the use of diagrams. From the production schedule we can draw a picture of the different input combinations that will produce a given output. Figure 3 is the exact counterpart of Table 4. In it the smooth curve indicates the different combinations of labor and capital that yield an output of 346 units. This could be called a "production-indifference curve" by analogy with the consumer's indifference curve of the Appendix to Chapter 23. But a more expressive name would be to call it an "equal-product" curve. (The reader should be able to draw in on Figure 3, as a dotted curve, the corresponding equal-product curve for output equal to 490. He should realize that an infinite number of such equal-product contour lines could be drawn in, just as a topographical or weather map could

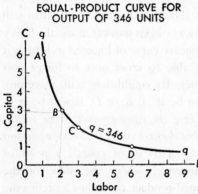

EQUAL-PRODUCT CURVE FOR
OUTPUT OF 346 UNITS

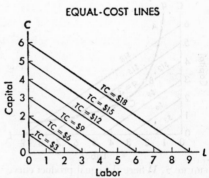

EQUAL-COST LINES

FIGURE 3. All the points on the curve represent the different combinations of capital and labor that can be used to produce 346 units of output.

FIGURE 4. Every point on a given line represents the same total cost. The lines are straight because of constant factor-prices, and they all have a numerical slope equal to the ratio of labor price to capital price.

be covered with an indefinitely large number of equal-altitude contour lines or equal-barometric-pressure lines.)

Given the price of labor and capital, the firm can evaluate the total cost for points A, B, C, and D or for any other point on the equal-product curve. Obviously, it will be maximizing its profits only when it has found that optimum point on the equal-product curve at which it reaches Least Cost. Purely as a graphical trick, the firm might try to save itself much tedious arithmetical computation by evaluating once and for all the total cost of every possible factor combination of capital and labor. This is done in Figure 4, where the family of parallel straight lines represents all possible equal-cost curves when the price of labor is $2 and the price of capital $3.

To find the total cost for any point we have simply to read off the number appended to the equal-cost line going through that point. The lines are all straight and parallel because the firm is assumed to be able to buy all it wishes of either input at constant prices. The lines are somewhat flatter than 45°

because the price of labor P_L is somewhat less than the price of capital P_C. More precisely, we can always say that the arithmetic value of the slope of each equal-cost line must equal the ratio of the price of labor to that of capital—in this case $\frac{2}{3}$.[1]

It is now easy to recognize the optimum equilibrium input position of the firm at which total costs are minimized for the given output. The single equal-product curve has superimposed upon it the family of equal-cost lines. This is shown in Figure 5. The firm will always keep moving along the heavy concave curve of Figure 5 as long as it is able to cross over to lower cost lines. Its equilibrium will, therefore, not be at A, B, or D. It will be at C, *where the equal-product curve touches (but does not cross) the lowest equal-cost line*. This is, of course, a point of tangency, where the slope of the equal-product curve just matches the slope of an equal-cost line and the curves are just kissing.

We already know that the slope of the equal-cost curves is P_L/P_C. But what is the slope of the equal-product curve? This slope is a kind of "substitution ratio" between the two factors, and it depends upon the *relative* marginal-physical-products of the two factors of production—just as the rate of substitution between two goods along a consumer's indifference curve was earlier shown to equal the ratio of the marginal or extra utilities of the two goods (Appendix to Chapter 23).

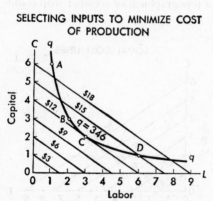

SELECTING INPUTS TO MINIMIZE COST OF PRODUCTION

FIGURE 5. Where the equal-product curve touches (but does not cross) the lowest total cost curve is the Least-Cost optimum position. This tangency means that factor-prices and marginal-physical-products (or "substitution ratios") are proportional.

[1] The careful reader will notice the parallel between the geometry of this section and that of the analysis of consumer equilibrium in the Appendix to Chapter 23. Each equal-cost line indicates all of the possible different quantities of labor and of capital that the firm might buy for any given cost outlay. Each line is straight since its equation is $TC = \$2L + \$3C$. In Chapter 23's Appendix, the consumer is buying goods, not factor services; otherwise his "consumption-possibility line" exactly parallels the equal-cost lines we are now discussing. We can explain similarly why the slope of an equal-cost line equals the ratio of the two prices involved.

But note this difference: The consumer was assumed to have a fixed budget; hence, he had but one consumption-possibility line. The firm is not limited to any particular level of costs; so it must consider many equal-cost lines before discovering its equilibrium.

LEAST-COST CONDITIONS

Thus, our Least-Cost equilibrium can be defined by any of the following equivalent relations:

1. *The ratio of the marginal-physical-products of any two inputs must equal the ratio of their factor prices.*

That is,

$$\text{Substitution ratio or } \frac{\text{Marginal-physical-product of labor}}{\text{Marginal-physical-product of capital}} = \frac{\text{price of labor}}{\text{price of capital}}$$

2. *The marginal-physical-product-per-dollar received from the (last) dollar of expenditure must be the same for every productive factor.*

That is,

$$\frac{\text{Marginal-physical-product of L}}{\text{Price of L}} = \frac{\text{marginal-physical-product of C}}{\text{price of C}} = \cdots$$

This condition holds for any number of inputs—for land as well as for labor and capital, etc. Relation 2 is discussed in detail in the main body of the chapter. (It could also be derived from relation 1 by transposing terms from one numerator to the other denominator, *i.e.*, by "interchanging means," as is always algebraically permissible.)

But the student should not be satisfied with any such abstract explanation. He should always remember the common-sense economic explanation which shows how a firm will redistribute its expenditure among inputs if any one factor offers a greater return for each last dollar spent on it. Finally, we may state the above Least-Cost relations in the form:

3. *Input prices and their marginal-physical-products must be proportional, the factor of proportionality being marginal cost.*[1]

That is,

MC of output × marginal-physical-product of labor = price of labor
MC of output × marginal-physical-product of capital = price of capital

and so on for any number of inputs.

---

[1] Why are these marginal-physical-products-per-dollar each equal to the reciprocal of marginal cost, or to $1/MC$? Because extra output per dollar is nothing but the upside down of extra dollars per unit of product, which is what we always have meant by MC.

MARGINAL-REVENUE-PRODUCT CONDITION OF BEST-PROFIT

The Least-Cost relationships 1, 2, and 3 are all equivalent. Each holds at every point along the total cost curve, *whatever be the output*. They do *not* tell the firm where it should finally produce.

But now we add the Best-Profit condition that $MR = MC$, and we recall the definition of marginal-revenue-product as equal to marginal-physical-product times marginal revenue. Then we can now combine the Least-Cost relations of 3 and the Best-Profit relationship to reach our final equilibrium condition:

Marginal-revenue-product of labor = price of labor
Marginal-revenue-product of capital = price of capital

and so on for any number of factors.

Thus, our graphical analysis has arrived at the same final result as our common-sense reasoning of this chapter—which tells us that we will stop hiring more of a factor only at the point where the marginal-revenue-product it brings just matches its market price. This is what lies behind every firm's demand curve for any productive factor.

QUESTIONS FOR DISCUSSION

1. Explain what is meant by a production function. Use it to describe the law of diminishing returns. What would the production function be like if there were three factors of production? How would you write it down?

2. If the price of capital increases from $2 to $3, what will happen to the parallel lines of Figure 4? Why will they be flatter? Why still parallel? What will happen to the new Least-Cost equilibrium point in Figure 5? Does this agree with common sense?

3. What is the relation between the slope of the equal-product curve and marginal-physical-productivities? Show that the tangency condition of Figure 5 is essentially the same thing as our previous marginal conditions for Least Cost. What trouble would tangency create for us if the equal-product contour were convex from above instead of being concave from above? (Hint: Would costs be at a minimum or maximum? What would you do about it?)

Chapter 27: PRICING OF

FACTORS OF PRODUCTION: RENTS

OF LAND AND OTHER RESOURCES

THE PRECEDING chapter showed how the derived demands for productive inputs are determined for each firm facing given market factor-prices. This chapter will show how the demands of all firms and industries are added together to form the aggregate market demand for the factor of production in question. Such a demand curve, together with the supply curve for the factor, will be found to determine its market price; in this way a market economy determines the distribution of income to owners of the different factors of production. The interesting special case of the rents to lands and to other resources serves to illustrate these general principles. The following chapters will provide still other important applications.

AGGREGATE MARKET DEMAND CURVES FOR OUTPUT AND FOR EACH INPUT

Figures 1a and 1b show how the demand for a given input, such as fertile corn land, can be derived from the consumers' demand curve for corn. This assumes, of course, that we hold constant the prices of such cooperating inputs as fertilizer, labor, and farm machinery. At each land-rent price prevailing in the market place, any small farmer must decide on the Least-Cost combination of the various inputs, and he must also decide on the Best-Profit scale of final output to throw onto the market. Therefore, each farmer will want to hire more and more of corn land up to the point where its marginal-revenue-product is equal to its market rental.

We are dealing with a competitive industry in which the single farmer is too small to affect the market price of corn. In such a perfectly competitive industry, no one need worry about spoiling the market for the previous units of corn being sold; consequently, marginal revenue and price are the same thing. It follows that marginal-revenue-product will be exactly the same thing as

COMMODITY DEMAND AND DERIVED FACTOR DEMAND

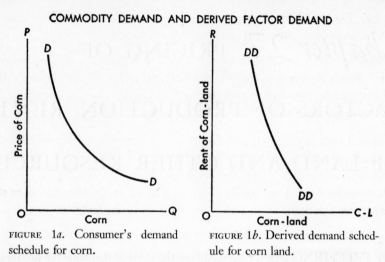

FIGURE 1*a*. Consumer's demand schedule for corn.

FIGURE 1*b*. Derived demand schedule for corn land.

marginal-physical-product times corn price. For such a special case of a perfectly competitive commodity market, economists often use the special name of "value of the marginal product" instead of marginal-revenue-product.

FOUR PRINCIPLES OF DERIVED DEMAND

We shall now develop four principles to show what the degree of elasticity of derived demand depends on.

Of course, the higher becomes the rent of corn land, the less of it will be rented, and the less will be the total corn produced. This reduction in the supply of corn will force consumers to move up their market demand curve in Figure 1*a*, and this will raise the price of corn. But the higher the price of corn, the less will farmers find it necessary to cut down on their purchases of corn land and other factors. Therefore, a comparison of Figures 1*a* and 1*b* shows us something interesting.

1. *If the demand for the product in Figure 1a is rather inelastic so that consumers will pay a much higher price before they cut down much on the amount they buy, then the derived demand for the factor of production in Figure 1b will also tend to be rather inelastic.*

If farmers are spending only a small fraction of their total costs on the renting of corn land, then a large increase in market rental rates would still increase the total costs of producing corn very little, and the increase in rent would thus have very little effect in raising corn price or in cutting down on corn production. Hence,

✻ 2. *The smaller is the proportion spent on a productive factor, the more inelastic the derived demand for it will tend to be.*

Sometimes this principle is described as "the importance of being unimportant." When we come to study how a trade-union for one small craft, such as the electricians, can often raise their wages and not suffer much unemployment, this same principle will be seen to be in operation.

Even if corn land is a rather unimportant element of total costs so that corn production is not appreciably changed, there will still be some decrease in total land demanded by the farmers; for, as the last chapter showed, the farmers' new Least-Cost combinations of productive inputs will require them to *substitute* whatever other factors they can for corn land. Hence,

✻ 3. *Other things being equal, the derived demand for any input will tend to be inelastic when the technical substitutability of other factors for it happens to be very low.*

If fertilizer or machinery or manpower can quite easily make up for any reduction in land area, then a small increase in land rent will result in a very great reduction of the amount demanded of it and its demand will be elastic. If substitutability is low, then our third principle tells us that lack of substitutes will make its demand inelastic.

Of course, we must not forget cross elasticity of demand. An increase in the price of corn land will tend to increase the demand for all of its substitutes. On the other hand, those inputs which "complement"—rather than "compete" with—corn land will have their demand reduced when the purchase of corn land is reduced. (Fencing might be an example.) And all factors, whether substitutes or complements, will tend to suffer a reduction in demand as a result of any output-effect on corn production necessitated by higher costs of production. All these effects can be expected to influence the prices of the other inputs.

The last of our principles can first be stated and then explained.

✻ 4. *The greater the changes induced in the prices of other factors, the more inelastic will tend to be the demand for the original factor whose price has initially changed.*

Thus, if an increase in land rent causes people to bid up eagerly the price of fertilizer, then there will not be so great a substitution of fertilizer for land;

or if a rise in the price of land causes the prices of fencing to be greatly depressed, then the combined cost of land and fences will not have risen so much, and there will not be so great a reduction in the use of land.

The above four principles governing the inelasticity or elasticity of derived demand were developed by Alfred Marshall, a distinguished English economist of some fifty years ago. They are important, and the reader should review them carefully. They apply principally to the cases at that time considered to be the most usual and important, namely, perfectly competitive industries.

Today, economists are aware of the great factual importance of imperfect or monopolistic competition. And for such situations a fifth principle may be added:

> 5. *The derived demand for any factor will tend to be inelastic when the imperfect competitors hiring it wish to pursue, and are able to pursue, price policies that cause their total production to change very little as a result of any increase in factor costs.*

On the other hand, if the monopolistic firm should greatly cut down on its output—either because its sales drop off rapidly when it increases its price or because it tries to pass on to the consumers a large part of the increase in its unit costs—then its demand for all factors is likely to decrease strongly in response to an increase in factor-price.

FACTOR-PRICE DETERMINATION BY SUPPLY AND DEMAND

Up until now we have worked only with the demand curve for a factor, taking its market price as given to the demanders. But obviously it is *all the firms together* who determine the factor's market price that each small firm faces. Now we must see how the total demand curve of all, for the factors, together with the total supply curve for the factor, will interact to determine the equilibrium price tending to rule in the market place.

Figure 2 shows the total demand curve for corn land, *DD;* it was arrived at by adding together each and every individual firm's demand curve. Now it is one of the peculiarities of land that, unlike most things, its total supply is relatively fixed by nature and cannot be augmented in response to a higher price for it, and its total cannot be diminished in response to lower land rentals. Of course, this is not strictly true. Land can sometimes be created by drainage, and the fertility of the existing land can be depleted by overcropping. Nonetheless, we can take the complete fixity of its supply as the characteristic feature of land. By tradition, we may confine our discussion to the "original and inexhaustible gift of nature" whose total supply is by definition *completely inelastic.* It was the price or return to such a factor that the classical economists of the last century called "rent." This differs from ordinary usage in which rent or rental is the money paid for the use over a period of time of anything— of a house, truck, etc.

In Figure 2, the supply curve for land SS is taken to be completely inelastic because of the fixity of its supply. The demand and supply curves intersect in the equilibrium point E. It is toward that factor-price that the rent of land must tend. Why? Because if rent rose above the equilibrium price, the amount of land demanded by all firms would be less than the existing amount that would be supplied; some property owners would be unable to rent their land at all; therefore, they would offer their land for less and thus bid down its rent. By similar reasoning, the rent could not long remain below the equilibrium intersection. If it did, the reader should be able to show how the bidding of unsatisfied firms would force the factor-price back up toward the equilibrium level. Only at a competitive price where total amount demanded of land exactly equals the total supply will there be equilibrium. It

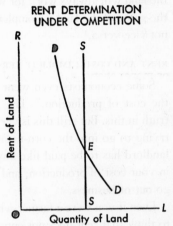

RENT DETERMINATION UNDER COMPETITION

FIGURE 2. Perfect inelasticity of supply characterizes the case of so-called "pure economic rent."

is in this sense that supply and demand determine any factor-price.

Note that the man who owns land does not have to be a particularly deserving citizen in order to receive this rental. A virtuous and poor landowner will be given exactly the same rental by competition as will a wealthy wastrel. It is the productivity of the land that is being paid for and not the personal merits of the landowner.

Even this productivity of the land is not something absolute. For example, what would happen if the price of corn were to fall greatly because people began to desire other goods? Then the derived demand for corn land would shift drastically downward and to the left. What will happen to the rentals received by landowners? After a time, rents must sink down to a new equilibrium intersection. The land is not less productive in a technical sense than it was before, and the landlords are neither more nor less virtuous than they were before. But factor supply and demand have changed.

A factor of production like corn land is said to earn a "pure economic rent" because: (1) its total supply is regarded as perfectly inelastic; and for the moment we shall assume that (2) the land *has no other uses*, such as the production of sugar or rye. Adam Smith's great follower in England of the early

1800's, David Ricardo, noted that the case of such an inelastically supplied factor could be described as follows:

It is not really true that the price of corn is high because the price of corn land is high. Actually the reverse is more nearly the truth; the price of corn land is high because the price of corn is high! Its total supply being inelastic, the land will always work for whatever is given to it under competition. Hence the value of the land is completely derived from the value of the product, and not vice versa.[1]

RENT AND COSTS: IMPLICIT VERSUS EXPLICIT RETURNS

Some economists even went so far as to say that "rent does not enter into the cost of production." The last paragraph shows that there is a grain of truth in this. But still this is very dangerous terminology. If you were a farmer trying to go into the corn-raising business, you would certainly find that the landlord has to be paid like anybody else. You would certainly figure in rent in your cost of production; and if you could not pay the rent, you would soon go out of business.

Even if you were a farmer who owned your own land, it would be a mistake to think that rent does not enter into your costs of production. After you had paid all your other bills, including wages to yourself at least as great as what you could earn elsewhere in the market, there would have to be left an amount at least equal to the market rental value of your land. For what if there were not such an amount? Then you would soon find that it would be better for you to rent out your farm on the open market and hire out your own labor to somebody else.

Sometimes economists call rent paid by a man to himself "implicit" rather than "explicit" rent. Very clearly, implicit rent is as much a part of long-run competitive costs as are any other costs, and the same can be said of the implicit wages or implicit interest earned on any other factors that you could sell rather than use personally.

RENT AND COSTS: RELATIVITY OF VIEWPOINT

We must avoid our old enemy the "fallacy of composition." What appears as a cost of production to each and every firm may *to the industry as whole* be really a derived price-determin*ed* expense rather than a price-determin*ing*

[1] Land is not the only factor whose return may be considered as economic rent. For an example where most of a wage payment is a "pure rent," see Chapter 28. And in the short run, the supply of a machine or plant may be entirely fixed; thus a hydroelectric plant takes a long time to build, still longer to wear out. The return to any factor in temporarily fixed supply is sometimes called a *quasi-rent*—"quasi-" because in the long run, its supply need not be fixed.

one. More than that, suppose we now assume that the corn-producing industry is just one of very many industries which can use the same land. Then to each *small* industry—such as the buckwheat or rye industry—the supply curve of land may appear to be almost completely horizontal or elastic. This is because that one industry may be too small a part of the total market picture to have any appreciable influence on land rents.

Now put yourself in the shoes of someone who takes the viewpoint of that industry as a whole. Will land then appear to be an element determining the price of rye? Or will it seem like a cost that is determined by the final price for rye? The answer must definitely in such a case be the former: To a small industry using relatively little of a factor, the factor-price is an important determiner of the industry's commodity price, and not vice versa. At the same time to the economy as a whole, the rent of a factor whose total quantity is inelastic can still be said to be more the *result* than the *cause* of the values of the various final products. To conclude: Whether rent is or is not a price-determining cost depends upon the viewpoint from which we look.

HENRY GEORGE'S SINGLE-TAX MOVEMENT: TAXATION OF LAND "SURPLUS"

In the last part of the nineteenth century, a western frontier still existed in this country. As more and more people came here from Europe, each acre of land had more and more people to work it. In a sense, therefore, the land became more productive. In any case its competitive rental value certainly tended to rise. This created handsome profits for some of those who were lucky enough to get in on the ground floor and buy land early.

Nor was this true only in agriculture. Men still alive in the Middle West can remember when towns first began. They will tell you how they might have been rich if only they had recognized 70 years ago that the corner of State and Madison would eventually become the center of town and would grow tremendously in value as a result of the tremendous increase in urban populations.

Sites with good locations earn rents in the same sense that fertile areas do. Many people began to wonder why lucky landowners should be permitted to receive these so-called "unearned land increments." Henry George, a printer who thought much about economics, crystallized these sentiments in the single-tax movement. This had a considerable following a half century ago or more, and there are still some adherents to it; but it is not likely that anyone running on the single-tax ticket will again come so close to being elected mayor of New York City as did George in 1886. Nor is it likely that anyone will soon come along and write so persuasive a bible for the movement as did Henry George in his *Progress and Poverty*, a book which sold millions of copies.

This is not the place to attempt any assessment of the merits and demerits of such a political movement. But its central tenet—that land rent is in the nature of a surplus which can be taxed heavily *without distorting production incentives*—can be examined to illustrate one principle of distribution and taxation.

Suppose that supply and demand create an equilibrium land rent, as in Figure

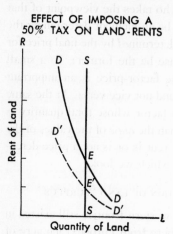

EFFECT OF IMPOSING A
50% TAX ON LAND-RENTS

Rent of Land

Quantity of Land

FIGURE 3. A tax on fixed land leaves rentals paid by users unchanged at E but reduces rent retained by landowners to E'.

3 at E. Now what would happen if we were to introduce a 50 per cent tax on all land rents? Mind you, we are not taxing buildings or improvements; for that certainly would affect the volume of construction activity. All we are taxing is the yield of the naturally fixed supply of agricultural and urban land sites, assuming that this can somehow be identified.

There has been no shift in the total demand curve for land; firms are still willing to pay the same amount as before for the same amount of land. Hence, with land fixed in supply, the market price that they pay must therefore still be at the old intersection E. Why? Because supply has not changed and neither has demand. Because at any higher price than before, some land would have to go without any demanders. And hence in the absence of any monopoly on the part of landlords, rents could not permanently be raised to land users.

Of course, what the farmer pays and what the landlord receives are now two quite different things. As far as the landlords are concerned, once the government steps in to take its cut of 50 per cent, the effect is just the same as if the net demand to the owners had shifted down from DD to D'D'. Landowners' equilibrium return *after taxes* is now only as high as E', or only half as high as E. The whole of the tax has been shifted backward onto the owners of the factor in inelastic supply! The landowners will not like this. But under competition there is nothing they can do about it, since they cannot alter the total supply and the land must work for whatever it can get.

Whether or not it is a fair thing to take away part of the return of those who own land is quite another question. Perhaps many voters will feel that such owners are not less deserving than are investors who have put their money into other things, but such a political question has no place in the present discussion. What is relevant is to point out that a similar 50 per cent tax, put upon a factor of production whose total supply is *not* completely inelastic, will certainly produce definite effects on the factor-prices charged in a competitive market. To some extent this tax would distort the pattern of production, and it would shift part of the burden *forward* onto the users of the factor and onto consumers. Thus, if the same acre of land were to be taxed differently when used for wheat rather than corn production, this would certainly have distorting effects on the price of wheat relative to that of corn.

SUPPLY AND DEMAND FOR ANY FACTOR

The competitive determination of land rent by supply and demand is only one instance of the general analysis applicable to any factor of production. How is the rental value per week of a tractor to be determined in a competitive market? We first sum up the derived demands of all business firms for tractors. (Of course, these derived demands have behind them marginal-revenue-product considerations as shown in the last chapter, but this behind-the-scenes relation need not now concern us as we observe the aggregate market demand for this factor.)

In addition to the *DD* curve shown in Figure 4, we must also have a supply curve such as *SS*. But there is now no reason why the supply curve should be perfectly vertical. It may now be positively elastic, rising upward toward the northeast—being dependent in the case of the tractors on their marginal costs of production. Or if the factor of production were labor, it might be that people would feel they could afford to work *fewer* hours as wages rise, so that the *SS* curve might eventually bend backward and northwestward from the vertical, rather than rising forward.

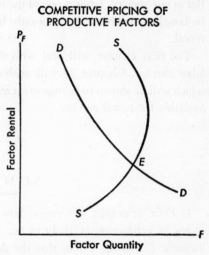

COMPETITIVE PRICING OF PRODUCTIVE FACTORS

FIGURE 4. Note that at high enough rentals factor supply "bends back."

In any case, whether the supply curve is vertically inelastic, positively elastic, or negatively elastic, there will be an *SS* curve as in Figure 4. Where the demand and supply curves intersect, the final equilibrium factor-price will be set. And if the demand curve for the factor shifts upward, its market price will tend to rise; on the other hand, if the supply offered of any factor increases, so that the supply curve shifts rightward, then the factor-price will tend to fall.

In a competitive market economy, therefore, factor-prices and the distribution of income are not determined at random. There are definite forces of supply and demand operating to create high returns to scarce factors that are very useful in producing the things wanted by people with purchasing power. But the price will drop if more of any factor should become available or if other close substitutes for it are found or if people stop wanting the goods that a factor is best suited to make. Competition gives and competition takes.

CONCLUSIONS

The same general principles determining land rent also determine the prices of all inputs; the rental of threshing machines or of trucks is determined in essentially the same way. We might even go so far as to say that wages are the rentals paid for the use of a man's personal services for a day or a week or a year. This may seem a strange use of terms; but if you think about it, you will recognize that every agreement to hire labor is really for some limited period of time. By outright purchase, you might avoid ever renting any kind of land. But in our society, labor is one of the few productive factors that cannot legally be bought outright. Labor can only be rented, and the wage rate is really a rental.

The next chapter will deal with the peculiar problems of wages and the labor market. Chapter 29 will analyze the problems of capital and interest, which will be shown to be important in determining the supply of durable goods available for rental and use.

SUMMARY

1. Four principles determine how inelastic the derived demand for any factor of production is likely to be. A factor's demand will tend to be very inelastic (a) to the extent that the demand curves for its final products are *inelastic;* (b) to the extent that it represents only a small, *unimportant fraction* of total costs of production of the finished products; (c) to the extent that it has no readily *substitutable* rival factors of production; and finally (d) to the extent that the *induced changes in other factors' prices* are ~~small~~ large. A fifth principle may be added in the case of imperfect or monopolistic competition: Demand for a factor will tend to be most inelastic when the firms hiring it tend to pursue price policies that keep their total *output from changing* very much.

2. We add all the derived demands for a factor to get the aggregate demand curve. This, together with the specified supply curve of the factor, can be expected to determine an equilibrium intersection. At the equilibrium market

price for the factor of production, the amounts demanded and supplied will be exactly equal—only there will factor-price have no tendency to change. Anywhere above the equilibrium price, suppliers will tend to undercut the market and to cause price to fall; anywhere below the equilibrium price, demanders will bid the price upward, restoring the equilibrium.

3. The unchangeable quantity of natural land is an interesting special case where the supply curve happens to be perfectly vertical and inelastic. In such a so-called *pure* rent case, competition will still determine an equilibrium market rental. But in this case, we are faced with a cost element that is more price-determin*ed* than price-determin*ing*; the land rent is more the result of the market prices for the finished commodities than their cause. Nonetheless, we must not forget that to any small firm, or to any industry too small to affect appreciably the total demand for land, rent will still seem to enter explicitly or implicitly into the cost of production just like any other expense. To such a small industry, rent appears to be as much price-determining as any other cost element.

From the standpoint of the community as a whole, the rent of an inelastically supplied factor will be reckoned in the national income at its full dollar value, like anything else. But below the veil of money, it still remains true that this factor would be willing to work for less if it had to, and in that sense its return is in the nature of a "surplus" rather than in the nature of a reward necessary to coax out the factor supply. This provides the basis for Henry George's "single-tax" proposals, aimed to tax the unearned increment of land value—and without any shifting forward of the tax to the consumer or distorting effects on production.

4. The general principles of supply and demand can also be used to explain the competitive price determination of all services other than those of land. In common everyday usage, we speak of rent or rental as the price paid for the use of any input, whether the factor's supply curve is inelastic or not. The rental of all inputs—including the wages that have to be paid for the use of the services of human beings—are determined in a competitive system by supply and demand. But there are special peculiarities to the labor market, and also there remain the special problems connected with interest rates and capital valuations.

The Appendix to this chapter uses the simple case of an island community to illustrate how the marginal-products of different factors interact to determine the general pattern of factor supply and demand. Those who wish to move on directly to the next chapters may omit this bird's-eye view of distribution reduced to its lowest terms.

QUESTIONS FOR DISCUSSION

1. The demand for permanent waves is rather elastic. What can you say about the derived demand for beauty operators? Which of the four principles of derived demand does this illustrate? Give an example of an industry of very inelastic demand and derived demand for factors.

2. Only a few drops of Angostura Bitters are used in a cocktail. Would you expect the demand for them to be inelastic or elastic? Why? Most of a laundry's expense consists of wages. Would this be a factor favorable or unfavorable to a union demand for higher wages? Why?

3. Few lubricants with the quality of oil exist. How is demand elasticity for oil affected by this fact? Why would a change in the price of oil from one state alone be expected to elicit an elastic demand?

4. Electricians in a textile plant realize that they are an unimportant part of total costs. This tempts them to ask for a wage increase. But they know that all the other unions in the plant will then insist on an equal pay increase. Use the fourth principle of derived demand to qualify the second principle of "the importance of being unimportant."

5. You work for a public utility whose price is fixed by law. Why will demand for your services be more inelastic than if you worked for a competitive company that could raise its price? Suppose the regulatory authority will permit the utility to raise its price as costs rise; how will your conclusion about inelasticity be affected?

6. You are given the following information:
a. It is difficult to substitute fertilizer or labor for land to any great extent in the growing of coffee.
b. Coffee is not a very important item in the family budget of coffee drinkers.
c. The coffee-growing industry is made up of many small producers.
d. The rental of land suitable for coffee growing is by far the most important item in the budget of producers.
e. The supply of other factors used in coffee growing is highly inelastic.
If these statements were correct, which of them would tend to make the demand for coffee land elastic and which inelastic?

7. "Value of the marginal-product" is defined as MPP × price of the product; "marginal-revenue-product," as MPP × marginal revenue. Which of these two values is lower for a firm in an imperfectly competitive industry? In a perfectly competitive industry?   (MPP: marginal-physical-product.)

8. Define the "pure rent" case. Explain the sense in which the price of such a factor is "price-determined" rather than "price-determining." Show that, nonetheless, an

increase in the availability of the rent-earning factor will depress its return and lower commodity prices that use much of it.

9. What was the Henry George single-tax movement all about? Use a diagram to show what the effect would be of taxing pure rent.

10. The rental of oil tankers and other ships is determined in a competitive market. Illustrate how supply and demand intersect. What about wages, which are the rentals of the services of human beings?

APPENDIX TO CHAPTER 27
BIRD'S-EYE VIEW OF MARGINAL-PRODUCTS
AND DISTRIBUTION IN THE SIMPLEST CASE

The supplies and demands for all factors interact with each other and with the supplies and demands for all commodities. The result of this competitive process is a set of equilibrium factor and commodity prices and a set of equilibrium quantities for all inputs and outputs. No more than this need be said in an introduction to economics. However, many people feel happier about a new subject if they can work out carefully a simplified case. That is the purpose of this Appendix.

BASIC ASSUMPTIONS

Imagine an island newly discovered off the coast of Europe. Suppose it consists of 1,000 square miles of land of uniform quality, well-suited to the production of food. Think of food as being a single, composite commodity, and imagine that it is the only commodity anyone ever wants to produce and consume. Only two productive factors are needed to produce this food: land and labor. A known quantity of food will always result whenever any given quantity of land is worked by any given quantity of labor. We can assume that the ownership of the newly found land has already been determined. It will not matter if the owners live on the island or if they are absentee landlords; the laborers who work on any parcel of land will operate efficiently in a routine manner without the need of any management.

If the island is conveniently near Europe so that workers can move back and forth across the water easily—travel cost is negligible, and it is as pleasant to live on the island as elsewhere—then the wage rate set in Europe will also be the wage rate that will ultimately have to prevail on our island. This may take a little time, since people will have to move to the island whenever wages there are higher than in Europe and back to Europe when wages are higher there than on the island. The island is not nearly big enough to change the general level of wages in Europe (just as a small bay in the ocean is so small that the level of water in it is determined by the level of water in the wide ocean rather than vice versa). The common level of wages can be thought of as being paid in units of food. Or if we use a one-dollar market basket of food for our unit of food, we can think of real wages as being paid in ordinary dollars. For example, a man can be thought of as earning $1.000 per year or as earning 1,000 units of food per year.

DETERMINATION OF EQUILIBRIUM

Now our stage is set. Initially, there are no workers at all on the island. But confronted with a $1,000 annual wage rate at which people can be drawn from Europe, the owners of land will now be able to arrive at their individual demands for labor. The total amount of labor demanded will be 1,000 times the amount demanded on each square-mile farm. This is because we are making the important special assumption that it is only the *proportion* of land to labor that counts, and not the absolute *scale*. Two hundred men, working on 2 square miles of land, would produce exactly twice the quantity of food obtained when 100 men work on 1 square mile.

But what determines the demand for labor on each unit of land? Our theory of production earlier told us that every prudent employer will add labor to his land up to the point where labor's marginal-revenue-product is just equal to its wage rate. Because food is our only product, and because its price is perfectly fixed at the defined level of $1, it is clear that marginal-revenue-product and marginal-physical-product are exactly the same thing: the former is one times the latter, and for brevity we can speak simply of marginal-product. So to find the demand for labor, we must first investigate marginal-product.

LAWS OF MARGINAL-PRODUCT

Figure 5 shows the extra production of food that results when we add successively more units of labor to the same square mile of land. The first few men have a very great marginal-product, about 3,000 food units or dollars per year, as shown by the very tall vertical slab marked (*a*). Because of the law of diminishing returns, we know that adding more men to the same unit of land will cause their marginal-product to fall. This is shown by the shorter vertical slab marked (*b*). As we add still more units of labor, the marginal-product falls still lower and lower. Finally, when we have 100 units of labor working, the very last unit of labor has a marginal-product of only 1,000 food units or dollars; and at 200 units of labor, marginal-product has fallen to less than 800 food units.

This marginal-product curve in Figure 5 tells us all there is to know about our simple production function—the law which determines the quantity of food to be had from different quantities of land and of labor. We can read off from Figure 5 not only *marginal*-product but *total* product, thus: When there is zero labor, the food product is zero. When one man is put to work, we get a product of about 3,000 units as represented by a very thin slice on the left-hand side of slab (*a*). When 20 men are at work on our square mile of land, what is the total product? It is the sum of all the vertical slices making up the area of slab (*a*). Similarly, the sum of areas of the slabs, (*a*) + (*b*) + (*c*) + (*d*) + (*e*), must equal the total product that is being produced on each square mile by the joint cooperation of land and the stated quantity of labor, 100 units. This total works out to 150,000 units of food produced on 1 square mile of land by 100 workers.

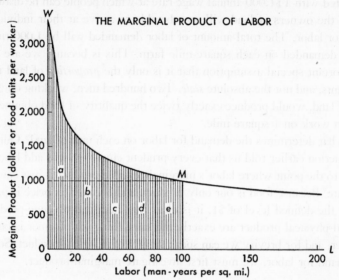

FIGURE 5. Each extra man adds less and less to total product, as shown by the shorter and shorter vertical slabs. Summing all of these vertical slabs gives us the total product as an area.

The law of diminishing returns has told us that this total product is increasing as we add labor, but increasing at a decreasing rate. If we had wanted to avoid any diminishing returns, we should have had to increase land at the same time that we increased labor, so that the whole scale would have grown together with no change in any proportions.

IDENTITY OF MARGINAL–PRODUCT CURVE AND DEMAND FOR LABOR

Now we can determine the demand for labor on each farm. Recall the rule that the prudent landlord must follow in our simple case: Hire labor up to the point where labor's marginal-product is just equal to the wage. Confronted with any wage rate that he must pay for the hire of labor, our landlord will simply go to the marginal-product curve of Figure 5. At a high real wage, he will hire little labor; but if the wage level in Europe and elsewhere should fall it will pay him to put more labor to work. And since the rule is to equate marginal-product with the wage, the marginal-product curve and the demand curve are one and the same. Thus, if the Europe-set wage were 1,000 dollars or food units annually, then 100 laborers would be hired on each square-mile farm, as shown at the point M in Figure 5.

TOTAL DEMAND AND SUPPLY

Now we can derive the island's total demand for labor. It is *DD* in Figure 6. Since there are 1,000 square miles on the island, this curve is nothing but a 1,000-fold scale enlargement of the Figure 5 curve of labor's marginal-product on a single unit of land. Because of the law of diminishing productivity, this demand curve is a declining one.

The long-run supply curve of labor can be indicated by *SS* and must be drawn horizontally at the wage level set to our island by Europe and the rest of

DETERMINATION OF EQUILIBRIUM IN THE LABOR MARKET

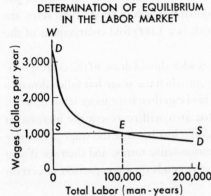

FIGURE 6. Summing the marginal-product curves for all of the 1,000 square-mile farms gives us the total demand curve for labor. The supply curve is given by the wage-rate abroad.

DIVISION OF THE NATIONAL PRODUCT

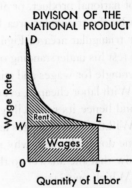

FIGURE 7. The residual left over after wages are paid goes to rent.

the world. Where the curves of supply and demand intersect is our equilibrium *E*. It tells us in this case what we already know—that wages will be at the world-set level of $1,000 per year. But it tells us more than that: It also tells us exactly how many people will be employed on our island and how much will be the total production.

The equilibrium quantity of labor for the island will be 1,000 times the equilibrium amount demanded at the going wage by each 1-square-mile unit of land (or a total of 1,000 times 100 laborers = 100,000 laborers, as shown below *E* in Figure 6). The equilibrium total product, or national income, will be 1,000 times the sum of all the vertical slabs of Figure 5, or 1,000 times $150,000 = 150 million dollars.

Figure 7, which is a redrawing of Figure 6, shows the total of national product as the shaded area *ODEL*. Of the 150-million-dollar total, it turns out that exactly two-thirds, or 100 million, goes as wages to labor; this is because each of the 100,000 laborers had to be paid 1,000 dollars or food units a year. Wages are shown by the area of the rectangle $OWEL$, its altitude being the wage and its base the number of workers.

Who gets the rest? Obviously, on each square mile of land, whatever product is left after the workers get paid off must go as a *residual* to the owner of the land. Who else could claim it under a system of private property? Each farm yields 50,000 food units to the landowner after 100 laborers each receive 1,000 food units.

One thousand times the rents received on each unit of land gives us the total rents received by all landowners. This is the remaining one-third of the total of national product, or 50 million dollars' worth of food. Total rents are shown by the triangular area WDE, which is a 1,000-fold enlargement of the similar triangular area of Figure 5.

(To test his understanding of this, the reader should draw in the corresponding rectangle for wages and triangle for rent when the wage has fallen down to $800. With labor cheaper, every unit of land can then have more labor to work on it and hence its rent will go up. What area will represent the increase in rent? Will the *total* of wages have to go down just because the wage *per worker* has gone down? Explain why not in common-sense terms, and then see if you can show that the answer to this question depends on a comparison of certain areas. Which ones?) [1]

RENT AS A DIFFERENTIAL [2]

In the above theory we assumed that all land is equally fertile and equally well located. What would happen if there were many different grades of land varying in their fertility? Figure 8 shows what would happen if two other kinds of land were to be discovered on our island in addition to our original land, which we may call Grade I. Grade II land is less productive than Grade I, but more productive than Grade III. This is shown by the fact that its marginal-product curve lies lower than does that of Grade I, but higher than that of Grade III.

At a very high wage, like S, only Grade I land will come into cultivation. As the wage drops, more and more labor is added to Grade I land, until finally, the marginal-product on Grade I land drops down to the marginal-product of the very first labor units applied to Grade II. A further drop in the wage causes labor to be added to both Grades I and II in such a way as to keep their labor marginal-products always equal to the going wage and to each

---

[1] It happens in this example that the share of rent in the national product remains at about one-third after the increase in population and lowering of wage. This is a special case: A reduction in wages would always increase the absolute total of land rent, but total product might change by a greater or lesser percentage than did rent.

[2] The following section may be skipped without loss by beginning readers.

other. Grade III still is not in cultivation at all, until the critical wage level U is reached. Below this level, labor is added to all three kinds of land—in such a way as to keep the marginal-product of labor everywhere equal to the same market wage.

Around 1820 the marginal-product analysis had not yet been invented; economists like David Ricardo did not use such diagrams. But they realized that workers had to get the same wages wherever they worked. And they reasoned as follows:

**DEGREE OF UTILIZATION OF THREE GRADES OF LAND
AT VARIOUS GIVEN WAGE RATES**

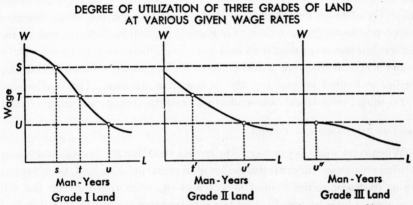

FIGURE 8. At each common wage, men are allocated to the different types of land up to the point where their marginal-products are just equal to the wage.

Find, if you can, some low-grade "frontier" or "marginal" land where a worker can just earn his wage, leaving nothing left over to the landowner. Then you can use such marginal no-rent land to measure the rent that will be earned on good land. Thus you can imagine three identical brothers: The first works on a small unit of Grade I land, the second brother works on a small unit of Grade II land, and the third works on a small unit of Grade III land. The general wage rate is assumed to be just high enough to leave nothing left over to the landowner on III, or to be at U. Grade III would then be called "no-rent" or "free" or "marginal" land. The classical economists then set down the following rules:

All identical workers must get the same wages. This wage rate must be equal to what is produced by the third brother who works on the marginal land which is just good enough to remain in use and just bad enough to be free. The difference between what Brother I produces on the good land and what III produces on the "margin" must be attributable to the fertility of Grade I land worked by Brother I, and that difference must be the rent of Grade I land that will be brought about by competition. Also, the difference between what Brother II produces on his piece of Grade II land and what his identical Brother III produces at the margin will be the competitively determined rent of the Grade II land. Thus, *all land rents can be measured as a differential between what nonland factors produce on the land in question and what those same factors would produce if working out on no-rent marginal land.*

This theory of differential rent is not untrue. But it is rendered unnecessary by the analysis of the last sections. Except that it calls attention to certain relations that will exist under competition, the theory of differential rent does not tell us much. After all, what land will be marginal: I, II, III, . . . ? The theory is silent on this. And if all land is exactly alike, the theory becomes completely mute. (Some followers of Ricardo broke this silence by making the nonsensical statement that, if all land were alike, there could be no differential —and hence all land rent would be zero. As long as the uniform land of one quality is limited in quantity, this is complete nonsense. The land on our 1,000-square-mile island was uniform in quality, but it still earned rent.)

RENT AS THE MARGINAL-PRODUCT OF LAND

When economists began to realize around 1900 that the law of diminishing returns creates an "internal margin" within every piece of land, they stopped trying to detour to the frontier in search of an explanation for rent. But still they were a little bothered by the fact that land rent seemed to be determined as a *residual* while labor's wage was made equal to its marginal-product. This was really nothing to be terribly bothered about; for after all, the laws of private property do hold, and rent was a well-determined residual. But still their sense of logic or of aesthetics was troubled by the different treatment given to land and to labor.

After all, what would happen if each 100 men in our earlier example were to organize a company and to rent land from the open market? How much would they demand? Would not the same marginal-product reasoning now be applicable to the extra product due to land? Let us see.

What would be the market rental of land facing our small group of cooperative workers? Surely, the rental rate would be 50,000 food units or dollars per square mile per year. This is because no landowner would be tempted to part with land for less, as we have already seen. At this market rental, how much land would be demanded to work with our 100 units of labor? Obviously, any bit of land that added more in production than its market rental would be hired, and land would cease to be hired once its marginal-product fell to below its market cost.

Figure 9a shows the marginal-product curve resulting when we add different amounts of land to a fixed number of 100 men. Note that, with everything a matter of proportions only, an increase in *land relative to labor* is exactly the same thing as a decrease in *labor relative to land*. To move rightward in Figure 9a is exactly the same as to move leftward in Figure 5. Land's marginal-product curve is defined by our production function, and hence it must be

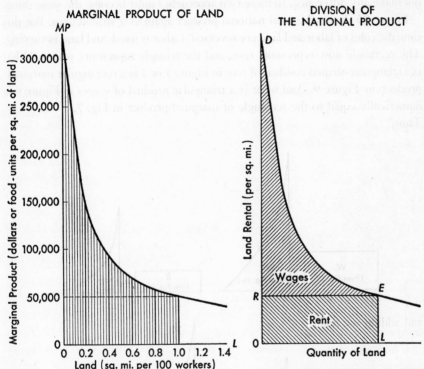

MARGINAL PRODUCT OF LAND

DIVISION OF THE NATIONAL PRODUCT

FIGURE 9a. Variable land is added to fixed labor. The sum of the diminishing vertical slabs gives total product. (Note symmetry with Figure 5.)

FIGURE 9b. Each and every little unit of land is paid the marginal-product of the last little bit of land. Now wages appear as a residual triangle—what is left of total product after rent is paid.

consistent with the data of Figure 5. At the market rental, exactly 1.0 square miles of land will be demanded by this firm of 100 workers. (Compare this diagram with the similar diagrams of Figures 5 and 6, and be sure you see why this is so.)

The firm or labor cooperative will produce $150,000 worth of food units, and after paying land the market rental of $50,000, it will have $100,000 to be divided up among the 100 workers. Hence, from this way of looking at it, the $1,000 of wages is a residual. But it is at the same time equal to marginal-product of labor—as our earlier way of looking at the problem made clear. If the two ways did not come out the same, it would either pay workers always to hire land or landowners always to hire the workers. Under equilibrium in perfect competition, legal technicalities of who hires whom must not make any difference, so these two approaches must become the same thing.

Figure 9b shows the total national product again as a shaded area. But this time the roles of labor and land are reversed. Labor is fixed, and land is varying. The rectangle now represents rent, and the triangle represents wages. What is a triangular-shaped residual of rent in Figure 5 or 7 is a rectangular marginal-product in Figure 9. And what is a triangular residual of wages in Figure 9 is numerically equal to the rectangle of marginal-product in Fig. 7. Thus,

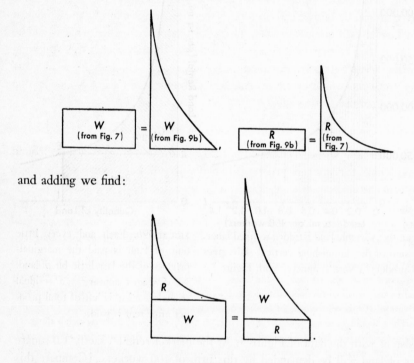

and adding we find:

MORE THAN TWO FACTORS OF PRODUCTION

Thus, there is perfect symmetry between land and labor. Supply and demand determine the equilibrium remuneration of each, and this can be interpreted either as a residual or as a marginal-product. The same would be true if we had more than two factors of production. In the simple case where proportions rather than scale are important and where the factors are continuously substitutable in producing a single national product such as food, the demand for each factor is an aggregate curve of marginal-products, drawn up with other factors held constant. The total of national product paid to the varying factor can be represented as the rectangular area defined by the equilibrium intersection point and the two coordinate axes. The triangular residuum is what goes to all the other factors. But the share of each other factor can equally well be represented as a rectangular area on its own curve of marginal-product. Each factor can be held constant or varied, and the result must, in this ideal case, be always the same.

This simple theory of distribution is often attributed to J. B. Clark, an American economist at the turn of the last century. In advanced courses, it is shown rigorously that under our simplified conditions the different ways of looking at the factor return do, indeed, add up to the total product.[1] (This is more than can be said of certain foolish theories, which claim that each factor should get the difference between what is produced with it and what would be produced if *all* of that factor were taken away. Usually such a rule of giving each factor its *average* rather than *marginal* product will promise *to each and every factor* the whole of the product; the different factor shares would add up to more than the total product.)

GENERAL SUPPLY AND DEMAND FOR LABOR OR ANY FACTOR

Up until now we have reasoned in terms of the special case of a horizontal supply curve for labor. The classical economists of more than a century ago also concentrated on such a special case, but for them this was supposed to be brought about by Malthus-like population behavior. If real wages rose, people were supposed to reproduce themselves until diminishing returns brought real wages down. This iron law of wages was represented by a horizontal long-run

[1] Without going into higher mathematics, it is possible to indicate why the total of rent as determined on a piece of land by the triangular area of Figures 7 and 5 must be rigorously equal to the marginal-product that would be lost if that 1 unit of land were taken out of cultivation. If this square mile of land were taken away, what would its 100 units of labor do? They would have to move out and work on the frontier—if there is such a thing. Or more generally, in a world where all land was homogeneous, they would be spread evenly over all the remaining 999 square miles. What will the loss of product be? These shifted labor units will no longer be producing the high marginal-products of (*a*), (*b*), (*c*), (*d*), etc. Instead they will all produce at the marginal-product level of *E* (which for a small change in land will not appreciably be changed on any of the other 999 units). The loss in product due to land must therefore be exactly the triangular surplus represented by the areas of the vertical slabs above the 1,000 line in Figure 5—which shows that the marginal product of land is indeed equal to its residual rent. This explanation is a literary rendition of what is called Euler's theorem in mathematics, and it rests on the assumption of constant returns to scale.

supply curve for labor. It is no longer very realistic among Western peoples. For this reason, it seemed better in this Appendix to introduce such a horizontal supply curve by means of the assumption that laborers could migrate back and forth to and from our island.

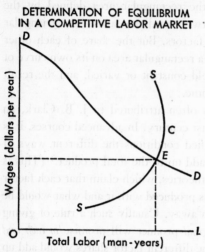

DETERMINATION OF EQUILIBRIUM IN A COMPETITIVE LABOR MARKET

FIGURE 10. This is similar to Figure 6, except that the supply curve is determined domestically.

Even this is not very realistic in these days of passports and immigration restrictions. Also, it would be much more interesting to show how the level of wages is determined instead of our accepting such a wage level from abroad. The time has come therefore to drop the assumption of a horizontal supply curve for labor. Let us suppose that our island prohibits all further immigration from the rest of the world and that it is fortunate enough to have more land per capita than is true elsewhere. Its real wages will then be higher than in the rest of the world, but there is nothing that workers elsewhere can do about it.

Exactly how are the prices of labor and land worked out in this case? Now we draw in some kind of nonhorizontal supply curve for labor, such as SS in Figure 10. At higher wages, the population of the island may at first choose to work more hours per week; perhaps at still higher wages, they may feel that they can afford more leisure and less hours of work per week—as shown by the bending back of the supply curve above the critical point C.

Just as before, we proceed to the intersection at E of SS and DD. At this wage and no other, the total amount of labor demanded is just equal to the total amount supplied. The amount of rent can also be determined by the usual triangle (Note that, if population were to grow, thus increasing the labor supply and moving the SS curve of Figure 10 bodily to the right, the equilibrium point E would occur lower down on DD and the triangle of rents earned by landowners would be greater. Landlords would benefit when laborers multiplied like rabbits, but each worker would not.)

The supply curve of labor might even turn out to be perfectly inelastic—just like the case of land. Such a supply curve would, of course, mean that labor is ready to work in the same total amount, regardless of what it gets paid. But supply and demand would still determine distribution.

Instead of making labor like land as in the last paragraph, we could reverse the process. We can make land like labor by dropping the assumption that land's supply curve is perfectly inelastic. Perhaps at higher rentals people would turn hunting parks into cornfields or drain swamps. In any case, we must still arrive at a new equilibrium where both wages and land rentals are simultaneously determined by equality of their market supplies and demands. In an introduction to economics, it would not be appropriate to work all this out in detail. But it would not be hard to show how the derived demand for one factor *shifts* whenever the quantity and price of the other factors change and to show how these cross-elasticity interactions do lead to a unique final equilibrium.

INTERCOMMODITY SUBSTITUTION

It would also not be hard to show what happens when we drop the simplified case of a single product. As any factor, such as machine tools, becomes more plentiful, its rental will tend to fall. Not only will more of it tend to be substituted for other factors in each line of production—in addition, those special goods which happen to use much of this factor in their production will fall in price more than will prices generally. This relative price drop will tend to cause consumers to buy more of such cheapened goods, and in this way the derived demand for the factor will become even more elastic. Thus, *in addition to intracommodity technical substitutability between factors, there is also intercommodity substitutability resulting from differential price effects.* (This suggests how distribution will be determined even when the continuous substitutability assumptions of the marginal-product theory of production break down. If factors must be used in fixed-proportions, their derived demands are still perfectly well determined. These demands, together with supply relations, will determine all prices. Intercommodity substitutions now become extremely important, as do the supply conditions for the factors.)[1]

[1] An example illustrates how intercommodity substitutions can determine factor prices even in the worst case of fixed-proportions, *e.g.*, where 1 unit of machinery *and* 1 unit of labor are needed to produce a unit of wine and where 1 unit of machines *and* 2 units of labor are needed to produce a unit of bread. Assume that wine sells for $10 per unit and bread for $12. Bread differs from wine by $2 in price and cost; and in terms of inputs, it differs by 1 extra unit of labor. Hence wages must be exactly $2 per unit, and machines must be priced at $8 per unit (= $10 − $2, or $12 − 2 × $2). So from commodity prices we can obtain factor-prices—even in this fixed-proportions case.

You will realize that the prices of wine and bread had also to be determined by supply and demand and will depend in part upon how much income goes to hungry laborers and thirsty machine owners and upon the initial supplies of the factors. For example, imagine that we started with a supply of 200 machines and 300 laborers, and let us summarize the resulting general equilibrium.

If we had started with factors in a 1 : 1 ratio—say 200 of each—and *if* we require them

As a concluding note, it may be mentioned that to understand the different aspects of the problem of distribution in our island community is to begin to understand much of the history of the classical and modern theories of distribution and of competitive pricing. But it does not tell us much about the cases of monopolistic competition: (1) where there may be economies of scale that lead to a few firms gaining semimonopoly power and (2) where consumers may develop a special preference for products that can be produced only by factors owned by a single firm. As Chapter 30 shows, in these cases the firms may earn "monopoly profits" or "monopoly rents" which the attempted competition of other firms cannot take away from them. To "natural scarcity" is then being added artificial or "contrived scarcity"—brought about by someone's holding in his supply for fear of "spoiling the market."

SUMMARY TO APPENDIX

1. In a simple world where food is produced by land and labor, the curve of labor demanded by the owner of one unit of land will be the curve of falling marginal-product of labor. The total demand curve for labor will be a 1,000-fold enlargement of the demand on each of the 1,000 square miles. Where the supply curve of labor intersects with the demand curve will be the equilibrium wage and quantity of labor. The total product left over from the harvest after the laborers have all been paid their wage is the *residual* left over for rent. Rent is represented by a triangular shape on labor's marginal-product diagram, while wages are represented by a rectangular area.

2. But the factors can all be treated perfectly symmetrically. We can hold labor constant and add land to it. Workers' demand for land at any given rental will be limited by the marginal-product curve of land. The aggregate demand for land is the magnification of the demand of each group of workers, the extent of the magnification depending upon the total number of workers. The

---

to be fully employed, they would *all* have to go into wine production. We could not possibly produce any bread and still keep all our factors employed. Similarly, if our factor totals were in a 1:2 proportion—say 200 machines, 400 laborers—we should have to produce nothing but bread.

But we start with a halfway ratio—200:300. Common sense and simple algebra tell us that we must then split our machines half and half between the two industries, thereby using up the total of both factors in producing 100 wine units and 100 bread units. The prices of these supplies of goods would be then determined by the interplay of competitive supply and demand for the two goods and for the two factors, and thus we end up at the above equilibrium prices for goods and services.

resulting equilibrium between the supply and demand for land must yield exactly the same marginal-product rental for land as was arrived at by the residual method. Otherwise, it would no longer be a matter of indifference as to whether (a) landowners hire labor or (b) laborers hire land.

3. Ricardo and other classical economists of a century ago emphasized that, when land is of different grades, the workers on it must nevertheless receive the same wages. Therefore they attempted to measure the rent of any piece of land as a differential—equal to the surplus produced on the piece of land in question over and above what the variable factors working it would be able to produce out on the frontier or on marginal no-rent land. This theory of differential rent is but a special case of the general theory of competitive bid and offer for productive factors. It has little to say about most of what is interesting in distribution theory, so that it has been superseded or amplified by the recognition that diminishing return creates an internal margin on every piece of land, whether of highest fertility and location or of lowest.

4. When many products are brought into the picture, we can go beyond the possibility of *intracommodity technical substitution* of other factors for a factor which has become relatively dear. In addition, there will now be *intercommodity substitutions* by the consumer, who will begin to buy less of the now dearer goods using relatively much of the expensive factor and who will buy more of the now cheaper goods using relatively little of it. Even in the worst case where the factor proportions are fixed within each industry, these differential commodity price changes can, together with the supply conditions for the factors, determine the pattern of distribution. Hence, the general theory of competitive supply and demand transcends the theory of marginal products but in no way contradicts it.

QUESTIONS FOR DISCUSSION

1. Explain in detail how we can read off total product from the marginal-product curve. Show that this would not be quite true if total output did not begin at zero when labor is zero.

2. "Constant returns to scale" means that increasing all inputs in exactly the same proportion will increase output in exactly the same proportion. What would you suppose "increasing returns to scale" then means? "Decreasing returns to scale"? Show that constant returns to scale is not inconsistent with the good old law of diminishing returns.

3. Suppose the wage rate abroad rose from $1,000 to $1,500. Describe the new equilibrium level of employment, rent, total product, etc. Show that almost the same

result could be created on the island even if the world wage level did not change but instead immigration was restricted. By about how much would it have to be restricted? Would landowners like this?

4. Show that either of the two factors can be thought of as earning a residual. Explain why it is plausible to believe that this residual is the same thing as the factor's marginal-product. (Hint: Observe the behavior of a fixed number of workers who are confronted with a given market rental for land. Show that with workers the fixed hiring factor and land the variable hired factor, the same final production and factor-price equilibrium must emerge. Illustrate with rectangles, triangles, etc.)

5. Suppose land and labor both have inelastic supplies. Which factor return is a pure rent? Is the resulting equilibrium determinate? Why and at what level?

6. Suppose there are three factors of production. What then?

7. Write a two-page essay on the general logic involved in the differential theory of rent.

8. "If the demand for anybody's factor or good is not infinitely elastic, then the equilibrium of perfect competition must be modified." What is the general nature of the needed modifications? What conditions of tastes, returns, and factor ownership might give rise to less than perfectly infinite elasticity of demand?

9. What is meant by "technical substitution between the factors"? Give examples. What is meant by intercommodity substitutions? When different commodities use the factors in different relative degrees, show that an increase in any one factor will cause more of it to be used even if there is no technical substitutability. (Hint: As its price falls, goods which use much of it will be greatly cheapened and will have their sales greatly expanded.)

10. In the wine-bread footnote, what would happen if we changed the price of bread to $15? What if we also increased our machines and labor by 100 units apiece, ending up with 300 machines and 400 laborers. (Hint: Unless all the extra factors go into the wine industry, all of both factors cannot be fully employed.)

11. Again with regard to the wine-bread footnote: What would the new equilibrium be (a) if bread's price ceased being higher than wine's, (b) if the total supply of labor dropped to less than the supply of machinery? (Warning: This is very difficult; one factor becomes free.)

Chapter 28: COMPETITIVE

WAGES AND COLLECTIVE

BARGAINING

A MAN is much more than a commodity. Yet it is true that men do rent out their services for a price. This price is the wage rate, and of all prices it is by far the most important. For the vast majority of the population, the wage is the sole determinant of family income; and when we remember that much of the income of farmers and of nonincorporated enterprises is in actuality a form of labor income, we realize that wages must constitute at least 80 per cent of the national income.

When the price of coffee or of typewriter ribbons changes, it is easy to remain calm and dispassionate; the effects on our welfare are relatively minor. But let my wage be cut by 5 per cent and I change from an affable philosopher into a raging malcontent. Because wages are prices that arouse vital human emotions, they are the proper study of the psychologist as well as the economist. The sociological importance of wages has economic implications which a student of the labor market must always keep in mind.

WAGE LEVELS AND DIFFERENTIALS

Wage rates differ enormously. The average wage is as hard to define as is the average man. An automobile executive may earn one-half million dollars a year at the same time that a postal clerk earns $3,000 and a farm hand $1,200. In the same factory, a skilled machinist may earn $80 a week while an unskilled man gets $40. Part of any theory of wages must explain these differentials.

But important as these wage differences are, we must not overlook the vital question of the general wage level. Wages of virtually every category of labor are higher than they they used to be half a century ago. Why? Wages are higher in the United States than they are for similar categories of labor in Europe, and they are higher in Europe than they are in Asia. Why?

What is supposed to determine wages under competitive conditions? This is the first problem we shall tackle. Then, in Part B of this chapter we shall investigate the effect of deviations from competitive conditions and analyze the economics of collective bargaining between trade-unions and employers.

A. *WAGE DETERMINATION UNDER PERFECT COMPETITION*

EQUALITY OF WAGE—FOR IDENTICAL LABOR

Let us begin by examining the simplified case of wages paid to a particular category of laborers all exactly alike in skill, effort, and every other respect.

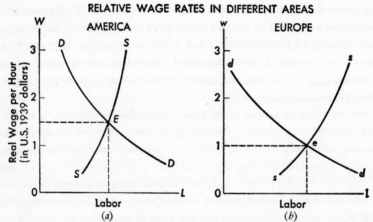

FIGURES 1a and 1b. Supply and demand determine a higher competitive wage in America as compared with Europe.

Then competition will cause their wage rates per hour all to be exactly equal. No employer would pay more for the work of one identical man than he would pay for his twin, and no worker would be able to ask more for his services.

How is this single market wage determined? If we know the supply and demand curves for these laborers—as in Figure 1a—then the competitive equilibrium wage must be at E, the intersection point. The reader can by now supply the details of the process whereby wages are bid up or down to this equilibrium level. (It is important to note that we are interested in *real wages*— in what the wage will buy and not just in its money amount. Therefore in Figures 1a and 1b we express wages in money units whose purchasing power over goods is held constant at the level of some particular year and place, *e.g.*, in terms of American dollars of 1939 purchasing power.)

Imagine that Figure 1*a* represents the state of affairs in America and Figure 1*b* that in Europe. Why are wages so much higher in America than in Europe? Is it because we have unions and they do not? Or because we have passed higher minimum wage laws than the Europeans? Obviously, such factors have nothing to do with our simplified competitive world. A true, but superficial, answer would be: Supply and demand are such in America as compared with Europe as to lead to a higher wage here.

But *why* are supply and demand such as to lead to high American wages? What lies behind these schedules?

NATIONAL RESOURCES AND HIGH PRODUCTIVITY

In the first place we note that the derived demand schedules for labor slope downward and to the right, going from northwest to southeast. One reason for this will occur to you at once: The law of diminishing returns suggests that adding more and more labor to the same American natural resources and land area will tend to diminish labor productivity and wages. Suppose you let American population increase so as to shift the supply curve *SS* far to the right in Figure 1*a*. Then the wage might fall to the European level or even lower.

One important explanation of high American wages, therefore, lies in the sphere of economic geography: *Compared with the size of our working population, we are generously supplied with land, with coal, with iron, with oil, and with water power.* The per capita supplies of these vital sinews of modern industrial production are less in Europe and still less in many other parts of the globe.

TECHNOLOGY, CAPITAL, AND HIGH PRODUCTIVITY

But economic geography does not tell the whole story. Two regions may be exactly alike in endowment of natural resources; but if one of them uses superior technological methods, its productivity and real wages may be much higher than the other's. In part, using superior technological methods involves better know-how, better applied science, and better work methods; in part, it is made possible by the relative abundance of capital goods—of man-made machinery, materials, and plants.

Just why the United States developed a superiority in know-how and capital availability is not well understood by economic historians. But the facts of this superiority are not subject to much dispute.

IMMIGRATION AND RESTRICTIONS OF LABOR SUPPLY

This raises an obvious question: Why do not Europeans move from their low-wage area to our higher wage area? We all know the answer from our history books. People did migrate to this country in great numbers during the three centuries prior to World War I. A few came to seek religious freedom, many came because they liked our system of government, but by far the greatest number came to the United States because they expected to better their economic condition here.

After World War I, laws were passed severely limiting immigration. Since then only a trickle of immigrants has been admitted. The reasons for the restriction of entry were primarily sociological rather than economic. The ethnic groups from Southern and Eastern Europe began to dominate the stream of immigration in the decades before World War I. Because of ensuing political resentments, quotas were set up, sharply limiting *all* immigration but greatly favoring Western Europe where most immigrants had come from in the earlier centuries.

This is our first example of interference with the free play of competition in the wage market. By keeping supply down, immigration policy tends to keep wages high. Let us underline this basic principle:

> *Limitation of the supply of any grade of labor can be expected to raise its wage rate; any increase in supply will, other things being equal, tend to depress wage rates.*

Note that this principle holds for wage *rates*, paid per hour or year to any class of workers; it most certainly need not hold for the *total* of wages, paid to the class of workers as a whole. If we admit millions of migrants into this country, hourly wage rates might fall; but with so many more hours of labor being worked, it is quite possible—indeed, likely—that total dollars of wages earned would rise. As long as the demand curve for the workers in Figure 1*a* has an elasticity greater than one, lowering their wage rates per hour can be expected to increase rather than decrease their total payroll earnings. (What if the elasticity were equal to one? Less than one?)

THE COUNTERLAW OF INCREASING RETURNS

At this point we must be careful not to overstate the law of diminishing returns. Working against it, for a range at least, is a counterlaw: *the law of increasing returns* or of *economies of mass production*. One of the reasons the United States is so prosperous is that ours is so *large* a free-trade area. Modern technology increasingly requires larger and larger plants: unless you can produce a thousand electric refrigerators per *day*, you will not realize the full economies of mass production. So, with trade barriers in Europe, a small country like Belgium, which cannot be sure of selling even a thousand re-frigerators per *month*, finds it difficult to have an efficient domestic industry.

Look to the automobile industry for a still more striking example of the importance of large-scale operations. General Motors, Chrysler, and Ford all produce in tremendous quantities. Even the smaller independents, like Studebaker or Nash, can be efficient only because they are able to buy tires, headlights, and countless parts from factories that sell to all the automobile companies. The British automobile industry keenly feels the competitive disadvantages that result from lower volume outputs.

All this raises a question: Would the United States be better off in the 1950's if our population were cut by one-third, so that we had scarcely 100 million people? If you apply the law of diminishing returns uncritically, you will answer "yes." But in view of the counterlaw of increasing returns, the answer is very much in doubt. Are we already regretting the bulge in births immediately following World War I? Will the revival in the birth rate after World War II tend to lower real wages in the future? Probably not, I should guess—provided we are able to import raw materials from abroad on a relatively free-trade basis.

Is postwar Europe overpopulated? Certainly some agricultural areas of extreme population density are. And if urban areas like the United Kingdom must for reasons of defense and security depend upon their own agriculture for much of their food, then a balanced reduction in population might increase their per capita welfare. But if a peaceful pattern of world trade can be re-established, will much be gained by moving people from European towns to Australian and Canadian towns? Nobody knows the answer—but that in itself suggests we must not expect too much from such a policy.

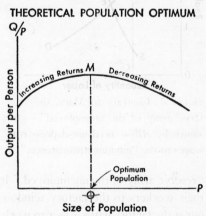

THEORETICAL POPULATION OPTIMUM

FIGURE 2. At the point where decreasing per capita returns begin, output per person is at its very highest.

THEORY OF THE OPTIMUM POPULATION

All this suggests a rather interesting theory of population. Why not have the best of both situations? Why not take advantage of increasing returns per capita as well as of diminishing returns? Specifically, why not aim at letting population grow up to the exact point where increasing returns end and decreasing returns begin? This point will give the highest level of real wages or real incomes and is called the "optimum population." Figure 2 illustrates how the optimum population is defined at the very top of the productivity curve.

Unfortunately, no economist knows in terms of actual numbers what the curve of increasing and diminishing returns looks like. Perhaps we in America should for purely selfish reasons welcome millions of new immigrants and births. Or are we already beyond the point of optimum population? What if Congress were to appropriate a billion dollars in order to make a controlled experiment? Could it find out the answers to these important questions? Why not?

THE IRON LAW OF WAGES: MALTHUS AND MARX

At the beginning of this book, in Chapter 2, we encountered the Malthusian theory of population. According to this theory, you should draw in on Figure 1*a* a *horizontal* long-run supply curve of labor. This should be drawn in at the wage level corresponding to the lowest standard of living at which people will just reproduce their numbers. (Draw in this minimum level *SS* curve in Figure 1*a*, and show why wages fall to the minimum of subsistence.) A century and a half ago, economics was called "the dismal science" because many classical economists believed that wages tended toward the bare minimum of subsistence. In our survey of the growth of populations by births and deaths, we have seen how unrealistic for the modern Western world is this notion of a bare-minimum long-run supply curve of labor.

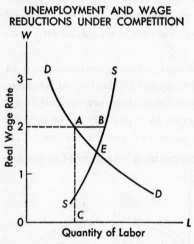

UNEMPLOYMENT AND WAGE REDUCTIONS UNDER COMPETITION

FIGURE 3. Contrary to Marx, the "reserve army of the unemployed" — as shown by *AB* — need not depress real wages to the "minimum subsistence."

A quite different version of the iron law of wages was provided by Karl Marx. He put great emphasis upon the "reserve army of the unemployed." In effect, employers were supposed to lead their workers to the factory windows and point to the unemployed workers out at the factory gates, eager to work for less. This unhappy spectacle, according to Marx, would be enough to depress wages to the level of a subsistence minimum.

Let us try to show this on our diagrams. Figure 1*a* is redrawn as Figure 3. Suppose that the wage is at $2 per hour and employment is at the level indicated by the point *A*. Sure enough, there will be unemployment just as was alleged. The amount of unemployment would be represented by the distance between the labor supplied and demanded AB. In our simple, idealized model of competition, such unemployment could certainly be expected to put downward pressure on wages.

But does the basic Marxian conclusion follow? Is there any tendency for real wage rates to fall to a *minimum subsistence level?* None at all. There is absolutely no reason why in our simple model real wage rates should ever fall below the equilibrium level at E. In a country well endowed with capital and natural resources, this competitively determined equilibrium wage might be a very comfortable one indeed as compared with wages in history and in most parts of the present-day world. In a less fortunate country, we should expect it to be lower.

Thus we reach an important principle: If competition in the labor market were really perfect, there would be no necessary tendency for wages to fall to any minimum subsistence level.

Employers might prefer to pay low wages. But that would not matter. In a competitive market they are unable to set wage rates as they would *like*. As long as employers are numerous and do not act in collusion, their demands for any grade of labor will bid its wage up to the equilibrium level at which the total forthcoming labor supply is absorbed. The workers may aspire to still higher wages, but under competition they do not get what they would *like* either—as long as they do not act collusively to limit the labor supply, their wishes will not serve to keep wages from falling to the competitive level.

SHORTER HOURS AND SMALLER LABOR FORCE

The law of diminishing returns makes it easy to understand why the trade-unions have favored restrictions on immigration. The same analysis helps to explain why they have pressed for (1) a shorter and shorter working week and more days of vacation per year; (2) restrictions on child labor, encouragement of early old-age retirement, and exclusion of women from some areas of labor; and (3) restrictions on degree of effort and speed-ups.

The old labor jingle

> Whether you work by the week or the day
> The shorter the work the better the pay

expresses the hope that workers can travel upward on the demand curve for labor.[1]

---

[1] Union policy today is by no means uniform in pressing for these restrictions upon supply. Of recent years, many unions have revised their views on retirement age; they now oppose compulsory retirement at sixty-five. The AFL has recently gone on record in favor of a more liberal immigration policy for the United States. Some unions still featherbed, but others encourage increased productivity.

THE LUMP-OF-LABOR FALLACY

It would be wrong to think that this economic analysis alone explains why unions pursue policies to restrict labor and effort. There is a related and still more powerful reason why workers fight for shorter hours. They fear unemployment; they tend to think *the total amount of work to be done is constant in the short run.* So what happens if a foreigner is put to work? Or a woman comes into the labor market? Or an old man refuses to retire? Or a fellow worker begins to work too efficiently? Or a machine replaces a man? The worker is apt to think that each and any of these events represents a threat to his own job and livelihood.

This attitude is sometimes called by economists the "lump-of-labor fallacy." We must give this notion its due. To a particular group of workers, with special skills and status, the introduction of technological change may represent a real threat. Viewed from their personal standpoint, the lump-of-labor notion may not seem so fallacious.

True enough, in a great depression, when there is widespread unemployment for years at a time, one can understand how workers may yield to lump-of-labor philosophy. But the lump-of-labor argument implies that there is only so much useful remunerative work to be done in any economic system, and that is indeed a fallacy. If proper and sound monetary, fiscal, and pricing policies are being vigorously promulgated, we need not resign ourselves to mass unemployment. And although technological unemployment is not to be shrugged off lightly, its optimal solution lies in offsetting policies that create adequate job opportunities, and not in restrictions upon production.

A THIRTY-HOUR WEEK?

There are, of course, still other arguments for or against cutting working hours from, say, 40 per week to 30. As our standards of living and productivity rise, it is only natural that we should feel we can afford more leisure. Historically, working hours have been progressively shortened, as we have already seen. But at this stage of history—in the 1950's—would American workers really wish to purchase 10 extra hours of leisure if this meant foregoing a sizable fraction of real and money income—say 20 per cent of what potentially might be earned? I wonder. The last decade of full employment has seen a great reduction in the agitation for the 30-hour week; this suggests that the *unemployment* rather than the *leisure* argument really carries more weight.

Moreover, when a union leader favors a shorter week, he at the same time asks that there be no cut in take-home pay. What worker could be against a free present of more leisure? We shall investigate a few pages later the degree to which unions can squeeze higher wages out of employers; so we need not discuss here these same arguments which are also used to favor the 30-hour week. But there is one argument that does bear directly on the question of hours. During World War I and after, it was found that, when the working day was cut by 1 hour in 10, output did not fall by 1 in 10. Why not? Because output *per hour* increased. This suggests that a 25 per cent cut, from 40 to 30 hours a week, might not require an equivalent 25 per cent cut in take-home pay. But this is a far cry from the claim that workers can take an extra day per week off and not reduce total production. The Bureau of Labor Statistics has made careful studies of the available evidence, and these lend little credence to the extreme claims of proponents of the 30-hour week.

Saturday work will no doubt become rarer and rarer in American industry. Probably there will be a trend toward increased vacations with pay—not so much because the vacation will improve workers' productivity during the rest of the year but rather because people get a great deal of enjoyment out of summer and winter vacations. Taking more time off will be probably one of the ways in which we shall choose to enjoy the fruits of technological progress. No doubt, too, our grandchildren will choose to work a still shorter week than we do now.

GENERAL SUPPLY CURVE OF LABOR

Let us return to our case of perfect competition. What is the supply curve of labor like? How does the wage rate affect population? How does it affect people's desire for a longer or shorter average working day? How does the wage level influence the number of people *not* in the labor force (via age of retirement, years of schooling, women workers, etc.)? Will higher wages enable and motivate people to work more effectively, or will they feel they can afford to take things easier?

These questions show that the supply of labor involves at least four dimensions: (1) population, (2) proportion of the population actually in the labor force, (3) average number of hours worked per week and year by workers, and (4) the quality and quantity of effort and skill that workers will provide.

Of these four labor-supply dimensions, the third is most subject to purely economic causation. We have already seen that, in the Western world, population has become dependent on sociological as well as economic forces. Deep-seated customs and laws seem, also, to determine which population groups are in the labor force of the gainfully occupied.[1] While economic factors have

[1] For a discussion of the relationship between labor force and total population, see "The Labor Force and Economic Change" by Clarence D. Long, in *Insights into Labor Issues*, R. A. Lester and J. Shister, editors (Macmillan, New York, 1948). The labor force tends to

some influence on the morale and incentives of workers, increasingly we are recognizing the vital contribution that the psychologist and social anthropologist can make to the study of team productivity in a factory.

"SUBSTITUTION-EFFECT" VERSUS "INCOME-EFFECT"

This leads us to the interesting economic question; What effect will wage rates have on the number of hours worked per year? We have already touched on this in earlier discussions. A diagram may help to make the issues clear. Figure 4 shows the supply curve of total hours that a group of people will want to work at each different wage. Note how the supply curve rises at first in a northeasterly direction; then at the critical point C, it begins to bend back in a northwesterly direction. How can we explain why higher wages may either *increase* or *decrease* the quantity of labor supplied?

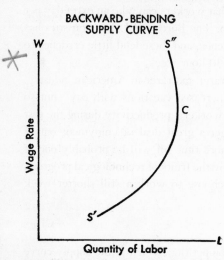

BACKWARD-BENDING SUPPLY CURVE

Wage Rate

Quantity of Labor

FIGURE 4. Above the critical point C, raising the wage rate reduces labor supplied.

Put yourself in the shoes of a worker who has just been offered higher hourly rates and is free to choose the number of hours worked. You are torn two different ways: On the one hand, you are tempted to work some extra hours because now *each hour of work is better paid.* Each hour of leisure has become more expensive—hence you are tempted to substitute extra work for leisure. But working against this so-called "substitution-effect," there is an opposing "income-effect." With the wage rate higher, you are, in effect, a richer man. Being richer you will want to buy more clothes, more insurance, better food, and more of other consumer goods. But most important for the present problem, *you will tend also to buy more leisure!* Now you can afford to take Saturday off if you want to; now you can have a week's vacation in the winter or an extra week in the summer.

grow in depression: when a husband is thrown out of work, his wife and children may seek jobs. Tending to cancel this is the fact that women and other workers are, under prosperous conditions, attracted into jobs by plentiful employment opportunities.

[1] See Chapter 23 for a discussion of "substitution-effects" and "income-effects" in connection with consumption.

Which will be more powerful, the substitution-effect or the income-effect? Or will they just balance each other and cancel each other out—so that the supply curve neither rises forward nor bends backward, but rises perfectly vertically and inelastically? There is no one answer. It depends upon the individual. In Figure 4, from S' to C the substitution-effect outweighed the income-effect. But from C to S'', the income-effect was the more important.

RENT ELEMENTS IN WAGES OF UNIQUE INDIVIDUALS

Generally, one could expect that, after people receive a comfortable margin over what they consider to be conventionally necessary, further increases in wage will not bring forth further hours of work. This was tested by a tax lawyer who studied his professional and business friends in New York City to learn the effect on them of the heavy wartime taxes. Somewhat to his surprise, he discovered that taxes seemed to make them work harder so as to maintain their previous standards of living. Apparently, the short-run income-effect was more powerful than the substitution-effect. But probably most powerful were their nonmoney drives—their desire for achievement and their liking for their work.

As we shall see in Chapter 30 on profits, the most harmful effects on incentives of our increasingly high tax rates seem to be in connection with risk taking and venture capital rather than in connection with the supply of effort by gifted people.[1] And as we saw in Chapter 27, all things considered, most of the high earnings of outstanding individuals can probably be classified as "pure economic rent." Joe DiMaggio earns more than $100,000 a year playing baseball, something he likes to do anyway. Outside the field of sports it is doubtful if he could have counted on earning more than, say, $5,000 a year at most. Between these two limits his supply curve is almost completely *inelastic*, and so we should term the excess of his income above the alternative wage he could earn elsewhere *a pure rent*, logically analogous to the rent of nature's fixed supply of land.

EQUALIZING DIFFERENCES IN WAGES

Let us now turn from the problem of the supply of labor in general and investigate the vital problem of *differentials in competitive wages* among different categories of people and jobs. Supply conditions now become all-important in explaining the tremendous wage differentials observed in everyday life.

When you look more closely at the differences among jobs, some of the observed pay differentials are easily explained. Jobs may differ in their un-

---

[1] According to many medical authorities, successful businessmen and professional people probably work too hard for their own good—as indicated in such groups by the high incidence of ulcers, coronary thrombosis, and similar diseases.

pleasantness; hence wages may have to be raised to coax people into the less attractive jobs. Such wage differentials that simply serve to *compensate for the nonmoney differences among jobs* are called "equalizing differences." Steeple jacks must be paid more than janitors because people do not like the risks of climbing flagpoles. Workers often receive 5 per cent extra pay on the 4 P.M. to 12 P.M. "swing shift" and 10 per cent extra pay for the 12 midnight to 8 A.M. "graveyard shift." For hours beyond 40 per week or for holiday and week-end work, one and a half times the base hourly pay is customary. When you observe a doctor who earns $8,000 a year, you must remember that at least a part of this is an equalizing difference needed to induce people to incur tuition costs and endure the lack of pay during 10 or more years of training.

Jobs that involve dirt, nerve strain, tiresome responsibility, tedium, low social prestige, irregular employment, much seasonal layoff, short working life, and much dull training tend to be less attractive to people. To recruit workers for such occupations you must raise the pay. On the other hand, jobs that are especially pleasant or attractive find many applicants, and remuneration is bid down. People like white-collar jobs, and so clerical wages tend to be low.

To test whether a given difference in pay is an equalizing one, ask people who are well qualified for both jobs: Would you take the higher paying job in preference to the lower paid one? If it turns out that they are not eager to make such a choice, then it is fair to conclude that the higher paid job is not really more attractive when due weight is given to all considerations, nonmonetary and monetary.

NONEQUALIZING DIFFERENTIALS: DIFFERENCES IN LABOR QUALITY

If all labor were homogeneous, every observed competitive wage differential could be explained as an equalizing difference. But turn to the real world. True, some of the observed differentials can be regarded as equalizing. But you know that the vast majority of higher paid jobs are also *more*, rather than less, pleasant. Most wage differentials cannot therefore be of the equalizing type. What then are they due to?

Are they perhaps due to the fact that competition is imperfect? Undoubtedly some observed differentials are of this type. Trade-unions or minimum-wage laws or a monopoly by the workers in a particular occupation can explain part of the existing nonequalizing differentials. If you removed these obstructions due to monopolistic or imperfect competition, people would flow into some of the higher paid jobs and bring pay in these jobs into equality with that prevailing elsewhere. We shall analyze these interferences with competition in a moment.

But never forget that many of the observed differentials in wages have little to do with the imperfections of competition; they would still persist if there were no monopoly elements. Even in a hypothetically perfect auction market, where all the different categories of labor were priced by supply and demand, equilibrium would necessitate tremendous differentials in wages.

This is because of the tremendous *qualitative* differentials among people. You would not expect the competitive wage of a man to be the same as that of a horse or that of a horse to be the same as that of another mammal such as a cow. Then why should you expect one man to receive the same competitive wage as another man or as a woman? A zoologist may call us all members of the same *Homo sapiens* species, but any personnel officer who is trying to equalize the marginal-physical-product per dollar expended in every direction knows that people vary tremendously in their abilities and their contributions to a firm's dollar revenue.

There are about 65 million people in the American labor force. There is no single factor of production called labor; there are thousands of quite different kinds of labor. If you are hiring men to shovel railroad trains out of a blizzard, it will probably pay you to lump together as one indistinguishable factor of production all adult males of certain ages who appear to be reasonably healthy, muscular, and sober. Similarly, the labor market will always group people into certain general classifications for purposes of wage determination. Even after these groupings have taken place, there still remain myriads of different categories of labor, and wage rates of the different categories will have a tremendous spread.

"NONCOMPETING GROUPS IN THE LABOR MARKET"

About 80 years ago, economists began to call these different categories of labor "noncompeting groups in the labor market." Instead of one single factor of production, labor was recognized to be many different factors. Economists expected as many different wage rates would result as there were noncompeting groups. Their instinct was sound, but there is some danger of misunderstanding their terminology.

In the first place, we must not think that in a perfectly competitive labor market the so-called noncompeting groups would disappear. We should still have different categories of labor—just as in the wheat market we have winter wheat, spring wheat, grade 2 red wheat, etc. Second, no one can doubt that these different groups are in some sense competing with each other. Just as I decide between hiring a horse or a tractor, so I must decide between hiring a very skilled, fast-working, high-paid worker and a lower wage, less skilled one.

The essential point then is this: The different categories compete with each other; yet they are not 100 per cent identical. They are *partial rather than perfect substitutes* for each other.

Workers can to some degree cross over from one category into another. If welders' wages were to become $100,000 a year, I might study the art and quit being a teacher. Or if I did not, others would. Therefore, even when the wages of the different categories of labor are different, quantitative wage differences are still subject to the laws of supply and demand. "Cross elasticity" of supply becomes very important: The wage amount that you have to pay to recruit foundrymen depends on what the near-by automobile industry is paying to men on the assembly line.

Or take the case of skilled surgeons. They receive high pay in all countries compared with butchers. Why? Because their work is important? Only in part on this account. For suppose (1) that every year as many babies were born with the capacity necessary for a surgeon as are born with the capacity necessary for a butcher, (2) that someone learned how to train surgeons in no time at all, and (3) that a surgeon's activities and responsibilities were not regarded as less pleasant or more taxing than those of a butcher. Then do you really think that surgeons would continue to receive higher earnings than butchers? And if you think the sanctity of human life is the important explanation, how do you account for the fact that the best plastic surgeons are higher paid than the best abdominal surgeons?

GENERAL EQUILIBRIUM OF LABOR MARKET

In real life as we know it, things are not black or white. There is some mobility between different jobs; differences in wages will gradually over a long period of time tend to encourage greater and greater mobility; and it is never necessary for all workers to be mobile—a few may suffice. But there will still remain certain permanent barriers to mobility that depend upon the irreducible differences in biological and social inheritance. Hence, wage differentials will still persist even in the long run.

How big will these differentials be? Suppose we made it easy for people to get the education they are fitted for and to travel from one region to another where their skills can be better used. And suppose we provided people with the best possible information about job opportunities and about their personal potentialities. Then undoubtedly, the differentials would be considerably reduced.

But such differentials as remain, how exactly are they determined? The answer is provided by supply and demand. *The market will tend toward that equilibrium pattern of wage differentials at which the total demand for each category of labor exactly matches its competitive supply.* Then and only then will there be general equilibrium with no tendency for further widening or narrowing of wage differentials.

Table 1 sums up our conclusions.

TABLE 1. *Competitive Wage Differentials*

	Situation	Result
1	People all alike—jobs all alike	No differentials
2	People all alike—some jobs differ in disutility	Equalizing wage differentials
3	People differ, but each type of labor is in unchangeable supply ("Noncompeting groups")	Wage differentials that are "pure economic rents" or "surpluses"
4	People differ, but there is some mobility between groups ("Partially competing groups;" "cross elasticity" important)	General equilibrium pattern of wage differentials as determined by general demand and supply. (Includes 1–3 as special cases)

B. *IMPERFECTIONS OF THE LABOR MARKET AND COLLECTIVE BARGAINING*

Real-world labor markets are far removed from the ideal model of perfect competition. You can grade wheat into neat market categories, but you cannot do that with human beings. No auctioneer allocates workers to the highest bidders. Studies of areas such as New Haven, Connecticut, show that workers often have only the most imperfect knowledge of near-by wage rates. Nationwide studies show that there are considerable short-run and long-run immobilities: Through ignorance, inertia, or attachment for a particular locality or job, workers may fail to move to higher paying jobs, so that wage differentials persist.

Two tests indicate that the labor market is imperfect. When there is a considerable increase in unemployment—as in the recession of 1938—do wage rates drop as they would in a competitive market? History answers "no." You may be every bit as capable as someone who has a job, and yet there is no way that you can take his job away by underbidding him. Just imagine going to General Electric or any large corporation when the next depression comes, brandishing your degrees and certificates of I.Q. and excellence, and offering to work for less than they are paying. Could you get a job that way?

The fact that a firm of any size *must* have a wage policy is additional evidence of labor market imperfections. In a perfectly competitive market, a firm need not make decisions on its pay schedules; instead it would turn to the morning newspaper to learn what its wage policy would *have* to be. Any firm, by raising wages ever so little, could get all the extra help it wanted. If, on the other hand, it cut the wage ever so little, it would find no labor to hire at all.

But just because competition is not 100 per cent perfect does not mean that it must be zero. The world is gray, not black or white—it is a blend of (1) competition and (2) some degree of monopoly power over the wage to be paid. If you try to set your wage too low, you will soon learn this. At first nothing much need happen, but eventually you will find your workers quitting a little more rapidly than would otherwise be the case. Recruitment of new people of the same quality will begin to get harder and harder, and you will begin to notice slackening off in the performance and productivity of the people who remain on the job.

Availability of labor supply does, therefore, affect the wage you set under realistic conditions of imperfect competition. If you are a very small firm, you may even bargain and higgle with prospective workers so as not to pay more than you have to. But if you are any size at all, you will name a wage for each type of job, then decide how many of the applicants will be taken on; and in terms of the number of applicants who respond, you may alter your wage rate over time. Even in the absence of unions, you will find that it is a perplexing task to decide on an optimal wage policy.

Is it best for you to try to pay the so-called "going wage"? (And if so, what exactly is meant by a "going wage"?) Or, like many large and prosperous companies, should you aim for the cream of the local labor market by paying higher than average wages? Or are you in a highly competitive industry so that you must try to squeeze what work you can out of low-paid people, who will leave you once they can get another job?

THREE WAYS THAT UNIONS TRY TO RAISE WAGES

Dropping the oversimplified picture of perfect competition, we can use economic theory to analyze how trade-unions operate. How might unions hope to raise wages in a particular industry? There are three main methods, and all of them are closely interrelated. (1) Unions can reduce the supply of labor. (2) They can use their collective bargaining power to raise standard wage rates directly. (3) They can cause the derived demand curve for labor to shift upward. These three devices are much alike and often reinforce each other, but there are also significant differences between them.

1. *Restriction of Labor Supply.* We have already seen that a union may restrict the supply of labor in order to travel upward on the derived demand

curve for labor. Immigration barriers, maximum-hour legislation, high initiation fees, long apprenticeships, refusal to admit new members into the union or to let nonunion members hold jobs—all these are obvious restrictive devices that have been used in the past. In addition, there are other, more subtle restrictions on labor supply: explicit union limits on work loads (number of bricks per day, width of paint brush, stand-by orchestras, number of looms attended, "featherbedding," and the like) and implicit understandings forcing a slow-down of the working pace.

2. *Raising Standard Wage Rates.* Direct limitations on the labor supply are today no longer so necessary to unions, except to reinforce the ability of the

TWO WAYS OF RAISING WAGES

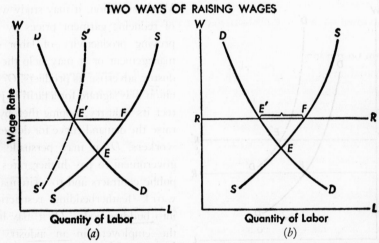

FIGURES 5*a* and 5*b*. Raising the standard wage to *RR* in (*b*) has exactly the same effect on wages as reducing the effective supply from *SS* to *S'S'* in (*a*); the workers from *E'* to *F* are excluded from employment in either case.

union to secure a high standard wage rate and to enforce it. Union leaders have learned this important economic fact: If you can persuade or force employers to pay a high standard wage, then the supply of labor will take care of itself. At the standard rate, employers will hire the number of men they want, and any surplus job applicants will be *automatically excluded* from the labor market.

Figures 5*a* and 5*b* contrast *direct* restriction of labor supply and *indirect* restriction via a high standard wage. In Figure 5*a* the union cuts down supply from *SS* to *S'S'* by insisting on long apprenticeships and high training fees. The wage consequently rises from *E* to *E'*. (Test your understanding of this: Explain the effects on doctor's earnings of a policy that reduced the number of students relative to total population going through medical schools.)

Alternatively, in Figure 5*b*, the union gets all employers to agree to pay wages no lower than the minimum standard rate, as shown by the horizontal line *RR*. Note that here, too, the equilibrium is at *E'*, where *RR* intersects the employer's demand curve. The workers from *E'* to *F* are as effectively excluded from jobs as if the union had directly limited entry. What is it that now limits supply? It is the lack of job opportunities at the high standard wage rate.

This helps explain what used to puzzle many observers of modern unionism. At the same time that unions were liberalizing restrictions on union membership, wage rates were being pushed up by collective bargaining.

3. *Shifting the Derived Demand Curve Upward.* A union may hope to increase wages by any policy that improves the demand for labor. Thus, like the International Ladies' Garment Workers Union, it may study ways of reducing garment prices by improving productivity of labor and management or it may help the industry advertise its products. Or the union may agitate for a tariff to protect its industry, hoping thereby to raise the demand curve for domestic workers. Or it may persuade the government to pay higher rates on public contracts and to write make-work featherbedding restrictions into building codes. Or it may help the employers in an industry to maintain a high monopoly price, with some of the extra profits going into higher wages.

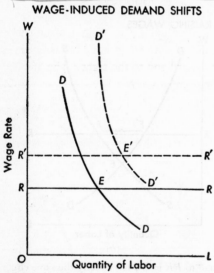

WAGE-INDUCED DEMAND SHIFTS

FIGURE 6. Raising wages (from *RR* to *R'R'*) in this case shifts the curve of demand productivity upward (from *DD* to *D'D'*), with employment actually increasing (from *E* to *E'*).

Moreover, if collective bargaining raises wages, and if increased wages increase the productivity of labor, then labor will have shifted its own demand curve upward. Figure 6 depicts the case in which an increase in the wage from *RR* to *R'R'* itself results in an upward shift in the demand curve for labor—from *DD* to *D'D'*. Note that at the new equilibrium *E'*, both wage and employment have increased.

In the old days, the standard example of this was the case where workers were being paid so little that they were malnourished and therefore inefficient; higher wages might then have made them more effective and thus might have resulted in lower rather than higher production costs. Today in this country, few workers can be thought of as physiologically undernourished, but psychological elements are often as important as physiological. Many an employer has found that too low wages are bad business even from a hard-boiled dollars-and-cents standpoint.

Moreoever, it is often argued that high wages have a favorable "shock effect" on the employer's efficiency in the use of labor. One of the reasons advanced for the high productivity of American industry, even back in the nineteenth century when unions were unimportant, was the fact that high farm earnings made it necessary for industry here to develop good machine methods in order to be able to pay high wages and still stay in business. There is something to this shock-effect argument, but just how much nobody knows. It should, at any rate, be used with caution.

WAGE INCREASES AND REDUCTIONS IN EMPLOYMENT.

If raising wages means simply that you climb up the existing demand curve for labor, then employment will decrease in consequence.[1] This is because demand curves almost always slope downward and to the right.[2] The amount of unemployment created in a particular occupation by wage increases would depend upon the elasticity of the demand curve for that particular category of labor. We saw in earlier chapters that a factor demand is a "derived demand,"

[1] Intermediate economics texts and texts on labor problems show that, where an employer was previously possessed of monopoly-buying-power over labor, collective bargaining can—if not pushed to excess—right the balance, leading to both increased wages *and* increased employment. An employer with monopoly-buying-power is called a "monopsonist" after the Greek words for "single" and "buyer." Before unionization, the monopsonist who is on his toes will set his equilibrium wage at MM in Figure 7. This will always be lower than the so-called competitive wage at E. Why will the monopsonist's equilibrium always be at a point like m? The monopsonist will not want to travel upward from m to E because he realizes that any wage increase beyond m will raise the wages paid to *already hired workers* by more than the extra revenue resulting from hiring the new men.

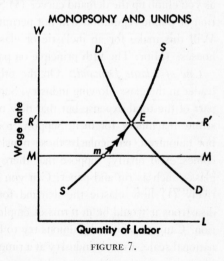

MONOPSONY AND UNIONS

FIGURE 7.

When the union raises the wage toward E by collective bargaining, we travel up the SS curve. Note we do not travel up the demand curve DD. Wages and employment both rise together. (Query: What if collective bargaining raises the standard wage to a level $R''R''$ that lies *above* E? What then will happen to employment? Draw in the arrows on the demand curve.)

[2] Some economists have noted cases where, in the short run, demand is virtually completely inelastic.

and Chapter 27 discussed the four or five conditions that determine how elastic or inelastic the demand for labor might be. The following two cases will help to review and apply those principles.

Case of Inelastic Derived Demand. Suppose that a particular building-trades union, such as the electricians', raises wages. (1) Note that, in the short run, employers cannot substitute other factors—such as machines or plasterers for electricians. Review the five principles to see which of them tells us that the drop in employment of electricians will as a result tend to be small in the short run. (2) Do not forget *the importance of being unimportant:* The total cost of a house will be little affected by a change in the wage rate of electricians alone. Will this fact tend to cause a strong or mild reduction of employment as a result of an increase in their wages? (3) Suppose there is a great housing shortage so that people feel they need homes desperately. How will inelasticity of demand for the final product, housing, affect the derived elasticity for electricians? (4) Suppose that all practicing electricians must be in the union so that an increase in wages is not followed by a great increase in the supply of nonunion labor. Will this inelasticity of supply of rival factors tend to make the demand for union electricians a steep one—or a relatively horizontal, elastic one which registers a great drop in employment as you climb up the demand curve? (5) Suppose finally that imperfect competition or public regulation will not permit the prices of houses to change much. Will this make for an inelastic or elastic demand for the factors that build houses? (Hint: The fifth principle on page 558 bears on this question.)

Case of Elastic Demand. On the other hand, suppose you were a union leader in the glass-blowing industry. Suppose that labor costs are an important part of the total expense but that new mechanized processes exist which substitute machinery for men. Suppose, too, that a large part of the industry is not unionized, particularly those nonskilled workers who run the new machines. And finally, suppose that there are many commodity substitutes for glass—such as tin and paper. Can you apply our principles to show qualitatively (1) how elastic the demand for labor would then be and (2) how disastrous it would be in terms of employment to raise wages in such a situation? Can you show why unions try to bargain collectively on an all-inclusive national scale, a whole industry at a time? (Hint: The demand for the products of *all* firms in the industry will be more inelastic than the demand facing any one firm alone, and also the threat of nonunion competition will then be less.)

UNION WAGE POLICY

Actually the glass-blowers' union did belatedly see the need for wage cuts. Similarly, in 1931 the hosiery workers' union accepted a wage cut in order to stem the tide of nonunion competition. The shoe industry in Massachusetts has been losing firms to other less unionized rural areas; in the postwar period the union has taken account of the implied elasticity of demand for its laborers and has accepted lower earnings than would otherwise have been the case. On the other hand, John L. Lewis' United Mine Workers' Union provides a clear-cut example of a union raising hourly wages—even though this means a reduction in hours of work and a large increase in the sale of oil as a substitute for coal.

Some unions do take account of the effect of their wage demands on employment. But such self-imposed limits by unions on their own demands for wage increases operate feebly to the extent that (1) workers regard an increase in wage rates as always a good thing; (2) the union has regard exclusively for the interests of the workers who will continue to be employed after the wage increase, disregarding the interests of those who will become underemployed or the interests of those workers who potentially might be in the industry but are hardly aware of the possibility; and (3) the demand curve for labor is actually inelastic *or is thought to be* inelastic.

MANAGEMENT AT THE COLLECTIVE BARGAINING TABLE

Just as unions sometimes realize it would not be to their interest to get higher wages, managements sometimes take the view that an increase in wages would improve their long-run corporate earnings. But both of these views are exceptional. Usually at any collective bargaining conference, the workers are pressing for higher wages than management wishes to pay.

Thus, workers in a certain tool company may be receiving about $2 an hour base pay. The old collective bargaining contract with the union may be running out; a meeting has been called between the vice-president of the company in charge of industrial relations and the union bargaining representatives. The union asks for a 10 per cent wage increase, or 20 cents per hour. The employer offers a 5 per cent increase, or about 10 cents an hour. Perhaps the union does not expect to get the full 20 cents, and the company may know that it will have to increase wage by more than 10 cents.[1]

THEORETICAL INTERDETERMINACY OF COLLECTIVE BARGAINING

What will be the terms of the final agreement? Unfortunately, this is one important subject that economic theory can tell us little about. The result depends on psychology, politics, and a thousand other intangible factors. As far as the economist is concerned, the final outcome is in principle indeterminate—

---

[1] In 1951, part of the 20-cent wage demand might take the form of a demand for pensions and a welfare-insurance fund, but the same principles apply.

almost as indeterminate as the haggling between two millionaires over the price to be paid for a rare oil painting.

In this case the final wage agreement might be anywhere between $2.10 and $2.20. Six main arguments will be appealed to during the bargaining: (1) If the cost of living is rising, the union economist will talk a great deal about the workers' *standard of living;* but if prices are falling, it is the employer who will bring up this fact. (2) If the company and industry have been prosperous, the union will stress *ability to pay;* but if the industry has been unprofitable, the employer will emphasize this fact. (3) If *productivity* has risen or fallen in the industry, this will be brought into the negotiations by one of the interested parties. (4) If other firms in the same area are paying *going wages* higher or lower than this firm, this fact will be brought out. (5) Labor will extol the philosophy of high wages as a means of bolstering *purchasing power* and national prosperity; management will emphasize the higher cost aspects of wage increases. (6) If a *national pattern* of "fourth- or *n*th-round" wage increases of so much per hour has already been set by a few "key bargains" in large industries such as coal, steel, or automobiles, that will have great weight in the deliberations.

Most often labor and management will arrive at a new yearly contract after some days of negotiation; perhaps $2.16 will be the final wage reached by collective bargainers in our example. But sometimes they will get stalled— between, say, $2.15 and $2.17. A government mediator may try to narrow down the 2-cent disagreement. Or there may be an understanding that a disinterested "arbitrator" will render a decision, which both parties will accept. Unfortunately, economic theory cannot tell us how such an arbitrator will arrive at his final decision. All the previously mentioned factors will be weighed in his mind, plus the all-important question: What decision is likely to be acceptable to both sides?

STRIKES AND COLLECTIVE BARGAINING

Usually, there will not be a strike or lockout. But at all times, everybody will be realizing that failure to reach agreement will mean a costly strike. Still, it may ultimately come to pass that management refuses to go above $2.15 while labor refuses to take less than $2.17. A "work stoppage" will result. Should we call this an "employees' strike" or an "employer's lockout?" In popular speech, it will certainly be referred to as a strike. But since either party knows it can end the work stoppage by agreeing to the other party's terms, it does not matter which we call it.

A strike hurts both parties badly: The workers may lose several weeks' pay; the employer's plant is almost sure to be completely shut down for the same period of time. Worse than that: The public generally suffers if the two parties cannot get together peacefully.

Radio news commentators ask why workers go out on strike just because of a 2-cent disagreement; they point out that it might take two or three years for the workers to recover—at 2 cents an hour—their loss of earnings during the strike. But the workers look at it differently. To them the employer caused the strike by his stubbornness. They point out that the employer will lose more by the strike than the extra 2 cents would cost him in many years' time.

Why then do both parties let the strike occur? The explanation lies in this vital truth: A strike is *not* really over just the last 2 cents of wage disagreement! The workers believe that the employer would not have been forced from $2.10 up even to $2.15 except for the threat of a strike, which hangs over the negotiation like a time bomb. It takes agreement by both parties to keep the bomb from going off. (Of course, this is brutal language. We all sincerely hope that the day will arrive when language far removed from conflict and strife will adequately describe the facts of industrial relations. But as would-be scientific observers we must not let our wishes sway our judgment.)

Threats become hollow unless occasionally carried out; a gun known to be loaded with blanks frightens no one. Both parties must show that they are truly prepared to incur at some point the costs of a strike. Thus, suppose the employer was deprived voluntarily or by law of the right to refuse any wage demand if it would bring on a strike. Would this cost him only 2 cents an hour? Obviously not. There would then be no reason why the union might not hold out for a 50- rather than a 17-cent wage increase. Similarly, if the union could never exercise the right to strike, why should not the employer offer $1 rather than $2 per hour if he can get labor at that rate?

COLLECTIVE BARGAINING AND THE PUBLIC INTEREST

Within the framework of present legislation, the government does not interfere. Collective bargaining is usually carried on by voluntary cooperation of labor and management. The result is far from ideal, but it is not at all clear in the judgment of experts that more active government regulation and control would improve things. Nonetheless we do all know that collective bargaining in important and vital industries, such as transportation and steel, is "heavily affected with the public interest." To every labor dispute there are three parties, not two. When labor and management fight in key industries, the *public* is vitally harmed. Therefore, in every emergency situation, the voluntary conduct of collective bargaining will always be superseded whenever it leads to a tie-up of the nation's economy and a threat to the nation's security. The government will take over the railroads to keep them running; the courts will issue injunctions; the President may even threaten to draft men into the armed forces.

But once the government has superseded voluntary collective bargaining, what principles are to be used in setting wages? Fact-finding boards are appointed, but that only reframes the question. Moreover, is the problem of defining a "fair wage" simply a factual question of economics? Or is it simply a political question of what public opinion will accept as a fair settlement? There are no easy answers that an economics textbook can set down in italic type. But we must emphasize that a stable and progressive economic system requires all participating parties to use self-control in exercising their political powers.

QUALIFICATIONS

1. *Has unionization raised wages?* The advocates of organized labor claim that unions have raised real wages; the critics criticize unions for having done so and having thereby distorted the efficient use pattern of economic resources. Despite this agreement that unions raise real wages, the facts are not at all clear.

Since 1933, for example, low-paid, nonunionized occupations (such as domestic service and farm work) have shown greater percentage wage increases than have most unionized trades. Moreover, in this same period of tremendous organization of labor, there has been a general tendency toward higher wages—but with the differentials remaining about the same in *absolute* terms. This means that the percentage differentials are diminishing. (For example, suppose you are a unionist earning $2 an hour, and I earn $1 in a nonunion trade. Now let us both get a $1 increase; this leaves the absolute differential unchanged; but no longer do you get twice my wage—instead you receive $3 to my $2.)

It is true that the average wage in unionized industries is higher than the average wage in nonunionized industries. But that in itself does not prove that unions are responsible for the difference. The industries that are unionized tend also to be those dominated by large rather than small enterprise and by firms which use workers of higher than average skills. Even before they were unionized, these same industries paid higher than average wages.

Professor Arthur Ross of the University of California has studied the change in wage rates since 1933 in union and nonunion industries.[1] He finds that the industries most recently unionized do seem to show a slightly greater wage increase since 1933 than do similar industries either that have never been

[1] Arthur M. Ross, *Trade Union Wage Policy* (University of California Press, Berkeley, 1948).

unionized or that had already been unionized prior to 1933. (That is, if we examine industries *A*, *B*, and *C*, all of which were paying about the same wages in 1933, then *A*, the recently unionized industry, seems to show a slightly greater wage increase than does *B*, the never-unionized industry, or than does *C*, the industry unionized before 1933).

One warning: Such statistics on the differential movements of union and nonunion wages cannot give the whole answer to the question whether unions have raised wages. Labor spokesmen claim that unions help raise wages for the unorganized workers. Thus, a nonunion industry's policy may be to follow any changes in the wage scale hammered out in unionized plants near by. If an industry raises wages in order to keep the union out, the union will get no credit for its influence in the figures. On the other hand, if the targets for union organizers are profitable, expanding, high-productivity, concentrated industries, then the union might be riding aboard a moving demand curve and given credit for wage increases that would have occurred even in its absence. Which is cause and which is effect?

If we had a laboratory like the chemist, we might hope to set up experiments to determine which hypothesis is more nearly correct; but the social sciences being what they are, we can only wait for more data to accumulate and hope that they will throw light on this important question. The statistics on national income do not seem to reveal any great shift in the fraction of national income going to labor as compared with the preunion era.

2. *Pitfalls in the concept of a general demand for labor.* A second important warning must be given. It is legitimate to draw up a demand curve of the usual general shape for one small labor market; as long as all other prices and wages are more or less unaffected, it is indeed true that a higher money wage is the same as a higher real wage; it is true also that employment can be expected to fall off somewhat.

But we must never forget the fallacy of composition. What is true for any small sector of the economy need not be true for the whole aggregate. If all wage rates rise, it is preposterous to suppose that commodity prices will remain constant. Thus, doubling all money wages *might* well result in a doubling of all prices. Were that the case, the real wage would not be changed at all. And hence, in a diagram like that of Figure 1, we should be moving neither upward nor downward on the demand curve. (Turn back to Figure 1 and note that the vertical axis represents real wages in dollars of *constant purchasing power.*)

We must never forget that wages are not simply costs: they also represent *incomes* of most of the population. Therefore, the sales revenue of business enterprises is vastly affected by a substantial change in wage levels. Since the demand for labor is a demand derived from the demand for business products, it is clear that every change in wages generally must shift the general demand curve for labor. Hence, it is exceedingly dangerous to argue in terms of an unchanged demand curve for labor.

To illustrate this pitfall, let us ask ourselves the following question: In 1932 when there was widespread unemployment, would an all-round decrease in money wages have *increased* employment? Or, as claimed by the trade-unionists, would a decrease in general money wages have decreased "purchasing power" and *decreased* employment? To the extent that a halving of wages would result in a halving of all prices, all money incomes, and all money spending, the answer must be obvious. Such a completely balanced deflation would neither help nor hurt the unemployment situation. This serves as a warning against accepting the superficial claims of those critics of labor who argue in terms of simple *DD* curves and of those friends of labor who argue in terms of "purchasing power."

This whole subject is one of the most complex in all of economics, and it obviously cannot be settled in an elementary textbook—or for that matter in a newspaper editorial or after-dinner speech.[1] The CIO in the Robert Nathan report of 1946 claimed that higher money wages provided an important key to full employment; the AFL and Leon Keyserling of President Truman's Council of Economic Advisers have made similar pronouncements. On the other hand, for a century wage cuts have been extolled as a panacea for depression. Both views may be wrong; the truth is that economic *theory* provides no conclusive answer.

[1] Today most economic theorists believe that the favorable effects of any over-all general wage cut will depend upon how it affects the balance of saving and investment, or total real demand. If (1) lower wages cause prices to drop and (2) people's cash and holdings of government bonds do not drop in proportion, then the increase in people's *real wealth* may have favorable effects on the real propensity to consume and on employment. But falling prices may aggravate debts and bankruptcy and, by making people pessimistic, may harm investment; consequently, most advanced textbooks in economics seem to advocate expanding people's real wealth and real consumption schedule by means of expansionary bank and financial policy rather than by deflation. This is one of the rare cases where economists are more in agreement on policy than they are on analysis.

SUMMARY

A. COMPETITIVE WAGE DETERMINATION

1. In perfectly competitive equilibrium, if all men and all jobs were alike, there would be no wage differentials. The equilibrium wage rate would be determined by supply and demand. To the extent that country A (1) has more natural resources per worker than a country B and (2) better productive methods (because of capital availability and technical knowledge), to that extent the competitive wage in A is likely to be higher than in B.

2. The law of *diminishing returns* suggests that a reduction of labor relative to natural resources might be expected to raise real wages. While this principle lies back of labor's immigration policy and similar restrictions, historical examples of economies of mass production point to the operation of a counter-law of *increasing returns*. In abstract theory the "*optimum* population" size is at the point where diminishing returns just begins to overbalance increasing returns.

3. Under modern technological and institutional conditions, there is no tendency for population growth to push real wages to a minimum subsistence level. According to theory, pressure exerted on real wages by the so-called "reserve army of the unemployed" tends to depress real wages only to the *equilibrium* level. In the Western world at least this equilibrium wage is much above the physiological *subsistence* level and is increasing with every decade.

4. Fear of unemployment sometimes leads to acceptance of the "lump-of-labor" fallacy. This belief that there is only a fixed amount of useful work to be done may result from the experience of technological unemployment or depression. It lies behind much of the agitation for a 30-hour week, protective tariffs, and featherbedding work rules. But the problem of widespread unemployment calls for public and private policies to furnish adequate job opportunities, and not for defeatist restrictionism.

5. The supply of labor has four dimensions: population size, percentage of people gainfully employed, average number of hours worked per week and per year, and quality of effort of workers. Of these, the wage rate affects primarily the number of hours worked. The others depend intimately on sociological factors.

6. As wages rise, there are two opposite effects on the supply of labor: The "substitution-effect" tempts each worker to work longer because of the higher pay for each hour of work; the "income-effect" exerts influence in the opposite direction—since higher wages mean that workers can now afford, if they

wish it, more leisure along with more commodities and other good things of life. Each individual person's tastes will determine which effect will dominate. But it is likely that for most people there does exist *some* critical wage; above this wage further increases are likely to make the supply curve bend backward. The supply labor of very gifted, unique people is probably quite inelastic; their wages are likely to contain a large element of so-called "pure economic rent."

7. Once we drop our wholly unrealistic assumptions concerning the uniformity of people and jobs, we find that substantial wage differentials will characterize even a perfectly competitive labor market. "Equalizing wage differences," which compensate for nonmonetary differences in disutility between jobs, explain some of the differentials.

8. But differences in quality of various grades of labor are probably largely the most important cause of wage differences. Although it cannot be claimed that labor consists of wholly "noncompeting groups," it is nonetheless true that there are innumerable categories of partially competing groups. When the relative wage of one category rises, there are substantial cross-elasticity effects on labor supply as some people switch to the improved-pay occupation. The final pattern of wages is determined in a perfectly competitive labor market by the general equilibrium of the interrelated schedules of supply and demand. (The student should reread Table 1 to see how the different special cases fit into this pattern of general equilibrium.)

B. IMPERFECT COMPETITION AND COLLECTIVE BARGAINING

1. In real life, labor markets are not perfectly competitive. Employers usually have some control over wages, but their wage policy must always be conditioned by the available supply of labor.

2. Unions try to affect wages by (*a*) restricting labor supply, (*b*) establishing standard rates via collective bargaining, and (*c*) following policies designed to shift upward the derived demand schedule for labor. Of these methods (*b*) is by far the most important today.

3. Relative increases in wages will in most industries usually result in less employment in those industries. This is based on the assumption of a movement *along* a given demand schedule (*i.e.* there are no shifts in demand due to higher productivity, etc.). If the relevant demand curve is elastic, a given percentage increase of the wage rate will cause a *greater* percentage reduction in employment, and hence the total of wages earned will decline. If, however, demand in the operative range is inelastic, higher wages, though still resulting in *less* employment, will nevertheless mean an *enlarged* payroll. The five

principles of Chapter 27 indicate what factors help to determine the degree of elasticity in any particular instance.

4. At the collective bargaining table the following are some of the determining factors around which argument is likely to center: (a) cost and standards of living, (b) ability to pay and profits, (c) productivity trends, (d) "going wages" paid elsewhere in the locality and in the industry, (e) the influence of higher wages on purchasing power and on the level of costs, (f) the "national pattern" as determined by "key bargains" in important industries. Economic theory cannot tell what the final wage bargain will be; the terms of wage settlement are theoretically indeterminate.

5. Usually a compromise settlement will be possible, without government intervention, formal arbitration, or a strike. But the *threat* of strike is ever-present and conditions the whole bargaining procedure. Strikes hurt labor, management, and the public; but if either labor or management unilaterally gave up the right to strike or to veto wage increases, it would seriously weaken its own bargaining power. In vital industries, however, the interest of the public transcends the individual interests and rights of the disputing parties; consequently, voluntary collective bargaining is on trial in such strategic areas and is subject to government controls whenever damaging work stoppages occur.

6. Historically, the extent to which unions have succeeded in raising wages is in doubt. Since 1933 union membership has greatly increased, but in this same period wage differentials seem to have remained about the same in absolute terms. This suggests a decrease of percentage differentials. While it is true that *recently unionized* industries seem to show slightly greater wage increases from 1933 to 1950, the quantitative difference is not great. Moreover, it is not clear as to which is cause and which effect. Heavily concentrated and expanding industries may have been targets for unionization, and the high wages may have been the result of factors associated with or causing unionization rather than the result of unionization as such.

7. A final warning is in order: We must beware of the fallacy of composition; we must be careful in ascribing to the *demand curve for labor in general* the shape characteristic of the *demand curve for one small category of labor*. Wages are more than costs; they also constitute much of the income of consumers, and they heavily react back upon the demand for the products of business. A general change in money wage rates can be expected to have important effects on prices. It is even possible that real wages will not change at all. To the extent that a general wage change is balanced by an equivalent percentage change in *all* prices, little substantive effect upon unemployment or jobs

may result. In actual fact, a general wage change may have nonneutral effects on saving and investment and may harm or help employment. But this is one of the most thorny parts of advanced economic theory. Only a warning of the complexity of the problem need be given in an introductory work.

QUESTIONS FOR DISCUSSION

1. Explain how wage differentials would disappear in a perfectly competitive market where all people and jobs were exactly alike.

2. What factors of technology, economic geography, and legislation help to determine the level of real wages?

3. Show how diminishing returns and countertendencies are linked up with the theory of optimum population. Be critical in making applications.

4. Is the Marxian iron law of wages the same as the Malthusian? Discuss and appraise.

5. How would you prepare a brief (a) attack on and (b) defense of the "lump-of-labor fallacy." Bring in immigration, 30-hour week, and technological change.

6. Upon what do the various dimensions of the supply of labor depend? Show why the substitution-effect tends to increase labor supply when wages are raised while the income-effect has opposite influence. Could the latter ever be so strong as to cause the supply curve to bend back and touch the vertical axis? Why not? (Hint: If the backward-bending supply curve ever becomes elastic, higher wages will be decreasing money income rather than increasing it.)

7. Define and contrast "equalizing and nonequalizing differences in wages." Which of these two concepts would be exemplified by high wages that contained much "pure economic rent"? What about noncompeting groups?

8. Prepare a systematic outline showing how pure rents, noncompeting groups, equalizing and nonequalizing differentials fit in with general equilibrium in competitive labor markets.

9. Give a list of imperfections in the labor market. Show that not all are related to monopoly power or to trade-union organization.

10. State arguments purporting to show that there is or is not "equality of bargaining power" between employer and employee. What was implicitly assumed by the theory of competitive wages?

11. Give three ways that unions try to influence wages. Contrast the first two, and appraise their importance. How important in your judgment is the method listed as No. 3 in the chapter?

12. "Unions can raise real and money wages in a particular industry, but the result will be less employment." Evaluate the degree of truth in this statement, illustrating with cases of great or little elasticity of demand for labor.

13. Review Chapter 27's five principles of derived demand to show their relevance for Question 12.

14. Give a journalistic account of how collective bargaining might work in a given industry. Be sure to report the important economic facts and arguments that bear on the result. How is the public interested in voluntary collective bargaining?

15. Write a short essay showing why it is difficult to answer the important question: Do unions raise wages?

16. Explain the dangers involved in treating the general demand for labor just like the demand for a particular group of laborers. Show that wages are both costs and sources of demand, so that no satisfactory theory has yet been found to reconcile these elements.

Chapter 29: INTEREST AND CAPITAL

CAPITAL is one of the most interesting parts of economic theory. It is also one of the most difficult. In this chapter we shall sketch in broad outline how supply and demand for assets determine the market rate of interest. To the Appendix is left a discussion of some of the theories of the effect of the interest rate on saving and capital formation.

DIFFERENCES BETWEEN INTEREST RATES

Part of each year's national income is received in the form of interest earnings on assets. A $100 railroad bond will pay you $3 a year if you mail in the coupons attached to it. Or a savings account in a bank may be paying you 2 per cent per annum. Or you may own a share of common stock in a well-known company: the company has not missed a dividend for the 90 years of its existence, and you receive each year through the mail $2 for every share that you own, which happens to be about 4 per cent of today's market value of $50 per share. You lend $100 and receive back $106 at the end of the year. You own a corner lot whose market price is $1,000 and which yields you a net rental of $50 a year.

All these examples illustrate two facts: First, financial assets—such as bonds, mortgages, stocks, saving accounts, life insurance policies, and promissory notes—all tend to yield a money return of so much per year or per 6 months; so if you have twice as many bonds or twice as much of any given security, you can expect to receive twice the dollar return per year. Consequently, each type of asset tends to yield a certain *percentage rate of return per year*. Such a percentage rate of return is in the nature of what we call an *interest rate per annum*.

A second fact revealed by our above examples is that different types of assets usually yield different rates of return. In the above examples we encountered interest rates that varied from 2 to 3 to 4 and up to 6 per cent. If you turn to the financial page of today's paper, you will notice even greater differentials in the quoted rates of interest yield. (The arithmetic by which the newspaper computes the percentage yield of a bond is a little complicated and need not concern us here. Only remember this: If the market price of a bond rises while its dollar coupons do not, then its "yield" falls.)

Moreover, if you compare today's paper with a newspaper of 25 years ago, you will find that at that time, too, there were differentials in interest rates. Some of the differentials will appear to be rather similar to those prevailing today, e.g., the securities issued by new and risky companies will usually be found to promise a higher interest yield than those of old-established and consistently profitable companies. But there will also be differences in the pattern of differentials between yields of different securities then and now; e.g., the yields of short-term gilt-edged bonds of the federal government or reputable companies will be found today to be much lower relative to the yields of long-term bonds, and bonds will generally be found to have much lower interest rates relative to common stock yields than used to be the case in the 1920's.

In addition, compare the whole general average level of interest rates in the 1950's with those that prevailed in the 1920's or before World War I. You will be struck by the fact that the average of interest rates is now lower, by as much or more than one-third. From this you will suspect that (1) there are certain general economic forces tending to establish the average rate of interest, around which the pattern of yields fans out, and (2) there are certain economic forces determining at any time the dispersion and spread of the interest-rate structure.

EQUALIZATION OF INTEREST YIELDS IN ABSENCE OF UNCERTAINTY

In earlier chapters we discussed why it is that people are willing to hold some of their assets in the form of zero-earning idle cash, which yields no interest return. What is the major reason for holding cash in excess of what is needed for transaction purposes? The answer was seen to lie in the fact of *uncertainty*. People know that stocks can crash in price, bond prices may decline and bonds may go into default and fail to pay interest or principal, and the real-estate market may get frozen so that property can hardly be disposed of at any price. This same fact of uncertainty helps explain most of the differentials in interest rates. Riskier assets have to promise a higher yield.

If people were absolutely sure that a $100 Asset A would yield them 5 per cent next year while a $100 Asset B would yield only 4 per cent, then they would certainly all want to buy the higher yielding asset. But when they all tried to buy A, they would tend to bid up its market price. And as long as A still paid $5 per year, this increase in its market price would be exactly the same thing as a decrease in its percentage yield. Similarly, as all investors shied away from the Asset *B* which had promised only 4 per cent, its market price would fall. Its percentage yield would therefore rise. Where would this process stop? If there were no uncertainty, obviously only when the percentage yields of the two assets had become equal—perhaps at 4.6 per cent or some other intermediate interest tate.

Under conditions of perfect certainty, there could be only *one interest rate* prevailing for the coming year. Bonds, common stocks, land, mortgages, promissory notes, and even the deed to a machine tool would be priced in the market place so as to earn exactly the same per cent interest on each dollar invested in them. Otherwise, there would not be a competitive equilibrium.

MARKET CAPITALIZATION OF ASSETS EQUALS THEIR PRESENT DISCOUNTED VALUE

Under conditions of absolute certainty, anyone can borrow or lend as much as he wishes at the single competitive market rate of interest. Every asset must be yielding that same market rate of interest. As we have just seen, this equality of yield results from the way competitors bid up or bid down the market price of any asset—whether it be a bond, a stock, a patent, a going business, a corner lot, or any earning stream of net rentals whatsoever.

What exactly is the formula for the capitalized market value of any asset? This was discussed in Chapter 3, and our answer here can be brief:

Under absolute certainty, every asset will be capitalized *by the price bids of buyers and sellers* in the market place at the *present discounted value* of all its future net receipts.[1] These dollar receipts cannot simply be added up regardless of the date when they are received. The further off in the future is a given dollar receipt, the less it is worth today. Why?

Because the positive market rate of interest means that all future payments must be *discounted*. A building far off looks tiny because of space perspective. The interest rate produces a similar shortening of time perspective. Even if I knew you would pay my heirs $1 in 999 years from now, I should be foolish to advance you a cent today. Let us review the arithmetic of this discounting process.

At 4 per cent interest I can set aside about 96 cents today and it will grow to $1 within the year. Hence, the *present discounted value* of $1 payable a year from now is only 96 cents (or to be exact $100/1.04 = 96^{16}/_{104}$ cents). The present discounted value of $1 payable in 2 years' time is only about 92 cents [or $\$1/(1.04)^2$]. Similarly, any table of compound interest will show that

---

[1] By *net* receipts we mean all the dollar rentals received from the asset *minus* all cash outlays for materials, repairs, etc. The method of calculating net receipts is discussed more fully under the heading "Net Productivity of Capital" in the Appendix to this chapter (see especially the footnote to that section).

money, invested and reinvested at 4 per cent compound interest, more than doubles itself in 20 years' time. Then what must be the market value today of $1 payable in 20 years? The present discounted value is less than 50 cents.[1]

You may raise the following objection: "It is all very well to know how to evaluate a single dollar payable at some specified date in the future. But most assets involve a bundle of dollars payable in some instalment pattern over future years. How does the market place evaluate such assets?"

This is a perfectly valid question. An asset such as a bond does pay equal instalment coupons for a long time and then pays you back your principal. A truck probably gives you a bundle of receipts that decrease as it gets older and begins to need repairs. A piece of land may be paying you a certain rental, not once, but in every year. Except for single-payment loans, we must always evaluate a bundle of receipts.

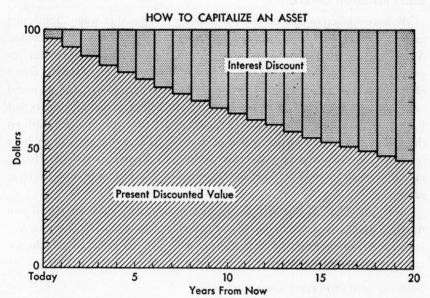

HOW TO CAPITALIZE AN ASSET

FIGURE 1. The present value of a machine earning net annual rentals of $100 for 20 years (with interest rate given as 4 per cent) is shown by the remaining lower area.

But the way to arrive at any asset's present discounted value is straightforward. We let each dollar stand on its own feet; we evaluate the present

[1] The general rule for present discounted values is the following: To figure out the value today of $1 payable n years from now, ask yourself how much must be invested today at compound interest to grow into $1 at the end of n years. Now we know that at 4 per cent compound interest any principal grows in n years proportionally to $(1 + .04)^n$. Hence, we need only invert this expression to arrive at the final answer. Therefore, the *present discounted value* of $1 payable n years from now is only $\$1/(1 + .04)^n$. What if the interest rate were 6 per cent? Or i per cent?

worth of each part of the stream of future receipts—giving due allowance for the discounting required by its payment date. Then we simply *add together* all these separate present discounted values. And thus we have arrived at the asset's capitalized market value—or what is often called its present discounted value.

Figure 1 shows this graphically for a machine that earns steady net annual rentals of $100 over a 20-year period and has no scrap value at the end. Its present value is not $2,000 but only $1,359. Note how much the later dollar earnings are scaled down or discounted because of the time perspective we have been talking about. The total area remaining after discounting (the diagonally shaded area) represents the total of the machine's *present discounted value*—its capitalized market value.

RENTS REGARDED AS INTEREST

We have spoken of national income as being composed of wages, rents, and interest. Or briefly we can speak of it as labor incomes and property incomes. Moreover, the total of property incomes can, under ideal conditions, be regarded as interest! The reason is as follows: After any rent-producing factor of production—land, machinery, or any other—has been capitalized, its rental earnings will appear in the form of interest. The $40 of annual net rentals that I received from a parcel of land will appear as a 4 per cent interest return on the $1,000 capitalized market value of the land. The rental earned net by a truck will likewise appear in the guise of interest on its capital value. To the investor, these interest returns are indistinguishable from any other interest earnings.

This shows that all property incomes could be expressed as interest. From this viewpoint, we could think of the national income simply as *wages plus interest*.[1] (The important thing is not to count any net rents twice: Do not count in land rents and *also* the interest on the money invested in land.)

INTEREST DETERMINATION UNDER CERTAINTY

Because interest theory is the most difficult part of economics, initially we must be content to examine the problem under the simplest possible conditions. Divide and conquer is our motto; consequently we shall at first sidestep all problems raised by "uncertainty." Capital and interest are difficult enough even under idealized conditions of perfect certainty, where everybody has a crystal ball clearly revealing the pattern of future events.

Our approach will treat interest as a market rate to be determined by supply and demand. Who are the demanders? *Business firms* of all kinds. What is it

---

[1] As a matter of fact, if we could legally buy and sell human beings and the rights to their future earnings, then wages, too, might be capitalized. After that was done, *all* the national income might be called interest.

that they need or demand? We shall see that they have a need or desire for assets; these tangible or intangible assets represent the present discounted value of a stream of future money rentals or receipts.

Who are the suppliers and what do they supply? The suppliers are *households* —families and individuals. It is households which supply the equity capital and debt capital that businesses need. One might crudely put matters this way: Households supply their past savings to business, which demand these accumulated savings to finance ownership of machines, etc. (Beware of getting supply and demand reversed. In this analysis, *do not* think of businesses as the suppliers of securities and households as the demanders of securities. In our terminology, businesses are the demanders and what households supply is a willingness to hold earnings-assets.)[1]

We begin by sidestepping all the complications introduced by (1) nonprofit organizations such as universities that are owned by nobody, (2) trust funds, (3) such financial intermediaries as banks and insurance companies. We may suppose that all households do their own financial investing themselves: Either they hold common stocks of business concerns, or they hold bonds and notes of business. Under conditions of certainty, where people have no need to hoard idle cash, the breakdown between debt and equity financing of business would be a matter of complete indifference. Only the total of earning assets held by households would matter.

Table 1 illustrates our division of the economy into businesses and households. We recall the fundamental identity of every balance sheet: The *assets* on the left-hand side of the balance sheet must be matched on the right-hand side by *liabilities and net worth*. The left-hand side shows business assets; the right-hand side shows households' equity ownership or debt claims to those assets.

TABLE 1. *Division between Business and Households (In billions)*

Business Concerns (Consolidated)		Households (Families and individuals)	
Current assets (inventory, etc.)....	$150	Liabilities (bonds, notes, etc.).....	$100
Fixed assets (machines, land, etc.)..	200	Capital (equity ownership: com-	
Intangible assets (patents, good will,		mon stocks, etc.)	300
etc.)	50		
Total business demand for asset-financing	$400	Total household supply of earning-asset holding	$400

[1] Sometime in the past, when the business was formed or as it grew, households supplied it with cash in return for financial earning assets (stocks and bonds, etc.). The business presumably used the cash to acquire productive assets such as machinery, inventory, and intangibles. But all that is in the past, and the cash is no longer the important part of the picture.

In drawing up our hypothetical balance sheet, we have disregarded and canceled out all interbusiness liabilities and claims. (Thus, suppose Corporation *A* owes Corporation *B* 1 million dollars; then in our consolidation of the two together, we shall cancel out the note held on *A*'s left-hand side against *B*'s right-hand note-payable. The debt and equity claims of households against business will not cancel out but are shown as totaling 400 billion dollars.)

Businesses do not own themselves; it is people who own them. In their desk drawers, people hold the stock shares and certificates of indebtedness indicating this ownership. In fact, people own very little else: we can even think of them as all renting their homes from business concerns—albeit in many cases from self-owned business concerns. The only other asset that people could hold would be money. Such cash would be a nonearning asset; and if you knew you could with certainty count on 5 or 6 per cent interest yields on earning assets, you would, except for transaction purposes, not hold cash. So we may forget about such nonearning assets until we return to uncertainty and the theory of liquidity preference.

HOUSEHOLD SUPPLY OF EARNING-ASSET HOLDING

How do supply and demand depend on the interest rate? That is our next problem. The reason why households are willing to hold stocks and bonds— the reason why they are *willing to* supply asset holding—is the *interest rate* paid by earning assets. The amount of their supply of asset holding will depend upon the interest rate. For example, we can write down the hypothetical schedule shown in Columns (1) and (2) of Table 2.

Later we shall examine in detail the nature of this household supply relationship; here we need only note that a fall of the interest rate from 6 to 4 per cent causes the amount of asset holding supplied by households to fall from 450 billion to 400 billion dollars; a further drop in interest to 2 per cent causes the supply of earning-asset holding to drop way down to 100 billion dollars.

TABLE 2

Interest rate, per cent per annum	Earning-asset holding that would be supplied by households, billion dollars	Earning assets that business would wish to have financed, billion dollars
(1)	(2)	(3)
6	450	300
4*	400*	400*
2	100	600

* Equilibrium position.

Now let us turn to the demand side of the picture. How will the interest rate affect the needs of business for capital financing? This is the same thing as asking: How will the market rate of interest affect the total of assets that businesses will demand?

Columns (1) and (3) of Table 2 illustrate this demand relationship. When businesses have to pay 6 per cent on their borrowings and equity capital, they will find it profitable to own and operate only 300 billion dollars of machinery, land, patents, raw materials, etc. But when the market rate of interest falls to 4 per cent, businesses will be able to earn that lower return on 400 billion dollars of total assets. And at 2 per cent, businesses are shown to have a demand for assets of 600 billion dollars.

Why does the value of the assets demanded by business increase with each fall in the interest rate? When the rate of interest falls, the total assets shown on all balance sheets will rise for two separate reasons.

1. *Recapitalization upward of existing assets.* The lower interest rate means an immediate increase in the capitalized values of all existing assets. At 2 per cent rather than 4 per cent, a smaller discount will be applied to the same future receipts. In fact, as we saw in Chapter 3, the capitalized value of land or other perpetual income streams will double if the interest rate is permanently halved.

2. *New projects become feasible.* The second reason for increased asset value is more subtle. At the lower interest rate new assets will come into being. Many investment prospects exist which did not pay at the 4 per cent rate; but when the rate drops to 2 per cent, they will now turn out to be profitable. Numerous examples could be given, but one will do.

Suppose you could build an irrigation canal that would yield a permanent stream of dollar earnings. Suppose the cost of the canal cannot be recovered by the total of the earnings until many more than 25 years go by; to be definite, let us say the canal will yearly earn only one-fiftieth of its construction cost. Then at 4 per cent interest, can you afford to build the canal? Since Chapter 3 showed that 4 per cent per annum is the equivalent of "25 years' purchase," you most certainly can*not* afford to build the canal. But if the rate of interest drops to 2 per cent—to $1 \div \frac{2}{100} = 50$ years' purchase—what then? You can now profitably issue bonds or stock to build the canal.

We may summarize the two reasons why demand for assets rises with a lowering of the rate of interest: The market value of the earnings of all existing assets is capitalized upward because of less discounting, and the lower interest

[1] The last half of the Appendix to this chapter develops these relations in greater detail.

rate will make it profitable now for the first time to invest in assets and capital projects involving greater durability and more time-consuming methods.

In summary: Lowering interest rates increases the assets demanded by business and their need for additional equity or loan capital from households.

EQUILIBRIUM OF BUSINESS DEMAND AND HOUSEHOLD SUPPLY

Putting together the business demand schedule and the household supply schedule, we go back to Table 2 and find it obvious that the equilibrium interest rate must be 4 per cent. At 4 per cent, households are content to provide all the financing that is demanded by business. At 2 per cent, businesses want more financing than they can get; therefore they will go around to households and bid up the interest rate. At 6 per cent, households would want to hold more stocks and bonds than businesses can provide. This excessive willingness of families to hold earning assets will bid up their market prices and depress the market rate of interest on loan and equity claims.

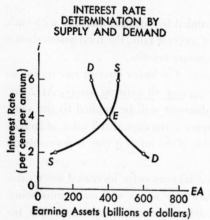

INTEREST RATE DETERMINATION BY SUPPLY AND DEMAND

FIGURE 2. At the equilibrium interest rate, households are willing to hold earning assets (stocks, bonds and other securities) just equal to the desire of businesses for financing.

GRAPHICAL DETERMINATION OF EQUILIBRIUM INTEREST RATE

Figure 2 illustrates this same process graphically. DD is the business demand curve for assets. SS represents households' willingness to hold earning assets. They intersect at the equilibrium interest rate at E. Why cannot the interest rate remain lower than E? Why not higher than E?

The reader can ask himself: What happens to the interest rate when the demand curve of business shifts rightward (*e.g.*, because of invention of a new process requiring much capital)? What would happen if the demand curve shifted leftward? What would happen to interest if people became eager to supply more earning-asset holding? (Hint: Shift the SS curve rightward.)

BRIEF RÉSUMÉ

This completes the bare outline of the theory of interest rate determination *with uncertainty assumed absent*. Is this a difficult theory? To some degree, it is. To understand it, we must keep firmly in mind the relationship of (1) assets on the left-hand side of business balance sheets to (2) the ownership of those assets provided by households—as shown on the right-hand side of the business balance sheet. The demand schedule of businesses for assets, *i.e.*, their desire and need to have so much financing from households, depends on the interest rate they must pay on their borrowing or equity capital. Similarly, there is a supply schedule showing the willingness of households to hold earning assets (stocks and bonds.) This willingness, too, depends on the interest rate.

What determines the equilibrium rate of interest? At the intersection of the supply and demand curves—where the amount of financing desired by business is just matched by what people are willing to provide—there will be the equilibrium market rate of interest.

Note that all this is expressed in terms of dollars and cents. We never have to try to add together heterogeneous items—such as nuts and bolts, looms and printing presses, land sites and patents. The market place gives every asset a *present money value*, and only these financial sums need to be added.

THRIFT AND CAPITAL ACCUMULATION: CASE STUDY 1

Let us now put our theory to work. We may first use it to explain how a society progresses when people are thrifty and thereby promote the growth of the nation's stock of capital goods. That will be Case 1. Then after we have qualified Case 1 and discussed the so-called "liquidity-preference" theory, we can examine a more unconventional Case 2, in which the banking system and monetary authorities bring about the same result in a quite different manner.

In Case 1 we imagine that people are willing to save a considerable fraction of their incomes. Their accumulation of savings means that the SS curve in Figures 2 and 3 is shifting rightward at a fast rate as the years pass by. Earlier in Chapter 13 we saw that there can sometimes be a "paradox of thrift": If unemployment is permitted to develop, people's at-

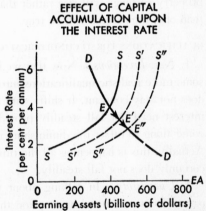

EFFECT OF CAPITAL ACCUMULATION UPON THE INTEREST RATE

FIGURE 3. As people save over the years, their supply curve of willingness to hold earning assets shifts, the interest rate falls, and capital and income grow.

tempts to be thrifty might become self-defeating, and actual capital formation might be reduced rather than increased. Here in Case 1 let us suppose that our economy is a well-running one where this is not permitted to happen.

Sound private and public policies are followed, so that attempts to save do indeed result in capital formation.

Thus, as our *SS* curve shifts rightward, we travel southeastward along the business demand curve *DD*. The rate of interest is falling lower and lower; and as it falls, it encourages a brisk rate of business investment or capital formation. Investment projects that were not profitable at 4 per cent now become profitable at 3 per cent. When all these are used up, lowering the interest rate to 2 per cent brings forth a continued flow of new capital-formation projects.

As the nation's stock of machinery and other capital goods grows, what happens to national product? To wages? To interest earnings?

The nation is becoming more and more prosperous; national product rises because laborers and land can now work with more and more capital goods; so hourly wage rates and total real wage earnings both increase. As long as no new inventions are admitted into the picture, what will happen to interest yields when there are more capital goods to work with the same land and the same population? The law of diminishing returns suggests that the interest rate received by the capitalist class must be falling. But now as a class, the total of their principal is greater—as shown by the movement to the right along *DD*. And as long as the *DD* curve has an elasticity greater than one, the increase in principal will outweigh the decrease in interest rate—so that total property earnings will rise rather than fall. Where *DD* has an elasticity less than one, the reverse will be true.

QUALIFICATIONS FOR TECHNOLOGICAL CHANGE AND UNCERTAINTY

1. *New Inventions.* Now that we have described Case 1, we can introduce some more realistic qualifications into our theory. In actuality, the *DD* curve does not stay constant. It shifts with every technological change. The rate of interest need not fall steadily provided that new "capital-using" inventions come along to offset the diminishing returns to the growing stock of capital.[1] Actually, this is happening all the time; over a century the interest rate most certainly does not fall steadily.

2. *Uncertainty.* In talking about technological innovations we have departed from our initial assumption that everybody can read the future with certainty. And it is about time that we do introduce the important all-pervading fact of uncertainty. Realistically, the business demand curve for capital assets

---

[1] The demand for capital could even shift leftward; this would result from new inventions which make it less necessary to use durable goods and time-consuming, roundabout methods than before. The example often given of such a "capital-saving invention" is wireless or radio communication which supposedly made it less necessary to rely on expensive telegraph poles and underground cables.

is a very volatile thing. It is not solidly based upon objective facts. It is only a highly subjective evaluation of future dollar earnings. It depends very much on the business outlook and on waves of pessimism and optimism.

Suppose 20 per cent of the labor force were to become unemployed suddenly; suppose production were to fall to below-capacity levels. Then the demand schedule for capital would certainly shift very violently. And—as we saw in earlier chapters—extreme reductions in the rate of interest might fail in periods of depression and pessimism to bring forth any appreciable volume of capital formation.

MONEY AND INTEREST: LIQUIDITY PREFERENCE

With uncertainty in the picture, we can no longer put off the relation of money supply to the interest rate. People in real life never know what the future will do to stock prices, bond prices, real estate, or any other earning asset. They may very well decide to pass up a second-grade railroad bond that seems to promise them an 8 per cent return; or because of their fear of a decline in the value of gilt-edge marketable government bonds, they will forego a 2 per cent return, preferring to put part of their total wealth into nonearning (but safe!) cash. This we earlier called liquidity demand.[1]

Now we know one important element lying behind the households' *SS* supply schedule of willingness to hold earning assets. At each promised market interest rate, every investor has to decide how he will divide his wealth between (1) earning assets and (2) nonearning cash. How will the interest rate enter into his decision? Raise the interest rate yielded on earning assets, and what will happen? Other things remaining the same, the investor will be tempted to shift out of cash and to hold more earning assets when interest rates are high.

Lower the interest rate, and what will tend to happen? The investor will now find he foregoes less income when he holds idle cash, and hence he will shift from earning assets to cash.

In short, the *households' supply schedule of willingness to hold* earning assets is almost the mirror image of its curve of *liquidity preference for money*. Each *SS* curve is drawn up on the assumption of a specified total of *M*—the total supply of currency and checkable demand deposits. An increase in the money supply will shift the supply schedule rightward in Figure 2 or 3 and thereby reduce the rate of interest. Thus we arrive at the same result as does the liquidity-preference theory.

---

[1] The Appendix to Chapter 16 discussed liquidity demand for money.

RECONCILIATION OF THE LIQUIDITY-PREFERENCE AND EARNING-ASSET APPROACHES

The two theories are equivalent. The *earning-asset* theory of this chapter speaks of business demand and household supply of earning assets as determining the rate of interest. Or we can equally well adopt the *liquidity-preference* wording and say: The supply and demand for money-holding determines the rate of interest.[1] But although the two theories are equivalent, we shall later use the earning-asset approach to show that interest is not *solely* a monetary phenomenon as some liquidity-preference theorists claim.

CHEAP-MONEY POLICY AND CAPITAL FORMATION: CASE STUDY 2

Very briefly we can illustrate the importance of money by a second case study. Let us depart from Case 1, where personal thriftiness led to capital formation. Suppose the Central Bank begins vigorously to promote easy money by a so-called open-market operation. It buys bonds from people and commercial banks, paying for them with newly printed currency or by its

[1] Graphically this can be seen as follows: Figure 4a compares the liquidity-preference approach with the asset approach. When the total supply of currency and demand deposits increases from M_1 to M_2, we move downward on the liquidity-preference curve from e_1

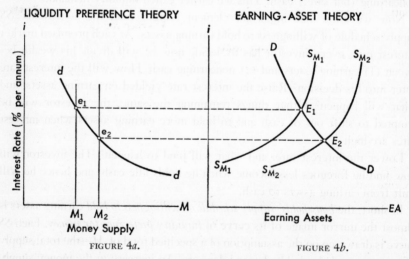

FIGURE 4a.   FIGURE 4b.

to e_2. Figure 4b shows how the same increase from M_1 to M_2 produces exactly the same drop in interest rates. The supply schedule depends upon M in such a way that it shifts just enough to lead to the same new equilibrium rate of interest. (In a more advanced discussion, we should have to recognize that the dd curve itself depends on the slope of the DD curve rather than simply mirroring the SS curve. This is an additional reason why the present total-asset approach is more fundamental than the more derivative liquidity-preference approach.)

checks. Bond prices will rise; interest rates will fall. Investors who have sold bonds will be holding more cash; they will now look at common stocks and consider them a better buy than the reduced-yielding bonds. This will tempt them to buy stock shares; this will lower the yields of common stocks and make it easier for businessmen to raise equity capital.

In addition look at the commercial bankers. They now have higher *excess cash reserves* than before. They will therefore tend to be more lenient in lending to their customers, and through competition they will tend to drive down interest rates on mortgages and loans.

How does all this look to the business community? In Figure 5, the *SS* curve is shifting rightward because of the cheap-money policy and interest rates are falling. (Note that Figures 3 and 5 are almost *identically* drawn.) Businessmen who need equity and loan capital do not know whether this results from thriftiness or from Central Banking operations. It is not their business to know this, nor would they particularly care if you told them.

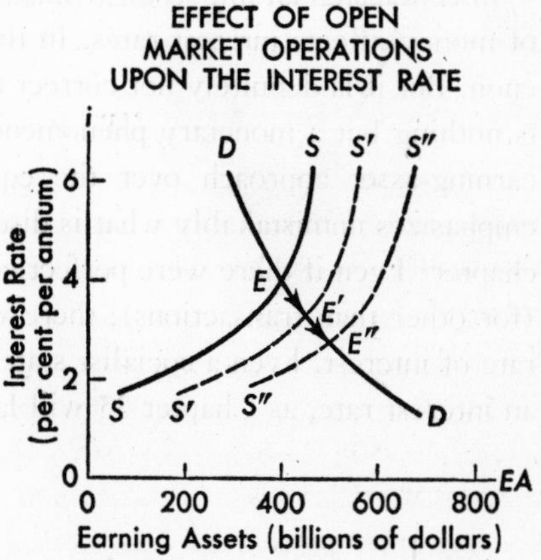

Just as in Case 1, (1) capital formation will rise; (2) the stock of capital

EFFECT OF OPEN MARKET OPERATIONS UPON THE INTEREST RATE

FIGURE 5. When the Central Bank makes capital funds more freely available, the interest rate falls, and there is more rapid real capital formation, much like that shown in Figure 3.

will grow; (3) national product will grow; (4) wage rates and total real wage earnings will tend to rise; (5) interest rates and property yields will fall; (6) total property earnings will rise or fall depending upon whether the *DD* curve is elastic or inelastic.

Quite possibly such an easy-money policy might succeed too well. For if unemployment is already low, the increase in investment will have to bid resources away from other uses and the familiar inflationary spiral may set in.

To control inflation one of two things must happen: The cheap-money policy must be reversed, or else *fiscal policy* will have to step in to cut down on government expenditure and to raise taxes. How large will these increased taxes have to be? Large enough to cause people to release as much economic resources from the field of consumption as are required by the stepped-up rate of the capital-goods industries.

Case 2 is all too familiar all over the postwar world. It differs greatly from the classical picture in which some *prior* act of thrift is supposed to provide the money and real financing of capital formation. In the present case study of an investment boom brought about by an easy-money policy, increased taxation rather than thrift was the instrumentality that performed the function of releasing economic resources from the consumption to the investment sphere. This is an interesting contrast to Case 1.

INTEREST NOT SOLELY A MONETARY PHENOMENON

In conclusion an important truth must be stressed. It is true that the supply of money affects interest rates. In that sense interest is a monetary phenomenon. But it is definitely not correct to go from this to the belief that interest is nothing but a monetary phenomenon. Herein lies the one advantage of the earning-asset approach over the equivalent liquidity-preference theory. It emphasizes unmistakably what is discussed at the end of the Appendix to this chapter: Even if there were perfect certainty and no demand to hold idle cash (for other than transactions), there would in all likelihood still be a positive rate of interest. Even a socialist state would have to introduce something like an interest rate, as Chapter 35 will later show.

Why will there never be a zero interest rate?

SUMMARY

1. A number of different interest rates coexist at any one time. This spread of rates must be explained in terms of varying degrees of uncertainty and risk. For if there were perfect foresight on the part of everyone, competition would bring the interest yields of every asset into perfect equality by the bidding up or bidding down of asset values.

2. If there is perfect certainty, the interest yields of all assets are equalized. The market place capitalizes every asset at the *present discounted value* of its future receipts. Discounting comes in because the market interest rate brings about a time perspective much like visual space perspective. The present discounted value of any payment is equal to that smaller amount of money which must be invested today at compound interest in order to grow to equality with the future payment. The greater the interest rate, the greater the discount. At a zero interest rate there would be no discounting at all.

3. We can speak of the national income as composed of wages, rents, and interest. But if we like, we may take note of the fact that all rentals will be capitalized at the market rate of interest. And hence under conditions of certainty, we could reduce *all* property income down to interest if we wished to.

4. We can divide up the economy into sectors: the *business sector*, whose balance sheet shows assets that must somehow be financed, and the *household sector*, which owns the stocks and bonds of business and provides the equity and debt capital for business enterprises.[1]

5. We can think of the interest rate as being determined by (*a*) the aggregate business demand for financing of asset holding interacting with (*b*) the aggregate net supply by households of earning-asset holding.

At each interest rate, firms will find it profitable to invest in time-consuming processes—up to the point where any further extension of their investment would yield them less than the market rate of interest at which they can borrow. At each interest rate, households will be willing to hold or own some total amount of earning assets. Competition will gravitate toward that equilibrium rate of interest where aggregate household supply just intersects with aggregate business demand.

Those not wishing to go behind the supply and demand schedules for assets may skip the Appendix and go on to later chapters.

QUESTIONS FOR DISCUSSION

1. Give some examples of differences in interest yields. Show why and how these differences would disappear if there were a perfect capital market and absolutely no uncertainty concerning the future.

2. A positive interest rate means that all future receipts and costs must be discounted. What does this mean? How is the discounting done for a particular interest rate and future payment? For an asset which has several future payments at different dates? Illustrate with United States savings bonds.

3. What would be the present discounted value of the machine depicted in Figure 1 if the interest rate were 0 per cent? If interest were 6 per cent? Suppose such a machine cost between $1,300 and $1,400 to build. If the market rate of interest were 10 per cent, would the machine be bought? Why not? At about what rate would it just become profitable to buy?

4. Investments *A* and *B* have the same present discounted value. Most of the receipts from *A* accrue in the near future; most of those from *B*, in the more distant future. The rate of interest falls. Will *A* and *B* continue to have the same present value? If not, which will now be the more valuable and why?

---

[1] We cancel out all the interbusiness claims in the consolidated balance sheet; similarly we cancel out all interhousehold loans; and in reckoning the final net totals, we have canceled out any consumption borrowings from businesses by households.

5. "Rather than say that national income equals wages, rents, and interest, it would be more correct to say that it equals wages and rents or wages and interest." What is the speaker driving at?

6. The price of a bond can be thought of as determined by the supply of bonds issued by business firms and the demand for them by households. Show that in this chapter we have been interested in showing how the bond's interest rate is determined, and not the bond's price, which is the inverse of its interest rate. Show that for this reason we have reversed the roles, making householders the suppliers and businesses the demanders. Show how the interest rate equilibrates the business demand for financing of their real capital assets with the households' willingness to hold the bonds and stocks of business. (Be certain you understand that, whenever we speak of the "*supply of* asset holding provided by households," what we have in mind is their willingness to own the stocks and bonds of business concerns.)

7. Show that, at any interest rate lower than the equilibrium one, businesses will want more capital than householders are willing to supply and the rate will tend to rise. What if the initial interest rate had been above the equilibrium rate?

8. Write a few paragraphs comparing and contrasting the way capital grows and interest falls as a result of an increase in people's thriftiness and as a result of a Central Bank and Treasury easy-money policy. (Throughout, assume that adequate other measures are taken to ensure against unemployment or inflation.)

9. Suppose that a wave of pessimism sweeps over a business community. What do you think will happen to the interest rate—or can you tell? In terms of the earning-asset approach, what happens to the demand curve? To the supply curve if the public is also pessimistic?

10. "People's liquidity preference for non-interest-earning cash depends very much on the realistic fact of uncertainty. Therefore, the interest rate is actually very much dependent on uncertainty. Nonetheless, a positive rate of interest could still persist even in a world without uncertainty and where liquidity preference was of negligible importance." Do you disagree? Defend your position.

APPENDIX TO CHAPTER 29
THEORY OF SAVING, INVESTMENT,
AND INTEREST

Behind the demand curve for assets are certain basic technological facts concerning capital's net productivity. Behind the shifting of the supply curve are certain basic subjective facts concerning people's attitudes toward thrift and saving. Let us begin with theories of saving.

INTEREST RATES AND SAVING

Factual Studies.   We saw in Chapters 10 and 12 that the level of a family's income is a most important determinant of how much it will consume and save. The level of interest—whether 2, 4, or 6 per cent—probably has a minor effect on the fraction of their income that people will want to save.

Statisticians have pored over the historical records to see whether years of high interest rates were closely associated with high or low rates of thriftiness. No conclusive findings result. The influence of interest rates is not strong enough to stand out, even after allowances are made for changes in other complicating factors (such as business activity or degree of optimism).

Also, people have been sent questionnaires and families have been interviewed. But again they have not revealed any clear-cut tendency to save more or less of their incomes at higher interest rates. People seem to fall into three categories: (1) Most families claim that they would save the same fraction of their incomes at high or at low interest rates. (2) Some families are saving to meet specific goals—old-age retirement, vacations, college education for their children, etc. When the interest rate on their saving rises, they do not have to save quite so much in order to meet these goals. (3) A third category of families feel that the higher interest rate gives them a slightly higher incentive to save for the future. Their response tends to cancel out the response of those in (2).[1]

All in all, it appears that interest is not so important as other economic and noneconomic factors in determining saving. A few of these other factors may be briefly listed: family income, accumulated past savings, custom and habit, life-insurance commitments, expectation that the dollar's future buying power will decline, etc.

---

[1] In the last chapter on wages we met this same clash between "substitution-effect" and "income-effect" in connection with the supply of labor. One further technical point should be mentioned: With a higher interest rate, the *rentier* class will have more income, and this should enable it to save more.

Theories of Saving. Since the facts are so inconclusive, economists often turn to logical reasoning to see whether they can determine any pattern of saving. They ask this question: If a man can get back $1.04 in the future for each $1.00 that he takes away from today's consumption, why will he not keep on saving all his dollars?

With respect to the dollars being spent on current consumption, people are often said to have "time preference"; *i.e.*, in consuming $1.00 now rather than $1.04 next year, people seem to be overestimating the present as compared with the future. Economic theorists usually give three general reasons for this time preference.

1. *Risk of death.* We may not live to enjoy $1.04 next year; thus the uncertainty of human life provides one rational reason for time preference.

2. *Irrational subjective discount of the future.* Like children or animals, we may tend to concentrate on the here and now through sheer inability to visualize our future needs and satisfactions. Some would call this "irrational" time preference.

3. *Diminishing marginal utility.* Often it is claimed that your last dollar when you have $5,000 a year gives you less satisfaction than your last dollar when you have only $1,000 a year. This helps explain why you will *not* save all of today's dollars. The less you consume today, the more valuable will each last remaining consumption dollar be; and the more you consume next year, the less valuable will each of next year's consumption dollar be. From this it follows that you will soon refuse to give up an extra high-utility present dollar —even if you are offered more than one of next year's low-utility dollars for it. (Query: If you have a wealthy spinster aunt with a weak heart, can you show that it might be rational to borrow today at a very high interest rate? Hint: How valuable to you are today's dollars in comparison with those of the future?)

This completes our factual and theoretical survey of the motives which determine how rapidly savings will be shifting the supply curve of asset holding over the years. The level of interest does not appear to be an important causal factor. The elasticity of saving with respect to interest appears to be very low.

CONSUMPTION LOANS AND USURY

The primary role of the interest rate is in connection with the community's need for productive capital goods. This was not always so. Back in the Middle Ages, most loans were consumption loans. Loans made by the rich to the needy poor always tend to be rather unpopular. We feel sorry for Esau who sold his birthright for a mess of pottage, and he came to feel sorry for himself.[1]

But in any case, in the last half-dozen centuries, borrowing for business purposes became dominant over borrowing for consumption purposes. So gradually people began to alter their view of interest as constituting unethical usury.

THEORY UNDERLYING THE DEMAND FOR CAPITAL

We have seen that behind the supply curve of asset holding there lie all the past decisions between consuming income and saving it and all the present-moment decisions between holding nonearning cash and interest-yielding assets. We now must ask, What lies behind the demand curve? Why will business firms pay interest on loans? Why will there exist tangible and intangible assets evaluated in the market place so as to yield a flow of money income to their owners?

The answer has to lie in the empirical fact that there is *a superiority in time-consuming methods of production* great enough to make businessmen want to incur the interest costs of such methods. Or, to put the same thing in a different way, we may state as an empirical fact: Capital goods have a *net productivity* in a very definite sense.

Here are some illustrations of this important principle underlying the demand curve. Why does a farmer borrow from the bank at 6 per cent in order to fatten a hog for sale in the market 5 months from now rather than sell it today? Why does not a woodman cut down his young trees and put the proceeds into paying off his debt at the bank or into buying a bond? The answer must lie in the fact that *time itself is productive in many processes*—productive of more final output, of output that is better in quality, and most important of all, of output that will sell for more dollars.

NET PRODUCTIVITY OF CAPITAL GOODS VERSUS GROSS PRODUCTIVITY

This productivity of time-consuming or roundabout methods of production can be taken as a basic technological fact. This fact was known to the first cave man who caught no fish during the morning in order to spend that time in making a spear to catch more fish in the afternoon. Or we may illustrate it by considering a particular bit of fixed capital—a machine tool or hammer. Its services can be rented out in the market place for so many dollars per day or

---

[1] Under proper competitive conditions, consumption loans might benefit both the borrower and the lender, and the interest rate might be as necessary in dovetailing supply and demand as are the prices of food and clothing in a barter between bakers and tailors.

week according to the principles of derived demand worked out in earlier chapters.

The fact that capital goods are productive and earn rents might by itself appear to be enough to explain why capital goods have some kind of net productivity. But we must take care. The big question is this: Are the net dollar rentals earned by the machine over its life greater than the dollar cost of maintaining and constructing it? Does the machine really have a *net* productivity *over and above its maintenance and depreciation charges?* Its rentals constitute only a *gross* productivity; by themselves, they are not enough to guarantee that a net productivity really exists of so much per cent per annum.

In all our examples, we must look for net rather than gross productivities. For the cave man's spear to have a net productivity, it is not enough that it helps him catch fish; it must enable him to catch fish in excess of what he could catch by devoting all his time to fishing with his hands. And when a farmer spends some months in fattening a hog, we must first make sure that the extra pork will sell for more than the cost of the extra feed; then only can we speak with certainty of the net productivity of time itself.

Fortunately, we shall be able to verify that a net productivity of capital does empirically exist over and above all expenses that have to be paid out. But our examples have warned us that this is not such a simple problem, to be disposed of quickly and lightly. It would be oversimple to think of capital goods as if they were rabbits or self-multiplying bacteria.

A DIGRESSION ON RABBITS

But consider the far-fetched case where rabbits are the only capital goods. It will serve to point up how important it is to distinguish between capital's net rather than gross productivity. Let us suppose that rabbits initially grow in our back yards without our ever having to expend any labor on them. If rabbits double every year, the rate of interest will be 100 per cent per year— but only at the beginning. For suppose that, instead of consuming all the annual increment of rabbits, we thriftily plow some of it back into capital formation. Then the density of rabbits to land will be steadily increasing. The biological theories of Malthus and Darwin come into play and activate the economic law of diminishing returns. As food becomes scarce, the net reproductive rate of rabbits will drop from 100 per cent down to, let us say, 10 per cent per annum.

As students of economics you know what this means. It means that land is now a *scarce* factor. As rabbit capitalists, we shall now be willing to pay rent to get more land to grow our rabbits on; and under competition, the landlords will make it their business to ensure that we pay them part of the 10 per cent gross harvest of rabbits as rentals for the use of land. The *net* productivity of capital is now less than the gross 10 per cent per annum—less by the amount of rent that must be paid.[1]

NET PRODUCTIVITY OF CAPITAL

The clue to the magnitude of the net productivity of capital goods lies in the good old law of diminishing returns. Other things being equal, the larger becomes the stock of any capital good the lower will be the amount its services can rent for, and the lower will be its gross productivity. If the stock of any particular kind of machines were to be increased beyond a certain point, its dollars of gross productivity would fall to below its maintenance and replacement expenses and its percentage net productivity might even fall to zero.[2]

---

[1] You might even wonder whether land rent could not reduce the net product down to zero per cent. As long as the market rate of interest remains positive, this can never happen. Thus, if we have to pay 4 per cent interest on loans, we will make sure that our stock of rabbits will have grown only up to a definite critical point. At this critical capital-to-land ratio, land rents will absorb exactly 6 of the 10 per cent of gross rabbits produced—leaving exactly 4 per cent to equal the market rate of interest. But if the market rate drops to 2 per cent, rabbits will be accumulated until diminishing returns (and rising rents) again bring capital's net productivity into equality with the market rate of interest. Needless to say, in all the above, any change in the price of rabbits has been ruled out.

[2] The exact definition of an asset's "net productivity" is as follows: The net productivity is that *percentage rate per annum* which will bring the asset's present discounted value into exact equality with its initial cost of construction; in other words, an asset's net productivity equals the highest rate of interest at which it could profitably come into existence. (The 20-year asset of Figure 1 of this chapter will illustrate this. Draw its *un*discounted receipts as a rectangle. Now apply different rates of discount—such as *A, B, C, ...* Each will leave a different *present discounted value*—shown by a chopped-off area.

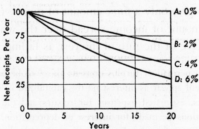

For one of these rates of discount—say that of *C*—the remaining area of present value will just equal construction costs. Hence, the rate shown in *C* is the asset's net productivity.)

If the market interest rate is above the net productivity, the asset will not come into existence. You would not be able to earn the market rate of interest on the principal you have put up to buy the asset. If the market rate is below, so many of the assets will be bought as will bring their net productivity finally down to the market rate. If the asset cannot be readily reproduced at constant costs, or if competitors cannot freely enter to duplicate it, the owner

EQUALITY OF INTEREST AND NET PRODUCTIVITY

But businessmen will never knowingly push their investment so far. They will aim at the following equilibrium position:

> In an ideal capital market where businesses can borrow and lend at a given market rate of interest, they will carry their demand for assets up to the point where the net productivity of capital assets equals the interest rate.

It is this fundamental equilibrium condition between capital's net productivity and the interest rate which lies behind the demand curve for assets. The lower the market rate of interest becomes, the further will businessmen find it profitable to push their investment into capital projects of every kind—the more machinery they will buy, the longer lived will be the machinery they choose, the more time-consuming will be their investment projects, the greater will be the capitalization of existing net rentals, etc. All these factors cause the *DD* curve to slope downward and to the right.

A ZERO INTEREST RATE POSSIBLE?

In a world of perfect certainty, it is hard to see how people could ever save enough to bring the net productivity of capital all the way down to a zero interest rate. As long as there is a single hilly railroad track left, it would pay at a zero rate of interest to make it level. Why? Because in enough years, the savings in fuel would pay for the cost. As long as any increase in time-consuming processes could be counted on to produce any extra product and dollars of revenue, the yield of capital could not be zero. (1) As long as any land or other asset exists with a *sure perpetual net income*—and (2) as long as people are willing to give only a *finite* amount of money today in exchange for an infinitely large amount of income spread over the whole future—then (3) we can hardly conceive of the rate of interest as falling all the way to zero.[1]

---

of the asset may enjoy a permanent surplus or rent; this will be capitalized like any other stream of receipts and will appear as interest on the capitalized value.

In calculating receipts, estimated expenses for repairs and the like must of course be deducted. Should deductions be made for interest or depreciation? No. Because interest is *already* being taken account of in the discounting process, we must not count it in again among the expenses. Depreciation is represented by the decline in present discounted value as the asset gets nearer and nearer the end of its life; it would also involve illegitimate double counting to subtract some estimated depreciation expense from receipts in arriving at the correct net receipts figure. More advanced economic theory lies behind this warning, and the beginning student is not expected to comprehend its significance.

[1] Under realistic conditions of uncertainty, we must qualify the above. Before you have recovered the costs of leveling the roadbed of the railway, airplanes might make them

A zero rate of interest is a little like an "absolute zero of temperature" in physics. We can imagine getting close to it, but we can hardly imagine actually reaching the limiting state of a zero rate of interest. Thus, interest is a basic phenomenon that would not disappear even in the most ideal economic world.

SUMMARY TO APPENDIX

1. Statistical studies of history and present-day studies of families suggest that the interest rate is a minor determinant of the fraction saved out of a given income.

2. Theory attempts to explain why you have a "time preference" for spending $1 on today's consumption when you could invest it at interest and get more than a dollar's worth of future consumption. Three reasons are suggested: (a) rational subjective preference for the present because of the uncertainty of life; (b) so-called irrational neglect of the future through simple inability or unwillingness to visualize future needs and pleasures; (c) recognition of the law of diminishing marginal utility: if you plan to consume too much in the future and too little today, the future dollars will have so little utility that even getting more of them will not compensate for the further loss of present-day high-marginal-utility dollars.

3. Behind the business demand for assets lies a basic technological fact: Time-consuming roundabout processes, involving much durable equipment, will enable you to get more than 1 unit of future production for every unit of present-day production sacrificed. To put it differently: As long as capital goods are scarce, they will have a *net productivity* of so much per cent per year.

4. Investment projects and capital-goods accumulation will proceed up to the point where diminishing returns has finally brought their net productivity into equality with the market rate of interest. The lower the market rate of interest, the further can the accumulation of capital and efficient roundabout processes proceed. A zero rate of interest can, under the most ideal statical conditions of certainty, probably be approached but never quite be reached.

obsolete—or earthquakes might undo your work. In 1932 people expected and experienced zero or negative returns from most capital projects.

QUESTIONS FOR DISCUSSION

1. What facts and what theories suggest that the proportion of incomes saved may not depend so much on the interest rate as it does on other factors? What other factors?

2. What are the reasons underlying subjective time preference and saving?

3. Describe carefully and distinguish between the gross and net productivity of capital. Is net productivity defined in dollars? How then? Does it depend on dollar prices?

4. Show that any asset with a net productivity greater than the market rate of interest will be produced and that one with a net productivity lower than the market rate of interest will not be produced. Show that in many cases "free competitive entry" will force down any asset's net productivity to the market rate. (But note that, if the owner of this factor is in a unique position, he may be able to earn a permanent "rent," which will be capitalized.)

5. Defend or attack the thesis that a zero rate of interest is possible or probable.

Chapter 30: PROFITS AND INCENTIVES

IN ADDITION to wages, interest, and rent, economists often talk about a fourth category of income: profit. Wages are the return to labor; interest the return to capital; rent the return to land. What is profit the return to? Economists do not always agree on the answer. A graduate student recently checked over a number of modern textbooks and came up with 14 different answers!

What shall we do? Examine all 14 answers? Add a fifteenth? The obvious thing is to give a common-sense description of what people generally mean when they speak of profits. Let us call a spade a spade. If profit is a miscellaneous catchall category, let us recognize it as such. And let us be satisfied to notice what are some of the important elements contained in the usual definitions of profit.

We shall discuss the four main definitions of profit. The usual profit figures bandied about will not check with any of the four as we shall see.

REPORTED PROFIT STATISTICS

When a U.S. Department of Commerce or United Nations statistician gives newspaper reporters a figure involving profits, what does he usually mean? First, he means *corporation earnings*—whether they are paid out as dividends or retained as undistributed profits. (In some reports he includes and in some he excludes corporate profit taxes, and sometimes he "adjusts" corporate profits for changes in evaluation of inventories due to price-level changes. So you must be careful in using published statistics.) He may also give the reporters a second figure that has the flavor of profits about it, namely, *income of unincorporated enterprises* (of farmers, of the self-employed, of doctors, of partnerships, etc.).

We know how he arrived at such a statistical figure of profits for a corporation or unincorporated enterprise. From the sales revenue of the firm, he sub-

639

tracted the firm's costs: its cost of materials, wage payments to employees, bond interest, land rents, etc. What is left goes into the figures as profit.

FIRST VIEW: PROFIT AS "IMPLICIT" FACTOR RETURNS

But obviously, part at least of what is left may be merely the return to the owners of the firm for the capital supplied by them. Part may be the return to the personal work provided by the owners of the firm—by the farmer and his family, by the doctor, by the various partners, or by corporate executives who also happen to be principal stockholders. Part may be the rent return on self-owned natural resources.

This shows us the first principle about profit: Much of what is ordinarily called profit is really nothing but interest, rents, and wages under a different name. *Implicit* interest, *implicit* rent, and *implicit* wages are the names economists give to this part of profit—*i.e.* to the earnings of self-employed factors.

SECOND VIEW: PROFIT AS THE REWARD TO ENTERPRISE AND INNOVATION

Suppose we lived in a dreamworld of perfect competition, where we could read the future perfectly from the palms of our hands and where no innovations were permitted to disturb the settled routine of things. Then there would really be no profits at all. The statistician might still report some profit figures to the press; but we know that, under these ideal equilibrium conditions, the *implicit returns* to the labor and property supplied by owners *would exactly swallow up all the profits reported.* Why? Because owners would hire out their factors on the market if they did not get equal rewards from using them in their own businesses. And because people who previously were hiring out their labor and property services would soon go into business for themselves if they knew they could earn more in that way.

We do not live in such a dreamworld. We never shall. In real life somebody must act as boss and decide how a business shall be run; somebody must coordinate the work of the different factors. Competition is never perfectly perfect. Somebody must try to peer into the future to decide whether there will be a demand for shoelaces or what will be the price of wheat. And in the world as we know it, there is a chance for a man with a brand-new idea to invent a revolutionary machine or a softer soft drink—to promote a new product or find a way to lower costs on an old one.

Let us call the man who does any of these things an *entrepreneur* or *innovator.* Although it is hard to draw the line, let us distinguish him from the bureaucratic executive or manager who simply keeps an established business running. Many economists—such as the late Joseph Schumpeter, Harvard's Austrian-born economist—do not think of profit as simply the wages of management. They think of *profit as the return to innovators or to entrepreneurs.*

Today it is easier for us to understand this distinction than it used to be half a century ago. We are all acquainted with huge corporations that are run by managers who own less than 1 per cent of the common stock. Even though these executives run the business, they are paid wages much like anybody else. Management of this type is a skill not fundamentally different from other skills—such as being able to keep books or supervise a production process. People who possess this skill are bid for in the market place, and like any other factor, they move into those jobs where they will receive the highest wages.

The innovator is different. Though he may not always succeed, he is trying to carry out new activities. He is the man with vision, originality, and daring. He may not be the scientist who invents the new process, but he is the one who successfully introduces it. Maxwell developed the scientific theory of radio waves, Hertz discovered them experimentally, but Marconi and Sarnoff made them commercially profitable. On the other hand, De Forest, who discovered the triode tube, also sought to put his inventions into commercial use. But he went broke a number of times and on each occasion disappointed the hopes of investors who had put money into his enterprises.

Many try; a few succeed. The dollars earned by the successful innovators are defined by some economists—like Schumpeter—as profit. Usually these profit earnings are temporary and finally are competed out of existence by rivals and imitators. But while one source of innovational profits is disappearing, some new clever innovation is being born. So altogether these profits do not ever have to disappear completely.

THIRD VIEW: RISK, UNCERTAINTY, AND PROFIT

If the future were perfectly certain, there would be no opportunity for a bright young man to come along with a revolutionary innovation; everything would be already known. This shows that innovators' profits are closely tied up with risk and uncertainty. Frank Knight, a famous University of Chicago economist of the last 30 years, has an important theory that *all true profit is linked up with uncertainty*.[1] Innovators' profits, such as we have discussed in the preceding section, represent one important category of uncertainty-induced profit.

Go to Knight with the story of a broker who guessed that wheat would rise in price and who thereby made a million dollars over the week end. Knight probably would nod and say, "That's what I mean. If the future were perfectly certain, the market would have discounted in advance the coming shortage of wheat and these profits would not have arisen." Or go to Knight

[1] FRANK H. KNIGHT, *Risk, Uncertainty and Profit* (London School of Economics and Political Science, Series of Reprints of Scarce Tracts, No. 16, 1933).

with the story of a broker who lost his shirt betting wheat would rise in price. Knight would probably reply, "Profits can be negative as well as positive. Uncertainty causes a spread between what people *expect* will happen and what *does actually* happen. The amount of this discrepancy is profit (or loss)."

In examining any profit figures, we must always keep uncertainty and risk in mind. We saw in the last chapter that some low-grade risky bonds may appear to be yielding 8 per cent at the same time that high-grade safe bonds yield only 3 per cent. But if the chances are that 1 out of 20 low-grade issues will default on their principal in the coming year, then you are kidding yourself if you think that these bonds are a better buy. Actually, the extra 5 per cent is no more than enough to cover the risk of default.

While the people who buy lottery tickets face uncertainty, the promoter of the lottery faces no risk. He knows that he will come out ahead. Similarly a large insurance company may rely on mathematical laws of probability to reduce its relative riskiness. Why? Because the different risks tend to be canceled off against each other if the numbers are large enough. To the extent that we can eliminate uncertainty by pooling risks, the problem of profits fails to arise. It arises only for the irreducible minimum of riskiness that remains.

In some years, the total of losses may be greater than the total of profits. Risk bearers then as a whole have paid out to labor, to capitalists, and to land-owners more than those factors would have earned if the future had been certain. In another year, the algebraic total of Knight-defined profits may turn out to be positive—so that the factors of production have then received less than they would have if the future were certain. A big question is this: Are risk bearers on the whole overly optimistic? As a class do they lose money and subsidize the other factors of production? Or are risk bearers as a class overly pessimistic—as claimed in most economics textbooks—so that profits represent a positive payment for the service of risk bearing?

Knight does not claim to know the answers, and neither does anyone else. But this much is clear: If we regard profit as the return caused by uncertainty, then profit is not simply a fourth factor return like wages, interest, or rents. Profit is *part* of these factor returns. A worker who is unlucky enough to have picked a trade that becomes obsolete can also suffer losses. Glass blowers displaced by the machine are a standard example of the difference between what actually happened and what people expected to happen. Or a man who by chance studied nuclear physics may find himself unwittingly playing the role of a lucky entrepreneur. Because of uncertainty, a landowner may also experience windfall gains or losses; and in that sense, part of his rents may be positive or negative profits. The same is true of the capitalist interested in investing his principal.

These "capital gains or losses" are bred by uncertainty, and they cannot be predictably expected to recur again and again. Many experts would not admit that they are income; in England, capital gains as such are not taxed at all. In this country, as of 1951, they receive very special treatment: Capital gains on assets owned more than 6 months can never be taxed at more than a 25 per cent rate, whereas ordinary income can be taxed as much as 80 per cent or more.

FOURTH VIEW: PROFIT AS A "MONOPOLY RETURN"

The author once discussed in a classroom these three aspects of profit: (1) profit as *implicit* rents, wages, and interests; (2) profit as the temporary return to daring, but unforeseen *innovations;* and (3) profit as the divergence—thrown up by the fact of *uncertainty*—between what people had *expected* to happen and what actually happened. A student came up to him after class and complained: "Your discussion has confused me. Now I don't know what it is that I'm against."

Probably he, like many men in the street, had in mind a fourth notion about profit. He thought of *profit as the earnings of monopoly.* Like most people, he probably had a grossly exaggerated notion of how much of each dollar that we spend on an automobile or pork chop goes to profit receivers—according to any of our definitions. Most likely, he thought that about 50 per cent of each dollar goes to wealthy monopolists; the truth is that, even in terms of the catchall statistical definition, corporate profits after taxes are less than *one-fifth* of their wage payrolls.

PERFECT COMPETITION REDEFINED

Still if we are to be objective, we must not close our eyes to this fact: In the world as we know it competition is not "perfect." Let us recall again what perfect competition means as rigorously defined by the economist. It does not simply mean that there should be at least two sellers of a product. It is not enough that two companies should compete over the radio in proclaiming the superlative merits of their respective goods; it is not enough that there be partial substitutes for the products sold by any particular business firm. Even if the firm is trying desperately to expand its production and sales at its publicly quoted price, this does not ensure perfect competition in the economist's strict sense. Perfect competition is a much stricter condition than any of these—or than all of them put together. *Perfect competition means that each seller has absolutely no control over price*; it means that his demand curve is perfectly horizontal and *infinitely* elastic; it means that no person is able to control any significant fraction of the total of any category of productive resource.

We have seen in Chapter 24 and elsewhere that this is a far cry from the real world. Almost all firms, except farmers, can raise or lower their prices without losing or gaining *all* the customers in the market. Instead their demand curves are somewhat tipped, and there is a discrepancy between price and marginal revenue. Most market situations are imperfectly competitive—a blend between competition and monopoly. But this near-universal condition is by no means necessarily illegal or immoral. When we go on to examine the ownership of productive factors, we see that no two factors are quite alike. Your abilities as a worker and those of your neighbor are somewhat different. If we define your precise pattern of abilities as a separate factor of production, then we must admit that you do own and control an appreciable fraction of the total of that unique factor of production—100 per cent, in fact. Or you may be the sole owner of the patent to a particular process. Or you may own the only site where the river narrows down to its most suitable place for a bridge. Or there may be no acre of Iowa farm land quite like yours.

Let us see how this ties in with imperfect competition. Your neighbors are a little different from you certainly. But in all probability they are enough like you so that the wage rate for your services would not be appreciably different even if you *withheld* some from the market. You really do not possess any appreciable monopoly power because the demand for the factor you own is for practical purposes infinitely elastic.

The same is true of your acre of good Iowa corn land. If you let half of it stand idle, the price of corn would not be affected; and the derived price for your land would be unchanged even though you and your family know that there is really no other farmstead quite like it.

And note this: If the land is sufficiently fertile, you will, of course, be making quite a living off your farm. Perhaps you may even be in the top 2 per cent of the income distribution. Even though competition is perfect, this rent return to the land you own can*not* be competed away by rival farmers. As long as the Good Lord made only a limited amount of fertile Iowa farm land, it will earn a rent for its owner—regardless of how he originally acquired title to the land. *Competitively determined rents are the results of a natural scarcity.*

"CONTRIVED SCARCITIES" VERSUS "NATURAL SCARCITIES"

It is quite a different matter if the demand for one of your factors of production is negatively inclined rather than infinitely elastic. (Let us review what this means: It means that, when you raise your price, you still can sell *some* of your factor; this is the sense in which you have some monopoly control over price.) If you are the sole owner of an important patent, it will pay you to charge a price so as to limit its use. If audiences swoon to your singing as to nobody else's, then you will have to remember that, the more you sing, the lower will be the price that the market will pay for your singing. If you own the best site for a bridge, then you must be careful not to sell anyone else the lot next to it; otherwise, he will be able to offer the bridgebuilders a site that is nearly as good as yours, and this will limit the dollars you can derive from yours.

What does all this add up to? It means that, *as soon as there is an appreciable deviation from perfect competition, it will pay you to take account of the fact that you will spoil the market the more you offer of your factor.*

Any prudent firm takes account of the loss on all previous units resulting when it sells an extra unit of product, and it is its marginal revenue—lower than price because of the loss on previous units—which a prudent firm concentrates on. So with you as the owner of a factor. You are interested in the *marginal* or *extra revenue* that the factor brings you. You will not withhold *all* the factor from the market—that would bring you in *no* revenue at all. Nor will you provide so much of the factor that it becomes a free good and brings in no revenue. As a quasi-monopolist or imperfect competitor, what should you do? You will withhold just so much of that service as will bring its marginal revenue down to zero.[1]

Our principle is this: *Under imperfect competition, it pays people to limit the supply of their factors.* By definition, natural scarcities are such that nothing can be done about them. But under imperfect competition, we encounter in addition so-called *contrived scarcities.*

MONOPOLY EARNINGS AS THE RETURN TO "CONTRIVED SCARCITIES"

Hence, the fourth view of profits as a monopoly return is often reformulated in the economic textbooks to read as follows: *Part of what is called profit is the return to a "contrived scarcity."* This return takes the form of rent, wages, or interest, depending on the nature of the factor in question and on the contractual relations set up to handle the particular situation. (For example, an investor may buy the bridge-site land at the full-capitalized value of its monopoly earning power. To him, the return will seem to be interest.) So monopoly profits are inextricably tied up with wages, interest, and rent.

ETHICAL ATTITUDES TOWARD PROFITS

Any sampling of public opinion shows a fairly widespread hostility toward profit. A scientist recently asked a random sample of businessmen if they

---

[1] Of course, there may be some discomfort to you in rendering the service, or you may have the opportunity of selling the service in some other market—as in the case where you could use your bridge site to grow corn. In these cases, you will obviously equate marginal revenue to some defined marginal *cost* rather than to zero.

"tried to maximize their profit." To a man they all denied this firmly, perhaps because they pictured a profit maximizer as some kind of chiseling extortionist or miser. But then the scientist asked the same businessmen whether they thought any change in their present price policies could be counted on to make them better off in the long run. To a man, they all replied that they were already doing as well as they could hope to do.

It is misleading to talk about "a profit system." Ours is a *profit-and-loss* system. Profits are the carrots held out as an incentive to efficiency, and losses are the penalties paid for using inefficient methods or for devoting resources to uses not desired by spending consumers.

Within the framework of law and custom—where it is both illegal and uncustomary to put sand in sugar—what does the pursuit of profit mean? It means that the businessman, like anybody else, is trying to get as much as he can for the resources at his disposal. This is not different from what a worker is doing when he changes occupations or joins a union. If competition is perfect, the businessman will end up with no *excess profits*. If competition worked perfectly, the attempt by all to reap excess profits would result in none succeeding. Competitors would have to run hard in order to stay in the same place! This is a paradox, but it is true nonetheless.

Does the disappearance of profits mean that the businessman's land, acumen, sweat, and financial investment will go without reward? No, certainly not. Even under perfect competition, his factors will earn wages, interest, and rent. Much of the hostility toward profit is really hostility toward the extremes of inequality in the distribution of money income.

THE IMMEASURABILITY OF PROFIT

How important are these four different categories of profit? We have no way of knowing. It would be nice if we could say that so many billion dollars of the reported total of profit is implicit wages, so many billions implicit interest, and so many billions implicit rents and, of the remainder, so much is innovator's profit and so much is the algebraic total due to uncertainty generally. It would be nice, too, if we could divide the total of all factor incomes into two separate parts: (1) the return to so-called contrived scarcities and (2) the competitive rent return to so-called natural scarcities.

But probably we shall never be able to do this with precision. And what good would it do us if we could? Well, for one thing, some reformers believe that, if only Congress could easily identify every situation of an illegally contrived scarcity, it might hope to bring about a more efficient use of resources.[1]

[1] Wherever contrived scarcities exist, they distort the optimum pattern of resource use. They may also create high earnings for the people involved. But high earnings do not always

Or some citizens may think that, if Congress could identify the temporary profits due to innovation, it might try to tax them more heavily. And some may agitate for reversal of the present light treatment of capital gains and propose that Congress tax the profits arising from uncertainty more heavily than it taxes ordinary income.

EFFECTS OF TAXATION ON PROFITS

But even if you are opposed to high profits, you know that taxing profits will raise grave problems. Such legislation will have many effects on the economic system, and we had better examine these effects hardheadedly before making up our minds on how far to go in this direction. Let us examine some of the effects of taxing each of the four different kinds of profit.

1. Suppose you pass a law taxing a corporation's implicit interest more heavily than the explicit interest it pays out to bondholders. What are the consequences likely to be? To answer this question, we do not have to put ourselves into a trance, for the American corporation income tax is just such a law.

Standard Oil has to pay the government 47 cents out of each dollar earned on the capital supplied by its stockholders; on the capital it raises through bond flotations, it does not have to pay corporate taxes. (That is, Standard Oil can deduct from its taxable income each dollar of bond interest, but it *cannot* deduct any dollars paid out in dividends or plowed back as undistributed profits). What is the result? If Standard Oil is just indifferent between bond or stock financing, it will tend to rely on bonds in order to make its capital earnings show up as explicit rather than implicit interest. (The reader may work out the following similar problem: When I quit my job for a week in order to paint my house, I switch from explicit to implicit wages and the latter is not taxed as personal income. What tendencies would you attribute to this feature of our tax system?)

2. The case of taxing innovators' profit is even clearer. Taxing a retired innovator's income may seem to have no distorting effects. But we must not forget the young innovator who can then no longer look forward to reaping a tidy sum from his new ideas. He may decide to take that civil service job or to remain the thirteenth vice-president of a bank. You cannot tax the results of an old innovation without affecting the prospects of an as-yet-unborn in-

follow. Thus, under imperfect or monopolistic competition, there may be many taxicabs or grocery stores. Each owner may have a sloping demand curve and may be setting a price in excess of marginal cost. Yet there may be so many imperfect competitors that none of them is earning more than he could get in a perfectly competitive industry. Wiping out the imperfections and illegally contrived scarcities might improve the pattern of production, but it still might not have much effect on the relative distribution of income.

novation. (Incidentally, this provides a partial defense of patents. Society deliberately gives a man a monopoly; this permits him artificially to keep something *partially* scarce. But society hopes that the offered bribe of monopoly will encourage the invention of things that would otherwise be 100 per cent scarce).

3. If Congress taxes risky activities more heavily than routine activities, what can any reasonable person expect to happen? People will naturally tend to avoid venturous fields and to gravitate toward routine, steady ones. But all of us—rich and poor alike—have a great stake in promoting vigorous exploration of new ways of doing things. Not only has scientific and technological innovation been the secret of our material progress, but in addition the investment associated with venturesome projects is just what the doctor orders to avoid depression and mass unemployment.

As we have seen, our present tax system already discriminates against venture capital. It is true that income taxation is being improved by introducing systems of "averaging income" over more than one year; but until further reforms are made, it remains partially a case of "heads I lose, tails the government wins." The losses brought to me by uncertainty cannot be fully offset against my gains, and taxing profits still more heavily would increase the harmful effects on venture capital.

4. In advocating taxation of monopoly profits you may think you are on more solid ground. But how can you decide what fraction of any company's profits are attributable to these so-called contrived rather than natural scarcities? In 1920 the American Viscose Company dominated the rayon field with its patents, and it earned 156 per cent on its capital. Perhaps the courts might identify cases like this as monopoly profit; perhaps not. But such simple cases are the exception, since we have seen that returns to alleged contrived scarcities are intermingled with all factor returns. Monopoly profits may already have been capitalized and may appear in the guise of interest, or they may take the form of high wages.

Moreover, the best cure for monopoly is not to transfer its earnings to the state, as King Louis XV and other despots used to do with their salt and match taxes. If a factor is not naturally scarce, why keep it artificially scarce? Where the government can recognize illegal monopoly, it should deal with it by court action or by public-utility regulation. It would seem sounder policy to wipe out excessive monopoly profits by price cuts rather than to transfer them by taxation.

WARTIME EXCESS-PROFITS TAXES

The pattern of supply and demand is tremendously altered by any major war. The government enters the market as a huge-scale purchaser of war materials, and these expenditures cause a surge of demand in almost every line of activity. With or without the imposition of price controls and "governmental renegotiation of contracts," earnings in many industries shoot far above their peacetime levels. Common justice suggests that nobody ought to reap windfall gains at a time when other men are asked to risk their lives on the battlefield.

The excess-profits tax in force in early 1951 may be used to illustrate the nature of excess-profit taxation. Suppose my corporation has an income of $125,000. *All* of this is subject to corporate income tax: on the first $25,000 I pay 20 per cent, and on the $100,000 in excess of $25,000 I pay (20 + 27) per cent. Altogether I pay $52,000 of corporate income taxes on ordinary profits.

But not all of my $125,000 income is treated as excess profits. Only the dollars over and above some established earnings base represent excess profits. Thus, if my "base" is $75,000, then I have $50,000 of excess profits and on this I must pay 30 per cent, or $15,000, of additional excess-profits tax.

Obviously I want to have as high a base as possible. How is it computed? I have two choices and can pick the better one of the two: (1) I calculate my average positive corporate income in the three best years of the period 1946–1949 and take 85 per cent of this as my base; or (2) I calculate certain percentages of my "invested capital."[1]

In a time of emergency, when patriotic motives are to the forefront and winning of the war is the paramount objective, such a temporary tax may be heavy and still have little distorting effect upon incentives or production. Nevertheless, if long prolonged, the tax is likely to involve inequities. A growing concern, which had struggled along in pretax years with low earnings, is hit far more heavily than an established firm with a comfortable profit record. As the tax persists, unfortunate and unintended effects may emerge. A firm may incur expenditures it would not have dreamed of making in the absence of the tax; if the money were to go into the profit account, the government would take practically all of it anyhow. The longer that heavy excess taxation continues, the greater become its distorting effects upon efficiency and progress.

INCENTIVES, SURPLUSES, AND EQUITY

Throughout the Western world voters show themselves often to be in favor of measures that tax the rich relatively more than the poor and that tend to reduce the inequality of income distribution. Within the framework of con-

---

[1] The details are complicated and subject to changes. Also there are elaborate relief provisions for growing companies, depressed companies, public utilities, new investment, etc. No firm ever has to pay more than 62 per cent of its income in total taxes, and every firm has a "base" of at least $25,000. In early 1951, the outlook is for an increase of some 8 per cent in the corporate income tax rate.

stitutional government, it is the privilege of the electorate to press for what they regard to be ethically the good life; but in weighing what they consider to be the ethical advantages of a more equal distribution of income, the public should rationally face what may be some of the concomitant effects—(1) reduced venturesomeness and risk taking, (2) distortion of efforts, and (3) reduced thriftiness. These last two have been discussed in the two previous chapters. Perhaps it is fair to conclude that the effects on venture capital are the most serious of all.

PROFIT NOT NECESSARILY A SURPLUS

The prevailing hostility toward so-called profits shows that there is a fifth—and fallacious—definition of profit running around in the back of most people's minds. They think of profits as being *the unnecessary surplus* that factors earn. Our earlier discussion of the rent earned by inelastically supplied land show that "taxable surpluses" may indeed occasionally exist. And if we examine the case of *any* factor of production, it must be clear that, every time you raise prices in order to coax out the last or marginal unit, you are in part creating kind of an extra surplus for all the factors already employed.[1] (Thus in World War I the government raised the price of copper so as to bring inefficient mines into operation; in doing this, it created high earnings for the more efficient mines.)

Every factor income, therefore, has in it both elements of (1) *surplus* and (2) *incentive payment*. But that does not mean that you can take the 250 billion dollars of national income and divide it up into two parts—say 100 billion dollars of taxable surplus and 150 billion dollars of incentive payments. *The two are hopelessly intertwined;* and unless you were to make a study of each and every factor or commodity unit and were to name a different price for each unit—as was done by OPA for the copper industry in World War II—you would have no way of hitting at the surplus without at the same time doing damage to incentives. The fifth notion of profit as a surplus must therefore be handled with the greatest care.

When we come to survey the features of different economic systems, we shall return again to the issue of incentives.

[1] In more advanced texts, Alfred Marshall and others term this "producers' surplus," which is closely analogous to "consumers' surplus."

SUMMARY

1. Profit is a highly miscellaneous catchall category. In national income statistics, it is the total of lumped-together corporate earnings and the income of unincorporated enterprises. But really four different concepts of profit must be carefully distinguished.

2. Much of what is called profit is really *implicit* interest, rent, and wages payable for the productive factors provided by the owners of the business.

3. The special category of *high temporary earnings resulting from innovation* is often termed profit by many economists. Routine management earns wages, they say, but profit may accrue to genuine entrepreneurship.

4. *Uncertainty* is the all-pervading fact of life. This makes innovation possible, and it also creates positive and negative divergences between what factors expect to earn and what they actually end up earning. Frank Knight and other economists define profit and loss as the *unforeseeable discrepancies created by uncertainty.* Whether the algebraic total is positive or negative will depend upon luck, upon events, and upon the unanswerable question: Are people on the whole overoptimistic so that they accept too many risks? Or are they overpessimistic so that a positive price is being paid for the limited supply of risk bearing, as many textbooks claim?

5. Still another definition of profit is: the return accruing as the result of a monopoly position. This concept is sometimes varied to describe profit as part of the return resulting from a "contrived scarcity." This return may appear in the form of rent, wages, or interest.

6. The taxation of any of these categories of profit can be expected to have definite repercussions, many of them undesirable from any viewpoint. The fifth notion of profit as *an identifiable and taxable surplus rather than incentive payment* is dangerously oversimple. If the public wishes to pursue what it calls equity or an ethically more desirable distribution of income, let it face and weigh what some of the costs may be—particularly in the important field of risk taking.

QUESTIONS FOR DISCUSSION

1. Explain why what is usually called "profits" is made up of different things. Define "implicit" and "explicit" factor earnings. Illustrate.

2. The second and third views of profit are closely related to each other. Why? Show that they have little to do with the notion of implicit earnings.

3. Give examples of innovation. How might they be affected by taxation? Do the same for risk taking.

4. What is meant by imperfect competition? By perfect competition? Is it possible to point to a monopoly profit which everyone will think "bad"?

5. Why attempt to distinguish between natural and contrived scarcities? Is it easy to do so in any case?

6. What are the ethical and incentive aspects of heavier taxation of what is called profits or of higher incomes generally?

7. A tax on corporate profits tends to push a corporation into bond financing rather than stock financing. What undesirable effects, if any, do you see in this method of financing?

8. Under perfect competition, profit would disappear (except in the short run) but the businessman would still earn a return in the form of wages, interest, and rent. Does this mean that the establishment of perfect competition (assuming this to be possible) and the elimination of profit would be a desirable objective for society? Why or why not?

PART FIVE

International Trade

and Finance

Chapter 31: THE BALANCE OF
INTERNATIONAL PAYMENTS

IN THE earlier chapters of this book we have taken international trade more or less for granted. Here in Part Five we wish to analyze explicitly the interesting economic problems arising as soon as an economy begins to engage in foreign trade. The present chapter and its Appendix deal with the monetary mechanisms involved in international trade. In the following chapter we put these principles to work to help us understand the contemporary international economic scene. Then in the two final chapters of Part Five, we concentrate on the basic real factors that underlie international trade and are often obscured by the monetary veil which covers all international transactions. These basic real factors are involved in any rational appraisal of the problems raised by tariffs and other barriers to the international division of labor.

FOREIGN EXCHANGE RATES

If I buy maple sugar from Vermont or pig iron from Pittsburgh, I naturally want to pay in dollars. Also, the farmers and steel producers in question expect to be paid in dollars, because their expenses are all in dollars and because their living costs are all in dollars. Within a country, economic transactions are simple.

But if I wish to buy an English bicycle, matters are more complicated. I must pay in British money, or what is called "pounds sterling," rather than in dollars. Similarly, an Englishman must somehow get dollars to an American producer if he wants our merchandise. Most Americans have never seen a British pound note. Certainly they would accept pounds only if they could be sure of converting them into American dollars—dollars to spend or save.

Clearly, therefore, exports and imports of goods between nations with different units of money introduce a new economic factor: the foreign exchange rate, giving the price of the foreigner's unit of money in terms of our own.

Thus, the price of a British pound is in 1950 about $2.80. There is, of course, a foreign exchange rate between American money and the currencies of each and every country: 50 cents for a Philippine peso, less than 1 cent for a French franc, etc.[1]

Given the foreign exchange rates, it is now simple for me to buy my English bicycle. Suppose its quoted price is £20 (*i.e.*, 20 British pounds). All I have to do is look up in the newspaper the foreign exchange rate for pounds. If this is $2.80 per pound, I simply go to a bank or post office with $56 and ask that the money be used to pay the English bicycle exporter. Pay him what? Pounds, of course, the only kind of money he needs.

Whether I use the post office or a bank or a broker is of no particular importance. In fact it is all the same if the English exporter sends me a bill requesting payments in dollars. In any case, he ultimately wants pounds, not dollars, and will soon trade the $56 for £20. (Needless to say, we are neglecting commission charges and the cost of money orders.)

The reader should be able to show what a British importer of American grains or automobiles has to do if he wants to buy, say, a $2,800 shipment from an American exporter. In this case pounds must be converted into dollars. Why? How?

THE INTERNATIONAL BALANCE OF PAYMENTS

So much at present for foreign exchange rates. Unless you are an expert, you need not worry further about mechanical details. Still your knowledge will be incomplete unless you understand the basic economic forces working behind the scenes. How are banks, post offices, and brokers always able, here and abroad, to exchange pounds for dollars and dollars for pounds?

The answer lies in the fact that international trade is largely a two-way street. Goods are being traded for goods, just as in a horse swap. When we import, we offer dollars for pounds. When we export, the English offer pounds for dollars. Let us see why this is all so by examining the balance of international payments.

Official records are kept of all international transactions during a year: of merchandise exported and imported, of money lent abroad or borrowed, of gold movements, of tourist expenditures, of interest and dividends received or paid abroad, of shipping services, etc. They all go to make up the balance of

---

[1] There are also foreign exchange rates between the pound and the French franc, etc But these rates between other countries need not interest us much, particularly since in a free competitive market the pound-franc rate can be simply calculated from the pound-dollar and franc-dollar rate, because sharp-eyed international arbitragers see to it that relative rates do not get out of line.

international payments, which is simply a double-entry listing of all items, drawn up in such a way that it must always show a balance.[1]

The balance of international payments is usually presented in three sections:

1. Current items:
   Merchandise (or "trade balance")
   Invisibles:
   Transportation (shipping services, etc.)
   Travel expenditures
   Income on investments (interest and dividends)
   Government and other unilateral transfers (including gifts, immigrant remittances)
2. Gold movements (in and out)
3. Capital movements (in and out)
   Government
   Other

The totality of all items under (1) is sometimes referred to as the "balance on current account." Centuries ago, when merchandise items predominated, writers used to concentrate on them alone: If merchandise exports were greater than merchandise imports, they spoke of a "favorable balance of trade"; if imports exceeded exports, they spoke of an "unfavorable balance of trade." This is not a very good choice of terms, since we shall see that a so-called unfavorable balance of trade may be a very good thing for a country.

In addition to the so-called visible merchandise items, we must not forget the important role played these days by the "invisibles." These consist of such things as shipping services which we provide for foreigners or which they provide for us, American tourist expenditures abroad, our earnings from abroad, and charities or the gifts our government makes or that immigrants send back home. If you think about it, you will realize that an invisible item like the expenditure of an American for a drink in Paris has the same effect on the final balance of payments as does his import of French wine to be drunk here at home in America. And if we provide shipping insurance service to foreigners, that acts just like one of our merchandise exports.

A good way to decide how an item should be treated is to ask the following question: Is the item like one of our merchandise exports, providing us with more foreign currencies? Or is it like one of our merchandise imports, causing us to use up our stock of foreign currencies and making it necessary to get

[1] Smuggling and some other items elude the record keepers, so it is almost always necessary to introduce a miscellaneous category of omitted items just large enough to show a formal balance.

more foreign currency? The first, or export-type, item is called a "credit item"; the import-type item is called a "debit item."

To show how this rule works, ask the following question: How shall we treat income on investments received by Americans from abroad? Clearly they are credit items like exports in that they provide us with foreign currencies. The reader can reverse the argument to show that the interest and dividends which foreigners receive from us must be treated like debit items—like imports, they use up foreign currencies.

It is to be stressed that the balance of trade and the balance of current items do not necessarily have to be in perfect balance. Only the *total* balance of international payments must be always in balance. This is because any lack of balance of current items must be exactly matched by an opposite balance of the capital and gold items. Why? Because whichever of our sales abroad are not matched by swaps against goods and gifts must be paid for by gold or must be owed to us.

It should be noted that our balance of payments is with all the rest of the world and not with just one country. Our total balance of payments must always be in balance, but there is no reason why there must be a balance with any one country, such as Britain. On the contrary, it is usual and desirable for us to sell more to Britain than we buy from her; for Britain to sell more to the East Indies than she buys from them; and for the East Indies to sell more to us than we sell to them. This example of triangular trade is just one instance of the profitability of multilateral trade. As discussed in a later chapter, standards of living all over the world would deteriorate if international trade were pressed into the mold of bilateralism, with a perfect balance being insisted upon between every pair of countries.

Table 1 presents the official Balance of International Payments of the United States for 1949. In Column (1) the various current items (merchandise and invisibles), gold, and capital items are listed by name. In the three remaining columns, the quantitative figures are listed for each item. Column (2) lists all the "credit items"; *i.e.*, all the international transactions that are just like exports and enable us to get hold of foreign currencies. Column (3) lists all so-called "debit items," *i.e.*, all transactions that are just like imports and require us to give up dollars for foreign currencies. Column (4) gives the net difference between credits and debits.

This is well illustrated by the merchandise item. Our merchandise exports were 12,337 million dollars in 1949; because foreigners had to pay ultimately for these in dollars, foreign currencies were made available to us in this amount. Therefore, this is listed as a credit item in Column (2). Our imports were only 7,144 million dollars; and since we had to pay for these in foreign currencies,

TABLE 1. *Balance of International Payments of the United States, 1949 (In millions of dollars)*

Items	Credits (items— like exports— providing America with foreign currencies)	Debits (items— like imports— using up foreign currencies)	Net credits (+) or debits (−)
(1)	(2)	(3)	(4)
Current merchandise and service:			
1. Merchandise (adj.)	$12,337	$7,144	+5,193
2. Transportation	1,289	768	+ 521
3. Travel expenditures	363	688	− 325
4. Income on investments (interest, dividends, etc.)	1,323	329	+ 994
5. Miscellaneous services	644	786	− 142
Unilateral transfers (net):			
6. Private	. . . .	. . . . .	− 515
7. Government	. . . .	. . . . .	−5,304
8. Net balance on current account	. . . .	. . . . .	+ 422
9. Net gold exports (+) or imports (−)	. . . .	. . . . .	− 164
Capital: Net exports of our I.O.U.'s (+) or net imports (−): long-term and short-term:			
10. U.S. government	. . . .	. . . . .	− 643
11. Other	. . . .	. . . . .	− 591
12. Total net exports of capital (+) o. net imports (−) . .	. . . .	. . . . .	−1,234
13. Errors and omissions			+ 976

SOURCE: Department of Commerce.

this is listed in the debit column. With our exports in excess of imports, we had a favorable balance of trade of 5,193 million dollars ($12,337–$7,144). This is listed as a plus item in the net credits. The reader should go through all the remaining items one by one to be sure he understands their true nature.

Table 1 illustrates the striking characteristic features of our postwar balance of payments. Taking into account merchandise and invisible items, we were exporting much more than we were importing. The rest of the world spoke despairingly of a great "dollar shortage" or "dollar gap." This gap was symptomatic of the fact that they wished to import from the United States much more than they were able to export to us. How was our tremendous "export surplus" financed? Row 7 in Table 1 shows that this was financed in large part by 5.3 billion dollars of gifts by the American government—the so-called Marshall plan aid and other similar aid programs.

But even with such a tremendous program of direct government aid, the final item in row 8 shows that we still had a favorable balance on current account of 422 million dollars. How was this financed? Row 9 shows that in part it was financed by having foreigners send us gold. In the years just before and just after World War II, these gold imports bulked even larger as an item in our balance of payments.

However, it is clear that not enough gold came in to cover all our favorable balance on current account. How was the remainder financed? The third part of Table 1 shows that private Americans and the United States government were lending money abroad. Instead of foreigners having to pay us by sending us exports of goods and services, they were sending us exports of their promissory notes—their I.O.U.'s. (Hint: Instead of thinking of America as "exporting capital," you will always find it easier to keep from getting confused by thinking of every capital movement as a movement of I.O.U.'s. These I.O.U.'s can always be recognized as being either credit or debit items by treating them exactly like the movement of merchandise or of gold: An import is a debit, and an export a credit.)

Exactly how do foreigners borrow from us? Suppose that we have an export surplus which is to be balanced by our importing foreign I.O.U.'s. There are various ways in which this capital movement can take place: Foreigners or their government might (1) borrow from a New York bank or (2) sell bonds in the New York market or (3) borrow from the United States government's Export-Import bank or (4) sell some of their shares of stock in American or foreign companies or (5) fail to renew an old loan that they made to us years ago or (6) use up a deposit that they hold in an American bank, etc. The reader should go through the opposite steps when we borrow from abroad and describe some of the ways that this might take place.

To summarize: If a nation's exports of goods and services on current account exceed her imports and unilateral gifts, then she will have to be paid either by an import of gold or by foreign promises to pay.

Figure 1 shows the excess of America's exports over imports in postwar years. Note how government gifts, government loans, and private loans financed the discrepancy. Note, too, how by 1950 the dollar gap began to close. The Korean war caused our imports to grow; and in addition, as is

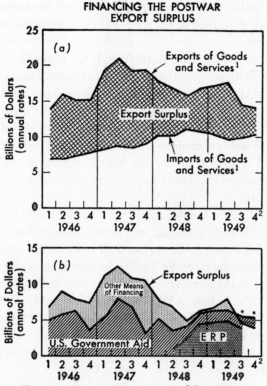

FIGURE 1. SOURCE: Department of Commerce.

discussed later, the 1949 world-wide devaluation or depreciation of the pound-dollar exchange rate (from a \$4 price for £1 to a \$2.80 price for £1) seems to have helped to close the gap.

STAGES OF A COUNTRY'S BALANCE OF PAYMENTS

Historically, the United States has gone through three of the four stages typical of the growth of a young agricultural nation into a well-developed industrialized one.

1. *Young and Growing Debtor Nation.* From the Revolutionary War era until just after the Civil War, we imported more than we exported. England and Europe lent us the difference in order to build up our capital structure. We were a typical young and growing debtor nation.

2. *Mature Debtor Nation.* From about 1873 to World War I, our balance of trade appears to have become favorable. Aside from tourists' and immigrants' items, this was made necessary by the growth of the dividends and interest that we had to pay abroad on our past borrowing. These invisible items kept our balance on current account more or less in balance. Capital movements were also about in balance, our new lending just about canceling off our borrowing.

3. *New Creditor Nation.* In World War I, we expanded our exports tremendously. At first, private American citizens made loans to the warring Allied powers. After we got in the war, our government lent money to England and France for war equipment and postwar relief needs. We emerged from the war a creditor nation. But our psychological frame of mind had not adjusted itself to our new creditor position. We passed high tariff laws in the early 1920's and again in 1930. Because America refused to import, foreigners found it difficult to get the dollars to pay us interest and dividends, much less repay the principal.

So long as we remained in this third stage of being a new creditor country; so long, that is, as we kept making *new* private foreign loans all through the 1920's, everything momentarily appeared all right on the surface. We could continue to sell more than we were buying, by putting most of it "on the cuff." The rest of the world met our export surplus by sending us gold, and by sending us I.O.U.'s. As long as Wall Street bankers could interest Main Street in foreign bonds, everything seemed rosy. But by 1929 and later, when Americans would no longer lend abroad, the crash finally came. International trade broke down. Debts were defaulted. America, as much as the rest of the world, was to blame.

4. *Mature Creditor Nation.* America has not yet succeeded in moving into the fourth stage of being a mature creditor nation. England reached this stage some years ago. As is usual in such cases, her imports exceeded her exports. Before we feel sorry for her because of her so-called "unfavorable" balance of trade, let us note what this really means.

Her citizens were living better because they were able to import much cheap food, and in return did not have to part with much in the way of valuable export goods. The English were paying for their import surplus by the interest and dividend receipts they were receiving from past foreign lending.

Fine for the English. But what about the rest of the world? Weren't they worse off having to send exports to England in excess of imports? Not necessarily. Normally, the capital goods that England had previously lent them permitted them to add to their domestic production—to add *more* than had to be paid out to England in interest and dividends. Both parties were better off. Nineteenth-century foreign lending was twice blessed: it blessed him who gave and him who received. Of course, things were not always quite so smooth. Some investments proved unwise. Political problems of colonies and nationalism complicated the situation. And as we shall see, after World War I, the whole process broke down.

BASIC SIGNIFICANCE OF INTERNATIONAL CAPITAL MOVEMENTS

Let us return now to the problem of capital movements. If political problems of nationality and domestic problems of unemployment did not enter the picture, then the fundaments of international lending would be easy to understand. We could easily cut through the fog of money and finance and concentrate upon the real aspects in terms of goods and resources.

How does capital grow within a country? By our diverting labor, land, machinery, and other resources away from the production of current consumption goods. Instead, we plant trees, drain rivers, build new machinery and buildings. All these add to our future national income and levels of future consumption.

We are postponing present consumption for future consumption; in fact, for an even *greater* amount of future consumption. Where does the increase in future consumption come from? From the fact that *capital goods have a "net" productivity*. This net productivity of capital is the real side of the interest rate.[1]

In countries with much labor and many inventions, the rate of interest tends to be high. But as more and more capital is produced—as more seeds are added to the same acres of land and more tools are given to a limited number of people—the law of diminishing returns sets in. The rate of interest drops from 6 to 5 to 4 and even below 1 per cent. Now that businessmen can borrow at a lower rate of interest, projects that were before unprofitable do become profitable. Investors wish for inventions or for new labor and resources.

Different parts of the world have different amounts of resources: labor, minerals, climate, know-how, etc. Were it not for ignorance or political boundaries, no one would push investment in North America down to the point of 3 per cent returns *if elsewhere there still existed 6 per cent opportunities*. Some capital would certainly be invested abroad. This would give foreign labor higher wages, because now the foreign worker has more and better tools to work with. It would increase foreign production. By how much? Not only by enough to pay for the constant replacement of used-up capital goods, but in addition by enough to pay us an interest or dividend return on our investment. This interest return would take the form of goods and services which we receive from abroad and which add to our standard of living. An all-wise

[1] See Chapters 3 and 29.

scientist would probably approve of the process. It would make sense to him because capital is going into the regions where its productivity is highest.

When would we be repaid our principal? So long as we are earning a good return, there is no reason why we should ever wish to have it repaid. However, the once backward country may finally become rather prosperous. It may wish to pull in its belt as far as consumption is concerned, and to use its savings to buy out our ownership in its factories, farms, and mines. But suppose that we are rich, with plenty of savings and with so much capital at home that our rate of interest is low. We will not particularly wish to sell out or be repaid. We will raise the selling price of our farm and factory holdings abroad. Or in other words, we will be content with a smaller percentage interest return. Thus, there is no necessary reason why a country should ever be paid off for its past lending, unless it has become older and poorer than the rest of the world.

When nationalism rears its ugly (or beautiful) head, matters change. Within the United States, interest and dividends may stream from South to North and West to East until doomsday. A few people may grumble about absentee ownership; but the courts and police are there to see that property rights are respected. Not so between nations. When a country is poor, it may be anxious to borrow. After it has become richer, it becomes unhappy to have to pay dividends and interest abroad. It chooses not to remember that its prosperity stemmed in part from its past borrowing. More than an economic burden is involved; politically, countries don't like the principle of absentee ownership by "furriners." Therefore, they are prone to insist upon getting rid of their international liabilities—paying them off at a fair price, at an unfair price, or often by outright default.

Economics and politics mix in ways too complicated to discuss in this book. Some say "trade follows the flag." Others say the flag follows trade. Some say the pursuit of economic gain is the primary motive behind the imperialistic search for colonies. Others claim that national power (offensive and defensive) is an end in itself; that economic well-being is sacrificed to this end; and that economic resources are sought for their contribution to military strength (offensive and defensive) rather than for their contribution to economic well-being. According to this view, without wars and nationalism, anyone could invest and trade anywhere; all sensible people would prefer to live in small countries unhindered by costly military establishments and colonial administration. At the opposite extreme is the view that victory in battle, rather than comfortable living, is the only worthy end in life; the foreigner is of no importance compared with the fatherland; he can be stripped of his goods and land, and he can be made to work for the "super-race," so that the latter can have its cake and cannons too. The world of the last few centuries lies some-where in between these extreme cases.

FINANCIAL VERSUS REAL ASPECTS OF FOREIGN LENDING

Let us turn from politics back to economics, to see how these processes take place in financial terms. Money throws a veil over the real aspects of capital movements. Usually a foreigner borrows *money* from us rather than capital goods directly. He gives us an I.O.U. in the form of a bond, note, or stock certificate. We give him dollars. If he simply holds the dollars or puts them in an American bank or invests them in an American security, then there has been no net capital movement at all. We have some form of his I.O.U.; he has some form of ours. In the capital movements section of the balance of international payments, the difference just cancels out. Only when he uses the receipts of the loan to import goods and services (or gold) in excess of his exports to us, only then has a real and a financial capital movement taken place.

When the time comes for interest payment, the foreigners must sell us more goods than they buy in order to get the extra dollars to remit to us. Our balance of international payments then will show an import surplus, balanced by the invisible credit item, interest and dividends.

Should we feel glad or sorry when we are exporting more than we are importing? If we never had to worry about unemployment, we would certainly regret having to give away goods that might better serve our own well-being, Only the consolation of later receiving goods in return could serve to compensate us for this present loss. If we could look into a crystal ball and see that the investment were sure to go sour later and never be repaid either in principal or interest, then we should certainly conclude that the capital movement was a bad and not a good thing.

Why then do people seem to become so happy over a so-called "favorable" balance of trade when they are giving away more goods than they get? Why does a congressman's heart bleed when we have an "unfavorable" balance of trade and are receiving more in goods than we give? The answer is partly stupidity. The congressman has not thought the matter through. But that is only the smallest part of the story.

The answer is also partly selfishness. Particular businessmen and laborers may benefit by our shutting out imports and encouraging exports—even though the country as a whole is worse off. Suppose that the 60 million workers in the United States are always fully employed. Then it will be to our greatest advantage to put our resources to work in those industries where we have the greatest *relative* advantage. This may mean that it is better for us to produce automobiles and trade them for watches rather than to produce watches; better to produce machine tools and import wool rather than produce both; better to take advantage of all possibilities to get goods cheaply from abroad.

But that is looking at the matter from the standpoint of all the country and of all consumers, from the standpoint of real wages of American labor as a whole. But what about the watchmakers and the wool growers? The tariff may be subsidizing them, and they will put pressure on their congressmen not to lose that subsidy. If it were a question of a sudden removal of all tariffs or of national defense, arguments could be made on both sides. But certainly there is no strong *economic* argument against a gradual reduction of protective tariffs, so that as workers died off and transferred from relatively inefficient industries, there would be a shift to American industries with greater long-run efficiency.

The above all holds, assuming that total spending is always just sufficient to keep us at full employment. When investment outlets are so brisk as to lead to inflation, the argument that a country should want to import rather than export is even more powerful. When total spending tends to be higher than the value of goods that can be produced, people who leave watchmaking and wool growing can find new jobs with relative ease. The more we import of goods and the less we export, the greater is the stock of goods available for our money to purchase. Also, the more efficiently we allocate our resources, the more goods will we be producing. The greater the flow of goods compared to the total of spending, then the better our ability to control inflation. The time, therefore, to reduce tariffs gradually is during booms—such as the years immediately following World War II. Special interests will still squawk. But they need not then be given excessive attention.

It is when we drop the assumption of full employment that we find that there is something more than ignorance or special pleading to explain the mad frenzy of nations to give away rather than receive goods. We then begin to move in a never-never land of non-Euclidean axioms, where black appears white and parallel lines meet, where individual wisdom appears as social folly, and where even social folly seems to have some of the aspects of social wisdom. The next chapter deals with international trade and jobs in the years ahead.

SUMMARY

1. The balance of international payments summarizes all the credit and debit items for a nation, including merchandise items, invisibles, gold, and capital movements. The balance of payments of the United States during the late 1940's reveals the important role of government in meeting the postwar "dollar gap."

2. As a nation passes from the "young debtor" to the "mature creditor" stage, its balance of trade and balance of current items undergo a series of changes which the reader should understand.

3. No problem in international finance is more important than that of understanding the real and the monetary aspects of capital movements, in their effects both upon the industrial development of nations and upon the problem of unemployment.

QUESTIONS FOR DISCUSSION

1. Draw up a list of items that belong on the credit side of the balance of international payments, and that belong on the debit side. Divide the statement into three parts: current, gold, and capital movements.

2. What is meant by a favorable balance of trade? How does the trade balance differ from the balance on current accounts? Why the term "invisible items"? What is the difference between short-term and long-term capital movements?

3. Construct hypothetical balance sheets for (a) a young debtor country, (b) a mature debtor country, (c) a new creditor country, (d) a mature creditor country.

4. America buys from the East Indies; England buys from America; England sells to the East Indies. How might the balance of payments between any two of these countries look? Between any country and all the rest of the world? (Hint: Instead of having a single column of credits, of debits, and of net credits, introduce new columns for each country traded with.)

5. A Canadian railroad company floats bonds in England and uses the proceeds to buy tracks and locomotives. How would the English balance of payments be affected by this capital movement? Later the loan is repaid with interest. How would the balance of payments be affected?

6. "Foreign lending causes war. Foreign giving postpones war. Free foreign trading prevents war." Comment.

7. Comment on Stuart Chase's "common-sense formula":

> "The stuff we produce, as a nation,
> Plus the stuff we import,
> Less the stuff we export,
> Is a measure of our standard of living."

8. Comment on his description of international finance in the 1920's:

> "American investors loaned dollars abroad.
> Foreigners used the dollars to pay for
>   American exports.
> The exports stimulated production and
>   employment in America."

But

> "Foreigners got the goods, while
>   American investors lost their shirts."

9. Write a two-page essay describing what is meant by the "postwar dollar gap." How have events since June, 1950, affected it? Why?

APPENDIX TO CHAPTER 31
A FEW MECHANICS OF INTERNATIONAL FINANCE

Without going into details, we may briefly survey how exchange rates, prices, and trade are determined (1) under *freely flexible* exchange rates and (2) under the *gold standard* or some other regime of stable exchange rates.—

FREELY FLEXIBLE EXCHANGE RATES

From 1919 to 1925, the price of the pound fluctuated from day to day, going from almost $5 down to $3. Such a rate is determined by the interplay of competitive supply and demand for foreign exchange. When Americans wish to import or travel, their demand for pounds tends to push up the rate— say from $3 to $3.10. Any other American debit item, such as our desire to lend abroad, has the same effect.

Any credit item, on the other hand, such as our exporting to Britain, adds to the supply of pounds, because foreigners then need dollars. This tends to depress the price of foreign exchange or pounds. Brokers and bankers keep their ears glued to the telephone in order to follow the tug of war of supply and demand acting on flexible exchange rates.

We need not go into details of the exact mechanism, except to note one important tendency: When the price of foreign exchange rises, there are usually strong forces making for self-correction and helping to keep it from rising indefinitely. Similarly, there are self-correcting forces tending to limit a decline in the exchange rate.

Thus, if our imports become too large, we bid up the price of pounds. But at $4 per pound rather than $3, Americans find that British dishes and cloth have greatly increased in cost. Our imports are discouraged, which tends to correct the situation or at least to keep the exchange rate from rising further. More than that. Now an Englishman can get more dollars for his pounds. Consequently, even if American industries do not change their dollar price tags, the British will be encouraged to take more of our exports once the dollar has depreciated. This is an additional factor operating toward restoring the equilibrium of exports and imports and limiting the magnitude of the exchange-rate variation.

The reader should show that, just as a depreciation of the dollar tended to create an American export surplus and to correct an import surplus, so will an appreciation of the dollar tend to encourage American imports and discourage American exports and to be self-correcting and self-limiting. (Hint: Let the pound fall to $2.50. Why will it not fall farther?)

DETERMINANTS OF SUPPLY AND DEMAND

It is all very well to say, as we have just been saying, that supply and demand determine a flexible exchange rate. But if we want to probe deeper behind the scenes to ascertain what makes supply and demand act as they do, we shall find that the level of the exchange rate depends upon at least the following four fundamental factors.

1. The *strength of our desires* for foreign goods and services relative to their desires for our goods and services: the greater our desire for their goods, the higher will be the price of foreign exchange be bid. The dollar will tend to depreciate in value and the pound to appreciate.

2. *The more our national income rises*, the greater will be our demand for imports. This will tend to make the dollar depreciate. On the other hand, high foreign national income makes the dollar appreciate, or what is the same thing, makes the price of foreign exchange cheaper for Americans. All this comes about because a country's "propensity to import" increases with national income in much the same way that its willingness to consume does.

3. The higher our *prices* and *costs* are, relative to the foreigners', the greater will be our imports, relative to exports. Therefore, high American prices and low foreign prices usually mean a high price for foreign exchange. After World War I this third factor, then considered most important of all, was called the "purchasing power parity" theory of exchange rates. According to this theory, the relative change in exchange rate between two countries will—other things being equal!—be proportional to the relative change in our prices compared to those abroad. Or,

$$\text{Foreign exchange rate} = \frac{\text{American prices}}{\text{foreign prices}}$$

This theory is most useful when one of the two countries has suffered a tremendous inflation which has tended to raise most of its prices by almost the same percentage. If now everything else is exactly the same, except that it takes one hundred times as much foreign money to buy things, then we should expect that the exchange rate (the price of a unit of foreign currency) would probably have to find its level at about one one-hundredth of the previous rate.[1]

4. Finally, the foreign exchange rate will be higher, the more Americans wish to lend abroad, the greater the payments we have to make on past debts

---

[1] The fall during inflation of the German mark, the Greek drachma, the Italian lira, the French franc, and the Chinese dollar, and other foreign exchange rates are all good examples.

or on war-punishment reparation payments, and the less willing foreigners are to hold dollars. When our investors develop a desire to hold foreign I.O.U.'s, bonds, stocks, bank deposits, or currency—then they will bid up the foreign exchange rate. The reader can work out the reverse case, where payments into the United States tend to lower the foreign exchange rate.

This last factor of capital movements is intimately tied up with *speculation* in foreign exchange. If only merchandise exports or current items were involved, the foreign exchange rate might be sluggish and change very little. Unfortunately, when the price of the pound drops from $3 to $2.96, many people begin to be afraid that it may fall still farther. Therefore, they try to get out of pounds and into dollars. But the increased sale of pounds and reduced demand for pounds, resulting from jittery short-term speculative capital movements, tends to push the pound down farther. Thus, small movements of the exchange rate are often amplified in a self-aggravating way by "hot money," which rushes from country to country with every rumor of war, politics, and exchange rate fluctuation. When such "capital flight" gets started in one direction on a large scale, the exchange rate may move chaotically and in extreme degree.

DISADVANTAGES OF FLEXIBLE EXCHANGE RATES

There is much to be said for flexible exchanges. Each country is free to pursue its own internal economic policies, leaving the exchange rate to take care of itself. However, there are also important disadvantages. With the exchange rate varying wildly from month to month, the volume of international trade and lending is greatly discouraged. A producer of goods would naturally prefer to sell and buy at home rather than to be betting continually upon the foreign exchange rate.[1]

A further disadvantage of fluctuating exchange rates results from the fact that each change in rates disturbs the existing situation in export and import markets. When suddenly the dollar depreciates, our exporters are helped and our importers are hurt. When the dollar appreciates, the reverse happens. This contributes toward unemployment, windfall profits and losses, and general instability.

STABLE EXCHANGE RATES

For these reasons, nations usually try to introduce some stability into the exchange rate. The simplest way to do this is, not to pass a law or edict, but rather to come into the market with a big enough supply or demand for

---

[1] In Chapter 22 on speculation, the possibility of reducing risks by "hedging" in a "futures market" is discussed. Unfortunately, foreign exchange markets have not been well enough organized to make this very helpful.

foreign exchange to keep the rate stable. Usually governments do this through so-called "exchange stabilization funds." There is no reason why a wealthy eccentric private citizen might not attempt to stabilize, say, the dollar price of Belgian francs. He, or any governmental fund, would have to start out with a huge pile of both dollars and Belgian francs (or with commodities like gold or wheat which could be converted by sale into either currency). Then to stabilize the price of the franc, he would simply instruct his brokers to bid dollars for francs whenever the price tended to fall, and to sell francs for dollars whenever the price tended to rise. So long as he did not run out of either francs or dollars, and so long as he stood ready both to buy and to sell francs at a given dollar price, then the franc-dollar exchange rate would be perfectly stable at that level.

Of course, even a multimillionaire might not be rich enough to do this for very long. A government, or the International Monetary Fund, is in a more powerful position. However, even the most powerful government will not be able to stand up against the ocean's tide and maintain any given exchange rate—unless it is able to influence prices, costs, and other conditions *so as to make private supply and demand for foreign exchange just about balance at the "pegged" rate*. Otherwise it will eventually be drained of all its holdings of one of the currencies—and then bingo! the rate can no longer be held steady.

Historically, the so-called "quasi-automatic gold standard" was a still more important method of stabilizing exchange rates and of thereby facilitating international trade. Let us turn to it.

WORKINGS OF THE GOLD STANDARD

To go on the gold standard a country need consult no one. Its Treasury must do two simple things: (1) agree to buy all gold brought to it at a given price—say $35 an ounce, in the case of the American Treasury—and (2) be willing to sell gold freely to all comers at the same price of $35 per ounce. The result: the dollar price of gold becomes perfectly fixed, at a level called "mint parity."

As far as a single country is concerned, that is all there is to it. But where does the foreign exchange rate enter the picture? As soon as a second country (say Britain in addition to the United States) goes on the gold standard, then the *price of gold in terms of pounds* is also stabilized. To keep the arithmetic simple, let us work this out using a $3 rather than $2.80 pound.[1]

Of course, things equal to the same thing must be equal to each other. If a dollar is $\frac{1}{35}$ ounce of gold and a pound is $\frac{3}{35}$ ounce of gold, then the price of a

---

[1] Thus instead of using the true 1951 price of £12½ per ounce, imagine that the United Kingdom buys and sells gold freely at 35 ÷ 3 pounds or £11⅔ per ounce.

pound in terms of dollars must be 3. This is not simply a question of arithmetic, but of hard practical business sense. If I want to buy pounds in order to import from Britain, I will never pay more than $3 for them. Why? Because I can take three crisp American bills and get from the United States Treasury $\frac{3}{35}$ ounce of gold. I ship this gold to London, where the English Treasury gives me a crisp pound note. The reader should be able to work out the reason why an Englishman will never supply pounds for less than $3.

Thus, with each currency tied to gold, they become tied to each other at a fixed exchange rate. But with one minor qualification. There is approximately a 2-cent shipping, insurance, and interest charge involved in transporting gold between New York and London. Therefore, supply and demand can bid the pound price up to $3.02 before it becomes profitable for Americans to export gold. This is called the American gold-export point (or the British gold-import point). As an exercise, the reader may show that the British gold-export point is at about $2.98, and that the exchange rate is free to wobble around the hypothetical $3 mint parity point within the range set by the two gold points.

THE EQUILIBRATING SPECIE-FLOW-PRICE MECHANISM

Up to this point the process has been completely mechanical. But the thoughtful reader will worry, as the "mercantilist" writers of the seventeenth and eighteenth centuries did, over this: What prevents the exchange rate from always being forced to the gold-export point of one of the countries until the one-way drain finally uses up all its gold reserves and forces it off the gold standard? The answer was first discovered just two centuries ago by the Scotch philosopher, David Hume. He claimed there was an automatic self-correcting "specie-flow-price" mechanism at work. According to him, Americans need not worry if they are importing more than they are exporting and are losing gold or specie. (1) The gold pouring into England will proportionately increase the amount of English money. (2) The increase in English money will (via the quantity theory of money and prices) cause a proportionate inflationary increase in British prices. Also, (3) the gold flowing out of America will cause a proportionate contraction of our money supply. (4) Again, via the quantity theory, this will cause a proportionate deflationary fall in American prices.

As a result of these four steps, there will be a double-edged tendency toward correcting the outflow of gold. (5) With British prices high relative to our own, Britons will begin to buy more of our exports. (6) Similarly, with our low prices, it will now pay us to buy less of their imports. Thus, the situation will finally correct itself. The changes in relative price levels caused by the flow of gold will restore the adverse trade balance and choke off the one-way flow of gold before it has gone very far. Therefore, said Hume, there is nothing to worry about.

Today we are not so sure. England may not want to have an inflation, and America may not like the idea of having a deflation just because the impersonal gods of the gold standard dictate it.

Besides, since Hume's time, banking and finance have become more elaborate. Now that gold coins are no longer the important part of our money supply, the process is not automatic. Instead the Treasury and the Central Bank are supposed to "follow the rules of the gold-standard game." When gold flows out, this is to be a signal for us to put on the deflationary brakes. For example, we should (1) increase tax collections relative to expenditure; (2) discourage private investment by raising the "rediscount" and other interest rates; (3) tighten up on bank reserves by Federal reserve open-market sales of securities or by raising legal reserve rates; (4) put downward pressure on wages and prices. In short, we should deliberately create a depression and deflation.

The reader should be able to list the inflationary steps that the rules of the game would impose on the country receiving gold. He will then be in a position to understand how, and why, countries refused to play the rules of the gold-standard game in the years after World War I. They did this to avoid inflation or deflation. But, as a further result, the one-way drains of gold were not corrected, and finally the gold standard broke down.

However, the breakdown was due not simply to the willful disregard by nations of the rules of the game, but also to the fact that the gold standard is a "fair-weather system" that works best only when small strains are placed upon it. In the jittery, troubled period between the two wars, with erratic capital movements, the strains were anything but small.

Finally, from a technical economic viewpoint, we are no longer so optimistic as Hume was about the efficacy of the specie-flow-price mechanism. The weaknesses of the quantity theory have already been pointed out in earlier chapters. Also we have seen that prices and costs are often sticky in capitalistic countries. Still worse, there is a possibility that the Hume price changes could make the situation worse rather than better if international demands turn out to be inelastic rather than elastic. In such cases, lowering the prices of American export goods will not expand our sales much; therefore, Englishmen will actually offer fewer pounds for dollars rather than more pounds. Similarly, if the American demand for British goods should be very urgent and inelastic, raising British prices may force us to demand more pounds rather than less.

Thus, the price reaction to a depreciation of the dollar may be a perverse rather than an equilibrating one: The dollar would have to depreciate still further.

THE 1949 CURRENCY DEPRECIATION

In the middle of 1949, the British pound and numerous other currencies all over the world went through a dramatic price depreciation relative to the dollar. The price of a pound was adjusted downward from $4 to $2.80. This represented a greater drop than most experts had foreseen.

It is too soon to tell what the results of this move have been. But on the surface it appears to have had results in accord with orthodox expectations. Before the depreciation, a country like the United Kingdom had a tremendous desire for American imports, far in excess of her ability to send and sell exports here. She had to apply stringent import controls. Her citizens needed a license to make most purchases in the United States. Nevertheless, her reserves of dollars began to dwindle. Rats leave a sinking ship, investors were afraid that the pound would fall in price, and so they did what they could to sell pounds. In addition, early in 1949 the United States was having a slight cyclical downturn; our imports from the United Kingdom dropped tremendously. British reserves of dollars fell to a dangerously low figure.

At last the British government took the decision to depreciate the pound. This they did. What was the result? The "terms of trade" turned against the United Kingdom; i.e., her import prices rose relative to her export prices. American goods became so expensive that British citizens decreased their physical imports of American goods, thus helping to curb the dollar gap. Less certain was the favorable effect upon British dollar receipts resulting from the fact that her goods could now be bought by Americans for cheaper dollar prices. True, we bought more goods in physical terms, but also we paid a lower dollar price for each unit. On the whole, our demand may have been sufficiently elastic for there to have been some improvement in Britain's dollar receipts.

In any case, the rats began to come back to the ship, the American recession proved transitory, and the Korean war helped greatly to reverse the flow of dollars. The United Kingdom, therefore, showed a great improvement in the position of her dollar reserves in the year following the depreciation—in accord with orthodox theory.[1]

[1] It is true that there was upward pressure on her wage and price level, but the trade-unions supported the Labor government's program and restrained their wage demands. As of late 1950, the outlook is for no further depreciation of the pound.

For all the reasons earlier discussed, the gold standard probably would have broken down and been abandoned long ago, were it not for an important equilibrating process not dreamed of in Hume's specie-flow-price philosophy. In recent years economists have emphasized that *income changes in the two countries help to restore equilibrium*. If our exports go up, then even without any price changes, we now have a higher national income. Part of this higher income we shall want to use to buy more imported goods. Thus, (1) to some degree, an increase in exports will directly induce an increase in imports via income, no matter what happens to prices. But, (2) when we analyze in detail the full multiplier effects of our increased income, we shall see that the induced increase in imports is only *partial* rather than being equal to the original increase in exports. There is still some need for prices or exchange rate changes to restore equilibrium. The details of the argument follow; but they can be skipped at a first reading.

Let us turn then to the multiplier analysis of foreign trade. We have seen that new domestic investment creates primary jobs and income and that the spending and respending of this new income give rise to a chain of secondary multiplier effects. New exports have exactly the same multiplier effects. They raise incomes directly, but in addition they set up a chain of further spending and respending.

Thus, a billion dollars' worth of new export orders to New England machine-tool factories will create 1 billion dollars of primary jobs and income. Then workers and owners may respend perhaps two-thirds of their new income on the consumption products of Indiana and California; two-thirds of this extra income is in turn respent, etc. The process comes to a halt only when the total adds up to $1 + \frac{2}{3} + (\frac{2}{3})^2 + \cdots = 1/(1 - \frac{1}{3})$ times 1 billion dollars, or to 2 billion dollars of secondary consumption expenditure in addition to the 1 billion dollars of primary expenditure.

Besides introducing a multiplier effect of exports into the picture, international trade has a second important effect. Higher American national income will increase our imports, let us say by one-twelfth out of every extra dollar. This means that our chain of induced domestic purchasing power will peter out quicker than in the above example. At each step, these imports act as "leakages," just like the marginal propensity to save.[1]

Therefore, out of the original 1 billion dollars of income in the export in-

---

[1] If the reader applies the foreign trade multiplier analysis to a small city or country, he will find that the secondary multiplier effects upon the workers of that region are almost negligible, since almost all of extra income leaks out to other regions.

dustries, perhaps only $\frac{7}{12} (= \frac{2}{3} - \frac{1}{12})$ rather than $\frac{8}{12}$ will be respent on *American* consumption goods (in Indiana, California, and so forth). And so it will go at each stage. The whole multiplier will now add up only to

$$1 + \frac{7}{12} + (\frac{7}{12})^2 + \cdots,$$

or only to $2\frac{2}{5} = 1 \div (1 - \frac{7}{12}) = 1 \div \frac{5}{12}$ instead of to 3. This is because $\frac{1}{12}$ of our extra $2\frac{2}{5}$ billion dollars of generated income—or $\frac{1}{5}$ of a billion dollars in this case—tends to go abroad for extra imports.

It would be wrong to look upon this leakage of purchasing power abroad as simply a nuisance. Disregarding unemployment and looking at matters from the standpoint of stable international finance, we must rather regret that 1 billion dollars of new exports has only induced $\frac{1}{5}$ of a billion dollars of imports.

If we look at our multiplier formulas we find that this is a general rule:

So long as some fraction of income at every stage is leaking into domestic savings, a new dollar of exports will never be able to lift income by enough to call forth a full dollar of new imports.[1]

[1] Suppose that each extra dollar of income is always split up into the three fractions: c for American consumption goods, b for America's propensity to import goods from abroad, a for the remaining amount going into saving. Then let exports go up by one unit. The multiplier tells us that our income will go up by $1/(1 - c) = 1/(b + a)$. Multiplying this extra income by the fraction b, we get induced imports of $b/(b + a)$, which is certainly less than our original one of new exports—to the extent that the marginal propensity to save, a, is positive. If there is any induced domestic investment, it can be thrown in with c and our result will still hold for any "stable" system with positive "leakage," a.

Chapter 32: POSTWAR

INTERNATIONAL ECONOMIC

PROBLEMS

WE MUST now turn to the main international economic problems facing the United States and the rest of the world in the 1950's. How can we understand the important facts? Which economic policies must we avoid? Which policies must we follow?

EXPORTS AND JOBS

Talk to a businessman whose memory goes back 40 years. He will point out that exports have always been a stimulating factor along with domestic private or public investment. He will recall the years 1915 and 1916, before we entered World War I, when France, Russia, and England suddenly became avid customers for our exports. We sent them goods in return for barren gold and fancy gilt-edged certificates. The result: a shift from American depression to great prosperity. Or in the period after we entered World War I, when our shipments of useless shot and shell increased, again there resulted all the apparent trappings of prosperity booms, *i.e.*, high prices and plentiful jobs.

During the 1920's when we were making many foolish private loans to the rest of the world and whooping it up for tariffs allegedly to "protect the American workers' standard of living," one of the contributing factors to our favorable balance of saving and investment seemed to be heavy foreign lending. Like domestic private investment or government deficit expenditure, the foreign trade balance was adding more to total money spending than it was subtracting. The hard-boiled businessman sums it up: "Of course, many of our foreign loans later turned sour and investors lost their money. But while we are shipping goods abroad, jobs are created. It doesn't matter as far as *current* jobs and prices in the twenties are concerned whether the loans 10 years later will turn out good or bad, or whether they represent public or private gifts." Or, as the late president of the First National Bank of New York put it: "It is better to have lent and lost than never to have lent at all."

What is the true cost to the American people of the goods we are throwing away? If unemployment were always at a minimum, the answer would be clear. The cost of devoting resources to unwise domestic investment, to public leaf raking, and to throwing goods abroad would be the useful goods and services that we could be producing by applying those same economic resources to useful lines. This is the fundamental real cost to keep in mind— not some confusing financial figure.

What happens to this cost analysis if there is unemployment, if the alternative to shipping goods abroad is idle factories and idle men? If we accept this hopeless assumption, then everything is changed. The extra production seems to cost us nothing, since it is produced with resources that would otherwise be rusting and champing in wasteful idleness. The lucky (or shall we say unlucky?) foreigners get our goods; but that doesn't mean that we are forced to consume any less than before. Drawing up our national score card, we might state that (1) we ship one million dollars of exports abroad receiving no worthwhile goods in return; (2) our production has gone up by a million dollars; (3) our jobs and sweat have increased, and the evils of idleness have slightly decreased; (4) our total consumption seems to have remained the same.

Now if we believe that the proper end of economic activity is the consumption of goods and services, our verdict would seem to be, "We are neither better off than before nor worse off." Actually, this is wrong. We have forgotten something very important.

When workers and capitalists in Lynn, Mass., receive extra income from producing generators for export, they will spend part of that income upon new American consumption goods. When export producers have received an extra million dollars of income, they will respend perhaps two-thirds of it upon consumers' goods produced in Pennsylvania or Iowa. Now there is an extra $666,667 of production, jobs, and income in those states. Two-thirds of this will be spent upon other American consumers' goods. And so it goes. The "multiplier" analysis of Part Two applies just as much to international investment as to anything else. By the time the process has worked itself out, American production and employment have gone up by 3 million dollars: 1 million of primary exports plus another 2 millions of secondary consumption.

Our national score card reads as follows: (1) total production and employment up by 3 million dollars; (2) total domestic consumption up by 2 million dollars. Thus, even those interested only in consumption as an end of activity must admit that, as compared to twiddling our thumbs in depression idleness, throwing away goods has made us better off rather than costing us something! To this our businessmen will say, "See, I told you so, even though I didn't know the economists' fancy language and couldn't spell out all the details."

So far so good, even though the whole process reminds us of the first savages who had to burn down a house to roast a pig. International "boondoggling"— for that's just what it is—is no better or worse than scattering leaves and raking them; but if it were the only alternative, it might be better than nothing.

But why assume that the only alternative is doing nothing? Surely, a third alternative, other than (1) inaction or (2) international boondoggling, can be found. In addition to the 3 million dollars' worth of jobs and the 2 million dollars of second-round consumption, we should also be able to get something useful for our 1 million dollars of work on the first round. Instead of throwing useful goods into the ocean, so to speak, why not use them for domestic consumption or domestic capital formation? Or if we feel that it is to our national interest and preference to help out the consumption and development of foreign nations, let us make sure that it does really help them out. (This is just common sense, just as it is clearly better for the government to build useful dams and hospitals rather than to rake leaves or construct pyramids. Both policies may lead to extra jobs and extra induced private consumption, but one leads to a greater total of useful production than the other.)

BEGGAR-MY-NEIGHBOR POLICIES

In an earlier chapter we learned the paradox of thrift: the attempt of individuals to increase their saving will, in a world of unemployment, often result in *less* actual saving and investment because of the harmful effects on income and employment. Here we have just come to understand what might be called the "paradox of international charity": *As compared to doing nothing toward curing depression unemployment, it may be better to increase exports and refuse imports; better not just from the standpoint of jobs, but from the standpoint of domestic consumption.*

A little knowledge is a dangerous thing. Suppose that you are a congressman who has grasped this possibility. You might immediately set about to create a favorable balance of trade for the United States. You might begin to do one or all of the following beggar-my-neighbor policies:

1. Increase protective *tariffs* on our imports and promote "Buy American" campaigns.

2. Better still, pass a law setting low *import quotas*, so that not more than a specified amount of each good can be shipped to us.

3. Or, taking a leaf from Hitler's Nazi book, introduce comprehensive

exchange control: so that every import must receive a special license; exports are to be subsidized; bilateral trade agreements are made with each country, limiting the direction and degree of trade and serving as a political weapon of intimidation or bribery. An elaborate system of regulations is set up, according to which foreigners have to pay different prices for the dollars they need for each different kind of good—depending upon what you think the "traffic will bear," etc. (As this is written, in 1951, most nations still have extensive exchange control.)

4. *Depreciate the dollar* as much as possible, so that foreigners can buy our imports very cheaply, while pounds and francs are made so expensive as to discourage our importing. In other words, the more we succeed in depreciating the dollar compared to all foreign currencies, the greater the exports we are able to give away and the fewer are the imports we are willing to take. One way to depreciate the dollar is to raise our buying price for gold. If other countries do not retaliate, this "devaluation of the dollar" will cheapen the dollar relative to foreign currencies and will enable us to give away exports in return for useless gold imports.

(A fifth way that a country can expand its exports relative to its imports is to offer foreigners sound or unsound *international loans* at low rates of interest; or even more, to make them huge gifts—financed by the Treasury or by gullible private investors. But the foreign country is not necessarily beggared as a result.)

A good congressman should be able to think up a few more devices, but these are the most important policies to be followed by a country that hopes to solve its unemployment problem at the expense of its neighbors: *i.e.*, by a country whose motto is "A short life and a merry one. Export and be happy, even though an international financial crash is brewing."

Any intelligent person who agrees that the United States must play an important role in the postwar international world will strongly oppose the above policies, because they all attempt to snatch prosperity for ourselves at the expense of the rest of the world. Such a person would think it unfair of us to try to export our unemployment, so to speak, on to our neighbors.

But suppose we are hard-boiled; or to put it crudely, selfish. We must still regard these beggar-my-neighbor policies as rather foolish. Why?

One does not need much intelligence to see that foreign nations will not stand idly by while we attempt these policies. They too have economics textbooks, and legislators. They, too, during a great depression will be following beggar-my-neighbor tactics; they too will be raising tariffs and introducing import quotas and exchange control; they will be trying to depreciate the pound (or the franc as the case may be) so that the dollar will appreciate in value. In short, they will be trying to increase their exports and reduce their imports.

What is the result when all countries try to beggar their neighbors in this way—when all try to climb on each other's shoulders to see the parade? Obviously, we cannot succeed in exporting to England more than she is importing to us, while *at the same time* England is succeeding in exporting to us more than she is importing. Our mutual attempts to develop favorable balances of trade are worse than canceling. International trade drops to the lowest level of exports and imports. Both nations are worse off.

Again, how can we succeed in getting the pound-dollar foreign exchange rate up to $4 per pound (a "depreciation" of the dollar) at the same time that the English are succeeding in depreciating their pound down to far below $4 per pound? We both can't succeed. Because depreciation and appreciation are relative things, no one is better off. To elaborate the obvious further, how can we lend to Britain (net) in the next depression at the same time that she is lending (net) to us? In fact, if the legislators of both countries are on their toes, we cannot even succeed in giving away goods to each other. For, if free supplies began to come in from abroad, more American workers would be thrown out of jobs—a condition that no red-blooded American could ever permit to happen.

What is the final moral? Obviously, that a strong, important country like the United States cannot sensibly regard international trade as a way of solving its unemployment program. We cannot. And we should not if we could. But we cannot. Other countries will retaliate to our beggar-my-neighbor tactics, with the result that we shall all be much worse off.[1] Between 1950 and 1970, our choice should not be between (1) doing nothing about unemployment or (2) trying to export our unemployment abroad by restrictive trade policies in the hope of getting favorable secondary multiplier effects. Instead we must aim at a superior third choice whereby (3) we conquer the problem of unemployment by domestic policies and use international trade only to increase our present and future standards of consumption, or to serve our political aspirations and responsibilities.

POSTWAR INTERNATIONAL COOPERATION

Economic isolation will not work. On this, if on no other proposition, $99\frac{44}{100}$ per cent of all economists are agreed. Nevertheless, economic isolation may again rear its head, because nations who ignore history are con-

---

[1] If our neighbor abroad has overfull employment and inflation while at the same time we have unemployment, the above beggar-my-neighbor policies may then paradoxically be pleasing to both of us.

demned to repeat it. Let us turn to the problems that the United States must face in the postwar world.

Let us assume that we all want to aim at the twin goals: full and efficient employment at home, with a rising standard of living and productivity; and peaceful, profitable trade relations with our neighbors on a durable basis. To achieve these goals we must face and solve the following eight main problems.

PROBLEMS OF POSTWAR INTERNATIONAL FINANCE

1. *Full Employment at Home.* The United States can make its greatest single contribution to sound postwar economic relations by adopting such domestic public and private policies as will keep its real national income high and growing. In the past, America has long been the important plague center of unemployment. By letting our national income slump off, we permit our imports to fall to low levels, while still striving to export. As a result of trying to solve our unemployment problem through a favorable balance of trade, we deflate and impoverish the rest of the world. This invites retaliatory foreign restrictions; and all nations lose in the mad game of beggar-my-neighbor.

If we do a pretty fair job in the postwar of keeping American employment and income high—by means of *domestically created* purchasing power!—other nations will be able to pay us for our exports by their exports. With reasonably full employment at home, we shall be in a position to welcome goods sent to us as dividends and interest on our past investments and as repayment of principal. With full employment, we can welcome anything that enables us to raise our living standards by importing more *cheaply* and fully. With full employment, we can gradually reduce our artificial protective barriers and subsidies to relatively inefficient American industries.

2. *The European Balance of Payments Problem.* In addition to relief, countries such as Britain and France have been given reconstruction loans. The British loan was for 3½ billion dollars to be spread over 1946–1951 and to be repaid with interest in yearly installments thereafter. Aside from her bombed cities and factories, Britain suffered tremendous losses of her foreign investments as a result of the war. Before lend-lease and Pearl Harbor, she had to sell almost all her holdings of American stocks and bonds; we sent her guns in exchange for her giving us back our old I.O.U.'s. The same thing happened with respect to England's relations to Canada, Australia, India, and the Empire. England now owes them, instead of being their creditor. Not being able to pay them on demand, she has "blocked" or frozen their right to receive payment. They can use these balances only to buy goods in Britain. Our loan and Marshall Plan aid may eventually help toward unfreezing the so-called "blocked sterling balances" owed by England abroad.

More directly, our loan did enable Britain to pay for the food imports that used to be paid for by her interest and dividends from abroad. The war has revolutionized Britain's creditor position—her net interest and dividends have been greatly reduced. If her standard of living and her food imports are to be maintained, she must greatly expand her volume of physical export trade, to 175 per cent of prewar levels. Our loan to Britain was to tide her over the transitional postwar period and enable her to improve her technology so as to be able to expand her production. Note that Britain's exports must expand, not to make jobs but rather to make imports. "We must export or die" really means for her "We must import or die. No longer enjoying extensive returns on foreign investments, we must export in order to import."

3. *Foreign Lending and the International Bank.* The United States is more developed industrially than the rest of the world. South America, the Orient, and other regions of the world could profitably use our capital for their industrial development. Such capital could be expected to increase their production by more than enough to pay generous interest and repay the principal.

But private American citizens are not willing to lend. Substantial private lending died some time in 1929, perhaps forever. Yet American citizens have savings which they would be glad to lend if such capital transactions could be made safe; and the American nation would benefit by a higher future standard of living from such sound foreign lending, provided we arrange our affairs so as not to have to worry about extensive future unemployment.

Therefore, the leading nations of the world (except Soviet Russia) have come together to form the International Bank for Reconstruction and Development and its sister institution, the International Monetary Fund. As its name implies the International Bank is formed to provide sound long-term loans for reconstruction and development. (The International Fund is concerned, as we shall see shortly, with short-term credit and the cooperative stabilization of foreign exchange rates.)

The International Bank is easy to understand. The leading nations subscribe to its initial 9 billion dollars of capital stock in proportion to their economic importance. The United States quota is about one-third, or 3 billion dollars. The bank can use its capital to make sound international loans—to people or countries whose projects seem economically sound but who cannot get private loans at reasonably low interest rates.

So far, each country has been called upon to put up only 20 per cent of its full quota, and it is not planned that the members will have to put up the remaining 80 per cent. Obviously this is not much money on international standards. The International Bank's true importance arises from something greater than the loans that it can make out of its own capital. More important is the fact that it can float bonds and use the proceeds to make loans. The bonds are safe because they are backed by the credit of all the nations (up to their 100 per cent of quotas). Also, the International Bank can *insure* loans in return for a $\frac{1}{2}$ or 1 per cent premium; private parties can then put up the money knowing that the Bank's credit is behind the loan.

As a result of these three ways of extending long-term credits, we can expect to see goods in the years ahead flowing out of the United States whose ultimate purpose will be international reconstruction and development. If sound, these loans will be repaid in full. If some go sour, the loss will be paid out of the Bank's interest or premium earnings. If still more go sour, the loss will be spread over all the member nations—not on Uncle Sam alone. While the loans are being made, Uncle Sam will be getting jobs (and if spending is already too great, some increase in its inflation problems). When the loans are being "serviced" or repaid, America will be experiencing an import surplus of useful goods.

In addition to the International Bank to which many nations belong, the federal government has set up its own Export-Import Bank. This also makes foreign loans: *e.g.*, an American exporter who wants to sell machine tools to Brazil may be helped to do so by the Export-Import Bank. Many of these loans are "tied loans"; *i.e.*, our Congress has insisted that the proceeds all be spent *directly* in this country. We criticize this sort of restrictive practice in others but, obsessed by the job aspects of international trade, we practice it ourselves.[1] Table 1 indicates the main postwar loans of the United States.

4. *Stable Exchange Rates and the International Monetary Fund.* When exchange rates vary from day to day, the risks of international trading become so great that its volume is greatly reduced. World specialization and productivity is reduced. Also, when every nation tries to engage in a race for competitive exchange depreciation, all end up worse and world trade ends up on its back.

The gold standard, while it operated, kept exchange rates constant. But (as is shown in the Appendix to the last chapter) it made each country a slave rather than a master of its own economic destiny. As long as we stuck to its rules, we had to inflate ourselves whenever the rest of the world said inflate; and deflate ourselves when the rest of the world had a depression. Of course it had some advantages, but alas, poor gold standard! It was a casualty of

---

[1] Not only do tied loans distort the direction of international trade, but in many cases they are quite unnecessary. If part of our loan is used abroad, say in England, rather than here in the United States, then the extra dollars put in the hands of the British will probably cause them to take some of our exports. International trade is multilateral rather than bilateral.

TABLE 1. *U.S. Government Grants, Loans, and Other Transfers to Foreign Countries, 1947–1950 (Millions of dollars)*

Type of aid	1947 total	1948 total	1949 Total	1949 First quarter	1949 Second quarter	1949 Third quarter	1949 Fourth quarter	1950 First quarter	1950 Second quarter*
A. Unilateral payments:									
UNRRA and post-UNRRA	761	84	2	2					†
Civilian supplies distributed by the armed forces	1,009	1,448	1,059	287	253	334	185	109	†
Transfers to Philippines	91	130	203	52	44	59	47	40	†
Chinese aid		168	109	49	43	12	5	16	†
Korean aid program			30	3	11	4	12	22	†
Greek-Turkish aid	74	348	171	52	43	41	35	34	†
International Refugee Organization	15	89	71	18	17	18	18	17	†
Interim aid	12	546							
European Recovery Program		1,398	3,732	906	1,119	940	767	771	
Other	288	135	182	39	46	39	58	40	
Total unilateral payments	2,250	4,344	5,559	1,409	1,576	1,447	1,127	1,049	†
Less unilateral receipts	303	183	255	27	19	156	53	41	†
Equals: Net unilateral payments	1,947	4,161	5,304	1,382	1,557	1,291	1,074	1,008	1,100
B. Long-term loans and investments:									
Lend-lease credits		2	4	1	1	2		1	†
Surplus property including ship sales	273	192	24	16	8				
Export-Import Bank loans	797	454	163	50	42	35	36	51	†
United Kingdom loan	2,850	300							
Subscription to									
International Bank	317								
International Monetary Fund	2,745								
European Recovery Program		476	425	281	98	16	30	54	
Other	161	18	59	11	12	22	14	15	
Total long-term loans and investments	7,143	1,442	675	359	161	75	80	121	†
Less repayments	294	443	205	64	55	41	45	49	†
Equals net long-term loans and investments, including International Bank and International Monetary Fund	6,849	999	470	295	106	34	35	72	100

* Estimates based on incomplete data, by Council of Economic Advisers.
† Not available.
SOURCE: *Economic Report of the President,* July, 1950.

World War I, and since then all the king's horses and all the king's men couldn't put it together again, and many wouldn't want to if they could.

The International Monetary Fund along with the International Bank grew out of some international conferences held in Bretton Woods, N. H., in 1944. The Fund hopes to secure the advantages of the gold standard without its disadvantages; *i.e.*, exchange rates are to be relatively stable, but international cooperation is to replace the previous automatic mechanism; also, countries are to be spared the need for making adjustments by deflating themselves into unemployment.

Early in 1947, the Fund set initial postwar exchange rates for most of its members. (Thus the dollar was set equal to 0.889 gram of gold and the British pound to 3.581 grams, with a resulting dollar-pound exchange rate of $4.03 per pound.) But king gold is tolerated only as a constitutional, rather than an absolute, monarch. And in 1949 Britain, most of her Dominions, and much of Western Europe depreciated their currencies by 30.5 per cent, so that the pound has been stabilized at $2.80.[1]

It is too much to expect that there will be a perfect balance of international transactions in the troubled postwar period. Quite clearly, some countries, such as the United States, will for a while sell more abroad than they buy— even after taking into account long-term foreign lending and aid programs. Other countries will be running into adverse trade balances and debt. How then can stable exchange rates be maintained?

Here is where the International Fund comes in. It provides short-term credits for the debtor countries. The Fund tries to set up rules and procedures to keep a country from going on year after year, getting deeper into debt. After a country has been piling up debts for a considerable period, certain financial penalties are applied. More important, the Fund's directors consult with the country and make recommendations for remedying the disequilibrium. However, they do not tell a country that it must create a depression for itself in order to cut down its national income to such a low level that its imports will finally fall to within its means. Instead, the country is permitted on its own hook first to depreciate its currency by 10 per cent. This will tend to restore equilibrium in its international trade by expanding its exports and contracting its imports.

If this is still not enough to correct the so-called "overvaluation" of the debtor country's currency, the Fund authorities may, after proper consultation, permit still further depreciation of the debtor country's exchange rate. But note this: all changes in rates take place in an orderly way. Most of the time, we have international stability. But there is also provision for flexibility

[1] This incident was more fully discussed in the Appendix to Chapter 31.

when needed—which is better by far than waiting for a big international blowup or breakdown.

Let us discuss briefly and without going into the mechanical details how the International Fund is able to extend short-term credits. First, all the member nations must pay in certain initial quotas, which are set in proportion to national income and the volume of international trade. The United States quota is about one-third of the total and equals $2\frac{3}{4}$ billion dollars. At least 75 per cent of each country's quota is payable in its own currency; the rest is payable in gold, but not beyond 10 per cent of a country's official holding of gold and American dollars.

Ordinarily a country will go along paying for its imports by means of its exports or long-term borrowing. But suppose these are not large enough, and the country—say, England—is in need of short-term credit from the Fund. How does the Fund enable such a debtor country to get hold of, say, dollars? It does this by extending "purchasing rights." It simply permits the British to buy with British currency some of the Fund's own holdings of dollars. To keep the Fund from getting loaded up with pounds and stripped of its dollars, in any 12-month period, the British are not permitted to buy an amount greater than one-fourth of their original quota. And the Fund will never hold more than twice the original quota number of British pounds.

After the British balance of payments has improved, they are expected to buy back with gold (or with dollars) the pounds they have sold to the Fund. Thus, the Fund need never run out of dollars or any other currency; especially if it leads to corrective action to prevent continuing disequilibrium.

No more need be said here of the technical mechanics of the Fund. It is enough to emphasize that the Fund helps to establish stable—but flexible—exchange rates; that it provides short-term credits toward this end; and that it works toward international equilibrium by cooperation, coordination, and consultation and attempts to work against trade restrictions.

5. *European Recovery Program.* We have come out of the war with more resources than ever before. Other nations—such as Holland, France, England, and Norway—suffered very extensive war damage. If the peace is to be durable and if democracy is to flourish, we ought to send these countries food and goods for relief and rehabilitation purposes. We must do this because of our generosity—or some will argue, because of our power politics—but not because gifts make jobs on our farms and in our export industries.

Because of the painful lesson learned from the World War I debts, we have been smart enough to cancel off immediately our lend-lease debts with England, France, and other allied powers. By having their men fight the enemy with our guns, planes, and ships, we saved American lives. Let us leave the matter there, and not let interallied war debts lead to the bad feeling and economic collapse of the previous postwar period.

Even though UNRRA (United Nations Relief and Rehabilitation Administration) ended with 1946, America is still finding it necessary and desirable to send further relief supplies abroad. Relief, as such, should be recognized as a gift, not as a loan.

Communism thrives on economic chaos abroad. Disorganization and privation in Europe constitute a threat to the peace and security of the United States. For this reason President Truman and George C. Marshall, then Secretary of State, asked the countries of Europe to get together and draw up plans for helping themselves to economic recovery, so that we could intelligently aid them in this task. Sixteen nations—excluding the satellites of the Soviet Union, who all declined to participate—met at Paris in the summer of 1947 and drew up an important economic report pointing out the roads to cooperative recovery over the following 4 years and indicating how American financial aid would be necessary to help them help themselves in becoming again self-supporting. They pointed out the great and universal "shortage of dollars," which is the financial counterpart of the great need in Europe for the food, fertilizer, and capital equipment that only America can provide.

Despite the fact that high postwar spending in the United States kept goods scarce and prices high, both political parties pledged their support to the European recovery program—for reasons of charity, for reasons of political security, and to head off the spread of European communism. The Marshall plan has been a great success, amply fulfilling every expectation. What will happen after 1952, when it is due to expire, the future must tell.

6. *European Rearmament Program.*   Just as the end of the Marshall plan was in sight, American aid to European countries for their rearmament began to grow appreciably. Earlier the "Truman Doctrine" had provided for aid to Greece and other countries in danger of Soviet domination. Especially after the outbreak of the Korean war in mid-1950, the United States realized the need to help build up the military establishments of the Atlantic Pact nations to some kind of minimum position of strength.

This additional monetary aid, plus the increase in American imports resulting from the booming of our domestic activity in the wake of our own post-Korean armament program, has, as we have earlier seen, greatly altered the whole dollar-gap problem of Europe.

7. *Point Four: The Bold New Program.*   Aside from providing substantial material aid to foreign countries, there is one thing we can do that may help them a great deal and yet cost us very little, namely, help other countries acquire the technical know-how that will enable them to increase their levels

of productivity and living standards. This program has hardly yet got under way. It is known as the Point Four program because it was first enunciated as the fourth point in the 1949 inaugural address of President Truman. Congress early in 1950 made an appropriation of 35 million dollars to be used toward this end. Since this important program still exists largely on paper, there is no better way to describe it than to quote from Truman's original enunciation.[1]

Fourth, we must embark on a bold new program for making the benefits of our scientific advances and industrial progress available for the improvement and growth of undeveloped areas.

More than half the people of the world are living in conditions approaching misery. Their food is inadequate. They are victims of disease. Their economic life is primitive and stagnant. Their poverty is a handicap and a threat both to them and to more prosperous areas.

For the first time in history, humanity possesses the knowledge and the skill to relieve the suffering of these people.

The United States is pre-eminent among nations in the development of industrial and scientific techniques. The material resources which we can afford to use for the assistance of other peoples are limited. But our imponderable resources in technical knowledge are constantly growing and are inexhaustible.

I believe that we should make available to peace-loving peoples the benefits of our store of technical knowledge in order to help them realize their aspirations for a better life. And, in cooperation with other nations, we should foster capital investment in areas needing development.

Our aim should be to help the free peoples of the world, through their own efforts, to produce more food, more clothing, more materials for housing, and more mechanical power to lighten their burdens.

We invite other countries to pool their technological resources in this undertaking. Their contributions will be warmly welcomed. This should be a cooperative enterprise in which all nations work together through the United Nations and its specialized agencies wherever practicable. It must be a world-wide effort for the achievement of peace, plenty, and freedom.

In addition to these government plans, we have been privately exporting our "know-how" abroad. Many of our largest companies are establishing branch factories abroad; often the capital is largely raised abroad, with Americans supplying the technical knowledge. Some shortsighted people raise their hands in horror at the thought of our helping foreign nations to become our industrial competitors. They seem to forget the statistical fact that international trade is largest between developed industrial nations, not between us and backward countries.

[1] President Truman's Inaugural Address, Jan. 4, 1949.

8. *Freer Multilateral Trade.* We have already discussed the postwar problems of (1) domestic full employment in America, (2) the European balance of payments, (3) foreign lending and the International Bank, (4) stable exchange rates via the International Fund, (5) the Marshall plan, (6) the rearmament of Europe, and (7) the Point Four program for international development. To the extent that these problems have been met—or at the least, after a good start has been made on them—can we attain the final goal of freer international trade. Only then can the Roosevelt-Hull program of reciprocal trade agreements be successful in reducing (1) tariffs, (2) import quotas, (3) exchange control, (4) monopolistic international "cartels," (5) restrictive international commodity agreements by governments, and other forms of protectionism. Only then can the newly created ITO (International Trade Organization) and the Economic and Social Council of the United Nations succeed in combatting bilateralism in favor of mutually beneficial multilateral trade. Because World War II was so vast and devastating, we must expect and be patient with slow progress toward these goals.

SUMMARY

1. One way of increasing the level of domestic income is to engage in an extensive foreign investment program. Not only does this directly increase the number of jobs and the flow of income, but in addition it sets up a familiar multiplier chain of secondary respending.

2. However, a country like the United States has no need to achieve its full employment in this way, since there are always adequate programs for maintaining adequate demand by domestic means. Foreign investment should be undertaken for its own sake or in terms of our political and moral responsibilities; it should not be used simply to make jobs.

3. During the great depression a vast variety of beggar-my-neighbor tactics were used by countries in their attempt to export their unemployment to other nations.

4. World War II is not long past, yet a remarkable amount of progress seems to have been made by the international economy in moving toward a solution of the half-dozen principal postwar international economic problems.

QUESTIONS FOR DISCUSSION

1. "In 1935 it was better to export goods in exchange for useless gold than to do nothing." Discuss critically. Would your answer be different in 1942 or 1948?

2. How does the multiplier analysis apply to international trade?

3. Define, describe, and criticize beggar-my-neighbor policies.

4. Contrast and compare the International Bank and the International Fund.

5. Draw up a list of what you consider our most important postwar economic problems. If you were in Congress, what would you do about them?

6. Why would you expect that a post-Korean boom in the United States would improve the dollar position of Europe?

7. "Not one single American industry should be sacrificed in the name of the ITO's program for realizing freer multilateral trade." Do you agree?

8. Describe the extent of our postwar aid to the rest of the world. Was this merely "generosity"? Did generosity play an important role?

9. What is your Point Five program for the future?

Chapter 33: INTERNATIONAL TRADE AND THE THEORY OF COMPARATIVE ADVANTAGE

AGAIN and again we have seen how specialization increases productivity and standards of living. Now we must show exactly how this works out in the field of international or interregional trade, going behind the façade of international finance. Why did the United States specialize a century ago in the production of agricultural goods and exchange these for the manufacturing output of Europe? Why is she today able to export highly complex mass-produced goods to the far corners of the globe? Why is the agriculture of Australia so different from that of Austria or Belgium? How great would be the costs of complete self-sufficiency to a modern country? How do all countries benefit from trade?

The key to the correct answers to such questions, and many more, is provided by the theory of comparative advantage or comparative cost. Developed more than a century ago by David Ricardo, John Stuart Mill, and other English followers of Adam Smith, the theory of comparative advantage is a closely reasoned doctrine which, when properly stated, is unassailable. With it we are able to separate out gross fallacies in the political propaganda for protective tariffs aimed at limiting imports. At the same time, it helps us to identify the germs of truth that sometimes pop up in the heated claims for protection.

Like much of the reasoning of the classical economists, the theory of comparative advantage can be best understood and defended if we agree in advance to apply it only to a Euclidean world where there is substantially full employment. If this seems objectionable to the reader in view of the grave problem of unemployment, let him be referred to the preceding chapter where the effects of international trade on domestic employment were discussed and where we agreed that a country like the United States must not depend upon beggar-my-neighbor international economic policies to solve her domestic problem of unemployment.

DIVERSITY OF CONDITIONS BETWEEN REGIONS OR COUNTRIES

For simplicity, therefore, let us imagine two countries or continents, each endowed with certain quantities of natural resources, capital goods, kinds of labor, and technical knowledge or know-how. The first link in the comparative-cost chain of reasoning is the *diversity in conditions of production between different countries*. Specifically, this means that the production possibilities of the different countries are very different. Although people could try to produce something of every commodity in any region, it is obvious that they would not succeed; or, if they did succeed, it would be only at a terrific cost. With hot-house procedures and forcing methods, wine grapes could perhaps be grown in Scotland; but the cost in terms of economic resources would be exorbitant, and the resulting product would hardly be fit to drink anyway.

Even if by chance two countries can both produce the same commodities, they will usually find that it pays for each to concentrate its production especially on some goods and trade them for other goods. If we consider trade between, say, the northern temperate zones and the southern tropics, this proposition will seem true and trite. Of course, resources near the equator are more productive in the growing of bananas, and of course northern resources are better designed for wheat growing. Everyone can readily see that in this case specialization and trade will increase the amount of world production of both goods and also each country's consumption of both goods.

It is not so immediately obvious, but it is no less true, that international trade is mutually profitable even when one of the two countries can produce *every commodity* more cheaply (in terms of all resources) than the other country. One country has an *absolute advantage* in the production of every good; the other country has an absolute disadvantage in the production of every good. But so long as there are differences in the *relative* efficiencies of producing the different goods in the two countries, one can always be sure that even the poor country has a *comparative advantage* in the production of those commodities in which it is relatively most efficient; this same poor country will have a *comparative disadvantage* in those commodities in which it is more than averagely inefficient. Similarly, the rich, efficient country will find that it should specialize in those fields of production where its absolute advantage is comparatively greatest, planning to import those commodities in which the highly inefficient country has the least absolute disadvantage.

Thus, trade between America and Europe in food and clothing is mutually advantageous even if America should be able to produce both of these items more efficiently (in terms of all economic resources). Moreover, barter between America and Asia is especially advantageous to us even though the Chinese laborer receives only a fraction of the real wages going to productive American labor. We shall see in a moment how this paradoxical situation is possible.

A traditional example used to illustrate this paradox of comparative advantage is the case of the best lawyer in town who is also the best typist in town. Will he not specialize in law and leave typing to a secretary? How can he afford to give up precious time from the legal field, where his comparative advantage is very great, to perform typing activities in which he has an absolute advantage but in which his relative advantage is least? Or look at it from the secretary's point of view. She is at a disadvantage relative to him in both activities; but her relative disadvantage is least in typing. Relatively speaking, she has a comparative advantage in typing.

A SIMPLE CASE: EUROPE AND AMERICA

Let us illustrate these fundamental principles of international trade by a simplified example. Consider America and Europe of a century ago, and concentrate on only two commodities, food and clothing. Now in the Western Hemisphere land and natural resources were then very plentiful relative to labor and capital, whereas on the Continent, people and capital were plentiful relative to land.

This contrast is best seen if we look at the *intensive* agriculture of a country like Belgium. There, in order to get the greatest possible output, small plots of land have to be cultivated assiduously by many people and much fertilizer. Compare this with the extensive agriculture of the early United States, where one family cultivated many acres and where national product was maximized by each man "spreading himself thin" over the virtually free land. A Belgian farmer would have thought this wasteful. But in view of the relatively high cost of American labor or capital and the low cost of land, it was not. Actually, it was prudent.[1]

Of course, if surplus population could have all migrated from Belgium to the United States, real wages here would have tended to fall toward equality with rising wages there; and high land rents there would have fallen toward

---

[1] This disregards the practice of burning out the natural fertility of the soil by overuse, and also the destruction of forests, giving rise to floods and soil erosion. From a social point of view, such exhaustion of natural resources undoubtedly represented a tremendous waste. Even today conservation programs in the lumber, oil, and agriculture fields leave much to be desired.

equality with rising rents here. Actually, this would have tended at the same time to increase *total world production*, because the transfer of workers from their poor Belgian farms to rich American farms would entail a gain in their productivity. All this follows from the fundamental law of diminishing returns, discussed earlier.

But let us be selfish and hard-boiled. Let us suppose that immigrants from abroad are to be kept out of the United States in order to keep labor scarce here and wages high. From this same selfish point of view, should the United States also impose a protective tariff designed to keep out imports from abroad? Or should it not? To answer this important social question we must measure carefully the amounts of food and clothing that will be produced and consumed in each country (1) if there is no international trade and (2) if trade is permitted to follow its own course.

AMERICA WITHOUT TRADE

In Chapter 2, we saw that every economy has a production-possibility (or transformation) schedule indicating how much of one commodity such as food, can be produced if all resources are diverted to it; also how much of the other commodity, clothing, can be produced if all resources are diverted to its production; and how either good can be transformed into the other—not physically, but—by transferring resources from the production of one to the other.

For simplicity, let us suppose that food can always be transformed into units of clothing in America at the *constant ratio* of 10:3. For each 10 units of food sacrificed, we can always secure 3 units of clothing. Let us further assume that, when all resources are diverted to the production of food, America will have altogether 100 (million) units of food.

TABLE 1. *Production-possibility Schedule of America (10:3, Constant-cost Ratio)*

	A	B	C	D	E	F	G	H	I	J	K
Food (millions)	100	90	80	70	60	50	40	*30	20	10	0
Clothing (millions)	0	3	6	9	12	15	18	*21	24	27	30

Then, clearly America can, if she chooses, have 90 (million) units of food and 3 (million) units of clothing, 80 (million) and 6 (million), . . . , or finally 0 (million) of food and 30 (million) of clothing. We may put this in the form of a schedule, as shown in Table 1.

This may be plotted in Figure 1, just as was done in Chapter 2, Figure 3.

The solid line *AK* is the production-possibility curve. But something about the diagram looks a little different from that of Chapter 2. This new production-possibility curve is a straight line whereas the earlier one was rounded, being of a convex curvature when looked at from above.

The straight-line production-possibility schedule has been introduced in order to keep the argument simple; any tendency toward what is called "increasing costs" has been deliberately assumed away. The returns of food for clothing sacrificed are instead always to be given by the constant-cost ratio 10:3, instead of having relative costs rise in a more realistic fashion. Constant costs have been assumed only to simplify the argument—to relieve the student from having to remember many different cost ratios. As will be seen later, this will not seriously affect the validity of the argument. Where a few qualifications are needed, they are later made in the Appendix to this chapter.

So far we have been talking only about production. However, if the United States is isolated from all trade, what she produces is also what

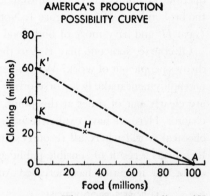

AMERICA'S PRODUCTION POSSIBILITY CURVE

FIGURE 1. The constant-cost line *AK* shows America's domestic production possibilities. The new line *AK'* indicates an increased ability to produce clothing, and means that America can move northeast from *AK*, enjoying more of both goods.

she consumes. Let us suppose, therefore, that the starred quantities, *H*, of Table 1 and Figure 1 represent the amounts produced and consumed by America in the absence of trade; or in numerical terms America then produces and consumes 30 (million) units of food and 21 (million) units of clothing.

Why was this particular combination decided upon rather than one of the other possibilities? We have seen in Chapter 3 that in a competitive system nobody "decides" upon this, but that the price mechanism, operating through supply and demand for goods and services, determines What shall be produced, How, and For Whom. Well, the starred quantities are the What. Very little need be said here about the How, except for the obvious remark that agricultural food production will require more land relative to labor than will more highly fabricated clothing output. As to the For Whom, we need only repeat that scarcity of labor in the United States will mean rather high wages for workers, while superabundance of land here will mean low rents (per acre) for landlords.

Let us proceed to introduce Europe into the picture. Before doing so, it will pave the way for the later argument to interject a question. What would happen if some American (perhaps Eli Whitney, inventor of the cotton gin, will do as an example) should make a clever invention so that each 10 units of food could be transformed into 6 rather than 3 units of clothing. Would America be potentially better off? The answer is obviously "yes." The production-possibility curve has shifted outward and upward and is now shown by the broken line, AK', in Figure 1. Note that America could now go from H to (say) H' and have more of both food and clothing.

Of course, someone may rise to the floor and ask, "What if the invention throws people out of work? Will America be better off? May not technological unemployment make her worse off?" These are not stupid questions, but they are clearly out of order at this point. They belong to Part Two or to the last chapter. Here we have explicitly asserted that we move in a happy, Euclidean, classical world where all resources are fully employed, either as a matter of luck or as a result of sensible public and private domestic policies. Without a doubt, the invention has increased America's *potential* production or her full-employment national income—whatever it does to her realistic chances of attaining or maintaining full employment.

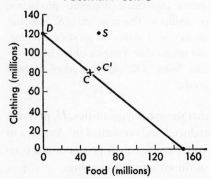

EUROPE'S PRODUCTION POSSIBILITY CURVE

FIGURE 2. Before international trade, Europe is on her domestic production-possibility curve at C, consuming just what she produces. (Disregard the points C' and S until later in the chapter.)

EUROPE WITHOUT TRADE

We can now do for Europe exactly what was done above for America; but with an important difference. Europe's plentiful endowment of labor relative to land would give her a different cost or transformation ratio between food and clothing. She would have less of a comparative advantage in food and more in clothing. For her each 10 units of food may be transformable into, say, 8 units of clothing.

She gets 5 more than was true of the United States because of her comparative advantage in clothing. However, in terms of food, America gets $1\frac{0}{3}$ or 3.33 units for each unit of clothing sacrificed; while Europe's comparative disadvantage in food production gives her only $1\frac{0}{8}$ or 1.25 units of food for each sacrificed unit of clothing. *The important thing to concentrate upon is the difference in the two cost ratios: 10:3 for America and 10:8 for Europe.*

Let us still keep the two continents isolated from each other. What is Europe's exact production-possibility schedule? Let us suppose that Europe's population is so large and her land area is such that before trade she was producing and consuming 50 units of food and 80 units of clothing. This fact, plus the constant-cost ratio, 10:8, tells us all we have to know in order to draw up Europe's complete production-possibility schedule as in Table 2. Check these data against the correct production-possibility line shown in Figure 2.

TABLE 2. *Production-possibility Schedule of Europe (10:8 Constant-cost Ratio)*

	A	B	C	D
Food, millions	150	100	*50	0
Clothing, millions	0	40	*80	120

THE OPENING UP OF TRADE

Now, for the first time, let us admit the possibility of trade between the two continents. Food can be bartered for clothing at some *terms of trade*, i.e., at some *price ratio*. To dramatize the process let us suppose that in mid-ocean there stands an impersonal auctioneer, whose business it is to balance supply and demand, offers of clothing, and offers of food. He does this by calling out to both countries an exchange rate or price ratio between food and clothing. Until supplies and demands are balanced, he keeps the bidding going. When he finally hits on the equilibrium price level *at which supply and demand balance*, then he raps his gavel three times and says, "Going, going, *gone!*" But only then.

Probably, he will suspect in advance that Europe is going to specialize on clothing production, in which she has a comparative advantage, and will wish to export part of her clothing production in exchange for food imports. But he has no idea what the final price ratio or "terms of trade" between clothing and food will be—whether the final food-clothing price ratio will be 10:3, 10:8, 10:5, 10:6, or anything else. For that matter, if the auctioneer is very new at the game, or very stupid, he may think that the final equilibrium exchange level or terms of trade will be 10:1 or 10:12.

Actually, neither of these last two can be the final exchange ratio. He would soon learn this from bitter experience. For let him tell America and Europe that they can get all the clothing they want in exchange for food at the rate of only 1 unit of clothing for every 10 units of food. What will America do? By producing at home, she can get 3 units of clothing for each 10 of food. Clearly she will not be sucked into trading food for clothing on those terms; she would rather remain self-sufficient.

That is only half the story. Why shouldn't America go to the other extreme and export clothing in exchange for food imports? Each 1 unit of clothing gets her 10 units of food from the auctioneer. What will 1 unit of clothing get here at home in domestic food production? Obviously, from Table 1 and Figure 1 only $1\frac{0}{3}$ or 3.33 units of food. At 10:1, therefore, America should certainly shift all her resources to clothing production; she should export some of her surplus clothing in return for food imports.

Now, what about Europe? At home she gets only $1\frac{0}{8}$ or 1.25 units of food for each unit of clothing. At 10:1, she too will want to trade clothing for food. We see, therefore, what a green hand the auctioneer was. By calling out 10:1, he brings a flood supply of clothing on his head and only demands for food. Since he has no supplies of either good up his sleeve, he must now change his tactics. He must raise the price of food relative to the price of clothing. He had better try the ratio 10:2, or perhaps even 10:9. The student is now in a position to reason out why neither of them will do: why 10:2 will still bring out a tidal wave of clothing; and, on the other hand, why 10:9 represents the opposite error, in which there is a tornado of food.

Clearly, then, *the final exchange ratio cannot be outside the original two-country limits of* 10:3 *and* 10:8! Anywhere in between is a possibility—with America following her comparative advantage and specializing in food, and Europe following her comparative advantage and specializing in the production of clothing.

We are now at a breathing space. Let us summarize exactly what has been proved:

1. If nature endows two regions unequally with factors of production, the *relative* costs of transforming one commodity into another domestically will be different for the two regions.

2. Under international trade, goods will be exchanged for each other at a price ratio somewhere *intermediate* between the domestic cost ratios of the two countries.

3. Each country will specialize in the commodity in which it has a comparative advantage, exporting its surplus of the product for imports from abroad.

4. Each country is made better off by trade and specialization: if America can get, say, 6 units of clothing for each 10 units of food traded, she is certainly better off than when she domestically transforms 10 units of food into only 3 units of clothing; Europe does better when she trades 6 units of clothing for 10 units of food than when she must domestically transform 8 of clothing into

10 of food. The same would be true if we had picked any other trading ratio than 10:6—just so long as it lies between the limits 10:3 and 10:8.

5. Trade is *indirect* production. Trade is efficient production. Efficient production is always better than inefficient production. (The reader should note that the advantage of trade has nothing to do with *relative wage rates*. Under free trade, wages in each country tend to be pulled up to the higher levels of productivity of its export industry and not down to the low efficiency level of the import industry.)

EXACT DETERMINATION OF THE FINAL PRICE RATIO

Just where in between the domestic cost ratios will the terms of trade settle down? David Ricardo, the English economist, to whom the comparative-cost theory is usually attributed,[1] got just up to this point but no further. Some of his immediate followers were foolish enough to say, "We split the difference between the two countries' cost ratios, or in this case pick 10:5½ as the equilibrium rate."[2]

Actually, as John Stuart Mill, the third great classical economist (after Smith and Ricardo) showed a little later, *the exact final level of the terms of trade in between the two cost ratios will depend upon the strength of world supply and demand for each of the two commodities.* If people have an intense desire for food relative to available supplies of food and clothing, the price ratio will settle near the upper level of 10:8; if clothing is much demanded by both countries, it will settle nearer to 10:3.[3]

Mill did what our auctioneer would have to do. He drew up a schedule showing supply and demand at *each possible price ratio*:[4] how much food America would wish to export and how much food Europe would want to import; and at

[1] DAVID RICARDO, *Principles of Political Economy and Taxation* (1817) Chap. VII.

[2] Or would they have said halfway between 1⅔ and 1⅛, giving us 11¾₄ or 10: 4.5⅚? Both answers are equally foolish.

[3] Also, if America were very small relative to Europe, so that its supplies made hardly a "dent" on the market, then the price ratio might even stay at 10:'8. America would then be specializing in food and importing clothing, but all of America's food exports would amount to so little that Europe would still have to produce some food for herself. This is possible only at a price of 10:8. America would in this case get all the gains from international trade. It pays to have a large (different!) neighbor.

[4] This schedule would differ from the ordinary supply and demand schedules for wheat, tea, or automobiles observed in Chapter 20 only in the fact that the price of, say, food is not expressed in money terms, but in barter terms, *i.e.*, in terms of clothing. Similarly, it is not money that is offered for food but clothing. We can either say that America supplies food and Europe demands food, or we can just as well say that America demands clothing and Europe supplies clothing.

the same time, how much clothing Europe would be willing to export at each price ratio in comparison with the amount of clothing America expected to import. At one, and (usually) only one, intermediate price ratio, exports and imports will balance. At this equilibrium price, exports and imports will "mesh" (or match), quantitatively as well as qualitatively; the auctioneer and Mill will heave a sight of relief, and trade will continue indefinitely until tastes or technology have changed.

For our numerical problem it has been assumed that the equilibrium terms-of-trade ratio is 10:6, a little nearer to Europe's pretrade ratio than to America's.

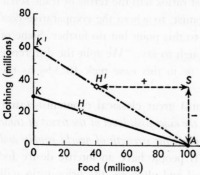

AMERICA AFTER INTERNATIONAL TRADE

America concentrates its production completely on food. In Figure 3, America is production-wise at A. But since she can trade freely at 10:6, America is not limited to her old production-possibility curve. By trading, she can now move on the dotted line AK' *just exactly as if a fruitful invention had been made.* Is America made potentially better off by trade? Indeed she is. Just where she will stop on this broken line, which we may call her new *consumption*-possibility curve, depends upon the workings of her internal price system. It has been assumed that this causes her to stop at the point H', where 40 (million) units of food and 36 (million) units of clothing are consumed. The dotted arrows show America's exports $(+)$ and imports $(-)$.

FIGURE 3. The heavy line AK represents America's domestic production-possibility curve; the heavy broken line AK' her new consumption-possibility curve when she is able to trade freely at the price ratio 10:6 and in consequence has decided to specialize completely in the production of food (at A). The dotted arrows from A to S and S to H' show the amounts exported $(+)$ and imported $(-)$ by America. As a result of free trade, she finally ends up at H' with more of both goods than before at H.

All this is summarized in America's rows of Table 3. This important table should be studied very carefully, because to understand it thoroughly is to understand the doctrine of comparative costs.

As a result of specialization and trade, America has become better off; she has more food and more clothing to consume. The same is true of Europe. What is the black magic by which something seems to have been got for nothing? The rows marked World, which represent the sum of the American and European rows give the answer. *World production of both goods has been stepped up by specialization and trade.*

TABLE 3. *Summary Table Showing Specialization and Gains from Trade According to Comparative Advantage (All data in millions of units)*

	Price ratio of food and clothing	Food produc- tion	Food con- sump- tion	Food exports (+) or imports (−)	Clothing produc- tion	Clothing con- sump- tion	Clothing exports (+) or imports (−)
Situation before trade							
America......	10:3	30	30	0	21	21	0
Europe	10:8	50	50	0	80	80	0
World	None	80	80	0	101	101	0
Situation after trade							
America......	10:6	100	40	+60	0	36	−36
Europe	10:6	0	60	−60	120	84	+36
World	10:6	100	100	0	120	120	0
Gains from trade							
America......	—	—	+10	—	—	+15	—
Europe	—	—	+10	—	—	+4	—
World	—	+20	+20	—	+19	+19	—

Actually, the second World row gives the data in which the auctioneer would be most interested. He is assured that equilibrium has been reached by two facts shown there: (1) World consumption of each product is identically equal to world production with no goods lost in transit; and (2) the amounts that each country exports are just balanced by the amounts that the other country wishes to import. Thus the price ratio 10:6 is the right one.[1]

This completes our explanation of comparative advantage. The reader might test his full understanding by filling in on Figure 2 for Europe everything that has already been filled in for America on Figure 3. Why does Europe's new

[1] The auctioneer could have made up a whole book full of such tables, each page corresponding to a different price ratio. But only one page is the right one because at all other prices the algebraic total of exports and imports · ould not cancel out. Thus, at 10:7, America's desire for clothing imports would surpass Europe's willingness to export clothing. The world as a whole would be trying to consume more clothing than had been produced. Since the auctioneer has no inventories draw upon, he would have to turn the pages toward a higher price for clothing. On the right page the price ratio would be an equilibrium one, and exports and imports would be in balance.

consumption-possibility line, made possible by trade, pivot around the point D on the vertical axis? Draw in the arrows to S representing the amounts exported $(+)$ and imported $(-)$ as was done in Figure 3. Note that Europe's arrows match America's but are opposite in sign. Why is this quantitative meshing of exports and imports necessary at equilibrium?

SUMMARY

1. If two countries have different production conditions so that the costs of converting one commodity into another are different, it is clearly to their separate selfish advantages to trade regardless of whether their wage levels are different. Each country specializes in the commodity in which it is relatively most efficient. The commodity producible at a comparative disadvantage in a country will of course be wanted in some amount by its consumers; but the country in question will find it more efficient to take resources out of *direct* domestic production of that commodity and put them instead into the lines of greatest advantage. Such diverted resources can be thought of as creating the wanted goods *indirectly*, in the sense that exports turned out by them can be more advantageously bartered for the wanted goods in question. A country following comparative advantage is simply acting like any prudent business firm which buys things from outsiders if it cannot produce them as cheaply itself.

2. In international exchange one country does not gain at the expense of another. The benefits from trade are mutual. All countries gain. This is possible because the total of world production is increased by international specialization along the lines of comparative cost.

3. Precisely how these total gains will be split up between the participating nations depends upon the reciprocal supply-demand situation. We can state with confidence that the final terms of trade, or price ratio, will fall somewhere within the divergent domestic cost ratios of the two countries. Whether it will fall near to one's original cost ratio and thereby give most of the benefits to the other, cannot be told in advance.

Moreover, as tastes and technology change, the terms of trade may turn in favor of or against a particular nation. For example, after World War I, surplus agricultural supplies turned the terms of trade against the backward, debtor, agricultural countries of the world. This is typical of depressions, whereas the reverse is usually true in time of prosperity and boom. In the recent postwar period the terms of trade were turned strongly in favor of agriculture, as every food purchaser was bitterly aware.

QUESTIONS FOR DISCUSSION

1. List some products that the United States exports or imports. What other countries are involved?

2. "If a country can buy a good cheaper abroad than it can produce it at home, it is to its advantage to do so." Is this consistent with the theory of comparative advantage?

3. State in a single page the meaning of the theory of comparative advantage.

4. How would you apply that theory to trade between people within a country?

5. Can you rewrite Table 3 assuming that the new final price or trading ratio is 10:5 rather than 10:6, and that America ends up consuming 35 units of food?

6. Exactly what did John Stuart Mill add to David Ricardo's theory of international trade?

7. Which of the following two statements is absolutely false?

a. "Even if the United States can produce every product with less labor and capital hours than Czechoslovakia, it may still pay both of us to trade."

b. "Even if the United States can produce every product for fewer *dollars* than they can be imported for from abroad, it will still pay us to trade—provided only that some commodities have relatively higher import prices than others."

How do the statements differ? What are the implications of the valid statement for real wages here and abroad?

8. Why shouldn't the United States use international trade to get rid of her unemployment?

9. List some qualifications to the simplest theory of comparative advantage. (For this and the following questions, see the Appendix.)

10. Compare and evaluate multilateralism and bilateralism.

11. "If there are more than two commodities or two countries, the whole theory of comparative advantage has to be scrapped." Discuss.

APPENDIX TO CHAPTER 33
SOME QUALIFICATIONS TO THE DISCUSSION
OF COMPARATIVE ADVANTAGE

Very briefly we must now show what happens when we remove some of the oversimplifications made in the above discussion. The conclusions are not essentially changed, and even the changes in details are usually not too difficult.

MANY COMMODITIES

First note that up until now we have simplified the discussion by considering only two commodities: food and clothing. Obviously, food stands for many different items (beef, milk, etc.), and the same is true of clothing. Moreover, the advantages of exchange are equally great when we consider the thousand and one commodities that can and do enter into international trade.

As is shown in advanced textbooks in international trade,[1] when there are many commodities that are producible in two countries, they can be arranged in order according to their relative advantage or comparative cost. For example, the commodities, automobiles, flax, perfumes, watches, wheat, and woolens might be arranged in the following comparative-advantage sequence:

AMERICA ◄———┼————┼————┼————┼————┼————┼———► EUROPE
Wheat, Automobiles, Flax, Watches, Woolens, Perfumes

This means that wheat costs are lowest relative to all other commodities in America; Europe has its greatest comparative advantage in perfumes; its advantage in watches is not quite so great, etc.

From the beginning we can be almost sure of one thing. The introduction of trade will cause America to produce wheat and Europe perfume. But where will the dividing line fall? Between automobiles and flax? Or will America produce flax and Europe confine herself to watches, woolens, and perfumes? Or will the dividing line fall on one of the commodities rather than between them, so that, say, flax might be produced in both places at the same time?

The reader will not be surprised to find that the answer depends upon the comparative strength of international demand for the different goods. If we think of the commodities as beads arranged on a string according to their comparative advantage, the total demand and supply situation will determine where the dividing line between American and European production will fall. Then,

[1] For example, G. HABERLER, *Theory of International Trade* (Macmillan, New York, 1937).

an increased demand for automobiles and wheat, for example, may tend to turn the terms of trade in direction of America and make us so prosperous that it will no longer pay us to continue to produce our own flax. Also, there is the possibility that a new scientific discovery permitting America to grow flax on the desert might rearrange the order of the comparative advantages of the different commodities and alter the pattern of specialization and trade.[1]

[1] This ordered array of goods might have arisen from the following numerical data, which are presented only for the curiosity of the more advanced reader and which have nothing to do with the above discussion. As before, it is not necessary to measure costs in terms of money or labor but only in terms of the relative commodities into which any good can be "transformed." Suppose that we choose to measure the costs of every good in both countries in terms of woolens, which is selected arbitrarily because it comes last alphabetically. Then our data might be as arranged alphabetically as in the accompanying table:

Goods	American cost ratio, in terms of woolens	European cost ratio, in terms of woolens	Comparative European costs, in terms of American costs
Automobiles............	1,000	3,000	$\frac{3,000}{1,000} = 3.0$
Flax.................	0.8	1.6	$\frac{1.6}{0.8} = 2.0$
Perfumes.............	5.0	3.0	$\frac{3}{5} = 0.6$
Watches..............	50	75	$\frac{75}{50} = 1.5$
Wheat...............	0.2	0.8	$\frac{0.8}{0.2} = 4.0$
Woolens..............	1.0	1.0	$\frac{1}{1} = 1.0$

This means that in America one must give up the production of 1,000 units of woolens to get 1 automobile, while in Europe the cost of 1 automobile is the sacrifice of 3,000 units of wool production. Therefore, the comparative cost of automobiles in Europe is three times that in America, and so forth for the other goods.

Obviously, Europe's relative cost advantage is greatest in perfumes and least in wheat; in between, the commodities are arranged as shown above in the text. The fact that the figures in the last column are predominantly greater than 1 in no way reflects on the efficiency of Europe, but results from the accidental fact that we chose woolens as out common denominator in which to express costs. Had we selected wheat or watches, the opposite would have been the case and yet none of our results would be any different—except for a "scale factor" (such as converts inches to feet or yards).

MANY COUNTRIES

So much for the complications introduced by many commodities. What about many countries? Europe and America are not the whole world. And even they include many separate so-called sovereign nations.

Introducing many countries need not change our analysis. As far as any one country is concerned, all the other nations with whom she trades can be lumped together into one group as "the rest of the world." The advantages of trade have nothing specially to do with state boundaries. The principles already developed apply between groups of countries and, indeed, between regions within the same country. In fact, but for historical accident, they would be more applicable to trade between our Northern and Southern states than to trade between the United States and Canada.

From the standpoint of pure economic welfare, the slogan "Buy American" is as foolish as would be "Buy Wisconsin," or "Buy Oshkosh, Wisconsin," or "Buy South Oshkosh, Wisconsin." Part of the great prosperity of the United States has resulted from the fortunate fact that there have been no restrictive customs duties within our vast 48 states, and we have constituted the world's greatest free-trade area.

There is, however, one new aspect introduced by the existence of many countries. America may find it very profitable to trade indirectly with Europe. America sells Europe much, including finished commodities like automobiles. It buys little from Europe. But it does buy rubber and raw materials from the East Indies. They in turn do not usually buy goods from America. However, they do buy clothing and other goods from England. Thus, we have a very advantageous triangular trade, as shown in the accompanying diagram.

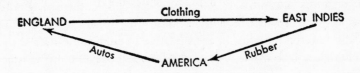

The arrows indicate the predominant direction of exports.

What would happen if all countries tried to sign bilateral trade agreements with each other, so that America could not and would not buy from the Indies unless they bought an equal amount from America? And so forth with every two countries? Very clearly, trade would be cut down severely. Imports would balance exports, but at the level of whichever was the lower. Everyone would be worse off.

Just how tragic to all countries bilateralism would be is indicated by Figure 4, showing the advantageous international pattern of world multilateral trade.

**THE SYSTEM OF MULTILATERAL TRADE,
AS REFLECTED BY THE ORIENTATION
OF BALANCES OF MERCHANDISE
TRADE IN 1938**

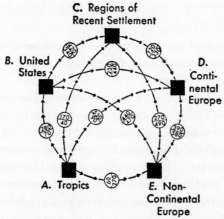

FIGURE 4. SOURCE: League of Nations.

INCREASING COSTS

Returning again to two countries and two commodities, we must now drop the assumption that costs are constant. The production-possibility curves of Figures 1, 2, and 3 should really have been convexly bent, as they were in Chapter 2. It is no longer possible to specify a single cost figure for each country.

America is better endowed on the whole for food production than Europe; still after a great amount of American food is produced, the cost of *extra* food will begin to exceed that of Europe. Even after American competition has drastically lowered the price of food relative to clothing, a little of the best land in Europe will be able to hold its own in food production. In the same way, that first little bit of American clothing production which can be produced at low costs will continue even after international trade has reached an equilibrium level. However, any attempt to expand American clothing production further would entail higher extra costs and competitive losses.

We may summarize the modifications in international trade made necessary by increasing costs as follows:

As a result of international trade, each country will tend to specialize, as before, in the commodity in which it has the greatest comparative advantage; and it will export some of that commodity in exchange for the other country's surplus exports. But because of increasing costs, specialization need not be complete: something of both commodities may still be produced in either country, because even the less favored commodity may have low enough costs to compete when its production is small.[1]

INTERNATIONAL COMMODITY MOVEMENTS AS A PARTIAL SUBSTITUTE FOR LABOR AND FACTOR MOVEMENTS

Having acknowledged the existence of the law of increasing costs described in Chapter 2, we must also examine the implications of the law of diminishing returns within the two countries.

After international trade takes place, resources in Europe flow from food to clothing production. Because clothing requires relatively much labor and little land, the pressure of population on the limited land of Europe is relieved. Land is no longer so relatively dear; rents fall compared to wages. In America the reverse happens after trade: concentration upon food production in which labor is economized and land heavily utilized tends to raise rents relative to wages.

In every case the free international movement of goods has effects which are

[1] For the geometrically minded, Figure 5 may be helpful, although most of us will probably do better to skip over it. It shows America's condition before and after trade when increasing costs prevail. The production-possibility curve is now convex. Before international trade, America is consuming and producing at the starred point, H. The domestic price ratio is 10 : 3, just equal to the ratio of extra costs of getting (at H) a little more clothing for a little sacrificed food. This is shown by the slope of the AK curve at H.

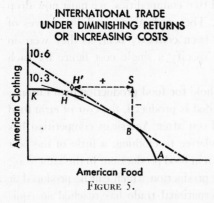

INTERNATIONAL TRADE
UNDER DIMINISHING RETURNS
OR INCREASING COSTS

American Food

FIGURE 5.

After trade, when the common price ratio is 10 : 6, American production shifts to B, toward less clothing but not away from clothing altogether. The new production point, B, will be reached as a result of competition, because the slope of the curve there —*i.e.*, the ratio of costs of extra clothing for extra food—is 10 : 6, or just equal to the common international price ratio. At B, and only there, will the value of America's national product (weighted by the 10 : 6 price ratio) be at a maximum.

The straight line represents the new consumption-possibility curve to which America can get as a result of trade. It is straight and not bent because the auctioneer offers to trade freely, giving America at the 10 : 6 ratio as much or little clothing for food as she wishes. The final levels of consumption, determined by supply and demand, are given by the point H'. As before, the arrows indicate exports and imports.

There are still gains from trade. But because of diminishing returns and increasing costs, there is not so much specialization as before and not quite such large gains. Note that at the equilibrium point, where no further trade is possible, relative (extra or "marginal") production costs in the two countries are equal, each to the common price ratio 10 : 6.

partly like those following from the free international movement of factors of production. Just as the movement of labor from Europe to America would relieve the scarcity of labor in America and of land in Europe, so the movement of clothing from Europe to America and of food from America to Europe tends to make the superabundant factor in each country less abundant, and the scarce factor less rare.

The person who has most clearly emphasized how commodity trade partially relieves the scarcity in all countries of the less abundant factors of production is the Swedish economist and public financier, Ohlin (pronounced O'Lean).[1] He has made the following important addition to the classical doctrine of comparative cost:

> Free movements of labor and capital between countries will tend to equalize wages and factor prices. *However, even without any movements of productive factors across national boundaries, there will often result a partial (but not necessarily complete) equalization of factor prices from the free movement of goods in international trade.*

It is clear, therefore, that, although international trade increases national product in England, it may at the same time so reduce the share of particular groups that they are made worse off. Thus, the large British landowners who a century ago constituted the backbone of the Conservative or Tory party may have been selfish in opposing the famous repeal of the English corn law tariffs in 1846, but they were not necessarily unintelligent in making their unsuccessful last-ditch fight to retain protective tariffs on imported grains.

DECREASING COSTS AND INTERNATIONAL TRADE

If economies of mass production are overwhelmingly important, costs may decrease as output expands. This would only strengthen the case for international exchange of goods. In fact, decreasing costs are a second great factor— in addition to differences in comparative costs—which explains why specialization and trade are profitable. For, as was discussed in Chapter 3, large-scale specialization is most fruitful when there is a widely expanded market. In fact, even if there were no differences in comparative cost between two countries, it would pay for them to toss a coin to decide who was to produce each of two goods subject to increasing returns or decreasing costs. Complete specialization would increase world production of both goods.

This may be illustrated by our example in Chapter 3 of the two identical

[1] BERTIL OHLIN, *Interregional and International Trade* (Harvard University Press, Cambridge, Mass., 1933).

Indian twins who, despite their similarity, still find it advantageous to specialize so that they may reap the efficiencies of mass production.

Moreover, there is one very practical aspect of international trade under decreasing cost. Peculiarly under such conditions is competition likely to break down and be succeeded by monopoly or monopolistic competition. By excluding foreign competition, protective tariffs only serve to consolidate the position of the monopolist. This is recognized in the old slogan: "The tariff is the mother of trusts." Freer international trade is often an effective, and an efficient, way of breaking up such monopoly positions.

DIFFERENCES IN TASTES OR DEMAND AS A REASON FOR TRADE

Two reasons have been given thus far for international trade: (1) differences in comparative costs between regions and (2) decreasing costs. For completeness, a third obvious possible cause for trade may be mentioned. Even if costs were identical in the two countries and increasing, trade might take place as the result of differences in *taste*.

Thus, it might pay both Norway and Sweden to produce fish and meat in about the same amounts. If the Swedes have a relatively great fondness for fish and the Norse for meat, then a mutually profitable export of fish from Norway and meat from Sweden would take place.

Both parties gain from this trade. The sum total of human happiness is increased, just as it is when Jack Spratt trades fat meat for his wife's lean. Both get some "consumer's surplus" from the swap.[1]

TRANSPORTATION COSTS

Up to this point, we have neglected the whole problem of transportation costs. The economic costs of moving bulky and perishable goods lessens the extent of profitable regional specialization. The effects are like those produced by the passage of artificially restrictive tariff legislation. As is discussed in the next chapter, many of these effects are harmful to national economic welfare. In the case of transportation costs, the evil is unavoidable, whereas protective tariffs or artificial barriers to interregional trade within a nation are squarely the responsibility of man.

---

[1] Even two individuals with identical amounts of two goods and the same tastes may in rare instances trade. Two sailors, each with a fifth of rye and a fifth of gin, might toss a coin to decide which is to have 2 fifths of gin and which 2 fifths of rye. The reader should reason out why the same might be true of herring and chocolate, but not of corned beef and cabbage. This fourth cause of trade is primarily only a curio.

Chapter 34: THE ECONOMICS

OF TARIFF PROTECTION AND

FREE TRADE

IT would be absurd to try to decide whether God exists or not by counting on one hand all the arguments in the affirmative, and on the other hand all the arguments in the negative—and then to award the decision to the side with the greater number of points. It would be no less absurd to evaluate the case for tariff protection by a simple numerical counting of unequally important pros and cons.

Indeed, there is essentially only one argument for free or freer trade, but it is an exceedingly powerful one: namely, the fact that *unhampered trade promotes a mutually profitable international division of labor, greatly enhances the potential real national product of all countries, and makes possible higher standards of living all over the globe.* This was elaborated upon in the previous chapter.

The arguments for high protection against the competition of foreign imports take many different forms. They may be divided into three categories: (1) Those which are definitely economically false, some so obviously and palpably as hardly to merit serious discussion, but some whose falsity can be detected only by subtle economic reasoning. (2) A few arguments for protection which are without validity in a "classical" static full-employment world but which contain some kernels of truth in a world of underemployment and economic development. (3) Finally, certain noneconomic arguments which may make it desirable national policy to sacrifice economic welfare in order to subsidize certain activities admittedly not economically efficient.

NONECONOMIC GOALS

Let us begin with the latter for they are most simply disposed of. If you ever are on a debating team and are given the assignment to defend free trade, you will strengthen your case at the beginning by conceding that economic welfare is not the only goal of life. Political considerations are also important. Thus, it may be necessary to become partially self-sufficient in certain lines of activity at great cost because of fear of future wars.

An example is the production of synthetic rubber. Even if the original plant costs are charged off as a military expense of World War II, it is doubtful whether we can as yet produce rubber from petroleum or grain alcohol at less than, say, 15 cents a pound. In the early years of the 1950's, world demand for rubber is high enough to keep its price above the variable unit cost of synthetic production, so that both it and natural rubber will continue to be produced. But if the price should finally fall, what then? During the great depression, the price of rubber fell to about 2 or 3 cents a pound in the East Indies, and still supplies were forthcoming. Apparently it is not yet possible for synthetic rubber to beat out natural rubber on a price basis, although the synthetic product will always continue to be used for some special purposes even at a higher price because of its peculiar physical properties.

If, therefore, synthetic rubber capacity is considered necessary for national defense and if the needed amount of capacity is not able to survive under free trade, the economist cannot assert that national policy should be against protection to this industry. But he can insist that a *subsidy* to domestic production would be preferable to a tariff: This would bring the domestic price down to the international price instead of raising the price to the consumer up to the domestic cost; also the subsidy would show clearly what the total costs of national defense are and would better enable the public to decide whether the game is worth the candle.

The question of a national policy to foster the American mercantile marine is a similar one. Without a doubt the United States does not possess a comparative advantage in building or operating a merchant fleet. As soon as American seamen, through trade-unions or on their own, insist upon living conditions and wages remotely resembling those in Detroit factories, then we cannot compete with English, Dutch, Japanese, and Norwegian ships. If we give no weight to America's "glorious seafaring tradition"—a long way back!—and consider purely economic welfare, the correct policy is obvious. If America has a comparative advantage in factory production, let men go to Detroit factories where their real productivity is high. American international trade will not suffer by being carried in other countries' bottoms.

However, if national defense makes a large merchant marine necessary, that is another matter. Mail subsidies and complete writing off of the costs of ships built during World War II may then be justified. Still, there is reason to believe that a fraction of such outlays spent in scientifically preserving Liberty ships over the years might be a partial substitute.

The problem of deciding how much to spend in peacetime on national defense is always a perplexing question, especially since armament races are both *cause* and effect of international disunity. The economist can claim no special competence to advise on this problem. He can point out that selfish economic interests often wrap themselves in the flag and try to justify uneconomic projects in terms of national defense. With less confidence, the economist can point out that mutually profitable international trade may help to promote international understanding and unity and that political interferences with trade have in the past provided some of the frictions that made war inevitable.

In conclusion, it is well to point out other noneconomic goals that may deserve consideration. Society may feel that there is some special sanctity about farm life, or something worth preserving in the way of life of the "stout agricultural yeoman or happy peasant." (It is to be doubted that all people who rhapsodize in this fashion have ever lived on a farm.) Or some groups may agree with the Soviet Union and the church that rural living is worth fostering because the country has a higher birth rate than the cities. Or the day may arise when decentralization of population will be necessary because of the threat to our concentrated eastern seaboard cities of self-guided atomic bombs. In all such cases subsidies rather than tariffs seem called for. A tariff is simply one rather indirect clumsy form of subsidy which draws attention away from the evil in need of a remedy.

GROSSLY FALLACIOUS ARGUMENTS FOR TARIFF

Keeping Money in the Country. To Abraham Lincoln is sometimes attributed the remark, "I don't know much about the tariff. But I do know that when I buy a coat from England, I have the coat and England has the money. But when I buy a coat in this country, I have the coat and America has the money."

There is no evidence that he actually ever said this. But it does represent an age-old fallacy typical of the so-called "mercantilistic" writers of the seventeenth and eighteenth centuries who preceded Adam Smith. They considered a country lucky which gave away more goods than it received, because such a "favorable" (!) balance of trade meant that gold would flow into the country in question to pay for its surplus of exports over imports.

In this day and age it should be unnecessary to labor the point that, while an increased amount of money in the hands of one person will make *him* better off, doubling the money in the hands of everybody in a full-employment economy will only serve to raise prices. Unless the single individual is a demented miser like King Midas, the money makes him better off, not for its own sake but for what it will buy or bid away from other individuals. However, for society as a whole, once full employment is reached, new money cannot hope to buy any new goods.[1]

A Tariff for Higher Money Wages.   Today it is agreed that extreme protection can raise prices and attract gold into one country, if all other countries do not retaliate with tariffs. The tariff may even increase *money* wages. But it will tend to increase the cost of living by more than the increase in money wages, so that *real* wages will fall as labor becomes less productive.

One could go on endlessly giving examples of protectionist fallacies which every thoughtful person can explode in a minute by subjecting them to analysis. This does not mean that such crude fallacies can be dismissed as unimportant. Actually, they are most important of all in shaping legislation, the other fancier arguments simply being used as window dressing.

Tariffs for Special-interest Groups.   The single most important motivation for protective tariff is obvious to anyone who has watched the "logrolling" that goes on in Congress when such legislation is on the floor. It is the well-known "give-me." Powerful pressure groups and vested interests know very well that a tariff on their products will help them, whatever its effect on total production and consumption. Outright bribery was used in the old days to get the necessary votes; today powerful lobbies are maintained in Washington to drum up enthusiasm for the good old crockery, watch, or buttonhook industry.

SOME LESS OBVIOUS FALLACIES

A Tariff for Revenue.   First, there is the claim that the tariff should be used to raise government tax revenue. Actually, a customs duty on imports is only one form of sales tax, and a peculiarly obnoxious one. The sales tax, itself, is often regarded as one of the least desirable forms of taxes because of its inequitable and "regressive" burden upon the poor. A custom duty or tariff is especially bad because in addition to its regressive impact, it distorts economic resources away from their best uses. If the people who advance the revenue argument were really sincere, they would advocate a sales tax which would also fall on domestic production. But this would provide no protection at all.

To clinch the point, only remember that a really prohibitively high tariff, which perfectly "protected" us from imports, would collect no revenue at all! Back in 1890, the so-called "billion-dollar Congress" found itself with a surplus of tax revenue over expenditure. Since there was no debt to retire, Congress found the situation embarrassing. It finally solved the problem of excessive tariff revenues not by lowering tariff rates but by raising them so high as to reduce the total of revenue collected.

[1] Of course, the gold might be spent abroad. But this perfectly sensible way of improving welfare by importing was precisely what the mercantilist "bullionists" were arguing against.

Tariffs and the Home Market.   A second argument, which by itself is on the whole false but whose fallacy is rather difficult to spot, goes as follows: "Farmers should support a tariff for industry because that will gain them a large home market for their products." Henry Clay, the perennial candidate who turned out to be neither "right" nor "President," often advanced this argument a century or more ago.

Its falsity can be seen from different points of view. First, by cutting down industrial imports we are really at the same time indirectly tending to cut down our farm exports. Thus the farmer is hurt directly. "But," Clay might remonstrate, "what about the extra home market for farm produce?"

Well, what about it? Our detailed example of comparative cost showed that isolation from international trade decreases the total of national product or real income. The total domestic demand for farm products will certainly be less at a low level of real income than at a high level. So unless it can be buttressed by one of the quite different arguments for protection to be discussed later, the slogan about "creating a home market" is seen once again to be fallacious.

Competition from Cheap Foreign Labor.   A third argument for protection has been the most popular of all in American history because it appealed to the large number of labor votes. According to its usual version, "If we let in goods produced by cheap pauper foreign labor—by Chinese coolies who live on a few cents' worth of rice per day or by low-paid Czechoslovakian shoe workers —then the higher standard of living of American workers cannot be maintained." So stated, the argument cannot stand up under analysis.

We have seen that trade is mutually profitable even if one country can produce every good more cheaply in terms of resources than the other. The important thing is comparative advantage, not absolute advantage. In the last analysis, trade boils down to two-sided barter. One country cannot indefinitely undersell the other in every line of merchandise.

Earlier we have shown that full employment at home does not, or at least should not, depend in the long run on foreign trade. If, then, everyone in this country remains fully employed at his most suitable occupation, is it not to *our selfish advantage* for the workers of other countries to be willing to work for very little? Or to put the matter another way, the comparative-cost doctrine shows that we benefit most by trading with countries like China or the tropics which are very different from ourselves, rather than with countries like England or Germany which are like our own industrial economy.[1] As a further

---

[1] This argument must be qualified and amplified. Backward countries, so poor that they have little real purchasing power with which to import, at best can export little to us. Most trade today is between industrialized countries. As a backward country advances industrially, it buys more from industrial countries, and not less; but perhaps not proportionally more, and perhaps there is less surplus per dollar of trade accruing to both parties.

criticism of the pauper-labor argument, there is the remarkable fact that the analysis of comparative advantage, summarized in Table 3 of the last chapter, did not concern itself at all with the wage rates in either country. Wages had nothing to do with the increase in national income that resulted from trade.

So much from a theoretical point of view. If we turn to the real world, we find the arguments to be even more incorrect. In Europe and in China the workers beg for tariffs saying, "Protect us from the 'unfair competition' of high paid, efficient American workers who have skill and machinery far better than our own." The rest of the world lives in mortal fear of competition from American mass-production industries. The English protectionist claims that the American worker in Bridgeport, Connecticut, who is paid $1.50 per hour is more than three times as efficient as the English worker who gets paid 60 cents an hour. This is perhaps an overstatement but it is near to the important truth: high American real wages come from high efficiency and do not handicap us in competing with foreign workers.

Thus far we have had nothing but adverse criticism for the "cheap pauper foreign labor" tariff argument. To be perfectly honest, and without honesty there can be no science, we must admit that it may have an iota of possible truth. The Ohlin proposition of the Appendix to the preceding chapter suggested that free trade in goods may serve as a partial substitute for immigration of labor into the United States. This implies that labor scarcity in the United States could be alleviated by our international specialization on labor-economizing products and that real wages might actually fall under free trade. Real national product would go up, but the relative and absolute share of labor might go down.[1]

Although admitting this as a slight theoretical possibility, most economists are still inclined to think that its grain of truth is outweighed by other more realistic considerations. Of course, particular laborers such as Waltham watchmakers might be hurt by removing a tariff. Nobody denies that. But since labor is such an important and flexible factor of production with many alternative uses, it seems likely that other laborers would gain more than they lose and that labor as a whole would share in the increased national product resulting from trade.[2]

[1] The advanced student may be referred to the paper by W. F. Stolper and P. A. Samuelson, "Protection and Real Wages," in *Readings in the Theory of International Trade* (Blakiston, Philadelphia, 1949), p. 333 (reproduced from *Review of Economic Studies*, Vol. 9, November, 1941, pp. 58–74).

[2] It would be inappropriate to discuss in an elementary textbook the theoretically valid argument that by *limited* protection a country may turn the "terms of trade" in her own favor, and so to speak "make the foreigner pay the duty." The reader is referred to G. Haberler, *Theory of International Trade* (Hodge and Company, London, 1936), p. 290, for a discussion

A Tariff for Retaliation.   Some people admit that a world of free trade would be preferable to a world of tariffs. But they say that so long as other countries are so foolish or so wicked as to pass restrictive tariff legislation, there is nothing that we can do but follow suit in self-defense. Actually, however, a tariff is like an increase in transportation costs. If other countries were foolish enough to let their roads go to ruin, would it pay us to chop holes in ours? The answer is No. Similarly, if other countries hurt us and themselves by passing tariffs, we should not add to our own hurt by passing a tariff.

To make sure that he grasps the point that our tariff harms us as well as the foreigner, the student should realize that there are four gains when the Hull trade-agreements program succeeds in getting another country and ourselves to lower tariffs reciprocally. The other country's tariff reduction bestows gains (1) on us and (2) on them. Our tariff reduction adds two more gains, (3) upon ourselves and (4) upon them.

The only possible sense in the argument, therefore, that we should retaliate when a foreign country raises tariffs, is that our threat of retaliation may deter them from raising tariffs; and our promise to reduce tariffs may persuade them to reduce theirs. This would justify our passing an occasional tariff as a bluff; but whenever our bluffs do not seem to cause foreigners to reduce their tariffs, we should give them up.

Most realistic students of political science believe from their studies of history that retaliatory tariffs usually cause other countries to raise theirs still higher, and rarely provide an effective bargaining weapon for multilateral tariff reduction.

The "Scientific" Tariff.   This is one of the most vicious arguments for a tariff; vicious because it often sounds plausible and moderate, but if taken literally, it would mean the end to all trade. According to the usual form of this argument, tariffs should be passed to "equalize the cost of production at home and abroad." We saw in the preceding chapter that all of the advantage from trade rests upon *differences* in cost or advantage. If tariffs were passed raising the costs of imports to that of the highest American producer, no goods would come in at all.[1]

There is nothing scientific about such a tariff. It is a grave reflection on the economic literacy of the American people that this least defensible of all

---

of this theoretical possibility. Even if we grant it practical importance, we must consider it a beggar-my-neighbor policy which will invite retaliation and which cannot be simultaneously *adopted by everybody with profit.*

[1] With nonconstant cost the scientific tariff formula is indeterminate. No tariff at all may equalize foreign costs with those of a very few of America's most efficient producers. Where should the line be drawn?

protectionist arguments has had tremendous political importance in our history, and has even been written into law upon occasion.

ARGUMENTS FOR PROTECTION UNDER DYNAMIC CONDITIONS

At last we are arriving at a point in the protection versus free trade debate where those in favor of tariffs can begin to score some weighty points. Two important arguments fall in this category: (1) that a tariff may help to reduce unemployment and (2) that temporary tariff protection for an "infant industry" with growth potentialities may be desirable.

Tariffs and Unemployment.   The first of these arguments need not be discussed in this chapter, because we are here assessing the effects of international trade on a country's potential or full-employment income. This does not mean that the "tariff to aid unemployment" argument is unimportant. Actually a main theme of this book is the problem of full employment. We can no more neglect the influence of international trade on total purchasing power or effective demand than we can ignore the possibility of "technological unemployment." For international trade, like scientific discovery, can conceivably increase a nation's *potential* level of total product and at the same time tend to. lower the *actual* level of production, consumption, and employment attained. Such a gap between actual and potential production would represent the frittering away of our gains in the form of unemployment and overcapacity. We cannot shirk the task of devising policy measures aimed at closing the gap between actual production and attainable full-employment production.

But beggar-my-neighbor international policies are not the proper methods. In Chapter 31, the favorable multiplier effects of exports on jobs and the unfavorable "leakage" effects of imports were discussed. However, the short-sighted character of such beggar-my-neighbor tactics, which invite retaliation and leave everyone worse off, was also stressed.

Tariffs for "Infant Industries."   This is, however, the time to discuss the "infant-industry" argument for protection. Alexander Hamilton in his famous "Report on Manufactures" stated it very clearly; it is also associated with the name of a nineteenth-century German economist, Friedrich List; and it has received the cautious blessing of John Stuart Mill, Alfred Marshall, Frank W. Taussig, and other orthodox economists.

According to this doctrine, there are many lines of activity in which a country would really have a comparative advantage, *if only it could get them started.* If confronted with foreign competition, such infantile industries are not able to weather the initial period of experimentation and financial stress. But given a breathing space, they can be expected to develop economies of mass production and the technological efficiency typical of many modern processes.

Although protection will at first raise prices to the consumer, once the industry grows up, it will be so efficient that costs and prices will actually have fallen.

There is certainly something to this, at least as a theoretical possibility. The late Professor F. W. Taussig in a careful historical study[1] came to the tentative conclusion that the American silk-manufacturing industry represented a successful case of the infant-industry argument. That is, silk manufacturing finally developed a comparative advantage; it finally grew up so that it could stand on its own feet even were the tariff to be removed. But the same could not be said about the woolen worsted industry. This industry came into being because of tariff protection; but seemingly it never did reach the point where it could utilize our so-called "Yankee mechanical ingenuity" as effectively as other industries. It represented, therefore, a baby that never grew up.

Unfortunately for the practical importance of this argument, even promising baby industries cannot swing many votes. It is not they who tend to receive protection from Congress but rather the old and powerful vested interests who have never shed their diapers for, lo, these many years.[2]

The "Young-economy" Argument.   Probably, the infant-industry argument had more validity for America a century ago than it does today, and has more validity for present-day backward nations than for those which have already experienced the transition from an agricultural to an industrial way of life. In a sense such nations are still asleep; they cannot be said to be truly in equilibrium. All over the world, farmers seem to earn less than industrial workers. Consequently, there is everywhere a relative growth of industry and a decline of agriculture. Populations migrate cityward, but this movement is not rapid enough to achieve an equilibrium of earnings and productivity. A strong case can be made for using moderate protection to accelerate these economically desirable long-run trends. Such a defense of protection might more appropriately be called a "young-economy" argument rather than an infant-industry one.

One final word. Please note that the infant-industry or young-economy arguments are not contradictory to the principle of comparative advantage. On the contrary, their validity rests upon the presumption of an induced, dynamical

[1] F. W. Taussig, *Some Aspects of the Tariff Question* (Harvard University Press, Cambridge, Mass., 1931, rev. ed.).

[2] Perhaps an exception to this rather cynical view is provided by certain war industries such as chemicals and optics which got a start when World War I cut off German competition. After the war these "war babies" demanded and received protection even though American scientific progress in these fundamental fields had been clearly inferior to that of Germany. However, now that Germany has lost her best scientists, it is likely that we enjoy a comparative advantage in these fields. Even if we didn't, military security might make subsidies to them necessary.

shift of the production-possibility curve outward and in the direction of a new comparative advantage in the lines requiring temporary protection.

This completes our discussion of the tariff controversy except for its implications with respect to unemployment which have already been discussed. No fair-minded reader who takes the trouble to think the matter through can fail to see how shallow are most of the economic arguments for tariff protection. The only serious exception is the infant-industry or young-economy argument. It is not surprising therefore that economists—who are supposed to agree on almost nothing—were unanimously opposed to the extreme tariff rates in the Smoot-Hawley Tariff of the early thirties and have been overwhelmingly in favor of the Hull Reciprocal Trade Agreements and the postwar ITO (International Trade Organization) aimed at lowering trade barriers.

SUMMARY

1. The case for freer trade rests upon the increased productivity which international specialization according to the law of comparative advantage makes possible. Higher world production is made possible, and all countries can have higher standards of living. Trade between countries with different standards of living is likely to be especially mutually profitable.

2. Most of the arguments for tariff protection are simply rationalizations for special benefits to particular pressure groups and will not stand up under analysis.

3. An important exception is provided by the need to favor certain uneconomical lines of activity for reasons of national defense. Perhaps an outright government subsidy would be preferable in such cases.

4. The only other exception of any practical importance, aside from the argument for a tariff to relieve unemployment, is provided by the case of infant industries or young economies which need some temporary protection in order to realize their true long-run comparative advantages.

QUESTIONS FOR DISCUSSION

1. What do you think is the single most favorable argument for a tariff?

2. Make a list of fallacious tariff arguments. How would you outline the various arguments for and against tariffs?

3. Briefly describe the tariff history of the United States.

4. "Import quotas are much like tariffs." Discuss.

5. Comment critically on the infant-industry and young-economy arguments. What is their relation to comparative advantage?

6. Mention some noneconomic considerations relevant to tariffs.

7. Show that the arguments against tariffs are even more applicable against exchange control.

PART SIX

Epilogue

Chapter 35: ALTERNATIVE

ECONOMIC SYSTEMS

THE CRISIS OF CAPITALISM

AFTER World War I, new governments were set up all over Europe. By 1927 any impartial observer would have said that the future of the capitalistic way of life appeared serene and assured. Yet within a half-dozen years, country after country succumbed to dictatorship; totalitarian fascist governments covered the map of Europe. The depression decade of the 1930's finally ended in a great world war.

A half-dozen years after World War II, what is the outlook? The world is divided into two great blocks: Soviet Russia and Siberia with her satellites of Eastern Europe and Asia stand within the Iron Curtain; and outside is the rest of the world. But the nations outside the Iron Curtain are far from homogeneous. Labor-Socialist governments are now ruling, or have recently been ruling, in Britain, in Australia and New Zealand, and in all of Scandinavia. Various forms of dictatorship still linger on in Spain and Latin America. France, Germany, and Italy have within them noisy and articulate left-wing political parties. The awakening nations of Asia and Africa do not view the world with laissez-faire-tinted glasses.

Only the United States and Switzerland and a few other countries remain as islands of capitalism in an increasingly collectivized world. And even here, the scene is drastically changed: ours is a mixed system of private and public initiative and control; and in these disturbed days, a mixed system of a peace and a war economy.

Every new dispatch reminds us that the capitalistic way of life is on trial. Not only must it perform adequately—more than that, it is required to perform superlatively. Mass unemployment here at home would have disastrous repercussions upon our prestige abroad, to say nothing of the internal political unrest that a slump would involve.

A. *FASCISM, COMMUNISM, AND SOCIALISM*

A BOUQUET OF ISMS

Men have always had visions of a more perfect society. Plato's Republic, Sir Thomas More's Utopia, Marx's Dictatorship of the Proletariat, and so on without number. It is only too easy to look at concrete present-day imperfections and then to contrast them with the ideal features of a vaguely defined utopia. Beyond agreeing on the faults of the present order, different schools of reform have very little in common.

At the one extreme, we have the anarchists who believe in no government at all; at the other, the apologists for an all-powerful collectivized, totalitarian, communistic social order, where the first person singular is all but replaced by the first person plural. Within the field of socialism itself, we find many subdivisions: Christian socialism, state and Marxian socialism, guild socialism, Fabian (or evolutionary) socialism, and many others. In the popular mind, socialists are characters who meet in a cellar lit by a candle thrust in an empty wine bottle to plot a bloody revolution, or at least to brew bombs sent in laundry parcels to government officials and capitalists. Or the term "socialist" is frequently used as a disparaging stereotype to discredit anyone who believes in social security, progressive taxation, bank deposit insurance, some other social improvement, or free love.

Whatever the strength of radical parties abroad, in America no third party has ever been able to develop in any strength.[1] The American Socialist party runs a candidate for the presidency every election—along with the Prohibition party—but gains only a negligible fraction of the vote. The Communist party has never been able to gain any sizable vote, either under its own name or in disguise.

If we look at the picture in Europe, we find the names of almost all the parties have the word "socialism" in them. But this does not mean much: a party like France's Radical Socialists turns out to be anything but radical, being one of the extreme conservative parties. Even Hitler's fascistic party took the name of "National Socialism." Often, however, the leading European "liberal" parties can be characterized as "social democrats." For example, the

---

[1] Theodore Roosevelt's 1912 Bull Moose party was primarily an offshoot of the Republican party. Old Bob LaFollette's 1924 Progressive party was by far the most successful third-party effort, and yet he was able to carry only his home state, Wisconsin. Henry Wallace's 1948 Progressive party was a complete failure.

Labor party in Britain, the pre-Hitler German Social Democratic party, the presently ruling parties in Sweden and Norway—all of these claim to be in favor of gradual, nonrevolutionary extension of socialism by peaceful and democratic methods.

It is clear, therefore, that we do not have to master all of the thousand and one different "isms" in order to understand the world today. It is enough to understand something of (1) relative *laissez faire* or private enterprise, (2) socialism, (3) communism, and (4) fascism. There is no hard and fast boundary between these; it is all a matter of degree. Moreover, we cannot even range these along a line, with fascism at the extreme right wing and communism at the extreme left wing. In some ways—although neither would admit it—communism and fascism have much in common.

Most of this book has been concerned with describing the capitalistic system, so we may turn to the others.

FASCISM

This is easier to characterize politically then economically. Whether in Hitler's Germany, Mussolini's Italy, Franco's Spain, Salazar's Portugal, or Peron's Argentina, fascism is usually characterized by a one-man dictatorship, by one political party with all others abolished, by the disappearance of civil liberties of the type granted in our Bill of Rights. Fascistic movements are always highly nationalistic, often with the emphasis placed upon a vaguely defined "master race" which exploits and persecutes minority groups. In the words of Mussolini, fascists are urged to "live dangerously"—to value war and national power as ends in themselves. The individual is to be secondary to the state.

On the economic side, Mussolini's fascism happened to toy with the notion of a "syndicalist" or "corporate" state; each industry and group of workers was organized in a syndicate, and these were to meet and bargain and plan how the economy should be run. However, this syndicalism has never come to much and has not been especially characteristic of other fascist regimes.

Almost all of them are against free and militant trade unionism; almost all give the central government great regulatory power over every sphere of economic life. Some work hand in glove with religious authorities; others are antichurch. Often capitalists and the lower middle classes contribute to the initial strength of fascist movements; but later when the fascist movement begins to take on—as they sometimes do—revolutionary aspects, the capitalists may regret the Frankenstein's monster that they have helped to create. Their only consolation lies in the fact that one of the earmarks of a fascist regime is opposition to communism; often it sails into power by exaggerating the immediate likelihood of a bolshevik revolution, and after coming into power the threat of communism is used as an excuse for the suppression of all democratic processes.

MARXIAN COMMUNISM AND SOVIET RUSSIA

Travel eastward from New York, and if you continue long enough you will return to it from the west. Move far enough to the right and you will round the circle and encounter the extreme left-wing communist movement. For three quarters of a century after Karl Marx and Friedrich Engels issued their 1848 Communist Manifesto, numerous international socialist conferences were held; but outside the British Museum, not much was accomplished.

In 1917, the big moment arrived. Czarist Russia was knocked out of the war by the Germans. Lenin, a follower of Marx, was transported in a sealed railroad car across Germany and into Russia. Aided by Trotsky, a one-time New York inhabitant, Lenin's Bolsheviks snatched power from the more moderate regime that had overthrown the monarchy. Preaching peace, promising land for the peasants, and a dictatorship of the proletariat, the followers of the red hammer and sickle forcibly took power and gained adherents in the navy and army.

There then followed what John Reed (later buried in the Kremlin) called "10 days that shook the world." The meeting of the democratic Constituent Assembly, only few of whose elected representatives were procommunist, was forbidden. An army was organized and trained by Trotsky, and successive towns were won over to the revolutionary forces—often by strategic capture of the water and power supply alone. Subsequently there followed a great civil war between the Red and White armies, the latter aided by Poland and Western powers. In the end, the officers of the White army ended up chiefly in Paris, driving taxicabs and drinking vodka to the memory of Czar Nicholas II.

The world expected a Russian collapse. But the communist regime persisted —not without experiencing horrible famines, in which literally millions perished. Aristocrats and bourgeoisie were ruthlessly "purged" and "liquidated"—new words for age-old processes. The Communist party was the only permitted political party; only a few per cent of the population could belong to this elite group; it elected the members of local "soviets" of factories and farms. These soviets elected representatives to still higher soviets, until at the very top over all the autonomous federated Union Republics, stood the Council of People's Commissars of the Supreme Soviet of the USSR (Union of Socialist Soviet Republics).

The Soviet leaders had no blueprint to guide them. Marx had confined himself largely to the faults of capitalism, revealing very little of what the promised land was going to be like. It was not even on the timetable that backward Russia, which had hardly emerged from feudalism into capitalism, should experience its revolution before the downfall of the top-heavy industrialized nations. During the 1920's, Lenin compromised with capitalistic enterprise in the NEP (New Economic Policy). But in 1928–1929, the first Five-year Plan for industrialization of factories and collectivization of agriculture was introduced. This was followed by a second Five-year Plan.

Because of the rapid pace of capital formation, war preparedness, and the state of Russian technology, consumption was severely rationed throughout these years. Workers had ration cards that were honored at specific stores, but money continued to be used. Excess money income could be spent only upon special goods at higher prices than the basic ration. Real and money wages differed between occupations with piece rates and incentive pay for higher productivity becoming more and more dominant.

Joseph Stalin, one among many of Lenin's lieutenants, finally won out in the struggle for power after Lenin's death in the early 1920's. Trotsky and other old-line revolutionaries were accused of plotting with foreign powers against the Soviet Union, and in the middle 1930's a tremendous purge of generals and officials culminated in the sensational Moscow trials—sensational because all the defendants vied with each other in beating their breasts and avowing their own guilt. After the Chamberlain-Hitler Munich appeasement pact, Nazi Germany and Soviet Russia in 1939 signed a nonaggression pact, which lasted until Hitler—flushed with his victory over Poland, Scandinavia, and France—attacked Russia.

With the aid of fanatical patriotism and United States lend-lease, the Russians traded their blood for the Germans' until few Germans were left. After the defeat of the Axis, the short-lived comradeship with the Western powers flickered out, and the world now stands in the shadow of the atomic bomb with Russia trying to spread her influence over Europe, and with Britain and ourselves bent on stopping her.

So much for this thumbnail sketch of Soviet political development. Economically, the Communist regime is far removed from any profit system of individualism. A State Planning Commission—the Gosplan—deals with two of the three basic economic problems: What goods to produce, and How to produce them. It is concerned with the location of industry, with the relation of industry to agriculture, and the relation of consumer goods to producer goods. Factories, land, and capital equipment are owned by state enterprise. Private property is limited to dwelling houses, furniture and personal effects, and anything the workers may save from their earnings. The problem of For Whom rests with an Economic Council, which sets wage rates. Piecework rates are widely used, with an elaborate system of incentive bonuses, as a stimulus to increased output. Inequality of incomes, wealth, and inheritance is presumably less than in a capitalist society, although other inequalities may arise through the special privileges granted to party members and the like. Prices of consumer goods are set by the government and sold by state stores and cooperatives.

The Russians claim that they have "industrial democracy." This is clearly a different commodity from political democracy as we know it. Even defenders of the Soviet Union will admit that expressions of opinion against the government or the Communist party will not be tolerated. Free press—in our sense— is forbidden. Possibly a majority of the Russian people prefer their form of government, but no one should blind himself to its great differences from our own concepts of democracy and freedom.

SOCIALISM

In defining fascism or communism, we were able to point to Nazi Germany or Soviet Russia. Socialism cannot be so easily described. Of course, we can describe the Swedish socialist government or the British Labor party's program, but these do not have such dramatic contrasts with our system. They represent a middle way.

Nevertheless, there are at least a few elements that seem to characterize socialist philosophy:

1. *Government Ownership of Productive Resources.* The role of private property is gradually to be lessened as key industries such as railroads, coal, and even steel are gradually nationalized. Unearned profits from increases in land value are also limited.

2. *Planning.* Instead of permitting the free play of profit motives in a laissez-faire market economy, coordinated planning is to be introduced. Sometimes the program of "production for use rather than profit" is advocated; advertising expenditure on gadgets is to be wiped out; workers and professional people are to develop instincts of craftsmanship and social service so that they will be guided by other motives than those of our "acquisitive society."

3. *Redistribution of Income.* Through government taxing powers, inherited wealth and swollen incomes are to be reduced. Social security benefits and welfare services provided by the collective purse are to increase the well-being of the less privileged classes.

4. *Peaceful and Democratic Revolution.* As distinct from communism, socialism often advocates the peaceful and gradual extension of government ownership—revolution by ballot rather than by bullet. This is often more than a tactical move; rather a deep philosophical tenet of faith.

We may briefly discuss the British case as illustrative of one socialist program in operation. In Britain, the coal, electricity, gas, transport, and communications industries have all been nationalized; so also have been parts of others such as ordnance, engineering, building materials, and wholesaling. Nationalization of the steel industry probably aroused more protest than any of the preceding. The coal industry, for example, was clearly demoralized at the close of the war, and nationalization was accepted for the lack of any better solution, but steel was far more efficiently run. The steel case led to a demand for restatement of the Labor party's policies.

The most important force behind these policies has been the Trades Union Congress. This body had argued for public ownership and control of natural resources and services—more specifically: (1) nationalization of land, mines, and minerals, (2) nationalization of railways, (3) extension of state and municipal enterprise to provide social necessities and services, and (4) participation of the workers in management of public services and industries.

These proposals could be interpreted as a very sweeping socialist program. But in 1950, Labor presented a more qualified picture of its scope of operations. Here its spokesman was Herbert Morrison, a leader of the party "moderates." He suggested that modern economic activity tends to divide itself naturally into two segments, public and private. The former, Mr. Morrison argued, comprises roughly 20 percent of the sphere formerly left to private enterprise and is made up of the "public utilities" and "natural monopolies." The remaining 80 per cent should remain private, except in cases where such enterprise is incapable of supplying the necessary service.

In Britain, the owners of industries to be nationalized have been given compensation. And anyone who opposes the Labor government—as most English newspapers do—is free to express his opinion and organize politically.

POLITICAL FREEDOM AND ECONOMIC CONTROL

Degree of public economic direction is a trait that ranges from a laissez-faire society through a collectivist communist regime. But a survey of history shows that this classification must not be confused with the degree of political freedom and democratic civil liberties. Fascist regimes have often passed socialistic measures, and communist bureaus have suppressed personal freedom. On the other hand, Britain, Scandinavia, and other socialist countries have retained all the familiar civil liberties and individual political freedoms that are guaranteed by our own Constitution.

It is one thing to tell a corporation what it may charge for electric power, and quite another thing to tell a man what he can say, what he can believe, or how he must worship.

B. *THE USE OF AN OVER-ALL PRICING SYSTEM UNDER SOCIALISM AND CAPITALISM*

This is an introduction to economics rather than a book on social movements and comparative political systems. Let us turn, therefore, to see how our economic analysis of pricing can be applied to a noncapitalistic system.

In analyzing the problem of pricing in a planned socialist state, we kill two birds with one stone:

1. We get one of the best possible reviews of the over-all working of an ideal *capitalistic* price system.

2. We gain an introduction to problems of "welfare economics," *i.e.*, to the study of what is considered right and wrong concerning any economic system. This depends, of course, upon ethical points of view, which are themselves a-scientific. But the economist, as a disinterested observer, may help to throw light upon how successfully an economic system realizes any suggested ethical goals.[1]

A DILEMMA FOR CENTRALIZED PLANNING

The earlier chapters of this book have shown how a system of market prices operates so as to solve the basic economic problems of What, How, and For Whom. To drive home a better understanding of what all this really means, make a mental experiment. Suppose you were given the job of writing down the blueprints of a completely planned economic system. How would you set about this problem?

First, let us suppose that you are interested in giving people what they want and not in telling them what they ought to want. Obviously, you cannot give them everything they want: land, labor, capital goods, and technological knowledge are limited in amount. So you will have to make compromises and choices.

You may say to yourself: This is obviously a complicated mathematical problem, calling for the use of lots of high-powered electronic high-speed calculating machines. But remember that you will have to deal with the millions of items that are to be found in department stores, with thousands of

---

[1] For example, he may be personally opposed to an equal distribution of income, but that doesn't prevent him from measuring the degree of success in reaching this ethical goal.

grades of productive factors, and with numerous individuals and families. The number of unknowns of the mathematical problem will be in the millions, and the number of steps in its solution in the billions of billions. No known set of calculating machines can begin to tackle such a problem.

You are stumped. And discouraged. Perhaps you will lower your sights and stop being a perfectionist. Instead of giving people exactly what they think they want, you may decide that there will be only a few types of, say, shoe styles and sizes, and so forth, so that the calculation problem will be simplified. Or you may start to give people goods that you find it convenient to give them.

One thing is clear: If centralized planning means that one centralized person must have in his mind all the myriad intricacies of detail, then it is an impossible job to do with any efficiency. So you will naturally begin to experiment with various devices to decentralize the job. And quite probably you will finally end up by introducing a pricing system in many ways like that of capitalism. How might such a pricing system work?

The following pages attempt to answer this question by describing a socialist's utopian pricing mechanism. They are to be regarded as an extended parable and not as a program that any community is likely to institute or that would represent a practicable or desirable goal for reform. Often the economist uses the example of Robinson Crusoe to illustrate economic principles; this does not mean that we should aim to live alone on islands. Similarly, a hypothetical socialist system represents a device for indicating how a market mechanism operates.

PRICING IN A SOCIALIST STATE: CONSUMPTION GOODS PRICES

Many socialists have insisted that, in their new society, the consumer should still have *freedom of choice* and would not have dictated to him the relative amounts of different commodities which he is to "enjoy." As in the capitalist system each person will receive a sum of money or abstract purchasing power which he can spend among different commodities as he wishes. Thus, vegetarians will not have to eat meat, and those who most prefer meat will be able to exert their preference.

How will relative prices between salmon and Spam or any other consumers' goods be set by the socialist state? Generally speaking, they will be set with the same double purpose as in a capitalist society: (1) just high enough to ration around the existing supplies of consumers' goods, so that none are left over and none are short; and also (2) just high enough to cover the socially necessary extra costs of producing the goods in question—or, in technical terms, prices are to be set equal to relative "marginal utilities" and "marginal costs."

THE DISTRIBUTION OF INCOME

So far the process has worked much like the capitalistic system. However, socialism, almost by definition, means a society in which most land and capital goods or nonhuman resources of all kinds are owned collectively by society and not individually by people. In our society an Astor who owns 500 parcels of New York City land which each produce $2,000 of net rents per year will receive an income of 1 million dollars per year—which may be 1,000 times what a night watchman is able to earn, and 200 times what the average skilled engineer can earn. With most property owned collectively and not distributed with great inequality among different individuals, an important source of inequality of the distribution of income would be removed.

Many people profess to hold the ethical and philosophical belief that different individuals' wants and needs are very much alike, and that the present market mechanism works inadequately because the rich are given so many more votes in the control of production than the poor as to make the market demand for goods a poor indication of their true social worth. Such people with a relatively equalitarian philosophy will welcome the great reduction in the spread of incomes between the lowest 90 per cent of all families and the highest 10 per cent. They will argue that taking away $1,000 from a man with an income of $100,000 and giving it to a man with an income of $2,000 will add to social well-being. After the distribution of income between families has been determined correctly, according to society's fundamental (a-scientific) value judgments, then and only then will it be true that the dollars coming on the market will be valid indicators of the value of goods and services; and only then will they be serving to direct production into the proper channels and goods into the right hands.

How is what is considered the proper, ethical distribution of income to be achieved aside from the negative act of wiping out unduly high property incomes? Perfectionists have two answers: (1) in part by letting people get some of their income in the form of wages; but (2) in large part by having these wages supplemented by receipt of a lump-sum *social dividend payment*. This cash payment would presumably be pretty nearly the same for most average families; but even in an equalitarian society, there might be differences to compensate for different numbers of children, different age and health status, and so forth.

It is an ethical rather than a scientific question as to just how large each person's final income ought to be. As a science, economics can concern itself only with the best means of attaining given ends; it cannot prescribe the ends themselves. Indeed, if someone decided that he preferred a feudal-fascistic kind of society, in which all people with little black moustaches were to be given especially high incomes, the economist could set up the pricing rules for him to follow to achieve his strange design best. He would be told to determine his social dividend payments so as to achieve the required optimal distribution of income, after which each dollar coming on the market could be regarded by the economist as correctly representing (that eccentric person's) true social values.

The social dividend differs from a wage because it is to be given to each individual *regardless of his own efforts*. That is why it is called a "lump-sum" dividend. Any bonus based upon productivity or effort is to be treated as a wage. We have not yet seen how wages are to be determined. But before doing so let us first turn to another important problem.

PRICING OF NONHUMAN PRODUCTIVE RESOURCES AND INTERMEDIATE GOODS

What should be the role of land and other nonhuman productive resources as an element of cost in an ideal socialist state? Some people would say that such nonhuman resources should not enter into cost at all; that only human sweat and skill is the true source of all value; and that any extra charges based upon the cost of land or machinery represent a capitalistic surplus which the owners of property are able to squeeze out of the exploited laboring masses by virtue of the private monopoly of ownership of the means of production. This view is sometimes loosely spoken of as the "labor theory of value," and it is usually attributed to Karl Marx, the intellectual father of communistic socialism. Learned scholars dispute over just what Marx meant by the "labor theory of value," and whether he intended it to be applied to a socialistic economy in the short or long run.

We need not enter into this dispute. However, it is important to note that, in its simple form, the labor theory of value will lead to incorrect and inefficient use of both labor and nonlabor resources in even the most perfect socialist society. So long as any economic resource is limited in quantity—*i.e.*, scarce rather than free—the socialist planners must give it a price and charge a rent for its use. This price need not, as in the case of the Astor millionaire under the capitalistic system, determine any individual's income. It can be a purely bookkeeping or accounting price set up by the planners, rather than being a market price. But there must be a price put upon the use of every such resource.

Why? First, we must price nonhuman resources to ensure that society is deciding *how* goods shall be produced in the best way, so that we really end up out on the true production-possibility curve of society and not somewhere inside it. It would be absurd to get rid of the capitalistic system with its alleged wastes due to unemployment, and then by stupid planning end up far inside of society's true production potentialities.

Related to the above point is the second need for all resources to be given a value if correct prices are to be charged to consumers for final goods that use up a great deal of scarce resources. In other words, for society to find itself in the best of all possible positions along the production-possibility curve, we must price such consumption goods as food and clothing so as to reflect their true relative (extra or marginal) costs of using up scarce resources. Otherwise, the free choice exerted by consumers on their dollar spending will not truly reflect their own or society's best preferences.

THE EXAMPLE OF LAND RENT [1]

These two reasons are difficult to grasp. However, let us try to make the necessity for land pricing clear by considering a single example. Suppose there are two identical twins in a farming utopia. What if one were to produce wheat on an acre of good land, and the other to produce less wheat by the same year's work on an acre of bad land. If they are identical twins, working equally hard, we would certainly have to say that their wage rates should be the same. Now, if wages were to be treated as the only cost, in accord with the labor theory of value, then the same price could not be charged for the two different outputs of wheat, even though the kernels of wheat were identical. The good-land wheat would have involved low labor costs and will have to sell for less than the poor-land wheat.

This, of course, is absurd. A well-wishing social planner might try to get around the dilemma by charging the same price for both, perhaps losing money on the poor-land wheat and gaining on the other. Or what is almost the same thing, he might say "Let us pay the twin on bad land lower wages than his brother, so as to keep the costs of the two wheats the same; but then let us make the richer brother share his wages with the poorer."

Such a solution is not absurd, but it falls short of achieving the desired best results; maximum production and equal pay for equal human effort. In particular, it fails to shift more labor on to the more productive land.

The only correct procedure is to put an accounting price tag on land, the good land having the higher tag. The prices of both kinds of wheat will be equal, because the land cost of the good-land wheat will be just enough higher than that of the poor-land wheat to make up the difference. Most important of all, the socialist production manager must try to minimize the combined labor and land cost of producing each kind of wheat. If he does so according to the marginal-product principles discussed in Part Four, he will accomplish something new and important and undreamed of by the simple believer in the labor theory of value.

[1] If desired, this section may be omitted without interrupting the continuity of the chapter.

He will find it pays to work the good land more intensively, perhaps with the time of $1\frac{1}{2}$ men until the extra product there has been lowered by the law of diminishing returns so as to be just equal to the extra product of the $\frac{1}{2}$ man's time on the poor land. Only by putting a price upon inert sweatless land are we using it, and sweating breathing labor, most productively! The price or rent of land rises so as to ration its limited supply among the *best* uses.

Note too that the most finicky humanitarian will have nothing to complain of concerning our solution. By transferring labor from one plot of land to the other until its marginal productivity has been made equal, we get the largest possible total production of wheat.[1]

The two brothers are paid the same wages because they have worked equally hard. But their wages are not high enough to buy all the wheat since part of the cost of the wheat has come from (bookkeeping) land charges. However, the people through their government own the land equally. The land's return does not go to any property owner, but is available to be distributed as a lump-sum dividend to both brothers according to their ethical deserts. By putting a proper accounting price or rent on land, society has more consumption than was otherwise possible.

If we turn now to the production of more than one consumer's good, it will be obvious that their cost prices must be made to reflect the amount of socially limited land and machinery which they each use up. A field crop like potatoes requires little labor and much land as compared to an intensive garden crop like tomatoes. If each commodity were priced on the basis of labor costs alone, potatoes would sell for too little and too much land would be forced out of tomato production. Everyone would end up worse off.

One last point concerning the final determination of a product's cost and price. After the costs of all necessary factors of production have been added together to arrive at total cost, the planning authorities must set their prices at the extra or marginal cost of new units of production. Or more accurately, the socialist managers of a plant must behave like a perfect competitor: they must disregard any influence that their own production might have on market price, and must continue to produce extra units up to the point where the last little unit costs just as much as its selling price. For many industries, such as railroads where unit costs are constantly falling, setting marginal costs equal to price will imply that *full* average costs are not covered. In a noncapitalistic

---

[1] As the discussions of marginal productivity in an earlier chapter have shown, *total product will be at a maximum only when labor has been transferred from the poor land* (where its marginal product is low) *to the good land* (where its marginal product is high). Every such transfer must necessarily yield us extra product, until finally no further increases in output can result when the marginal-products have been equalized in the two uses.

society the difference would be made up by a (accounting) grant from the state. For if a railroad system is worth building, it is worth being utilized to the full.[1]

To summarize: Correct social planning requires that all scarce resources, whether human labor or not, be given accounting prices at least. The final costs of consumers' goods should include the sum total of *all* extra costs necessary to produce each good; or, in short, should equal *marginal cost*. The demand for consumers' goods is really an indirect demand for all productive resources, a demand which can be kept in proper check only by putting appropriate valuations on productive resources.

Otherwise, society's valuable nonhuman—and human!—resources will be incorrectly allocated, and the market pricing of finished goods will not lead to maximum consumers' satisfaction. It is to be emphasized that the accounting prices of land and other nonhuman resources need not, in a socialist state, be part of the incomes of anyone. In the language of the visionary critic of private enterprise: no one is "exploited" by having a property owner skim off part of the final product. Instead, the contribution of capital and land to production is given to people in the form of the *social dividend*.

THE ROLE OF THE INTEREST RATE IN A SOCIALIST STATE

We have seen that the interest rate has an important function in a capitalistic, socialistic, or any other kind of economic system. Capital goods have a "net productivity." So long as resources can be invested for the present or the future, it will be necessary to make important decisions with respect to capital. Shall we apply present land and labor to the production of a corn crop this year or to apples 15 years from now? Shall we have grape juice today or wine 10 years hence? Shall we replace a worn-out printing press by a new expensive one which yields its services over a period of 20 years, or buy a cheap one that will only last 14 years? Every one of these questions can be answered only by using an interest rate to relate future and present economic values. Without such an interest rate, the existing stock of fixed and circulating capital cannot be devoted to its best uses; and whatever amount of national income society has decided to invest in capital formation cannot be embodied in the best form without such an interest rate.

---

[1] The long-run question as to whether to build a railroad in the first place may involve an "all-or-none decision," which cannot be made step by step. In such a case, there must still be a balancing of the extra (or marginal) advantage and extra cost to society of the enterprise. But for such a big step, price is no longer a good indicator of total welfare, since—as we saw in Chapter 23—there is always an element of consumer's surplus in the total amount of goods that a person consumes, over what he has paid for them. Welfare may go up as price and total value go down.

The interest rate acts as a sieve or rationing device: all projects that can yield 6 per cent over time are undertaken before any that yield only 5 per cent are started.

It should be added that most economic writers on socialism do not think that the rate of interest should also determine—as it does in our economy, to some degree—the rate at which capital growth is to take place at the expense of current consumption. The decision as to how much should be saved would be determined by the state "in the light of national and social needs" and not by the "haphazard" notions of individuals with respect to the future. But the level of social saving and capital growth once having been determined, the interest rate must be used to allocate scarce "capital supplies" optimally and to determine the order of priority of alternative projects.[1]

WAGE RATES AND INCENTIVE PRICING

We must now return to the problem of how the socialist planners would set wage rates, and then we are done. If the amounts of labor of all kinds and of all skills were perfectly fixed, there would be no reason why labor should not be given accounting prices just like any other productive factor. Workers would receive no wages at all. They would then receive all the national income in the form of an enlarged *social dividend*.

However, if people are to be free to choose their own occupation and if they are to be given a choice between working a little harder and longer in return for extra consumption goods, then it will be necessary to set up a system of *actual market wages* at which people can sell their services. These rates may differ depending upon the irksomeness and unpleasantness of the job; and unlike our system, the pleasanter jobs may be the lower paid, and the ditch-diggers or garbage collectors may have to be higher paid to attract people into their jobs. Occupations that require much training and skill will receive high pay, but much of that pay may be spent by the state in providing the education necessary to acquire those skills. Piece rates may often be used under socialism, and a worker with a 10 per cent higher productivity may receive higher wages. Workers will in every case be offered wages equal to their marginal or extra productivity.

Therefore, it is not necessarily true that all incomes will be at a dead level in the socialist state. They will differ somewhat as a result of two distinct factors: (1) society's appraisal of the "needs and worth" of different individuals—as reflected primarily in the size of the individuals' lump-sum *social*

---

[1] There is no logical reason why individuals who are willing to forego present for future consumption should not be permitted to do such voluntary extra saving and receive an interest return equal to the net productivity of capital.

dividends, and (2) the need for wages to differ to provide incentives and to compensate people for extra disutility and effort. Incomes would not differ, however, because of inequality in the ownership and inheritance of property.

SUMMARY OF SOCIALIST PRICING

1. A socialist system could make use of four different kinds of pricing: (1) consumer-goods prices, (2) wage and incentive rates, (3) accounting prices of intermediate goods, and (4) final lump-sum dividends (when positive, subsidies; when negative, taxes). The first three groups of prices would be determined by supply and demand.

2. To give people free choice between consumers' goods, market prices would be set for such goods. Similarly, to provide freedom of choice of occupation, to give people incentives, and to provide compensation for differences between occupations, wage rates would have to be set to correspond to (marginal) productivities and disutilities.

3. Accounting prices would have to be set on all nonhuman productive resources to ration them in their best uses where their (relative) marginal productivities are equal and highest. Similarly, there would have to be a rate of interest to ration the existing and growing stock of capital among its best uses. Any consumption good would be produced up to the point where the full marginal cost of production (necessary to attract all resources from other uses and from leisure) is just equal to the price.[1]

4. Lastly, the final distribution of income would be made to correspond to what society regards as the ideal distribution pattern by means of a payment of a lump-sum social dividend to people, depending upon "need and wants" but never—like a wage—on effort or performance. Presumably in a socialist society, it would be felt that a much more nearly equal distribution of income will be necessary before the dollar votes of consumers can be expected to reflect true social preferences. However, this is a nonscientific, ethical question.

5. None of these processes except the last requires detailed comprehensive planning by a central agency. Mathematicians would not have to be called in to solve thousands and thousands of simultaneous equations. Instead, the decentralized planners would proceed by successive approximation, by trial and error—setting provisional market and accounting prices and cutting them or raising them depending upon whether available supplies are piling up or running short.

It would be naïve to think that any actual socialist society would succeed in

---

[1] The decentralized managers of industries would achieve this result by seeking to maximize their net algebraic profits, measured in accounting points or actual dollars, but with *all* prices taken as given parameters.

reaching the ideal equilibrium positions described above. Errors of foresight would inevitably be made. Existing vested interests, anxious to preserve their security in a dynamic world of change, would resist and sabotage such change in the same qualitative fashion as they have done in historical societies. There is great reason to doubt that politicians and the electorate would pay much attention to the incentive mechanisms outlined in the preceding pages. The importance of this discussion is that it teaches us how to appraise the mechanical efficiency of pricing in a *non*-socialist society!

WELFARE ECONOMICS IN A FREE-ENTERPRISE ECONOMY

On the basis of the above general principles of pricing, we are in a position to see what friendly and unfriendly critics think is wrong in our present system, or not necessarily right from various ethical viewpoints. The possible deviations from the social optimum may be briefly listed as follows:

1. The existing distribution of property, income, education, and economic opportunity is the result of past history and does not necessarily represent a perfect optimum according to the ethical philosophies of Christianity, Buddhism, paganism, the American creed, or other ideologies. Defenders of the capitalist system point out that such deviations from the optimum distribution of income can be corrected by appropriate tax policies, if that is what is desired. There are always, however, some costs to be incurred in our capitalistic system from such policies because of effects upon incentives, risk taking, effort, and productivity.

2. The widespread presence of monopoly elements in our system and the limited appearance of perfect competition mean that production is rarely being pushed to the optimum point of equality of marginal cost to price; because the elasticity of demand is not infinite under imperfect competition, production is pushed only to the point of equality of marginal cost to marginal revenue. Because of the fear of "spoiling the market," monopoly price is too high and monopoly output is too low.

This is related to a further evil under monopolistic competition when entry of new firms into an industry is very easy. There may then tend to be an inefficient division of production among too many firms; the price charged is too high, but because of wasteful use of resources, no one is making any profits.[1]

[1] Another evil, discussed in more advanced economic writings, is the fact that individual firms, in making their decisions, never take into account the possible effects of their production decisions on other firms or industries. In digging his oil well, Pat doesn't realize that he may be robbing Mike's oil pool; and the same with Mike—with the result that less oil is obtained in the end, and with more cost. Because of such so-called "external diseconomies" (or occasionally, "external economies") apparent "private marginal costs" do

3. Finally, of course, as shown in Part Two, under a laissez-faire system, there may be great wastes due to unemployment and the business cycle. Consumers, labor, farmers, and business together with public fiscal and monetary policy must be mobilized in a never-ending war against this greatest of modern scourges—this poverty that has no real cause but stems only from our intricate monetary society.

These imperfections can be ameliorated within the framework of our traditions. In any case, many—perhaps most—Americans will feel that the dynamic vitality of our mixed-enterprise system outweighs its disadvantages.

AN OPTIMISTIC LAST WORD

In earlier chapters we have seen how our modern economy operates. Throughout, we have subjected the economy to a searching examination, pulling no punches when it came to taking note of friendly and unfriendly criticisms of the working of the economic system. In this chapter we have glanced briefly at the alternative systems of communism, fascism, and socialism. In setting down how a socialist economy might use a pricing system, we have gained new insight and respect for the operation of a pricing system in our own mixed system. The system is not perfect. No system is. But its imperfections can certainly be ameliorated within our existing framework of ideas and institutions.

I should like to conclude on a note of profound optimism. The American economy is in better shape in the 1950's than it ever was in the past. At the present time, possessing only 6 per cent of the world's population, it produces some 40 per cent of the world's income. And with all its defects, it has behind it a record of the most rapid advance of productivity and living standards ever achieved anywhere. Our mixed economy—wars aside—has a great future before it.

---

not reflect true "social marginal costs"; and certain lines of activity deserve to be contracted and others to be expanded. Compare A. C. Pigou, *Economics of Welfare* (Macmillan, New York, 1932).

SUMMARY

A. FASCISM, COMMUNISM, AND SOCIALISM

1. Out of the multiplicity of social movements and philosophies, these three constitute the important challenge to our present order. Perhaps most significant are the noneconomic issues involved in a comparison of capitalism and alternative systems. We have not more than touched upon the question of the extent to which a socialist society might, or might not, be able to develop among its people new attitudes to replace capitalistic incentives, such as instincts of professional good craftsmanship and social service, which put emphasis upon production for use rather than for profit. Nor have we been able to set down final answers to the crucial problems of the relationship between individual freedom and social control in different economic systems.

Can a socialist society preserve the civil rights and political freedoms for the individual? What is the importance of political democracy without economic democracy? How can capitalism be made to function better? A number of references are suggested below for those interested in further readings.[1]

B. PRICING IN SOCIALISM AND CAPITALISM

2. In a pure unmixed competitive society, the economic problems of What shall be produced, How, and For Whom are solved in an intricate, interdependent manner by the impersonal workings of the profit-and-loss market system. Every economic variable depends upon every other, but all tend to be simultaneously determined at their general equilibrium values by a process of successive approximations involving adjustment and readjustment.

3. Unless a socialist economy were uninterested in efficiency and economizing, or in freedom of choice of goods and jobs, it would have to institute a system of pricing. However, some prices would be purely accounting or bookkeeping figures; in addition, the final determination of the distribution of income would involve an outright social dividend, given to everyone by the explicit a-scientific decision of government and society.

[1] R. H. TAWNEY, *The Acquisitive Society* (Harcourt Brace, New York, 1920); F. A. HAYEK, *The Road to Serfdom* (University of Chicago Press, Chicago, 1944); D. M. WRIGHT, *Democracy and Progress* (Macmillan, New York, 1948); H. C. SIMONS, *A Positive Program for Laissez Faire*, Public Policy Pamphlet 15, University of Chicago Press, Chicago, 1934); A. C. PIGOU, *Socialism versus Capitalism* (Macmillan, New York, 1939). For further information on welfare economics, see J. E. MEADE and C. H. HITCH, *An Introduction to Economic Analysis and Policy*, (Oxford University Press, New York, 1938).

4. From the standpoint of welfare economics, it is seen that our own capitalistic system may depart from what is considered a social optimum in three main ways: through improper distribution of income, through monopoly, and through fluctuations in unemployment. It is the present writer's belief as exemplified throughout the book, that all these evils can be ameliorated by appropriate policies, within the framework of the capitalist system.

It is too easy to compare the obvious imperfection of our known system with the ideal perfections of an unknown planned order. And it is only too easy to gloss over the tremendous dynamic vitality of our mixed free enterprise system, which, with all its faults, has given the world a century of progress such as an actual socialized order might find it impossible to equal.

QUESTIONS FOR DISCUSSION

1. Make a list of a number of isms, describing each and outlining its history.

2. Describe your own vision of Utopia. Does it differ from the present order?

3. Compare and contrast fascism and communism. What is the relation of socialism and capitalism to each?

4. Discuss the development of the Labor party in England, and its postwar activities.

5. "I'd rather starve in free America than live off the fat of the land under totalitarian communism." Are these your sentiments? Why?

6. "For all its talk of planning and production for use, Soviet Russia employs its resources less efficiently than the United States and has a slower rate of progress than we do." Discuss.

7. Summarize how a pricing system works to solve the three fundamental economic problems. Illustrate the interdependence of these three problems.

8. Discuss the four kinds of prices in a planned, socialist state.

9. List what you consider to be economic imperfections in the present economic order. What are its virtues?

10. In January, 1951, prices and wages were temporarily frozen in order to check inflation. Describe the problems this might create for What, How, and For Whom. Suggest remedies.

Index

A

Abilities, distribution of, 72, 594–597
Absolute advantage, 694–695
Acceleration principle, 389–392
Accounting, elements of, 134–148
  balance sheet, 135–137, 141–142
  depreciation, 139–141
  good will, 146
  income statement, 137–139, 141–142
  intangible assets, 146
  inventories, 136
  profit-and-loss statement, 137–139, 141–142
  reserves and funds, 143–146
Advertising, 214
  and monopolies, 523
Aged, job opportunities for, 72–75
Agriculture, decline of, 80–81
  government aid to, 84–88, 448–453
    Brannan plan, 451–453
    crop restriction, 449–450
    parity prices, 450–451
  income from (see Farming)
  instability of, 83–84
  long-run solution to, 88–89
  poverty in, 82–83
Allen, Frederick Lewis, 466n.
American Federation of Labor (AFL), case study of collective bargaining by, 190–192
  and discrimination, 75, 189
  history of, 193–194
  organizational structure of, 189–190
Antitrust policy, 524–526
Arbitrager, 56n., 462
  and foreign exchange rates, 656n.
Assets (see Accounting, elements of, balance sheet; Interest rate, determination of)

B

Bagehot, W., 385n.
Baker, John C., 96
Balance of (international) payments, 656–661
  and calculation of NNP, 245
  capital movements, 660
    monetary vs. real aspects of, 665–666
    significance of, 663–665
  current items (trade balance and invisible items), 657
  European postwar problem, 683–684
  and flexible exchange rates, 669–671
  and gold standard, 672–675
  historical stages of United States, 661–663
  and multiplier analysis of international trade, 676–677
  and specie-flow-price mechanism, 672–675
  and stable exchange rates, 671–672
Balance of trade (see Balance of payments, current items)
Balance sheet in accounting, 134–137, 141–142
Bank of England, 316n., 324, 339, 344
Bank deposits, considered as money, 55, 308
  creation of (or multiple expansion of), 326–333
    qualifications concerning, 333–335
  insurance of, 325
  multiple contraction of, 332–333
Banking, branch, 314, 333
  as business, 316–317
  control of, 324–326
    (See also Federal reserve system)
  development of, 313–319
  fractional reserve, 319–321, 323–324
    paradoxes of, 323–324
  "monopoly," 332–333

747

we are the freest when
we realize our limitations!